Growing Toward Unity

L T H

THE LIVING THEOLOGICAL HERITAGE
OF THE UNITED CHURCH OF CHRIST

Volume 1. Ancient and Medieval Legacies

Volume 2. Reformation Roots

Volume 3. Colonial and National Beginnings

Volume 4. Consolidation and Expansion

Volume 5. Outreach and Diversity

Volume 6. Growing Toward Unity

Volume 7. United and Uniting

THE LIVING THEOLOGICAL HERITAGE

OF THE UNITED CHURCH OF CHRIST

Barbara Brown Zikmund
Series Editor

L T H

VOLUME SIX

Growing Toward Unity

Edited by Elsabeth Slaughter Hilke, with a Postscript by Thomas E. Dipko

The Pilgrim Press
Cleveland, Ohio

The Pilgrim Press, 700 Prospect Avenue E.,
Cleveland, Ohio 44115-1100, U.S.A.

Printed in the United States of America on acid-free paper

06 05 04 03 02 01 5 4 3 2 1

Library of Congress Cataloging-in-Publication Data
The living theological heritage of the United Church of Christ /
Barbara Brown Zikmund, series editor.
p. cm.
Includes bibliographical references and index.

Vol. 1, Ancient and Medieval Legacies ISBN 0-8298-1064-1
Vol. 2, Reformation Roots ISBN 0-8298-1143-5
Vol. 3, Colonial and National Beginnings ISBN 0-8298-1109-5
Vol. 4, Consolidation and Expansion ISBN 0-8298-1110-9
Vol. 5, Outreach and Diversity ISBN 0-8298-1111-7
Vol. 6, Growing Toward Unity ISBN 0-8298-1112-5
Vol. 7, United and Uniting ISBN 0-8298-1113-3

Contents

The Living Theological Heritage of the United Church of Christ

Remember me, O LORD, when you show favor to your people; help me when you deliver them; that I may see the prosperity of your chosen ones, that I may rejoice in the gladness of your nation, that I may glory in your heritage.

Psalm 106:4–5 (NRSV)

The United Church of Christ is a microcosm of the history of Christian theology. Although the UCC was not officially "born" until 1957, it draws upon a long-standing and rich theological legacy. A living theological heritage has shaped, and continues to support, its common life.

Unfortunately, a perception exists that the UCC is without any roots, that it is unsure about its faith. Lutherans quote the works of Martin Luther; Methodists revere the ideas of John Wesley; Episcopalians have the divines of the Church of England. But members of the United Church of Christ often seem uncertain about their theological heritage and identity.

The United Church of Christ was created out of a mid-twentieth-century ecumenical passion to heal the divisions of the Christian church. Its focus was on the future, not on the past. Nevertheless, it has a remarkable theological and historical legacy. This volume, and others in this series, offers resources from Congregational and Christian history and German Evangelical and Reformed traditions, along with many hidden histories, to leaders and members of the United Church of Christ and to the wider society. We hope that these materials will strengthen the denomination and inform those seeking a better understanding of the past and present life of the UCC.

For example, New England Congregationalism leaned on the theological insights of key English separatist thinkers in the late sixteenth and early seventeenth centuries. Participants in American frontier religion developed six theological principles to guide their Christian witness. The theological work of John Nevin and Philip Schaff shaped and reshaped the German Reformed Church. German Evangelical immigrants brought with them a theology forged by a European church-union movement. Few people know this heritage, and when they look for more information, it is difficult to find the sources.

Ten years ago the Office for Church Life and Leadership and the Board for Homeland Ministries of the United Church of Christ authorized *The Living Theological Heritage of the United Church of Christ.* They designed this series of seven volumes to enable the United Church of Christ to recover its theological past and strengthen contemporary faith and practice. The series is offered to the churches and their members to enable them to move beyond their theological inferiority complex and to claim their heritage.

• • •

The series brings together key materials that undergird UCC faith and practice. A team of thirteen editors, guided by an editorial board of seven, presents these volumes as a quarry of resources to be mined by the churches for years to come.

The design of each volume does three things:

First, it gathers together important materials that have shaped the theological identity of the United Church of Christ—ancient christological discourses, sixteenth-century treatises by Reformation theologians, the Heidelberg Catechism, writings and sermons from colonial Congregationalism, the Cambridge Platform, mission statements, popular hymns, prayers, official ecumenical materials, resolutions from wider church meetings, minority reports, and even protest literature. Some of the materials are obvious and known, some are fugitive, and some are new discoveries. The editors chose all of them, from the first century to the twentieth century, not simply because they are part of the historical record, but because the editors believe that these documents have shaped the theological identity of the UCC.

Second, each volume contains brief introductions to individual documents or groups of source materials, giving the reader background information needed to understand what is printed. Who wrote it? When was it written? Why was it written? What was the result? These document introductions help make the materials understandable in and of themselves.

Third, each volume has one or more introductory essays to highlight broader insights and theological interpretations of the materials. Obviously, any selection of documents can distort by highlighting some things and excluding others, but the editors have attempted to make the selections as inclusive as possible. The introductory essays, written by the editors, weave the materials into meaningful patterns and gather up the collective wisdom of the UCC to make it more accessible in the present.

• • •

The Living Theological Heritage of the United Church of Christ has seven volumes.

Volume 1, *Ancient and Medieval Legacies,* grounds the theological life of the United Church of Christ in the search for unity and theological clarity within the ancient and medieval church. As a Protestant denomination, why should the UCC concern itself with pre-Reformation theology and history? Because not to begin with the early church betrays its understanding of Christian unity. This volume explores the themes of unity ("united"), ecclesiology ("church"), and Christology ("Christ") from the time of Jesus to the Reformation. It highlights the fact that the United Church of Christ stands in a long line of faithful Christians who have sought to understand and name their faith from the first century to the present.

Volume 2, *Reformation Roots,* explores the theological legacies of the United Church of Christ found in the sixteenth-century Protestant Reformation. From reformers like Erasmus, Zwingli, Luther, Calvin, English separatists, and the irenic leaders of the Palatinate, the UCC has forged its theological core. Volume 2 provides a collection of Reformation materials especially meaningful to the United Church of Christ.

Volume 3, *Colonial and National Beginnings,* examines the development of early Congregationalism and German Reformed theology. It lifts up the ideas and concerns that motivated colonial thinking and demonstrates how they evolved with the migration and increasing diversity of the population.

Volume 4, *Consolidation and Expansion,* documents the story of the Christians and the German Evangelicals on the American frontier and tracks later developments in Congregational and German Reformed history. It illustrates how the Christian movement brought together Methodists from North Carolina, Baptists from New England, and Presbyterians from Kentucky. It reveals the contributions of German Evangelicals on the Mississippi frontier. At the same time, it follows the development of German Reformed and Congregational faith and practice as the nation matured and people migrated west.

Volume 5, *Outreach and Diversity,* brings together a mix of materials flowing from the mission outreach of all of these groups. It also explores the experiences of minority and immigrant communities. The call to evangelize, educate, and serve stretched the theological mind of those groups that later created the UCC. African American contributions, encounters with indigenous peoples, social witness, and new immigrants raised new theological issues and encouraged a pattern of theological engagement with the world.

Volume 6, *Growing Toward Unity,* celebrates the long-standing commitment of the UCC to an ecumenical vision and the search for Christian unity. It steps back from the complex history of peoples and ideas documented in the earlier volumes to examine the vision of Christian unity that eventually gave birth to the United Church of Christ. It is a theological heritage that takes seriously the prayer of Jesus "that they might all be one."

Volume 7, *United and Uniting,* documents the evolution of the United Church of Christ's theological identity since 1957. It looks at over four decades of UCC life and gathers up its theological treasures. It recognizes that the theological journey of the UCC has been wide-ranging, one that has produced a distinctive living theological heritage. It also invites the UCC to become more theologically self-conscious.

• • •

We hope that *The Living Theological Heritage of the United Church of Christ* will enable those who are members of the UCC to find new courage to speak with pride about their UCC faith and theological inheritance and will give those who are not members of the church a clear understanding of this unique community of Christians.

Acknowledgments

The editor of volume 6, Elsabeth Slaughter Hilke, would like to extend special thanks to several people who were especially helpful to her research: Kay Schellhase and Diane Russell at the Evangelical and Reformed Historical Society in Lancaster, Pennsylvania; Lowell Zuck and Bill Kerr at the Evangelical Synod Archives at Eden Theological Seminary in St. Louis, Missouri; Connie Keller at the Elon College Archives in Elon, North Carolina; Joan Blocher at Chicago Theological Seminary Library; Harold Worthley at the Congregational Library in Boston; and Eldon Eisenach of the University of Tulsa, Oklahoma. Extraordinary help and support were given by Tom and Jane Hamilton, who shared their excellent library on the Southern Christians; Joe Burgess and John Thomas, who offered unfailing collegial support; and Jurgen Hilke, who added to his professorial responsibilities by becoming administrative assistant to the project as a thirtieth anniversary present.

BARBARA BROWN ZIKMUND
Series Editor

Growing Toward Unity

The United Church of Christ claims and celebrates the varied contributions made by the four streams that originally came together to make it a *united* church—Congregational, Christian, Evangelical, and Reformed. At the same time, an important part of its present identity is formed by its commitment to move toward the future as a *uniting* church, seeking to make the unity of Christ's church more visible. It is as a uniting church that it belongs to the World Council of Churches (WCC), sharing with other members of the World Council a commitment to strive for "unity in one faith and in one Eucharistic fellowship expressed in worship and in common life in Christ . . . in order that the world may believe" (WCC Constitution).

Why did the United Church of Christ become a united church, and why does it feel called to continue uniting? The answer to these questions begins with the New Testament mandate for unity given to all Christ's followers. It continues in the history of those followers who sought to realize this mandate throughout church history, through the histories of the four denominations that came together to form the United Church of Christ, and into the history of the United Church itself. It extends also through the development of the worldwide ecumenical movement founded explicitly in response to a New Testament mandate for unity.

The New Testament Mandate

The New Testament attests to a fundamental sense of unity among early Christians that was grounded in the revelation of God in Jesus Christ.

"There is one body and one Spirit, just as you were called to the one hope of your calling, one Lord, one faith, one baptism, one God and Father of all, who is above all and through all and in all" (Eph. 4:4–6, NRSV). New Testament Christians believed that in God's revelation in Jesus Christ and in the church's witness to that revelation, believers were and ought to be "one." They were bound together in one Christian faith for the forgiveness of sins, and in one community of faith, the body of Christ, the church. "We, who are many, are one body in Christ, and individually we are members one of another" (Rom. 12:5, NRSV).

From the beginning, early Christians recognized that there were differences among Christians—differences such as race and class, Jew and Gentile, Greek and barbarian, slave and master. But they also realized that these *differences* should not lead to *divisions* between them that would contradict their unity in Christ. They considered the diverse gifts and functions within the Christian community to be the work of the one Spirit, necessary for the church's well-being.

At the same time, even as the early Christians celebrated their unity, they considered unity to be a goal. Christians were one in Christ, to be sure; but Christ gave them a mandate to make that oneness more visible in the world, so that the world might believe the gospel (John 17:20–21). This tension between unity as a gift already given and unity as a goal to be achieved runs throughout all Christian history, providing a connecting thread and fostering movements to make unity more visible.

The Meaning of "Ecumenical"

The English world "ecumenical" is derived from the Greek noun *oikoumene,* which in turn is derived from the Greek verb *oikein,* "to inhabit." Scholars who study the word note that it was used in a secular context from the time of the Greco-Roman empire to refer to the empire itself, or to the whole *civilized* world, that is, the realm of Greco-Roman *culture,* as opposed to the barbarian world.

In the New Testament, *oikoumene* sometimes refers to "the whole world," without any political or cultural connotation at all. At other times it points to a world governed by God, as, for instance, where the expected reign of God is spoken of as the "*oikoumene* to come" (Heb. 2:5).

Later, the term gained widespread usage in the church to describe the Christian community within the empire. By the fourth century, the *oikoumene* had come to mean "the Christian world," with the double meaning of the "Christian empire" and the "whole church."

In the fourth century, Christian leaders meeting in Constantinople in 381 C.E. referred to the Council of Nicea that met in 325 C.E. as an "ecumenical council." Although the council was convened by the emperor and met under his authority, the decisions of an ecumenical council were understood to possess general authority and validity over all. If something was "ecumenical," it was for the whole church. Eventually, several councils that made definitive dogmatic statements came to be called ecumenical councils: Nicea I (325 C.E.), which defined Christ as being of the one essence with the Father; Constantinople I (381 C.E.), which proclaimed the divinity of the Holy Spirit; Ephesus (431 C.E.), which defined the unity of the person of Christ; and Chalcedon (451 C.E.), which defined the two natures, divine and human, in the person of Christ. When Christianity split into Orthodox and Roman Catholic churches, these divisions continued the early usage of "ecumenical." However, after the sixteenth-century Protestant Reformation spawned numerous doctrinal camps and regional churches, the term "ecumenical" fell into disuse in the Protestant churches.

Recent years have produced a new "ecumenical movement" dedicated to reclaiming the unity of the early church. Through the work of the World Council of Churches, "ecumenical" has come to describe "the whole task of the whole church to bring the gospel to the whole world." Thus, to call something "ecumenical" today reminds Christians of the unity and the mission of the church all over the world.

The Ecumenical Movement in the United States

The development of the ecumenical movement in the United States during the nineteenth and twentieth centuries was a product of secular and religious "unitive forces" intertwined with the increasing complexity of denominational life. New forms of communication, over the telegraph and later the telephone, allowed people to communicate across great distances, shrinking the globe and giving people around the world a new sense of closeness and familiarity. Travel from country to country, by train, by steamship, and later by plane, became increasingly possible, making travelers aware of being connected to people all over the world. Furthermore, the destruction and despair caused by the American Civil War, World Wars I and II, and the Korean War exposed military personnel to people who were different from themselves. People everywhere began to see themselves as part of one worldwide human community.

"Unitive forces" also emerged during the eighteenth and nineteenth centuries among Christians, reminding them of the unity of the church and leading toward the development of a worldwide movement dedicated to making Christian unity more visible. First, in the early nineteenth century, great frontier revivals began to blur denominational loyalties. A new concern arose for missionary outreach within all the churches. Many missionaries, however, found that competitive denominationalism seriously hampered their effectiveness. The earliest missionary societies, such as the American Board of Commissioners for Foreign Missions, founded in 1810, initially involved Christians from many denominations. At the World Missionary Conference in Edinburgh in 1910, hundreds of participants caught a new vision of Christian cooperation and unity through their common confession of "One Lord, One Faith, One Baptism."

Up until the early twentieth century, most Protestant attempts to reclaim the unity of the church broke down over doctrinal differences between the denominations, especially in matters pertaining to the sacraments or issues around ministry. For this reason, at the 1910 Missionary Conference in Edinburgh, theological discussions were deliberately excluded from the program out of concern that they would lead to unhelpful dissension. Charles H. Brent (1862–1929), a missionary bishop of the United States Protestant Episcopal Church serving in the Philippines, wanted something more. He recognized that church unity would never be achieved unless divisive theological issues were addressed. Therefore, he suggested that churches ought to send representatives to another conference—a World Conference on Faith and Order—where Christians could discuss theological matters. In the end, 385 men and nine women representing 108 churches from all over the world met in Lausanne, Switzerland, in 1927. Although this first World Conference on Faith and Order reached agreement on a number of significant issues, the agreements were not as significant as the new hope that the conference raised among the churches that they might eventually be able to witness together to the "one faith" proclaimed in the Bible.

A second unitive force was expressed through the development of interdenominational youth work. The Young Men's Christian Association (YMCA), founded by George Williams in London in 1844, provided religious activities for youth from many denominations. By the late nineteenth century, the Student Volunteer Movement for Foreign Missions was founded in 1886, and finally the World Student Christian Federation, bringing together Student Christian Movements that had sprung up in countries all over the world between 1890 and 1910, was established in Sweden in 1895 by an American, John R. Mott (1865–1950), and Karl Fries of Sweden. Nondenominational youth organizations had a seriousness of purpose and a willingness to try new solutions, giving future religious leaders firsthand ecumenical experiences.

A third unitive force was the formal development of national and global Christian organizations of cooperation and federation. In 1905, four thousand delegates from thirty United States denominations came together for an Inter-church Conference on Federation, which by 1908 developed into the Federal Council of the Churches of Christ in America. Many Christians began to nurture a compelling vision that the one church spoken of in the Bible might be attainable in the United States. Their vision broadened still further between 1910 and 1938 when United States delegates attending various international conferences returned home full of great ecumenical enthusiasm.

During the early decades of the twentieth century, serious Christians all over the world came together to wrestle with questions of shared faith and order, and to pool resources to engage in common life and work. The resulting Faith and Order Movement and Life and Work Movement gave new opportunities for ecumenical experience. The Edinburgh Conference of 1910 was followed by two worldwide Conferences on Life and Work, where many delegates from the United States were inspired to seek unity: the Stockholm Conference in 1925 and the Utrecht Conference in 1938. During the same years, a Faith and Order Movement convened two World Conferences on Faith and Order: the Lausanne Conference in 1927 and a second Edinburgh Conference in 1937. All of these international conferences were important precursors of the World Council of Churches.

During the 1930s there was a growing desire to establish a truly international global ecumenical organization, but because of World War II, the World Council of Churches did not hold its first meeting until 1948, in Amsterdam. It was the first worldwide Christian organization, committed to calling Christian churches "to the goal of visible unity in one faith and one Eucharistic fellowship expressed in worship and in common life in Christ, and to advance toward that unity in order that the world may believe." Inspired by these words, Christian leaders made dramatic commitments to work and study together to determine how the goal of visible unity might be understood and achieved.

The Goal of Visible Unity

Christians all over the world were enthusiastic about the World Council of Churches' goal of "visible unity in one faith and in one Eucharistic fellowship expressed in worship and in common life in Christ," but some felt that it remained ambiguous, and none agreed on all the implications. They debated: "How much agreement is necessary in striving toward unity?" "How much diversity is possible and legitimate?" "Is the World Council of Churches proposing that all the churches become one church? Or, if not, how do separated churches still share in the church's unity?" Although forms of these questions had been asked by many Christian denominations for many years, they received fresh attention within the global ecumenical movement.

Some churches in the World Council felt that the sense of "spiritual unity" already existing in the churches was sufficient for mutual respect and for cooperation in mission and service. Others felt that they needed some agreement on the basic convictions of faith as a basis for the formation of a federation of churches. Still others argued consistently for organic or corporate unity, as suggested by the Pauline concept of the "body of Christ." Although these categories were sometimes used to judge various efforts at unity, authentic Christian unity took all forms. Christians wondered at times whether they should strive for one "universal world church" spanning all countries and cultures. And realistically, they also wondered whether such a universal church was even possible.

In 1961, the third assembly of the World Council of Churches, at New Delhi, formulated an important statement on unity. It affirmed that the unity of the church has been given in Jesus Christ once and for all. This foundation has not been lost, but it has been obscured by the divisions of church history. Therefore, unity is "God's gift and our task." The church is called continually to make its essential unity more visible—to manifest it in fellowship, witness, and service. After the assembly this led to an emphasis in the churches on the unity of "all in each place" in "fully committed fellowship."

Seven years later, in 1968, the World Council assembly in Uppsala continued the emphasis on "all in each place," but added to it the principle that all of the churches constituted the church universal. Finally, the 1975 World Council assembly in Nairobi offered yet another interpretive layer to the notion that all the churches in every place constituted the church universal by describing the fellowship of these churches as a "conciliar fellowship."

> The one church is to be envisioned as a conciliar fellowship of local churches which are themselves truly united. In this conciliar fellowship each local church possesses, in communion with the others, the fullness of catholicity, witnesses to the apostolic faith, and therefore recognizes the others as belonging to the same church of Christ

> and guided by the same Spirit. . . . Each church aims at maintaining sustained and sustaining relationships with her sister churches, expressed in conciliar gatherings whenever required for the fulfillment of their common calling. (World Council of Churches, *Breaking Barriers, Nairobi 1975,* ed. D. Paton [Grand Rapids: Eerdmans, 1976], 60)

By the late 1970s there were more than three hundred member churches in the World Council of Churches, and it was growing. How could such diverse constituencies be truly represented in conciliar fellowship? Furthermore, where could such a council take place? The ancient image of a council assumed that an assembly came together in a specific place with a specific form. Christians wondered: What place and format could possibly accommodate twentieth-century diversity?

Seeking an answer to this question, Herbert Froehlich, in an article in *The Ecumenical Review* in July, 1986, suggested that a council did not need to be seen as one representative assembly in a specific place, time, or form. Instead, it might be envisioned as an ongoing process, or several processes, developing and addressing new issues in new ways in new historical periods. Furthermore, the processes by which people and churches journeyed toward the hoped for universal council were part of the conciliar process. Every group, no matter how small, could participate, provided it engaged with one or more groups seeking to overcome barriers caused by politics, economics, culture, or religion.

The Ecumenical Heritage of the United Church of Christ

As the denominations that came together to make up the United Church of Christ moved toward union with one another, unity was at the core of their commitment and part of their growing self-understanding. Unity still stands at the center of the identity of the United Church of the Christ. Every individual, group, or antecedent denomination that became part of the United Church of Christ developed a more mature understanding of the Christian faith and the unity of the church over time. Persons and groups were formed by their experiences—by the books they read, sermons they heard, teachers and mentors who influenced them, ethnic and racial experiences, and the special denominational histories that now are part of the United Church of Christ. Ecumenical progress takes place when various persons and groups decide to enlarge their individual boundaries to form more inclusive common boundaries. In every case, individuals or groups open themselves to new positions and try to broaden their own boundaries to include new positions. The final boundary for the journey is the whole inhabited earth, the *oikoumene.*

In some periods of history, churches have been able to heal divisions through common devotion to one leader, such as a patriarch or pope. At other times, the focus has been upon the ways in which one baptism in the name of the triune God binds all Christians together. Protestants have been encouraged to recognize that "being catholic" is an essential mark of the church in all times and all places. And in certain instances individuals and groups have indicated a willingness to let go of, even "to die" to, particular denominational traditions in order to participate in the larger unity of all Christ's followers.

The journey toward unity in the United Church of Christ also transcends boundaries. Individuals and groups first seek to determine and understand the boundaries of their convictions, and then they move to broaden the boundaries and include perspectives and positions quite different from their own. At times, they may feel that they are unable, in good Christian conscience, to move to more inclusive positions, but they keep struggling toward the goal.

Again and again, in efforts to embrace Christian unity, they wrestle with recurring questions:

- Is church autonomy compromised by fellowship or connectionalism?
- Is the historic episcopate the only way to authorize ministry?
- Is baptism for infants or only for adults?
- Can baptism with water mean sprinkling or does it require immersion?
- When does the preservation of denominational identity prevent the unity of the church?

In 1957, when the Congregational, Christian, Evangelical, and Reformed traditions came together to form the United Church of Christ, none of these questions vanished. They continue to appear again and again in new forms, alongside emerging "ecumenical" questions about inclusiveness and accessibility. The journey toward unity stands at the center of the history of the United Church of Christ, and it is clear that the journey toward unity will continue to shape its future.

PART I

The Ecumenical Journey of the Congregational Churches

Although Congregational churches burst into the twentieth century convinced that the gospel they proclaimed compelled them to work toward the unity of the church, church union had not always seemed so pressing. In fact, early Congregationalists in colonial North America were much more concerned to keep their churches *separate* from others than to *unite* with them.

Congregationalism grew out of a protest movement against the Anglican Church in England, which produced sixteenth- and seventeenth-century English Puritanism (see vol. 2:26–32). Committed to simplifying the organization and worship of the church, Congregationalists were more Bible-centered and more experientially oriented than Anglicans. A small handful formally separated from the Church of England, but most tried to establish their own congregational polity, or church order, while remaining in communion with the "mother Church."

Early Congregationalists affirmed the Bible as the ultimate source and authority for Christian truth, while relying on the powers of human reason to interpret that authority. They found in the Bible a theology centered in the concept of a covenant of grace, initiated by God and granting forgiveness of sin and new life in Christ. Christian life was the grateful response of the people of God to this gift of the covenant, made in the context of the locally gathered congregation.

When Puritans migrated to colonial North America and began to establish churches, they wanted nothing in the arrangement of the local church to stand in the way of their free response to God's Word. Hence, they insisted that each congregation remain completely autonomous, unrestricted by any ecclesiastical authority that might interfere with that response (see vol. 3:1, 6, 7). Connections to other local congregations or other denominations were seen as a threat. For over two hundred years local Congregational churches were fiercely independent, holding no regular national meetings, but calling one occasionally when there was something specific to discuss. In those early years, working for union with other Christian groups would have seemed an intolerable threat to their cherished autonomy.

By the nineteenth century, however, Congregational principles had increasing importance. When people spoke of "autonomy," it was no longer used just in discussions of church polity. Instead, "autonomy" was linked with "individual rights" and "freedom" as central principles of political life in the United States. By the late nineteenth century, "autonomy" became almost synonymous with the new life force of democracy. Congregationalism gained new status as an ecclesiastical form of democracy (see vol. 4:80–81).

Second, as New England Congregationalists encountered the forces of expansionism and spread west, they began to feel the need for some organizational structures to help them establish new congregations and to strengthen cooperative relationships. In 1801, the Presbyterians and the Congregationalists signed a "Plan of Union" to guide their mission work in the West (see vol. 4:71). Ministerial associations were developed for the support of the clergy, and voluntary gatherings for the churches known as unions, conventions, and, occasionally, associations were established.

Third, by the early nineteenth century, religious revivals sweeping the country began to emphasize a convert's contribution to the society. Whereas the First Great Awakening had focused primarily on an individual's experience of the totally undeserved action of God in salvation, nineteenth-century revivals preached that Christians are sent into the world to better the conditions of those less fortunate. Nationwide voluntary organizations blossomed to aid Christian converts in their Christian responsibilities (see vol. 5:1–5).

Congregationalists also came to a new realization that the gospel charges them to work for the unity of the church for which Christ prayed. In fact, many Congregational leaders argued that Congregationalism was uniquely suited to the task of bringing about church union.

The first official statement articulating the way in which Congregationalism saw its ecumenical responsibility was produced in 1865 in Boston at the second national gathering of Congregational churches (see vol. 6:1; vol. 4:82). On behalf of the business committee, Alonzo Quint presented what came to be called the "Burial Hill Declaration." The ecumenical emphasis of this statement was unprecedented among the Congregationalists. It asserted "that division . . . is a sin against the unity of the body of Christ, and at once the shame and scandal of Christendom." Recognizing that the essential unity of the church was already given, and that they were "but one branch of Christ's people," those who signed the declaration committed themselves "to hold fellowship with all who acknowledge Christ and to act efficiently in the work of restoring unity to the divided Church."

The 1865 Boston meeting fostered a new spirit of unity and common mission among Congregationalists, leading to the organization of the National Council of the Congregational Churches in the United States, which held its first meeting in Oberlin, Ohio, in 1871. Alonzo Quint proclaimed the council "a great step . . . toward Christian union." However, the "Declaration on the Unity of the Church" (what came to be called the "Oberlin Declaration"), approved the day after a new denominational constitution was adopted, expressed the commitment of Congregationalists to Christian unity most eloquently (see vol. 6:2). The declaration was considered so significant that provision was made for it always to be printed in connection with the constitution. This was done for forty years, until a new constitution was adopted in 1913.

Early Efforts to Create a United Church

Although the Burial Hill Declaration (1865) and the Declaration on the Unity of the Church (1871) issued a clear mandate to the churches to "act efficiently to restore unity to the divided Church," years passed before Congregationalists were able to develop the experience and rationale for effective ecumenical work. In fact, at times their ecumenical commitments seemed in conflict with their sense of themselves as members of completely autonomous local churches. This ambivalence was evident during negotiations for church union begun in 1904 between the Congregationalists, the Christians (who soon dropped out), the Methodist Protestants, and the United Brethren. In spite of the enthusiasm of Congregational leaders for union, Washington Gladden, chair of the joint committee, reported early on in the negotiations that the issue of autonomy had become a weakness for the Congregationalists. Congregationalism, he noted, had failed to develop fully the principle of fellowship (or, connectionalism) in tandem with its commitment to autonomy (see vol. 6:3). In spite of Gladden's concern, a plan of union was proposed, and a Council of the United Churches scheduled to meet in Dayton, Ohio, in 1905. Demonstrating an extraordinary spirit of unanimity, this council of representatives from the Congregationalists, Methodists, and Church of the Brethren was able to agree on a "Declaration of Faith" and on a statement of the "Committee on Polity and Vested Interests" that seemed to balance issues of autonomy and connectionalism. Participants were thrilled that prospects for church union seemed almost within reach.

When the Council of the United Churches met a second time in Chicago in 1907, participants adopted, almost unanimously, an "Act of Union," which included the "Declaration of Faith" already endorsed in 1905 (see vol. 6:4). The plan was then sent to all three denominations with hopes that a vote to approve the union would take place at the next national meeting of each denomination.

The Methodist Protestants accepted the proposal unanimously, while the United Brethren approved it with slight alterations. The Congregationalists, however, were unable to act, trapped by the tension that Washington Gladden had lamented in 1904. Individuals and churches that had remained silent throughout the union negotiations suddenly became very uncomfortable. A few objections were made about the different "temperament" of the other denominations. But most objections raised concern about potential violations of autonomy—either the way in which the "Declaration of Faith" might violate individual freedom of belief, or the possibility that the "Act of Union" could violate the autonomy of a local congregation.

By June of 1907, William Hayes Ward, chair of the Committee on Comity, Federation and Unity (CCFU) of the National Council of the Congregational Churches published an articulate defense of the "Act of Union" and a detailed explanation of why neither autonomy nor the right of the local church to ordain its pastor were threatened. He also expressed his outrage over the dissent that had suddenly appeared after years of public discussion of the proposals. But it made no difference.

Although the 1907 National Council remained convinced that the proposed union should go forward, it admitted that "divergent opinions" had surfaced among Congregationalists. Congregational leaders sought to avoid an outright vote on the plan by inviting the other two denominations to join them in referring the "Act of Union" back to the General Council of the United Churches for "restudy" so that the section on the autonomy of the local churches and associations might be strengthened. In effect that killed the plan. Neither of the other two denominations was open to further conferences. Both turned immediately to plans for union with other denominations. In 1910, the CCFU tried to fan the embers of union by asking the National Council of Congregational Churches to send back to the other two denominations the "Act of Union" as previously formulated, but with an "Explanatory Statement" assuring the Congregationalists of their right to autonomy. Again, neither denomination responded.

Why did this effort fail? William Hayes Ward noted a weakness in the way Congregationalists did their ecumenical work. Most of the opponents of the union were totally uninformed because there were few denominational structures devoted to keeping people in the churches informed on and educated about issues related to church union. Nor were there any "ecumenical officers" whose specific job was to give time and strength to engineering church union. The ecumenical work of the Congregationalists simply was immature. Some Congregationalists might have been clear about what they wanted to do, but they were not so clear about the specific mundane steps necessary to do it.

Furthermore, a deeper theological issue underlay the failure. The principle of "local church autonomy" had been conceived by the Puritans as a way of protecting local churches from ecclesiastical authority interfering with their response to the Word of God. However, as the nineteenth century progressed, "autonomy" was no longer used simply in discussions of church polity. Autonomy had become one of the cornerstones of democracy. Some Congregationalists, who had come to identify themselves by the principle of absolute autonomy, failed to notice that autonomy was no longer used in its original way—to safeguard the freedom of a local church to respond to God's Word. Autonomy had become an absolute value, disconnected from its theological rationale. In fact, autonomy concerns ended up haunting the efforts of Congregational churches to realize their ecumenical vision for many years. In the 1940s and 1950s, when certain members and congregations within the Congregational Christian Churches decided that they could not come together with members and congregations in the Evangelical and Reformed Church to create the United Church of Christ, they resisted for the same reason: they feared that church union would destroy the absolute autonomy of the local congregation.

Coping with the Historic Episcopate

In 1888, the Lambeth Conference of the Anglican churches around the world adopted what came to be known as the "Lambeth Quadrilateral." Drafted by the Protestant Episcopal Church in the United States in 1886, it has stood ever since as the statement of the basic elements that the Anglican Church wishes to have honored in all its efforts for reunion with other churches (see vol. 6:5).

When the Quadrilateral was sent to churches in the United States, the Congregationalists began a series of union discussions with the Episcopalians. Their conversations continued intermittently for thirty-seven years, and much of the dialogue revolved around the "fourth essential for the restoration of unity" as outlined in the Quadrilateral—the historic episcopate.

Congregationalists initially maintained that the earliest episcopate in the church had to do with the governing of the church, not the authority of its priests; hence, it should not be understood as part of the essential substance of the faith. Furthermore, Congregationalists protested against the implied judgment that because they did not have bishops, they did not have a valid ministry and were not a valid church of Christ.

In 1895, Congregationalists stated their opposition to the historic episcopate more emphatically: "No union of denominations is possible on any basis which includes what is meant by the historic episcopate. The ordination of the various churches must be accepted as valid, and their bishops as regular." Moreover, most Congregationalists felt that they could never approve of any governing authority that would undermine the autonomy of the local congregation. On this basis preliminary negotiations between the two denominations were called off. At that time the National Council of the Congregational Churches in the United States proposed its own four-point proposal for union—sometimes called the "Congregational Quadrilateral" or "The New Jersey Platform" (see vol. 6:6).

Congregationalists reiterated their opposition to the historic episcopate repeatedly during the next decade. Nevertheless, when the Lambeth Conference of 1908 called for a world conference of "all Christian communions" to promote better mutual understanding, and the Protestant Episcopal Church in the United States called for a worldwide conference to consider questions touching faith and order, both the Episcopalians and the Congregationalists set up committees to consider further contacts (see vol. 6:7). Even a grassroots proposal for the union of an individual Congregational church and an individual Episcopal church was received as offering "some happier adjustment of . . . existing differences" (see vol. 6:8).

Nearly all remaining optimism for cooperation with the Episcopalians, however, was quashed in 1918 when the Protestant Episcopal House of Bishops rejected a proposal by Newman Smyth and Williston Walker, representatives of the Congregational "Commission on Unity," that suggested cooperation between the two denominations in ministering to soldiers and sailors in the armed forces. The bishops rejected the idea because the differences between the communions were not concerned simply with ordination, but with "a revelation of God's mind and will." The bishops further reminded the Congregational "memorialists" (referring to the way Congregationalists viewed the eucharist as a memorial meal rather than a sacred sacrifice) that since every Congregationalist church was independent with regard to doctrine, discipline, and worship, there was not even a central authoritative body with which the bishops could meet to discuss questions of intercommunion! They concluded that if the Protestant Episcopal Church were to declare itself willing to ordain or commission a chaplain "from whatever church," it would be tantamount to denying that "*any* truth—even the Trinity or the Incarnation—was important or necessary!" Relations between the two churches fell to a new low.

Still not ready to give up, a few members of the Protestant Episcopal Church and the Congregational churches, acting individually, advanced another proposal. They proposed that the Protestant Episcopal Church adopt a concordat permitting its bishops to give Episcopal ordination to non-Episcopal ministers. The concordat was to state that any Congregational or otherwise non-Episcopally-ordained minister could receive Episcopal ordination at the hands of the bishop of the diocese in which he or she lived under certain specified conditions. The minister thus reordained would be able to officiate in any diocese or missionary district of the Episcopal Church when licensed by its ecclesiastic authority. Eventually, two conferences were held between the relevant Episcopal and Congregational committees concerned with church union. An impressive position paper containing various proposals for reunion was written by Congregationalists Newman Smyth and Williston Walker (see vol. 6:9). Finally in 1923 a proposal was approved by the General Convention of the Protestant Episcopal Church that gave constitutional provision for reordaining non-Episcopal ministers with an Episcopal ordination.

The Congregationalists were concerned about how much authority the concordat would have over the actions of individual bishops. Their concern increased when, in a well-publicized test case, the highly regarded Professor Roland Bainton of Yale Divinity School was refused ordination by the Episcopal bishop of Connecticut. With that turn of events, many Congregationalists came to the sober realization that the concordat they had greeted with such enthusiasm was not, in the end, of much use to them. The Episcopal General Convention was even less positive, refusing to reappoint a commission for further discussion with the Congregationalists.

When the National Council of the Congregational Churches met in Springfield, Massachusetts in 1923, great discussion about the concordat ensued. William E. Barton, who earlier had been on the committee negotiating with the Episcopalians, offered a strong "Declaration on Unity" based upon traditional Congregational principles (see vol. 6:10). It affirmed the "valid, apostolic, prophetic and priestly" ministry of the Congregational churches in direct response to the Episcopal insistence on the historic episcopate. It also brought to a conclusion thirty-seven years of effort on the part of the Congregationalists to find a basis for union with the Episcopalians.

The Global Ecumenical Influence

Few Congregationalists were ever aware of how many negotiations concerning union were carried out by their leaders between 1886 and 1931. Dozens of papers were written explaining church union to Congregationalists and outlining the nature of Congregationalism for other Christians. Strong leaders like Alonzo H. Quint, William Buddington, William Hayes Ward, Washington Gladden, Newman Smyth, Williston Walker, William E. Barton, Charles E. Burton, Nehemiah Boynton, and Frank K. Sanders nurtured the Congregational commitment to church union. In spite of the fact that they had no concrete successes for almost fifty years, they kept the ecumenical spirit alive.

Ecumenical advances in the wider church further helped to broaden the ecumenical vision of the Congregationalists. For example, *The Congregationalist and Christian World* (*C&CW*) gave extensive coverage to the participation of United States Congregationalists in the International Congregational Council (ICC), founded in 1891. Through the ICC, Congregationalists gained important experiences working with people from other countries.

In 1908, Congregationalists applauded the merger of churches related to Presbyterian and Congregational missions in South India, creating the South India United Church (see vol. 6:11). As a "Pioneer Interdenominational Union," it was an important step toward the goal of an indigenous, self-governing, and self-propagating Indian church. Furthermore, it kept Congregational dreams of church union in the United States alive.

More than participation in the International Congregational Council or the founding of the South India United Church, however, it was the participation of Congregational leaders in the World Missionary Conference held in Edinburgh in 1910 that really showed them the meaning of the *oikoumene*. Those who went reported, "Men who spoke in various tongues, who held a wide variety of beliefs and who had been trained in different customs of worship assembled from every part of the world . . . these strangers who were meeting as brethren *saw one another* . . . [they] *heard one another*. . . . The almost lost art of communion may be recovered by the assemblies where saints see and hear one another praising God" (see vol. 6:12).

Congregationalists were involved in numerous ecumenical ventures. In

1908, they played a central role in the founding meeting of the Federal Council of the Churches of Christ in America. They welcomed the Federal Council as a useful advisory organization for denominational ministries, "the mouthpiece of the Churches on all matters of social, religious and political interest."

In 1920, Congregationalists took a bigger step toward organic union by endorsing a "Plan of Union" proposing the "United Churches of Christ in America," which had been adopted by the Interchurch Council on Organic Union in February of that year. Unfortunately, this initiative was not successful anywhere because most of the other participating national organizations declined or deferred involvement (see vol. 6:13).

Ecumenical accomplishments in other countries did not go unnoticed. In 1925, when the United Church of Canada came into being through an amalgamation of four groups of Canadian churches—the Congregationalists, the Presbyterians, the Methodists, and a number of churches that had already participated in local unions (so-called Local Union churches)—Congregationalists in the United States celebrated. It was said that forty distinct Christian bodies were finally made one through nineteen distinct acts of Church union. Congregationalists in the United States believed that Canada had blazed a trail that they hoped one day to travel (see vol. 6:14).

Finally, the international Lausanne Conference on Faith and Order in 1927 made an extraordinary impression on Congregationalists in the United States. More than eighteen different articles about Lausanne were published in *The Congregationalist*—more coverage than any other ecumenical event had received in years. There were scholarly articles by professors, followed by candid impressions from local pastors, alongside pronouncements by the seven women delegates on the place of women in the church (see vol. 6:15). The Congregationalists felt that they were taking their place on the world ecumenical stage.

Learning from New Voices

During the same period, Congregationalists learned a great deal from their relationships with various foreign-language groups flooding into North America, some of which were formally connected with Congregationalism—Scandinavians, Japanese, Armenians, and Germans. Early in the twentieth century, the National Council of the Congregational Churches established a Commission on Cooperation with Foreign Speaking Churches to formalize closer ties with these churches. The relationship was difficult. Most long-standing Congregationalists did not speak any foreign language, and they believed that foreign newcomers simply should learn English and blend into the melting pot. New immigrants, however, resisted. They wanted to preserve links to their homelands, their languages, their cultures, and their religious practices. Two groups of German-speaking Congregationalists stretched the hospitality and enriched the ecumenical understanding of all Congregationalists.

The first group was the Evangelical Protestants (see vol. 6:16). They did not come to America as part of one particular religious group, but brought with them instead a particular religious attitude—one that valued freedom of thought, an open mind, and respect for those whose beliefs were different.

In the eighteenth century, members of these churches, and other Germans with similar liberal attitudes, immigrated to the United States and founded the first German Evangelical Protestant church in Pittsburgh in 1782. Eventually, other similarly independent and tolerant German churches grew up in this area, each church valuing its own autonomy as an expression of its respect for diversity of opinion and freedom from external control. And, like the early Congregationalists, they were hesitant to band together in groups or synods.

Harold W. Barkhau, a pastor of one of their churches, also identified this spirit with the tolerant and irenic position of the Church of the Prussian Union, founded in 1817 by the king of Prussia to bring Lutheran and Reformed Churches in his area together. Some of these churches were called Evangelical Lutheran, others Evangelical Reformed, some simply Evangelical. They were known particularly for their tolerant attitude and liberal position, and in some sections of Germany they were called Evangelical Protestant churches.

By 1912, most Evangelical Protestant churches had become English-speaking, and those that had not affiliated with another denomination created a union with one another. Recognizing that their small size limited their ability to participate in the wider mission work of the church, they began looking to join a larger denomination that valued local church autonomy and personal freedom of thought. In 1922, they entered into union negotiations with the Congregationalists, and in 1925, the Evangelical Protestant Church of North America became part of the National Council of the Congregational Churches in the United States.

A second group of German-speaking Congregationalists enriched the ecumenical awareness of Congregational Churches—the Germans from Russia (see vol. 6.17). Nearly all of these Congregationalists were from families that had moved to Russia in the late seventeenth and early eighteenth century following special inducements from the Russian government. While they were in Russia, they had lived in tight German-speaking communities on the shores of the Volga River and the Black Sea. In Russia they had resisted pressures to assimilate with the Russian people, maintaining a hard and simple farming life, and devoting themselves to spiritual revivals, prayer meetings, Bible studies, and meetings of praise, prayer, and song within a pietistic lay organization called the Brotherhood. A hundred years later, when the Russian czar decided to rescind their privileges and "Russianize" them, more than three hundred thousand German-Russian immigrants came to the western frontiers of North America.

Ironically, these Germans from Russia were befriended by the Congregationalists rather than by one of the many German church groups on the frontier. They found that Congregational polity granted them the freedom to continue the Brotherhood's practices of holding revivals, prayer meetings, and worshiping in the German language. They also continued to live in the same kind of tightly knit, pietistic, and hardworking German-speaking communities in which they had lived in Russia, becoming remarkably stable and self-sufficient. By 1925, German Congregationalists from Russia had their own college, seminary, and publishing house, and they worshiped in churches led by well-trained German-Russian-American ministers. George Eisenach, a professor at their Yankton Seminary in South Dakota, wrote many articles interpreting this community to other Congregationalists.

Predictably, as second- and third-generation German Congregationalists raised their children in the United States, changes in language and culture began to erode the uniqueness of their church life. Nevertheless, many strong Congregational churches in the Midwest look back proudly to their roots in nineteenth-century German-speaking Russian immigrant communities.

Through relationships with Germans, Scandinavians, Armenians, and Asians, Congregationalists came to understand that the issues and dynamics of social and cultural identity and indigenization were much more complex than they had previously thought. They learned to value contacts with such groups for the richness that their differences contributed to Congregationalism. They found strength as they became a more multicultural church.

The Congregational-Christian Union

Congregationalists and the Christians were first linked as prospective union partners in 1894, when the Christian Convention issued the "Haverhill Resolution" proposing a cooperative union between Christians and Congregationalists "and any other denominations seeking union" (see vol. 6:36); and again in 1897, when commissions concerned with Christian unity in both denominations agreed on a "Craigville Proposal for Union between Congregationalists and Christians," which, unfortunately, was dropped the next year by the Christians (see vol. 6:18).

Twenty-five years later, in 1923, when union talks were reopened between the two denominations, the Congregationalists and the Christians were much more experienced. Each denomination had learned a great deal from its own ecumenical history. Each knew how to educate and inform local church members, answer questions, and publish information about leaders and articles on each other's history and beliefs (see vol. 6:19). Furthermore, the Congregationalists made some good-faith actions to show their commitment to church union. In 1927, as conversations toward union progressed, they made two concessions to further the possibility of union with the Christians. First, they decided unilaterally to drop references to the Kansas City Statement in the negotiations lest the Christians, who were always very protective of religious liberty, worry that it might impose some form of creedal authority. Second, they declared their willingness to forgo using the name "Congregational" and return to the name "Churches of Christ" if that would further negotiations.

In the end, the union was consummated without many problems. In 1931, the National Council of the Congregational Churches and the General Convention of the Christian Church met in Seattle and accepted a new constitution creating the General Council of the Congregational and Christian Churches. An editorial in the new *Congregationalist and Herald of Gospel Liberty* expressed the exhilaration and the hopes that everyone had for the new denomination. "The Seattle Council has been a great Council. It has passed into history, but the history of it is not past. It will go on in the actions that it inspires, in the newer and larger meanings of fellowship and association, in the vital thrust of Christian ideals into the lives and environments of a million Congregationalists and Christians."

Congregationalists, who three hundred years earlier had founded colonial congregations in each New England town, naming them the "First Church of Christ in . . . ," were comfortable with their new partners from the Christian Convention, who had always insisted that churches should put away denominational bickering and simply call themselves "Christians" (see vol. 6:20).

From Protecting Autonomy to Seeking Church Union

1. An Ecumenical Vision:
"The Burial Hill Declaration"

(1865)

During the seventeenth and eighteenth centuries, the Congregational churches in colonial North America formed quite a homogeneous entity, held together by their common origin in England, their common home and culture in New England, and their common theological heritage as heirs of John Calvin. By the nineteenth century, Congregationalism confronted several challenges that changed it greatly. Geographically, Congregationalism had expanded beyond New England to include new churches and ministries to people on the expanding western frontier. By the end of the Civil War, Congregationalists saw additional responsibilities and opportunities in the South. Theologically, the Unitarian controversy in the East and contrasting religious situations in the West and South brought a new diversity to Congregational theology. Moreover, formal disestablishment (the end of state financial support for Congregational churches in New England) had created a new and practical need for Congregationalists to compete with other denominations for members and congregations. Congregationalists began to feel a new urgency to define and identify their polity and theology more precisely.

A second national gathering of representatives from Congregational churches was called in 1865 (the first was held in Albany, New York, in 1852) in Boston, Massachusetts, to address issues of polity and faith. A preparatory committee had prepared a comprehensive statement of

---

Source: "Declaration of Faith" ["The Burial Hill Declaration"], in *A Manual of the Principles, Doctrines and Usages of Congregational Churches,* comp. J. E. Roy (Chicago: Church, Goodman and Donnelly, 1869), 17–19.

church polity modeled after the 1648 Cambridge Platform of Church Discipline (see vol. 3:6). In 1865, however, differences in perspective between eastern leaders, who stressed the church's autonomy, and western leaders, who were appreciative of connectional structures and cooperative agencies, led the council to prepare a brief substitute statement stressing the independence and the communion of the churches while rejecting any hierarchical conception of the structure of ministry.

A pre-council committee had also prepared a broad "Declaration of Faith" reaffirming the allegiances of the Cambridge Platform and the Savoy and Westminster Confessions (see vol. 2:32). The council sent this declaration for consideration to a committee of its own, which in turn prepared a more elaborate statement including a statement of the churches' common acceptance of Calvinism. A heated debate developed over whether it was correct to describe the prevailing theology within Congregationalism in 1865 as Calvinist. The day's meeting adjourned without a vote on the declaration.

The next day, the whole council took a trip to Plymouth, Massachusetts, for a meeting at Burial Hill commemorating the many Pilgrims buried there. Overnight, Alonzo H. Quint, a noted Massachusetts pastor, chair of the business committee, and future moderator of the National Council of the Congregational Churches, prepared a substitute declaration of faith, writing the last lines on the train to Plymouth using his tall hat as a writing table.

This declaration, known as the "Burial Hill Declaration," made broad affirmation of the faith of the Puritans as expressed in earlier Calvinist confessions (without using the word "Calvinist"). In addition, the declaration affirmed the unity of the church as already given. It decried divisions among churches as "a sin against the unity of the body of Christ, and at once the shame and scandal of Christendom." Finally, it committed the Congregationalists to extending "to all believers the hand of Christian fellowship," and to fulfilling their responsibility "to act efficiently in the work of restoring unity to the divided Church." (This document is found also in vol. 4:82.)

Standing by the Rock where the Pilgrims set foot upon these shores, upon the spot where they worshiped God, and among the graves of the early generations, we, Elders and Messengers of the Congregational Churches of the United States in National Council assembled—like them acknowledging no rule of faith but the Word of God—do now declare our adherence to the faith and order of the Apostolic and Primitive Churches, held by our fathers, and substantially embodied in the confessions and platforms which our Synods of 1648 and 1680 set forth or re-affirmed. We declare that the experience of the nearly two and a half centuries which have elapsed since the memorable day when our sires founded here a Christian commonwealth, with all the development of new forms of error since their times, has only deepened our confidence in the faith and polity of those fathers. We bless God for the inheritance of those doctrines. We invoke the help of the Divine Redeemer, that, through the presence of the promised Comforter, he will enable us to transmit them in purity to our children.

In the times that are before us as a nation, times at once of duty and of danger, we rest all our hope in the Gospel of the Son of God. It was the grand peculiarity of our Puritan fathers, that they held this Gospel, not merely as the ground of their personal salvation, but as declaring the worth of man by the incarnation and sacrifice of the Son of God; and, therefore, applied its principles to elevate society, to regulate education, to civilize humanity, to purify law, to reform the Church and the State, to assert and defend liberty; in short, to mold and redeem by its all-transforming energy, every thing that belongs to man in his individual and social relations.

It was the faith of our fathers that gave us this free land in which we dwell. It is by this faith only that we can transmit to our children a free and happy, because a Christian commonwealth.

We hold it to be a distinctive excellence of our Congregational system, that it exalts that which is more, above that which is less important, and by the simplicity of its organization facilitates, in communities where the population is limited, the union of all true believers in one Christian Church; and that the division of such communities into several weak and jealous societies, holding the same common faith, is a sin against the unity of the body of Christ, and at once the shame and scandal of Christendom.

We rejoice that, through the influence of our free system of Apostolic order, we can hold fellowship with all who acknowledge Christ, and act efficiently in the work of restoring unity to the divided Church, and of bringing back harmony and peace among all "who love our Lord Jesus Christ in sincerity."

Thus recognizing the unity of the Church of Christ in all the world, and knowing that we are but one branch of Christ's people, while adhering to our peculiar faith and order, we extend to all believers the hand of Christian fellowship upon the basis of those great fundamental truths in which all Christians should agree. With them we confess our faith in God; in Jesus Christ, the incarnate Word, who is exalted to be our Redeemer and King; and in the Holy Comforter, who is present in the Church to regenerate and sanctify the soul.

With the whole Church we confess the common sinfulness and ruin of our race, and acknowledge that it is only through the work accomplished by the life and expiatory death of Christ, that believers in him are justified before God, receive the remission of sins, and through the presence and grace of the Holy Comforter are delivered from the power of sin and perfected in holiness.

We believe also in an organized and visible Church, in the ministry of the Word, in the sacraments of Baptism and the Lord's Supper, in the resurrection of the body, and in the final judgment, the issues of which are eternal life and everlasting punishment.

We receive these truths on the testimony of God, given through Prophets and Apostles, and in the life, the miracles, the death, the resurrection, of his Son, our Divine Redeemer,—a testimony preserved for the Church in the Scriptures of the Old and New Testaments, which were composed by holy men as they were moved by the Holy Ghost.

Affirming now our belief that those who thus hold "One Faith, one Lord, one Baptism," together constitute the one Catholic Church, the several households of which, though called by different names, are the one body of Christ; and that these members of his body are sacredly bound to keep "The unity of the Spirit in the bond of peace," we declare that we will co-operate with all who hold these truths. With these we will carry the Gospel into every part of the land, and with them we will go into all the world, and "Preach the Gospel to every creature." May He to whom "All power is given in heaven and earth" fulfil the promise which is all our hope: "Lo, I am with you alway, even to the end of the world." To Him be praise in the Church forever. Amen.

2. Bound Together in Unity: *"The Oberlin Declaration on the Unity of the Church"*

(1871)

The successful nationwide meetings of clergy and lay delegates from established Congregational churches in Albany in 1852 and Boston in 1865 helped the Congregationalists to appreciate the benefits of working together on their common tasks and to gain a sense of Congregational identity and purpose. Since the beginning of Congregationalism, regional and national gatherings of representatives from the churches had been ad hoc; that is, no plans were made for future meetings, and no permanent nationwide organization was established. Thus, when enthusiasm gathered in the wake of these meetings for creating a permanent and regularly occurring national gathering, it was a sign of a growing denominational sense among Congregationalists.

As 1870 approached—the 250th anniversary of the landing of the Pilgrims in Plymouth, Massachusetts—the Congregational Church of the Pilgrimage in Plymouth, Massachusetts, invited all the churches to send delegates "to consider the appropriateness of particular action in celebrating this fifth jubilee." The time was ripe to make a national structure a reality.

Consequently one of the first "particular actions" of those who gathered in Plymouth was to call upon the state associations of the Congregational

---

Source: "Declaration on the Unity of the Church" ["The Oberlin Declaration"], in *Minutes of the National Council of the Congregational Churches of the United States of America, First Session, Oberlin, Ohio, November 15–21, 1871* (Boston: Congregational Publishing Society, 1871), 31–32.

churches to work toward the establishment of a permanent national body. The churches set about the task quickly, and a call was issued for churches to send representatives to a founding meeting in November 1871 in Oberlin, Ohio. The meeting resulted in the formation of the National Council of the Congregational Churches of the United States.

The constitution established by the council took care to respect the polity and theology of historic Congregationalism, "indicating the direct responsibility of each congregation to the Lord Jesus Christ, the One Head of the church universal and of all particular churches," and ensuring the consequent right and responsibility of government residing in the local churches. The christological center of every Congregational church required the autonomy of the local church so that it could affirm the unity of the churches already given to all as part of "Christ's catholic church." The National Council was established to foster the "substantial unity" of the churches in doctrine, polity, and work, and to facilitate their working together to develop resources, pursue evangelism, and conduct their relations "to all parts of the kingdom of Christ."

This mandate for church union was reinforced on the day after the constitution was completed, when the council heard a paper on "The Unity of the Church" presented by Rev. Dr. William I. Buddington. Affirming the unity of the church of God already given, it committed the Congregational churches to promoting a more visible unity in the future by participating in the "growing unity of counsel and of effort among the followers of Christ." The concluding paragraph of the paper seemed to express the burgeoning ecumenical sentiments of the council most succinctly, for it was quoted for many years by Congregational leaders as the central affirmation of their ecumenical mandate. In fact, the National Council made provision that the entire paper, entitled "Declaration on the Unity of the Church," always be presented in proximity to the constitution. As a consequence, until the next constitution was written forty-two years later, this ecumenical "Oberlin Declaration" was regarded as "part of the basis of the body."

The members of the National Council, representing the Congregational churches of the United States, avail themselves of this opportunity to renew their previous declarations of faith in the unity of the church of God.

While affirming the liberty of our churches, as taught in the New Testament, and inherited by us from our fathers, and from martyrs and confessors of foregoing ages, we adhere to this liberty all the more as affording the ground and hope of a more visible unity in time to come. We desire and purpose to cooperate with all the churches of our Lord Jesus Christ.

In the expression of the same catholic sentiments solemnly avowed by the Council of 1865, on the Burial Hill at Plymouth, we wish, at this new epoch of our history, to remove, so far as in us lies, all causes of suspicion and alienation, and to promote the growing unity of counsel and of effort among the followers of Christ. To us, as to our brethren, "There is one body and one spirit, even as we are called in one hope of our calling."

As little as did our fathers in their day, do we in ours, make a pretension to be the only churches of Christ. We find ourselves consulting and acting together under the distinctive name of Congregationalists, because, in the present condition of our common Christianity, we have felt ourselves called to ascertain and do our own appropriate part of the work of Christ's church among men.

We especially desire, in prosecuting the common work of evangelizing our own land and the world, to observe the common and sacred law, that in the wide field of the world's evangelization, we do our work in friendly cooperation with all who love and serve our common Lord.

We believe in "the holy catholic church." It is our prayer and endeavor, that the unity of the church may be more and more apparent, and that the prayer of our Lord for his disciples may be speedily and completely answered, and all be one; that by consequence of this Christian unity in love, the world may believe in Christ as sent of the Father to save the world.

Early Efforts to Create a United Church

3. Applied Christianity:
"A Proposal for Church Union"

(1904)

Washington Gladden

Washington Gladden (1836–1918) was one of the last survivors of that intrepid group of Congregational ministers who, in the last two decades of the nineteenth century, sought to turn the light of the enlarging knowledge of science and history upon the faith to illuminate what was most essential and pressing for the next generation. At the cost of ridicule, hostility, and sometimes loss of position, he and his associates, called "the rampageous preachers," stood for the broadening and unification of Christianity and for its vigorous application to social, industrial, and international problems.

These preachers found in the Bible a liberal, christocentric theology that came to be called "the New Theology." From it they developed a notion of the immanence of God in the world that understood divine creation to be not simply a past event but an ongoing process in which the divine was at work both in natural and in human life and history. Providing a compelling basis for the solidarity of all humanity, it allowed them to be open to the insights of the new biblical scholarship of the time, and at the same time freed them to build what they saw as a more modern faith that issued from the harmonizing of the new evolutionary science and religion. Thus, Gladden was one of the first to introduce the laity of the church to the insights of biblical "higher criticism" in his volume Who Wrote the Bible? A Book for the People. *He also developed a Christian interpretation of Darwinian evolution through which he preached a*

Source: Washington Gladden, "A Proposal for Church Union," *The Congregationalist and Christian World,* 11 June 1904, 819–20.

basically optimistic view of human nature and an understanding of the forces of the natural world as evidence of the very presence of God.

It was the connection Gladden made between theology and action in society, on the one hand, and work for the union of the churches, on the other, that made him an ecumenical leader. He called this connection "Applied Christianity." At its core was the notion that a theology centered on Christ sent all Christians into society to bring the realm of God on earth. He pressed this agenda in an address to the 1889 National Council on "Christian Socialism," and continued it as moderator of the National Council of Congregational Churches in 1907, laying the foundation for the formation of a national Council for Social Action some thirty years later. Gladden's "Applied Christianity" also drove him to work within the church to realize that unity of Christ's followers. He actively participated in the group preparing the earliest proposal for union between the Congregationalists and Christians, the Craigville Proposal of 1897 (see vol. 6:18), and was chair of the joint committee that prepared the (ultimately unsuccessful) Act of Union between the Congregationalists, Methodist Protestants, and United Brethren in 1904. Gladden was one of the earliest Congregational leaders to recognize that the "balance" between autonomy and fellowship in Congregational self-understanding had become out of balance in the direction of autonomy, and he foresaw that this imbalance, if not corrected, would become a problem in the future.

[At their recent meeting in Washington. D.C., Methodist Protestants indorsed the plan for union with Congregationalists and United Brethren. One of the most notable of the addresses on the subject before the conference was that of Dr. Washington Gladden, chairman of the joint committee which proposed the plan, portions of which are printed herewith. —EDITORS.]

People who are in the habit of attending church in these days know that the old lines of division between the various evangelical churches are practically obliterated; you can not tell, one time in twenty, from the preaching to which you are listening, whether you are in a Presbyterian church, or a Methodist church, or a Baptist church; the controversies with which the air was filled when some of you were boys no longer enlist the interest of earnest Christians.

It is possible that if these three Christian bodies should come together in one there would be found in that larger fellowship some greater variety of opinion than now exists in any one of them; but I am persuaded that with this greater variety there would also appear a deeper and stronger unity. We should be constrained to seek for points of agreement, to emphasize the things wherein we are at one, and our unimportant differences would only serve to throw into a brighter light our essential unity.

Something More Than Federation Contemplated

One definite question is submitted to you, as to the other two national bodies—the question whether you are ready to unite with the others in calling together a General Council, to which shall be committed the task of working out the problem of unity. The business of that council would be to consider and formulate plans by which the unity toward which we are reaching out could be progressively realized. It would signify something more than federation, for federation, as I understand it, contemplates the maintenance intact of all the parts and organs of each of the denominations taking part in it. None of them makes any sacrifices of its own life, they only try to find some outside work in which they can co-operate. This General Council proposes to do much more than this. It proposes to find ways in which the three denominations shall immediately become one in certain important parts of the work which they are now carrying forward.

A Common Work to Do

It will address itself first, perhaps, to the question whether much of our missionary work cannot be consolidated with good results. Take the entire foreign missionary work. Why should it not be carried on by one missionary organization, in the direction of which all these denominations should be represented? Could we not by uniting our forces in this great field of the world secure some important economies, increase the missionary enthusiasm of all our churches, and push the work with far more efficiency? Might not the General Council formulate plans by which there should be a merger of the three foreign missionary organizations in one?

This would be something more than federation, it would be a step and a long step in the direction of organic union. Take also the great work whose urgency is increasing—the work for the neglected races on this continent, the Negroes, the Indians, the Chinese. It is a work of education and of evangelization; a work which appeals to every man who loves his country and his kind. There never was a time, I think, when the Negro needed the friendship of Christian people so much as he needs it now. For the great responsibilities of freedom he was utterly unfit, and his possession of it has proved, in a vast number of cases, an injury more than a benefit to him. He must not be re-enslaved, he must be fitted for freedom and citizenship. There are many good men and women in the South who see this and will do what they can; but it is a task too heavy for them, it demands the united wisdom and devotion of all who love humanity. Each of these denominations is doing something, I suppose, in this great field; could we not wisely unite our efforts? Would there not be strength in union here? Might not the General Council of the united churches work out a plan by which the people of these three Christian bodies could join their forces for the wise prosecution of an enterprise which bears such a vital relation to the welfare of the nation?

I doubt not also that men of good will, consulting together in this council, could find ways by which in our Sunday school work and our educational work and our publishing work we could consolidate and co-ordinate some, if not all our agencies, with great gain to all the denominations. And if in such work as this we were able to join, we should come to feel that we were indeed one. It would be something more than a federation; it would be taking on continually more and more of the character of an organic union. We should be contributing to a common treasury; we should be working side by side in many fields; in all our largest interests and endeavors we should have a common responsibility and a common pride and a common enthusiasm.

Now it would be the business of this General Council to bring about such consolidations as these in the activities of the three denominations. It would have no power over any of them; its functions would be only advisory; its recommendations would have to come back to the three bodies for approval and adoption. It would need to proceed cautiously and tentatively; no step ought to be taken without full deliberation and the practically unanimous consent of all the three bodies.

Our Administrative Systems Should Not Become Fetiches

There was once much argument to show that the administrative machinery employed in the several denominations was of apostolic origin, but not much emphasis is put on these arguments nowadays; it is pretty clear that the apostles employed very little machinery, and had no thought of establishing any fixed system of polity; they supposed, as evidently their Master intended, that methods of work, in every age, could be adapted to the conditions and needs of the age. That is what has happened. Different groups of workers, in successive periods, have shaped their administrative machinery to suit their own purposes. There is nothing sacrosanct about any of these methods. Yet something like this seems to be in the minds of a good many of us. I find Congregationalists, and I dare say that you find Methodist Protestants who have a kind of feeling that any change in forms, of church government would be something like apostasy. It is important that we recognize the fact that this is an exaggerated feeling. The worship of the idols of the tribe, as Bacon has told us, is a common form of idolatry, against which we need to be warned. These systems of polity are the work of our own hands, and we must not too highly exalt them. It is not at all improbable that those portions of them which we most strenuously assert and most passionately cling to, represent our weaknesses. That is almost the uniform fact with individuals. If you find a man taking especial pride in any trait of his character, pluming himself on the possession of any quality, you almost always find that that is the particular thing from which he needs to pray to be delivered. I am inclined to believe that this is true of religious sects.

Where Congregationalists Are Weak

Speaking as a Congregationalist, I feet quite sure that it is true of my own people. The one, thing of which we have boasted is our independency. It has become our weakness. The other principle of fellowship which ought to have been co-coordinated with it has not been normally developed. What is true of Methodist Protestants I do not know, but I dare say that some of you may be aware of the existence of similar conditions. The truth is that any change which can be made in our administrative methods by which our work can be better done ought to be made with no hesitation.

The practical question before us in working out the problem of organic unity is what measure of autonomy shall be conceded to the local church. The Congregationalists exalt the principle of autonomy; they even exaggerate it, as I have admitted; or, at any rate, they have put so much more emphasis upon it than upon their other cardinal principle of fellowship that the result has been detrimental to the organization. Yet the principle of autonomy seems to be gaining ground in all the denominations. The local church in all the stronger governments is taking more and more control of its own affairs. The Methodist Episcopal local churches are asserting every year a larger degree of self-government; they practically choose their own ministers and keep them as long as they please; the supervision of the presiding elder, in all their strong churches, is more a matter of form than of power. I think that the same thing is true of the United Brethren. In your own body the amount of local self-government seems to vary; larger liberty is allowed to the local church in some parts of the country than in others.

Autonomy an Essential

Now, I think it would be only fair to say that in the working out of this problem of organic unity it will probably be found that this principle of the autonomy of the local church will have to be pretty definitely recognized. I do not believe that Congregationalists would surrender the substance of their own most distinctive principle, and I am inclined to think that a great reason why this movement for unity finds friends in the United Brethren and Methodist Protestant churches is that there are a great many among them who desire that their local churches shall have a larger measure of autonomy.

Supervision Also Desirable

And yet there are many among us who feel that in the interest of the weaker churches and in the planting of new churches and in the promotion of the larger co-operations to which we ought to be giving our strength, some more systematic supervision is necessary. There is much that the stronger among us could do and want to do for the weaker which we fail to do because of this lack of some co-ordinating agencies. And it seems to me that we might well use in some modified form some of the methods by which the Methodist Protestant and the United Brethren keep their churches supplied and their ministers at work. Perhaps they can teach us how to make more effective our cardinal principal of the fellowship of the churches. At any rate some of us are ready to join with you in calling this General Council and in making through it a most earnest attempt to see whether adjustments can not be made by which these three bodies of Christians can become one body.

The Cow and the Moonshine

One of my Methodist brethren in Columbus once told me of a little experience of his, as a farmer's boy, in getting a cow into her stall. It was a moonlight evening, and when the stable door was opened and the cow had got her head inside she saw directly across the passage way that led to her stall what looked to her perhaps like a bar of solid silver. It was a beam of moonlight, revealed by the floating dust which lay across the stable, the light coming in through an aperture in the wall. The cow stopped short before this barrier. Doubtless it appeared to her insurmountable. She may even have been impressed in her bovine way with the notion that it was a barrier placed in her path by heaven itself, and that it would be sacrilege to break it down or jump over it. But constrained thereto by a little vigorous prodding from the boy who was driving her she at length made a desperate lunge and found her way to her stall and was soon rejoicing in her fodder. My friend said that the surprise of that cow in her discovery that a barrier so formidable could be overcome so easily was something remarkable.

I suspect, my friends, that if there be only among us a real desire for union, it will turn out that many of the difficulties in our path are mainly moonshine.

4. Clarifying Convictions:

"Act of Union" and "Explanatory Statement"

(1907 and 1910)

William Hayes Ward et al.

The 1865 Burial Hill Declaration and the 1871 Declaration on the Unity of the Church appended to the constitution expressed eloquently the goal of the new National Council of the Congregational Churches that it should "act efficiently in the work of restoring unity to the divided Church." Nevertheless, years would pass before the Congregationalists developed the negotiating experience and knowledge needed effectively to inform and enlist their constituency in ecumenical causes. They were also slow in gaining an understanding of how their own denominational identity was supported by their ecumenical calling.

As in many things, experience was the best teacher. Significant learning came through almost twenty-one years of proposals for union with the Methodist Protestants—including a seven-year-long Tri-Union series of discussions between the Congregationalists, the Methodist Protestants, and the United Brethren.

The National Council of the Congregational Churches first appointed a committee to correspond with the Methodist Protestant Church in 1889, though it was not until 1903 that meetings were held with the Methodist Protestants and the United Brethren (the Christians also participated in one meeting) to discuss the difficulties and advantages of union.

Source: William Hayes Ward et al., "Act of Union" (1907) and "Explanatory Statement" (1910), in "Report of the Committee on Comity, Federation, and Unity," in *Minutes of the National Council the of Congregational Churches of the United States, Fourteenth Triennial Session, Boston, Mass., October 10–20, 1910* (Boston: Office of Secretary of National Council, 1910), 259–63.

From the beginning debate surrounded the issues of "autonomy," so important to the Congregationalists, and "connectionalism," equally important to the Methodist Protestants. The denominational media supported the idea of this three-way union with great enthusiasm, suggesting that the denominations involved should study one another's history, character, and "the genius of their work." The Congregationalists proposed an exchange of pulpits, joint conferences, missionary fellowship meetings, and various other methods to promote Christian friendship and cooperation.

Calling themselves "A Council of the United Churches," representatives from the three denominations met in 1905 and agreed unanimously on a Declaration of Faith and a Statement on Polity and Vested Interests. A second Council of the United Churches, meeting in Chicago, adopted—almost unanimously—an Act of Union providing for a federation of the three churches. This federation stipulated that each denomination would remain intact in all local affairs, with the option of joining united local associations and state conferences if they so chose, while a National Council would be created to further the combined work of the churches in a purely advisory capacity. Ordination and ministerial standing would be handled in annual conferences, except where it was preferred that such things be done by local bodies.

As this proposal took shape, concern increased among the Congregationalists. Some worried about the different "temperament" of the other denominations, but most Congregationalists were uneasy because they feared that the autonomy of the local church would be compromised. The chair of the National Council Committee on Unity, William Hayes Ward, explained that the objections were groundless, but he was not successful in stemming a growing tide of opposition. When it came time for the Act of Union to be voted upon, the National Council of the Congregational Churches was unable to act. Instead, it referred the matter to a committee of twenty-eight. The committee, while expressing confidence that the union eventually would go forward, acknowledged "divergent opinions" among the Congregationalists and proposed that the Congregationalists invite the other two denominations to join them in returning the Act of Union to a General Council of the United Churches for further work, with the results to be reported back to the national bodies of the denominations.

In the end, neither the Methodist Protestants nor the United Brethren responded. Even when the Congregationalists tried to revive the issue in 1910 by sending each of them the Act of Union with a new "Explanatory Statement" appended containing additional guarantees on the autonomy of the local churches, the other denominations were not interested.

Act of Union

Between the Congregational Churches, the Church of the United Brethren in Christ, and the Methodist Protestant Church

We, the representatives of the Congregational Churches, the Church of the United Brethren in Christ, and the Methodist Protestant Church, believing that we can do more to promote the work of our Lord Jesus Christ in the world by uniting than by continuing our separate existence as denominations as heretofore, and being of one accord in the desire to realize our Lord's prayer, "that they all may be one," having already at the first meeting of this council entered into a common Declaration of Faith hereinafter set forth, do now, in order to bring about an organic union, propose to our respective denominations the Articles of Agreement hereinafter set forth.

Declaration of Faith

We, the representatives of the Congregational Churches, the Church of the United Brethren in Christ, and the Methodist Protestant Church, rejoice at this time to enter into union with one another, through the grace of our Lord Jesus Christ, in the love of God, and for fellowship in the Holy Spirit. In this solemn act of faith and obedience towards the great Head of the Church, we do most humbly and confidently make confession of our faith and heartily renew the consecration of our lives to Him and to the service of mankind.

1. Our bond of union consists in that inward and personal faith in Jesus Christ as our divine Saviour and Lord on which all our churches are founded, also in our acceptance of the Holy Scriptures as the inspired source of our faith and the supreme standard of Christian truth; and, further, in our consent to the teaching of the ancient symbols of the undivided Church, and to that substance of Christian doctrine which is common to the creeds and confessions which we have inherited from the past. But we humbly depend, as did our fathers, on the continued guidance of the Holy Spirit to lead us into all the truth.

2. We believe that God, the Father and Lord of all, did send his Son Jesus Christ to redeem us from sin and death by the perfect obedience of his holy will in life, by the sacrifice of himself on the cross, and by his glorious resurrection from the dead.

3. We believe that the Holy Spirit, the Spirit of God and of Christ, moves in the hearts of men, calling them through the gospel to repentance and faith, awakening in them spiritual sorrow for past sin and confidence in the mercy of God, together with new desires and a new power to obey his will.

4. We believe that those of the sons of men who, hearing God's call of divine love, do heartily put their trust in the Saviour whom his love provided, are assured by his word of his most fatherly forgiveness, of his free and perfect favor, of the presence of his Spirit in their hearts and of a blessed immortality.

5. We believe that all who are through faith the children of God constitute the Church of Christ, the spiritual body of which he is the head; that he has appointed them to proclaim his gospel to all mankind, manifest in their character and conduct the fruit of his Spirit; that he has granted them freedom to create such offices and institutions as may in each generation serve unto those ends, and that for the comfort of our faith he has given to his church the sacred ordinances of baptism and the Lord's Supper.

6. We believe that, according to Christ's law, men of the Christian faith exist for the service of man, not only in holding forth the word of life, but in the support of works and institutions of pity and charity, in the maintenance of human freedom, in the deliverance of all those that are oppressed, in the enforcement of civic justice, in the rebuke of all unrighteousness.

Possessed of these convictions, both as truths which we do most firmly hold, and acts of faith which spring from our hearts, we do, therefore, in the happy consummation of this union, and in the name of all the churches which we represent, commit ourselves, body, soul, and spirit, to the faith, love, and service of him who made us and saved us, the everlasting God, our Father, Redeemer, and Lord. To him be ascribed all praise, and dominion, and glory, world without end. Amen.

Articles of Agreement

Article I

The name of this organization shall be The United Churches, comprising the Congregational Churches, the Church of the United Brethren in Christ, and the Methodist Protestant Church.

Article II

For the purpose of realizing the fellowship of the churches, and to provide for their cooperation, they shall be organized into District Associations, Annual Conferences, and a National Council.

Article III

District Associations shall have their boundaries, composition, duties, and prerogatives defined by the Annual Conferences, of which they shall be subdivisions.

Article IV

1. State Associations of the Congregational Churches and Annual Conferences of the Church of the United Brethren in Christ, and of the Methodist Protestant Church, shall be recognized and continued as Annual Conferences under this organization until such time as the National Council may, by the consent of the parties concerned, arrange new boundaries. They shall have the right to maintain intact their present modes of organization and operation in local affairs, but they shall be known and styled as Annual Conferences of The United Churches, comprising the Congregational Churches, the Church of the United Brethren in Christ, and the Methodist Protestant Church: and they shall make effective this union by cooperating with the National Council in all matters affecting the general interests of the churches.

2. Two or more State Associations, or Annual Conferences, may, by mutual consent, unite to form one Annual Conference with power to make rules and regulations for its organization and operation in local affairs.

3. All Annual Conferences shall have power to make rules and regulations for their organization, and for the conduct of all their local affairs.

4. Ordination to the ministry and ministerial standing shall be in Annual Conferences except where it is preferred to delegate or leave these to local bodies.

Article V

The National Council of Congregational Churches, and the General Conferences of the Church of the United Brethren in Christ and of the Methodist Protestant Church, shall continue their legal existence as long as may be deemed necessary.

Article VI

1. The National Council of The United Churches, comprising the Congregational Churches, the Church of the United Brethren in Christ, and

the Methodist Protestant Church, shall assemble in . . . . on the third Thursday in May . . . . and regularly thereafter on the same day every four years. It shall be composed of representatives as follows: Each Annual Conference shall be entitled to one ministerial and one lay representative for every five thousand members and major fraction thereof, within its bounds, to be elected as itself may prescribe. *Provided,* that each Annual Conference shall be entitled to at least one ministerial and one lay representative; and *provided,* that the National Council may at any time change the ratio of representation.

2. A majority of the representatives in attendance shall constitute a quorum of the National Council, and ordinary questions shall be determined by a majority vote; but no vote shall be passed contravening or modifying this Act of Union unless a majority of the representatives from each denomination represented in the union agree thereto. And whenever requested by a majority of the representatives of any one of these denominations, the vote shall be by denominations, and a majority of each shall be necessary to carry the question pending.

3. The National Council shall elect at every quadrennial meeting a president, a secretary, a treasurer, and such other officers as may be deemed necessary, who shall hold office until their successors are elected; and who shall perform the usual duties of their office and such other duties in the service of the churches as the Council may determine.

4. The National Council at its first meeting shall proceed to organize societies and boards for the conduct of the general business of the churches: such as missionary, evangelistic, educational, church building, Sunday-school, publishing, and other benevolent work; or it may adopt for any of these purposes societies and boards now existing if a majority of the representatives of each denomination consent.

5. In organizing these societies and boards the National Council shall name for membership therein those who now constitute such societies and boards in the denominations represented in this union wherever similar societies and boards exist; and in others, membership shall be distributed among the denominations in due proportion. This arrangement, however, shall be only temporary and for the purpose of facilitating the combination of the interests involved and preventing confusion and interruption in the work of any existing society. As soon as may be, consistently with the interest of the work, the membership of these societies shall be reduced to a basis of economy and efficiency of administration, and the National Council shall at every quadrennial meeting determine how many and who shall constitute these societies and boards.

6. All societies and boards now existing in the churches represented in

this union shall, as soon as possible after the adoption of this Act of Union and the organization by the National Council of the societies and boards indicated in this article, cease their active operations in collecting funds from the churches. They shall hand over to the corresponding societies and boards organized in pursuance of this article the income of all their funds and use of the property and equipment now used in the prosecution of their work, wherever this may be lawfully done pursuant to their corporate purpose; and in general it is understood that they will cooperate in carrying out the true intent and purpose of this union to consolidate all the active operations of the three denominations in general church work. But nothing herein contained shall direct nor authorize any diversion of trust funds from the spirit or the purpose for which such funds were donated.

7. The societies and boards organized by the National Council shall meet at the call of the president of the Council as early as practicable after the adjournment of the Council, and elect officers. They shall secure charters in pursuance of the instructions of this article and appoint secretaries and agents for the prosecution of the work assigned them. They shall arrange for the visitation of churches and Annual Conferences by their agents in the interest of their work and take full charge of all the work now performed by corresponding societies and boards in the denominations represented in this union. They shall make a full report to each regular meeting of the National Council and shall be responsible to that body.

8. The National Council shall make rules and regulations for the conduct of its business and for the prosecution of all the general work of the church; it shall counsel, warn, and appeal to the churches on questions of religious and administrative concern, and, in general, shall represent the churches; *provided,* that nothing be done in contravention of this Act of Union.

Article VII

Ministers in good standing in any denomination represented in this union shall be ministers in this organization. Licentiates shall retain their standing for the period of their licensure. Ministers under censure must look to their own denomination for relief.

Article VIII

This union shall be consummated by the adoption of this Act of Union by the denominations represented in accordance with their rules and regulations, and when the moderator of the National Council of Congregational Churches, the bishops of the General Conference of the Church of the United Brethren in Christ, and the president of the General Conference of the Methodist Protestant Church shall have announced that this Act of Union has been adopted by the proper bodies representing their respective denominations, these officers shall unite in filling the blank in Article VI, Section 1, fixing the place and time for the meeting of the National Council, and publish the same, together with a call for the election of representatives, according to Article VI.

Explanatory Statement

This Act of Union we approve with the understanding on our part, and asking the concurrent understanding on the part of the United Brethren and Methodist Protestants, that the three bodies of churches in entering into this union do not yield or forego their accustomed liberty of action in the conduct of their ecclesiastical affairs, but that each is at liberty to maintain its principles of self-government, with all that is involved of autonomy or connectionalism, so that our Congregational churches may continue to observe their practices of local government in fellowship with other churches; and equally that churches of the United Brethren and the Methodist Protestant bodies individually or in their larger organizations reserve their right to maintain their customs and methods of administration unhampered by any interpretation that may be put on the provisions of this "Act of Union."

William Hayes Ward
Washington Gladden
Henry C. King
W. Douglas Mackenzie
Charles H. Rutan
James W. Strong
Lucien C. Warner
William Horace Day

Coping with the Historic Episcopate

5. A Global Issue: *"The Lambeth Quadrilateral"*

(1886)

The Lambeth Quadrilateral is a four-part statement of the basic elements that the Anglican Communion wishes to be honored in any plans for reunion with other churches. It was sent out to the churches by the Lambeth Conference of the Anglican Communion in 1888. Since then, it has been considered by Anglicans to be "the substantial deposit of Christian faith and order committed by Christ and his apostles to the church unto the end of the world."

The first Lambeth Conference occurred in 1867, when the Anglican Communion—expanded to worldwide proportions as a fellowship of independent provinces itself expressing unity within diversity—felt the need to initiate a worldwide conference of Anglican bishops to discuss domestic concerns within and between various Anglican churches around the world. There was no indication at the time of the immense significance the Lambeth Conference would come to have in the ecumenical world in later years. It was a conference only of Anglicans, with no right to pass binding decrees, and no authority but a spiritual one.

A second conference was held in 1878, a somewhat broader agenda involved the question of Moravian Orders and the relationship of the Anglican Communion to Old Catholics and others in Europe who had renounced their allegiance to the Roman Catholic Church and wanted to form some connection with the Anglican Church. By the third Lambeth Conference in 1888, the ecumenical importance of the gathering began

---

Source: "The Chicago-Lambeth Quadrilateral," in *Journal of the General Convention* (1886), 80, in *A History of the Ecumenical Movement,* vol. 1, ed. R. Rouse and S. Neill (Geneva: World Council of Churches, 1953), 264–65.

to emerge, with committees appointed to consider the Scandinavian Lutherans, the Reformed Churches, the Old Catholics, the Eastern Churches, and the Free Churches in Scotland.

The most significant work of the Lambeth Conference, however, turned out to be a report from a committee on "Home Reunion." At Lambeth the bishops on the committee had before them a report prepared by the General Convention of the Protestant Episcopal Church in the United States, which had met in Chicago in 1886. This report, with slightly altered wording and the addition of the Apostles' Creed to the second article, eventually was accepted by the committee as supplying "a basis on which approach may be, under God's blessing, made toward Home Reunion."

After being endorsed by the Lambeth Conference, it came to be called the "Lambeth Quadrilateral." It has served as the basis of all Anglican negotiations with non-Episcopal churches, and has been used by the wider ecumenical movement as a reasonable basis on which to build church union agreements.

Originally, the four points were regarded as a necessary prerequisite for discussion considering union. Over time, however, there has been considerable controversy within the Anglican Communion itself when some have interpreted the Quadrilateral, in itself, as a sufficient basis for union. For most Protestant churches in the ecumenical movement, including the Congregational churches, the fourth point, which insists on the importance on the historic episcopate, has always been the most controversial.

We do hereby affirm that the Christian unity now so earnestly desired . . . can be restored only by the return of all Christian Communions to the principles of unity exemplified by the undivided Catholic Church during the first ages of its existence; which principles we believe to be the substantial deposit of Christian Faith and Order committed by Christ and His Apostles to the Church unto the end of the world, and therefore incapable of compromise or surrender by those who have been ordained to be its stewards and trustees for the common and equal benefit of all men.

As inherent parts of this sacred deposit, and therefore as essential to the restoration of unity among the divided branches of Christendom, we account the following, to wit:

(a) The Holy Scriptures of the Old and New Testaments, as "containing all things necessary to salvation," and as being the rule and ultimate standard of faith.

(b) The Apostles' Creed, as the Baptismal Symbol; and the Nicene Creed, as the sufficient statement of the Christian Faith.

(c) The two Sacraments ordained by Christ Himself—Baptism and the Supper of the Lord—ministered with unfailing use of Christ's words of institution and of the elements ordained by Him.

(d) The Historic Episcopate, locally adapted in the methods of its administration to the varying needs of the nations and peoples called of God into the unity of His Church.

6. The New Jersey Platform: *"The Platform of Union"*

(1896)

William Hayes Ward et al.

After the Lambeth Quadrilateral was sent out to the churches, a decade passed in which the Congregationalists conducted their first round of discussions on the Quadrilateral in general and the historic episcopate in particular. By 1895, the Committee on Union with Free Baptists and Other Denominations announced to the National Council of the Congregational Churches that acceptance of the historic episcopate would require all other denominations to "accept the order of bishops as officially superior to the ministry, and to receive ordination through bishops who claim uninterrupted apostolic succession." Therefore, the committee concluded, although the proposals remained as one of the evidences of the longing for unity pervading the Christian church, "as practical proposals they no longer need to be considered." The experiment was in the end a failure, and the field was open for other proposals that did not "involve submission."

Taking its own advice, the committee offered an alternative proposal for unity later called the "Congregational Quadrilateral," which it offered to other Protestant Evangelical Churches.

Source: William Hayes Ward et al., "The Platform of Union" ["The New Jersey Platform"], in *Minutes of the National Council of the Congregational Churches of the United States, Ninth Session, Syracuse, N.Y., October 9–14, 1895* (Boston: Congregational Sunday School and Publishing Society, 1896), 294.

We propose to other Protestant Evangelical Churches a union based on:—

1. The acceptance of the Scriptures of the Old and New Testaments inspired by the Holy Ghost to be the only authoritative revelation of God to man.
2. Discipleship of Jesus Christ, the divine Saviour and Teacher of the world.
3. The Church of Christ, which is his body, whose great mission it is to preach his Gospel to the world.
4. Liberty of conscience in the interpretation of the Scriptures and in the administration of the Church.

7. Pessimism Overwhelmed by Hope:
"The Barrier to Union," "For a Conference of All Bodies," and "The Congregational Attitude"

(1910)

When the Anglican Communion sent the Lambeth Quadrilateral out to the churches in 1888 (see vol. 6:5), the young National Council of the Congregational Churches began a discussion of and with the Protestant Episcopal Church that continued intermittently and with great fluctuations in enthusiasm for thirty-seven years.

The Quadrilateral laid out four elements as requisite for union. Of these, it was the fourth, "the Historic Episcopate, locally adapted in the method of its administration to the varying needs of the nations and peoples called of God into the unity of His Church," that caused the Congregationalists the most difficulty.

According to the Congregational reading of church history, the earliest episcopate had to do with the governing of the church, not the authority of its priests. After careful study, the Congregational Committee on Christian Unity called the episcopate "an impassable barrier" (1892), and declared, "No union of denominations is possible on any basis which includes what is meant by the historic episcopate. The ordination of the various churches must be accepted as valid, and their bishops as regular" (1895).

Source: "The Barrier to Union," *The Congregationalist and Christian World,* 10 September 1910, 329; "Noteworthy Documents on Unity: The Episcopalian and the Congregational Deliverance," *The Congregationalist and Christian World,* 29 October 1910, 637.

An editorial, "The Barrier to Union," explained that the Congregational position was based on the Reformation notion of the priesthood of all believers. For Congregationalists, the historic episcopate was a barrier as "impassable" as it had ever been.

However, when a commission of the Protestant Episcopal Church in the United States asked prayers of all the churches on behalf of the union movement, and invited churches to appoint independent but cooperating commissions that would work out plans for a World Conference on Faith and Order, the Congregationalists responded enthusiastically by setting up a special commission of five to consider any overtures that might come as a result of the conference. Efforts were made to reinterpret the fourth element of the Quadrilateral, and some Congregationalists continued to hold on to their hope for union with the Episcopalians.

The Barrier to Union

The influence of such an assembly as the World Conference at Edinburgh toward the union of Christian churches is already felt everywhere. To the compulsion of need for a united front of believers in Christ in their advance on all mission fields is now added a new and mighty impulse of fellowship awakened by the coming together of representatives of Christian communities in every country. The idea of unity will take on new interest, not only in interdenominational assemblies, but in the official conferences of various bodies, such as the National Council of the Congregational churches in Boston and the General Convention of the Protestant Episcopal Church in Cincinnati next mouth.

What real barriers are keeping these two denominations apart, how can they be removed, and is it desirable to consider propositions looking toward organic union? A definite answer to this question at this time, admitted by all parties to be fairly stated, might not only prevent much waste of time in discussion, but might save the waste of these awakened impulses to fellowship which are impressing the world anew with the greatness of Christian love and the unity of Christian faith.

A definite step toward church union was made when in 1887 the bishops of the Anglican Church, meeting in Lambeth Palace, London, offered as a basis of union what has become known as the four Lambeth proposals. The first three, concerning the Holy Scriptures, the Apostles' and Nicene Creeds and the sacraments of baptism and the Lord's Supper, would probably at that time have been accepted as such a basis by nearly all Protestant churches. The insistence on the fourth, called "the historic episcopate," was the apparent cause of the failure of the movement, though the discussion aroused by it has not yet fully ceased.

What was meant by the historic episcopate? The way in which these proposals originated suggests an answer. They were first formulated in substance at the Episcopal General Convention in Chicago in 1886. Rev. Phillips Brooks offered in the convention a resolution of fraternal greetings to the National Council of Congregationalists then in session in the same city. The resolution, though adopted in the Lower House, was voted down in the House of Bishops. The bishops presumably were not unfriendly toward the assembled Congregationalists.

But they believed themselves to be the highest of three orders of the ministry essential to the constitution of the church of Christ. They believed that no one could belong in these holy orders except by the laying on of hands of men qualified for this act, as they themselves were, by having received ordination through successive generations of men so consecrated, traced back directly to the twelve apostles. The Episcopal Church holds that such men have exclusive possession of certain gifts and graces thus transmitted to them from our Lord Jesus Christ. The Episcopal bishops at Chicago were restrained from greeting the Congregational National Council lest they should thus seem to admit that Congregational ministers might possess these gifts and graces.

But Congregational ministers do not claim to possess the gifts exclusively assumed by a priesthood. One chief reason for the existence of Congregational churches, as all know who are familiar with their history, is that they regard it essential to the purity of Christian faith and life to maintain that all true believers in Christ are the priesthood. No external union, if it were possible, of two bodies holding these two opposing views would be to the advantage of Christianity. It would intensify the discord of opponents holding the same loyalty to one Lord.

But the Congregationalists at Chicago welcomed the unsent resolution as a step in approach toward fellowship. *The Congregationalist* at that time said of it, "That it should have been made at all even by a man of Dr. Brooks's liberality marks a decided change within recent years in the attitude of the Episcopalians toward other Christians. . . . Dr. Brooks and those of his way of thinking also may be assured that Congregationalists cordially appreciate and reciprocate their courteous and Christian attitude."

The barrier preventing any organic union between the Episcopal and the Congregational denominations is as impassable now as it has ever been. Attempts have recently been made by some Congregational leaders, notably by Dr. Newman Smyth and other honored brethren in Connecticut, to propose Episcopal ordination of Congregational ministers as a *via media* for such a union. But the method of ordination practiced by the Episcopal Church is not regarded by Congregationalists as an obstacle to union. The barrier is the theory of the ministry held by the Episcopal Church. Congregationalists protest against the claim that they have not a valid ministry and are not a church of Christ because they refuse to attribute to any order of men or to any institution a power imparted by Christ to be the necessary intermediary between the soul and him.

What advantage would there be, then, to discuss in the Episcopal General Convention or the National Council the subject of organic union between these two bodies or between the Episcopal Church and other Protestant denominations? So far as our vision extends there would be none. Rather is it probable that mutual irritation would be awakened by it. Even the terms of discussion would be provocative. For Episcopalians claim to be *the* Church, and resent our speaking of them as a denomination as much as they resent the assumption by us that our denomination is *a* church.

What, then, on our side can be done to promote Christian harmony? We believe that notable steps toward it have been taken since those meetings in Chicago almost a quarter of a century ago. A growing proportion of Episcopalians regard Congregationalists as brethren. They are ready to admit, while claiming exclusive possession of divine gifts and graces for priests ordained according to the historic episcopate, that the fruits of grace have flowed through other than their priestly channels, and that these fruits have followed the labors of Congregational ministers. We, on the other hand, have no quarrel with them because of their claim of exclusive powers for their ministry. The satisfaction they find in the exercise of such powers we may not refuse to share so far as the results appear to strengthen the body of Christ, though we neither claim nor wish such powers for our ministers.

We honor and love the Episcopal Church for its spiritual life, for the devotion of its members and for its great and growing service in bringing the Kingdom of our Lord Jesus Christ to the world. We welcome its co-operation wherever its bishops are willing to co-operate with us. As Episcopalians are coming to acknowledge more and more the genuineness and fruitfulness of the labors of Congregationalists, it becomes easier for them and for us, each in our own organization seeking the same ends and rejoicing in each other's progress and triumphs, to say, "We are brethren."

Noteworthy Documents on Unity: The Episcopalian and the Congregational Deliverance

Herewith we print the two important actions on Church Unity taken last week by two representative religious bodies.

For a Conference of All Bodies

(Action taken by the Episcopalians at Cincinnati)

Your committee is of one mind. We believe that the time has now arrived when representatives of the whole family of Christ, led by the Holy Spirit, may be willing to come together for the consideration of questions of faith and order. We believe, further, that all Christian communions are in accord with us in our desire to lay aside self-will and to put on the mind which is in Jesus Christ, our Lord. We would heed this call of the Spirit of God in all lowliness and with singleness of purpose. We would place ourselves by the side of our fellow-Christians, looking not only on our own things, but also on the things of others, convinced that our one hope of mutual understanding is in taking personal counsel together in the spirit of love and forbearance. It is our conviction that such a conference for the purpose of study and discussion, without power to legislate or to adopt resolutions, is the next step toward unity.

With grief for our aloofness in the past and for other faults of pride and self-sufficiency which make for schism, with loyalty to the truth as we see it and with respect for the convictions of those who differ from us, holding the belief that the beginnings of unity are to be found in the clear statement and full consideration of those things in which we differ, as well as of those things in which we are as one, we respectfully submit the following resolution:

Whereas, there is today among all Christian people a growing desire for the fulfillment of our Lord's Prayer that all his disciples may be one, that the world may believe that God has sent him:

Resolved, the House of Bishops concurring, that a joint commission be appointed to bring about a conference for the consideration of questions touching faith and order, and that all Christian communions throughout the world which confess our Lord Jesus Christ as God and Saviour be asked to unite with us in arranging for and conducting such a conference. The commission shall consist of seven bishops appointed by the chairman of the House of Bishops and seven Presbyters and seven laymen appointed by the president of the House of Deputies, and shall have power to add to its number and to fill any vacancies occurring before the next general convention.

The Congregational Attitude

(Action taken at Boston last week)

Whereas the last Lambeth Conference of the Anglican Communion which was held in London in 1908 lifted up the ideal of church unity in these words: "We must set before us the Church of Christ as he would have it, one spirit and one body, enriched with all those elements of divine truth which the separated communities of Christians now emphasize separately, strengthened by the interaction of all the gifts and graces which our divisions now hold asunder, filled with all the fullness of God, we dare not, in the name of peace, barter away those precious things of which we have been made stewards. Neither can we wish others to be unfaithful to trusts which they hold no less sacred. We must fix our eyes on the church of the future which is to be adorned with all the precious things, both theirs and ours. We must constantly desire, not compromise, but comprehension, not uniformity, but unity."

And whereas the Anglican bishops further recommended that for this end conference of ministers and laymen of different Christian bodies be held to promote a better mutual understanding; and we on our part would seek, as much as lieth in us, for the unity and peace of the whole household of faith; and, forgetting not that our forefathers, whose orderly ministry is our inheritance, were not willingly separatists, we would loyally contribute the precious things, of which as Congregationalists we are stewards, to the Church of the future; therefore this Council would put on record its appreciation of the spirit and its concurrence in the purpose of this expression of the Lambeth Conference; and voice its earnest hope for closer fellowship with the Episcopal Church in Christian work and worship.

It is further recommended this matter be referred to the committee on overtures from the Episcopal Church to act as our representatives in carrying out the spirit and in furthering the intent of this resolution.

It was Voted, that in view of the possibility of fraternal discussion of Church Unity suggested by the Lambeth Conference of Anglican Bishops, 1908, a special commission of five representatives be appointed to consider any overtures that may come to our denomination as a result of this conference.

8. LOCAL UNITY:

"The Lenox Proposal"

(1915)

Although the work of the Commission on Comity, Federation and Unity of the National Council of the Congregational Churches was extraordinary in depth, breadth, and accomplishment (see vol. 6:20), the Congregationalists were well aware by the beginning of the twentieth century that their ecumenical work was not accomplished simply by denominational leaders on behalf of the people in the churches. Rather, every attempt of local individuals or churches to reach out to other churches with a view toward union was recognized as an important part of the ecumenical process.

It was in this context that Rev. Newman Smyth, on behalf of the Commission on Comity, Federation and Unity, brought to the National Council a proposal for the joint worship and work of an Episcopal parish and a Congregational church in Lenox, Massachusetts. After meeting together and discussing their mutual beliefs and teachings, the pastors had found that—without disloyalty to their respective theological traditions—they could find no essential differences between themselves. Thus, they appealed to the bishop of the Diocese of Western Massachusetts and to the Commission on Church Unity of the National Council of the Congregational Churches to find a way for them "to unite for work and worship in loyalty to the ecclesiastical standards of the communions" to which they belonged. They hoped that this grassroots effort might percolate upwards and lead to a "happier adjustment" between Congregationalists

SOURCE: "The Lenox Conference," in Newman Smyth, "Relations with the Protestant Episcopal Church," in "Report of the Commission on Comity, Federation and Unity," in *Minutes of the National Council of the Congregational Churches in the United States, New Haven, Conn., 1915* (New York: Office of the National Council, 1915), 330–33.

and Episcopalians. Unfortunately, the National Council's enthusiasm for this proposal was not shared by the Episcopal Diocese. Soon thereafter the Episcopal priest in Lenox was transferred to another church.

There has been presented to the Committee a request for conference concerning certain proposals for co-operation in work and service by a Congregational and an Episcopal clergyman in Lenox, Mass. It is typical of conditions which in many other localities are waiting for solution. It forces directly upon us the open shame and sin of the continuance of the inherited schism between the Episcopal and the non-Episcopal clergy and churches. A concrete case, such as this, has the advantage of taking out of the abstract and presenting for definite and practical determination the far-reaching questions involved in it. It seemed also to the Committee that a thorough consideration of it in all its bearings by a small conference, in an irenical spirit, might give promise of some happier adjustment of our existing differences. Until these unhappy divisions shall be confessed and healed the American Churches cannot confront the world in the full power of the love of God. On account therefore of the possible value of this concrete case in the preparation of the matters of faith and order which are to be laid before the World Conference, as well as for its immediate importance in defining our Congregational relations with the Episcopal Church, the Committee requested that such a conference be held, and we received from the official representatives of the Episcopal Church an appreciative and cordial response. We submit the following correspondence in explanation of the proposals presented to us, and the steps which have already been taken for a mutual study of the principles involved and their possible reconciliation in some working agreement.

To the Right Rev. Thos. F. Davies, D.D., Bishop of the Diocese of the Western Massachusetts, and to the Commission on Church Unity of the National Council of the Congregational Churches of the United States;

We, the undersigned, Rev. Arthur J. Gammack, rector of Trinity Church, and Rev. Leon D. Bliss, pastor of the Congregational Church, Lenox, Mass., conjointly lay before you the following statement and respectfully ask your counsel and advice.

In this town there have existed since the eighteenth century the Congregational Church and the Episcopal Church. Each has an honorable history and each meets a present need.

Between us, the pastors of these Churches, there exists the most cordial friendship. We have deliberately and constantly endeavored to co-operate for the moral and religious welfare of this community. Without disloyalty to our respective theological standards, we fail to find essential differences in our belief and teaching of the Christian faith. We believe that our congregations generally share our feelings, both of cordial good-will and of regret for the obvious waste of means and effort and, more than all else, deplore with us the reproach which falls upon the cause of Jesus Christ through the unhappy divisions of His Church. We believe that they are ready to follow our leadership into closer relations. We believe that the union of all our people for Christian work and worship, if it can be done consistently with the laws of the communions which we represent, would accomplish much more than the sum of their present results. Each of these Churches has undoubtedly a noble service to render but, by working together in all ways possible, each would strengthen and encourage the other and together they could accomplish much that is now impossible. We do not favor any scheme which would involve the absorption of either congregation by the other. Each church, we believe, should preserve its autonomy and continue to meet its own obligations.

We appeal to you then, authorized as you are to speak with authority, and we earnestly request you to consider whether or not a way may be found whereby we and the Churches under our care, without prejudice or detriment to either, can unite for work and worship in loyalty to the ecclesiastical standards of the communions to which we belong.

The things in which union seems to us desirable are:

1. The merging of the Men's Club of Trinity Church and the Congregational Brotherhood in one organization. The nature of these two bodies seems to involve only the question of expediency.
2. The combining of our Sunday Schools, each school remaining under its own teachers and using its own literature.
3. Bible study classes and mission study classes.
4. A weekly evening service for prayer and fellowship.
5. Combining of our choirs.
6. Union services on special occasions such as Thanksgiving Day, Christmas, during Holy Week, and so forth.
7. Union services throughout the year on Sunday evenings, the ministers preaching alternately, each assisting the other in the services.
8. Union services on Sunday mornings from November 1 to May 1.

During the remainder of the year, on account of larger congregations which neither church could accommodate at one time, each church to hold morning service in its own building. From November to May the services to be conducted alternately as at the evening services, each pastor having one sermon for the day.

This is the program along which, were the initiative left to us, we should work towards such specific and practical realization of unity as the circumstances seem to permit and call for. We lay the matter before you for consideration and decision. We devoutly hope and pray that no insuperable difficulties may be encountered. If there is not, we believe that such co-operation as we have outlined, would redound to the honor of Christ and the strengthening of His Church both here and elsewhere.

In His name, your servants and brethren,

LEON D. BLISS

Lenox, 12 Dec., 1914. A. J. GAMMACK

Bishop Davies cordially responded to our expression of our readiness to enter into the desired conference; and after his return from absence abroad, at his invitation Dr. Smyth and Professor Williston Walker met with him at his residence in Springfield on Feb. 25th. After due consideration it seemed to us that some larger consultation was desirable in view of the far-reaching nature of the issues involved. The following correspondence will explain the steps which have been taken by mutual consent to secure studious and thorough consideration of these important questions in further irenical conferences of representatives of both communions.

MY DEAR DR. SMYTH,

The proposition from Lenox is so far reaching in its effect, and involves, in my opinion, such serious conflict with the Canon Law of the Episcopal Church, that any immediate action on it, other than conference and deliberation, seems to me impossible.

If the Commission on Faith and Order of the Episcopal Church would discuss the underlying principles with your Commission on Unity, I should be happy to have it so, and have so written to Dr. Manning.

Believe me, Sir, with regard, sincerely yours,

THOS. F. DAVIES,

February 26, 1915. *Bishop of Western Massachusetts*

9. Congregational Convictions:

"A Statement of the Views . . . on the Church, the Eucharist, and the Ministry"

(1921)

Newman Smyth and Williston Walker

This statement on the church, eucharist, and ministry presented a succinct summary of the Congregational position vis-à-vis the Episcopal doctrine of the historic episcopate, while at the same time making several proposals to help surmount the apparent impasse between the two denominations.

No theologians could have been better suited for this task. Newman Smyth, longtime pastor of the prestigious Center Church in New Haven, had gained recognition for many books and articles in the New Theology and Social Gospel movements, and had been active in ecumenical work for many years. Williston Walker, renowned Professor of Ecclesiastical History at Yale, had written extensively on Congregationalism and church history. Together, they had just finished a book on Approaches Toward Church Unity. *They understood the sensitive issues between the denominations, and made some remarkably innovative proposals.*

The statement begins with the strong assertion that since the Congregationalists and Episcopalians are already included in the unity of the church already given in the church universal, neither denomination can, or should try to, exclude the other. They remind the Episcopalians that Jesus Christ has already given the grace of his presence through the

Source: Newman Smyth and Williston Walker, "A Statement of the Views Commonly Held by Congregationalists on the Church, the Eucharist, and the Ministry," in *Minutes of the National Council of the Congregational Churches of the United States, Nineteenth Regular Meeting, Los Angeles, California, July 1–8, 1921* (New York: Office of the National Council, 1921), 64–69.

Lord's Supper to the church universal as part of his priestly work, and the church continues to communicate this presence through the priesthood of all believers. Consequently, "no office or ecclesiastical ordinance or order" (such as those ordained to the Episcopal priesthood, or any other ministry) may claim to have higher authority (than Christ's) over the sacrament's validity or distribution.

From an ecumenical standpoint, the section on ministry was the most innovative. Every church had the right and obligation to determine its own procedure with regard to ordination, and this procedure ought to receive recognition by all other communions "in the ministry of the Church of God." "The Apostolic succession is the succession of the spiritual gifts residing in and continuing through the Church, not apart from it or superior to its being." Speaking to the Episcopal insistence that the only way for ordained Congregationalists to be acceptable was (re)ordination into the historic episcopate by an Episcopal bishop, Smyth and Walker noted that the "ordaining Council" in the Congregational system performs the same functions as the bishop in the Episcopal system. They invited Episcopalians to accept ordination by this "group episcopacy"(as it would come to be called later in the twentieth century) as a valid ordination.

Smyth and Walker examined the (1920) Lambeth proposal that the Episcopalians' Christian ministers of other Christian communions accept "a commission through Episcopal ordination, as obtaining for them a ministry throughout the fellowship." Episcopalians had said that in a reunited church they would publicly and formally seek "additional recognition of a new call to a wider service in a reunited Church," and would themselves willingly accept from the recognized authorities of other communions "a new commission for mutual ministry in the larger fellowship."

This seemed to imply that the Episcopalians were disclaiming the implications involved in notions of "reordination," or "conditional ordination" (namely, that the previous ordination had not been valid) and were offering to give and receive "a new commission for mutual ministry in the larger fellowship." If this was true, Smyth and Walker continued to propose plans for the new fellowship. They declared that the confessions and declarations of faith of their own and other Protestant churches would be a sufficient basis for a common fellowship in the ministry, and suggested that "a constitutional Episcopate" (an episcopate of governance, not of ministry) could oversee churches in this common fellowship.

Finally, in an apparent attempt to reinterpret the matter for Congre-

gationalists, Smyth and Walker lifted up the traditional Congregational custom of having an "installing council" examine a previously ordained minister prior to installing the minister in a new congregation. They suggested that in a united church the bishop might be charged with judging the fitness of clergy in such situations, similar to a Congregational installing council. If a candidate was willing to receive "the additional commission in accordance with the Lambeth proposals," the historic episcopate could be preserved. In fact, such a concordat allowing for a recommissioning of Congregational clergy was eventually accepted by the Protestant Episcopal General Convention in the United States, although when the Congregationalists attempted to test it through the request of Roland Bainton for reordination, the request was denied. In the end, the concordat was of little use (see vol. 6:10).

A paper presented by the Commission of the National Council of Congregational Churches to the Joint Conference in New York, March 29, 1921, for presentation to the joint sub-committee.

The Order of Topics in Their Relative Values: I. The Church. II. The Sacrament of the Eucharist. III. The Orders of Ministry.

I. The Church

1. There are no divisive differences in the Protestant creeds in their general definitions of the Church. There are differences of expression and of emphasis, but a common belief exists in the Church as the whole congregation of faithful believers, the Universal, the Holy Catholic Church, the body of Christ who filleth all in all.

2. The Unity of the Church was visible in the first company of disciples who with all that were added to them continued steadfastly in the Apostles' teaching and fellowship, in the breaking of bread and in the prayers.

3. The common obligation therefore is for each separate fellowship of believers so to hold its particular position and to act in relation to other communions that by its attitude no other part of the Church may be compelled to remain in separation from the whole Church; or by any act of attempted exclusion of others effectually to exclude itself from fellowship with the whole Body of Christ, or in its effort to make other bodies sectarian, itself to become a sect.

4. The historical continuity of the Church is the fulfilment from age to

age of the Lord's promise to be with his disciples always even to the end of the world.

5. The spiritual continuity of the Church has been made manifest through its vital power of adaptation and growth in its relation to the thought and the life of the world.

II. The Sacrament of the Eucharist

1. The institution of the Lord's Supper was Jesus' personal act in forming the fellowship composed of all his disciples and all who should be added to them until He comes.

2. Jesus gave the bread and the wine to the disciples while He was yet present with them. The elements then were not in any literal or physical sense his body, but they were intended to enable his disciples afterwards to realize his presence. In whatever sense they make His presence real to the communicant, they are sacramental.

3. There is no office, or ecclesiastical ordinance or order superior or essential to the sacrament which Jesus gave to the disciples in the upper chamber. The apostles could communicate it, but they could not limit or prevent the grace of Christ from going forth from it wherever partaken, that He may be present even where two or three are met in His Name. For it was not the ministering hand of that disciple who was nearest Jesus at the Last Supper who gave the bread to the other disciples, it was Jesus himself who made the bread and wine sacramental. When so given both in matter and in form, in the words which Jesus used, what right have we by any ordinance of ours to pronounce not valid the blessing of our Lord?

III. The Eucharist and the Priesthood

The subordinate but not necessarily divisive question arises concerning the priestly character of the ministration of the Eucharist.

1. It will be agreed on all sides that the Lord's Supper represented to the disciples the sacrificial death of Christ.

2. It follows consequently that in consecrating the elements the servant acts in accordance with the priestly office of the Lord. The sacrament in and of itself gives to the ministration of it a priestly character.

3. It is generally held among us that all the offices of Christ as prophet, priest, and king are committed to his Church; and in this particular the priestly office of Christ is continued in the common priesthood of believers. With all the other gifts of grace it is the endowment and heritage of no

single class or order, but of the Church which is his body. The first Church of Christ in Jerusalem held all things in common, and that included not material goods only, but all spiritual values as well.

4. While holding precious our own experiences of the grace of the sacrament, we would not limit the beliefs of others who have come to regard the Eucharist as the sacrament of the Altar. We would humbly recognize all the varieties of religious experience in the communion of the Lord's Supper, and whenever it is observed we would gladly partake of it ourselves, answering the Lord's last prayer that his disciples may be one.

IV. The Orders of Ministry

As we rediscover our fellowship in these greater matters of religious experience, we may find the way already opening before us through the lesser differences of our ecclesiastical polities.

1. General Agreements Respecting Ordination

a. *The qualifications of candidates for ordination.* There are no separative differences. Indeed if in the canonical requirements for the ordination of a priest in the Episcopal Church, for the word Bishop the words Ordaining Council be substituted, the usual Congregational procedure would be quite well described. So far as examination as to soundness of faith is concerned, while no particular creed is required, the candidate is asked to present a full statement of his beliefs, and is questioned with regard to it as the ordaining Council may see fit. The Congregational National Council recently adopted unanimously a declaration of their faith. The consent of the ordaining Council is necessary before the candidate may be regularly ordained and received into our ministry.

b. *Certified list of accredited ministers.* The names of the ministers recognized as belonging to the Congregational ministry are certified and registered in the Congregational Year Book.

2. What Is Visibly Set Forth in Ordination

a. *The regular and lawful ordering of the ministry.* Each communion may properly reserve to itself the right, as it is its obligation, to determine its own procedure with regard to its ministry.

b. Such ordination, includes a special consecration and prayer for the impartation of the Holy Spirit and the grace of God according to the obligation and the needs of the ministry.

c. It is essential that there be recognition of the fellowship of other communions in the ministry of the Church of God.

3. What Is Implicitly Recognized in Such Ordination

a. The intention of Ordination is understood as the setting apart and consecrating of the person ordained to the distinctive service of Christ for which he is ordained according to the teaching of the New Testament and the practice of the churches under variant forms from the time of the Apostles.

b. While we find no authority either in Scripture or in Christian experience for the assumption that there can be no spiritually valid administration of the Lord's Supper except by an ordained ministry, there is need of such ministry for the regular and orderly administration of the Lord's Supper.

c. Ordination involves the recognition of the ministry as an essential organ of the Church, that the church may continue in the Apostles' faith and teaching.

4. Differences Concerning Ordination

Differences arise from divergencies of views concerning the conference of grace through ordination.

a. According to one view it is held that a needful or enhanced degree of gracious influence may be inwardly and spiritually received as one has been set apart and consecrated to the Christian ministry. Of whom much is required, to him much is given. On the other hand it is held that, more than this, through the act of ordination some distinctive power or grace may be transmitted. According to this view, when carried to an extreme, it will be believed that such grace of orders may be tactually conferred by the Episcopal ordination of a priest, in the church.

b. These views when carried to an extreme seem to be so divergent that, like the two sides of a parabola, they could not recurve and meet though prolonged to infinity. Nevertheless these diverging conceptions are not necessarily so parabolic as they may seem. Possibly if more thoroughly thought out and measured by their values in religious experience they may be found, like an ellipse proceeding from its two foci, to meet in one large Christian comprehension.

c. The possible way of reconciliation is to be sought through a recognition each by the other of the partial truth for which each stands. The one view is predominantly the prophetic conception of the Christian ministry. The other, as distinguished from it, is the priestly view. One holds to the immediate personal experience of grace. The other rests on the corporate endowment of grace for the office of the ministry. Each of these positions, taken by itself alone, does not stand for the whole testimony of the Spirit in the history of the Church of Christ. The one tendency is centrifugal; if unbalanced it results in a multitude of sects. The other is centripetal; if left unchecked it tends to reduce the Church to a lifeless mass in which individuality is lost.

d. The Spirit of Christ, ever present and coworking throughout the history of the Church, has not suffered either of these tendencies to go too far without counteraction from the other, although for a season now one, now the other, may seem to be in the ascendant.

e. The conclusion follows that should any church or party within a church carry so far its distinctive tendency as to separate itself from the fellowship of other Christian communions, that would be for it to fall into the peril of sinful schism. The whole Church is greater than its parts; it is more also than the sum of its parts. It is to be orderly fellowship of all together in the liberty wherewith Christ makes free.

5. Differences Concerning the Conferring of Ordination

These are secondary to the differences just mentioned. But they are the most obvious stumbling blocks in the way to reunion of the churches. In accordance with the first principles set forth above, this difficulty would appear to be one left wholly within the power of men of good will in the several communions to remove as a wall of separation between us.

(1) For first, as stated above, the apostles committed all that they had received from the Lord to the churches which they founded. "All things are Yours," said the Apostle Paul.

(2) The Church of Christ has inherent power so to adapt its organs and functions that it may survive and bear fruit more abundantly from generation to generation. This is only saying that this Church is the living Church having in itself the Spirit of life from the Lord.

(3) The Apostles did not have, and as witnesses to Jesus could not have had, any personal successors. The Apostolic succession, which may be recognized, is the succession of the spiritual gifts residing in and continued through the Church, not apart from it or superior to its being.

The Congregational churches since their separation from the Church of England have maintained a regular succession of ordained ministers who have been chosen, set apart and accredited in their fellowship according to their usages. They hold that their ministers are episcopally ordained, and that they are ordained to the episcopate. They hold their ministry to be regular and valid also as rightly intended in accordance with the will of our Lord, and as abundantly justified and rendered acceptable unto God by the fruits of the Spirit. While not for a moment denying what they are well assured their God and the God of their fathers has blessed, they would hold their trust of ministry in willingness to receive as well as to give whatever may be lacking that Christ may be all in all.

V. Confirmation and Confession of Faith

A point of difference between the Congregational and the Episcopal churches is to be found in matters of Confirmation and Confession of Faith. In regard to none of the major rites of the Church has usage altered in historic times more than in regard to that of confirmation.

Unquestionably the majority of the earlier candidates received into the Church were those of mature years, and in connection with baptism, or shortly after baptism, it was customary that they should have hands laid upon them, as symbolizing, if not actually effecting the reception of the Spirit, as in the eighth of Acts. Baptism and the laying on of hands certainly constitutes one ceremony by the third century in the Church, as Tertullian asserts, and nothing which could be called a differentiation of confirmation from baptism then existed. In the course of time the Eastern and Western Churches went different ways, and their attitude is still different. The Eastern Church to this day regards confirmation as part of the baptismal service, and anointing by the priest with oil which has been consecrated by the bishop is distinctly a ceremony applicable to infancy. In western Christendom the custom grew up in the early middle ages of reserving confirmation to the bishop, though the age of the recipient and the proximity to the baptismal reception were long indeterminate. With the Reformation, Churches like the Anglican and the Lutheran maintained confirmation as a separate ceremony, though insisting generally upon an intellectual preparation on the part of the candidate. In the Anglican communion confirmation remained in the hands of the bishop; in the Lutheran, in that of any regularly established pastor. Comparatively modern times have witnessed in many communions an emphasis upon confirmations as personal assumption of baptismal vows made in behalf of the recipient in childhood as well as the gift of the grace of the Holy Spirit, which seems to have been its early significance.

The Congregational churches from their origin, instead of confirmation have emphasized confession of faith. They have regarded the believer as entering into a peculiar personal and intimate relation with his Lord through a mutual covenant, in which, after the model of the Abrahamic covenant of old, the disciple personally acknowledged the Lordship of Christ and his fellowship with Christ's people. This they have regarded as no one-sided acknowledgment, but one in which the Lord himself receives his sincere follower. As such the Congregational churches have always regarded confession of faith and entrance into the covenant, not indeed as a sacrament, but as the most sacred of all transactions in which a disciple might engage. It is fair to say that the Congregational churches, with this interpretation of entrance into the covenant relation between the believer and his Lord, regard the transaction as more solemn, intimate and vital, and as demanding far more of the human participant than is usually required in confirmation.

At the same time it would seem that the important elements in confirmation were preserved in the Congregational practice; for that is in the highest degree a personal assumption of vows made in one's behalf in infant baptism; and also the divine promise to those in covenant relation, "I will be a God unto thee, and to thy seed after thee," is a promise which may very properly be held to include the bestowment of all spiritual gifts.

VI. Further Proposals for Reunion

The Lambeth Appeal invites conferences for considering the possibility of taking definite steps to cooperate in a common endeavor, on the lines set forth in their Appeal, to restore the unity of the Church of Christ. This call lays upon us the obligation, as it opens to us the opportunity, of making new proposals to your Commission for conferences with you. In particular the overtures submitted to all their Christian Brethren by the Anglican Bishops concerning Ordination, ask them to accept "a commission through Episcopal ordination, as obtaining for them a ministry throughout the whole fellowship." They expressly declare that "in so acting no one of us could possibly be taken to repudiate his past ministry." They say, "We shall be publicly and formally seeking additional recognition of a new call to wider service in a reunited Church, and imploring for ourselves God's grace and strength to fulfil the same." And they further declare that "if the authorities of other communions should so desire, we are persuaded that, terms of union having been otherwise satisfactorily adjusted, Bishops and clergy of our Communion would willingly accept from these authorities a form of commission or recognition which would commend our ministry to their congregations, as having its place in our one family life. . . . We can only say that we offer it in all sincerity as a token of our longing that all ministries of grace, theirs and ours, shall be available for the service of our Lord in a united Church."

We on our part would recognize the fact that the spirit and the form in which these proposals are offered largely relieve difficulties arising from differences of convictions and inherited feelings. They disclaim, at least, the implications involved in such words as "reordination" or "conditional ordination," and offer to give and to receive in some possible way a new commission for mutual ministry in the larger fellowship.

We accordingly would submit for conference the following consideration:

1. The confessions and declarations of faith of our own and other protestant communions as a sufficient basis for a common fellowship in the ministry.

2. We would deem worthy of further consideration, the possible service that might be rendered by a constitutional Episcopate freely adapted to the polities of other churches in their common fellowship.

3. We recall the fact that our forefathers carried over from the Church of England habits and practices which they freely adapted their new conditions as independent churches. One such inherited custom of ours may be particularly pertinent in our present efforts to reach mutually acceptable practical proposals. When one of our ministers, who has been previously ordained, is called to the pastorate of another church, it is customary for that church to invite a Council of the neighboring churches to meet and advise with them as an Installing Council, and if it be deemed best in their judgment, after due inquiry, to install him over his new charge, and to commend him to the fellowship of our churches. It occurs to us that similarly to the functions of our installing Council, the bishop might be charged with the responsibility of judging, concerning the sufficiency of the faith and necessary personal qualification of a minister who was desirous of receiving the additional commission in accordance with the Lambeth proposals. Some general canonical provision to that effect, which you might deem efficient, leaving both the bishop and clergyman to come to a good understanding, might safeguard all essential interests, and be at once understood and acceptable to ministers of other communions. Some early precedents for such "orders of license" in the Church of England might be adduced.

On our part we would welcome from you, and submit to the serious consideration of our ministry and churches, any further proposals or canonical provisions which you may deem practical, and which may serve to promote the fellowship of the faith and the ministry of the whole Church of God.

10. The Useless Concordat:
"Additional Statement" and "The Springfield Declaration on Unity"

(1923)

Commission on Comity, Federation and Unity; William E. Barton

At the 1923 meeting of the National Council of the Congregational Churches, the Commission on Comity, Federation and Unity reported the conclusion of its thirty-seven-year-long negotiations with the Episcopal Church. In spite of the approval of a concordat by the General Convention of the Protestant Episcopal Church giving constitutional provision for reordaining non-Episcopal ministers with an Episcopal ordination, the application for Episcopal ordination made by Congregationalist Roland Bainton of Yale Divinity School had been refused by the bishop of Connecticut. An "Additional Statement" by the commission detailing the unfortunate case was appended to the report of the commission.

The National Council encouraged the commission to focus on more fruitful possibilities for union, instructed the commission to meet with any commission from the General Assembly of the Presbyterian Church in the U.S.A. on a plan for union, and approved the plan of union proposed by the American Council on Organic Union. Finally, the National Council adopted a "Declaration on Unity" presented by Rev. William E. Barton (1861–1930).

Source: Commission on Comity, Federation and Unity, "Additional Statement," in *Minutes of the National Council of the Congregational Churches of the United States, Twentieth Regular Meeting, Springfield, Massachusetts, October 16–23, 1923* (New York: Office of the National Council, 1923), 219–20; William E. Barton, "Declaration on Unity" ["The Springfield Declaration"], in ibid., 220–22.

Barton had long been recognized as an authority on Congregationalism, having written the widely quoted manual The Law of Congregational Usage *in 1916, and he had been a member of the Congregational Commission on Unity in the final negotiations with the Episcopalians. The declaration upheld somewhat defiantly the "valid, apostolic, prophetic and priestly ministry" of the Congregational churches. This became the conclusive response by the Congregational churches to those who insisted upon the historic episcopate.*

Additional Statement

In addition to its printed report, the Commission on Comity, Federation and Unity has to report that a recent event of much importance has thrown light on the question whether or not the Episcopal Bishops have power to act in any instance according to the agreements of the Concordat. This involves the serious question under what obligations to act the Bishops are laid in accordance with the agreements of the Concordat adopted by the Episcopal Convention. The Canon explicitly and positively states upon what conditions an applicant for additional ordination under the Canon may receive orders. It thus creates a certain right on the one side and a corresponding obligation on the other side.

The particular case which brings this question to a point of decision is as follows: Professor Bainton of the Divinity School of Yale University, with the approval of Dean Brown, asked of the Bishop of Connecticut such ordination. This instance was itself of more than ordinary local significance owing to its relations to the interests of religious education in the universities. The Bishop was unwilling to grant the request. Without reference to any personal or other considerations of which the Bishop must be the judge, the final reason which the Bishop gave for his refusal to grant this application at once renders this case a precedent for all such applications, and consequently it becomes a test case of the value of the Concordat to the ministry of other churches. For the Bishop stated that the House of Deputies had refused to concur with the House of Bishops in authorizing such changes in the form of ordering Priests as might seem advisable in the special ordinations authorized by the Concordat. Consequently the Bishop decided that he had no power to proceed for, he said, a "bishop must act under the law," hence, so far as this decision is accepted by the Episcopal Church, the offer to us of the Concordat does not hold good.

The Corresponding Secretary of the Commission, Dr. Smyth, then wrote to the Secretaries of the General Convention requesting them to send transcripts of any acts relating to this subject. Their answers made clear that the action of the House of Bishops favoring the Concordat was received by the Deputies on the afternoon of the day before the adjournment of the convention; and, on the next morning, was returned without concurrence to the Bishops just before their adjournment, after their routine business had been finished, and too late for any conference with the other House. Therefore no further action was taken. Consequently, as at present advised, subsequent action is the responsibility of the Episcopal Church.

In recording this apparent failure of the negotiations to find some solution of the problem of ministerial ordination, your Commission desires gratefully to record the progress that has been made towards mutual understanding. The significant fact should not be lost sight of, that the General Convention, both Houses concurring, amended the Constitution of the Episcopal Church so as to make constitutional provision for giving Episcopal ordination to men remaining ministers of other churches, thus recognizing the validity of the ministry of other churches. This is a long step in one direction towards the ultimate reunion of the English-speaking Church.

On motion the report of the Commission as a whole was adopted.

Declaration on Unity

The Congregational Churches of the United States, by delegates in National Council assembled, viewing with sorrow the sectarian divisions existing in Christendom, and earnestly desiring that in the midst of a divided and hostile world, there may be a friendly and united Church, hail with unfeigned joy every indication of approach to union in the visible body of Christ. Believing that in the present condition of opinion in the Church and in the world, a declaration of our own position as a branch of the Holy Catholic Church will have value both in preventing futile and ill-advised attempts at impossible and undesirable approaches to forms of uniformity without the spirit of oneness in Christ, and also in furthering every feasible approach toward an outward and visible expression of the unity of the Spirit which underlies all denominational differences, hereby set forth our historic and present attitude toward the unity of the Church of Christ.

I. We believe that the basis of all Christian unity is unity in the Spirit of Christ; and that all men who are in Christ are one, and are members of the Holy Catholic Church, however wide and deep may be their apparent separation in race, nationality or history in rite or ceremonial or creed. We believe that all external unity, if valid, must inhere in this fundamental unity. "There is one body, and one Spirit, even as we are called in one hope of our calling."

II. The Congregational Churches believe and affirm that they are true churches of the Lord Jesus Christ with a valid, apostolic, prophetic and priestly ministry; and we cannot recognize in any organization a more valid ministry or a higher ecclesiastical authority than that which we possess as a branch of the Holy Catholic Church. This faith, however, we hold in the broadest catholicity, affirming with those who established this National Council.—

"As little as did our fathers in their day, do we in ours make pretention to be the only churches of Christ. We find ourselves consulting and acting together under the distinctive name of Congregationalists, because, in the present condition of our common Christianity, we have felt ourselves called to ascertain and do our own appropriate part of the work of Christ's Church among men. We especially desire, in prosecuting the common work of evangelizing our own land and world, to observe the common and sacred law, that in the wide field of the world's evangelization, we do our work in friendly co-operation with all those who love and serve our common Lord. We believe in the Holy Catholic Church. It is our prayer and endeavor that the unity of the church may be more and more apparent, and that the prayer of our Lord for His disciples may be speedily and completely answered and all be one; and that by consequence of this Christian unity in love, the world may believe in Christ as sent of the Father to save the world."

III. We stand ready to meet any approach toward closer visible union with other branches of the Christian Church upon a level plane of mutual good will and mutual recognition of prerogative. We will meet any duly constituted church of Jesus Christ with full recognition of its authority and of the validity of a ministry ordained with intent to convey authority, to preach the gospel and administer the ordinances of the church in accordance with the commands of our Lord Jesus Christ. We will and do receive members from other churches as we receive them from our own churches. We will not and do not call common that which God hath cleansed, nor deny spiritual efficacy where God has manifested His Spirit. We hold in honor the name by which this group of churches has come to be called, a name descriptive of our form of government; but we will hold to no distinctive name if by mutual abandonment of denominational titles we may be permitted without apparent arrogance or misrepresentation to resume the name by which our churches historically were called, The "Churches of Christ" in their several localities. We hold dear certain forms in which we are accustomed to confess our faith, but we have never used and will never use a creed for purposes of division or exclusion.

We cannot by the abandonment of our name or the disregard of our historic symbols effect immediate union with other branches of the Church of Christ. But we are ready to go forward as the Spirit of Christ shall lead us, into the larger unities of the Kingdom of God.

As we cannot permit creeds to be imposed upon us, so we will impose no divisive creeds upon others. We will seek not every church its own things, but every church also the things of others. This only will we ask, and this we freely offer that unitedly we will confess and serve our common Lord, and love one another as He gave us commandment.

And if this vision tarry, even now and until it is fully come, will we live in the spirit and hope of its accomplishment. We will refrain from planting new churches that must compete with Christian churches already organized. We will treat all Christians as Christians, and all Christian ministers as ministers of Christ, and all Christian churches as churches of the Lord Jesus Christ; we will pray for and seek to promote the unity of the Spirit in the bond of peace, to the honor of our Lord and Saviour, Jesus the Christ.

The Global Ecumenical Influence

11. India:

"Real Union in South India"

(1908)

J. P. Jones

The South India United Church (1908) was the union of nearly all the Presbyterian and Congregational missions in South India: the Presbyterian Union of the churches of the United Free Church of Scotland in Madras and vicinity, the churches of the Dutch Reformed Mission in the Arcot district (the so-called Scudder Mission), and the Congregational Union of the churches of the missions of the American Board of Commissioners for Foreign Missions and the London Missionary Society in South India. These six missions comprised a Christian community of more than 140,000. The union had certain federal characteristics, allowing considerable independence in eight regional councils.

Although the union was sometimes denigrated for having been "engineered" by missionaries, it pointed toward the vision of an even larger Church of South India, in which all churches that accepted the supremacy of Holy Scripture might be united. In the minds of Congregationalists, such a union was not simply a hope or a vision but an actual possibility.

In the city of Madras, where Protestant missions were established nearly two centuries ago, and in the old Congregational church whose history of

Source: J. P. Jones, "Real Union in South India," *The Congregationalist and Christian World,* 12 September 1908, 333–34.

more than a century is replete with reminiscences of famous missionaries, was held a meeting, July 25–27, which will probably take a unique place in the annals of the church of God in India.

It was the occasion of the consummation of the plan of union of the South India United Church. This ecclesiastical union has for years been the subject of the earnest prayers and efforts of many of God's people. It was really the coming together of two ecclesiastical unions which had existed for a few years. The one was the Presbyterian Union of the churches of the United Free Church of Scotland in Madras and vicinity and those of the Dutch Reformed Mission in the Arcot district—the well-known Scudder Mission, which separated half a century ago from the Madura Mission of the A. B. C. F. M. The other was the Congregational Union of the churches of the missions of the A. B. C. F. M. and the London Missionary Society in South India.

Belonging to these six missions there is a Christian community of more than 140,000 souls. Of these more than 22,000 are communicants connected with the 118 organized churches.

This union meeting was one of unbroken harmony and of much enthusiasm. There were more than a hundred delegates, of whom about three-fourths were Indians, while the rest were foreign missionaries. The Declaration of Union was unanimously adopted. The two bodies came together while singing "All hail the power of Jesus' Name"; and, as soon as the declaration was read, the whole audience spontaneously rose and sang the Doxology. Much joy and enthusiasm were revealed in praise and fellowship upon reaching this result.

New Ecclesiastical Products

Ecclesiastically the consummation of this union is quite unique, for it involves more than a union of Presbyterians and Congregationalists. It represents a blending of two forms of Presbyterianism—those of the United Free Church of Scotland and of the Dutch Reformed Church of America. It also embraces the rigid Congregationalism of the American missions with the jealous individualism of English independency.

The product is a happier one than we had hoped for. It furnishes an elastic polity which wisely blends the excellence of all the systems involved. It recognizes three organizations—churches, church councils and the general assembly. It conserves to all who desire it the autonomy of the individual church, and at the same time it enables such churches as may wish it to seek advice and direction from the councils. Any church is at liberty to conduct its affairs by popular votes, by a committee or by a body of elders, just as it please.

The General Assembly possesses more the character of a Congregational Council than a Presbyterian General Assembly. Its functions are mainly advisory and not legislative. The terminology of the union is a blending of the Congregational and the Presbyterian, with an avoidance of the terms of either party in several instances.

A Liberal Intellectual Basis

The Confession of the United Church is brief and to the point. While it does not evade the statement of any important doctrine, it avoids any undue elaboration or detail. It has only five articles, and even these are preceded and followed by italicized notes, which soften their rigor and diminish their importance, and which comfort the nervous individualist, more anxious to be protected in his creed of tomorrow than in his confession of today.

It is an admirable illustration of the waning dominance of intellectual assent as a basis of union among men who are building up the Kingdom of God in a great heathen land. And may the day soon come when all creeds and confessions shall cease to have a place as a basis of fellowship and of organic life among those who love the Lord in sincerity and who desire to unite together in the cultivation of love, of mutual regard and of co-operation in Christian service.

An Indigenous Movement

This union must not be regarded as a movement created by, and representative of, the progressive spirit of the Indian Church itself. Some have preferred against it the charge that it is engineered by the missionaries. The charge cannot be denied, although all the leaders of the Indian Church, save a few connected with the churches of the London mission, have taken an active interest and have voted cordially in behalf of all the propositions. The Indian members of the General Assembly revealed genuine joy in the consummation of the union and will do everything they can in behalf of an ever-broadening fellowship and communion of life.

The prominence of the missionaries in this movement is striking and significant. Though they represent several denominations and denominational interests in the far-off lands, they are heartily sick of representing before this people a divided and divisive Christianity. It must also be claimed that in the creation of this union the missionary leaders have shown admirable spirit in the voluntary effacement of their own denominational peculiarities. There has been a most genuine desire among all to eliminate as far as possible everything that is distinctly of the West, western, and to give to the movement a thorough Oriental complexion and to make the United Church an Eastern Church so far as we of the West are able to apprehend the spirit and the need of the East.

Another fact needs emphasis, namely, that in this whole movement toward union the missionary has worked toward his own effacement. The United Church is distinctly an Indian Church. If the missionary is still needed for its highest development, it is also eminently true that it is built on a foundation whose superstructure must more and more become Indian, and in which the place of the missionary will find ever diminishing importance until his help is no further required, and he passes away and becomes to the Indian Church a vision of the past.

It is interesting to note that our Presbyterian friends have been perhaps the most ardent in the pursuit of this union. It is not because their Christian communities are comparatively very small. They are far stronger than their numbers indicate. They have shown a willingness to sacrifice much in behalf of this Christian ideal, and have allowed nothing to stand between them and the consummation of this purpose.

It is some of the churches connected with the London Missionary Society, especially those which have been unduly indoctrinated in the sweets of autonomy and in the glories of individualism, which have thus far stood outside the union. But there is every indication that these also will soon abandon their isolation and join the growing forces of union.

Problems Raised by the Union

The limitations of this movement must not be overlooked. The churches uniting in this compact are mission churches. Some of them are not self-supporting, and their financial and administrative affairs are partly in the hands of missions or missionaries. And yet in matters of self-support and of self-government the Indian Church is rapidly moving forward.

Some of the functions of the church itself are exercised by the missions. The support and conduct of training institutions, of public schools, of evangelistic effort, of magazines, with the erection and maintenance of buildings for all this work, has not yet become the serious care of the Indian Church. But it is the special merit of this new union that it plans to absorb gradually all these outward activities of the mission and make them its own. It will require time for this. But it is a definite part of the scheme of the United Church to take up all forms of mission activity in the day of its growing strength. Indeed, some of these, such as the union of our theological seminaries and of our magazines, are already a part of its immediate program of activity. And committees have already been formed for the purpose of creating uniformity, so far as possible, in such matters as the forms of divine service, conditions of church membership and marriage rules. There is much in this line which will tax the energies of the United Church for some time to come.

Some of the anomalies and difficulties of the new situation are apparent. What is the ecclesiastical relation of the missionary to this church? It was amusing to see the difficulty which embarrassed the missionaries of some of the societies as they tried to explain their ecclesiastical status or connections. None are connected definitely with the Indian Church. Some are distinctly connected with, and amenable to, ecclesiastical bodies in a foreign land. Missionaries of the American Board feel that ecclesiastically they are orphans, while some of our London Missionary Society brethren are even more loose-jointed than ourselves, and neither own nor desire ecclesiastical affinities in any land on earth! Evidently, therefore, the position of the missionary is anomalous and his relation to the United Church is both irregular and temporary.

In the past it has been generally understood that every mission was in honor bound to establish and perpetuate the ecclesiastical polity of the home church which supported it. But here are the churches of four separate denominations severing their connection with their ecclesiastical past and launching out upon a new union which is not the offspring of any denomination. It is encouraging to know that while these separate denominations in the homeland have no thought of uniting, they have thus far thrown no obstacles to the union of their churches and missions in the foreign field. And for this generous sympathy all who have had a share in the formation of this union are truly grateful.

Relationship to Home Societies

It is easy to see how, when the United Church begins to control the various departments of missionary activity within its territory, difficulties may arise among the societies that have thus far supported these missions. Shall they withdraw from it entirely, or shall they contribute their share, as in the past, for its maintenance? This will raise another question. Will the societies and the missions then relinquish the principle which they have so often proclaimed and cherished, namely, that the native church shall have control only of those funds which it raises on the field? Many have held this to be a sacred principle. But it seems likely that it must be abandoned in view of the progress of the United Church in the conduct of all work within its own territory.

We believe that all these difficulties will vanish as the years increase, and that the fervent heat of love and fellowship which this movement has engendered will burn away all barriers to its future success.

Another matter which received consideration from the General Assembly was a scheme of federation with churches of other missions which are not prepared to enter into organic union with us. For example, the General Assembly of the Presbyterian Church of all India sent its delegate with a special request that our body enter into negotiations with it with a view to federation, if not something more. That august body parted with great reluctance from its South India Synod, which entered into our union, and still desires to keep in close touch with the United Church. Then, delegates from the Wesleyans, the Methodists and the Baptists, while expressing their inability to unite with us organically, were nevertheless very anxious to draw into closer fellowship and common activity with us on lines of federation. A committee was appointed to further and to perfect any such schemes and to present the same to the next General Assembly.

Thus the spirit of Christian fellowship and union is manifesting itself with ever-increasing power and is spreading all over this great land. Pan-Anglican, Pan-Lutheran, Pan-Presbyterian and various other "Pans" are already at work cultivating mutual understanding and amity within the various branches of each denomination and looking amiably into other folds to discover incitements to a wider fellowship.

This union movement has found no warmer friends and advocates than those two revered fathers in Christ recently called to join "the General Assembly and church of the first born who are enrolled in heaven." Dr. Jacob Chamberlain was the first moderator of the Presbyterian Synod of South India, and Dr. James Duthie the first chairman of the General Assembly—the two bodies whose union has now been consummated. The former spent forty-eight years and the latter fifty-two years of noble service for the cause of Christ and of Christian union in this land. They both looked forward with eagerness to the fulfillment of their desire in this union. How glad would they have been to have a part in the consummation of their labors and ours. But their task was done, and they have gone to their reward: but the blessed work in which they had so distinguished a part will go on from strength to strength, spreading and sending down its roots, like the great banian tree, until it covers the whole land.

The Confession of Faith Adopted by the South India United Church

NOTE I. *As the Confession is a human instrument, it is understood that persons assenting to it do not commit themselves to every word or phrase, but accept it as a basis of union, and as embodying substantially the vital truths held in common by the uniting Churches.*

1. We believe in one God, who is a personal Spirit, the Creator, Sustainer, and Governor of all things, infinite in love, wisdom, power, holiness, justice, goodness and truth. We acknowledge the mystery of the Holy Trinity—the Father, the Son and the Holy Spirit.

2. We believe that God, who manifests Himself in Creation and Providence, and especially in the spirit of man, has been pleased to reveal His mind and will for our salvation in various ways with ever-growing fullness, and that the record of this revelation, so far as needful for our salvation, is contained in the Scriptures of the Old and New Testaments, which are therefore to be devoutly studied by all; and we reverently acknowledge the Holy Spirit speaking in the Scriptures to be the supreme authority in matters of faith and duty.

3. We believe that all men are made in the image of God, and are brethren. We acknowledge that all have sinned and come short of the glory of God, having in manifold ways offended against God's good and holy law; and that out of this condition no man is able to deliver himself.

4. We believe that, to save man from the guilt and power of sin, God the Father in His infinite love sent into the world His only begotten Son, who alone is the perfect incarnation of God, and through whom alone men can be saved; that the Lord Jesus Christ through words of grace, and through His perfect obedience even unto the death of the cross, did reveal the Father, and by His life, death and resurrection did establish a way by which men may obtain forgiveness of sins and the gift of eternal life; that the Holy Spirit, the Lord, the Giver of life, maketh us partakers of salvation, enlightening our minds, convincing us of our sins, persuading us to accept Jesus Christ, and working in us the fruits of righteousness.

5. We believe that the Lord Jesus Christ has established a Church for the realization of the Kingdom of God, in which Church all who follow Him in sincerity are members, and that He entrusted to the Church the duty of making known to all men the Gospel of salvation through His name; we also believe that He instituted the ministry of the Word and the

Sacraments of Baptism and the Lord's Supper; we believe in the Resurrection of the dead and in a Judgement through Christ whereby all shall receive according to the deeds done in the present life, whether good or bad.

NOTE II. *The South India Church reserves to itself the right to revise the general Confession of Faith whenever the consensus of opinion of the United Body demands it.*

12. Edinburgh World Mission Conference: *"The Communion of Saints"*

(1910)

The Congregationalist and Christian World

The World Missionary Conference in Edinburgh in 1910 gave those who attended it an expanded awareness of the Christian community. This awakening, described so eloquently in "The Communion of Saints," is one of the earliest witnesses in The Congregationalist *to what the twentieth century came to call "the ecumenical experience." It is known by all Christians as they discuss with one another, attend conference annual meetings, ministerial associations, study groups, and all the myriad sorts of meetings of the global ecumenical movement. In those settings, a disparate group of people, highly aware of all that separates them, come together for dialogue in a common cause, and barriers are broken. Persons of radically different opinions gain a greater awareness of the views that they share with others, rather than those that separate them. Persons of differing ethnic, racial, denominational, and national origins, and of differing political and sexual orientations discover, behind the eyes of the Other, a brother or a sister. They see one another; they hear one another; they teach and admonish one another. They find, present among them, uniting them, the Spirit of Jesus Christ.*

What is the communion of saints? Let the reader attempt to answer this question before proceeding further. Many profess to believe in it. What does their belief amount to?

Source: A. E. Dunning, "The Communion of Saints," *The Congregationalist and Christian World,* 10 December 1910, 877.

The communion we mean is the interchange of thoughts and feelings between those who seek to grow in the knowledge of God, our Father, and into the likeness of his Son, our Lord. It means sympathetic and helpful intercourse to this end with men and women living in this world. The usefulness, even the life of the Christian church, depends on the communion of saints.

How can this communion best be promoted? Is it not by the assembling of saints together? But often they gather in the same building without knowing what it is to be together. Instruction is only one of the objects for which Christians attend church. The worship of God by the individual is only one of these objects. Not second to either of these is the communion of Christians with one another.

An article in the *London Quarterly Review,* quoted by the *Churchman,* illustrates what this communion is. The writer is discussing the psychology of religious fellowship as it was manifested in the World Missionary Conference in Edinburgh last summer. Men who spoke in various tongues, who held a wide variety of beliefs and who had been trained in different customs of worship assembled from every part of the world. Of course Chinamen, Africans, Slavs and Anglo-Saxons could not at once enter into intimate relations of fellowship. But the processes by which during the ten days of those meetings every barrier to their communion melted away were worthy of consideration in every church.

First of all, these strangers who were meeting as brethren *saw one another.* The Assembly Hall is a peculiar work of architecture. Two of the three sections of seats on the floor face each other and those who sit in the third section can look into the faces of brethren on either side, while all have the platform full in view. Every person present had before his eyes the faces of hundreds of others. The conference saw itself in all its moods, intent, inquiring, responding to the speaker's appeal. Every emotion was shared by the whole assembly, the answering smile at a humorous saying, the sympathetic expression as another's trial was mentioned, the thanksgiving, hope, purpose, as the work done or to be done was described.

One reason for the failure of many church prayer meetings may be laid to the seating arrangement. Who could carry on an animated conversation with his neighbor gazing down the back of his neck? The communion of saints needs the sight of their countenances. Thoughts and emotions are communicated through the eye and face and kindling expression of those who thus reveal the spirit within to friends with whom they are holding communion.

Some changes of architecture, then, are called for in many of our churches and rooms for prayer and conference. The spiritual temperature of friendly intercourse is raised not by words alone, but even more by the thoughts and feelings expressed without words in the animated countenances of those moved by the same spirit. It is therefore necessary to their next full communion that they see one another.

Next, the saints in that World's Conference *heard one another.* They heard the speakers, of course. In that assembly from many nations some understood the language on the platform and others did not. But rarely during the sessions did a full hour pass without a hymn or prayer. The hymns chosen were few in number and often repeated. This was intentional, for not many hymns are found in English collections which appeal to Christians of all lands and express their feelings well. The favorite hymns were simple, personal, by the use of which one and all could pour forth their adoration of God, their confessions, their longings. The passion of such hymns was a common passion and in it the communion of saints was realized. The conference was another Pentecost where, whatever the language in which the song was written, every one heard in his own tongue the wonderful works of God. And when prayer took the place of song in worship there was the same result. United feeling bred united thought, and again the communion of saints was realized.

Much spiritual power is wasted in our churches by selecting from one to four persons to worship God in song and measuring the value of the worship by the degree of exactness with which it conforms to laws and rules of musical expression. The communion of saints, as the Apostle described it, is *"teaching and admonishing one another* with psalms and hymns and spiritual songs, singing with grace in your hearts unto God." The sight of others singing with hearts moved by penitence, love to God and joy in him moves the dullest to share in the experience and its expression. The almost lost art of communion may be recovered by the assemblies where saints see and hear one another praising God.

The art above referred to emphasizes as an important aid in the communion of saints frequent periods of *united silence.* A delegate to the Edinburgh assembly wrote, "The silences of the conference were more to me than any of its speeches." Another delegate noted, "The devotional use of silence in the conference is a contribution of the first order to the church's resources for united worship and united intercessions."

Silence of itself is of course not fellowship. Who has not been in a meeting of saints where the silence was complete, but where its discord was acutely painful because every soul was inwardly crying out in isolated impatience that something ought to be doing?

United silence must be *directed silence.* The leader must give the key to which every heart is to attune itself. It may be confession, intercession for the assembly itself, for special ends to be accomplished by it, for the whole church of Christ, or for the world to be brought to him. It may be joyful thanksgiving for the gospel, or for what is being done through proclaiming it. Evidently the conference at Edinburgh found psychological effects in such silence greater than those who attended it had realized in promoting the communion of saints. This is the life of the Christian church. The success of its plans, the accomplishment of its purposes, the extension of its faith depend on it.

May not each church expect blessed results to itself and to the community by bringing its members to express to one another their thoughts and feelings toward one another and toward God by their countenances, their voices of prayer and praise and their united silences?

Can you confess with confidence as the result of your church experience, "I believe in the communion of saints"?

13. United Churches of Christ in America: *"The Plan of Union"*

(1921)

The proposal for some sort of organic union among "evangelical" churches in the United States was originally made by the Presbyterian Church in the United States of America in May of 1918 at its 130th general assembly in Columbus, Ohio. The assembly voted to invite major Protestant churches to "meet and counsel together with a view to finding a way by which we may outwardly and concretely express the spiritual union which we believe already exists among the people of Christ."

Responding to this invitation, representatives of twenty-three denominations met at Philadelphia in December 1918 for a preliminary "Interchurch Conference on Organic Union" to discuss an appropriate basis for a practical plan of union. The conference proposed an "Ad Interim Committee" to the respective denominational bodies, which would be empowered to formulate a plan based on the discussion at the Interchurch Conference. The National Council of the Congregational Churches appointed Raymond Calkins, Hubert C. Herring Sr. (replaced after his death by Lucian C. Warner), and Williston Walker to the Ad Interim Committee.

In February of 1920, the Ad Interim Committee finally called an Interchurch Conference on Organic Union in Philadelphia to consider its proposals. This gathering, representing eighteen communions, discussed exhaustively the proposed "Plan of Union," and after slight revisions adopted it nearly unanimously, sending it to the constituent bodies for

---

Source: American Council on Organic Union of the Churches of Christ, "The Plan of Union," in *Minutes of the National Council of the Congregational Churches of the United States, Nineteenth Regular Meeting, Los Angeles, California, July 1–8, 1921* (New York: Office of the National Council, 1921), 49–51.

ratification. Although the plan did not actually intend a full "organic union," it did envision a more integrated structure than was already present in the Federal Council, and it encouraged collaboration in many mission areas as an important step toward fuller, organic union. In 1921, the National Council of the Congregational Churches approved the plan in substance and sent it to the churches for their approval. By 1923, 138 churches had voted their approval and only seven had disapproved, so the national Congregational leadership voted to send its endorsement to the other participating denominations. Unfortunately, most of the other participating denominations either declined or deferred their vote.

Preamble

WHEREAS: We (the Evangelical Churches of Christ in the United States) desire to share, as a common heritage, the faith of the Christian Church, which has, from time to time, found expression in great historic statements; and

WHEREAS: We all share belief in God our Father; in Jesus Christ, His only Son, our Saviour; in the Holy Spirit, our Guide and Comforter; in the Holy Catholic Church, through which God's eternal purpose of salvation is to be proclaimed and the Kingdom of God is to be realized on earth; in the Scriptures of the Old and New Testaments as containing God's revealed will, and in the life eternal; and

WHEREAS: Having the same spirit and owning the same Lord, we none the less, recognize diversity of gifts and ministrations, for whose exercise due freedom must always be afforded in forms of worship and in modes of operation:

Plan

Now, we the Churches hereto assenting as hereinafter provided in Article VI do hereby agree to associate ourselves in a visible body to be known as the "United Churches of Christ in America," for the furtherance of the redemptive work of Christ in the world. This body shall exercise in behalf of the constituent Churches the functions delegated to it by this instrument, or by subsequent action of the constituent Churches, which shall retain the full freedom at present enjoyed by them in all matters not so delegated.

Accordingly, the Churches hereto assenting and hereafter thus associated in such visible body do initially covenant and agree as follows:

I. **Autonomy in purely denominational affairs.**

In the interest of the freedom of each and of the cooperation of all, each constituent Church reserves the right to retain its creedal statements, its form of government in the conduct of its own affairs, and its particular mode of worship:

In taking this step, we look forward with confident hope to that complete unity toward which we believe the Spirit of God is leading us. Once we shall have cooperated wholeheartedly, in such visible body, in the holy activities of the work of the Church, we are persuaded that our differences will be minimized and our union become more vital and effectual.

II. **The Council.** (How Constituted.)

The United Churches of Christ in America shall act through a Council and through such Executive and Judicial Commissions, or Administrative Boards, working *ad interim,* as such Council may from time to time appoint and ordain.

The Council shall convene as provided for in Article VI and every second year thereafter. It may also be convened at any time in such manner as its own rules may prescribe. The Council shall be a representative body.

Each constituent Church shall be entitled to representation therein by an equal number of ministers and of lay members.

The basis of representation shall be: two ministers and two lay members for the first one hundred thousand or fraction thereof of its communicants; and two ministers and two lay members for each additional one hundred thousand or major fraction thereof.

III. **The Council.** (Its Working.)

The Council shall adopt and promulgate its own By-Laws and rules of procedure and order. It shall define the functions of its own officers, prescribe the mode of their selection and their compensation, if any. It shall provide for its budget of expense by equitable apportionment of the same among the constituent Churches through their supreme governing or advisory bodies.

IV. **Relation of Council and Constituent Churches.**

The supreme governing or advisory bodies of the constituent Churches shall effectuate the decisions of the Council by general or specific deliverance or other mandate whenever it may be required by the law of a particular state, or the charter of a particular Board, or other ecclesiastical corporation; but, except as limited by this Plan, shall continue the exercise of their several powers and functions as the same exist under the denominational constitution.

The Council shall give full faith and credit to the authenticated acts and records of the several governing or advisory bodies of the constituent Churches.

V. **Specific Functions of the Council.**

In order to prevent overlapping, friction, competition or waste in the work of the existing denominational boards or administrative agencies, and to further the efficiency of that degree of cooperation which they have already achieved in their work at home and abroad:

(a) The Council shall harmonize and unify the work of the United Churches.

(b) It shall direct such consolidation of their missionary activities as well as of particular Churches in over-churched areas as is consonant with the law of the land or of the particular denomination affected. Such consolidation may be progressively achieved, as by the uniting of the boards or churches of any two or more constituent denominations, or may be accelerated, delayed, or dispensed with, as the interests of the Kingdom of God may require.

(c) If and when any two or more constituent Churches, by their supreme governing or advisory bodies, submit to the Council for its arbitrament any matter of mutual concern, not hereby already covered, the Council shall consider and pass upon such matter so submitted.

(d) The Council shall undertake inspirational and educational leadership of such sort and measure as may be proper, under the powers delegated to it by the constituent Churches, in the fields of Evangelism, Social Service, Religious Education and the like.

VI. The assent of each constituent Church to this Plan shall be certified from its supreme governing or advisory body by the appropriate officers thereof to the Chairman of the Ad Interim Committee, which shall have power upon a two-thirds vote to convene the Council as soon as the assent of at least six denominations shall have been so certified.

VII. **Amendments.**

This plan of organic union shall be subject to amendment only by the constituent Churches, but the Council may overture to such bodies any amendment which shall have originated in said Council and shall have been adopted by a three-fourths vote.

Note: The Churches represented in the Council were the Armenian, Baptist, The Christian, Church, Christian Union of United States, Congregational, Disciples, Evangelical Synod of North America, Friends (two branches), Methodist (Primitive), Methodist Episcopal, Moravian, Presbyterian Church in United States of America, Protestant Episcopal, Reformed Episcopal, Reformed Church in the United States, United Presbyterian, Welsh Presbyterian.

The attention of the constituent Churches is called to the fact that the assent called for by Article VI of the Plan should be secured in conformity with the constitution of each constituent Church.

14. CANADA:

"Church Union in Canada: An Editorial Interpretation"

(1923)

After twenty-three years of negotiation, the United Church of Canada finally came into being on June 10, 1925. It was an amalgamation of the Presbyterian, Congregational, Methodist, and the Local Union Churches (churches that had already formed union on a national scale).

Negotiations began in 1902 when an invitation was extended by the Methodist Church to the Congregational and Presbyterian churches asking whether these three churches, which had so much in common, might not consider closer union. By 1904, representatives had passed a resolution declaring organic union both desirable and practicable.

The period of 1904–10 was taken up with the preparation of the doctrinal "Basis of Union," which declared allegiance to the "evangelical doctrines of the Reformation" and presented a deft statement mediating between the Arminian and Calvinist views on election. Shortly after the three churches assented provisionally to the Basis of Union, unrest began to grow within the Presbyterian fold, with twenty of the seventy presbyteries eventually opposing both union and the Basis of Union.

From 1917 to 1921, a truce was called by mutual agreement of the churches to try to convince this strong minority that they had nothing to fear. Some of the opposition related to theological and religious factors, including anxiety that the "grand old tradition of Presbyterianism faith and witness" would be jeopardized by the Basis of Union. Some others

---

SOURCE: "Church Union in Canada: An Editorial Interpretation," *The Congregationalist,* 28 June 1923, 806–7.

disliked the more emotive forms of Methodist worship; some objected to the stance taken by the Methodists against alcohol; some were simply opposed to change. Unfortunately, the proportion of objectors did not change during the truce period.

From 1921 to 1925, efforts focused upon obtaining enabling legislation from the Canadian Dominion Parliament and the Provincial Parliaments to ensure the legal validity of the action of the churches. In addition, once it became clear that a division within the Presbyterian Church could not be avoided, time was taken to ensure a fair distribution of property between those who chose to remain Presbyterian and those who entered the new united church.

Finally, the enabling bill received royal assent, and on June 10, 1925, in Toronto, the United Church of Canada was launched. Since then it has continued to stretch out a hand to those communions that remain separate, hoping that a great and truly catholic Church of Canada may one day come into being. Congregationalists in the United States watched from south of the border and were impressed. It was no small achievement that "such diverse elements as connexionalism and congregationalism, Arminianism and Calvinism should be brought together."

After twenty years of negotiation, with long and repeated delays and postponements, when the goal seemed near attainment, the Presbyterian General Assembly of Canada, as we reported last week, has at last definitely voted to proceed with union with the Methodists and Congregationalists, and has taken action to secure from the Dominion and Provincial Parliaments of Canada such enabling legislation as is necessary to make the union legal and effective.

The basis of union upon which this action has been taken has been settled, except for very minor modifications, since 1911, when it was almost unanimously approved by the Methodists and Congregationalists.

Final action by the Presbyterians has been delayed all these years by a series of causes. From the first there has been in the Presbyterian body a strong, aggressive, and irreconcilable minority opposed to union. In the face of this opposition, represented by a voting strength of about 25 per cent. in the General Assembly, progress was slow and cautious, partly from necessity and partly from the hope that the union movement would strengthen with time. In accordance with what was known as the *Barrier Act,* the question was sent down to the Presbyteries and Sessions. By the time this popular referendum had been taken, and the matter had come back to the Assembly for decision, the War was on. The unionists were then determined to proceed at once to the consummation of union, but the opposition was so intense, and the representation so strong that action of such moment should not be taken when so many Presbyterians were on overseas service, that a compromise was suddenly agreed upon postponing further discussion and decision until two years after the closing of the War. It was feared by many that this ecclesiastical armistice might have the effect of allowing a retrogressive movement to set in, or of delaying the whole matter beyond the psychological moment. However, the question was revived after the period agreed upon and progress has since been as rapid as it could have been in view of the administrative difficulties and the problems of final consummation. If the vote now taken upsets the hope that the opposition would weaken, it also disposes of the fear that the strong majority favorable to union would back down and withdraw from negotiations when confronted with the alternative of splitting the church.

Cleavage Inevitable

The determined and persistent course of the unionists, even in the face of this cleavage, as well as the language and temper of the discussions, reveal the moral idealism and spiritual vision that have inspired and characterized this movement. Lifelong Presbyterians, with generations of Presbyterian forebears, who have loved their church and revered its past, have felt none the less that Christian unity and co-operation were leading out into new paths. There has been little of the spirit of iconoclasm. Courage and decision have been evident, but there has been ever manifest a due sense of the seriousness of the issues, and a reluctance unnecessarily either to break with the past or to disrupt present institutions and fellowships—a reluctance equalled only, it appears, by the courage to do so where spiritual necessity demanded it.

On the other hand those opposed to union have been inspired by a spirit of raw, if very sincere, denominationalism. Their roots are very firmly in the past, and they believe so intensely in Presbyterianism that they are unwilling to compromise what they deem essential matters of polity, faith and tradition. While the great majority of the liberal and progressive men are for union the lines of cleavage are not between liberals or progressives, and conservatives. Some of the leaders who are most liberal theologically are in the anti-unionist group. The cleavage is rather between those who believe that unity and co-operation are the new duty and privilege of the Church, and those who are either sheer denominationalists, or who believe that denominational integrity should not be destroyed in effective new co-operations. Dr. Drummond, of Hamilton, for instance, offered a last moment amendment in the hope of avoiding cleavage, recommending that the movement for organic union be abandoned in favor of effort toward a confederation. It must be said, however, that a considerable part of the opposition to union has centered around the historic Confession of Faith and the demand for full subscription to it. The anti-unionists, while they have called on heaven to witness their sincerity, and to further their cause have appealed boldly and unmistakably to denominational passion, if not to denominational prejudice. The advertisement from the Toronto *Globe* which we reproduced in last week's *Congregationalist* was somewhat typical of the anti-unionist methods and appeal.

Differing Like Christians

The vote in the Assembly, 426 for union to 129 against, does not differ materially from that when the Assembly first divided upon the question. During all the years feeling has run deep and high, but there has been strong, and in the main successful, effort to keep the controversy within the bounds of Christian courtesy and mutual respect and confidence. It is particularly gratifying that in the final stages, where bitterness and recrimination might have been most expected, there has been apparent a deep and sobering sense of the seriousness of the issues and the responsibility. Reports of the Assembly meetings emphasize the absence of ill-feeling and rancor throughout the debate. "We have been contending for great principles and we have done it like Christian men," said Rev. Dr. Pidgeon, Chairman of the Committee on Church Union in moving the adoption of the report. Even in an Assembly so hopelessly divided it must have been a thrilling moment when Dr. Charles W. Gordon (*Ralph Connor*) in moving a resolution of thanks to the Church Union Committee, and others, said: "Wc have passed through one of the greatest crises in our history, and it is a matter of deep gratitude to God that nothing has occurred in this debate to mar the fellowship we have had one with another," and Dr. Sedgewick, of Hamilton, Ont., one of the ablest men in the Dominion and one of the foremost opponents of union, rose to second the motion. Stating that he could not see eye to eye with either Dr. Gordon or Dr. Pidgeon, Dr. Sedgewick none the less expressed appreciation of the faithful service that had been rendered and a tremendous ovation is said to have been accorded his concluding words: "Great events in religious or secular life are dumb unless through some personality they find a voice and evoke a popular response."

Opposition Still Determined

It would be a mistake to imagine that because the nobler-minded types have differed like Christians, and have determined the atmosphere of the Assembly, that there has been an entire absence of unseemly spirit everywhere and throughout the years of controversy. Nor should it be too readily concluded that the Assembly's action has ended the controversy. By an overwhelming majority the Assembly has rendered a final decision, but already the minority has issued a statement challenging the moral and legal right of the majority to make a decision which they claim is subversive of the covenant of union upon which the Presbyterian Church in Canada was consolidated in 1875. They claim that "the prevailing part in this general assembly by reason of their illegal action as aforesaid have subverted this assembly and have thereby in effect seceded from the Presbyterian Church in Canada," and they give clear warning that they will regard all effort on the part of officials, individually or collectively, to administer property and funds other than for the Presbyterian Church as "a breach of trust in open violation of law."

Will the various parliaments pass the enabling acts, and will these fully surmount the difficulties? There is apparent confidence among the friends of union that this will be the case, but recollection of the success of the "Wee Frees" in Scotland is disconcerting, and enabling legislation will probably be upon a basis that will accord large rights to the minority.

What the Union Means

Just what, it may be asked, is the significance of the Assembly's action when it shall have attained full effect and legal approval? It will mean that the Methodist Church of Canada, the Congregational churches of Canada, and the Presbyterian Church in Canada (in so far as the majority action determines its destiny) will cease to exist as such in name or organization, and will be merged organically in *The United Church of Canada.* The proposals for this United Church have already been described in *The Congregationalist,* and it may be recalled that broadly speaking the union has as its aim the preservation in the United Church of what was most distinctive and valuable in each of the three negotiating bodies, rather than a compromised arrangement. The union can hardly be said fully to solve the problem of unity in Canada, though the uniting bodies represent a total of 2,498,120 persons, or 29.56 per cent. of the people of Canada. The leading denominations still outside of the union will be: the Anglicans, 1,407,959; the Baptists, 421,730; the Lutherans, 287,484; the Greek Church, 169,822;

and the Roman Catholics, with the largest total of all, 3,383,663. (Figures are from the census of 1921).

From the standpoint of a profound belief in the validity, necessity and possibility of Christian catholicity we should be disposed to regard the coming Canadian United Church as the making of one larger and freer denomination out of three. It perpetuates too many of the traditional denominational elements to have the full simplicity and freedom of a truly catholic church. But the whole movement toward its creation has symbolized something larger than it itself expresses. It is no small achievement that such diverse elements as connexionalism and congregationalism, Arminianism and Calvinism should be brought together. The ideal of a great, free, national church, coterminous in spirit and purpose with the Kingdom of God, is not lightly to be regarded, especially when it inspires men to sacrifice for its attainment every lesser organization and end. Our Canadian brethren have blazed the way through tangled and overgrown regions. They have given to the Christian world an example, which only to surpass can justify the failure to emulate.

15. Lausanne:

" . . . *Candid Impressions of the Conference*" *and "The Call to Unity"*

(1927)

Margaret Slattery and Lausanne Faith and Order Conference

It was not long after the World Missionary Conference in Edinburgh opened the hearts and minds of many Congregationalists to the possibility of a global Christianity that Charles H. Brent (bishop in the Philippines) persuaded his own Protestant Episcopal Church in the United States to invite "all Christian communions throughout the world which confess our Lord Jesus Christ as God and Saviour" to a global meeting on the divisive issues of doctrine and church order (deliberately not treated in Edinburgh). It took seventeen years, during which countless letters were written, contacts made, and preparatory meetings held (with the intervention of a world war), to realize Brent's vision. Finally, in 1927, over four hundred participants representing 127 Orthodox, Anglican, Reformation, and Free Churches met in Lausanne, Switzerland, "to register the apparent level of fundamental agreements within the conference and the grace points of disagreements remaining."

Discussions were held under the following rubrics: (1) the call to unity; (2) the church's message to the world—the gospel; (3) the nature of the church; (4) the church's common confession of faith; (5) the church's

---

Source: Margaret Slattery, "Lausanne: Candid Impressions of the Conference," *The Congregationalist,* 10 November 1927, 588–89; Lausanne Faith and Order Conference, "The Call to Unity," in *Creeds of the Churches,* 3rd ed., ed. John H. Leith (Louisville: John Knox Press, 1963), 568–69.

ministry; (6) the sacraments; (7) the unity of Christendom and the place of the different churches in it.

Although Brent reiterated frequently that the aim of the conference was not to achieve complete agreement or construct a plan for a united church, but simply to register agreements and disagreements, many participants who were not broadly experienced in ecumenical discussion came with such high expectations that the "careful registration of agreements and disagreements" was a disappointment. Nevertheless, the conference unanimously adopted a statement on "The Call to Unity," and received reports from sections 1 through 6. In addition the conference voted "A Common Confession of Faith," approved without one dissenting vote. The global ecumenical movement was on its way!

Lausanne: Candid Impressions of the Conference

[EDITOR'S NOTE: Miss Slattery has written the following article on the Lausanne Conference at the urgent solicitation of "The Congregationalist." It was not her intention to write anything concerning the conference, but in conversation with the Editor she expressed certain impressions which seemed to us so valid and so important that we urged her very strongly to give these impressions to our readers. This seems to us, by all means, the best article that has appeared on the Lausanne Conference. It deals with the whole situation with the complete frankness that the facts seem to demand. There is not in it a line of unworthy compromise, yet at the same time Miss Slattery has preserved the constructive values of criticism in the finest way conceivable. If the conference at Lausanne has failed, there is all the more reason that the great purpose that led the Congregational fellowship of America to participate in that conference should not be abandoned, but that our efforts should be directed toward making these purposes effective in quarters where unity may be possible on the simple basis of devotion to Christ.]

While one must be loyal to what he sees, and something within compels him to report an experience as he saw it and felt it, yet he is forced to question his own conclusions when he finds that they do not agree with those of his fellow observers in whose judgment he has confidence. I have been questioning my conclusions ever since the close of the three-weeks' Conference on Faith and Order held at Lausanne. Yet there they stand. I have read with intense interest the reports of others as they have appeared in interviews in the press and in the denominational papers. I have listened to reports of delegates as given to interested groups. But with the exception of the major part of the report given by Mr. Arthur Porritt in *The Christian World* and one or two others, I find in my own impressions fundamental differences. This is not because I am a woman, for most of the other women delegates are in agreement with the general reports.

I try to analyze the rebellion of soul which dominated me during the three weeks of addresses and discussions. I think it can be explained, in part, because I had just come from a year of work with youth and I had spent the month of July with youth in Geneva. I had been very conscious of *The Present,* with its demand that all men everywhere face the real issues vital to all humankind. At Lausanne I became immediately conscious of *The Past*—a long-gone Past. I had to attempt to respond in experience and thought to that Past. It was almost impossible to feel that the issues brought forward were important. Occasionally in some address Today would flash out, and in three brief moments Tomorrow challenged us. With this attitude of mind brought over from the atmosphere of youth's frank, direct, searching method of attacking problems, it was perhaps inevitable that I should feel no satisfaction in the outcome of a Conference on Faith and Order whose members, representing practically the entire Protestant Church, found it quite impossible, because of the Past, to participate in the Holy Communion or the Lord's Supper together in the name of the Christ whom they repeatedly declared had so earnestly prayed that "they all may be one."

Similar Difficulties in Other Conferences

In all fairness it must be said that if critics of the Church, looking upon Lausanne, are strengthened in their criticisms, they must be reminded that the same fate which met the heroic effort made there overtook also other conferences in Europe. For the various nationals meeting in the great Populations Conference to have come to any united conclusions, had they attempted it, would have been impossible. The Past had a mighty grip there, too. The educators of the world, meeting at Locarno, found very little common ground in method, material, or goal. The representatives within the same nation were wide apart in policy and practice. The conference of surgeons, of journalists, of boards of commerce, of women—all felt the power of the Past. In the League of Nations Council and Assembly, common meeting-ground is hard to find, and in tense moments when the fate of the organization hangs in the balance, the fierce grip of the Past is felt. Interracial conferences struck many a snag—the naval conference dissolved; even peace conferences could not agree as to methods of bringing peace to the world. A long-distant future may look upon our day as "The Age of the Dawn of Unity" and deem its accomplishments as great as we do those of the early Renaissance. In that case, what took place at Lausanne will share the honors of the difficult task of creating something like unity for the human race.

Yet one wished for the *Church* something more than could be accomplished by other bodies. One hoped that it would show the way of escape from the things that divide. One hoped that it might break down barriers by the very force of its Spirit; that its Christ might overrule the organizations created in his name; that it might greatly *dare;* and that it might

> Walk out toward the unknown regions
> Where neither ground is for the feet nor any path to follow,
> No map there, nor guide. . . .

One cherished the hope that the leaders of the Churches gathered at Lausanne might cry:

> Passage to you, your shore, ye aged fierce enigmas,
> Passage to you, to mastership of you, ye strangling problems!
> For we are bound where mariner has not yet dared to go.

But we did not dare at Lausanne. It was a cautious conference. So one hoping for a *great venture,* as he climbed the steep hill to the cathedral for the opening service, was deeply disappointed in the outcome of Faith and Order at Lausanne.

The High Barriers

It is true that almost insurmountable barriers divided us, and in fairness we must face them. There was the *barrier of language,* of which we were conscious every moment. It was almost as difficult to make stand the various brands of the English tongue as to overcome the handicap of German, French, Arabic, and Old Latin.

One morning, a Swedish delegate standing in our group was asked, "Do you speak English?" With a smile and a shrug, he said, "What shall I use to test my English? I have heard four English tongues this morning."

The conference in its general sessions of the eighteen days during which I was present laughed heartily three times. But of course, it is difficult to have a sense of humor in five or six languages or to appreciate one—and the various cultures have never agreed upon what constitutes a sense of humor.

Not only were there these varied language backgrounds and cultural backgrounds, but also there were delicate *political backgrounds* that, though no hint of them was given in words, were easily detected in action and reaction during discussion. With these serious handicaps only the challenging, inspiring personnel of the conference could have made at all possible the persistent, generous spirit of fair play that characterized almost every session.

If there was anything of which one can feel certain, it was that the power to develop beautiful and Christlike character in the individual does not belong to any special Church. No one could look into the faces of certain Greek Orthodox, Lutheran, Anglican, Wesleyan, Quaker, Methodist, Presbyterian, and a score of other delegates, and not realize that. It was evident, even in heated moments, that God has developed, and is developing, the spirits of men through creedal avenues as far apart as the poles—*or perhaps in spite of them.* There were many men bigger than their dogmas.

In the devotional services, whether the prayer was in German, French, or English, one often felt deeply the spiritual force. It did not seem to matter that one sang in English, while his neighbor on the left sang in French, and the one on the right in German. These experiences were like narrow planks in a bridge of union—but when it came to completing the bridge, it could not be done.

One heard again and again in the main sessions and in the group discussions and special reports the phrase *"the divided body of Christ,"* and always the phrase was followed by the confession of *"shame and reproach"* because of it. Yet even the slightest attempt to form *concrete statements* looking toward *union in fact* met with instant defeat. Only when words and phrases were changed, amended, emasculated until they might mean anything, could they be agreed upon, even to the point of presentation to the conference as a whole. There they must be further modified and at last *received.* Had a motion to accept or adopt been attempted, it would have been altogether impossible.

In vain Bishop Brent, a generation and more ahead of the great majority of us, both in the intellectual and spiritual appreciation of the meaning of *religion,* tried to keep Jesus Christ in the center. In his eager, earnest prayers, in his patient pleas, in his words of solemn warning, he tried to put there in the midst of all these words and phrases the challenging Christ in his glorious simplicity. But the majority in the conference seemed at all times more interested in safeguarding with scrupulous care what past generations had said about him.

One rainy afternoon when discussion dragged on over two words that, left to themselves, seemed simple and clear enough, there suddenly flashed into my mind a very vivid picture of my visit to a great temple in the old walled city of Nanchang in China, where I saw Tradition and Superstition maintaining their terrible grip upon the bodies, minds, and spirits of Chinese citizens. Despite all that the small group of intelligent, thoughtful Chinese men and women of the *present* could do, there were their fellows in the Temple of the Hells.

A second later there came another vivid picture—a broken dish, scattered food, harsh words of reproach from the lips of an Indian to a lower-caste child whose shadow had fallen across the food and polluted it.

The high-minded Indian graduate of Oxford, widely traveled and familiar with many cultures, tried to justify the entire caste system as we discussed it. I knew that the same old battle with Tradition and Superstition was being fought there in the aula at Lausanne. Human spirits, despite all that Today has learned, were still held in that mighty grip of a thousand years and more. Today seemed out of place in our midst, and Tomorrow always an intruder. We might have come together upon great principles of truth, but what Yesterday said about them proved our undoing.

One began to look with even deeper admiration upon the Nicene Creed as he realized the surrender of words and phrases that must have gone into its making by the Christendom of that older day. He longed to have this discussion eventuate in something as significant and as costly to our day as the Nicene Creed was to its own. But he was brought suddenly back to the aula by the continued discussion of the sacraments. Days later, he again lived in the past in the intense discussion which left no hope that the conference might close with a Communion service in which all should share.

Among the hundreds of delegates there were only a few of the extreme militant type of defender of the faith. Only on one or two occasions was there even a hint in voice or face of the old spirit of the inquisitor. No one cried, "They shall burn!" as in that other older day. Most of those who found it impossible to agree were deeply regretful. Many were eager to find a way, searched for words, were patient with points of order. Many of the delegates were willing to follow the example set by Chinese Christians and openly declare themselves "agreed to differ, but resolved to love." In these things one felt Christianity had made some gains. But in formal united statement these things could not be expressed.

The high moments of the conference—Bishop Brent's opening address, Prof. Adolf Deissmann's report, Rev. John Banninga's sincere, compelling record of a young man entering the ministry, the delegates from the Orient in their pleas for reality in union, the plea for youth and the Church that is to be, the young Lutheran's declaration for liberty, and other brief moments—pulled us up and away from meaningless generalities. To these, others have repeatedly referred. They were tiny rays of light cast, perhaps, with prophetic power upon the pathway of the future.

The Way to Unity

As I go over in memory the experiences at Lausanne, and re-read the words spoken there, I am profoundly convinced that if there shall be in future a United Church it will not come through conferences or councils of ecclesiastics and theologians, as such. I am convinced that it will not come through machinery set up by Church officialdom. Such a Church, I believe, even if it could be organized, would prove anything but a blessing to the cause of religion. Lausanne revealed such a divergence in thought about the Church and its ordinances, its ministry and its message, that, for long years to come, any attempt along similar lines to lead the various groups into a harmonious unit would be futile.

I had not thought these things until I stood face to face with *division.* I had heard so many fine words spoken about unity that I almost believed that it was coming. I am convinced that Lausanne has rendered a service to the Christian Churches by compelling them to acknowledge the fact of division. I do not believe that any delegate to the Conference on Faith and Order can ever sing again:

> We are not divided, all one body we,
> One in hope and doctrine, one in charity.

I am convinced that the experience at Lausanne may help us to attempt the simple federation of churches which do not present wide divergence in thought and practice. I believe it may help us to get together at the bottom, where lasting foundations after all are laid. I believe there are in many local communities churches willing to merge, that the Greater Church may live. I believe that such may pave the way to a spirit of unity which will, one far-away day, bring us together on a platform to which, all these centuries, Christ has been calling us.

If the Christian churches of communities of a few thousand souls having the same interests, pledging allegiance to the same nation, speaking the same language, cannot worship together, pray together, share the Lord's Supper and the Holy Communion and work together against the common enemies of the Spirit, how futile must be the efforts for the union of all Churches everywhere!

I am profoundly convinced that, until the Churches of England unite first in spirit and then along whatever lines time may develop; that, until German churches, Swedish, French, Orthodox in the Balkans and the Near East, the Churches of China, Japan, and India so unite; that until the Churches of America, in simple sincerity of spirit, cease their endless competition and so unite, *there can be no united Christendom.* Lausanne convinced me of the truth of these statements.

I believe that we must begin the process of uniting where it is always difficult to begin anything—*at the beginning* in our own souls and within our own communions.

There was not at Lausanne the slightest attempt to force unity—it would have meant immediate disaster. There was no attempt to keep any group from the fullest self expression—it would not have been tolerated. Attempts made by individuals to speak for their groups were resented and demands made that the individual assume responsibility for his statements. *For all these things one is deeply grateful.* That forms and phrases, traditional shibboleths, fine shadings in word meanings, hair-splitting, mint, anise, and cummin should have kept us from giving a united clarion call to the heart of a distraught world—these things filled my soul with rebellion. I longed to call to these officials, leaders, rulers in the Churches: "Wait a moment, the conference is almost over. What shall I say about the Church to the great mass of the unchurched? More important than that, what shall I say now to the youth whose keen eyes are turned searchingly upon every organization on earth?"

But my questions died upon my lips. I watched them go—long hair, flowing robes, clerical garb, business suits, picturesque headgear, girdles, gaiters, crosses large and jeweled, crosses small and simple, staff and insignia of high office, plain Quaker gray. I joined them. I saw hands clasped and heard farewells spoken in many tongues with deep regret. So many of us who had been strangers had become friends.

The courageous words of our leader, who had given all he had—body, mind, and soul—to this great dream, followed us down the steep steps and along the market place. After all, perhaps "something had got hold of us." There was a hurt in the hearts of large numbers in this group, a sense of deep disappointment that we had not been able to leap over the barriers and stand shoulder to shoulder in the midst of our fellow men to meet their need and that of each other. The divided household of Christ hurt us. Were we not all fellow human beings facing the grim realities of life and death in a confusing, baffling day? How amazing that we should permit the words of centuries dead and gone to divide us in our search for a deeper experience of God! It may be that as the years pass there shall be born out of disappointment a new passion for unity, a unity better than anything Lausanne even dreamed—a unity of the spirits of men and women of the Church that nothing can defeat. When it comes we shall have the beginning of the Kingdom of God on the earth.

In Christ there is no East or West,
In him no South or North,
But one great fellowship of love
Throughout the whole wide earth.
—*John Oxenham.*

The Call to Unity
Faith and Order Conference [Lausanne], August 20th, 1927

God wills unity. Our presence in this Conference bears testimony to our desire to bend our wills to His. However we may justify the beginnings of disunion, we lament its continuance and henceforth must labour, in penitence and faith, to build up our broken walls.

God's Spirit has been in our midst. It was He who called us hither. His presence has been manifest in our worship, our deliberations and our whole fellowship. He has discovered us to one another. He has enlarged our horizons, quickened our understanding, and enlivened our hope. We have dared and God has justified our daring. We can never be the same again. Our deep thankfulness must find expression in sustained endeavour to share the visions vouchsafed us here with those smaller home groups where our lot is cast.

More than half the world is waiting for the Gospel. At home and abroad sad multitudes are turning away in bewilderment from the Church because of its corporate feebleness. Our missions count that as a necessity which we are inclined to look on as a luxury. Already the mission field is impatiently revolting from the divisions of the Western Church to make bold adventure for unity in its own right. We of the Churches represented in this Conference cannot allow our spiritual children to outpace us. We must gird ourselves to the task, the early beginnings of which God has so richly blessed, and labour side by side with the Christians who are working for indigenous Churches until our common goal is reached.

Some of us, pioneers in this undertaking, have grown old in our search for unity. It is to youth that we look to take the torch of unity from our failing hands. We men have carried it too much alone through many years. The women henceforth should be accorded their share of responsibility. And so the whole Church will be enabled to do that which no section can hope to perform.

It was God's clear call that gathered us. With faith stimulated by His guidance to us here, we move forward.

Learning from New Voices

16. Progressive Germans:
"The Evangelical Protestant Church"

(1945)

Harold W. Barkhau

Among the various groups that immigrated to the United States in the late eighteenth and early nineteenth century and finally found a home among the Congregational churches, the Evangelical Protestant Church has a very distinct story. The first Evangelical Protestant church was founded in Pittsburgh in 1782, and was soon joined by others in that area. However, the churches were hesitant to band together. They placed such a high value on the freedom of personal thought, respect for others with different opinions, and the autonomy of the local church that they were unwilling to risk interference by external authority that might result from joining together.

Gradually, however, as new generations grew up in these churches—speaking English and blending into North American society—Evangelical Protestant Churches recognized their similarity to the Congregational churches and asked to affiliate with them in 1925.

The strange story of a liberal German group which united with us in 1925

To be properly understood, the Evangelical Protestant Church must have its background traced to its European origin. The political, social, and economic forces that were forming an authoritarian Germany were also

---

Source: Harold W. Barkhau, "The Evangelical Protestant Church," *Advance,* September 1945, 11–13.

evidenced in religious life. In the early Sixteenth Century the Reformation in Germany was under the domination of two men—Martin Luther in north Germany, founder of the Lutheran Church and Huldreich Zwingli in south Germany, leader of the Reformed Church. Even during the lifetime of these two great leaders an attempt was made, through the Marburg Colloquy, to unite the two churches of the reformed movement in Germany. Of the fifteen cardinal points of doctrine and church polity, both Luther and Zwingli could agree upon fourteen. The one on which they could not agree and upon which the attempted union ultimately failed was the Sacrament of the Lord's Supper. Luther accepted literally the statement "This is my body," whereas Zwingli gave it a symbolic meaning, contending that when Jesus broke the bread, He meant "This symbolizes my body." If the Marburg Colloquy had succeeded, the Protestant Church in Germany would have been united long before the Pilgrim Fathers landed on Plymouth Rock.

In the year 1817, on the 300th anniversary of the Reformation, the King of Prussia, by royal decree, summoned representatives of the two denominations to form a union. After the union became effective in Prussia, it spread to other parts of Germany. Some of these united churches were called Evangelical Lutheran, others Evangelical Reformed and some merely Evangelical. All, however, embraced the principle of granting to communicants the right to interpret the significance of the elements of the Lord's Supper according to their different points of view. Some of those who fostered a more tolerant attitude and favored a more liberal position came to be known in some sections of Germany as the Evangelical Protestant Church, whereas those who inclined to a more orthodox view chose to designate themselves as Evangelical Lutheran, Evangelical Reformed or simply Evangelical. They grouped themselves gradually into synods known by these various names. The Evangelical Protestant churches were not so prompt in associating themselves together as their less liberal brothers and particularly was this true of many of these pioneer churches in America. Here, separated by great distances, each church came to develop a quite independent spirit and to insist upon absolute autonomy. The principle of revolt against authoritarianism is clearly stated in their old constitutions. Aside from principle, the churches lacked the funds necessary to organize with widely scattered churches of similar faiths. Most of our churches in the Evangelical Protestant groups were in themselves a merger of Lutheran, Reformed, Evangelical and even other denominational backgrounds.

The Smithfield Church in Pittsburgh, which is the oldest Evangelical Protestant Church in the world, had its inception as a dual denominational group—the Lutheran and the Reformed. This church, which received its property by grant from the heirs of William Penn, began by holding separate services in the same building for those of these two denominations. In 1812 the two united, forming the German Evangelical Protestant Church of Pittsburgh. The church which the author served in Madison, Indiana, received its charter from the State with the name, "The German Evangelical Lutheran and Reformed Church."

It has been estimated that there were at one time at least 1,000 churches of the Evangelical Protestant persuasion on American soil. They were located largely in the areas of Pittsburgh, Cincinnati, Columbus, St. Louis and the small towns throughout the Middle West; some having been discovered as far west as Nebraska. It was not until 1870 that the first attempt by a group of strong, liberal ministers was made to form these churches into a union and this, unfortunately, failed. Haengaertner worked for the organization of churches from the 90's on and had been ousted from the fellowship for so doing. Then the laity was organized apart from the ministers and on this basis the churches were organized. By the time the Evangelical Protestant Conference was formed in 1912 the number of these churches had dwindled amazingly. This may be accounted for by a number of factors.

1. The churches were bound together not by any creed or similar doctrine, but by one language—the German. During the time of the great influx of German immigrants into this country (1840–1870) they increased in number and membership. When the immigration began to fall off there was no further source from which to draw.

2. Since the only ministers who could serve these churches in America were those who could speak German and since there were no German theological seminaries in America, all of the ministers had to be obtained from the Mother country. It became increasingly difficult to attract the right kind of men from a state supported church in their native land to a small rural church in America, where the means of livelihood were much less certain. Consequently, small churches whose ministers left or died remained for long periods without pastors, so that many churches perished for want of leadership or were swallowed up by other larger and better organized groups.

3. The exclusive use of the German language contributed to this decadence. The new generation growing up in America learned not German but English. But the churches, realizing that a common language had originally been their strong bond of union, were very reluctant to introduce the use of English into their services.

The author was told an interesting and amusing story in his first pastorate apropos of this situation. In one of the churches in the rural section of Indiana a confirmation service had been conducted the first time in English. A relative of one of the children from another more staunchly German neighborhood seemed greatly disturbed and following the service asked the minister if he thought our Lord could understand a service in English.

4. One of the chief reasons for the decline in the number of Evangelical Protestant churches may be attributed to their ultra-independent spirit and unwillingness to organize themselves more closely. Having no theological seminary of their own in this country, churches were often required to look to their better organized, albeit more conservative brethren, for their ministerial supplies. This led to many churches becoming affiliated with the denomination the minister represented.

Having formed a union among those few remaining strictly independent Evangelical Protestant churches in 1912, their leaders began to look about for a still wider affiliation. What they desired was a fellowship association which would neither require them to give up their local autonomy nor demand of them adherence to a rigid creed or more orthodox interpretation of their faith. They found everything they desired in the church of the Pilgrim Fathers and in 1925 became united with the National Council of Congregational Churches. The question has often been raised—Why did this group of German background unite with a group of traditionally English background? In reality they had many things in common, a few of which I shall mention here.

1. Congregational government. This was the most cherished possession of our Evangelical Protestant churches and the traditional practice of Congregationalism.

2. An educated ministry. Although most of the ministers of the Evangelical Protestant group were trained in Germany, they were nevertheless for the most part very well educated men. In Congregationalism they found the rock from which the American educational system has been hewn.

3. In point of theology, the Evangelical Protestant church had always cherished its liberal position. It embraced within its fold those who prided themselves on being unitarians as well as strictest trinitarians. Congregationalism is similar in this respect.

4. In culture the Evangelical Protestant adherents enjoyed and profited by the music of the great Germanic masters—Beethoven, Mozart, Schubert, Bach and many others. In literature they feasted upon the works of Goethe, Schiller and Lessing. In Congregationalism they found a kindred cultural background, although of a different nature.

Even in their dissimilarities they found a reason for union. Most of the ministers of the Evangelical Protestant persuasion recognized that one of their greatest weaknesses was the lack of a missionary spirit. One needs scarcely to mention that the missionary movement and first missionary society in America came out of the Congregational church.

Evangelical Protestantism contributed its traditional rite of confirmation so that in recent years it has been adopted by many of the so-called old-line Congregational churches. The more effective use of choral and group singing is being used more widely.

Finally, the specific observance of the Lenten season, which some Evangelical Protestant churches adopted from their Lutheran association, is now more widely practiced in Congregational churches throughout America.

If it is possible to determine the results of something so significant as a church union in the short span of twenty years, then one must be justified in saying that "surely this marriage has been a happy one and has borne much rich fruit."

17. Germans from Russia:

"Our German-Speaking Churches" and "Centennial Report from Lincoln, Nebraska"

(1938 and 1988)

George J. Eisenach; Herbert E. Wenz, Oleta Ernst, and Donald Ernst

Several groups that immigrated to the United States in the nineteenth and early twentieth centuries eventually found a home in Congregationalism. Among these were German-speaking Russian Congregationalists.

In "Our German-Speaking Churches: Outlook and Forecast," George Eisenach (1900–1969) tells the story of the German-speaking Russian Congregationalists. For this particular community, the process of settlement was not an easy one, because the community treasured its own language, culture, and religion, and resisted becoming part of North American culture. Eisenach recognized and mourned the inevitability of the assimilation process, but noted that with the Congregationalists the Germans from Russia had found a people who shared their strong sense of the autonomy of the local church. With the Congregationalists they would be allowed to cherish and preserve their ethnic heritage and identity.

Eisenach, born into a Russian Congregational community in McCook, Nebraska, served as pastor and professor to the wider German-Russian community and interpreted this community to the wider society. He served parishes in Wisconsin and South Dakota, where he became professor of theology at Yankton College and Seminary. After 1960, the seminary

Source: George J. Eisenach, "Our German-Speaking Churches: Outlook and Forecast," *Advance,* 1 December 1938, 547–48; Herbert E. Wenz, Oleta Ernst, and Donald Ernst, "Centennial: First German Congregational Church United Church of Christ, May 1, 1888–May 1, 1988," in the 1988 Church Directory of the First German Congregational Church UCC, n.p.; used by permission.

merged with the Mission House Theological Seminary of the Reformed Church in the United States, where he served as professor of historical theology.

The First German Congregational Church United Church of Christ in Lincoln, Nebraska, is a German-Russian congregation proud of its distinctive heritage and eager to retain it. Its centennial in 1988 allowed it "to record some of our history before it is forgotten."

Our German Speaking Churches: Outlook and Forecast

The German-speaking churches constitute the largest foreign group in our Congregational Christian fellowship. In addition to those churches, eight in number, which have their membership in English associations, we now have 197 German congregations, with an aggregate membership of 22,166, served by 109 pastors. During the ninety-two years of the history of this field of Christian service, since 1846, a total of 518 churches were organized, forty per cent of which are in existence, and they have been served through the years by a host of 454 ministers.

At present the German churches are organized into nine conferences or associations which are grouped together as the General Conference. Most of the churches, 84 per cent, are located in rural communities, and the vast majority of their members live on the soil. Many of the organizations are small numerically, particularly in rural areas, and as a rule these are combined into circuits or parishes. A rather large proportion of the churches, on the other hand, have developed considerable strength, provided themselves with substantial buildings, and are carrying on extensive and ambitious programs. The average membership of all congregations is 103, ranging all the way from five to 2,050. On the basis of averages there is one minister for every two organizations.

Not long after the inception of Congregationalism among this immigrant group, it became evident that the German-speaking churches had to have organization for themselves if the work among them was to prosper. This need found expression in the organization of state conferences and a General Conference, in the appointment of a general superintendent and general missionaries (field secretaries or pastors-at-large), and in the founding of a theological seminary and the establishment of a publishing concern. (That effective and intelligent work among this German immigrant population could be done only in connection with their mother tongue and their native characteristics, at least in the early years, was generally acknowledged.) The churches, scattered over a large area, stood in deep need of mutual sympathy, counsel, and stimulus, a need which gave rise to separate conferences. A medium that united the congregations into a closer bond of sympathy and inspired them with zeal was the publication of a German denominational paper. Other publications soon followed, and the establishment of a separate publishing concern became a necessity. No American theological seminary was equipped to supply ministers for these churches, so the founding of a separate institution was called forth.

This branch of Congregationalism found its period of greatest expansion after it made contact with the relatively recent immigration of Germans from within the bounds of the former Russian Empire. Fresh from the fields of pietism—the entire round of German colonies was swept by a series of religious revivals for a period of almost 80 years—imbued with deep religious zeal, liberty-loving, and loyal, a large proportion of this German population found in our fellowship a congenial church home. Its autonomous government gave them the freedom for which they hungered when in their German villages in Russia, and the work among them met with hearty response and bore fruit rapidly.

In this country they manifested the same religious zeal and devotion, the same enthusiasm and sincere piety, which characterized their religious life in the homeland. It was a personal religion, free from the forms of the letter and filled with the life of the spirit. True to their convictions, they organized meetings of prayer patterned exactly after those held in Russia, which in turn became the nuclei for German Congregational churches.

Approximately 95 per cent of the total membership of the German-speaking churches today are made up of Germans from Russia and children of such parentage. This is significant. So the answer to the question, "What of the German Congregational churches tomorrow?" is most likely to be found in the answer to these other questions, "Who are these Germans? and who are they today?"

They are children of Germans who, following the inducements held out by the Russian government, left their native country after 1763 and settled along the shores of the Volga in the southeastern part of Russia and along the north shore of the Black Sea. These colonists, well on the outskirts of civilization and cut off from the main stream of Russian life, were made the object of intense persecution, with the result that they became molded into compact groups. Living during a period of 160 years in their exclusive German villages, retaining their own language, customs, and religion, being influenced but slightly by the life about them, and untouched almost entirely by the great forward movement in the world at large—these colonists developed a distinct and unique civilization. Notwithstanding all the pressure put upon them, they successfully resisted every attempt to assimilate with the Russian people. Most of them never learned enough Russian to carry on a conversation. They did not mingle with and become merged in the mass of the nation.

When in the early seventies of the 19th century the Czar put an end to all privileges enjoyed by these Germans—local self-government, freedom of religion, freedom from military training, etc.—and was determined to make full-fledged Russians of them, thousands sought a land of liberty, and America was the magnet which drew most of them. Emigration began at once, but it was not until after 1890 that they came in large numbers, after which there was a continuous influx until 1914. By 1920 there were 303,532 of their number first and second generation, in the United States.

For a period of about 56 years the activities of the German department of our denomination have been carried on among this immigrant population with major emphasis upon the German language and traditional religious practices. In all of these churches this emphasis is still primary. We will do well to remember that we have to do here in the main with a unique immigrant group. In glancing through the years in retrospect, a number of factors stand out very sharply along the way. First to attract our attention is the fact that, although these German churches are scattered over a wide area, they are united by unseen ties and maintain their existence as an entity even though there is little opportunity for intimate fellowship among them all. Alike in birth, in education, in profession, and in social status, holding with great tenacity to their mother tongue and manifesting a strong desire to preserve their traditional religious faith, these Germans from Russia are united by a strong bond of common feeling and sentiment, faith and ideal. Here are mighty forces at work which must be reckoned with. In a sense they are the very life of these people.

Conspicuous is also the fact that in general the young people make little or no effort to break away from the traditional religious background of their elders. Indeed, they would find it extremely difficult to do so. Even though they are American-born, they have immigrant backgrounds, and they are bound to the religion of their parents by ties which are not apparent on the surface. A few may develop an under-current of resentment toward their own people, yet they have no escape from them. Occasionally, too, some become rebellious and attempt to reject completely the religion of their parents, and in order to compensate for this feeling they join English-speaking churches. It is significant, however, that they hardly ever feel at home in such churches. Almost invariably they either come back to the church of their parents or go to no church at all. There are exceptions, to be sure, but this holds for the vast majority. To their discomfort they make the unhappy discovery that intimate outside relations prove to be formal and cold. By and large the youth of the German churches accept the religious beliefs and practices of their elders and will maintain themselves as a distinct population group for many years, yes, even after the change from the German to the English language has completely taken place.

There is another side, of course. Strong influences are at work which are affecting not only certain individuals, but rather the German churches in their totality. For example, the influence of the English language is making a deep impress at the very foundation of German Congregationalism. The influence of "modern" forms of religious expression are having the same effect. Moreover, the ties of common nationality which have played such a significant role in uniting the churches and forming them into a distinct and unique organization are gradually giving away as the youth are being taken up into the full stream of American life. Then, too, there are some young people in almost every church who want to enrich their religious life through wider contacts than those afforded by the church to which they belong by birth. With these operative forces in the background, the question, "What of German Congregationalism tomorrow?" is finding lodgment in many minds.

It is evident that after the distinctive features of the individual churches are worn off or lived down, these organizations, most of them at any rate, will be absorbed by English associations and conferences. Until then, however, the German conferences will continue to be the only medium which will be able to hold the churches together and afford them the opportunity of intimate fellowship. Differences in culture, specifically in language and spiritual outlook, do not at present permit intimate Christian fraternity between English-speaking and German-speaking churches; a sharing of religious experience is at present inconceivable.

In view of these human elements in this German immigrant population, the absorption of the German churches by the English conferences must necessarily be very gradual.

So far as future numerical growth of German Congregationalism is concerned, it must be called to mind that the pioneering days of following up the new German settlements, days that were characterized by rapid organization of churches, are over. There are of course a few new communities born every year, but in broad outline it is possible to set some reasonable bounds to probable expansion; and on the whole the available churches are fairly adequate to care for any probable growth.

Furthermore, the processes that have been decreasing the number of congregations in rural areas, in almost all denominations, have also affected the German churches. For example, in an earlier day a large number of churches were present in parishes of two, three, four, five, and even six or seven churches each. In many instances these organizations were established in a time when difficulties of transportation made a large number of congregations in a single community a necessity. But the introduction of modern means of conveyance has appreciably altered that situation. with the result that some churches have been dissolved and others merged.

But German Congregationalism still has frontiers; not physical so much but spiritual. If spiritual progress is born in adversity, then surely the time for it has come. We are living in a day of frustrated hopes. Personality and spiritual values are being subordinated and submersed to the demands of a mechanistic order. The certainties of an earlier day are disappearing. Over against these adverse circumstances there is inherent in German Congregationalism a dynamic power which will give birth to spiritual progress for many years. The momentum of the many religious revivals of the past and present and the moving force of the prayer meetings within the churches are powerful enough to overcome those ugly materialistic barriers which are defeating the fulfillment of that fullness of life to which men are entitled.

Jesus Christ Our Sure Foundation

First German Congregational Church
United Church of Christ
Lincoln, Nebraska
May 1, 1888–May 1, 1988

A Message from the Pastor

The year of 1988 is very special for the members and friends of First German Congregational, United Church of Christ, in Lincoln, Nebraska. For 100 years fathers, mothers, young adults, youth, and children have worshiped together affirming God's faithfulness and living Presence. The Gospel of Jesus Christ has been proclaimed, the sacraments administered, the rite of confirmation performed, marriages consecrated and funerals have celebrated the lives of loved ones deceased for their faithfulness to God, the family, the church and to society. For all our blessings we give thanks to God.

One hundred years is a significant milestone in the life of this congregation. There has been a lot of change, yet this congregation has remained faithful from meager beginnings through better times till today. Lives have been nurtured in God's love resulting in a positive influence in society. May God continue to lead us to be faithful as we enter our second century of service to him and humankind.

Respectfully,
HERBERT E. WENZ
Pastor

Centennial
First German Congregational Church
United Church of Christ
May 1, 1888–May 1, 1988

The history of First German Congregational Church could not be written if it were not for a group of faithful, German people who accepted the invitation from Catherine the Great in Russia, who ruled from 1762–1796, to come to Russia and settle along the Volga River. The invitation came in 1763, and our Volga German forefathers and mothers, with their families, left Germany hoping to fulfill their dreams which could not be realized in their Fatherland.

Catherine was born in Prussia, the daughter of German parents. Her marriage to Peter the III of Russia, whom she despised, was a political arrangement. Peter died in a scuffle with the guards in 1762. Catherine was shrewd and knew that her fellow-German people were industrious and would be productive. Her assumption was accurate because they indeed made a bread basket out of the Volga region.

To make her invitation appealing, Catherine issued the following in her Manifesto:

1. Full religious liberty, with one exception: the colonists were forbidden to propagate their faith among native Russians;
2. Exemption from military service;
3. Grant of thirty (dessiatine) of land to every immigrant family; (One dessiatine equals 2.170 acres.)
4. Complete control over their own churches and schools;
5. Almost complete autonomy in local government;

6. Free transportation from Germany to their new home in Russia;
7. Tax exemption for ten years;
8. Interest free loans of 500 rubbles

   (Page 19 "Pietism and the Russian Germans in the United States," the late Dr. George J. Eisenach, printed by the Pioneer Press owned and operated by the German Congregational Churches which closed in 1964.)

Not only were the German settlers in the Volga region cut off from the rest of civilization, but they also suffered from the attacks of semi-savage nomadic tribes called Tartars, Bashkirs, Kirghiz and Kaimucks; and from famine, sickness and drought; nevertheless, they succeeded. The Germans had established 59 colonies on the east side and 45 colonies on the west side of the Volga with a population of 23,019 in 1768, and a population of 391,000 in 1895. (This information also comes from Dr. George J. Eisenach's book.)

When the freedom promised by Catherine began to slip away under the leadership of her successors and they began pressing the German men into military service, our forefathers and mothers sought freedom on the shores of North America and South America. They arrived in their new homeland virtuously [*sic*] penniless with the help of relatives and friends who came earlier.

The first German Congregational Churches were organized in Iowa with the help of the American Home Missionary Society of the (English) Congregational Church in 1847.

The first German Congregational Church in Nebraska was organized in Fremont in 1872 by the Rev. H. Mollenbeck. The next year he gathered a church at Bell Creek serving both churches until 1875 when they disbanded.

On August 1, 1873, the Rev. C. F. Veitz was commissioned to work among the German people in the vicinity of Crete, Nebraska. A church was organized at Olive Branch on March 26, 1875, and in Princeton, Nebraska on August 29, 1875. The Crete Church still continues today under the name of Plymouth Congregational Church, UCC. The Congregational UCC at Hallam also is a continuation of that effort.

On March 1, 1875, the Rev. H. Sallenbach, then pastor of the Muscatine and Pine Creek Churches in Iowa, was commissioned to come to Lincoln, Nebraska. He organized a church in 1876 with the wholehearted support of Superintendent H. N. Gates and the Rev. Lewis Gregory representing the English Congregational Church Missionary Society and the First (English) Congregational Church in Lincoln, respectively. The Rev. Messrs.

Emmanuel Jose and William Suess along with those mentioned previously were responsible for getting German Congregational Churches organized in the greater Lincoln area. But as stated previously also, only the Crete (Plymouth) and Hallam (Congregational) churches have continued. The rest disbanded for whatever reason.

It is important to state here that on September 1, 1878 a German Seminary was founded in Crete in affiliation with Doane College after two unsuccessful attempts to begin a Seminary in Iowa.

On November 13, 1879 the Nebraska German Conference was organized at the Olive Branch Church.

In the fall of 1882 the German Seminary moved from Crete to Chicago Seminary in Chicago, Illinois. In 1914, the German Seminary moved to Redfield College at Redfield, South Dakota. In 1932 the German Seminary moved to Yankton College, Yankton, South Dakota. By then the seminary was training both German and English speaking ministers. In 1961, Yankton School of Theology merged with Mission House Seminary at Sheboygan, Wisconsin to form United Theological Seminary at New Brighton, Minnesota, which now is one of our six closely affiliated United Church of Christ Seminaries.

In 1880, the first German Congregational church paper was founded (Der Kirchenbote).

On October 3, 1883, the General Conference of the German Congregational Churches was organized and the first General Superintendent was appointed in the person of the Rev. George E. Albrecht. The General Conference was disbanded at Zion Congregational Church in Lincoln, Nebraska at a Transitional Session held June 19–21, 1964 at which time it was recommended that local German background Congregational Churches join with the United Church of Christ. Most German State Conferences already had made that transition. The Centennial of the General Conference was observed 19 years after it was disbanded at Zion United Church of Christ, Lincoln on October 3–4, 1983 with your pastor coordinating that entire effort.

The above all is important to our history and the information was gleaned from the late Dr. George Eisenach's book "History of German Congregational Churches," now also out of print.

The worshipers who would form "Die Erste Deutsche Freie Evangelische Gemeinde Kongregationaler Verfassung" (The First German Free Evangelical Church with Congregational Constitution) met at (the old) Park School on May 1, 1888 for their first Worship Service. Student Adam Traudt from the German Department of Chicago Seminary and Superintendent M. E. Everz, who was the second Superintendent of the

General Conference of German Congregational Churches, led them in worship.

Dr. M. E. Everz and Student Adam Traudt assisted in helping 40 (men) charter members, to officially organize First German (as we will continue to refer to the Church hereafter) on June 10, 1888 in Park School where they had been worshiping. It seems proper to list the names of those 40 charter members: Peter Dreith, Conrad Schilleref, Heinrich Weckesser, Conrad Nazarenus, Adam Wolff, Christ Betz, Johannes Miller, Conrad Klamm, Johannes Krieger, Peter Heuser, Heinrich Schwarz, Heinrich Wolff, Heinrich Heuser, Johannes Rieger, Heinrich Betz, Conrad Wolff, Heinrich Hoffman, Heinrich Aschenbrenner, Peter Helzer, Johannes Feuerstein, Johannes Hoff, Heinrich Schleiger, George Eusel, Nikolaus Block, Wilhelm Wolff, George Schneider, Peter Wolff, Jacob Kildau, Friedrich Block, Jacob Gruen, Wilhelm Reiber, Conrad Ulrich, Heinrich Burbach, Johannes Block, Ferdinand Nicolai, Heinrich Amen, George Bauer, George Peter Butz, Heinrich Bender, and George Schaefer.

Under the leadership of Student Traudt, the congregation purchased a lot at 234 West "J" street and erected their first church building consisting of a sanctuary 28x48 feet and a Sunday School room 18x26 feet. The church facility cost $1,800.00 and was dedicated debt free on March 24, 1889 where the congregation worshiped and received Christian Education for 31 years. Dr. M. E. Everz recorded the experience of that day in the following words: "Brown were the happy faces, and hard the hands that greeted us on that day of dedication. We looked in vain for evidence of wealth, but not in vain for those of hard work and thrift. They were all common, hard-working people devoid of sealskin and satin, but not of devotion and love to God."

During the week ending on dedication Sunday, $675.00 was raised of which $550.00 was contributed by First (English) Congregational Church under the ministerial leadership of the Rev. Lewis Gregory. By the time of the dedication, the church had 60 members with a regular Sunday morning and evening attendance of 100 worshipers. The Sunday School had an enrollment of 80. From 30 to 50 men and women attended prayer meetings held Sunday afternoons, Wednesday evenings and sometimes Saturday evenings.

Pastors serving the congregation at the "J" street location were: Student Adam Traudt (1888–1889), the Rev. Johannes Lich (1889–1898), the Rev. E. C. Osthoff (1898–1900), the Rev. Gustave L. Henklemann (1900–1902), the Rev. Johannes Lich (1902–1906), the Rev. B. R. Bauman (1907–1910), the Rev. Gustave L. Henklemann (1910–1920 and then at 1st and "F" from 1920–1929). Dr. M. E. Everz requested that the Rev. Mr. Henklemann return for a second pastorate.

During the church's 32 years at Park School and at 234 West "J" street, there were 1250 baptisms, 407 marriages, 272 funerals and 336 young people were confirmed.

During that time also, in 1900, Pastor E. C. Osthoff was given the permission to leave with 43 families to form Zion Evangelical Congregational Church at 4th and "F" street. In 1927 Zion relocated to 9th and "D" street, its present location.

During that time also, families living in the north bottom of Lincoln around 9th and 10th street, who belonged to First German organized the Brown Church in 1901 which became Salem Congregational Church and today is Faith United Church of Christ. At one time there were four German Congregational Churches in the north bottom. Faith UCC and Immanual Reformed remain active yet today. Faith resulted from a merger of Salem and St. John Congregational Churches.

During that time also, February 15, 1907, some families left First German to organized Friedens Lutheran Church. Today the four churches in the south bottom are: First German Congregational UCC at 1st and "F," Zion UCC at 9th and "D," Friedens Lutheran at 6th and "D," and Ebenezer UCC, which grew out of Zion and was organized in 1915, at 8th and "B."

Decision to Relocation

It became apparent because of crowding due to a growing membership and the noise from trains at nearby tracks, that the congregation had to relocate. On January 8, 1917 they decided to purchase the property at 1st and "F" street. A two story house sitting on the corner was moved to the west end of the block on the north side of "F" street where it still stands today. World War 1 delayed the building program.

• • •

The chancel is a replica of the chancel of the church left behind in Balzar, Russia. The arch in the chancel area which appears to be wood is molded plaster. Contractors in the Lincoln area did not believe it could be done and came to witness the construction and the completed project. It is still intact today. A few years later a pipe organ was installed at the cost of $4,800.00.

Our forefathers and mothers worked hard raising large families, in some instances, and doing menial labor to support themselves. Even if it would have been available, they never would have gone on welfare.

For many years, families locked up their homes, boarded up the windows and in railroad box cars took their families to work in the beet fields in the panhandle of Nebraska and in Montana. Everyone worked in the field except a younger daughter who watched the baby(ies) back in the one room shacks where they lived. Back home in Lincoln, many of the men worked for the railroad companies. Living in the bottoms placed them near their work.

The Congregational-Christian Union

18. Union Envisioned: *The "Craigville Recommendations"*

(1897)

Negotiations between the Congregationalists and the Christians had their origin in 1894 when the New Jersey Christian Association recommended that a merger between the two groups be arranged. The next year, the Convention of the Christian Church invited a delegation of Congregationalists for a two-day discussion on all aspects of a potential merger. Subsequently, the Christian quadrennial convention adopted the Haverhill resolution approving a cooperative union between the Christians and the Congregationalists ("or between the Christians and any of the others"), "providing that the co-operative union not be based upon doctrinal tests" (see vol. 6:36). After a joint conference between the Congregational and Christian bodies the following April in Piqua, Ohio, discussed "measures of common interest," a few members of each of the commissions of the two bodies entrusted with union met in August, 1897, at Dr. Martyn Summerbell's cottage in Craigville, Massachusetts. The members present agreed unanimously to the "Craigville Recommendations" for a union between the two bodies. Subsequently, the proposal received a substantial majority from the complete committees on union of both denominations.

However, when the proposal came before the Christian Convention of 1898, there was said to be vigorous opposition from the southern and western delegates of the Christians, who accused the New England Christians of "selling out to the Congregationalists." The resolution was not adopted. Although Washington Gladden and William Hayes Ward on

---

Source: "Craigville Recommendations,"in *The Christians' Annual,* vol. 3, ed. B. M. Stoddard (Dayton, Ohio: Christian Publishing Association, 1899), 65.

the Congregational side, and Martyn Summerbell and J. B. Weston on the Christian side, continued to work for a merger, the idea was eventually dropped.

Resolved, That a union of the two bodies be recommended on the following basis:

1. Mutual recognition of the Christian standing of each other's churches and ministers, with no doctrinal test beyond the acceptance of the Bible as the only standard of faith and practice.
2. One name for the highest representative body, such as the General Council of Christian Churches.
3. Present organizations, institutions, and usages not to be disturbed by this action.
4. That it be advised that new enterprises or churches be established under such a name as "Christian" or the equivalent thereof.

As co-operative measures we recommend:

1. That ministerial associations of either body where there are also ministers who are members of the other body, invite such ministers into full membership.
2. That local conferences of churches and ministers, and state or district conferences or associations of either body invite churches and ministers of the other body into a full membership for purposes of local fellowship and co-operation, without disturbing their existing denominational relations.
3. That in state or any local home mission enterprises, the boards of the two bodies act together, in such a way that neither shall interfere with the work of the other, but that jointly they do that which shall best promote the interests of the cause of Christ.
4. That there be maintained between the churches and ministers of the two denominations such a fellowship and mutual understanding that when members of a church of one body remove to a place where there is no church of their own, but is one of the other, they be encouraged to take letters to such church of the other body; and that if a minister of one body accept a call to the church of the other he shall not thereby impair his membership or good standing in his own body.

The committee recommend the local or state associations or conferences in which delegates to the National Council or American Christian Convention are chosen, to authorize such delegates to act in a General Conference of Christian Churches, in case such a conference be advised by the National Council and by the American Christian Convention.

19. Union Encouraged:

"Union with the Christians" and "Catechism on Union with the Christians"

(1928 and 1929)

Charles Emerson Burton; *The Congregationalist*

When negotiations between the Congregationalists and the Christians reopened in 1923, the Congregationalists were much more experienced in wielding the tools of ecumenism than they had been in 1897. In the 1890s, commissions on unity from both denominations had agreed on recommendations for union, but there were objections from the Christian side (see vol. 6:18).

By the 1920s, both groups knew how to use their well-known leaders to educate their constituencies about the history and characteristics of the groups with which they were negotiating. They knew how to find out what was really concerning local church members related to union and to speak to those concerns directly.

"Union with the Christians" was contributed to The Congregationalist *in 1928 by Charles Emerson Burton, secretary of the Congregational Home Missionary Society from 1913 to 1921, and secretary of the National Council from 1921 to 1928. His positive endorsement was published alongside the proposal for organic union that had been made by the two commissions on union. Giving some of the background and history of the proposal, it focused on what the two denominations had in common in theology and polity.*

Source: Charles E. Burton, "Union with the Christians," *The Congregationalist,* 19 April 1928, 487–88; editorial, "Catechism on Union with the Christians," *The Congregationalist,* 23 May 1929, 707–8.

"Catechism on Union with the Christians," by the editors of The Congregationalist, *was published nearly a year later. It attempted to answer many of the more practical questions raised by Congregational churches about union with the Christians.*

Union with the Christians

The definite proposal for organic union of the Congregational and Christian Churches of the United States, as set forth in another column by the joint commission, will be heartily welcomed by Congregationalists who are acquainted with this congregationally organized group of churches.

Who Are the "Christians"?

In some parts of the country the Disciples of Christ are known as "Christians," but, technically, the name "Christian" belongs to the churches associated together in the "General Convention of the Christian Church," whose headquarters are at Dayton, Ohio. The report of the Census Bureau, soon to be published, will tabulate 1,044 churches, with 112,795 members. There are 182 churches in Ohio, 174 in Indiana, 151 in North Carolina, 88 in Illinois, 74 in Virginia, and 52 in New York, with smaller numbers in other states as far west as Kansas. There are some churches in New England, but the greater strength lies in the interior and in the South. The churches in Ohio and Indiana, for example, are in sections where there are only a few Congregational churches, and the same thing is true in the Southeast.

Another noticeable fact is that the Christian churches are located largely in rural communities, whereas the Congregational churches have centered more in cities. This has too often meant that Congregational churches had no feeders, and that the Christian churches necessarily lost their own people from the rural regions when they moved into the city.

To quote from the report of the Commission on Interchurch Relations to the Omaha meeting of the Council: "Their polity is Congregational; their organization is very similar to our own; they ordain their ministers in district gatherings comparable to our Associations. They support eight colleges and an active mission work. Many among them prefer baptism by immersion, but none hold exclusively to that form. Communion is open, and infant baptism is optional. Allegiance to Christ is with them the sole test of membership. They object to creedal statements which bind the individual."

Things in Common

A joint committee of the two denominations on June 17 drew up the following expression of things held in common:

1. Each Church has the congregational form of government.
2. In each, the individual church is the unit of authority.
3. Each Church accepts and practices representative government with regard to matters of common concern to the churches.
4. Each Church accepts the Bible as the rule of faith and practice, recognizing the right of free individual interpretation.
5. Neither Church holds to a creed which is binding upon individuals or upon churches.
6. Each is agreed upon the general foundational tenets of our common Christianity.
7. The Congregational statement of 1913 and the Principles of the Christian Church we find essentially in accord in evangelical temper and inclusive in their scope.

History of the Proposal

On March 1, 1924, the president of the General Convention of the Christian Church addressed to the Moderator of the National Council an official communication from the General Board of the Christian Church, setting forth various principles of Christian unity, and specifically requesting "a conference with representatives of your body to discover and discuss our common tenets, practices, and what adjustments may be possible in the interest of a closer relationship." This overture resulted in joint conferences, out of which came the proposals of the Congregational Commission on Interchurch Relations which were presented at Omaha in May, 1927, recommending in specific form the cultivation of closer acquaintance and the development of closer relationship. In consequence the National Council voted as follows;

> That the Council herewith express its approval of the recommendation of the Commission with reference to the Christian Church

and authorize the continuance of friendly conferences with a view to promoting the closest practicable relationship of our two Churches.

This action of the Council resulted in further joint conference and the prompt proposal by Dr. Coffin on behalf of the Christian Church that we should recommend actual organic union at the earliest possible date. This proposal from the Christian Commission met with a most hearty response on the part of the Commission of the Congregational Churches, and a tentative draft was at once drawn up of a communication to be presented to each denomination. This draft was revised in conference and referred to the individual members of the two committees, and later to the entire membership of both Commissions for careful revision and suggestion, so that the final form printed in this issue of *The Congregationalist* represents the hearty concurrence of the membership of both Commissions.

Meaning of the Proposal

The proposal is not a half-way step, but an actual proposition for organic union of the two denominations. Here, of course, the term organic is used as meant by Congregationalists. It would be quite possible to contend that Congregationalism is not organic in its own life. The proposal means that there should be as close union between what are now called Christian churches and Congregational churches as there is now between different Congregational churches.

The obvious next step in this connection is to have this proposal considered in our churches, our associations and our conferences, and finally at the Detroit meeting of the National Council in the spring or early summer of 1929. In this connection the important thing is that it should be approached in the right spirit. The right spirit means a broad-minded consideration of big things rather than the magnifying of small things. Any of us can find difficulties in the way of consummating such a union, but if the end to be attained is worthy we certainly can find the way to accomplish it.

Perhaps the first thing that our minds will leap to is the matter of the name. Here it should be borne in mind that the name "Congregational-Christian" would be primarily the name of a national organization and would not necessarily obtrude itself at all upon a local church; that is, instead of having a National Council of Congregational Churches and a General Convention of the Christian Church, we should have a National Council of Congregational-Christian Churches or a General Convention of Christian-Congregational Churches, or under whatever name might be decided upon.

The question of the closer relationship of state bodies, district bodies, associations and local churches would be left to those bodies themselves. The natural consequence would be the same kind of drawing together in the state and local bodies that is perfected in the national body.

Details cannot be entered upon in this connection. Of course, they will be considered very definitely and specifically as time goes on. Wisdom will prompt us to hold suspended judgment regarding details, and especially regarding difficulties. In the meantime it will contribute to the advancement of this proposal if those who are concerned will communicate to the office of the National Council any problems which arise in their minds, together with any constructive proposals which they wish to make.

If it seems to any that such a step should be taken not by two denominations alone, but by many, it should be observed that that proposal is at present being put up to a number of denominations whose polity is Congregational, and it would be by no means surprising if before these two denominations join hands definitely there might be several others that would be disposed to seek inclusion in a common family. If this should develop, then it would be quite possible to take a more pretentious name of the new body, such as The United Church of America or The United Christian Church; in fact, the question of the name is wholly open for the wisest conclusion that can be found.

Advocates of Christian union will welcome this step as promising much in itself and as challenging the followers of Christ generally to answer the prayer of the Master that they should be one.

Catechism on Union with the Christians

1. *Who are the Christians?* The body of the followers of Christ associated together in the General Convention of the Christian Church, with headquarters at Dayton, Ohio. They are to be differentiated from the Disciples frequently called "Christians." There are about 1,000 churches, quite largely rural, with a membership of approximately 125,000. They are strongest in Southern Ohio, Southern Indiana, Virginia and North Carolina.

2. *What is the basis of their fellowship?* Their churches subscribe to no creed but rather center their thought about the following principles: (1) Christ the only head of the Church. (2) "Christian" our only name. (3) the Bible our only creed. (4) Christian character the test of fellowship. (5) Individual interpretation of the Scriptures the privilege of every believer. (6) The union of all the followers of Christ.

3. *Are they like Congregationalists?* Very much so in polity, which

is wholly congregational, including liberty in theological thought. Being largely rural, they are most like the American rural churches of the congregational order.

4. *What ordinances do they observe?* The same as the Congregational churches, wholly open Communion; immersion is more frequently practiced and members are received under "spiritual baptism," where conscientious objections to external forms are professed.

5. *Are the Christian churches generally favorable to this union?* Yes, almost one hundred per cent, as revealed by extensive canvass.

6. *Does the union call for the changing of the practice of Congregational churches?* No, in no respect whatever.

7. *Are there not differences in tradition?* Yes, for example, the Christian churches do not share the Pilgrim tradition except indirectly, nor do large sections of the Congregational churches; likewise they would bring valuable traditions to the union which Congregational churches would gladly share.

8. *Is this a real union?* The plan does not propose *corporate* union, neither do the Congregational churches now enjoy corporate union. The National Council has no authority over the Conferences; the Conferences have no authority over the Associations or churches. We are united in *fellowship.* The proposition calls for an equally real unity in fellowship for these two groups. It also recommends full union in missionary work where union is most needed, and suggests actual unity of churches in competing or overlapping fields.

9. *Is a referendum to the churches, Associations and Conferences necessary?* Technically, no; practically, yes. Since there is in no sense any legislation suggested which imposes obligation on the churches, Associations or Conferences, there is no necessity for a technical referendum; practically, however, it is always wise to refer such questions to the appointing bodies. This has been done through reference of the question to state Conferences for their action, and through them to the Associations, and by correspondence with all the churches through their pastors; by request of all delegates to the National Council that they sound the sentiment of their constituents, and by repeated presentation in *The Congregationalist* and by releases to the public press whenever there are Congregational churches.

10. *Should union begin at the bottom?* This proposal did begin at the bottom with local churches and district bodies; in fact, a number of mergers of local churches have been arranged contingent upon this national unity. State and regional Conferences and Conventions have also planned actual mergers to be consummated on condition of national unification.

11. *Would it be better to delay final decision?* There are many details which could be postponed. To delay the decision of the main question would be rather disastrous, particularly to the smaller body, whose life and activity is greatly unsettled until this question is decided. Moreover, regarding the main question, there is scarcely anything further to be gained by further consideration, and as a matter of fact there are no steps proposed which could not be readily retraced should conditions clearly demand it.

12. *Are not the Christian churches willing simply to join the Congregational denomination?* No, they very properly feel that such a course would indicate that a small denomination can never unite with a larger denomination except by absorption, and that this would give a setback to the movement for unity rather than forward it.

13. *Are there possibilities that other denominations may follow this example?* Yes, some other denominations are now definitely considering the wisdom of seeking a share in this merger; in fact, the highest value attached to this movement lies in its pointing the way to a general movement toward Christian unity.

14. *Does the proposal mean a change of name on the part of Congregational churches or organizations?* No, not unless and until other denominations seek admittance to the union, at which time a general name acceptable to all could be adopted.

15. *What would we gain by this movement?* It is to be hoped that no Congregationalist asks this question from a self-centered standpoint. Clearly, however, there would be gain to the Kingdom in the fact that the rural membership of the Christian churches would find a church home in the cities to which they are constantly moving, and the city churches, which are largely Congregational, would receive by natural process this increment of strength. Congregationalists will gain also in the filling of the gap in those sections of the country where their churches are few. In some parts of the country where Congregational educational institutions are inadequate, the Christians have fine institutions which will supplement the Congregational ranks. Any overlapping there may be in the home mission field can be absolutely eliminated and mutual strength come from united administration.

16. *What can Congregationalists contribute to the Christian churches?* First of all, the satisfaction of the great passion of that body for Christian union. A sense of strength would be added to this comparatively small body in the realization that they were part of a nation-wide fellowship with a world-wide outlook. There would be a natural strengthening of their ministry, a grading up in the program of work along lines where Congregationalists are strong, an improvement in the output of helps for church

schools and other departments, easier access to enriched educational facilities, and a general quickening of the life of all the churches.

17. *What are the ministerial standards of the Christian churches?* Their ideal is ordination by conferences after college and seminary education. Being largely rural, the denomination has not been able to come as near reaching this standard as have the Congregational churches. They covet help in doing so.

18. *Would there be a tendency to lower the standard of the ministry?* This is hardly to be expected. Lists for the time being at least are to be kept entirely separate. Congregational Associations would still determine the standards for Congregational ministers. Churches might call, just as they can now, ministers from the Christian fellowship or from any other denomination. Some of the best Congregational ministers are from that fellowship, including at least two of our state superintendents. If we take counsel of our fears there would be, of course, opportunity for absorbing a few ministers with the lesser equipment.

19. *Would there be a tendency to lower ministers' salaries?* The average salary of the Christian ministers is about $1,000; that of the Congregational ministers about $2,000. The difference is mostly accounted for by the fact that Congregational churches are much more largely in the cities. There are by the last statistics 1,554 Congregational pastors receiving less than $1,500 salary; there are about 300 Christian pastors on full time receiving less than $1,500. The likelihood that many of these 300 would find their way into the higher paid positions of the Congregational Church is not very great.

20. *Would the Christian ministers share in the benefits of the Pilgrim Memorial Fund?* No, this is impossible under the charter of the Annuity Fund. Considerations of the question make it likely that similar provisions can be made by the Christian churches themselves and that pending the completion of these provisions such an arrangement as is now proposed for the unordained Congregational workers can be effected. Similar statement should be made regarding ministerial relief.

21. *Would the Congregational Home Missionary Society make appropriations to pastors of Christian churches from Congregational funds?* No, it is specifically provided that this should not be done, but rather that aid provided by Christian churches should be administered by the same board which administers Congregational home missions.

22. *Would the Building Society make grants to Christian churches?* No, building grants for Christian churches would likewise be provided by the contributions of the Christian churches themselves, but administered in common.

23. *Would there be likelihood of added charges on missionary accounts through the state treasuries?* The recommendation of the plan is that this shall not be the case, and the state superintendents of Congregational conferences give assurance that there would be no call for it. The answer to such questions does not mean that Congregationalists would forever be forbidden to lend a hand where most good can be done.

24. *Would Congregationalists ever provide funds for the help of what are now Christian churches?* The assurance desired is that missionaries and missionary work of either denomination shall not suffer in order that the calls of the other denomination may be answered. Having the guarantee that needed aid shall not be withdrawn from any in order to provide for others, there would be full liberty to assume new responsibilities in whatever direction the greatest call seemed to issue.

25. *Would the American Missionary Association be called upon to assume obligations for the relatively large Afro-Christians membership?* No, under the plan it is specifically provided that the Afro-Christian Convention shall be self-supporting aside from the continuance of the present assistance given to the single educational institution now supported.

26. *Would the vested interests of the denomination be jeopardized?* No, it is to be observed that no new corporations are provided for; that no authority is given to any body which could in anywise lay claim to any funds held by any corporation. These funds would all continue under their present control, their use being determined absolutely by the terms of gifts.

27. *Would there be any difficulty in maintaining the high standard of religious education of the Congregational churches?* The Christian churches hold the same ideals as the Congregational churches. Assurances of religious education leaders on both sides are fully reassuring.

28. *Is there danger of lowering the standard of religious education helps?* No, in the words of the editor of the Congregational helps, "I see no difficulty in arriving at a satisfactory basis."

29. *Would financial economies be realized?* Not at the start; ultimately there should be savings in overhead.

30. *Are there any difficulties connected with the official staff?* None have appeared. The Christians have no state superintendents; there are but few national paid officials. These should doubtless continue at least for the present, and the decision of that question under the plan rests with the General Convention, which is also responsible for the support of such officers.

31. *What are the obstacles involved?* While these do not seem to be very great from the Congregational standpoint, it is not to be thought that

there are no difficulties. From the standpoint of the Christian churches these difficulties are very much larger, but they are facing them with confidence. Congregationalists naturally face with some fear significant changes in traditions, associations, and sentiments. They may find themselves in association with people who do things in a different way. Shibboleths may need to change. Like all groups, Congregationalists have some pet phrases that might seem out of place. Some changes in organizations locally will be called for and various adjustments incident to the making of new acquaintances. These and any other difficulties which appear must be placed over against the importance which is attached to the unity of the body of Christ, of which this is a part, however small, and toward the larger unification of which it contributes in ideal and in practical form of realization.

PART II

The Christian Passion for Church Union

The Christian denomination was not a European transplant, as were the Congregational, Evangelical, and Reformed Churches. It was born on North American soil, sprung from the great ideals that flourished in the political and religious upheavals of the United States of America at the close of the eighteenth century.

Political patterns that had long been accepted were suddenly perceived as intolerable abuses. Galvanized by the great ideals of "individual rights," "autonomy," and "independence," the English colonists eventually rebelled against being ruled by a distant king. Soon after the revolutionary war was over, revivals swept the country and brought a heightened religious awareness. Citizens of the new nation began to explore how the ideals that had changed their political thinking could apply to their religious lives.

This highly charged political and religious climate produced three groups with remarkably similar convictions in three widely separated parts of the country—New England, the South, and the central Midwest (see vol. 4:1–6). The Christian movement in the South began about 1792 when a controversy arose in the Methodist Episcopal Church between its bishop, Francis Asbury, and a small group of ministers led by a brilliant young man named James O'Kelly. The dispute had to do with whether or not a local church or an individual minister could appeal a placement decision made by the bishop. According to the ministers, justice required that they have a say in where they would serve the church. According to the bishop, episcopal authority demanded that they accept his decisions. In the end, the bishop prevailed. The disgruntled ministers seceded from the church to form a group known first as the "Republican Methodists," and later simply as "Christians."

The Christian movement on the trans-Appalachian frontier began during and after the famous Cane Ridge camp meeting revivals that brought together thousands of unchurched pioneers in northern Kentucky. A group of Presbyterian ministers under the leadership of Barton W. Stone withdrew from their presbytery over issues of individual rights and denominational sectarianism. They, too, decided that they wanted to be known simply as "Christians," and to receive into their fellowship any sincere follower of Jesus Christ.

The New England Christian movement was the result of a revolt of two Baptists, Abner Jones and Elias Smith, against what they termed sectarian creeds and names. They believed that, in matters of Christian belief, every individual Christian should have the right to follow the dictates of his or her own conscience. The test for membership in the church should not be a particular creed or mode of baptism, but simply the Christian character of the believer.

These three movements had remarkably similar views about the right and freedom of individual Christians to decide for themselves, as guided by the Holy Scriptures, how they should believe, worship, and preach, unrestrained by church hierarchy, creed, or dogma. They also had a commitment to vital Christian piety as the only and sufficient test of church membership. Finally, they shared another important conviction. For them, the call to work for the unity of the church was not an addendum to their identity as Christians; it was central. The call to be Christian and the call to work for the unity of the church were simultaneous and inseparable. In fact, one might say that among the Christians, mission and evangelism took the form of ecumenism.

During the Cane Ridge revivals, Stone and his colleagues had been tremendously impressed by the sense of unity across denominational lines that the revivals had generated among the participants. Consequently, when the local churches argued about which churches deserved to keep which converts, and Stone's very own Lexington Presbytery scrutinized the sermons of the revival preachers for doctrinal irregularities to the point of launching a heresy trial, Stone and other Christian leaders were appalled. They feared that such dissension and wrangling would destroy the sense of unity among the people, which they believed was a sign of the God-given unity of the church.

Stone and his colleagues decided to separate from the Lexington Presbytery and set up their own "Springfield Presbytery." However, this new presbytery had a strikingly short life span. Its members began to worry that forming yet another presbytery was simply furthering the very sectarianism that they had left the Lexington Presbytery to avoid. They decided to disband, and drew up "The Last Will and Testament of the Springfield Presbytery," explaining their actions: "We *will* that this body die, be dissolved, and sink into union with the Body of Christ at large" (see vol. 6:20;

also in vol. 4:5). Thus united, they turned to the work of making the unity of Christ's followers even more visible.

The decision of Stone's group to let their presbytery "die" was particularly extraordinary given the wild proliferation of religious groups in the early nineteenth century. Most new splinter groups proclaimed their own new and more exclusive identity and declared narrower boundaries than the group from which they had separated. Stone's friends, however, moved in the opposite direction. They sought to enlarge their boundaries on behalf of the greater unity of Christ's church. They chose to be more inclusive rather than more exclusive. Although in 1791 they just wanted to be called "Christians," they could well have called themselves the first "uniting" church of Christ.

Elias Smith, of the New England branch of Christians, was sometimes labeled a cantankerous old curmudgeon, but he had a firm commitment to the unity of the church. In 1808, he began publishing the *Herald of Gospel Liberty,* the first religious newspaper in the United States (see vol. 6:21). Within a year the *Herald* was published every other Friday morning in Portsmouth, New Hampshire, "at his [Smith's] house on Vaughan-street, one door east of the bath house." Although the *Herald* was founded to further the cause of religious liberty, from the beginning it was a herald of ecumenism as well. In his first issue Smith published "The Last Will and Testament of the Springfield Presbytery." He also printed correspondence from James O'Kelly's group in Virginia. In the years that followed, the fact that the *Herald* published many letters and articles from members of all three groups greatly influenced their eventual union (see vol. 6:22).

The next step in the *Herald*'s ecumenical work was to print articles urging the newly united Christians to pursue union with other denominations. The *Herald* was filled with hymns to union, poems to union, impassioned sermons demanding union, and carefully reasoned articles requiring union. Between 1896 and 1897 alone, more than ninety-three articles on union appeared in its pages. There is simply no way of knowing how different the ecumenical history of the Christian denomination would have been without Elias Smith and his tireless determination to use his *Herald of Gospel Liberty* to unite the followers of Jesus Christ.

A Maturing Commitment to Union

The spirit and goals of the Christian movement were crystallized into six principles quite early on in its history: (1) the Lord Jesus Christ, the only head of the church; (2) the name Christian, to the exclusion of all party and sectarian names, sufficient for the followers of Christ; (3) the Holy Scriptures, or the Scriptures of the Old and New Testaments, the only creed, a sufficient rule of faith and practice; (4) Christian character, or vital Christian piety, the only and sufficient test of Christian fellowship and church membership; (5) the right of private judgment and the liberty of conscience, a right and a privilege that should be accorded to and exercised by all; (6) the union of the followers of Christ, to the end that the world may believe.

The first five principles were a banner behind which the Christians believed *all* churches could unite, and the sixth principle spelled out the goal and rationale for their ecumenical work. Unity was central. Nearly every issue of the *Annual of the Christian Church* (South) included a "Position on Christian Union" (see vol. 6:23).

The Christians pursued union with fervor. Between 1818 and 1923 they engaged in sustained negotiations—what they called "union courtships"—with five different groups: the Free Will Baptists, the Disciples of Christ, Unitarians, Christian Union people, and, finally, the Congregationalists. They also had brief discussions or local negotiations with several others. The Christians believed that they had a mission to bring about union, but fulfilling that mission turned out to be much more difficult than they ever anticipated.

In the early years of the movement, Christians were sometimes heavy-handed in their methods and overly polemical in their statements. They would "hold high the Bible" as the only rule of faith and practice (both metaphorically and literally) and refuse to sustain negotiations with any group that required assent to any creed or statement of faith for membership. They expressed great frustration, vocally and in print, at the inexplicable intransigence of people who thought differently from them! Many times they failed to realize how doctrinaire *they* were when they excluded groups that did not immediately drop their own theological or creedal principles and join them. Nor did they see that their commitment to the Six Principles functioned in the same way that a creed functioned for "creedal" churches. Yet, the Christians were deeply committed to church union, and as they understood themselves better, they became more accomplished advocates for their cause.

Since every Christian was committed to working for unity, many attempts were made at the grassroots level. The *Herald* regularly reported on local negotiations, local plans of union, and proposals for union created by concerned individuals (see vol. 6:24). In addition, accomplished theologians devoted themselves to making the case for Christian union: Martyn

Summerbell, W. M. Wellons, W. M. Hayes, Hermon Eldredge, W. A. Harper, J. F. Burnett, and F. D. Coffin (see vol. 6:25). By 1919, the Christians established a permanent Commission on Christian Union, which first pursued an unsuccessful "union courtship" with the Disciples and later led the enthusiastic Christians to a successful union with the Congregationalists. The commitment of the Christians to union was fundamental. It permeated everything they did, said, or sang (see vol. 6:26).

Blacks in the Christian Movement

Before the Civil War, black Christians in the South attended the same churches as white folks, but were frequently required to sit separately in the balcony. Immediately after the war, the Southern Christian Convention appointed three of their best ecumenical negotiators to assist the "Colored brethren" in organizing churches and conferences of their own. As a part of this effort, A. A. Bright, who later became field secretary for the black churches, prepared a *Revised Ritual of the Christian Church,* which was sensitive to the unique cultural legacy of the Christian movement among African Americans (see vol. 6:27).

Within a decade there were more than fifty "Afro-Christian" churches, three conferences, with forty ordained ministers. The initial concerns of these black churches were very practical. They were not focused on merging their churches with others, but on getting them built in the first place; they did not put much energy into educating members about ecumenism, but into giving them a basic education and job training for economic stability. As Joseph F. Mitchell wrote in the *Herald* in 1882, "The two great powers by which [my people] are kept back are powers that work like leprosy. They can see them, they can feel them. But then they don't kill at once, but slowly and slowly, so our people are deceived thereby. These two powers are . . . ignorance and poverty."

Afro-Christians learned their theology through oral tradition, sermons, and worship. It was a theology appropriate for an oppressed and struggling people, with a strong emphasis on Christian morality and ethical behavior, a strong call to endure through pain and hard times, and a vivid vision of eschatological hope. The establishment of a school for blacks in North Carolina, which eventually became Franklinton Christian College, was an important step in educating black Christians (see vol. 6:28).

Generally speaking, the ecumenical contribution of the early Afro-Christians did not consist in breaking down barriers between churches, but in breaking down barriers between races; in so doing, they helped many northern Christians realize that black people were brothers and sisters and part of the one body of Christ.

Courtship with the Disciples

From the beginning there was something ironic about the efforts of the Christians to unite with the Disciples. This was because such efforts were often more like family disputes than negotiations between strangers. After all, both groups had been founded on the conviction that the church of Jesus Christ was one, and ought not to have denominational divisions. Both groups deplored doctrinal statements as tests for church membership and declared that the New Testament was the adequate constitution for worship, discipline, and the governance of the church. Yet, early in their history there had been problems with what some people called a "union" between them, and others insisted was simply a "working agreement."

In Lexington, Kentucky, in 1832, some followers of Barton W. Stone met for worship with another group of frontier Christians who were loyal to Thomas Campbell, the founder of the Disciples. Believing themselves to be "on the same foundation" and "in the same spirit," they all pledged to unite their energies around the work of evangelism. The result was mixed. Originally, Stone took some pride in the fact that they had negotiated a union arrangement. This was, after all, what all Christians believed was right! On the other hand, Christians later became dismayed when hundreds of "Stonite" Christian churches in Kentucky, Illinois, Indiana, and Missouri did not stay connected to the Christian Convention, but became part of the Disciples of Christ. This loss was similar to the way many Congregational churches, founded under the Plan of Union of 1801 whereby Congregationalists and Presbyterians cooperated in frontier mission work, eventually became Presbyterian churches (see vol. 4:71). Stone returned to the fellowship of the Christian Churches in Illinois, but many of his followers did not. And the vague and fluid boundaries between the "Campbellites" and the "Stonites" left their descendants arguing for decades about whether and how much they shared common ancestry (see vol. 6:29.)

In spite of all the arguments about beginnings and names, the Christians and the Disciples continued to conduct a sporadic "union courtship." The two denominations had a great deal in common, and they knew it. However, they did disagree on whether baptism by immersion was a necessary requirement of church membership. This disagreement loomed large for many who could not bear for the other to believe anything that they could not believe themselves!

At the same time, the irony of their situation was not lost on either group. If, as one letter to the editor of the *Herald* asked, they could not unite with one another, who *could* they unite with? Still, learning how to move past their ambiguous history to claim real church union was difficult. The *Herald* published opinions on all sides of the union issue.

In 1919, a meeting was held between the Christians and the Disciples at which a prominent Christian leader, J. F. Burnett, suggested many practical techniques to prepare the Christians and the Disciples for union (see vol. 6:30). A year later, "the several Boards of the Christian Church," assembled in joint session, sent greetings to the Disciples at their international convention in St. Louis, Missouri, expressing the hope that the common life and thought of the two bodies might continue to draw them closer (see vol. 6:31). Hopes for getting beyond the immersion issue were further raised when the president of the Disciples, the great ecumenist Peter Ainslie, proposed to the Disciples that they advocate "acceptance by the Church of those whom Christ had obviously accepted, whether they were Baptized by immersion or not." Ainslie came under strong criticism from one group within the Disciples, and finally chose to decline reelection rather than stir up harmful controversy.

Alva Martin Kerr, the usually calm and irenic editor of the *Herald,* intentionally echoed the words of Ainslie when he expressed his frustration with the debate in print: "Either these unimmersed are Christian or they are not. If they are, it is a piece of utter and preposterous presumption for any church to refuse to receive into its membership those whom it admits Jesus Christ himself receives and approves" (see vol. 6:32).

Unfortunately, the Christians and the Disciples were not yet ready to agree with Ainslie and Kerr. The baptismal question remained for one hundred years, finding some resolution in the late twentieth century when the United Church of Christ and the Christian Church (Disciples of Christ) forged a partnership agreement generally affirming the concept of "open membership."

Learning from the Wider Church

Throughout their history the Christians were repeatedly impressed with worldwide movements toward federation and union. When the Federal Council of the Churches of Christ in America was founded in 1908, the Christians embraced it enthusiastically as standing squarely and unequivocally for the fundamental principles they had been advocating for a century (see vol. 6:33). They could affirm a federation easily because it produced none of the anxieties and stumbling blocks that usually surrounded discussions about organic union.

Outside the United States, successful church unions in South India and in Canada further inspired the Christians to regard their commitment to ecumenism with new hope. In 1920, they greeted with caution the Proposal on Church Union issued by the Lambeth Conference of the Anglican Church. Although Alva Martin Kerr's editorial on Lambeth in the *Herald* found a positive sign for ecumenism in the fact that the Episcopalians "admitted that the non-Episcopal communions are really churches," it concluded that it was idle for the Episcopalians to "deceive themselves with such a dream so long as they [hold] a position that never till the crack of doom will be accepted by the great body of Protestantism." He was referring to Episcopal understandings of ministry and the historic episcopate (see vol. 6:34; see also vol. 6:5–9).

The Christians were intensely interested in the World Conference on Faith and Order in Lausanne in 1927, even though they recognized that the attempt to find a basis for organic unity would inevitably involve efforts to agree on some common creedal statements. (See vol. 6:35) By the twentieth century, the Christians had become sophisticated in their ecumenical theology. They recognized that churches would never arrive at organic unity unless they had "the courage and the wisdom to face these differences and thrash them out in a Christian spirit."

The Congregational-Christian Union

After over one hundred years of various "union courtships" and deep involvement with the ecumenical movement of the wider church, the Christians finally found a partnership that worked: union with the Congregationalists. Union conversations between the two groups actually began in 1895, when the Christians proposed a cooperative union between themselves and the Congregationalists in the Haverhill Declaration (see vol. 6:36), and in 1898, when a conference between the two denominations produced the "Craigville Recommendations" (see vol. 6:18).

Although the two denominations had a lot in common, they also had a difficult time getting to know each other and learning to trust each other. The Christians were rural, the Congregationalists urban; the Christians were relatively poor, the Congregationalists relatively rich; the Christians were a very small denomination, the Congregationalists rather large. Nevertheless, they had enough similarities to make the "courtship" intriguing to both of them.

Each had an emphasis on local church autonomy, a toleration for variation in doctrinal beliefs, and an insistence that the individual had a right and a responsibility to hold to his or her own religious views without interference by ecclesiastical authority. Furthermore, both denominations had become quite experienced in the ecumenical methods needed to bring any denomination to union (see vol. 6:37; see also vol. 6:18–19).

When it was clear that the union was a real possibility, the Commissions on Union in each denomination jointly announced their recommendations in April 1928. They reassured the Christians and the Congregationalists that the autonomy of the local church and the right of each individual to follow Christ according to his or her own conscience would remain undisturbed (see vol. 6:38). Within a year, a Plan of Union was adopted by the National Council of the Congregational Churches and the General Convention of the Christian Church. Finally, in 1931, the headlines in a new joint periodical, *The Congregationalist and Herald of Gospel Liberty,* declared the consummation of the union and the birth of the Congregational Christian Churches. The publication of the "Preamble and Basis" of the new Constitution reassured those in the Christian denomination that the new union honored their heritage by clearly reflecting the treasured "Six Principles of the Christian Church" (see vol. 6:39).

Echoing "The Last Will and Testament of the Springfield Presbytery," W. A. Harper, president of Elon College, declared, "The Christian denomination will LOSE itself in a united movement with the Congregationalists, but both of these denominations will FIND themselves more alive than ever in a continuous and united service for the cause of Christian union in the nation and the world." This was precisely what the Christians had been aiming for all along.

From Rebellion to Reunion

20. Rebellion:
"The Last Will and Testament of the Springfield Presbytery"

(1804)

When great revivals began to sweep southwestern Kentucky in 1801, the Presbyterian Church was inclined to frown upon them because of the "excitement and strange manifestations" they brought on and because the revivalists were preaching the doctrine of "free grace" as opposed to a rigid Calvinist doctrine of election. Nevertheless, a Presbyterian minister, Barton W. Stone (1772–1844), and his colleagues Robert Marshall, John Dunlavy, Richard McNemar, John Thompson, and David Purviance of the Lexington Presbytery in Kentucky were soon caught up in the revival spirit and joined in preaching a doctrine of free salvation without election. They were struck by the sense of God-given unity across denominational lines that seemed to permeate the revivals, and saw this as a sign of the unity of God's church.

Soon, however, when the churches began to argue about which churches could keep which converts, and Presbyterian elders placed McNemar on trial for heretical preaching, Stone and his colleagues withdrew from the presbytery and set up their own, the Springfield Presbytery. In a short time, however, they began to worry that by forming another presbytery they were simply furthering the very sectarianism they had been seeking to avoid. So, they decided to let their presbytery "die . . . and sink into union with the Body of Christ," and drew up "The Last Will and Testament of the Springfield Presbytery" to explain their actions.

Source: "The Last Will and Testament of the Springfield Presbytery," *Herald of Gospel Liberty,* 1 September 1808, 2–3. (This document is found also in vol. 4:5.)

Their action went against the pattern of wild proliferation in frontier revivals among religious groups, whereby each group tended to chose its own new and more exclusive identity with narrower boundaries than the one from which it had separated. Stone and his group actually enlarged their boundaries on behalf of the greater unity of Christ's church, becoming more inclusive instead of more exclusive. At the suggestion of Rice Haggard, who was familiar with James O'Kelly's group in Virginia known simply as "Christians," Stone's group likewise chose to be known as Christians and to receive into their fellowship any sincere follower of Jesus Christ.

The *Presbytery* of *Springfield,* sitting at Caneridge, in the county of Bourbon, being through a gracious Providence, in more than ordinary bodily health, growing in strength and size daily, in perfect soundness and composure of mind; but knowing that is appointed for all delegated bodies once to die and considering that the life of every such body is very uncertain, do make and ordain this our Last Will and Testament, in manner and form following, viz:

Imprimis. We *will* that this body die, be dissolved, and sink into union with the body of Christ at large: for there is but one body, and one spirit, even as we are called in one hope of our calling.

Item. We *will,* that our name of distinction, with its *Reverend* title, be forgotten, that there be but one Lord over God's heritage, and his name one.

Item. We *will,* that our power of making laws for the government of the church, and executing them by delegated authority, forever cease; that the people may have free course to the Bible, and adopt *the law of the spirit of life in Christ Jesus.*

Item. We *will,* that candidates for the Gospel ministry henceforth study the holy scriptures with fervent prayer, and obtain license from God to preach the simple Gospel, *with the Holy Ghost sent down from heaven,* without any mixture of philosophy, vain deceit, traditions of men, the rudiments of the world. And let none henceforth take *this honor to himself, but be that is called of God, as was Aaron.*

Item. We *will,* that the church of Christ assume her native right of internal government—try her candidates for the ministry, as to their soundness in the faith, acquaintance with experimental religion, gravity and aptness to teach; and admit no other proof of their authority, but Christ speaking in them. We *will* that the church of Christ look up to the Lord of the harvest to send forth labourers into his harvest; and that she resume her primitive right of trying those *who say they are Apostles, and are not.*

Item. We *will,* that each particular church, as a body, actuated by the same spirit, chuse her own preacher, and support him by a free will offering without written *call* or *subscription*—admit members—remove offences; and never henceforth *delegate* her right of government to any man or set of men whatever.

Item. We *will,* that the people henceforth take the Bible as the only sure guide to heaven; and as many as are offended with other books, which stand in competition with it, may cast them into the fire if they chuse: for it is better to enter into life having one book than having many to be cast into hell.

Item. We *will,* that preachers and people, cultivate a spirit of mutual forbearance, pray more and dispute less; and while they behold the signs of the times, look up and confidently expect that redemption draweth nigh.

Item. We *will,* that our weak brethren, who may have been wishing to make the Presbytery of Springfield their king, and wot not what is now become of it, betake themselves to the rock of ages, and follow Jesus for the future.

Item. We *will,* that the Synod of Kentucky examine every member, who may be *suspected* of having departed from the Confession of faith, and suspend such suspected heretics immediately; in order that the oppressed may go free, and taste the sweets of Gospel liberty.

Item. We *will,* that Ja——— the author of two letters lately published in Lexington, be encouraged in his zeal to destroy *partyism.* We *will,* moreover, that our past conduct be examined into by all who may have correct information; but let foreigners beware of speaking evil of things which they know not.

Item. Finally we *will,* that all our *sister bodies,* read their Bibles carefully, that they may see their fate there determined, and prepare for death before it is too late.

Springfield Presbytery, (*L.S.*)
June 28*th,* 1804.
ROBERT MARSHALL,
JOHN DUNLAVY,
RICHARD M'NEMAR, *Witnesses*
B. W. STONE,
JOHN THOMPSON,
DAVID PURVIANCE.

21. The Power of the Press:

"The Herald of Gospel Liberty"

(1809)

When Elias Smith founded the Herald of Gospel Liberty *in 1808, it was the first religious newspaper in the United States, and it was published without interruption until it joined with* The Congregationalist *in 1931. Smith intended the* Herald *to espouse the cause of religious liberty, but from the beginning the* Herald *was a herald of church union as well. No one could pick up an issue of the* Herald *without understanding its conviction that union needed to be the pressing concern of the churches. In the last fifteen years of the nineteenth century more than seventy-five articles on Christian union were published in its pages. There were hymns to union and poems to union, impassioned sermons demanding union and carefully reasoned articles requiring union—even ad hoc proposals from individuals detailing how the union of the churches was to be achieved. What was most striking about the* Herald*'s union fervor was the way it enabled every man and woman in local churches to be grasped by the urgency of uniting the churches. It was an extraordinary phenomenon. They were sure that Christian union was right around the corner!*

Source: *The Herald of Gospel Liberty,* 8 December 1809, 136.

THE HERALD

IS PUBLISHED IN

PORTSMOUTH, N. H.

EVERY OTHER FRIDAY MORNING,

BY ELIAS SMITH,

At his House near Vaughan-street, one door east of the bath house

AT ONE DOLLAR PER YEAR.

[Postage paid by Subscribers.] Fifty cents in advance. Punctually forwarded to any part of the UNITED STATES where conveyance is practicable.

22. Wider Vision:
"Letters"

(1809)

William Guiry; Elias Smith

It was only four months after Elias Smith published news of "The Last Will and Testament of the Springfield Presbytery" (see vol. 6:21), written by Barton Stone's group of Christians in Kentucky, that Smith published a letter from Rev. William Guiry, of James O'Kelly's group of Christians in the South, informing the Christians in the North that they existed and had settled on very much the same ruling principles that Smith and Jones's group had chosen. Elias Smith's enthusiastic response in the next issue of the Herald, *suggesting that they ought to "join the wall," is one example of how central Smith's* Herald *was in bringing these union-minded groups together.*

From Guiry to Smith

Mr. Elias Smith.

SIR, I lately received a letter from a friend who informs me that there exists a body of people in New England who call themselves *the christian church,* that they have published a work entitled *the Herald of Gospel Liberty,* of which you are the editor. As I am exceedingly anxious to obtain

Source: William Guiry, "Letter to Mr. Elias Smith," *Herald of Gospel Liberty,* 19 January 1809, 43; Elias Smith, "Letter to Elder William Guiry," *Herald of Gospel Liberty,* 2 February 1809, 47.

information of this people, which my friend has not communicated, I hope you will consider this as a sufficient apology for troubling you with this letter; however, if any further apology should be necessary, I expect it will be included in the following communication.

In the year 1792 several hundred persons withdrew from the methodist church in consequence of their objections to the Episcopal form of government, the causes of the separation I have minutely related in a work entitled *the History of Episcopacy,* containing 381 pages.

After we became a separate people, three points were determined on. 1st. No head over the church but Christ. 2d. No confession of faith, articles of religion, rubic, canons, creeds &c. but the New Testament. 3d. No religious name but christians. For several years I have been a minister in this church and have traveled among the members from Philadelphia to the Southern frontier of Georgia. We have members in every State south of the Potomac, also a few churches in Pennsylvania; from the best information I can obtain I suppose there are about 20,000 people in the Southern and Western States who call themselves by the *christian name.* Our sentiments on doctrinal points have been sufficiently explained in a pamphlet entitled *an apology for renouncing the jurisdiction of the Synod of Kentucky, to which is added a compendious view of the Gospel, &c;* those persons who are the authors of the pamphlet have since their separation from the Presbyterians united with us. I believe on this and every other subject we are of one mind and of one heart except it be the subject of baptism. Many of our brethren who were formerly methodists or presbyterians are in favour of infant baptism. While myself and several others are of a contrary opinion. I have thought proper to receive baptism by immersion on a profession of faith, and have since my baptism baptized 3 or 4 of our preachers, others fear methodist reproach, &c. &c. I make this communication that you may know how far we agree and how we differ in sentiment.

I should be exceedingly glad to receive a letter from you stating the doctrines and government of the church to which you are united, and if there should not be any thing like Episcopacy or Calvinism in the way, my soul would exult if a union between us could be effected, should only a prospect of this kind present itself gladly would I pay you a visit the ensuing spring. From the title of your publication *the Herald of Gospel Liberty,* and from the name you have taken, the *christian church* I flatter myself the difference between us cannot be great.

Christian liberty how delightful the sound, but how little understood by the professors of christianity? "All acknowledge that the scriptures contain all things necessary to be believed, and practiced yet all make a number of ecclesiastical laws and creeds which the apostles never heard of." During the time I officiated as a minister in the church of England I had but faint ideas of christian liberty, and I am satisfied there are thousands in the world whose bigotry is so great in favour of the different human institutions in vogue among christians that they consider those who assert with Paul that all scripture is given by inspiration of God, and is profitable for doctrine, for reproof, for correction, for instruction in righteousness that the man of God may be perfect throughly [*sic*] furnished unto all good works, as fools or madmen.

May the Lord hasten the day when the little stone Daniel saw taken out of the mountain without hands shall fill the whole earth. Do my good sir favour me with a few lines directed to [Childsburg] Caroline County, Virginia, and because I consider you as the friend of christian liberty with pleasure I subscribe myself your sincere friend,

W. G.

From Smith to Guiry

DEARLY BELOVED IN THE LORD.

BEFORE this letter comes to you, the papers sent, will inform you that your letter is received and widely spread through the churches. Your communication has caused great joy among the brethren, and an intimation of coming this way the ensuing spring, has greatly increased a desire we had before that some of our ministering brethren at the south should make us a visit. The three things you mention; viz. 1. "No head over the church but Christ. 2d. No confession of faith, &c. but the New Testament. 3d. No religious name but christian," is what we have all agreed too, and are now agreed in throughout the whole Union.

We rejoice in the thousands of Ephraim here, and the twenty thousands of Manasseh there. We are happy to hear that you and many others understand New Testament *Baptism.* I wish it was more generally understood and practiced by our brethren at the *South.* I think they will attend to it more hereafter. The scholar who learns of the best master, does not learn all at once. In this part, our brethren I believe to a single individual, are agreed in baptism; believing it a burial with Christ, as you will see by the papers.

As to stating the doctrine and government of the churches here, I cannot do it in a letter, because we believe the New Testament, and that we ought to hear God's SON, JESUS, in all things. The two books sent, will give some knowledge of what we believe.

Brother Lanphier has sent me your sermon, "The pattern in the mount," which gives me joy, that you have found it, and are shewing it to others. The New Testament has been as the law once was, *among the rubbish.* Now we have found it, let us read it to the people from morning till evening.

You mention a visit this way in the spring if there is no "*Episcopacy* or *Calvinism* in the way" of an union. You may be assured, that if in this part we were as clear of every kind of babylonish ware, as of these two things; we should in reality resemble the church at Antioch in the days of Luke. *Episcopacy and Calvinism are as great an abomination to the brethren here, for ought I know, as a shepherd was to Egyptian in the days of Jacob.*

There is nothing to hinder a general union among the brethren from north to south, that I can see: but there is something to be done; that is, to let all our brethren through the whole know that we are striving for the same thing.

It is wonderful to me, that while I was labouring to convince men that Christ is all; not knowing there was another person on earth striving for the same thing, that others in the South should be doing the same. Had I known it before now, I might have leaned on them; but we have done like those in the days of Nehemiah; each built the wall over against his own house till they joined all in one, and set up the gates; while their enemies were saying, "What do these feeble Jews? Will they build? Will they make an end in one day?" But they meant them evil; saying, even that which they build if a fox should go up thereon, he would throw down their stone wall.

My Br. have we not built enough to join the wall? I think we have. With pleasure I look forward to a day, I hope, not far off; which I shall meet some of my brethren from the South, to join in *Christian Union,* endeavouring to promote harmony and love among thousands of our brethren widely spread throughout the United States of America!

If you make us a visit, I cannot promise you a reward of *gold* or *silver;* and as a christian, you do not wish for such an one; but if you come in the fullness of the blessing of the gospel of Christ, you may depend on an hundred fold of brethren and sisters, and multitudes to preach unto. Whenever you conclude to come, let me know, and the Lord willing, we will make arrangements to meet you, as far as *Providence* or *Boston,* where we may thank God, and I hope take courage.

It would be pleasing to me to journey into Virginia and see the brethren; but at present I see no way, my work calls me here.

Notwithstanding all the distress of nations, our prospects are glorious beyond expression. We are in a land of liberty, where the gospel of grace is sweetly, and extensively sounding; and sinners by thousands converted to God. We see the prophecies daily fulfilling,—and according to the sure word, the greater things for the believers to see, are near. O the glory before us!—"The resurrection of the just"—The thousand years of Christ's reign upon earth!—The new Heavens and earth, which we according to promise look for, when the New Jerusalem shall come down prepared as a bride adorned for her husband; in which the followers of the Lamb shall enter; there to dwell, having a right to the tree of life, where they shall drink of the water of life ever gliding between the golden banks! There *pain, night, death,* and the wicked are never seen! There each inhabitant shall eternally enjoy the presence of God and the Lamb!

Who would not be faithful unto death, while he has in view the promise, "A crown of life!" I forebear; and remain your brother and companion in tribulation, and in the kingdom and patience of Jesus Christ.

ELIAS SMITH

A Maturing Commitment to Union

23. Convictions Stated: *"Position on Christian Union"*

(1874)

A great many of the records from the early conferences of the southern Christians are no longer available; first, because the records before 1818 were usually burned publicly at the close of each session "lest they be used as established precedents in future conferences"; second, because there was no official organ devoted to the interests of the southern Christians until the Christian Sun *began publication in 1844; but also, because a fire tore through the library of Elon College on January 18, 1923, destroying nearly all of the painstakingly assembled archives of the Christian Church. Therefore, the* Annual of the Christian Church, *Southern Conference, published from 1870 to 1964/65, is an especially precious source of available information about the early southern Christians.*

From its inception, nearly every volume of the Annual *contained a "Position on Christian Union" indicating the commitment to union that the southern Christians had held since their founding by James O'Kelly, their recognition of the ordination of "all Evangelical ministers," their open pulpits and tables, and a formulation of the Six Principles of the Christian Church.*

Although the Annual *was intended for use within the Christian membership, its prominently displayed "Position on Christian Union" made a clear public statement of who they understood themselves to be and how they understood church union as their mission.*

Source: Southern Christian Convention, "Position on Christian Union," in *Annual of the Christian Church for 1874,* vol. 4, ed. W. B. Wellons (Suffolk, Va.: Christian Board of Publication, 1874), 77.

The Christians have always been the earnest advocates of union among the followers of Christ. They have ever practiced union, when practicable. They recognize all Evangelical ministers in their office, and their pulpits have been open to them. They are ready to worship and work with all believers in Christ, of every name. To the communion table, when spread by them, all believers are invited. Christian ministers are always ready to associate with all who love Christ, and to have fellowship with all who accept him as their Saviour. They cling to the name Christian, because there is nothing exclusive in it, and reject all party names because of their exclusiveness. They acknowledge no Head, no leader but Christ, because all believers are one in Him. They object to all creeds which cannot be expressed in the precise language of the Scriptures, because in a creed expressed in the teachings of Divine inspiration all may agree. They have adopted Christian character as their test of fellowship, believing that all who believe in Jesus and trust in him for salvation, ought to be received to christian and church fellowship. They, therefore, profess to receive all to their fellowship who give credible evidence that Christ has received them. They only require unity of sentiment in the essentials of religion, and extend to all the right of private judgment in things not considered essential to salvation.

These principles they cling to with much tenacity because the people of God may thus be united in feeling and practice. In the great, grand union movement of the day, the Christians find themselves in the front rank. But they are willing to be considered the most humble, and even absorbed, in the great army of union lovers and workers now concentrating upon the great principles which they have long cherished and practiced.

The Christians have taken the world for their field of labor, and are endeavoring to bring together in co-operation the liberal and good everywhere.

24. Local Negotiations:
"Christian Union" (Ohio)

(1886)

Among the Christians, where every church member was seriously charged with the responsibility of working toward Christian union, their periodicals always contained a profusion of local union negotiations, local plans for union, and proposals for union offered by impassioned individuals.

An article on "Christian Union" shared the preamble and resolutions adopted by the Southern Ohio Christian Conference at their Ministerial Institute in 1888. There, a committee composed of a Christian Union minister, a Christian minister, and a Christian layperson declared their approval of "a visible union and organic fellowship" with the Free Baptists and Christian Union peoples, and urged the executive board of their conference to send delegates to a forthcoming meeting of the Christian Union people.

A second article on "Christian Union" printed the preamble and resolutions adopted at a Columbus Grove, Ohio, meeting "between representatives of the Christian Church and the Christian Church, or the Christians and the Disciples of Christ," indicating their view that the differences between them were not as great as had been thought, and making several proposals for how the two denominations (and all others) could become closer.

Such grassroots initiatives were crucial to the ecumenical enterprise. They illustrate some of the early steps in the ecumenical movement

---

Source: Committee of the Southern Ohio Ministerial Institute of the Southern Ohio Christian Conference, "Christian Union," *Herald of Gospel Liberty,* 22 April 1886, 250; committees of the Christian Church and the Disciples of Christ, "Christian Union," *Herald of Gospel Liberty,* 14 October 1886, 651.

whereby groups learned to transcend their own boundaries and began to commit themselves to a larger shared Christian identity.

Christian Union

The following preamble and resolutions were adopted by the Southern Ohio Ministerial Institute, of the Southern Ohio Christian Conference:

Jesus' last prayer was an important one, and we do confess that it has been *too often* forgotten—"That they may all be one, even as thou, Father, art in me and I in thee, that they also may be one in us; that the world may believe that thou hast sent me." John 7:21. We believe that the one thing lacking for the full evangelization of the world, is the co-operation of God's children in the service of their Father. So long as we are human, so long as we are finite, so long as we are ignorant, so long as we are prejudiced, so long as we are separate, so long as we are in earth, it will be impossible for us all to agree as to matters of interpretation, in our intellectual conceptions or in the verbal statement of our belief. In the present state of the world and the church, we do not ask or expect uniformity of belief or interpretation, or of practice in regard to ordinances or ceremonies, but we do expect unity of heart, and unity of work, and unity of organization, and unity of life. To his own Master shall each one answer.

Let us, then, cease to judge one another, to debate with one another, and to disfellowship others as good as we, but let us cultivate a better acquaintance with one another, and as we come to know, we shall also come to love one another. We therefore rejoice to see the growing tendency of churches to unite, and we pledge ourselves to co-operate with all movements in that direction. We are especially pleased with the proposals for the practical union of the peoples known as Free Baptists, and the Christian Union and Christian connection. We are ready for a union with all men in Christ and his gospel, and we only caution ourselves not to organize some good Christians out at the same time that we organize some of us within our churchly associations; therefore,

Resolved, 1. That we favor a visible union and organic fellowship with the Free Baptists and Christian Union peoples, and all other Christian peoples on such terms as may cause no sacrifice of the rights of each separate individual conscience in matters of faith and doctrine; but we will willingly sacrifice any business forms or customs of our own that may in any measure interfere with the full consummation of the desired coalition.

2. We request the delegates of the Southern Ohio Christian Conference to the American Christian Convention to act as delegates to any meeting or convention that may be called.

3. In the meeting for consultation with the Christian Union people as called to meet at ______, Licking County, Ohio, April 14th, we request the executive board of the Southern Ohio Christian Conference to appoint suitable delegates to represent our conference and institute in that meeting, and do instruct them to vote so as to carry out the spirit of this report.

4. We do agree to set apart the 11th day of April, and such other days as may be appointed for consultation with any of God's children, in regard to better organization and co-operation in Christian union work, as days of special fasting and prayer to our common Father in heaven that he may lead us into ways of peace and unity, and that we may come to so love and work together "that the world may believe" in Christ Jesus and his gospel.

E. A. De Vore,
Christian Minister,
Lewis Richey,
Christian Union Minister,
S. R. Fairfield,
Layman in Christian Church,
Committee.

Christian Union

Preamble and resolutions adopted at Columbus Grove, Ohio, September 28, 1886, by representatives of the Christian Church and the Christian Church, or the Christians and the Disciples of Christ:

Whereas, a committee of two was sent by the Quarterly Conference of the Northwestern Ohio Christian Conference to the Yearly Meeting of the Disciples of Christ in Paulding County, Ohio, held at Hedges, Ohio, September 10–12, 1886, asking that a delegation of Disciples be sent to the annual meeting of the Northwestern Ohio Christian Conference to confer upon the question of Christian union; and, whereas, such a delegation of Disciples was sent to that conference for that purpose; and, whereas, a committee has now been appointed from the conference to meet with them and confer upon that subject; and, whereas, such joint meeting has now been held and a free and hearty Christian and brotherly talk has been had upon the subject of Christian union; therefore,

Resolved, 1. That as a joint committee we all in common recognize the great importance of the union of all the followers of Christ and the duty of seeking by every lawful means to bring about that union.

2. That we recognize that the two bodies of people here represented are for the present prevented from uniting together by differing convictions honestly cherished.

3. That we are impressed that some very important points of special sympathy exist between these two bodies, viz., (1) an earnest advocacy of the union of all Christians; (2) a rejection of all human authoritative creeds; (3) a rejection of all unscriptural names for Christians.

4. That we are impressed by our conference together that the grounds of difference are less than we had previously supposed.

5. That we recommend that the following things be done to prepare the way for Christian union: (1) That we of these two bodies speak of each other only by scriptural names for the followers of Christ, remembering that it is a point of conscience with both peoples to acknowledge such names only; (2) that we seek to acquaint ourselves more fully with each other's views; (3) that we speak of each other as brothers in Christ, and thus cultivate the spirit of brotherhood; (4) that we discuss our differences with a view to finding how near we can come together instead of with a view to magnifying differences; (5) that we seek acquaintance with each other by mingling in each other's meetings and exchanging pulpits.

6. That as far as possible we apply all these principles to the cultivation of Christian union among all who follow Christ.

L. GANDER,
D. LEPLEY,
E. A. DE VORE,
D. LOBAUGH,
G. B. GARNER,
Christian Committee.
J. M. ATWATER,
W. J. LHAMOR,
Disciple Committee.

25. Theological Reflections:
"Ten Practical Sides of Union Work"

(1897)

Martyn Summerbell

Martyn Summerbell (1847–1939) was professor of church history at Cobb Divinity School (1888–98), vice-president and lecturer at Defiance College (1898–1935), president of the Palmer Institute-Starkey Seminary (1898–1935), secretary of the Inter-Church Conference on Federation (1905), and member of the executive committee of the Federal Council (1905–39). Summerbell represented early Christian ecumenism at its best.

Summerbell was also one of the commissioners appointed by the Christian quadrennial convention at Haverhill, Massachusetts, October 9–14, 1895, to look into a cooperative union with the Congregationalists, "or any other denomination seeking such union," provided that the union not be based upon doctrinal tests (see vol. 6:36). After a preliminary conference between the Congregational and Christian bodies in Piqua, Ohio, in April 1896, the commissions on union representing the two bodies met in Summerbell's cottage in Craigville, Massachusetts, in August 1897, where they agreed to the "Craigville Recommendations" for union between the two groups (see vol. 6:18).

On the occasion of that meeting, Summerbell read a paper entitled "Ten Practical Sides of Union Work." The paper shows how far the Christians had come from their earliest days, when they were prone to "speechifying" on Christian union but very wary of any people different from themselves. Summerbell recognized the human weaknesses that so often stood in the way of union, as well as the simple and practical steps

---

Source: Martyn Summerbell, "Ten Practical Sides of Union Work," *Herald of Gospel Liberty,* 2 September 1897, 547–48.

whereby a denomination's ministers and members could choose to move closer to those in other denominations and have practical experience of one another's practices and behaviors.

[A paper read at the Union Meeting, at Craigville, Mass., August 8, 1897, and requested for publication by all the Christian ministers on the camp-ground.]

It is not necessary in this time and place to present arguments in favor of a closer union among the Lord's people than now exists; for the fact that we are here, indicates our conviction that each a consummation is devoutly to be wished, and, more than that, that we have some hope that means may be discovered for its accomplishment. For years the religious press has been teeming with pleas in favor of union, and several of the most conservative denominations have busied themselves in framing protocols and deliverances, explaining their interest in the subject, and their view of the methods by which it may be achieved. In the life of the Christians particularly, the idea of Christian union has been fundamental from the beginning of their movement, and the best pulpit efforts of their greatest preachers have been those in which they have set forth the sin of dividing the Lord's heritage, and the beauty of realizing the vision of our Lord in the visible unity of the discipleship. Possibly in nothing can any representative of the Christians be more loyal to the traditions and beliefs of the people with which he stands connected, than in forwarding in every possible way the speedy union of Christians.

And yet, strange to say, though closer union among Christians is so desirable, and is so heartily bepraised in the word, when we come to the fact of it, it is not achieved to any appreciable extent. The reason for this, as it seems to me, is that up to this time attention has been principally given to theorizing upon union, and that such plans as have been laid for bringing it to pass, have not been constructed with a view to actual conditions, and in consequence the difficulties encountered have been too serious to surmount. As a result many of these, which appeared to their projectors all that could be wished, have speedily "died a bornin'."

A word as to some of these difficulties, which in all our union planning will need to be reckoned with.

1. The first of these is the conservatism of established conditions. Whatever is, is. And because it is, it possesses the inertia of immobility. If it be a denominational tradition or institution, it is the holder in possession, and claims all the traditional nine points of the law. You propose change

to it, and in the nature of things it is bound to resist your suggestion, and the only way to effect a change is by bringing so strong a case that everybody is convinced of its value. But when you have won your contention by such general consent you have this advantage, that the forces of conservatism, which before were such an obstacle, now array themselves for its maintenance.

2. A second difficulty in securing the embodiment of our union eloquence, is the general suspicion which is made to attach to any plan for union, and to the leader, who offers it for the suffrages of his denominational confreres. Human nature is still human nature, notwithstanding all the influences of the gospel, and so it comes about that the question will be raised respecting the man who broaches a plan for union, as to what he is trying to make out of it. He may be trying for nothing but the glory of the Lord and his kingdom, and every plank in his platform may be sound and true, but for all that some one will surely insist that there is some occult intention, and the less it appears in evidence, the more certainly it must be there.

3. And this element of suspicion is all the more troublesome, since in some of our former union efforts mistakes have occurred, the memory of which lingers long. It is needless to say more of these than that they fall into the category of perfidy, organic or individual. Sometimes two denominations have arranged a compact of union, the one entering upon it in good faith; but the other playing the part of lion to the other's lamb, and making its meal to its own content, and to the other's detriment. Or, again, some man in high position, under pretense of union, perverts his influence to carry a church, or some other institution, which represents an investment of prayer and financial sacrifice, out of the denomination to which it belongs into some other; he, of course, having respect unto the recompense of reward. Such transactions, which have occurred too often, have developed among thoughtful men a sense of caution, when the subject of union is under discussion.

Obviously, therefore, any plan now to be proposed must make allowances for these difficulties. The map which shows the reefs, shows also the safe channels. If theorizing so far has amounted to little, there may be advantage in searching for the practical steps, which may also prove practicable.

1. I am of the opinion that any proposition for closer affiliation between the Christians and any other denomination must begin with the positive assurance that the integrity of the denomination shall not be disturbed. With the Christians there has been in the last ten or fifteen years, a very commendable advance in the spirit and fact of co-ordinate interest. What-

ever may be said about the profit of general Christian union, the Christians are coming to feel new courage as they grow into closer union with themselves. They will not consent to any alluring note of union with anybody or anything by piece-meal, which is equivalent to disintegration. Whatever they do, they will do together. They will insist on maintaining every denominational trust, and every denominational institution. Their present tendency is for more life, not less, in every agency and department of the church. Edification and not erosion, is the watchword of the hour. If the Christians consent to enter any parlor of union with other denominations, that parlor must be visibly furnished with windows all around, so as to admit plenty of light, and they must open clean down to the floor.

2. Starting with a plain and straightforward proviso of this nature, a second practical step toward Christian union, to be effected immediately, may be the frequent visitation of our ministry to the conferences and associations of a sister body. Such a tie of intimate fellowship may be emphasized by the associations of the one body electing the ministers of the other into honorary membership. This would confer a special grace, and yet it would not affect the voting interest, or imperil any denominational trust.

3. A third step toward a practical working union might be an interchange of membership between the Christians and the sister body. Frequently a church member, on changing his place of residence, finds no church of his own people. In such case he commonly selects a church according to personal convenience, and so is soon lost to his own people. I conceive that it would be a decided gain for the Christians and the Congregationalists, for example, to hold their membership within their own limits. Of course it is understood that no coercion could be practiced, for our American Christian will stand but little of that; but the brethren of the one body, in the case suggested, could be encouraged to unite with a church of the other, and so the chances of the return of such to their own churches, on a second removal, would be correspondingly increased.

4. A fourth step toward practical union would be a co-operation of the denominations named in pastoral settlements. What would be gained by this? Much more than is commonly supposed. For the first thing, a hold would be kept over ministers, whose services are now lost, when called outside their denomination. As affairs are, such is the struggle in crossing the denominational enclosure, as to rupture the former ties of sympathy. Under the proposed plan, however, the doors of separation would swing on a double hinge, both inward and outward, which would be a great gain. But the great advantage would be to the churches. Frequently now two weak churches of the two denominations are in close vicinage, neither being able to support a pastor alone. Under this plan they might call a

minister from either denomination, who should serve them both, each of the churches holding to its own doctrinal and denominational foundation, and sending its denominational contributions to its own denominational treasury, and enjoying the benefit of a grade of pulpit talent, which it could not obtain otherwise. The plan offers a solution of the problem of the rural church. God has set these little organizations all over our New England States. They are suffering now from a dearth of qualified ministers. An intense denominationalism tends to make them weaker and weaker.

But under the plan proposed, with a moderate denominationalism, which conserves all that is worth preserving, they might have a fresh lease of life and influence. Of course, where a minister serves two churches, it will require some grace on his part to dispense the gospel, and not dispense with it; and also to serve the church of the other denomination without attempting to engraft upon it the ways and usages of his own denomination. But if the plan is accepted, the influential men of both denominations will guard these matters, and in the long run what is lost in one place will be gained in another, and the just balance retained.

To what has so far been said, I may add that these four suggestions are embodied in the measure adopted by the Haverhill Convention. They do not imperil any vested interest, and would tend to aid the two bodies materially. And it is believed that if they were to work a little side by side, they would discover their supposed differences melting away, and would learn to recognize each other as truly brethren in the Lord.

26. HYMN:

"Union Would Save"

(1905)

O. B. WHITAKER

The early Christians talked, preached, wrote, and argued about union, as any glance at one of their newspapers revealed. But they also wrote their own hymns about union and sang them passionately. Hardly a month went by in the Herald *without the appearance of someone's poetic rendering of the biblical mandate, ready to be sung to some rousing and familiar tune. This fact more than any other shows how very dear to their hearts the union issue was. "Union Would Save" by O. B. Whitaker appeared in the* Herald *on January 5, 1905.*

(The following is a revision of this song. It is used in worship in Kansas, and is received with much favor. It can be secured of the author, Dr. O. B. Whitaker, Lincoln, Kansas, at 5 cents per single copy; 100 copies, $2.50.—Editor.)

(To be sung to tune of "Throw Out the Life-Line.")

The Church of our Savior was severed by man,
Vile mortals have wounded the Bride of the Lamb;
Division and schism, intestinal strife
Have wrest from the Church both her mission and life.

SOURCE: O. B. Whitaker, "Union Would Save," *Herald of Gospel Liberty,* 5 January 1905, 5.

Chorus—
The Church has been wounded, her life's blood is ebbing,
  Union her ruin would stay;
Thousands of souls all about us are dying,—
  Union would save them to-day.

Our Savior for Union most earnestly prayed,
That the world might believe it was God's Son that died:
"One fold and one Shepherd," He said there should be;
"One Master, and ye are all brethren," said He.

Chorus—
"Abomination," wrote Solomon's pen,
"Is he that sows discord 'mong children of men."
"How good and how pleasant," thus David's words fell,
"For brethren together in Union to dwell."

Chorus—
"One Lord, one faith, and one Spirit," said Paul,
"One body, one God, and one Father of all."
Then back to the Standard, the Bible—obey;
For why should division and sectism be?

Double Chorus—
The Savior commands it, the "Wise Man" hath said it,
  The Psalmist hath sung it of old;
God's prophets, apostles, disciples of Jesus,
  Call thee, "Come into the fold."
The Church has been wounded, her life's blood is ebbing,
  Union her ruin would stay,—
Thousands of souls all about us are dying;
  Union would save them to-day.

Lincoln, Kansas.

Blacks in the Christian Movement

27. Afro-Christian Worship: "Revised Ritual of the Christian Church"

(1901)

A. A. Bright

Until the close of the Civil War, black Christians worshiped in the same church as their white masters did, were received into its fellowship, and were ministered to by white pastors, although in worship they were often required to sit in galleries set off from the main room of the church by a railing. Children of slaves were gathered up by a Sunday school teacher and taught about the Bible, and some were even taught to read.

After Lincoln emancipated the slaves in 1863, and blacks were free to go into the world as free citizens of the United States, they often sought to express their new freedom by building their own independent, local black churches, often on the same property as the white church. Eventually, some of these black congregations organized themselves into a conference.

By 1866, a well-respected Christian leader, J. W. Wellons, introduced a resolution at a meeting of the North Carolina and Virginia Conference requesting the appointment of a committee to help the black Christians with plans to organize conferences, ordain deacons and elders, and license certain of their own people to preach.

Within a decade, black Christians had organized more than fifty churches, three conferences, and ordained forty ministers. By 1892, they had established a high school at Franklinton, North Carolina. And by 1900, many new churches had been established and the number of

---

Source: A. A. Bright, *Revised Ritual of the Christian Church* (Raleigh, N.C.: Raleigh Advocate Printers, 1901), 1–26.

ministers increased, with more young men asking to be licensed. New church buildings of better quality were built, and most congregations had Sunday schools for Bible study and religious education. Conferences were formed and soon organized the Afro-Christian Convention, composed of all the conferences of the black Christian churches. The high school in Franklinton had become Franklinton Christian College.

In 1901, A. A. Bright, soon to be field secretary for the southern division of the Afro-Christian Convention, answered the need in the black churches for a "Church Ritual" giving a brief history of their churches, a description of the fundamentals of the Christian church, basic rules for the organization and function of the local churches, the most fundamental theology, and words to hymns.

Preface

The Colored Christians have been needing a Church Ritual, gotten up for their use, that would give them some of the names of the fathers of their Church, to which they could refer in after days. This Church has struggled hard for existence against many opposing obstacles, but God has given it a better day.

Brethren, take this little book, and in the name of God, go forth and Christianize the world.

Yours for Heaven,
A. A. B. B. D.
[A. A. Bright]

Revised Ritual of the Christian Church

The Christian Church among the Colored people was originated from those who had been members of the white congregation before the surrender of the Southern Confederacy. After peace had been declared they began to congregate for the purpose of worshiping God. Their white brethren heard of them, and sent Revs. W. M. Wellons and W. M. Hayes to gather the scattered brethren together in a Conference. This assembly came together in the city of Raleigh, N.C., November 10, 1867. The following congregations were in the organization:

Christian Chapel, Pleasant Grove, Swift Creek Chapel, Raleigh, Pleasant Hill and New Berne.

The following preachers and delegates were present:

Revs. William H. Hayes and Samuel Foy. (J. J. Jeffreys and W. H. Hayes were ordained, and Samuel Foy and J. J. Jeffreys were licensed.) Delegates: John Kent, N. Horton, Berry Hank, Monroe Watson.

This Conference has had a steady increase. It established a college at Franklinton, N.C., in 1880, under the auspices of the North Carolina and Virginia Conferences. Its first president was Rev. George Young, of Carolize, N.Y.

Rev. Wilson, of Philadelphia, and wife, were great leaders in the establishment of this school for the uplifting of the young men and women of the Christian Church.

The Christian Church adheres to the following principles:

(1) Christ, the only head of the Church.

(2) The name CHRISTIAN to the exclusion of all party or sectarian names.

(3) The Holy Bible or the Scriptures of the Old and New Testaments our only Creed or confession of faith.

(4) Christian character or vital piety, the true Scriptural test of fellowship or church membership.

(5) The right of private judgment and the liberty of conscience the privilege and duty of all—upon Bible doctrine.

Chapter I

The Christian Church is composed of all who profess faith in the Lord Jesus Christ, and teach repentance through our Lord and Saviour Jesus Christ.

(2) Though he may belong to some other denominational Church, yet if he has been converted by the Son of the Living God, he is a Christian, and God accepts of him as one of His.

(3) God sent His only begotten Son into the world to establish one Church, not many; and all men who have been converted are brethren and members of this Church, of which Christ is the head.

(4) The Church is spoken of in the Scriptures as a household of which God, the Father, is the ruler, and such should not be divided against itself.

(5) All the principles and workings of the Church should be in harmony with the Scriptures, so that members may be brought together in one body.

Chapter II
Church Rules

It is the duty of every church to select a pastor to serve them in the holy things, and to preach to them the unsearchable riches of God's grace.

(2) The members shall provide for the support of the pastor, and shall pay their salaries in their monthly meetings, in which all the members are required to be present.

(3) No member who shall neglect to pay his or her salary dues for three consecutive meetings is a member in good standing, and before he or she can be restored to membership he or she must pay the arrearage.

(4) The members shall adhere to the decisions of the pastor, who shall ever make his decisions in accordance with the Word of God.

(5) The members shall meet weekly, and give support of the pastor's table, that he may be able to give all of his time to the preaching of the Gospel and looking after the needs of his flock. This amount shall not be included in his SALARY.

Now concerning the collection for the saints: "As I have given order to the churches of Galatia, even so do ye: Upon the first day of the week let every one of you lay by him in store as God hath prospered him, that there be no gatherings when I come." —*Cor. 16:1, 2.*

For the Scriptures saith: "Thou shalt not muzzle the ox that treadeth out the corn, and the laborer is worthy of his hire." —*1 Tim. 5:18.*

For it is written in the law of Moses: "Thou shalt not muzzle the mouth of the ox that treadeth out the corn. Doth God take care of the oxen!" —*1 Cor. 9:9.*

(6) The preacher's salary shall be three dollars for every male member annually, and two dollars for every female member. Children whose parents have to pay their salary dues, may pay such amounts as the members agree upon.

Chapter III
Reception of Members

A person may become a member of the church upon profession of his faith in the Lord Jesus. He shall come before the altar while a hymn is being sung. All candidates should be instructed in regard to the responsibilities of the church membership, of supporting the pastor, and the expenses of the church.

Q. (1) Have you sincerely and heartily repented your sins?

Q. (2) Do you believe in the Lord Jesus Christ as the Saviour of the world?

Q. (3) Is it your purpose through grace to live a godly life?

These questions being answered in the affirmative, the minister shall state the fact, and there being no objection, he or she becomes a member.

The Resurrection of the Dead

The Scriptures are clear on the point of the resurrection, both of the righteous and the unrighteous. The statement is plain, and though a man may try to satisfy his unbelief, yet it is true.

(2) Jesus Christ is our authority. He said unto Mary and Martha that "I am the resurrection and the life," and He could not be mistaken.

(3) The doctrine of the resurrection was not entirely new, because when Jesus spoke of it to Mary and Martha, Martha replying, said: "I know that he shall rise again in the resurrection of the last day."

"For the Father loveth the Son, and showeth him all things that himself doeth: and will shew him greater works than these, that ye may marvel. For as the father raiseth up the dead, and quickeneth them, even so the Son quickeneth whom he will. For the Father judgeth no man, but hath committed all judgment unto the Son; that all men should honor the Son, even as they honor the Father. He that honoreth not the Son, honoreth not the Father which hath sent him. Verily, verily, I say unto you, he that heareth my word, and believeth on him that sent me, hath everlasting life, and shall not come unto condemnation, but is passed from death into life. Verily, verily, I say unto you, the hour is coming, and now is when the dead shall hear the voice of the Son of God: and they that hear shall live; for as the Father hath life in himself, so hath he given to the Son to have life in himself. And hath given him authority to execute judgment also, because he is the Son of Man. Marvel not at this, for the hour is coming in which all that are in their graves shall hear his voice, and shall come forth; they that have done good, unto the resurrection of life; and they that have done evil, unto the resurrection of damnation." —*John 5:20–29.*

God hath appointed a day when He shall judge all the nations of the earth, and shall separate the good from the bad. Jesus Christ will sit on the throne, and before Him will be gathered all the nations, both great and small.

"When the Son of Man shall come in his glory, and all the holy angels with him, then shall he sit upon the throne of his glory, and before him shall be gathered all nations; and he shall separate them from one another, as a shepherd divideth his sheep from his goats." —*Matt. 25:31, 32.*

Administration of Baptism

The sacrament of baptism shall be administered by an Elder of Bishop, and it should not be delayed.

(2) The person or persons should present themselves for baptism, should stand in front of the minister while he shall read the following passages of Scripture:

"Then the eleven disciples went away into Gallilee into a mountain, where Jesus had appointed them; and when they saw him they worshiped him; but some doubted. And Jesus came and spake unto them saying, All power is given unto me in heaven and in earth, go ye therefore, and teach all nations, baptizing them in the name of the Father, and of the Son, and of the Holy Ghost, teaching them to observe all things whatsoever I have commanded you: and lo! I am with you always, even unto the end of the world. Amen." —*Matt. 28:16–20.*

"And he said unto them, Go ye into all the world, and preach the gospel to every creature. He that believeth and is baptized, shall be saved; but he that believeth not shall be damned." —*Mark 16:15, 16.*

After reading a suitable passage of Scripture, and the singing of an appropriate hymn, prayer should be offered; then the candidate should be led into the water. The minister, standing in the water, shall raise his right hand and say: "In obedience to the command of my Lord and Master, and upon the profession of thy faith, my brother (or sister), I baptize thee in the name of the Father, and of the Son, and of the Holy Ghost. Amen."

Administration of the Lord's Supper

The Lord's Supper should be served at least four times a year, making it three months between times.

(2) The most suitable time, perhaps, is on the Sabbath, directly after the sermon, of which notice should be given beforehand, that every member of the congregation may have his or her mind and heart properly prepared for this holy communion.

The elements should be set apart by prayer and thanksgiving, after which the minister shall break the bread before the people, saying in this manner: "Our Lord Jesus Christ, the same night in which He was betrayed, took bread, and when He had given thanks, He break it, and said: 'Take, eat; this is my body which is broken for you; this do in remembrance of me. This cup is the New Testament in my blood. This do ye as oft as ye drink it in remembrance of me.' "

After which a collection should be taken for the poor.

Deacons

It is plain from the Scriptures that the Deacons are distinct officers of the Church. Their duty is to supply the wants of the pastor, and take charge of temporal affairs of the Church.

(2) They should make suitable arrangements for the support of the pastor, and assist in administering the sacrament.

(3) One of the Deacons shall preside in the absence of the pastor, and shall strictly adhere to the rules of the Christian Church.

(4) They should counsel with the pastor in the government and spiritual affairs of the church, and conduct the public worship of the church when there is no one of higher authority present.

"Paul and Timothy, the servants of Jesus Christ, to all the saints in Christ Jesus, which are at Philippi with the bishops and deacons." —*Phil., ch. 1.*

"Likewise must the deacons be grave, not doubletongued; not given to much wine; not greedy of filthy lucre." —*1 Tim. 3:8.*

Licentiates

A LICENTIATE is one licensed to preach the gospel as a probationer, until he shall give full proof of his ability to teach efficiently the great doctrine of salvation.

(2) Great care should be taken that the candidate for license possess the moral and intellectual qualifications necessary to fit him for the responsible position to which he aspires.

(3) He shall therefore possess an unblemished Christian character, and a good English education, and be recommended by the church of which he is a member.

(4) He shall be examined on the doctrines and principles of the Christian Church, so that there shall be no doubt as to his qualifications to preach in the Christian Church.

(5) He shall be examined on the following branches, viz.: Reading, Spelling, Writing, Geography, Arithmetic, Grammar, Philosophy, History of the United State, Elements of Rhetoric and the Bible.

The Laying of a Corner-Stone

Wherever God's house is erected it should be marked in obedience unto Him who has enabled us to select a place in severance to His Holy name.

(2) "And they said, Let us rise up and build. So they strengthened their hands for this good work." —*Neh. ii:18.* "Surely I will not come into the tabernacle of my house, nor go up into my bed; I will not give sleep to mine eyes, or slumber to mine eyelids, until I find out a place for the Lord, an habitation for the mighty God of Jacob. We will go into his tabernacle; we will worship at his footstool." —*Ps. cxxxii:3–5, 7.* "Go up to the mountain and bring wood, and build the house, and I will take pleasure in it, and I will be glorified, saith the Lord; And the Lord stirred up the spirit of Zerubbabel, the son of Shealtiel, governor of Judah, and the spirit of Joshua, the son of Josedech, the high priest, and the spirit of all the remnant of the people; and they came and did the work in the house of the Lord of Hosts, their God." —*Hag. 1:8, 14.*

Apostle's Creed

"I believe in God the Father, Almighty maker of heaven and earth; and in Jesus Christ, His only Son, our Lord, who was conceived by the Holy Ghost, born of the Virgin Mary, suffered under Pontius Pilate, was crucified dead, and buried. He descended into hell; the third day He rose from the dead; He ascended into heaven, and sitteth on the right hand of God, the Father Almighty. From thence He shall come to judge the quick and the dead. I believe in the Holy Ghost, the holy Catholic Church, the communion of saints, the forgiveness of sins, the resurrection of the body, and the life everlasting. Amen."

Jesus before Pilate

"Pilate therefore took Jesus, and scoured Him; and the soldiers platted a crown of thorns, and put it on his head; and they put on Him a purple robe, and said, Hail, King of the Jews! And they smote him with their hands. Pilate therefore went forth again, and saith unto them, Behold, I bring him forth to you, that ye may know that I found no fault with him. Then came Jesus forth, wearing the crown of thorns, and the purple robe; and Pilate saith unto them, Behold this man! When the chief priests therefore, and the officers, saw him, they cried out saying, Crucify him! crucify him! Pilate sayeth unto them: Take ye him, and crucify him, for I find no fault in him.

The Jews answered him: We have a law, and by our law he ought to die, because he made himself the Son of God. When Pilate therefore heard that saying, he was the more afraid; and went again into the judgment hall, and sayeth unto Jesus," etc. —*St. John xix:1.*

Jesus Quieting the Storm

"And when he was entered into a ship his disciples followed him; and behold, there arose a great tempest in the sea, insomuch that the ship was covered with the waves; but he was asleep. And his disciples came to him and awoke him, saying, Lord, save us, we perish. And he saith unto them, Why are ye so fearful? O, ye of little faith! Then he arose and rebuked the winds and the sea, and there was great calm. But the men marveled, saying, What manner of man is this, then even winds and the sea obey him? And when he was come to the other side, into the country of Gergesenes, there met him two possessed with devils, coming out of the tombs, exceeding fierce, so that no man might pass by that way. And behold they cried out, saying, What have we to do with thee, Jesus, thou Son of God? Art thou come hither to torment us before the time? And there was a good way off from them an herd of many swine feeding: So the devils besought him saying, If thou cast us out, suffer us to go away into the herd of swine." —*Matt. viii:23–31.*

Be Watchful

"Watch thou in all things, endure afflictions, do the work of the evangelist, make full proof of thy ministry; for I am now ready to be offered, and the time of my departure is at hand. I have fought a good fight, I have finished my course, I have kept the faith. Henceforth there is laid up for me a crown of righteousness, which the Lord, the righteous Judge, shall give me at that day; and not to me only, but unto all them also that love his appearing. Do thy diligence to come shortly unto me. Lo, Demas hath forsaken me, having loved this present world, and is departed unto Thessalonica, Crescens to Galatia, Titus unto Dalmatia. Only Luke is with me. Take Mark and bring him with thee, for he is profitable to me for the ministry. And Lychicus have I sent to Ephesus. The cloak that I left at Troas with Carpus, when thou comest, bring with thee; and the books. But especially the parchment. Alexander the coppersmith, did me much evil: the Lord reward him according to his works: of whom be thou aware also; for he hath greatly withstood our words." —*2 Tim. iv:5–14.*

Marriage Ceremony

"My Friends:—Forasmuch as marriage was instituted by God Himself, and is honorable in all, it becomes those who would enter into this holy estate duly to consider the sacred obligations imposed thereby. You cannot therefore expect always to enjoy prosperity. Days of adversity will also come. But if you fear God, and keep His commandments, to do them, He will not forsake you. If, with full and free consent you desire to enter this holy relation, you will acknowledge the same by joining your right hands."

The minister then shall say:

"______ and ______, will you have each other, as husband and wife, to live together after God's ordinance, in the holy state of matrimony, to love, honor and cherish each other in health and sickness, in prosperity and in adversity, and forsaking all others to cleave to each other only, so long as you both shall live?"

28. Afro-Christian Education:

"The Education of the Colored People in the South"

(1909)

H. E. Long

Eight years after the 1863 Emancipation Proclamation, George Washington Dunn, a former slave who had become pastor of a black Christian congregation in Franklinton, North Carolina, decided he had to do something about the poverty and illiteracy of his people. Among his flock was Sanford L. Long, who was eager to further the education of his six children, who were being educated at home. These two men convinced the North Carolina Colored Christian Conference of the importance of establishing a high school in Franklinton, although they were unable to raise sufficient funds for the project. Finally, one of Sanford's sons, Henry Edward Long, opened a small private school in the Franklinton Christian Church. Tuition was twenty-five cents per pupil.

In 1880, an impassioned plea for funds for the school from George W. Dunn was printed in the Herald of Gospel Liberty. *It was the beginning of a fifty-year relationship between the* Herald *and the Franklinton school. By keeping its readers well-informed about the needs and progress of the school, and what they could do to help, the* Herald *raised everyone's awareness of unknown difficulties and broadened understanding of God's community. Over the years its readers responded with numerous gifts and contributions. George Young, a minister of the New York Eastern Conference, became principal of the Franklinton School, with*

Source: H. E. Long, "The Education of the Colored People in the South," *Herald of Gospel Liberty,* 2 September, 1909, 1108.

H. E. Long as his assistant. By 1882, a suitable school building was erected, sponsored by the American Christian Convention, and the school was incorporated as Franklinton Literary and Theological Christian Institute—changed in 1891 to Franklinton Christian College. Although the college never quite achieved collegiate level, it provided good high-school level instruction and a great deal of practical, biblical, religious, and theological training.

In 1904, Henry E. Long became president of the college, where he served with great distinction for thirteen years. His article "The Education of the Colored People in the South" continued the long reciprocal relationship between the readers of the Herald *and their southern brothers and sisters.*

The Franklinton school had an immense influence on the ministers and lay leadership in the black Christian churches. Most black ministers in the South who had any religious or theological training at all owed it to Franklinton. Although the school numbered eleven instructors and 104 students by 1922, it was not able to survive the Great Depression and closed in 1930.

Suddenly, the main source of trained ministers for the black Christian churches was cut off. Although Congregational and Christian seminaries were open to any blacks who could qualify, admission to them usually required a college degree, which was still rare among the southern blacks. It took several decades before black Christian congregations were able to overcome the loss of Franklinton.

Nearly a half century has passed since the negro set out as a free man to take a place in the march of progress as a citizen and to become a real part of the fabric of this government.

Just what position the negro should occupy as to his general status in the pursuits that make for advancement in the economic and material conditions in the common weal of a people, is still apparently a vexed question in the minds of some people. But in the light of the twentieth century civilization, in the midst of advancement in art, in science, in industrial pursuits, in commerce, in labor, it seems to my mind an easy matter to conclude that education for the negro as to his betterment is self-evident and at this late date it would be rather paradoxical to conclude otherwise.

There are those, however, who, while believing that education is a good thing, yet they would restrict him as to the kind.

We believe that every avenue should be open to him whereby he may become proficient along all lines, thus making not only a useful citizen but giving him the initiative element enabling him to bring things to pass.

The results of a Christian education exemplified in the negro's uplift are evidenced in many ways.

1. In his *economic life*. That is to say, he is applying scientific methods to the development of the soil, making the farm more intensely abundant in its yield and less extensive per acreage.

2. His manner of living is improved. The sanitary conditions of his home are in keeping with the progress of his education; the family health is less endangered; they care for their sick in a wise manner and are learning the cause and prevention of many of the common diseases. With certain classes cleanliness is next to godliness. Their homes are almost faultlessly kept clean and sweet.

3. The colored people are building for themselves larger and more comfortable homes. A sure sign of the upward march of any people. Rent money is turned into safe investment. The negro is fast becoming a factor in the commercial world, owning real estate whose value gives him standing as a financier.

As an outgrowth of this, there are many savings banks throughout the South founded, manned and successfully operated entirely by the negro. attesting his ability to handle large finances with fidelity and profit.

4. His moral and spiritual life has been quickened. The ownership of a home; the "cradle of virtues," lifts him morally; the church, the altar of worship quickens him spiritually; the school develops his intellect. The consciousness of responsibility in the maintenance of right principles, the acceptance of the gospel in its purity in his every day life is being more and more realized. Our father's faith in God during the dark days of slavery was unwavering, for they believed that God, in some way, at some time would deliver them and their children from bondage, and their faith was rewarded. Those of us who live in this age have enlightened faith which leads us to believe that better things are yet to come and that these better things are to be realized through right living—obedience to God and love toward our fellow man.

5. The negro is becoming capable of directing his own schools, universities, colleges and secondary institutions of learning, publishing houses and business in general. As ministers of the gospel they preach the Word with power and eloquence; they are successful in the professions and trades and in the various lines of endeavor.

These are some of the results of education. We are not unmindful, however, of his shortcomings.

6. If this much has been accomplished in less than half a century, what may we expect of the negro in the next half century? With these facts it must be a source of gratification to the friends North and South, who have spent money for the uplift of the grateful people.

While he is learning to help himself, the negro has not yet passed the point where he needs no help. Looking back he sees the place from which he has come and the progress made, he can now appreciate more the kind hand of friends of negro education in whatever way extended.

Our Needs

First of all we need the continued sympathy and encouragement of our friends North and South. We need better equipped schools. We cannot go far without encouragement and financial aid. As a race, we are too poor to stand alone; we need more money to educate men and women for leadership. The number of fit leaders among us is far too small. The masses of our people are still in darkness and ignorance.

The Outlook

That there is a bright future for our people we verily believe. Those who have had the advantages of education are doing the best they can for the enlightenment of their fellows; they are engaged in teaching, preaching and general Christian work. Franklinton Christian College stands for *Christian education* and *Christian workers.* Our young men and young women are doing noble work among their people.

The day of experimental work with the negro has passed. He has made full proof of his possibilities as a man. The educated negro in the South will yet be among the wonders of the world in his fidelity to his friends and those among whom his lot is cast, and in acting his part in the world's great drama.

Courtship with the Disciples

29. A Working Arrangement?

"Settling the History Muddle Between the Christians and the Disciples"

(1908)

W. D. Samuel and William J. Wright

This controversial exchange of letters in "Settling the History Muddle Between the Christians and the Disciples" is still under discussion by some denominational historians in the early twenty-first century. At issue is whether the early ancestors of the Christian denomination, including Barton Stone, founder of the Kentucky group calling itself "Christian," can legitimately be claimed by the followers of Thomas Campbell, who also called themselves "Christians" or "Disciples."

Both groups began during the frontier revivals of the early nineteenth century. Both believed that the church of Christ was one and should not have denominational divisions; that there should be no doctrinal tests for church membership or theological speculation in language not found in the New Testament; and that the New Testament was an adequate constitution for the worship, discipline, and governance of the church. Holding to common convictions, the two groups became interested in one another.

It seems that in 1832, representatives of the two groups had an unofficial "union" or "working arrangement" or "flowing together" that, variously interpreted, significantly changed the history of both denominations. The story goes back to Lexington, Kentucky, when some of Barton Stone's followers and some of Thomas Campbell's followers met for worship and

Source: W. D. Samuel and William J. Wright, "Settling the History Muddle Between the Christians and the Disciples," letters in *Herald of Gospel Liberty,* 19 March 1908, 364–65.

discussion. Finding that they had much in common, they decided to extend the hand of Christian fellowship and unite their energies by sharing the task of evangelism. They sent a follower from each group to ride together through the churches and to be supported by the united contributions of churches from both groups. The arrangement worked well for a time, but by the end of the century the vague and fluid boundaries between the two denominations meant that hundreds of formerly Christian churches in Kentucky, Illinois, Indiana, and Missouri affiliated with the Disciples of Christ.

Although Barton Stone later reclaimed his loyalty to the Christians, descendants of both groups kept arguing about whether they shared a common ancestry and whose congregations belonged to which denomination. Even as late as 1908, the issue was still hotly debated by descendants of Stone and of Campbell.

President Samuel's Letter

Piqua, Ohio, December 18, 1907.

Rev. William J. Wright,
Corresponding Secretary of the American
Christian Missionary Society, Cincinnati, Ohio.

DEAR SIR AND BROTHER:—Last October the Disciple Church of which you are a member and in whose missionary society you hold office of Corresponding Secretary, held its National Missionary Convention at Norfolk, Va. There was published in the booklet containing the program of that Convention under the head of "History" some statements to which I wish to call your attention as follows:

"The people known as Christians, or Disciples of Christ, first appeared as a distinct people in America in the early part of the Nineteenth Century. They sprang up almost simultaneously in various parts of the country and in various denominations.

Rev. James O'Kelly, of Virginia, a member of the M. E. General Conference, led off from that church a body of people, who refused to wear any name but "Christian," or consider any book other than the Bible as authority. In 1800, Rev. Abner Jones, a Baptist preacher in Vermont, started a similar movement. As a result, congregations were formed in all the New England and North Atlantic States. The Bible was the only book of authority, the historic creeds were rejected and the people and the churches bore no name but "Christian."

In 1803, Barton W. Stone and several other Presbyterian preachers withdrew from the Synod in Lexington, Ky., renounced all human creeds, took the Bible as their only guide-book, refused all names but "Christian," and proceeded to organize "Christian Churches."

These are some of the statements you made in that historical sketch as published in the booklet which contained the program of the Disciple's Convention held at Norfolk, Va., in October 1907.

Now, my brother, how a man holding the position you hold among your people, can make such statements concerning the history of your people, I cannot understand. You have not given the history of your people in one single instance in the statements referred to above. Instead, you have given the history of the Christian Church, the only church having a right to the name Christian by priority of dates, and by the principles to which you refer in your statements quoted above.

You refer to James O'Kelly as connected with your rise as a people. Mr. O'Kelly was never connected in any way with the people you represent and who were known in their early history as the "Disciples of Christ." Mr. O'Kelly was one of the founders of the Christian Church, but never has had anything to do with the "Disciples." He was never in any manner connected with the rise of your people.

The same is true of Rev. Abner Jones to whom you refer. He was connected with the early history of the "Christian Church," but never in any way, or manner, was he connected with the "Disciples."

You refer also to Rev. Barton W. Stone and several other Presbyterian preachers, who withdrew from the Synod in Lexington, Ky. This, my brother, was during what was known as "the Cane Ridge Revival." Following the time to which you refer, Rev. Barton W. Stone became a member of the "Christian Church"—not the "Disciple Church." About the year 1833, he and the founder of your church, Rev. Alexander Campbell, tried to form a union, but they failed. Mr. Stone associated and worked with the Disciples some after that, but never indorsed the doctrines taught by Mr. Campbell.

Now, my brother, allow me to set you right by quoting history correctly.

In the city of Baltimore, Maryland, in November 1792, the General Conference of the Methodist Church met. During that Conference the entire economy of that church was reviewed. It was at this time that James O'Kelly, Presiding Elder from Virginia, objected to some of the rulings of that body, and because of a permanent and serious disagreement, Mr. O'Kelly and a number of others withdrew from that conference.

It was a bold stroke for religious freedom, and yet for two years, though preaching the principles for which he had made so brave a stand, he and his associates called themselves "Republican Methodists." It was in 1794, August 4th, that he with a number of others met in Lebanon Church, Surry County, Virginia, for the further and larger development of the movement. In this meeting after much discussion, Rev. Rice Haggard, standing with the New Testament in his hand, said: "Brethren, this is a sufficient rule of faith and practice, and by it we understand the disciples of our Lord were first called Christians, and I move that henceforth and forever, the followers of Christ be known as Christians simply." The motion was unanimously adopted. From that time until now, we have had no other name. To this church, Rev. James O'Kelly, Rev. Abner Jones and Rev. Barton W. Stone belonged, and not to the people known as the "Disciples of Christ."

Allow me to quote from your founder, Rev. Alexander Campbell, as I find him quoted in a speech which was reported for, and published in, the *Millennial Harbinger* of which Mr. Campbell was the editor. He is speaking of the name of your people, and remember this was in 1839. Hear him:

"Our name—into what, or to whom have we been immersed? Into Calvin, Luther, Wesley, Campbell of Reformation? If not, then why nick-name us, or nick-name ourselves, when we assume or choose, such designation? Shall we be called Disciples of Christ, or Christians? Not because we have another leader than Christ, for he is our Teacher. We believe in him. We are immersed into his death, and have thus put on Christ. But we have been anticipated. The term "Christian" in New England and in some other sections of the land is chosen and appropriated by another party."

The other party to whom Mr. Campbell refers is the Christian Church.

This shows that Mr. Campbell chose for your people what he called "a more ancient name," the "Disciples of Christ." Further argument seems entirely unnecessary to establish this fact.

Now, my brother, you can plainly see that you have made statement sin your historical sketch which were and are incorrect and not only so, but these statements will do our people, the Christian Church, an injustice and injury.

I do not like to charge you with doing this thing knowingly, for it is hard to believe that any brother who believes "in justice to whom justice is due" would make statements so incorrect and misleading. However, your people are in the habit of causing this misunderstanding in many parts of the United States, so confusing our history with yours. You certainly know your history. Then why persist in infringing upon the rights of others?

As President of the American Christian Convention, embracing our work in the United States and Canada, I ask you to correct these statements over your own signature. I think justice to your people and to yourself, to say nothing of what you owe to us of the Christian Church, demands that you do it. As a Christian man, I must think you will willingly make the correction, giving us what justly and truly belongs to us.

Your correction will save me as the president of our Convention a great deal of trouble and bring a renewed sense of honor to yourself. Unless you do correct it, I shall be compelled to correct it myself through the press, both religious and secular, beginning at Norfolk, Virginia, where your historical sketch was printed and given wide circulation.

I strongly wish, however, that in the interest of truth and the cause of Christ I may be spared this trouble by your willingness to correct the error.

Awaiting your answer, I am, your brother in the bonds of love,

W. D. SAMUEL
President of the American
Christian Convention.

The Reply

Cincinnati, Ohio, December 28, 1907.

Rev. W. D. Samuel, Pique, Ohio.

MY DEAR BROTHER:—I am tardy in answering your long letter of December 12th. Prolonged absence from my office and great accumulations of mail account for delays.

Until I read your letter and editorial in the HERALD OF GOSPEL LIBERTY for December 12th, I did not suppose that any living being objected to the statement which you brethren criticise and ask me to correct. Even now, after several readings of the whole matter, I see no ground for your objections, though I do see your view-point more clearly than before.

I would not needlessly give offense to an enemy; much less would I knowingly offend you, my brethren. In this matter, I have lived before God in all good conscience even till this hour. I wrote only what I have heard and read a thousand times among our people; only what I believed to be every word true, and only what as I still see it, is the truth.

You and Brother Barrett object to my use of the name "Christian" and to my use of history. You say that I quote your history as being our own, and you want us to omit using the name "Christian" in describing our churches, conventions, etc., and use the name "Disciple" instead.

Both of you brethren speak of us as the "Disciple Church." There is no such organization in America. There never was such an organization in America. Of our nearly 12,000 congregations, only three are known to us as "Churches or Congregations of Disciples." Mr. Campbell never sought to fasten upon the movement the name "Disciple Church." When he said, "We call ourselves disciples of Christ," he referred to individual followers of our Lord, never to congregations or the movement in which he was a conspicuous figure. The congregations he always referred to as "Christian Churches," "Churches of Christ," etc., but never as Disciple Churches.

His individual preferences for the expression "Disciples of Christ" counts for nothing with a people just as free as he. Each congregation among us is absolutely independent and congregations and other organizations coming into existence selected whatever name seemed best. "Christian Church" is the chartered name of probably 9,000 or 10,000 of our congregations in America. Possibly 2,000 are named "Church of Christ" in their charters, while perhaps twenty are chartered as "Church of God" and three bear the name "Church of Disciples." Yet each individual of our million and a quarter members describes himself as "a disciple of Christ or a Christian."

Every one of our churches in and about this city is known and chartered as a "Christian Church." For example, there is the Central Christian church, Richmond Street Christian church, Walnut Hills Christian church, etc. This is fairly representative of conditions throughout the country: "Disciple Church" never; "Christian Church" seven times out of eight, including the churches in Wellsburg and Bethany, W. Va., in both of which the Campbells held membership.

Moreover, "Christian" is our name for all our institutions. We have the "American Christian Missionary Society" of which Alex. Campbell was president for seventeen years. Then there is our Foreign Christian Missionary Society with about 500 missionaries, teachers and helpers on the foreign fields; our "Christian Women's Board of Missions" which raised and disbursed nearly $300,000 last year. We have the "National Sunday-school Association of Christian Churches," the "National Benevolent Association of the Christian Churches," etc. It was these organizations, chartered under these names, not "Disciple," which held their recent conventions in Norfolk and reported having raised more than a million dollars last year.

Our papers bear the same name; these are some of them: "Christian Standard," "Christian Evangelist," "Christian Century," "Christian Courier," "Christian Worker," "Christian Union," "Pacific Christian," but "Disciple" never. Your own organ does not contain the word "Christian." Ours all contain it. How can it then, be yours and not ours?

Our institutions of learning commonly contain "Christian" in their chartered titles: "Texas Christian University," "Oklahoma Christian University," "Christian University," Canton, Mo., "Atlantic Christian College," "Virginia Christian College."

This is enough to show that the name Christian is of all but universal usage among us, and that we never use "Disciple" as you brethren use it. No one has or can have a patent or copyright on the name Christian. It is the inalienable right of every follower of our Lord and every organization of his followers. Priority can shut no man out of the use of that name. We wear it because it describes us. We are glad that we share it with you brethren. We would gladly share it with all who love God and worship him through Jesus Christ. What a great stride toward union if all the churches were simply Christian churches. It is our name, and thank God, it is your name too. I cannot change what I wrote under that heading. On that point, "What I have written, I have written."

As to using history for our own, I in part, plead guilty, for at places your history and ours are not simply parallel, but identical. We drank the same free spirit from the same earthen vessels, Stone, Jones, O'Kelly. That these men had something to do with the rise, direction and content of our movement, is of universal belief among us. Our books assert it; our professors and lecturers in the colleges declare it; our papers and magazines set it forth, and the ministers proclaim it from our pulpits. If I am wrong on that point, practically all our brotherhood shares my error.

I can select and quote a score practically as easily as one. Let one thoroughly representative man suffice, F. D. Power, Pastor of Vermont Avenue Christian church, (not Disciple), Washington, D.C. He taught for a time in the College founded by Alexander Campbell. He is in his thirty third year of the pastorate. He was chaplain to the National House of Representatives, was President Garfield's pastor and preached his funeral sermon. He has held the highest offices within the gift of our brotherhood. Hear him in Festival Hall, St. Louis, during the Louisiana Purchase Exposition:

"This was but one of a great number of movements on the part of godly men, deploring the evils that existed, and anxious for a restoration of Christianity on its original basis—the Haldanes in Scotland, O'Kelly and others in Virginia and North Carolina, B. W. Stone and his coadjutors in Kentucky, Walter Scott and others in Ohio, Bullard in the mountains of West Virginia—ministers of different denominations, unknown to each other, pleading for the Bible alone, without any addition in the form of creeds or confessions of faith. When Campbell, in 1823, began to plead for the original gospel and primitive order, and the union upon the apostles of all who loved the Lord Jesus Christ, these workers began to touch hands and blend together in one great common purpose and service. The most notable of these movements, that of Alexander Campbell in West Virginia and Pennsylvania, and Barton W. Stone in Kentucky, were united in 1831."

This is a sample of what I have read and heard, for 25 years. This particular statement is much stronger than mine. It was heard by a multitude. It was scattered in tract form by tens of thousands. It must have been perfectly acceptable to our people, for it was never criticised. It would not be difficult to fill a volume with similar utterances from preachers, teachers and writers, which fact shows that those things are universally believed among us.

We are a part of all preceding good. Others labored and we enjoy the fruits. We would be untrue to ourselves and to history not to give credit to the good men and great, who preceded the Campbells, and who were voices crying in the wilderness of extreme sectarianism of a hundred years ago.

Your position is that the O'Kelly, Jones and Stone movements merged and became the Christian Church sometimes called the Christian Connection. Our position is that the preceding movements were largely merged into the Campbell movement, but more particularly the Stone part of it. This is clearly stated in my article which you criticise. I say, "It was natural that when these men learned of the nearly identical character of the movements they headed, they should *seek* to unify their forces. The two greater forces, that led by Mr. Stone and that by Mr. Campbell, were brought into one, etc." Here I carefully distinguished between the success attending the efforts to consolidate.

Brother Barrett in his editorial grants that 52 of the congregations in the Stone movement were brought into the Campbell movement. I have personal knowledge of churches both from the Jones and O'Kelly movements coming into the larger movement headed by Mr. Campbell. That is, if one may believe the records of congregations and the testimony of old men and women in the churches. That O'Kelly was not an immersionist proves nothing. The Campbells did not start as immersionists. They were Presbyterians and were fully satisfied with the baptism of their church. Immersion was forced upon their attention long after the "Declaration and Address," was issued by Thomas Campbell in 1809.

From the best figures available it appears that about 300 congregations organized by the O'Kelly, Jones and Stone movements, came into our movement before 1840. Out of our present 12,000 congregations, 300 is not much; but in the days of our weakness, those congregations formed not far from 50 per cent of our strength. They helped mightily in those far gone times to lay the foundations of our present mighty structure.

I wrote history as my brethren are accustomed to writing it. I cannot write my own biography without writing parts of that of my brother who is ten years my senior. I cannot write United States history without embodying parts of the life story of England and Canada. Even the inspired writer, whose purpose it was to follow the destinies of Judah, was compelled to write the history of Israel.

We have much that is common with you, including a large part of our early history. "Honor to whom honor is due," demands that it be written about as I wrote it.

I assure you that in all this matter I have sought to have a conscience void of offense to man and God. I wish to be included among those who love their fellowmen, especially the household of faith. Love works no ill to his neighbor. I will never knowingly work ill to you. But I cannot change facts. Therefore, I can make no material change in what I wrote. May God help us to know and speak the truth.

May all his blessings abide with you.

Sincerely and fraternally,

WM. J. WRIGHT.

30. Courtship Analyzed:
"Letters" and "What Really Can Be Done?"

(1918–19)

Herald of Gospel Liberty; J. F. Burnett

Prior to a meeting on union held between the Christians and the Disciples in 1918, the editor of the Herald *asked his readers to express opinions about a potential union between the two denominations. In spite of eighty-six years of sporadic "union courtship" with the Disciples, intensive work by Christian leaders, and extensive efforts by the* Herald *to inform and educate its constituency, letters sent to the* Herald *were mixed. Some letters showed an impressive understanding of the main issues between the denominations—the Disciples' insistence on baptism by immersion as a requirement for church membership and the Christian claim that the Holy Spirit worked only through the Word. Other letters viewed the matter very personally or parochially—showing anger at alleged injustices endured by the Christians more than a century before, lifting up questions unrelated to the specific issues under discussion, sharing personal animosity based on local relationships, biblical prooftexting, and making pious requests for everyone to "trust their leaders" and "exercise sweet Christian spirit." When Christian leaders read these letters, they wondered if their many years of work had been in vain!*

J. F. Burnett's address "For the Christians" was one of two included in the Herald *article asking "What Really Can Be Done?" to achieve union*

Source: Letters to the editor, *Herald of Gospel Liberty,* 21 March 1918, 275; ibid., 28 March 1918, 300; J. F. Burnett, "What Really Can Be Done?" *Herald of Gospel Liberty,* 9 October 1919, 978–82.

between the Disciples and the Christians (the Disciples' address was by E. B. Bagby). Burnett, secretary emeritus of the General Convention of the Christian Church, was one of the most well-known of the Christian church leaders and ecumenists of the time. He believed that church union was possible and tried to rally the Christians around their great historic principles, especially their call to work toward the union of the church. Furthermore, Burnett proposed a series of practical suggestions for what could be done to bring the Christians and the Disciples closer together, suggestions that revealed not only the wisdom and experience of fifty years in the Christian ministry, but also many of the basic techniques of rapprochement between groups still used by church leaders a hundred years later. Unfortunately, it was to no avail. In the end, the Christians and the Disciples, who were so much alike, were not able to bring about church union with each other.

Letters

Another Woman Speaks Her Mind

I can never be a Campbellite! No, never! I am one of the fourth generation, rocked in a Christian cradle. I have also rocked my little ones in the same. I cannot cast my lot with a Church which is ashamed of its name, as I know this Church to be. Brethren, let us lend a listening ear to what Bro. Tarr has told us. The church he refers to is good evidence of truth, and that is not the only one they have taken. If we have ministers and college workers who wish to be Campbellites—the way is open; let them step over, and when they get there and are asked to what denomination do they belong, you say: "I am a Campbellite." Do not leave us and then wish to still wear our name. I believe in loyalty and I expect to be loyal to the Christian Church, if all others leave it. I am opposed to uniting with any Church on sectarian terms. What is the idea of uniting with the Campbellites? Will some one please tell us? —W.

Concerning the Union of the Disciples and the Christians

I have always favored a union of God's true followers. But it must be a real union and not a swallowing process of the weaker by the stronger. What is this we hear in favor of a union of the Christians with the Disciples? It is simply this: We know the Disciples have tried to rob us of our name, our history, our pioneer men, our members, and our churches, and to some extent they have succeeded. We propose to unite with them and thus place our stamp of approval upon the whole robbing business. We know we have thrust our heads into this hornet's nest before, and have never recovered from the sting we received, and yet we propose to thrust it in again. We know they are generally recognized as the greatest proselytes in the world, but we propose to endorse this by uniting with them. We know they have tried and are trying every day to filch money from our churches, even after repeated and persistent protests on our part, but we propose to show how well we like this by uniting with them.

We know their creed debars many of God's people from their membership, yet we propose to throw away our creed (the Bible), our right of private judgment, and our liberty of conscience, and swallow baptism by immersion only for the remission of sins, while they swallow us as the snake does the toad.

The charges made above are not born of malice, for I bear the Disciples no ill will, but these things are matters of history, are actual facts, and cannot be rubbed out.

There are many excellent Christian people among the Disciples and some of them are dear friends of mine, but on the part of the Church as a whole, let us see sincere repentance and a great reform, and then we will see what can be done, but until then *no, a thousand times, no.*

A. W. ANDES.

Harrisonburg, Va., March 19, 1918.

As I See It

I was much distressed (I should like to use a stronger term) by the very unchristian way in which some of our brethren spoke in a recent issue of THE HERALD in regard to the proposed union of the Christians and Disciples.

To me, such remarks are entirely out of place, because, as I see it, committees were appointed to confer one with the other, discussing various phases of church activities, beliefs, and propaganda. These men without doubt, named by The American Christian Convention, are true, loyal men, thorough Christians, and would take absolute care of our interests as a body, and to jump to the conclusion that our Disciple brethren have insincere motives is indeed premature, to say the least. Why speak disparagingly of and in a disrespectful way, before any principles have been laid down? I do not think our Christ would smile upon such an attitude.

Should one think a union could not be effected, a clean-cut, kindly discussion such as came from the pen of Rev. R. H. Gott, could not possibly be objected to, nor could it possibly give offense.

Personally, I have always preferred the doctrines and practices of a number of other denominations to that of the Disciples, but I certainly recognize that they are a splendid people, doing great things for the Kingdom, and do not consider for one moment but what a satisfactory medium might be reached as a union basis. At least let us exercise a sweet Christian spirit, and above all things refrain from saying things that will tend to create bitterness and strife.

I am very sure, were we to pick up one of the papers of the Disciples in which such radical statements were made, as some have been, that we would be angry.

Let us remember: "As ye would that men should do unto you, do ye *even so* to them."

May God help us to trust our leaders to meet the situation properly and in accordance with His will.

CARRIE B. BEAVER.

Advance, Indiana.

Should Disciples and Christians Unite?

Certainly they should. Not only *they,* but *all* other Christians. Why? Because the *Head* of the Church so earnestly requested this union, and why? That the *world* might be induced to *believe.* Is that not reason enough? Yes, you say, but on what platform can we all unite? The platform of the apostles and prophets, *Christ* as the chief Corner-stone. Why? Because it will thoroughly furnish unto all good works. If we are guided by the Holy Spirit, it will be into all truth, and all will be glad to make Christian character the only test for Christian fellowship, for a platform or creed that will *thoroughly* furnish will require no other furniture. Surely a *God*-made creed is perfect, while man-made creeds often need revising. What say you, brothers of every creed? Can we not unite on a God-ordained creed? If not, why not?

WM. L. CORYELL.

Kiowa, Kansas, March 19, 1918.

As a Missourian Sees It

DEAR HERALD:—I have waited (in the matter of renewing my subscription) to see how it may be decided as to letting the Disciples have the Christian Church. Living here, where they have said so much of our Church—where they have seemed to take every advantage of us, I know what a union would mean. You see if you were to let them have charge of our affairs, I would not be willing to take their literature—I know them too well, having lived among them for forty years. I would not choose their ways. Once they reported THE HERALD OF GOSPEL LIBERTY out of print. That grieved me very much. As it happened, I saw an article in *The Methodist Recorder*, taken from THE HERALD OF GOSPEL LIBERTY, and I was so glad that I sent for it and said, "I will never be without it while I live."

MRS. S. A. SNYDER.

Mill Grove, Mo.

Disciples and Christian Union

In playing checkers two things must be kept in mind. First, the game that you yourself are intending to play. Second, the game that your opponent plays.

Acting upon this theory, I took up the union question with a prominent Disciple recently. I secured results.

When I went into his presence I could almost hear myself purr, just as a well-fed kitten does when it is about to receive a bowl of milk. Why should I not congratulate myself, the little church in which I was born was soon, by a stroke of diplomacy which would make Kaiser Bill turn green with envy, to expand into a great brotherhood numbering almost two million souls. I had even figured it all out how certain of our prominent brethren were to be given high positions in this new brotherhood. Upon entering my esteemed Disciple brother's presence I told him how he was soon to be my full brother and not my brother by adoption.

He smiled and moved a man on the checker-board.

He asked two questions. First, "What is the belief and practice of your denomination regarding water baptism?" I told him. Second, "Does your denomination believe that the Holy Spirit operates only through the Word?" I told him. His conclusion was prompt. Viz.: "We would irritate you and you would irritate us." I thanked him.

"There is, however," said he, "much that can be done to create a better understanding between the two bodies. This ought to be done, and this is the subject which the joint committee soon to meet at Norfolk ought to discuss."

Whatever our esteemed commissioners may decide to do at Norfolk, this brother and I now are to play the same game. We are each trying to develop our respective fields and in our saner moments are trying to remember that each of us is a child of the selfsame Father, although reared in maturity in different families and under different conditions.

JOHN A. STOVER.

Danville, Ill.

What Really Can Be Done?

For the Christians
By Rev. J. F. Burnett, D.D.

To begin, in speaking for the Christians, I have to say that I do not know. The faith and practice of the Christians for all these years have debarred any one person the right to speak for the entire body in matters of faith. Any one individual may say how far he would go, but it is beyond his prerogative to speak for others, for with the Christians, to his own Master the individual standeth or falleth; and in all movements, discussions, or organizations, we have to recognize the divinely given right and responsibility of the individual. The Christians acknowledge no leader but Jesus Christ, and have never yet called any man master, nor acknowledged any man, or number of men, authority in doctrine, and it is safe to say they never will.

However, we may be assured of the endorsement of our constituency as far as it has expressed itself.

With desire, have the Christians desired the visible unity of all the followers of Jesus Christ. For this purpose were we born, and for this cause came we into the world. It has been the prayer of the saints, the voice of the singer, the theme of the preacher, the hope of the laity, the burden of all hearts, and the goal toward which we have striven. The Christian Church is a union church. Men and women, as individuals, came together in this fellowship, more than a hundred years ago, because they desired the fellowship of the saints. Some came from the Baptists, fresh from the wilderness of Judea; some came from the Presbyterians, leavened with the meal of Calvinism; some came from the Methodists, filled with a diversity of zeal, but all united in Jesus Christ. For that original idea of union the

Christian Church was born; for this it has lived, and for this it is willing to die.

The Christian Church declared in the beginning, declares now, and if possible will more emphatically declare in the future, that the basis of faith should be, not dogma, but Jesus; and the bond of fellowship, not subscription to a creed, but vital Christian piety—so that every one who accepts Jesus Christ as Savior and Lord, and lives his faith, whether he has a long creed or a short creed, or no creed at all, should be received without disputation and given the fellowship of a brother in Christ.

Our conference records are burdened with resolutions on Christian union; the pronouncements of our State and general bodies are all aglow with the heat of earnest hearts praying the prayer of our Lord over again *"that they all might be one."* The last, and perhaps the most impressive and significant of them all is the one adopted by The American Christian Convention, in session at Conneaut, Ohio, 1919. The Commission on Christian Unity submitted, among other things, the following, picked out here and there from its report:

> In these times, the great fundamentals are so urgent that we have no time to waste quibbling over differences. True religion tends to unite men; theological distinctions tend to separate them. We are living in a new age; old things have passed away; behold, all things are become new. Differences that were great and regarded as vital a few years ago have almost faded from the thought of the world. The glory won in the theological debates of the past has been dimmed by the radiance of the brotherhood of the present.
>
> There will perhaps never come to us again a more favorable opportunity for the unification of Christians than is ours today. The thought of the Church is vibrant with the life of a united brotherhood. The Federal Council of the Churches of Christ in America—the largest and most effective unit of expression the people of God now have—and many other organizations and movements clearly indicate the thought and desire of all Christians for a fuller fellowship. Of all the people of the world who ought to be glad and rejoice, it is the people here assembled, who for a hundred and more years have taught the things that are being taught to-day by the whole body of believers.
>
> The times demand unity of life and activity and the whole human race is calling to the church for light, for leadership, for guidance. In the presence of this insistent call, the church should and must be one.
>
> We note with gladness the drawing together of denominations similar in faith and polity. We should abet such fusions by every possible

act within our power. However, we recognize that unless this movement is carried on to its complete consummation, the result will be but fewer and larger groups equally denominationalistic in spirit. Federation is only a makeshift of the opportunist and a compromise with ecclesiastical arrogance. The gathering together of those affinitous in thought or method is but a sectarianism of broader gauge than that formerly followed. The ultimate must be unity, not into self-selective groups of common tastes, but by an inclusion so complete that not one true follower of Jesus Christ in all the world is omitted. In a divinely constituted brotherhood, there will be no exclusions of the Father's children. If there are such, the old human denomination, which has always been responsible for the divisions of the Church, is amply attested. A true union must be effected upon a basis that does not invalidate the authority of God, nor abridge the rights which He has given to the individual. The insertion of any presumptuous human authority or insistence upon group interpretations cannot make for real and universal union. We must subject our purposes to careful scrutiny. Since the days of Babel, movements to "make us a name" have come to a uniform end. A desire for unity for the sake of "bigness" is born out of unregenerate vanity. To unite because of congeniality is but gratifying our desire for personal or collective pleasure. There is but one motive sufficiently large to promote a genuine union and include all who should be a part of it—that is an absolute, loving commitment to the will and program of Jesus Christ without any reservations or prejudices injected from any source.

Upon this premise, the Christian Church, assembled in its quadrennial session of The American Christian Convention, hereby makes loving overtures to all true Christians everywhere, of whatever name or order, to unite by legal incorporation, placing all interests now owned and controlled by said Convention under the ownership and control of the amalgamated organization. The basis of union shall exclude all man-made exactions and interpretation, which have never been otherwise than both arrogant and divisive. It shall derive its government, always to be democratic, from the people composing it. All of its official gatherings shall be representative of the people and such representation shall be voted by them. No test of faith shall be established other than the acceptance of Jesus Christ as the Savior and the Word of God as a standard for the conduct of life and the guide of the church. No person, or group of persons, shall impose a dogma, form of worship, or practice of an ordinance upon any within

> its membership. The standing of all members shall be equal. They shall each be free to follow the Lord as His Spirit and Word direct them. Their standing in the church shall be based upon their Christian conduct—not upon the theological opinions of themselves or others. The designation of this body of believers shall be Scriptural, instead of derived from some feature of ecclesiastical practice. It shall be a union founded in fellowship solely upon righteousness in character and practice.

Following this recital, the following resolution was offered by the Commission on Christian Unity, which was unanimously adopted as was the recital:

> Be it resolved by The American Christian Convention, representing the religious body known as Christian, that we send greetings to all our brethren in the Lord, enjoining them to stand fast in the liberty wherein Christ hath made them free; that they be not again entangled with the yoke of ecclesiastical bondage. Also, that we hereby authorize the Committee on Christian Unity to seek and respond to conferences with any and all religious bodies desirous of union upon the basis herein stated.

While every member of the Christian Church understands perfectly well that no action of the General Convention binds the individual church, or obligates the personal membership to any extent beyond their willingness to go, yet it is safe to say that to the limit of the above pronouncement and the force of the resolution, our entire constituency will give endorsement.

But as dear to the heart of the church as Christian union is, there is one thing dearer still, and that is *truth.* Truth is more desirable than union. A union without truth would be a house of rotten straw in which would dwell all manner of impure things and crawling serpents. It would be a nest of unclean birds, the stench from which would be an offense in the nostrils of the Almighty. If union without regard to truth is what we seek, we had better all huddle back to the Roman Church. There millions of people are united under one head, bowing to one management, and obeying one mind, while the unity of the heart withers, bleeds, and dies at the feet of the Pope. The unity which the Scriptures require is a union in truth, in faith, in love.

> " 'Til we all come in the unity of the faith and the knowledge of the Son of God unto a perfect man, unto the measure of the stature of the fulness of Christ."

To a union of this sort the Christians are under promise, under bond, indeed to go their length to obtain, and in that effort they will not be found wanting. With the Christians it is not a question of what they may give up for the sake of union; but what they may give to the union—and they have ever been ready and willing to give themselves. I record it as my deliberate estimate of the people whom I serve, that they are ready to make the supreme sacrifice for the cause for which they live. They have understood from the beginning that they were born to die, but they have not feared death; for when the prayer of our Lord shall be answered, and they all shall be one in Him, it will be a glorious triumph to die in its realization.

I feel under obligation to say in fairness to all in general, and in justice to my own people in particular, that our constituency will not go far enough to endorse human creeds, or church interpretations; for by so doing, it would deprive the individual of the right to follow the Scriptures as he may conscientiously understand and believe their teaching. In a word, the Christians believe that

> "The Church of Christ is one: That it embraces all those who have been accepted of Christ as His real disciples; and, in its whole and its parts, it should be so organized, named, and governed as to include all and exclude none of those whom Christ has so accepted."

To this church is admitted the Baptist and the Quaker alike, without question or suspicion; and I do not believe that the Christian Church would now, or at any time hereafter, enter into any union, federation, or agreement which would accept the one and reject the other.

If William Penn and Roger Williams and John Wesley and Alexander Campbell can dwell together in unity up there, there is not a reason under the sun why their followers should not do the same down here, and it is a burning shame that they do not. (I sometimes think that we get the shame here, and we'll get the burning hereafter.)

When it comes to Scriptural declarations, our constituency will not be found wanting; but in matters of interpretation it must be excused.

For instance

> The Christian Church does not hesitate to say that to be baptized in the name of the Father, the Son, and the Holy Ghost is a Scriptural command, which should be obeyed. But will not say that baptism is three dips, face foremost, head down stream, after the candidate has knelt in the water; for that would be interpretation—and in-

terpretation belongs to the individual, and not to the church as an organization.

The Christian Church does not hesitate to say that men should repent, believe, and be baptized. But she will not say that faith precedes repentance, and that a few drops of water is as good as an ocean; for that would be interpretation—and the right to interpret belongs to an individual, and not to the church as such.

The Christian Church does not hesitate to say that men must be converted, for that is written in *the Book.* But she will not say that only he is converted who agonizes and groans, and then groans and agonizes, and then does both and shouts out, "I am saved," and then drops the subject indefinitely; for that would be very poor interpretation, even for an individual.

The Christian Church does not hesitate to say that Jesus Christ will come again, the second time without sin unto salvation, for that is a plain statement of *the Word.* But she will not say that it will be a literal, visible descent occurring on the 14th of October, 1920, for that would be interpretation, and that, too, of an event sealed up in the bosom of the Father.

The Christian Church does not hesitate to say that God is one, and that He is Father, nor that Jesus Christ is the Son of God, and that the Holy Spirit is our Comforter, for these are plainly stated in the Book. But the Christian Church will not say that these three constitute one divine, visible personality which men call the Trinity, for that is interpretation; nor will the church teach or declare the opposite doctrine of unitarianism—for the Book says Jesus Christ is the Son of God, and that is quite sufficient for a people who believe the Book.

The Christian Church will not hesitate to say there is but one church—*the Church* that Jesus is building upon the rock, and which He will present to Himself, a glorious church, not having spot or wrinkle or any such thing; for that is written in the Bible. But she will not say that the Roman Catholic Church is that one church, nor that only the immersed, or the sprinkled, or the white, or the black, belong to it; for that would be interpretation—and the Christian Church wants the Bible, and not man, to reveal the truth of God as it is in Christ Jesus our Lord.

It has been our interpretations, our definitions, our Latin, our Hebrew, and our Greek, that have separated us into classes and clans and sorely divided the family of God. We have nailed our Theses to the church doors;

we have proclaimed our Shibboleths; we have defined our *Belief,* and labeled ourselves the elect of God. We have eaten the husks of the sty, fed our souls on the definitions and interpretations of an age long since gone, while the fatted calf of a real Christian fellowship awaited our return. Let us return to our Father's house, where there is bread and to spare; let us say to Him, Father, we have sinned in Thy sight, and are no more worthy to be called the Bride—the Lamb's wife. We have defiled our garments with foul sectarianism, but we want to atone for our wrong in dividing the household of faith substituting human dogma for divine doctrine, and human names for the one Name above which there is none other—and our meeting here to-day is a testimony to our penitence for past offenses.

Standing as we are in the passing of denominational sectarianism, we can hardly realize that it played such sad havoc with the church, as we know it to have done. Within my lifetime such a meeting as this would not have been possible. Had we met, it would have been on the field of disputation, and the dry batteries of the Christians would have been set in battle array against the streams of doctrines poured out by the Disciples of Christ. Within my lifetime there have been ministers living on the north side of the street, who, while they were not prepared to say that the ministers living on the south side of the same street were sure to be damned, would nevertheless give it as their candid opinion that for the life of them they could not see how they could be saved. I have known a time when pulpit stormed against pulpit, and the shot and shell of the theological guns, and the whistle of the doctrinal minnie ball rattled and screamed and screeched through the sacred sanctuary hours at a time. But, thank God, I have come to a time when brethren dwell together in unity, and that, too, in a land that is soon to blossom as the rose. But even as bad as such a time as that was, it was tolerant compared to the earlier periods of denominational contention. There was a time when ministers and laymen alike were excommunicated if they failed to support and defend the distinguishing doctrines of the church to which they belonged. It was the glory of one pulpit to stand up those of diverse faith in the pillory of adverse public opinion and lash them with barbed-wire theology until with embittered spirit they rushed upon their opponents with a fury which our present thought cannot comprehend.

And back of that period was the time when for their faith men were set in dungeons, were tortured with rack and thumbscrew, cast to their death from great heights, falling through sharpened spikes on the way, burned at the stake, devoured by wild beasts, ripped up by ravenous dogs, and their bodies cast upon the dung heap to rot. But, thanks be unto God, such a time will come again no more.

The spirit that would unchristianize a disciple of the Christ because of his honest opinion touching the disputed points of theology regardless of his character, is entirely alien to the spirit of Him whose mission it was to show us the Father, and to teach mankind to love righteousness, and hate iniquity. Our fellowship may be deep enough, and high enough; but it is not broad enough, unless it extends itself to every child of God. There are no sects in the church of Christ. They are of the earth, earthy. Christ is not divided; He did not die to establish a divided church. There is no division or sectism in Him who loved us and gave Himself for us, and I earnestly ask why should there be among His followers. For myself I do not desire to know any difference between the servants of my Lord. We be brethren, differing, no doubt, one from the other; but in life, in spirit, in faith, in purpose, in desire, one, as our Christ and His Father were one. Is it not time for us to cease our wrangling, to eliminate our interpretations, to set aside our definitions—and loving the same Lord, being born of the same spirit, laboring in the same field, desiring the same results, and seeking the same reward, dwell together in the unity of the Spirit and the bond of peace.

The sort of union in which I believe and in which my constituency believes, is a union of hearts, and not of heads; a union in service, and not in forms. Differing if we may in intellectual conception, but agreeing in purpose, and uniting in service. When Jesus honored the home of Simon, the leper, with His presence, Simon, Mary, Martha, and Lazarus united to serve Him. Simon furnished the house, Martha prepared the meal, Mary furnished the perfume, and Lazarus listened. They might have disagreed as to the room in which the feast should be served, but they did not; they might have disputed about the things to be served, but they did not; they might have quarreled over the quantity and quality of the perfume to be used, but they did not; they might have found fault with Lazarus for keeping still, but they did not; and because they united in service, the Master was given a feast worthy of the occasion. No one of them all could have done what they all did when working together. Each contributed what he had, and the Master and they sat down together to eat and drink in delightful fellowship. I submit that we ought to be as wise and as religious as they.

And now I declare unto you that the Christians will come into your tents, will deliver to you their possessions, surrender to you their field, will be to you hewers of wood and drawers of water, will love you, honor you, serve you, and dwell with you in sweet and loving harmony, if only you will admit to membership in your local church such men as Martin Luther, Dwight L. Moody, Wilbur Chapman, William Penn, Abraham Lincoln, Robert F. Lee, and Woodrow Wilson.

I wish to submit a few practical things, which I feel sure the Christians will heartily endorse:

That Fraternal Messengers be sent to the State and national gatherings from each body, and that, when practical, exchange of pulpits be made, and co-operation in special evangelistic services.

That our denominational papers run occasional articles from writers of the other constituency, when dealing with subjects that would tend to deepen our appreciation of each other.

That we unite in the task of making clear to the public the identity of each body by according to each its name, its history, and its teaching.

That we unite on some definite task for a period of five years; for example, keeping a missionary in touch with the incoming foreigners at Ellis Island, or doing definite evangelistic work in cities where one or more of the two bodies have churches.

That where circumstances justify, local churches federate on a plan that will not disturb the identity nor the work of either. That is to say, that each receive members according to its custom, send its benevolences through its own channels, and do other things as it would do them did the federation not exist.

That we bury all suspicion and substitute hearty co-operation for competition wherever and whenever a common field is occupied.

That eight persons be named by the Disciples of Christ, to meet with the Commission on Christian Unity of the Christians—there being eight on that commission—these sixteen to form a joint committee, to discover wherein the two bodies agree and wherein they disagree, and make report jointly to a meeting of this character one year hence; and that said joint committee be asked to suggest a method whereby the differences may be minimized, and the agreements emphasized.

That should there be a congregation of both bodies in any one locality, one of which should be without a pastor, that the pastor then on the field care for both congregations until such time as a pastor is secured.

A careful survey of competing fields, with a view of such interchange of inactive, or weak, churches as might consolidate several such churches into one pastorate, and thus prevent needless duplication, and also conserve denominational energy and funds.

That there be mutual confidence in the Christian integrity of each, manifested in brotherly association and fellowship, resulting in respect for the field of work of each; and care in church extension not to foster un-Christian rivalry by seeking to plan missions, or churches, where it would cripple or endanger the organized work of the other.

That in Sunday-school work our general Sunday-school officers might exchange literature, and Sunday-school leaders of the one church attend and assist in the Sunday-school Conventions of the other.

31. Almost United:
"A Telegram"

(1921)

F. G. Coffin and J. F. Burnett

The "union courtship" between the Christians and the Disciples, begun in 1827 in eastern Ohio, reached its first high point in 1831, when a "working arrangement" was reached between Barton Stone and some of his followers with some of the followers of Thomas Campbell in Lexington, Kentucky. This was followed by "a wave of Campbellism" that swept hundreds of Christian churches into the Disciples camp, severely weakening the Christian presence in Tennessee and Kentucky and diminishing the number of Christian churches in Pennsylvania and Ohio.

In 1874, a committee of five Disciples met with a like committee from the Christians in Syracuse, New York, "to seek . . . for some basis of union in Christian work." They agreed to cultivate each other's acquaintance, exchange pulpits, and attend each other's conferences, associations, and missionary conventions in the hope that eventually a common ground for union might be found. Unfortunately, their hope was not realized.

Yet, in 1916 the two denominations tried again. In 1919, a meeting took place between representatives of both denominations to discuss practical steps leading to union, and by 1920, the prospects were looking surprisingly good. A telegram of greetings was sent in the name of F. G. Coffin, chair of the Commission on Christian Unity, and J. F. Burnett, secretary of the Commission, by the several boards of the Christian

---

Source: F. G. Coffin and J. F. Burnett, telegram to the International Convention, Disciples of Christ, St. Louis, Missouri, 19 October 1920, in *The Christian Annual,* ed. and comp. J. F. Burnett (Dayton, Ohio: Christian Publishing Association, 1921), 8.

Church assembled in joint session in Dayton, Ohio, to the International Convention of the Disciples of Christ, meeting simultaneously in St. Louis, Missouri, expressing the hope that "the common life and thought of our two bodies may continue to increase, drawing us ever closer together, until the prayer of our Lord shall be realized." Once again, union seemed within reach. Unfortunately, the issue of baptism by immersion, which had divided Christians and Disciples for one hundred years, still could not be resolved, and their hopes were not realized.

Upon the authority of the Boards, the following telegram was sent:

Dayton, Ohio, October 19, 1920

To the International Convention, Disciples of Christ, St. Louis, Mo.

The several Boards of the Christian Church, assembled in joint session, in Dayton, Ohio, send your Convention greetings in the confidence of a common Christian fellowship. We wish for you a Convention surpassing all previous sessions, and venture to express the hope that the common life and thought of our two bodies may continue to increase, drawing us ever closer together, until the prayer of our Lord shall be realized.

F. G. Coffin,
Chairman Commission on Christian Unity, Christian Church.
J. F. Burnett,
Secretary Commission on Christian Unity, Christian Church.

32. The Immersion Stumbling Block: *"Baptists and Disciples and Baptism"*

(1926)

Alva Martin Kerr

Alva Martin Kerr, D.D. (1875–1928), editor of the Herald of Gospel Liberty *from 1919 to 1928, was one of the most respected and beloved leaders in the history of the Christian Church. His sweetness and gentleness as a person and pastor and his courage in living with what was called "tuberculosis of the bone" for more than forty years combined in his writing to produce a thoughtful and irenic author who was bold and incisive in his thought but who never let that stand in the way of his respect for all of God's children. Succeeding an editor of the* Herald *who had stood "loyally and faithfully against Higher Criticism, the Darwinian Theory of Evolution, and the New Theology," Kerr brought the* Herald *into interdenominational prominence for his well-researched, balanced, and inclusive editorials, often stressing the necessity and the inevitability of union based on the inclusiveness of Christ's gospel and his respect for every child of God.*

The majority Disciples' position, that baptism by immersion be a requirement of church membership, had been a sticking point between the Christians and Disciples from the time of Barton Stone and Thomas Campbell. Even when a respected Disciples leader, Peter Ainslie, president of the Disciples General Convention, admitted that the Disciples insistence on immersion was inconsistent with its commitment to Christian unity, they clung to it.

Kerr felt that the Disciples' concern for immersion compromised their

---

Source: Alva Martin Kerr, "Baptists and Disciples and Baptism, *Herald of Gospel Liberty,* 11 March 1926, 219–21.

work toward union. With uncharacteristic vehemence he wrote, "Either these unimmersed are Christian or they are not. If they are, it is a piece of utter and preposterous presumption for any church to refuse to receive into its membership those whom it admits Jesus Christ himself receives and approves."

Unfortunately, most of the Disciples did not agree with Ainslie or Kerr, and the baptismal issue remained insurmountable. In fact, the issue was not resolved until the late twentieth century, when the United Church of Christ and the Christian Church (Disciples of Christ) forged a partnership agreement that generally affirmed "open membership."

The question of baptism is rapidly coming to the front as one upon which there must be some thoroughgoing clarification and decision before the Church of Jesus Christ can make very much further progress along the lines of Christian unity. This is inevitable. The hard logic of fact as well as of reason makes the conflict irrepressible. On the one hand is the indisputable fact that, by every test of practical evidence, Methodists and Presbyterians and others who have been sprinkled, and our friend Quakers who have practiced only spiritual baptism, are as genuinely Christian in all of their loyalties and sacrifices for Jesus Christ and unquestionably as much approved and blessed by him as are those who have been immersed. On the other hand is the compelling force of reason and consistency which is driving all but the hopelessly indoctrinated of the Disciple and Baptist churches to recognize the wholly indefensible inconsistency of acknowledging the unimmersed to be truly Christian, fellowshiping them both in life and in co-operative Christian work as Christian, and yet at the same time refusing to admit them into church membership only because they have not been immersed.

Under the inescapable impulsion of such logic of fact and reason, both the Disciple and Baptist denominations, especially among their younger and progressive elements, are finding their position less and less tolerable, and there is rapidly coming an irrepressible demand for what is known among them as "open membership." "There has now come to a head in both these immersionist denominations," declares *The Christian Century* in a long editorial under the above title in its issue for February 25, "an intense demand for complete emancipation from the bigotry and sectarianism of closed membership." With this intense demand The Herald is in complete sympathy; but we find ourselves decidedly at variance with our good friend, Dr. Charles Clayton Morrison, the author of the editorial, in his proposed method by which this "complete emancipation" is to be achieved. He insists that it will be both reasonable and sufficient for the Disciple and Baptist denominations simply to receive into membership those who come to them from other churches like the Presbyterian and Methodist without requiring a rebaptism by immersion, while at the same time these Disciple and Baptist pastors and churches themselves adhere to the practice of immersion only for all who are received by them upon confession of faith and not by letter. But we want to assure Dr. Morrison and our immersionist friends that the question can never be settled in such easy and superficial manner. It will require a far more complete and thoroughgoing readjustment of estimates and values than that—readjustments and estimates which reach down into the most foundational concepts of the Christian religion and involve the right and duty of churches as well as the very nature of Jesus Christ himself. Neither is it a question in which the immersionist churches only are interested and concerned. It involves the authenticity of the sprinkling of affusion churches and of the spiritual baptism of the Friends, and hence the standing of their members in the Church of Jesus Christ.

To Dr. Morrison it seems that open membership is not "a mere attempt to tinker with the ritualism of baptism" and that "open membership is not concerned with the right or wrong of the immersionist contention." And in similar vein, an advocate of open membership writing in *The Christian-Evangelist,* one of the finest of Disciple periodicals, contends: "The question of baptism does not enter into the discussion. We believe immersion to be the scriptural mode of baptism and we continue to practice it exclusively." But by no such sophistry of reasoning can the matter be separated from the question of baptism. Dr. Morrison and the other writer reflect it so in their own articles. Both give recognition of a superior type of baptism and contend that the Disciple and Baptist churches are justified in clinging to this type of baptism for their own elect, even if they must condescend to accept into their membership by letter those who have been sprinkled by other churches and pastors. To the Baptist and Disciple churches, immersion still remains the *"scriptural mode of baptism."* And therein is the whole crux of the situation. The Methodists, the Presbyterians, the Congregationalists, the Quakers resent the inescapable inference that they are less scriptural in their beliefs and practices than are the immersionists; and this question will never have tolerable and permanent settlement until we go down deep enough to decide what is scriptural. The whole matter hangs there. The *"constraint of conscience to practice baptism by immersion only"* which Dr. Morrison justifies and defends for the Baptist and Disciple open-membership churches, grows out of a basic conception of what it takes to constitute a "scriptural practice." They assume that in order to be strictly scriptural, one must follow the exact mode of baptism, even amid the snow and ice of the Occident, that Jesus practiced nineteen hundred years ago in the balmy Orient. But they do not apply this same rigid rule to other matters. Even in administering communion they do not recline at the communion table, nor do they do many other things in the identical manner which Jesus did. On every question under the sun except this one of baptism, they use a far more flexible and spiritual interpretation and adaptation to decide what is scriptural. Only by the most rigid form of extreme literalism and only by the extremist spirit of Judaistic ritualism can it be maintained that immersion is any more scriptural, in all of the finer and better sense of what constitutes being scriptural, than are the other modes of baptism. And it is futile to hope to promote the fullest spirit of Christian unity among all followers of Jesus Christ while some among them here and there assume themselves to be more scriptural than others simply because they have been immersed. This grave cause of schism in the Church can never be cured by any regulation regarding baptism which leaves room for a single vestige of this divisive attitude and spirit.

But the matter goes far deeper than that yet and finds its basic involvements in the question whether or not the Church of Jesus Christ is worshiping a dead Jesus, bound down to the environments and practices of the Orient nineteen hundred years ago, or whether we are following a living Christ who is so radiantly and triumphantly alive and abreast of the times that he can both sanction and bless the working out of his gospel into the modes and processes which best fit the clime and the conditions of our own land and generation—exacting only that profound love and loyalty which every one must admit are as intense and faithful among the affused and the Quakers as among the immersed. And never will this question of modes of baptism cease to disturb the peace and quiet of the Church, nor cease to be a source of the "bigotry and sectarianism" which Dr. Morrison so fervently deplores, until it is settled on that deep and foundational basis which recognizes the fact that Jesus is now a living Christ, more sane and more reasonable than the most reasonable of human beings; and that it is utterly incompatible with that concept of Christ to imagine for a moment that in his eyes one mode of baptism can be any more scriptural or acceptable than another.

Because this is true, the open-membership churches in the Disciple and Baptist denominations are pursuing a delusion and are doomed to disappointment if they hope to settle the question by receiving the sprinkled who come by letter, but insisting upon administering only immersion themselves. Out of a hundred years of a most unsatisfactory and distressing experience on this question, let the Christian denomination assure them that they will find neither satisfaction nor peace in such a halfway adjustment. Many of the churches of the Christian denomination have long tried the experiment—and they have found it a snare and a delusion. On the one hand this position sets up a sort of superior form of baptism, a first-preferred mode of baptism, which alone the church or pastor will practice. The natural and inevitable result is that many who have been baptized by this form will assume an air of "scriptural conformity," an attitude of more "formal correctness," over their brethren. It is a condition which we can testify is highly conducive to supercilious self-righteousness, with all of its manifold brood of evils. And it leads to interminable arguments and disunity over modes—a thing which is bad enough as between denominations but which becomes fearfully irritating and unendurable when it enters the confines of a local church membership or Sunday-school class. On the other hand, the children in such open-membership churches will grow to resent the fact that their own church does not grant to its own young folks a liberty of conscience which it extends to those coming from other denominations, but forces them either to be immersed or to go to some other church or some other pastor to secure the very sprinkling which their church and their pastor both accept and bless when it comes by a covering letter from another denomination. Formerly, by processes of rigid indoctrination, the Disciple and Baptist churches could teach their children to believe that immersion only was scriptural and right. But that day is forever past. The great student and other interdenominational gatherings and work now make such indoctrination impossible and such a doctrine ludicrous. And this is a situation which will be rapidly intensified through the closer contacts in the local church organizations where the sprinkled and the immersed are brought into fellowship with each other through open membership. Under such conditions, the inconsistency of the position becomes wholly untenable. For a man who believes in affusion to be placed under the necessity of going across the street to be sprinkled by a Presbyterian or Methodist in order to be properly equipped to unite with the open-membership Disciple or Baptist church to which his wife belongs is too great an absurdity long to be maintained in twentieth century thinking, and is in deadly conflict with that right of individual liberty upon which Protestantism is founded. How can the Disciples and Baptists hope to retain the high respect and admiration of their own young people under any such indefensible and halfway adjustment as the open-membership churches propose? The editor of *The Christian-Evangelist* rightly argues:

> If allusion is right as baptism when performed by one person, it is valid when performed by any other, and it should not be refused those who conscientiously desire it. This is the logic of the situation if one wishes to be consistent in his religious practices.

The same driving logic and sense of consistency make plain also that the Baptist and Disciple churches must either come to repudiate the unimmersed as not being truly Christian, and refuse longer to fellowship in federated councils and Sunday-school and Christian Endeavor and other interdenominational organizations with Methodist and Presbyterian and other bodies which practice sprinkling, or else these Baptists and Disciples must cease to shut out from their membership these unimmersed Christians. Either these unimmersed are Christian or they are not. If they are, it is a piece of utter and preposterous presumption for the church to refuse to receive into its membership those whom it admits Jesus Christ himself receives and approves. That is logic of a high and compelling sort also, a fact which *The Christian-Evangelist* has not so clearly distinguished, but which all but the highly indoctrinated immersionists are seeing and feeling with increasing clarity. This is true under ordinary circumstances. It becomes irresistible when one begins to think in the terms of isolated churches, where one church and one pastor must minister to a whole community made up of folks of every shade of training and belief, as pertaining to baptism as well as to other doctrines. How can any Disciple or Baptist church or pastor honestly presume to take care of such a community, or how can they ask to have territory either in the home or the foreign field allocated to them for their exclusive ministration, if they will administer nothing but immersion and refuse to recognize the conscience of the individual seeking membership? Surely Dr. Morrison was not thinking of such situations or in the terms of cooperative Christian effort which more and more is finding favor in modern Christian thinking, and of its practical application in allocated territories and churches in small communities, when he asserts: "It would seem sufficient to say that one good reason for continuing the established practice [of immersion only] is that there is no reason at all for abandoning it." One cannot think in these larger terms of applied Christian comity and Christian unity, either in the local field or in the vaster world task, without discovering that there is no place in the Kingdom of God for such a *baptism de luxe* as the immersionist churches and the "open-membership" churches are trying to adhere to, refusing to administer any other. Christian unity is blocked until all of the conscientious followers of Jesus Christ can have the freest access to the membership of his churches any time, anywhere. So long as Christ receives them, it is hardly believable or defensible that mere man should shut them out—by methods either positive or negative. To the Christian in the isolated field, the open-membership church which will administer no other baptism but immersion may easily become as exclusive as the closed-membership churches which acknowledge and receive nothing but immersion.

In conclusion let us reiterate our conviction that no man can put up an argument for immersion or any other particular mode of baptism and do it on the same high spiritual and intellectual plane on which he does his other thinking and reasoning—and rarely ever have we seen a more striking example of this than in Dr. Morrison's editorial. The most conspicuous and perhaps the most brilliant editorial writer in religious journalism today, a fearless liberal leader who brushes aside sophistries and delusions and writes with great force and clarity—his defense of the right of open-membership churches to administer only immersion furnishes an amazing contrast to the usual high order of editorials appearing in his great journal. No man ever has been or ever will be able to defend any one mode of baptism on the same high spiritual and intellectual plane on which he does the rest of his preaching and writing. It simply can not be done!

Learning from the Wider Church

33. National Union: *"The Obligation of the Christian Church to the Federal Council"*

(1920)

Frank G. Coffin

The Federal Council of the Churches of Christ in America was largely the brainchild of New England Congregationalist Elias B. Sanford (1843–1932). Drawing together the union ideas of Samuel Simon Schmucker (1799–1873) and Josiah Strong (1847–1916), Sanford formulated the plans for the Federal Council, held the preliminary hearings, and arranged for the groundbreaking Inter-Church Conference on Federation, held in Carnegie Hall in 1905, which drew up the constitution for the Federal Council. By 1908, the national assemblies of the constituent bodies had adopted the constitution, and the Federal Council officially came into being.

According to the constitution, the Federal Council was designed: (1) to express the fellowship and catholic unity of the Christian church; (2) to bring the Christian bodies of America into united service for Christ and the world; (3) to encourage devotional fellowship and mutual counsel concerning the spiritual life and religious activities of the churches; (4) to secure a larger combined influence for the churches of Christ in all matters affecting the moral and social condition of the people, so as to promote the application of the law of Christ in every relation of human life; and (5) to assist in the organization of local branches of the

---

Source: F. G. Coffin, "The Obligation of the Christian Church to the Federal Council," pamphlet published by The Commission on Christian Unity of the Christian Church, Dayton, Ohio, 1920.

Federal Council to promote its aim in their communities. It required that its member denominations recognize Jesus Christ as "Divine Lord and Savior."

In contrast to its nineteenth-century predecessor, the American Evangelical Alliance, representatives to the Federal Council were the denominations themselves instead of a voluntary collection of individuals. The Federal Council sought the cooperation of the high-church Protestant and Orthodox bodies instead of being specifically "evangelical." Finally, showing the influence of the Social Gospel movement in America, the Federal Council exhibited great concern for social problems rather than focusing primarily on issues of faith.

The Federal Council had no authority over the constituent bodies adhering to it, but exercised an advisory role in matters of interest to the churches. It also had no authority with regard to creed or form of government or worship, or anything else that might be seen to limit the autonomy of the participating churches.

During its half-century of existence, the Federal Council was blessed by the leadership of two remarkable ecumenists, Charles S. Macfarland, its first general secretary, and Samuel McCrea Calvert. By 1948, the Federal Council had grown to cover an extraordinary range of concerns in its various departments and commissions. It had major units in field administration, evangelism, international justice and goodwill, race relations, religious radio, Christian social and industrial relations, marriage and the home, just and durable peace, the ministry, religion and health, and worship.

The Federal Council's final contribution was through its increasing participation in the global ecumenical movement. After Edinburgh in 1937, the Federal Council founded its own Standing Committee for the Study of Christian Unity, and its leaders shared enthusiastically in the founding of the World Council of Churches in 1948. In 1950, it took the ecumenical risk of choosing its own demise by joining with many other representative church organizations in forming an even larger cooperative body, the National Council of the Churches of Christ in the United States of America.

The Christians greeted the founding of Federal Council in 1908 with enthusiasm, sure that it was a harbinger of great union events to come, and they supported it intensively throughout its existence. In 1920, when the Federal Council experienced a period of acute financial need, the Commission on Christian Unity issued "The Obligation of the Christian Church to the Federal Council" to raise the Christians' awareness of the Federal Council's accomplishments and their obligations to it.

Frank G. Coffin (1874–1941) was a pastor and educator in the Christian Church. He had served as president of the General Convention of the Christian Church (1914–1934), chair of the Commission on Christian Unity, which helped to bring about the union of the Congregational and Christian Churches, co-moderator of the General Council of the Congregational and Christian Churches (1931–34), and vice-president of the Federal Council of Churches.

The war brought a new word into general use. What it designates has been in the world since before history was written and seen in many areas. It carries a peculiar stigma and puts the one to whom it is attached under scorn as though it did not belong in the list of ordinary faults. That word is "slacker." It represents an uncondonable evasion of what one ought to do. The obligation to do the thing is presupposed, inherent and beyond all possibility of being an elective. It is something which in the nature of the case one with certain relations just ought to do.

All obligations are not regulated by contracts of mutual agreement between the parties concerned and specified in papers "signed, sealed and attested." They are unavoidably implied and binding in the nature of things. This is found in the relation between parents and children. Some of these obligations exist even when one party does not care to have them fulfilled as in the case of foreign missions, or when one party is opposed to their fulfillment as is the case of the drunkard when society is trying to make him a sober man.

When we become a part of an organization the obligation for the welfare of that organization is inherently ours. When we devote ourselves to certain ideas and principles the promotion of institutions which embrace these has an undeniable claim upon our support. It is almost always true that the work of such organizations can be made successful only when each one upon whom such an obligation rests discharges his full duty.

Christians generally need a quickened consciousness of obligation for good works. They should be alert, anxious and quick to respond to such duties. A way of evasion is easily found if it is being sought. There are always the "duties at home," "rumors by those who oppose," "inability to do much," etc. There is always a seemingly plausible justification if one prefers to "slack."

The Christian Church has obligations of a most binding character to the Federal Council. However they may seem to a few they are morally inescapable. They are written into the nature of things. The Christian Church is a part of the Kingdom of God. The whole is greater than any of its parts.

The theories maintained during our whole history would be outraged if we repudiate such obligations now. We can no longer be known by our words. Our deeds alone can speak for us. These obligations come from several considerations:

1. Being an organization to make effective the will of Christ among men there belongs to us the helping of every good possible. By the combined efforts of all God will save the world and build everywhere a new order of society. Every good cause needs all of its friends. Men should love opportunities to do good. The larger such opportunities are the greater delight should they awaken in those to whom they come. Their privilege is enhanced when they enable a church to do with others what would ever have to remain an impossibility without such mutual association. It's the accomplishing of the task that counts, not the location of the credit. It is also a fact that in the interest of their own spiritual enlargement Christians should do something from which they do not expect returns to themselves or their organization. Religion must have centrifugal quality.

2. The obligation of brotherhood expressed in a common, universal task. A load which is too great for another, or which can be better borne by our aid, is more than a challenge; it is an irresistible attraction for our efforts. Whether we have had anything to do in creating it is of no consequence. Whatever we can do to help bear it matters immensely. Common tasks are universal tasks. From them there is no exemption. They are not selected. Toward them there may be two attitudes—slacking or doing them. From the human side the world has no need surpassing that of brotherhood in both spirit and action.

3. The obligation for the Christian Church to render service in all fields. Without such a centralizing agency as the Federal Council we would have to think impotently and uselessly about much that the Lord wants done and has commanded us to do. There is so much which needs to be done on a gigantic scale to make the program of Christ effective in our day of modern social complications that no one denomination can do, and if all attempted it independently it would further complicate the whole situation. The Federal Council, which is twenty-nine denominations working together, can do what would have to remain undone without such an organization. With its maintenance of central offices at strategic territorial centers—New York, Washington, and Chicago and its numerous Commissions and Committees constantly at work a competent program can be devised and promoted throughout this country and the world. The field which it is occupying is one which is much in need of occupancy and one which would be entirely neglected but for this co-operative agency. Its departments of Research, Social Service, Race Relations, International

Justice and Goodwill, Relations with Religious Bodies in Europe, Mercy and Relief, Relations with the Eastern Churches, Financial and Fiduciary Matters, Army and Navy Chaplains, Council of the Religious Press are operating in fields almost untouched by other agencies. There are many other aspects in which the Council aids the organizations promoting them in a most effective way. The Council has shown an excellent spirit in promoting every phase of co-operative Christianity, whether under its own or other auspices. Its contribution to the enrichment of the fellowship spirit of all Christendom has been vast. It has direct contact with federated states, municipalities and many organizations. It keeps the denominations in step, strengthens morale and fuses strength. On all moral questions affecting the government at Washington its voice has a wholesome influence and is recognized as competent to speak for Protestant Christianity. It proceeds with carefulness and yet is fearless. It does not hesitate to incur criticism when its cause is just. It awakens Christian America to dangers and responsibilities which might be overlooked. Its general meetings are held quadrennially; its Executive Committee Meetings, annually; its Administrative Committee Meetings monthly and its staff meetings as frequently as there is need.

The Council now stands upon its record and not upon its theories. Its work in reform, improvement of social, industrial, racial, and international relations; its effort to awaken the conscience of the world already has such results to its credit as to make its value unquestionable.

4. The obligation because of results already attained has been implied in the preceding paragraph. Its program is commendable, but results alone speak with appeal. The church needs a clear voice today to speak for it in industry, temperance, law enforcement, war, interracial relations, etc. This it is getting at Washington and indirectly at the courts of the world through the Council. One sure evidence of the council's value is to be found in the sources of opposition to it. If it were not a formidable enemy to them the war promoters, scofflaws, industrial tyrants, and race hatred advocates would not be opposing the Council. When we compare the present with the situation of former years when there was no Federal Council, it is easily discerned that it has lent steadiness and aggressiveness to the church, provided a concert and effectiveness of movement in Education, Missions, Periodicals, denominational moderators and denominational agencies, Evangelism, Social Service, Moral reforms, etc. At the Stockholm Conference its contribution to co-operative Christianity was evidenced by the fact that it had already instituted and was operating most of the plans which European groups were looking forward to.

5. An added obligation to respond to the support of the Council just

now comes from the fact that it is being overlooked and crowded out by strenuous denominational programs. Quite every denomination is having the problem of keeping up the pace established by its recent promotional program. Enlarged programs were inaugurated from forward movement results. The income from these sources stopped but the programs were on. Tremendous overhead pressure has been necessary to maintain work so established. As a result all cooperative work has had difficulty in securing a hearing. Many enterprises of this kind would have had to close as a result had it not been for large individual donations. Then there is among many an increasing neglect of responsibilities due to minds already filled with other concerns, many of which are secular. It is doubtful if a more destructive thing could happen to present day Christianity than for its interdenominational agencies to be crippled.

Every member of the Christian Church should have something for the Council's support. It can do much more than if the twenty-nine denominations composing it were to attempt the same things independently. To support its program is wise benevolence.

6. Our obligation is accentuated by the Council's present pressing financial need. Its program has grown rapidly. This has increased its budget. The increasing expense in everything else is in religious work also. The purchasing power of the dollar that goes to church has decreased in like ratio with its fellows which go elsewhere. This situation has created a great deficit in the Council's treasury for which provision should be made. Yet, there are no limits to the possibilities of its program. Larger tasks should be undertaken. The time is ripening for its greatest possible contribution to the Kingdom. There should be enlargement, not curtailment, in its program. Its hands should not be tied, or limits placed upon its usefulness.

7. We are under obligation to the Council because of the benefits which we have received from it. It brings into our life the best from all sources. It makes the material gathered at their expense and by their experts available for our denominational use. Conversely it provides a channel by which the catholicity of the Christian Church may find entrance to many others. It places our ideals into a broader field and makes our principles known to the other denominations in a way which would never be possible by our independent action. In the Council we have always had all the recognition to which we were entitled. We have been adequately represented on its Commissions and Committees. We have been provided a delightful fellowship and have experienced an added feeling of strength because of this association. There has been no outside contact which has meant so much to our denominational life. Then there is no other agency moving us so effectively toward the goal of Christian Unity.

To discharge this responsibility more than a mere verbal endorsement is due. We want to continue this fellowship that we may both give and get the blessings which it confers. To continue to hold membership we must bear our part of its financial responsibility. In honor we cannot do otherwise. Only a slacker expects some one else to do the thing which rightfully belongs to him. It is for this reason that a generous annual contribution is asked from each congregation. This contribution is desired to cover our membership responsibility in the Federal Council and the expense of the work of promotion by the Commission on Christian Unity of the church.

34. The Anglican Challenge:

"The Lambeth Conference on Church Union"

(1920)

Alva Martin Kerr

The early Christians breathed the air of liberty, democracy, equality, and independence from their very origin at the close of the eighteenth century, and these principles remained central to their understanding of themselves and their church. It was not surprising, then, that they rebelled against the Episcopalian notion that ministers must be ordained by a bishop in a church that retained the historic episcopate. Elias Smith spoke out against this view vehemently and polemically in 1809 in a series of articles in the Herald, *in which he insisted that the episcopate was "exactly the opposite to gospel liberty; it brings all the people under a yoke of human bondage." James O'Kelly spoke out against it the same year in his "Plan of Christian Union," where he insisted that submitting to the episcopal form of government would be subjecting oneself to a human head and subscribing to an oppressive and unscriptural form of government. The Christians were unwavering in their opposition to the historic episcopate.*

Therefore, when the Lambeth Quadrilateral was first sent out to the churches in 1888, Martyn Summerbell responded with an article in the Herald *that continued the Christians' historic perspective: "To thoughtful Christians the assumption of priestliness is offensive, since it introduces into the Church the notion of caste or sect. Of all institutions in the world Christianity is the most firmly set against the presumptions of hierarchy and privilege" (see vol. 6:5).*

Source: Alva M. Kerr, "The Lambeth Conference on Church Union," *Herald of Gospel Liberty*, 23 September 1920, 917–18.

Nevertheless, by the twentieth century, the Christians had moved into the world of global ecumenism, and their commitments to union were much less polemical and much more sophisticated. Consequently, when the Lambeth Conference of 1920 sent out what seemed to be a more conciliatory statement to the churches, apparently admitting for the first time "that the non-Episcopal communions are really churches," the calm and irenic editor of the Herald, *Alva Martin Kerr, chose to address the issue of the episcopate once again. Kerr was heartened over the conciliatory tone of the new Lambeth statement, but he maintained nevertheless that the Episcopal insistence that non-Episcopally ordained clergy must submit to a reordination if they wished to be allowed to preach in an Episcopal pulpit meant that the Episcopalians had a long way to go before they could find a common meeting ground with denominations "which have been more thoroughly permeated with the spirit of democracy and which have an inbred intolerance to the idea of a priesthood."*

Since 1867 an assemblage of the Bishops of the Anglican Church has met from time to time in Lambeth Palace, London. Its deliberations are held in private and its public deliverances have always received universal attention. At a number of the latter meetings of this conference, the question of the reunion of the church has received extensive and sincere consideration, but its proposals have been so uniformly Anglican in their viewpoint and requirements that other denominations have looked upon them with unanimous disfavor. But a new note has been struck in the proposition for union which was issued by the conference which recently concluded its labors in London, and has aroused not only a very wide-spread interest both in America and Europe but also has been met with a far more generous response than any previous effort of the conference along this line. It is pointed out by a number of writers in the English press that for the first time in its history the Anglican Communion has admitted that the non-Episcopal communions are really churches, inasmuch as heretofore it has refused to concede to them this fact. The proposal in part says:

> We acknowledge all those who believe in our Lord Jesus Christ and have been baptized into the name of the Holy Trinity as sharing with us membership in the universal church of Christ, which is His body. We believe that the Holy Spirit has called us in a very solemn manner to associate ourselves in penitence and prayer with all those who deplore the division of Christian people and are inspired by the vision and hope of a visible unity of the whole church.

> The causes of division lie deep in the past and are by no means simple or wholly blameworthy. Yet none can doubt that self-will, ambition and lack of charity among Christians have been principal factors in the mingled process, and that these, together with blindness to the sin of disunion, are still mainly responsible for the breaches of Christendom. We acknowledge this condition of broken fellowship to be contrary to God's will, and we desire frankly to confess our share in the guilt of thus crippling the body of Christ and hindering the activity of His Spirit.
>
> The times call us to a new outlook and new measures. The faith cannot be adequately apprehended and the battle of the Kingdom cannot be worthily fought while the body is divided, and is thus unable to grow up into the fullness of the life of Christ. The time has come, we believe, for all the separated groups of Christians to agree in forgetting the things which are behind and reaching out toward the goal of a reunited catholic church. The removal of the barriers which have arisen between them will only be brought about by a new comradeship of those whose faces are definitely set this way.

In an effort to find a new approach toward such visible unity of the church, the conference put forth the following new "quadrilateral:"

> We believe that the visible unity of the church will be found to involve the whole-hearted acceptance of:
>
> The Holy Scriptures, as the record of God's revelation of Himself to man, and as being the rule and ultimate standard of faith, and the creed commonly called Nicene, as the sufficient statement of the Christian faith, and either it or the Apostle's Creed as the baptismal confession of belief.
>
> The divinely instituted sacraments of baptism and the holy communion, as expressing for all the corporate life of the whole fellowship in and with Christ.
>
> A ministry acknowledged by every part of the church as possessing not only the inward call of the Spirit, but also the commission of Christ and the authority of the whole body.

But for most Protestants in America, at least, the conference largely upsets its whole proposal by clinging to the importance of the episcopate. It says:

> May we not reasonably claim that the episcopate is the one means of providing such a ministry? It is not that we call in question for a moment the spiritual reality of the ministries of those communions

which do not possess the episcopate. On the contrary, we thankfully acknowledge that these ministries have been manifestly blessed and owned by the Holy Spirit as effective means of grace. But we submit that considerations alike of history and of present experience justify the claim which we make on behalf of the episcopate. Moreover, we would urge that it is now and will prove to be in the future the best instrument for maintaining the unity and continuity of the church.

It then proceeds by proposing that the ministry of all other Protestant churches should be willing to submit to a reordination by the Episcopal Church in order that these ministers may have recognition and standing and the freedom of the pulpits of that communion. In return for this concession from the non-conformists ministry, it is proposed that the Episcopal clergy be given some "form of commission or recognition" from the non-conformist churches. It insists that by such reordination no one could possibly be understood as repudiating his past ministry, but simply "publicly and formally seeking additional recognition of a new call to wider service in a reunited church." It declares, "We do not ask that any one communion should consent to be absorbed in another. We do ask that all should unite in a new and greater endeavor to recover and to manifest to the world the unity of the body of Christ for which He prayed."

On the whole the impression created by this Lambeth proposal is very favorable, inasmuch as it breathes both a spirit of deep earnestness and a new willingness for concession and recognition of the rest of the Protestant Church and ministry. But nevertheless, the Episcopal Church will have a long way to go yet before it finds a common meeting ground with denominations which have been more thoroughly permeated with the spirit of democracy and which have an inbred intolerance to the idea of a priesthood.

35. INTERNATIONAL FORCES:

"The Message of the Lausanne Conference on Church Unity"

(1927)

The World Conference on Faith and Order (Lausanne, 1927) had its inception seventeen years earlier at the World Missionary Conference in Edinburgh (1910), when Charles H. Brent, at that time the missionary bishop for the Philippines of the Protestant Episcopal Church in the United States, reminded his colleagues that Edinburgh, with its ordinance forbidding discussion of differences of opinion in doctrine and ecclesiastical structure and practice, was only a step along the way toward unity. It was imperative that the churches find a vehicle whereby they could discuss the causes of the divisions (of faith and order) between them, with the intention of removing them. Brent's suggestion came to the attention of the next meeting of the general convention of the Protestant Episcopal Church, and a resolution was passed appointing a joint commission to bring about such a conference.

After lengthy preparation, interrupted by the First World War, the conference took place in Lausanne in 1927. It focused on seven main issues: (1) the call to unity; (2) the church's message to the world—the gospel; (3) the nature of the church; (4) the church's common confession of faith; (5) the church's ministry; (6) the sacraments; (7) the unity of Christendom and the place of the different churches in it.

The editorial in the Herald *presenting the results of the conference, "The Message of the Lausanne Conference on Church Unity," identified*

SOURCE: Editorial, "The Message of the Lausanne Conference on Church Unity," *Herald of Gospel Liberty,* 15 September 1927, 852–53.

the issues of the nature of the church, the meaning and function of creeds (which had so long been anathema to the Christians), and the nature of the ministry and the sacraments as points on which there was the greatest divergence among the churches. At the same time, the article recognized that the greatest value of the conference lay not in agreements reached but in the experience of "brotherhood" felt by the representatives of churches from all over the world.

Perhaps the most significant part of the conference for the future of ecumenism lay in the fact that a worldwide "Continuation Committee" was appointed (with the president of the Christian denomination's Elon College, W. A. Harper, a member). This committee served repeatedly as a faith and order conference in miniature, drawing leaders of different communions into relationship and understanding, conducting a steady process of education in one another's beliefs, discussing major theological issues, and making decisions that greatly increased the long-term value and influence of the world conference that had already taken place. Even more significantly, the work of the committee directed the attention of all its participants toward the next world conference in Edinburgh (1937).

Many of the readers of The Herald are intensely interested in what was done by the World Conference on Faith and Order at Lausanne to promote the Christian unity for which the Christian denomination so long has prayed. Some of us feel that it is futile to attempt to find a basis for organic unity along the lines of creedal statements and definitions, such as were pursued by this Conference. But on the other hand, creedal and other such differences not only exist but are the one greatest obstacle to union and simply must be disposed of in some sort of way. The things which were discussed at Lausanne are the very things which come up the moment union is proposed between any two or more churches; and the churches can never hope to arrive at organic unity until they have the courage and the wisdom to face these differences and thrash them out in a Christian spirit. And the spirit at Lausanne was Christian and on the whole admirably fine.

The findings of the Conference cover several subjects, each studied by sections of the Conference and then adopted by the whole: The Church's Message to the World, The Nature of the Church, The Church's Common Confession of Faith, The Ministry of the Church, and the Sacraments. These reports, together with the Preamble adopted by the Conference, will be sent to the official boards of all of the denominations represented at the Conference. The Preamble, in part, follows:

This is a Conference summoned to consider matters of Faith and Order. It is emphatically *not* attempting to define the conditions of future reunion. Its object is to register the apparent level of fundamental agreements within the Conference and the grave points of disagreements remaining; also to suggest certain lines of thought which may in the future tend to a fuller measure of agreement. . . .

We thank God and rejoice over agreements reached; upon our agreements we build. Where the reports record differences, we call upon the Christian world to an earnest reconsideration of the conflicting opinions now held, and a strenuous endeavor to reach the truth as it is in God's mind, which should be the foundation of the Church's unity.

God wills unity. Our presence in this Conference bears testimony to our desire to bend our wills to his. However we may justify the beginnings of disunion, we lament its continuance and henceforth must labor, in penitence and faith, to build up our broken walls.

God's Spirit has been in our midst. It was he who called us hither. His presence has been manifest in our worship, our deliberations, and our whole fellowship. He has discovered us to one another. He has enlarged our horizons, quickened our understanding, and enlivened our hope. We have dared and God has justified our daring. We can never be the same again. Our deep thankfulness must find expression in sustained endeavor to share the visions vouchsafed us here with those smaller home groups where our lot is cast.

More than half the world is waiting for the gospel. At home and abroad sad multitudes are turning away in bewilderment from the Church because of its corporate feebleness. Our missions count that as a necessity which we are inclined to look on as a luxury. Already the mission field is impatiently revolting from the divisions of the western Church to make bold adventure for unity in its own right. We of the churches represented in this Conference cannot allow our spiritual children to outpace us. We must gird ourselves to the task, the early beginnings of which God has so richly blessed, and labor side by side with the Christians who are working for indigenous churches until our common goal is reached.

Some of us, pioneers in this undertaking, have grown old in our search for unity. It is to youth that we look to take the torch of unity. We men have carried it too much alone through many years. The women henceforth should be accorded their share of responsibility. And so the whole Church will be enabled to do that which no section can hope to perform.

It was God's clear call that gathered us. With faith stimulated by his guidance to us here, we move forward.

The Findings of the Conference

The statements upon the subjects mentioned above, and which will be sent out to the various churches as the findings of the Lausanne Conference, are too long for The Herald to print in full; but these will doubtless soon be made available in booklet form. As touching "The Church's Message to the World," there is little to which any group of Christians, perhaps, would take objection. It insists that "the message of the Church to the world is and must always remain in the gospel of Jesus Christ," and that this gospel is more than a philosophical theory, or a theological system, or a program for material betterment; that it is a joyful message of redemption and the "sure source of power for social regeneration" as well as the only way of salvation for the individual.

As to the nature of the Church, there was a great deal of division of opinion at the Conference, as there has always been throughout Christendom. It was agreed that the Church is "the communion of believers in Christ Jesus" and that there "is and can be but one Church, holy, catholic, and apostolic"; and that the Church on earth "possesses certain characteristics whereby it can be known of men." But some hold that one or the other of the existing churches is the only true Church; others, that the true Church is found scattered among all of the churches. Some hold that a particular form of church, and ministry is necessary; others, that no one form is inherently preferable; and still others, that no organization is necessary. These and many other very decided differences as to the nature of the Church not only gave rise to strong controversy at the Conference but compose some of the most foundational difficulties in the way of a united Church.

When it came to the statements of belief, there were fundamental differences of opinion. But the Conference was wise enough to make provision for such differences by declaring that, while it endorsed the Nicene and the Apostles' Creed, yet it should be "understood that the ways in which these creeds may be used shall be determined by the competent authority in each church" and that "the several churches will continue to make free use of such special confessions as they may possess." It even went so far as to affirm the conviction that the Holy Spirit, "in leading the Church into all truth, may enable it, while firmly adhering to the witness of these creeds (our common heritage from the ancient Church), to express the truths of revelation in additional forms according to the needs of future ages." And then the Conference proceeded to upset, logically and foundationally, all that it had said about these ancient confessions of faith by declaring:

> We desire at the same time to leave on record our solemn and unanimous testimony that no external and written standards can take the place of that inward and personal experience of union with the living Christ which is the only experience of spiritual vitality, and that the object of our faith is not any statement about Christ, but the Lord Jesus Christ himself.

When it said this, the Conference struck down to a bedrock principle which reveals the utter futility and folly of all of the clamor and clash which the churches have made down through the ages over their creeds and confessions, as the Conference thus admitted that in the last analysis it must be left to the individual himself and to his inward and personal experience with Jesus Christ. And that is just where the Christian denomination has always left it and insisted that it should be left by all the churches.

On the ministry of the Church there were also differences of the most fundamental kind—as to the nature of ordination, and the grace conferred thereby; the function and authority of bishops; the nature of Apostolic Succession, etc. The Conference believed that "the first step towards the overcoming of these difficulties is the frank recognition that they exist, and the clear definition of their nature," and it set forth some of these differences and something of their significance as obstacles to union. Reared as we have been in the atmosphere of a congregational church system, where there is an utter absence of the spirit of priestly authority and mysteries, it will be very difficult for us of the Christian Church to understand how sacred to others seem the priestly element of the ministry, the Apostolic Succession, and the special grace and authority which adhere in the ministry under these views. The two viewpoints seem irreconcilable; but there is ground for hope in the fact that Christian people of all churches are coming to recognize the validity of each other's faith and forms and to unite, as this Conference pleaded that they should do, "in the activities of brotherly service which Christ has committed to his disciples."

A Continuation Committee Appointed

The last section of the report deals with the sacraments; and here too there are vast differences—especially between the Orthodox Church of the East and the great body of Protestantism. The Orthodox Church holds that there are seven sacraments, and that in order to be valid these must be performed in a particular way and by a proper ministry. Others, like the Quakers, attach high value to the sacramental principle, but do not make use of the outward signs of sacraments but hold only to the spiritual content. Still others regard only baptism and the Lord's Supper as sacraments; and this Conference laid stress on these two, as they were the most generally acknowledged by the churches participating in this Conference. No attempt was made, however, to define and limit baptism by any special mode, nor to give any specific meaning to Holy Communion, about which there always has been such vast difference of opinion, even in Protestant bodies. The Conference contented itself with the assertion, "We are aware that the reality of the divine presence and gift in this sacrament can not be adequately apprehended by human thought or expressed in human language," and closed its statement on the sacraments with the prayer "that the differences which prevent full communion at the present time may be removed." In this prayer it would seem that every earnest-hearted Christian ought to join; for if there is any place the followers of Jesus Christ should be willing to come together, it certainly would seem to be around the table where they commemorate the suffering and death for them of their one common Lord and Master. It seems little less than a blasphemy on his name, and certainly it is on his spirit, that those who adore him should shut each other out from this sacred service.

Simply to read these findings of the Conference gives a sense of deep disappointment, as it is about such as any well-informed individual might himself have written. There is nothing that is new in it, and little that is clarifying—and certainly nothing that can be used to any great advantage in advancing the cause of Christian unity. But it must be remembered that the real value of this great and historic Christian assembly was not in any statement that it might issue, but rather in the mingling together of representatives of all of these churches in Christian brotherhood, and in frank discussion of the differences which hold them apart. Unquestionably this gathering has started trains of thought and feeling which will profoundly affect Christian understanding, and has begun processes which will work mightily for the advancement of Christian unity.

A world-wide Continuation Committee was appointed to carry on the work of the Conference, and we are happy to know that our own Dr. W. A. Harper was made a member of it. It is earnestly to be hoped that this Continuation Committee will find the way to perpetuate this quest for a closer rapprochement of the churches at the only place in which they are really divided—in the creeds and ceremonies.

The Congregational-Christian Union

36. An Invitation: *"The Haverhill Resolution"*

(1894)

The Christians sent out the "Haverhill Resolution" to the Congregationalists, "or any other denomination seeking such union," from their 1894 quadrennial meeting in Haverhill, Massachusetts. It was produced in the light of the Congregational proposal for union framed by the New Jersey Association and amended slightly by the Congregational National Council into what was sometimes called "The Congregational Quadrilateral" (see vol. 6:6). The resolution is interesting in several respects. First, after nearly a century of all kinds of union rhetoric, toward the end of which they had become a denomination in their own right, the Christians had become much more moderate in their language about union. The introduction to the resolution suggests "practical co-operation," not union or merger, and insists that "organizations of long standing" in the denominations must not be dissolved. Second, instead of identifying denominationalism directly with sectarianism and sin, as Christian leaders at the beginning of the century had done, the resolution speaks respectfully about denominations, insisting upon a distinction between sectarianism and denominationalism. It is admitted that denominations have the possibility of being faithful to Christ rather than being opposed to Christ's will. It proposed a system of fraternization and cooperation between people of different denominations in obedience to the gospel.

These milder and more nuanced Christian leaders valued their own denominational identity and were comfortable making a very

---

Source: Appendix II ["The Haverhill Resolution"], reproduced in *Minutes of the National Council of the Congregational Churches of the United States, Ninth Session, Syracuse, N.Y., October 9–14, 1895* (Boston: Congregational Sunday School and Publishing Society, 1896), 300–303.

moderate proposal of "co-operative union" between themselves and the Congregationalists "without detriment to any institutions at present constituted, such as churches, conferences, conventions, associations, publishing houses, mission boards, colleges and theological seminaries, and without impairing the vigorous prosecution of existing enterprises." Although the Christians were as committed to union as they ever were, they had begun to realize how much they might stand to lose by hasty action. These overtures led to the first proposal for a Christian-Congregational union, the "Craigville Recommendations" of August 1898 (see vol. 6:18).

The Congregationalist body is avowedly creedless. It stands on the Bible alone, allowing a large liberty of interpretation. It seeks to centre itself upon that which is simply Christian. The obvious fact that differences which, fifty years ago, separated them from the Christians and Free Baptists no longer exist, is recognized by them. This is brought about by changes in their own denominational attitude which have been going on for years. There has arisen among them an outspoken desire for closer affiliation with us and the Free Baptists. The overtures of the New Jersey Conference of Congregationalists are well understood. These have been indorsed by the Congregationalists of Michigan and elsewhere. Congregationalists have met in sessions of our own bodies in friendly interchange of Christian fellowship, and expressed their readiness for practical co-operation. Some of our Conferences have responded in a kindred spirit. The action of our New Jersey and Michigan Conferences will be presented to us by brethren representing those bodies.

Of our own attitude a few words are to be said. Our position has always and avowedly been against division in the Church of Christ on the lines of non-essential differences. We avow that the Church of Christ is *one;* that it consists of all those who are the disciples of the Lord Jesus Christ, accepted of him into his fellowship, regardless of personal beliefs or denominational relations; and that no conditions of fellowship should be held that will not *include all* and *exclude none* of those who stand in vital fellowship with Christ. Here we stand. We cannot reject overtures that come to us in harmony with this position. We cannot turn a cold shoulder on any Christian or body of Christians who propose to join us in work for Christ and the building up of his kingdom on ground of our own choosing. To do so would be to repudiate our own professions and turn our backs on all for which we have all these years contended. On the other hand, we have nothing to yield of the fundamentals of our position.

But we cannot consent to the putting up of any bars which would fence out any part of God's true children, even for the sake of a closer union with another part. Nor again, can we yield anything which is essential to true discipleship, anything which is essential to the nobility and completeness of human character, which the Gospel contemplates, and is in the world to effect.

We do not believe that, even for the greatest efficiency in united labor, it is necessary that existing organizations and vested interests should be surrendered. Organizations of long standing and permanent efficiency, especially such as hold important trusts, cannot be easily set aside. They need not be. They are necessary instrumentalities of efficient Christian work. The evil of different organizations does not come from the fact of their existence, but from the uses to which they are put. The existence of different fire companies is not in the way of efficiency in case of a fire, provided they all play to the same end—to extinguish the fire. The evil would come if too many companies were organized in the same town, so that none of them would have force enough to be efficient in action, or if they should turn their hose on each other when they ought to be playing on the fire.

The one end to be considered by us is, How can the cause of Christ be best promoted? How far, and in what way, are existing divisions in the way of its promotion? What does the best interests of the great cause demand? The dissolution of organizations or any of them? Or the combination of them in active work, in any and all ways which the higher interests of the cause demand? An army divided into companies, regiments, and corps is more effective than the same number of men in an agglomerated mass. We are here of different churches and conferences, but of one body. The army of Christ must have sub-divisions, demanded by location and by special work for special ends. There is all the difference in the world between sectarianism and denominational fidelity. It depends on whether the fidelity is for the denomination, for its own sake, to make it strong against rival denominations, or for Christ's sake, to create and give efficiency to an instrumentality to be used, subordinating its whole life and existence to Christ and his cause. When this latter spirit predominates, the question of denominational differences will lose its significance, and denominational, or rather Christian, likenesses in spirit and aims will draw all together; and co-operation—offensive, defensive, and aggressive—will be the natural result. Christians, in whose heart is the love of Christ, if they come together and work, will easily feel themselves one.

In this way and in this spirit, a system of fraternization and co-operation can be entered into at once between people of different denomination which really subordinate their work and fellowships to the high purposes of the Gospel. . . .

Our action should not limit itself to the members of any one body. Any Christian or body of Christians who will meet us, as we would meet them, to devise measures for interdenominational and inter-Christian fraternization and co-operation for Gospel work, shall have a sincere welcome. We hold and avow ourselves ready to work together with any body on conditions simply Christian for simply Christian ends. Your committee, would, therefore, recommend that this Convention express itself in the adoption of the following resolution:—

WHEREAS, It is a fundamental principle with our Christian body that the followers of Christ should not be divided, but united in a combined work for the upbuilding of the kingdom of righteousness, and

WHEREAS, Generally among Christians and bodies of Christians in recent times there is a strong tendency in this direction, so much so that recently direct overtures have come to us from the Congregationalists for closer fraternal relations and co-operative action, and

WHEREAS, We are in favor of any practical measures which promise greater good for Christ through wider co-operation among his disciples, therefore,

Resolved, (1) That the American Christian Convention approve the formation of a co-operative union between the Christians and the Congregationalists, or any other denomination seeking such union, or between the Christians and any one of the others, it being understood that the co-operating bodies are in parity of Christian standing, and that the co-operative union is not based upon doctrinal tests.

Resolved, (2) That the Christian bodies entering such co-operative union are to have common interest in spreading the gospel, and are to labor for the promotion of the common welfare; but that its work is to be conducted without detriment to any institutions as at present constituted, such as churches, conferences, conventions, associations, publishing houses, mission boards, colleges and theological seminaries, and without impairing the vigorous prosecution of existing enterprises.

Resolved, (3) That members of churches within such co-operative union, on change of residence to a community unprovided with a church of their own people, be encouraged to join some church within the co-operating bodies in preference to any other.

Resolved, (4) That should any ministers who are members of any of the co-operating bodies accept calls from any churches of any of the other bodies, their names may be held on the lists of members of their own bodies while in good standing and remaining within the union, *pro-*

vided that their names should not stand on corresponding lists of two bodies.

Resolved, (5) That we advise the appointment by this convention of a Commission of twelve members, to act in concert with similar commissions of other bodies on all matters pertaining to the interests involved.

Resolved, (6) That in any action of the commissions, the vote of one third of the members present, representing any one body, shall negative the action proposed so far as our body is concerned.

Resolved, (7) That this body approves the taking of similar action by State associations or Conferences or other subordinate bodies, but that all action may be subject to revision by the national bodies represented in any co-operative union.

Resolved, (8) That it is the opinion and sentiment of this convention that the ultimate ideal of Christian union is the union of all the followers of Christ in one body, in an organic union, inspired with the spirit of the Master, existing and acting with single reference to carrying on his work, building up his kingdom, and bringing the world to Christ; and we would encourage and co-operate with any and all measures looking to this end.

The Commissioners appointed were: Messrs. J. B. Weston, D.D., Stanfordville, N.Y.; J. J. Summerbell, D.D., Lewisburg, Penn.; Elisha Mudge, Briton, Mich.; Albert Dunlap, Columbus, O.; Robert Harris, Urbane, Ill.; T. M. McWhinney, D.D., Marion, Ind.; C. J. Jones, D.D., Norfolk, Va.; Martyn Summerbell, D.D., Lewiston, Me.; B. Mason, Springboro, Pa.; John Whittaker, Weaubleau, Mo.; the Rev. J. T. Phillips, Graysville, Ind., and E. L. Goodwin, Esq., Boston, Mass.

37. Getting beyond History: *"Christian Union a Primary Need" and "The Purposes of the Christian Unity Period"*

(1927)

W. A. Harper; Frank G. Coffin

When W. A. Harper wrote "Christian Union a Primary Need" and Frank G. Coffin wrote "The Purposes of the Christian Unity Period" in 1927, they demonstrated the seasoned wisdom about ecumenism to which 123 years of experience had brought the Christian denomination.

On the surface the two articles appear very different. Harper's address was given to ordinary people at a fellowship supper between two congregations, one Christian and the other Congregational, newly joined in a United Church in Raleigh, North Carolina. Coffin's piece was the official announcement of a denomination-wide, month-long "Christian Unity Period" set aside by the Christian leadership to broaden and intensify their members' commitment to ecumenism. Both, however, exhibited the clear-sightedness and a breadth of view that showed how far the Christians had come.

Each of these leaders revealed his conviction that what stood in the way of union was not so much the deficiencies of other people or denominations but the frailties of the Christians themselves: their habits of priding themselves on their own pedigrees and distinctiveness and showing prejudice and lack of appreciation for people different from

---

Source: W. A. Harper, "Christian Union a Primary Need," *Herald of Gospel Liberty,* 2 June 1927, 511–12; F. G. Coffin, "The Purposes of the Christian Unity Period," *Herald of Gospel Liberty,* 29 December 1927, 1226.

themselves; their tendency to allow elements of material wealth and status to loom larger for them than the "common welfare of the Kingdom."

Both men recognized that ecumenism must begin where each person "is," whether in a Raleigh fellowship hall or any other community where there is diversity of Christian expression. Only when the Christians were able to surmount these barriers to union would they be able to move on to find their place in the global ecumenical movement.

They recognized also that union could be achieved only by carefully "organized effort," with retraining away from familiar divisive patterns and education toward unitive patterns. What people have to say together needed to become more important to them than what they have to say separately.

In these two articles the Christians show an increased maturity in their understanding and pursuit of union. They were ready to join with another denomination in a unity larger than both of them together. They were ready to unite in the Congregational Christian Churches.

Christian Union a Primary Need

An address given at a Fellowship Supper held on May 5 between the Congregationalists and Christians in the new United Church at Raleigh, N.C.

I have great pleasure in bringing a word of greeting on this occasion and to give expression to the faith that stirs within me that it is God's will and Christ's earnest desire that the two Churches here met in fellowship tonight may take the step so necessary for Christian union, the formation of an organization which shall include them both organically and functionally in the interest of Christian union not only for themselves but for the whole world.

Christian union is the Church's primary need.

It is perfectly clear from the Scripture that we will never win the world to Jesus, that the world will never become Christian, until the Church of Jesus is united. Before his crucifixion Jesus prayed that his followers may be one; and he gives a reason for that prayer, "That the world may believe that thou hast sent me."

However discomforting it may be to those of us who profess to be his followers when we think of our divided condition, we cannot escape the truth that our divisions are responsible for the defeat of our Christian hope, and, what is more, that they are responsible for the failure so far of the mission of Jesus in the world.

We have been busy in important matters, we grant. Surely the work of our missionary departments, of our Christian educational institutions, of our orphanages, of our ministerial relief, of our hospitals, and of our other Christian enterprises is an important work; but these things are secondary to the primary obligation of the forces of Christ in the world. If we recognize him as Lord and Master, as surely we do, then we should not only continue to pursue the splendid work we have entered upon in his name but should make central and primary in our whole program the fundamental thing for which he prayed, and the failure to achieve it weakens our whole effort. Because we wish the Kingdom of Jesus Christ to prosper in the world we must enter upon a campaign for Christian union.

Let us learn a lesson from the American government. In 1772 we were thirteen colonies stretching along the Atlantic seaboard like a shoe string. Each colony was, so to speak, a separate denomination with its own ideals, plane, and purposes, but zealously devoted to the cause of democracy and freedom. Under stress of opposition these colonies came together; and in a little more than a hundred and fifty years these thirteen colonies have grown in power, in influence, and in prestige until today our government is recognized by all as one of the outstanding achievements of human progress in democracy. United we have stood through these years, and so progress and growth and success have come. There would have been a very different story to relate if we had continued separate and distinct.

In order to affect this union and to achieve this major experiment in democratic living, these colonies each had to give up something, but they have received far more than they gave up. Sacrifice always brings such rich reward, and the Church is no exception to this principle.

Why are we kept apart anyway in our Christian effort? It seems to me that there are three simple reasons for this and I may be privileged briefly to state them as follows:

1. Pride in our religious pedigree. If we knew less church history, we could more readily agree.

2. Insistence on distinctive things, the things for which we peculiarly stand, rather than the magnifying of things on which we are agreed. Theology is a voluminous science. It is not always luminous.

3. Property rights and official positions. The only man who turned away from Christ sorrowful was the rich young ruler. He had property and

held an office. If the church were over night bereft of all property and all officers, it would unite before six o'clock in the morning.

The final step in the realization of a reform measure is organized effort. First there must be consecration to the cause, then a genuine fellowship of prophetic souls, and finally organized effort to make effective the Christian purpose of the prophets of the new day. It, therefore, remains for churches like the Congregational and the Christian, one already in spirit and purpose, to become one in effective organization and then to attract to themselves still other Christian agencies, so that in the course of time and in fulfillment of the prayer of Christ the Christian world may be a whole and as a whole may achieve victory for Christ throughout the whole wide world.

The Purposes of the Christian Unity Period

The period from January 9 to February 6, 1928, is set apart in the calendar of the church activities for an emphasis on Christian Unity. The purposes to be served are:

1. To put the hearts and energies of our people into perfect unity with the spirit and purpose of Christ. A complete unity with Christ is the only possible basis, or even hope, of unity with others.
2. To devote ourselves to penitence and prayer for our own prejudices and the quickening of our appreciation of all fellow-Christians. It should be to each a period of self-discovery and self-improvement in Christian fraternity.
3. To study and pray so intensely over the needs of our day for the way of Christ in all things and the common welfare of the Kingdom of God that the great task may challenge us and God's spirit prompt us to a negligence of our minor differences.
4. To draw our own people East, West, North, and South into a more complete program of co-operation such as we idealize among others in our theories of Christian Unity.
5. To develop a more generous spirit and larger helpfulness to other churches in our own community and to make ourselves, wherever we may be located, a factor for unification in all community life. How can we love unity with others whom we have not seen if we love not a sister church whom we have seen?

6. To launch special study of the progress and programs of all co-operative movements of the Kingdom, discover our place of responsibility in them and for them, and begin immediate efforts to discharge the same.
7. To inaugurate a system of education and training which will lead childhood away from the prejudices which have hampered the past. If this is not done the period will have failed in its most strategic possibility.
8. To vision further steps to be taken in the interest of Christian Unity and co-operation, study the methods by which they may be accomplished, and enlist our whole church in effecting them.
9. To distribute literature, circulate our periodicals, educate through the church school, young people's organizations, sermons, prayer meetings, women's organizations, men's groups, etc., toward a closer affiliation of all Christian agencies.
10. To close the period with a substantial offering for the support of the Federal Council of the Churches of Christ in America and the maintenance of our membership therein, and to make possible the promotional work for union as authorized by the General Convention and conducted by the Commission on Christian Unity.

38. Unity Near:

"Christian-Congregational Meeting" and "The Congregational-Christian Proposal"

(1928)

When correspondence was reopened in 1923 between the Commission on Christian Unity of the Christian Church and the Commission on Interchurch Relations of the Congregational Churches, the two denominations were much more experienced in the ways of ecumenism than they had been at the time of the "Craigville Recommendations" for union between them in 1897 (see vol. 6:18). Although the Christians were largely rural and the Congregationalists largely urban, the Christians relatively poor and the Congregationalists relatively affluent, the Christians comparatively small and the Congregationalists comparatively large, they had important things in common. Each emphasized local church autonomy and a toleration for variation in doctrinal beliefs; each insisted that individuals had a right and responsibility to hold their own views without interference by ecclesiastical authority.

The Christians swung into preparing their people for a possible merger immediately. They published articles by their own and Congregational leaders explaining the history and beliefs of the Congregationalists and discussing union. They exchanged pulpits with the Congregationalists in local congregations and exchanged delegates to denominational meetings. In addition, they planned joint local and regional denominational

---

Source: Commission on Christian Unity of the Christian Church and Commission on Interchurch Relations of the Congregational Church, "Christian-Congregational Meeting," *Herald of Gospel Liberty,* 16 December 1926, 1192; idem, "The Congregational-Christian Proposal: Recommendations Relating to the Organic Union of the Christian and Congregational Churches," *Herald of Gospel Liberty,* 19 April 1928, 374.

meetings, so their members could come to know one another personally. When a joint meeting of the Commission on Christian Unity of the Christian Church and the Commission on Interchurch Relations of the Congregationalists adopted a joint declaration discussing union in 1926, every reader of the Herald of Gospel Liberty *could read the proposals. And when the recommendations for organic union made by the relevant commissions on union were finally published in 1928, the Christians as a whole were familiar with the Congregationalists, well-versed in the relevant merger issues, and ready to move onward toward union.*

Christian-Congregational Meeting

Last summer, committees from the Commission on Christian Unity of the Christian Church and from a similar commission of the Congregational Church met in joint session at Cleveland, Ohio, to discuss what might be done to deepen friendship and cooperation between the two bodies. The result of this meeting was the adoption of the following joint declaration. . . .

An informal discussion of the characteristics of the two denominations led to the following statements:

1. *As to relative size:* The Congregationalists number 901,660; the Christians 103,091. There are 5,826 Congregational Churches as against 1,134 Christian Churches; there are 6,000 Congregational Sunday-schools and about 1,000 Christian Schools.
2. *In organization:* Each communion is representatively governed.
3. *As to ordination:* Ministers of the Christian Church are ordained by a district gathering, virtually as Congregational ministers are coming very generally to be ordained.
4. *As to baptism:* The Christian Church uses all methods of baptism according to the desire of the candidates. Immersion still has the greater preference, though there is an increasing tendency toward sprinkling. Since Christian character alone is the basis of membership baptism is in no case the method of entrance into the church; therefore the Quaker is accepted without water baptism on an equal footing with the immersionist.

There would be opposition, perhaps quite strong, in the Christian Church to absorption by Congregationalism, but it would seem that the two churches could draw together in a very close fellowship which might in good time lead to some act of genuine union. The principal difficulty, aside from the matter of name, would arise in the fairly definite belief by many of the Christian denomination that Congregationalists insist upon a binding creed.

The ultimate results of the discussion were the following six [*sic*] findings:

1. Each church has the congregational form of government.
2. In each, the individual church is the unit of authority.
3. Each church accepts and practices representative government with regard to matters of common concern to the churches.
4. Each church accepts the Bible as the rule of faith and practice, recognizing the right of free individual interpretation.
5. Neither church holds to a creed which is binding upon individuals or upon churches.
6. Each is agreed upon the general foundational tenets of our common Christianity.
7. The Congregational statement of 1913 and the Principles of the Christian Church we find essentially in accord in evangelical temper and inclusive in their scope.

In view of the above and the added fact that it is our unanimous conviction that all Christian believers should now be brought into the closest possible fellowship and co-operation, the two subcommittees unite in making to their respective Commissions the following recommendations:

1. In view of the similarities in organization, belief, observance of ordinances and general practices between the Christian and Congregational Churches, and to the end that they may know each other better and enter definitely into a common fellowship, it is recommended that in States, districts, and towns where churches of both denominations exist side by side, they be urged to take steps toward close co-operation as an expression of the unity that ought to exist.

2. As steps in this direction, we recommend:

   (a) The holding in any one State of the state meetings of both bodies at the same date with some sessions in common;

   (b) We also suggest that a similar plan may be used in districts and in cities;

   (c) We further urge an exchange of fraternal delegates at every opportunity.

3. With regard to new enterprises, we recommend that the church extension agencies of our two bodies be urged to refuse to organize a new church of one body in a community already served by the other. We would urge that in cities all forward movements relating to the two denominations should be guided in accordance with the principles adopted in Cleveland by the Presbyterian and Congregational denominations.

4. We further recommend that where the members of either communion move into communities which do not have the church of which they have been members, they seriously consider the other denomination mentioned in these resolutions.

5. We recommend finally that in the whole missionary, educational, and publishing program of the two denominations, there be as far as possible an interchange of representatives so that each communion may quickly become familiar with the workings of the other.

With the informal expression of the hope that this meeting would lead to arrangements for a much more representative gathering which should have the very definite purpose of drawing the two denominations into as close a relationship as possible, the meeting adjourned with prayer by Dr. Peters.

The Congregational-Christian Proposal

Recommendations Relating to the Organic Union
of the Christian and Congregational Churches

The undersigned representatives appointed from the Commission on Interchurch Relations of the Congregational Churches and the Commission on Christian Unity of the Christian Church believe that the hour has come when, in the interest of the Kingdom of God and of the larger usefulness of their respective denominations, these two communions should immediately take steps toward an organic union.

We therefore recommend to our prospective Commissions, and through them, to the National Council of Congregational Churches and to the General Convention of the Christian Church:

1. That each of them at the earliest possible date take action endorsing an organic union between the Congregational and Christian Churches.
2. That the basis of this new relation shall be the recognition by each group that the other group is constituted of the followers of Jesus Christ. Each individual church and each group of churches shall be free to retain and develop its own form of expression. Finding in the Bible the supreme rule of faith and life but recognizing that there is room for wide differences of opinion among equally good Christians, this union shall be conditioned upon the acceptance of Christianity as primarily a way of life, and not upon uniformity of theological opinion or any uniform practice of ordinances.
3. That the autonomy of each local congregation and the right of each individual member to follow Christ according to his own conscience shall remain undisturbed.
4. That the United Church shall for the time being be called "Congregational-Christian," allowing each local church to continue the use of its present name if it so desires.
5. That as soon as this proposal shall have been ratified by the official bodies of the two organizations, a committee of equal number from each communion, adequately representative of each denomination, shall be appointed to study the whole situation carefully and to recommend a plan for the complete unification and management of their enterprises and program of work. In the meantime every possible step should be taken by the two Commissions to promote mutual acquaintance among the two constituencies and to canvass the practical questions involved in a merger.
6. That as soon as possible after the joint committee provided in the preceding paragraph is ready to report, a general convention including the two bodies shall be arranged, at which the report of the committee shall be acted upon. For this joint convention the executive committees of the two denominations shall make all arrangements.

7. The commissions recognize that numerous practical details will be involved. They are confident, however, that being united in purpose no insuperable obstacles will appear, and therefore propose that the two bodies go forward in mutual confidence.

FOR THE COMMISSION OF CHRISTIAN UNITY
FRANK G. COFFIN,
LEON E. SMITH.
FOR THE COMMISSION OF INTERCHURCH RELATIONS
FRANK K. SAUNDERS,
CHARLES E. BURTON.

These recommendations have now been approved by the Commission on Christian Unity of the Christian Church. The members of this Commission are:

Dr. F. G. Coffin, *Chairman of the Commission,* Iowa City, Iowa.

Dr. R. C. Helfenstein, Dover, Dela.
Dr. F. H. Peters, Defiance, Ohio.
Dr. Alva M. Kerr, Dayton, Ohio.
Dr. L. E. Smith, Norfolk, Va.
Dr. W. H. Denison, Dayton, Ohio.
Dr. W. A. Harper, Elon College, N.C.

39. Union Accomplished:

"Plan of Union," "The Preamble and Basis," and "Union Consummated"

(1929 and 1931)

Although there was much talk before and after the union of the Christians and the Congregationalists suggesting that the Christians were "lost" or "absorbed" in the union, a look at the documents forming the union reveals how careful the framers were to lift up and protect the identity and concerns of the Christians.

From quite early in the nineteenth century, the Six Principles of the Christian Church had been the banner behind which the Christians believed all churches could unite, and the Sixth Principle had spelled out the goal and rationale for all work toward unity. In the Congregational-Christian union the Six Principles did in fact provide the basis for union, if only because the two groups actually shared these concerns.

The second paragraph of section 1 of the "Plan of Union" shows how the planners protected the autonomy of the local church, as well as each individual's right to judge matters of faith according to his or her own conscience. The Bible is lifted up as the supreme rule of faith and life, and great toleration is urged for whatever differences in interpreting the Bible might occur. Even the Christian emphasis on Christianity as primarily a way of life, rather than a matter of doctrinal agreement, is preserved.

Moreover, when the new periodical Congregationalist and Herald of

---

Source: "Plan of Union of the Congregational and Christian Churches," *Herald of Gospel Liberty,* 14 November 1929, 890–92; "The Preamble and Basis" with editorial "Union Consummated," *Congregationalist and Herald of Gospel Liberty,* 9 July 1931, 923. (The Preamble and Basis compared to the Six Principles of the Christian Church prepared by Elsabeth Slaughter Hilke.)

Gospel Liberty *(1930) announced the adoption of the constitution of the new denomination and placed the preamble and basis to that constitution in a central position, anyone familiar with the historic Six Principles could see how these concerns remained central to the identity of the new denomination. The Christians had believed from the beginning that union meant giving up more parochial concerns and "sinking into union with the Body of Christ at large." They were proud to take such a major step in the movement toward the union of all Christ's followers.*

Plan of Union of the Congregational and Christian Churches

I. Sec. 1. That the National Council of the Congregational Churches and The General Convention of the Christian Church be united under the title of the General Council of the Congregational and Christian Churches (Unincorporated) looking toward complete union so soon as necessary legal steps can be taken, both national bodies to continue for the time being their organizations to meet legal requirements, while constituting the membership of the general organization. (Invitation is extended to other bodies to join this union. In the event of favorable action by one or more national bodies, it is agreed that a new and more inclusive name shall be chosen for the General Council.)

That the basis of this new relation shall be the recognition by each group that the other group is constituted of the followers of Jesus Christ. Each individual church and each group of churches shall be free to retain and develop its own form of expression. Finding in the Bible the supreme rule of faith and life, but recognizing that there is wide room for differences of interpretation among equally good Christians, this union shall be conditioned upon the acceptance of Christianity as primarily a way of life, and not upon uniformity of theological opinion or any uniform practice of ordinances

Sec. 2. The purpose of the General Council shall be to perform on behalf of the united churches the various functions heretofore performed by the National Council for the Congregational churches and the General Convention for the Christian churches, it being understood that where technical legal questions may be involved the action of the separate bodies shall be secured.

That for the first four years the Moderator of the National Council and the President of the General Convention shall be co-ordinate presiding officers, their service to be arranged by mutual agreement; that for the time being the National Council and the Secretary of the General Convention, while continuing their respective positions, shall be Secretaries of the General Council under such division of responsibility as shall be determined by the General Council or its Executive Committee.

That regular meetings of the General Council be held biennially in the spring or early summer of odd numbered years, and that these be so arranged as that necessary business meetings of the National Council and of the General Convention may be held for legal action and other necessary business.

II. That pending possible mergers among themselves, the larger units (i.e. the five Regional and the Afro-Christian Conventions, the Congregational "State" Conferences), and after merger the united bodies, shall severally be represented in the General Council by two delegates each, and each such Convention or Conference having churches whose aggregate membership is more than ten thousand shall be entitled to elect two additional delegates for each additional ten thousand members or major fraction thereof; provided that no conference with three or more churches shall be without representation.

III. That pending merger, local units (i.e. Christian conferences and Congregational district associations), and after merger the united bodies, be represented in the General Council on the basis of one delegate for every ten churches or major fraction thereof.

IV. That heads of church colleges and seminaries recognized by the General Council as affiliated with or co-operating with it, or with either communion, the National General Secretaries as defined in the by-laws and editors of national church periodicals, together with the officers of the national body, be members ex-officiis of the General Council.

V. That in order to conserve legal interest the charter of The General Convention of the Christian Church and that of the Corporation for the National Council of Congregational Churches be continued in force unless and until it becomes possible and seems wise to combine them.

VI. That the voluntary declaration of the representatives of each communion to the effect that they and their work ought not to be a charge on the financial resources of the other be recognized as the general principle to govern in adjustment of financial obligations; that therefore for the time being the miscellaneous expenses of the General Council shall be pro-rated on the basis of the relative membership of the two denominations, and that the expenses incident to continuing any officer, service, or missionary enterprise now carried by either denomination, together with present indebtedness, shall be met from the resources of that fellowship. Here, however, the fact is taken into account that there may be natural shiftings of constituency from one denomination to the other, as also changes in the work to be done which will call for corresponding adjustments. It is recognized, however, that where the arrangement at the start is equitable the combined constituency can be trusted faithfully to care for the combined work without fear of discrimination. It is contemplated that during the period of transition savings in overhead expense are not to be expected, but that gradually such will result. It is hoped, however, that all will think of such economics as making more kingdom building possible rather than as lessening the challenge to the grace of giving.

VII. That the promotion of income for missionary and educational work be committed to a Commission on Missions of the General Council consisting of the members of the jointly elected official administrative mission boards (that is, for the Congregational churches, the Prudential Committee of the American Board and the Directors of the Home Board), nine members-at-large (of whom at least one shall be from the Christian constituency) and the two presiding officers and the two Secretaries of the General Council ex-officiis.

VIII. That the functions of the General Council comparable to those now performed by the Executive Committees of the National Council and of the General Convention not otherwise provided for, be committed to an Executive Committee of the General Council composed of the members of the Executive Committee of the National Council (16 members), together with the President, Vice-President, Secretary, and Treasurer of the General Convention.

IX. That the functions of the Board of Missions of the Christian Convention in the foreign field and those of the Prudential Committee of the American Board of Commissioners for Foreign Missions be discharged by one body composed of identical members until such time as the constituent corporations may be legally merged.

X. That the functions of the Board of Missions in the home field, the Board of Christian Education and the Board of Publications of the General Convention, and those of the group of societies known as the Congregational Home Boards, be discharged by one body composed of identical members until such time as the constituent corporations may be legally merged.

XI. It is conceived that during the transition the provisions of IX and X shall be worked out substantially as follows:

1. Until corporate merger can be effected the Board of Missions of the Christian Church shall by necessary action constitute the Prudential Committee of the American Board its agent for the conduct of foreign missionary work, exclusive of that in Puerto Rico, and the American Board shall elect at least four members from the Christian constituency as full voting members of its Prudential Committee in the class of members-at-large.

2. That the Board of Missions, the Board of Christian Education, and the Board of Publications of the Christian churches shall by necessary action constitute the Board of Directors of the Congregational Home Boards, with its several Administrative Committees, their agents for home missions and church extension, Christian education and publication, and that at least four members from the Christian constituency be elected full voting members of the Board of Directors of the Home Board and a total of at least six members of the several Administrative Committees of the Home Board be elected from the Christian constituency, also two members of the Foundation for Education.

3. That Missionary Secretaries shall be appointed by the General Convention in such number as it may deem needful.

4. That the work of the Board of Missions of the Christian Convention in Porto Rico and at Franklinton College be transferred to the Administrative Committee serving the American Missionary Association, together with the resources for the maintenance of the same.

5. That agreeably with present practice responsibility for the work of home and foreign missions and church extension of the Afro-Christian Convention continue with that convention, its successor or successors, on the principle of self-supporting states among the Congregational churches.

XII. That the Christian Convention request the Administrative Committee on Ministerial Relief to further the cause of ministerial relief among the Christian churches with a view to bringing its ministry to a basis similar to that of the Congregational churches and in the hope of ultimate oneness of this work. Further: That whereas the Christian churches now give a certain amount of ministerial aid through local and regional conferences and understanding it to be the desire of the Christian churches to bring about as soon as possible national administration of ministerial aid, and that the Christian churches will welcome the leadership of the Administrative Committee on Ministerial Relief in perfecting an adequate plan for the aid of their own aged and retired ministers until such time as the merger shall become more nearly complete; and further,

That inasmuch as the Annuity Fund for Congregational Ministers seems to be legally forbidden to admit as members any except "Congregational" ministers, a movement be put on foot among the Christian churches to develop plans under which benefits comparable to those available for Congregational ministers shall be provided for ministers of the Christian churches, utilizing the experience and good offices of the Congregational Ministerial Boards.

XIII. That of necessity trust funds and moneys given for specific purposes must be administered strictly in accordance with the terms of trusts and the intention of donors so far as expressed. And further,

That until complete unity can be worked out all other moneys contributed by either group of churches shall be administered for the established work of those churches unless otherwise determined by the donors.

XIV. That the present status of educational institutions with reference to their denominational bodies be preserved, and that where mergers of educational institutions are possible they be encouraged.

XV. That the General Council name a commission on evangelism and devotional life to consist of the members of the Commission on Evangelism of the National Council, twenty-four in number, plus three persons chosen from the Christian Church constituency. This commission shall promote a program of evangelism and devotional life in all the churches. With a view to conserving all spiritual values, the Commission on Evangelism of the National Council shall be wholly free to adapt the general program to the needs of the Congregational churches and the representatives of the Christian Church shall be equally free to do likewise for the Christian churches. The work for life service, for which the Board of Evangelism is now responsible in the Christian Church, shall be committed to the Student Life Department of the Home Board.

XVI. The work of the Board of Finance of the Christian Convention in the field of benevolence being committed to the Commission on Missions, its responsibility for the finances of the General Convention itself and its share of the expenses of the General Council may be retained or committed to the members of the Executive Committee of the General Council who represent the Christian constituency, as may be determined by the General Convention.

XVII. That the business of publishing be combined as far as possible; that in particular a common Year Book shall be issued in the immediate future on the general tabular scheme of the Congregational Year Book and that in this Year Book for the time being at least all churches be published together for a given state or district, with separate sub-headings in each schedule for the Christian and Congregational churches, or with distinguishing marks as may be determined.

In case the Home Board as constituted above should deem it unwise to administer The Christian Publishing Association Building and printing plant in Dayton, Ohio, the General Convention shall be wholly free to make use of or dispose of this plant as it deems wise.

XVIII. That periodicals be merged as soon as the way is clear and to the extent found desirable. The Herald of Gospel Liberty and The Congregationalist may well be merged, possibly under a wholly new name. If, however, it should seem better to either group to continue indefinitely both periodicals, this may be done without breach of the spirit of unity, financial responsibility being carried by the respective constituencies.

XIX. That the Woman's Mission Board of The General Convention of the Christian Church shall be entirely free to determine its own course of action. The recommendation is strongly made, however, that its activities be applied to the whole program of the Church in co-operation with the Woman's organizations in the Congregational Church.

XX. That the appointment of bureaus and commissions be determined with the view of conserving all the recognized activities of both churches.

XXI. That a similar policy apply to representation in interdenominational and other bodies.

XXII. That in view of the requirement that beneficiaries of the C. B. M. R. and members of the Annuity Fund for Congregational Ministers must be Congregational ministers, ministerial ordination and standing be continued separately but with the endeavor to reach common standards as soon as possible.

XXIII. That regional, state, and local organizations of each denomination, being wholly self-determining, be free to continue as at present, with full fellowship in the General Council, but that conference with these bodies be had with a view to unification on lines comparable with the proposals for national union.

That in states or districts where the churches of one denomination are very few these might simply unite with the other body, retaining their name locally if desired; likewise, that in districts where the number is greater but still relatively quite few, these might be united with the other body as a unit, continuing their own name, as for example, the Christian Association of the Massachusetts Congregational Conference, thus retaining their denominational connection while uniting with the Congregationalists but without requiring the organization of a new state body. Likewise, for example, there could be the Congregational Conference in affiliation with the North Carolina Christian Convention or Conference.

Each local church may continue wholly unchanged in name and in organization. Any changes which seem wise may be made by the churches themselves, but it is recommended that the Joint Commission appoint an advisory commission, representative of the General Convention and the National Council, to assist conferences, associations, conventions, and churches on all matters involved in readjustment of their organization, legal affairs, and programs in line with this plan of union, this commission to be empowered to appoint local commissions for such adjustments whenever and wherever occasion may cause and such advise be sought.

XXIV. That The General Convention of the Christian Church and the National Council of Congregational Churches be requested to act on the proposals at the earliest possible date; that so soon as these or other plans are approved by the two Commissions, constitution and by-laws for the General Council be drawn up, embodying the principles decided upon, these to be offered to the National Council and to the General Convention for consideration.

XXV. In conclusion, these plans and recommendations of necessity deal with legal and technical details, but they have their justification in the spirit of unity which they presuppose and are designated to promote. If a desire for that unity for which the Master once prayed be the actuating motive of all plans and all acts, the way will become clear, as we proceed, where now it may appear filled with uncertainties, hesitation, and hindrance. We may be sure that no legal entanglements will be too difficult, no ecclesiastical customs too deeply fixed, no sentiments seem too precious to yield, no ambitions or personal commitments too intense, if the will to achieve be ours and the Spirit of God lead us. Going forward, thus led, we may ourselves secure, and may make plain to others, the road to joyous fellowship and enlarged usefulness.

The Preamble and Basis

The Congregational and Christian Churches of the United States, by delegates assembled, reserving all the rights and cherished memories of their historic past and affirming loyalty to the basic principles of unity and democracy in church polity, hereby set forth the principles of Christian fellowship immemorially held by these churches.

We hold sacred the freedom of the individual soul and the right of private judgment. We stand for the autonomy of the local church and its independence of ecclesiastical control. We cherish the fellowship of churches, united in district, state, and national bodies for counsel and cooperation. Affirming these convictions we hold to the unity of the Church of Christ, and will unite with all its branches in fellowship and hearty cooperation; and we earnestly seek that the prayer of our Lord for the unity of his followers may be speedily answered.

We find in the Bible the supreme rule of faith and life, but recognize wide room for differences in interpretation. We therefore base our union upon the acceptance of Christianity as primarily a way of life, and not upon uniformity of theological opinion or any uniform practice of ordinances.

United in these principles and in accordance with the Plan of Union adopted by their national bodies in 1929, the Congregational and Christian Churches in general council assembled agree in adopting the following constitution.

Union Consummated

Final Stage in Union of Congregational and Christian Churches. Constitution Adopted.

BY THE EDITOR

It was a momentous event when at noon on Saturday, June 27, in Plymouth Church, Seattle, the General Convention of Christian Churches assembled with the National Council of Congregational Churches, already in session in that auditorium, and Moderator Carl S. Patton, handing the gavel of office to Acting President D. B. Atkinson, gave to the latter the honor of putting the motion the adoption of which represented the final act in the organic union of Christians and Congregationalists.

Both Council and Convention had already adopted the proposed constitution for the new General Council, in their separate sessions, and now in joint session, Dr. Morris H. Turk, minister of the historic Williston Church in Portland, Me., where the Christian Endeavor Society had its birth, and acting for the time as chairman of the Congregational Commission on Interchurch Relations, in the unavoidable absence of Dr. Frank K. Sanders, the chairman, moved that the constitution be adopted and that "accordingly the said General Council be declared instituted and operative as of this date."

There was no staging of anything spectacular, no outward evidence of the momentous thing that was happening in creating the largest union of churches in history, but the great audience spontaneously burst into singing of *Blest be the tie that binds our hearts in Christian love;* and that was the most fitting symbol and expression of thankfulness and hope that could have been devised, had more studied preparation been made.

The adoption of the constitution in the Congregational group, and in the Christian group also, had previously been unanimous, and the same unanimity was in the joint meeting. For legal purposes National Council and Christian Convention will continue to exist, but over all and uniting all will be the new General Council, in which Congregational and Christian churches will hereafter be represented, not as separate nor as joint groups, but as one, having a common life and purpose and a common national and spiritual unity of fellowship in *The General Council of the Congregational and Christian Churches.*

The By-Laws relating to the new union, at this time of writing, are yet to come up for action seriatim, but the chief matter has been decided and the goal of prayer and hope in the blending of free churches, with a noble witness and heritage, into a common life and common tasks in witnessing to the freedom of the Christian spirit and in the manifestation of Christianity, in authority and action, as a way of life, is now determined. Let us meet the future and go on as those whose hearts and lives are bound in the blest ties of Christian love! May the fellowship of the Christians bound together in the General Council of Congregational and Christian churches be in every respect, and in every achievement of triumph, like to that above!

Comparison between . . .

The Preamble and Basis of the Constitution of the Congregational Christian Churches	*The Six Principles of the Christians*
We hold sacred the freedom of the individual soul and the right of private judgment.	5. The right of private judgment and the liberty of conscience, a right and a privilege that should be accorded to and exercised by all.
We stand for the autonomy of the local church and its independence of ecclesiastical control.	1. The Lord Jesus Christ, the only head of the Church.
We cherish the fellowship of the churches, united in district, state and national bodies for counsel and co-operation.	
We find in the Bible the supreme rule of faith and life, but recognize wide room for differences of interpretation.	3. The Holy Scriptures, or the Scriptures of the Old and New Testaments, the only creed, a sufficient rule of faith and practice.
We therefore base our union upon the acceptance of Christianity as primarily a way of life and not upon uniformity of theological opinion or any uniform practice of ordinances.	4. Christian character, or vital Christian piety, is the only and sufficient test of Christian fellowship and Church membership.
Affirming these convictions, we hold to the unity of the Church of Christ, and will unite with all its branches in fellowship and hearty co-operation; and we earnestly seek that the prayer of our Lord for the unity of his followers may be speedily answered.	6. The union of the followers of Christ, to the end that the world may believe.
	2. The name Christian, to the exclusion of all party and sectarian names, sufficient for the followers of Christ.

PART III

The Ecumenical Development of the Reformed Church in the United States

---

The Reformed Church in the United States was a descendent of the German and Swiss Reformed churches originating in the sixteenth century. In Switzerland, these churches were particularly indebted to theologians Ulrich Zwingli of Zurich (1484–1531), Heinrich Bullinger of Zurich (1504–75), and John Calvin of Geneva (1509–64). Zwingli, like Luther, was persuaded by the thought of Augustine and Paul that salvation was not dispensed by the medieval church, but by the sovereign grace of God in Christ (see vol. 2:10–11). Human beings might come to know this grace in Christ through the Word of God in Scripture, which was the sole authority for faith and practice, bringing the faithful person to knowledge of sin and of justification by faith alone. Zwingli was killed in battle during the early years of the Protestant Reformation. His work was carried on by Heinrich Bullinger, who further organized the Reformed movement and contributed greatly to its confessional background (see vol. 2:14). Calvin took Swiss Reformed theological writings to new heights. Trained in law and theology, Calvin gave the Reformed church guidance for its organization and polity, and a massive exposition of its Reformed faith in his *Institutes of the Christian Religion* (see vol. 2:15).

In Germany, the Reformed church was indebted to several early reformers from the Lower Palatinate on the Rhine river: Frederick III (the ruler of the Palatinate from 1559–76) and two young, relatively unknown, theologians, Zacharias Ursinus (1534–83) and Casper Olevianus (1536–87). After Frederick III converted to the Reformed faith from Lutheranism in 1560, he appointed Ursinus and Olevianus to facilitate Lutheran and Reformed cooperation in his domain by preparing a new catechism blending Lutheran and Reformed perspectives. The resulting Heidelberg Catechism (1563) became an important resource for the Reformed Protestants in central Europe for instruction of youth, family devotions, and worship (see vol. 2:21).

Ursinus and Olevianus also produced two other documents that helped delineate a new Reformed church: the Palatinate Liturgy (see vol. 2:22), which prescribed a simplified form of worship in which "altars were replaced by tables, baptismal fonts by zinc vessels, chalices by ordinary cups, and communion wafers by common bread"; and the Palatinate Church Order, which prescribed a presbyterial form of government for the church, functioning through a system of synods composed of laity and clergy.

Through their respect for the ancient ecumenical creeds, and their conviction that the one holy catholic and apostolic church consisted of "all the faithful in all the world and through all time" under a representative authority under Christ's headship, these Swiss Reformers affirmed that the church was one in principle. In an era when rivalries between reforming groups often led to judgments that Christians who did not worship or believe in "correct ways" were lost, the Swiss Reformed churches believed that where the Word was purely preached and reverently heard, and the sacraments administered according to the institution of Christ, the church was present. Diversity on nonessentials, they insisted, ought not be a cause for disunity. Yet, even among these Swiss Reformed Protestants there were theological, national, and linguistic differences that held them back from pursuing relationships with churches that were different.

The Swiss Reformed faith was established in colonial North America by Swiss German immigrants who came to Pennsylvania and other eastern colonies in the great migrations of the eighteenth century. Grinding poverty, frequent wars, an unstable economy, the invading armies of Roman Catholic France, and a period of severe winters drove thousands to flee central Europe—first to England, then to North America. Those who came were mostly farmers and laborers, craftspeople and shopkeepers—many without funds. Others were "redemptioners," who paid for their transportation by selling their labor for a certain number of years. These people dreamed of starting over in the New World, where their own initiative would be all that was necessary for building a better life. Although they were not accompanied by clergy as they settled in North America, they brought with them the piety of the Heidelberg Catechism, and their devotion to that catechism held them together in their new setting. In fact, the Heidelberg Catechism was "the plumb line of good theology, the lens for reading Scripture, [and the] fountain of piety" for what came to be known as the German Reformed Church in the United States (see vol. 3:30). This catechism was mild and irenic, with a devotional, heart-centered emphasis similar to the experiential piety of their Congregational neighbors in New England and related to popular eighteenth-century Pietism in Europe (see vol. 2:10, 21).

In 1725, John Philip Boehm (1683–1749), a schoolmaster and church leader from Worms, was asked to organize the earliest German Reformed congregations in Pennsylvania. When, three years later, Boehm was ordained by the Dutch Reformed Church through the Classis of Amsterdam, the German Reformed Church entered into a relationship with the Reformed church in Holland that lasted for sixty-five years. When the German Reformed congregations appealed to the Dutch Reformed Church for a German-speaking minister, a Swiss German minister, Michael Schlatter, was sent to them. Under the supervision of the Synods of North and South Holland, Schlatter organized German Reformed ministers and congregations into a "coetus," using a constitution devised by Boehm according to traditional Reformed principles. It provided for a consistory, strict church discipline, the instruction of children, adherence to the Heidelberg Catechism, and those lay offices necessary to the administration and spiritual affairs of a congregation.

As disgruntled colonists sought and gained political independence from the English in the mid-eighteenth century, German Reformed churches participated enthusiastically in the War for Independence. And by 1793, the Coetus of Pennsylvania declared itself independent of the church in Holland and adopted the title "The Synod of the German Reformed Church in the United States of America" (see vol. 3:22).

The Language Question

Members of this new denomination had both a proud German background and a deep commitment to their new country. Some were able to handle the transition from German to English with ease, but for others, the issue of the German language became a very divisive one. Many immigrants who came to North America after the revolutionary period did not see themselves as part of the United States. They clung to their ethnic identity and their German language. At the same time, church members who had been in North America for seventy-five years had come to feel like a part of their new country and to speak its common language.

For the more settled community, the Heidelberg Catechism was translated into English in 1810, and the German Reformed Synod officially stopped using the German language in its proceedings and minutes in 1825. By the 1820s, however, a new wave of Germans immigrated to the United States, strengthening those in the German community who saw their identity primarily in ethnic terms. In 1819, the synod responded to this situation by establishing area groups of churches, each group known as a "classis"—some spoke primarily English and some spoke primarily German.

As the century continued, there were ongoing debates within the synod about whether the "Germans" (who were of German ancestry and spoke German) and the so-called "English" (who were also of German ancestry but spoke English) should organize separate general synods and become independent bodies (see vol. 6:40). Critics of this proposal maintained that it was possible to honor the German language, culture, virtues, and character while maintaining "a thoroughly American spirit." The disagreement continued for years, intensifying in 1894, when a new constitution for the synod was rejected by the German classes, incurring the resentment of English-speaking members. In 1902, W. D. Happel expressed the sentiments of many when he warned in the *Reformed Church Messenger* that being a "German church" in the United States of America was ultimately unsatisfactory: it limited the Reformed Church's usefulness in the community and its contact with other denominations while narrowing the church's influence in the life of the nation. He recommended easing carefully and judiciously into the English language (see vol. 6:40). Time was on his side, and within a decade or two the conflict faded away as the process of assimilation led most "German churches" to adopt the English language.

Hospitality for New Immigrants

In 1890, while the Reformed Synod was still struggling to deal with its own problems as an immigrant church moving into mainstream society, it began doing missionary work among Hungarian Reformed immigrants.

Hungarians immigrated to North America in five waves between 1849 and 1956. Like most immigrants, the earliest Hungarians bonded together in ethnically based groups, some of which were religious. They came into contact with members of the (German) Reformed Synod and visited their churches in order to receive communion. As a consequence, in the nineteenth century the (German) Reformed Synod saw a need for missionary work among Hungarians and began a special ministry to them. First it sponsored Hungarian ministers and helped them organize congregations. The *Reformed Church Messenger* tried earnestly to familiarize its readership with the history and heritage of the Hungarians among them, publishing a series of articles by one the first Hungarian ministers, Gustav Juranyi (see vol. 6:41). By 1905, the General Synod of the Reformed Church in the United States approved the request for a separate Hungarian or Magyar classis.

Unfortunately, fourteen years after the Reformed Church in the United States began its "Hungarian work," the Hungarian Reformed Church back in Hungary sent an emissary to the United States to organize an "American Classis" among Hungarian immigrants. This classis was to serve Hungarian immigrants, but remain under the control of the Hungarian Reformed Church. When this happened there was considerable resentment among many (German) Reformed Synod members who had worked very hard to support their Magyar churches. At the same time, many of the Hungarians in the United States found the prospect of joining a new classis connected to their homeland church very attractive. They complained that the (German) Reformed Synod had not given them adequately trained Hungarian ministers, and they continued to be frustrated by the fact that the meetings and communications that they received from the Reformed Synod were always in German, which the Hungarians did not understand. An article in the *Reformed Church Messenger,* "The Hungarian Church Difficulties from an American Standpoint," documents the situation (see vol. 6:41).

In the end, when the outbreak of World War I made it unwise for Hungarians in the United States to return to Hungary, an agreement was negotiated between the Reformed Church in the United States and the Hungarian Reformed Church on behalf of "captive Hungarian immigrants." According to this agreement, called the "Tiffin Agreement" because it was signed in Tiffin, Ohio, the Eastern and Western Classes of the Hungarian Reformed Church in America were received into "organic, legal and ecclesiastical" relation with the Reformed Church in the United States. They were also assured of full privileges in the synod, payment of classis salaries in arrears, retention of their own properties, and free use of the Magyar language in their church life.

The (German) Reformed Church expected that eventually Hungarian ethnic congregations would undergo the same assimilation process that they themselves had undergone. However, many of the Hungarian Reformed congregations did not want to become part of any new "melting pot." They wanted to stay in ethnic churches that reinforced the cultural, linguistic, and ecclesiastical traditions of their homeland. By the second or third decade of the twentieth century, nearly all "German" Reformed congregations had moved from being ethnic-based congregations to seeing themselves as part of mainstream society. For this reason, many Reformed church members failed to understand why the Hungarians were not willing to do likewise. The experience of the Hungarians was different. As new waves of Hungarian refugees immigrated to the United States, Hungarian congregations guarded their ethnic identity even more jealously.

Years of misunderstanding and hostility on both sides of this situation made relationships within the (German) Reformed Church in the United States difficult. Finally, in 1939, after the Evangelical and Reformed Church was formed in 1934, a Magyar Synod was organized for the Hungarian congregations as a special "nongeographical" classis within the Evangelical and Reformed Church. During the next eighteen years there was another resurgence of concern on the part of Hungarians for a unified Hungarian Reformed community in the United States. Recognizing this legacy, in the early 1960s the newly formed United Church of Christ supported the Hungarians in their struggle to retain their Hungarian identity in second- and third-generation immigrant congregations. A successor to the Magyar Synod, the Calvin Synod, was recognized as an acting nongeographical synod within the United Church of Christ.

Hungarian congregations have made significant contributions to the United Church of Christ and have also been able to honor their own ethnic, cultural, and religious heritage. By providing ecumenical hospitality to Hungarian immigrants when many denominations could only focus upon preserving their own congregations or meeting their own internal needs, the (German) Reformed Church in the United States reached out to the Hungarian Reformed community, exhibiting a deep commitment to the oneness of the church and a gracious openness to church union.

Resisting Popular Culture

By the second decade of the nineteenth century, a special religious temper had developed in the expanding United States, nourished by the revivals of the Great Awakenings and inspired by the great ideas of human freedom and autonomy that fueled the struggle for political independence. This religious temper viewed the autonomy of individual religious experience as the criterion by which all things, even religious things, were to be judged. When this subjectively oriented religious temper met traditional German Reformed piety, turmoil ensued. The inwardness encouraged by the Heidelberg Catechism had always existed within the context of the church, where the promises of God offered in word and sacrament balanced subjectivist excesses. On the expanding nineteenth-century frontier, German Reformed people began to lose sight of this balance. Soon, some of them sought reassurance in the religious experiences generated by revivalist preaching.

This great emphasis on religious experience was common in all religions in the young nation. It led to an understanding of the church as a voluntary association of those with similar religious experiences. Devout Christians united with fellow believers in free association to create congregations. "The church" was made up of an aggregate of these congregations, an association that was both individualistic and democratic. As nineteenth-century frontier religion developed, the German Reformed Synod became increasingly convinced that it needed to balance this trend with a "well-organized and self-conscious church that possessed authority."

One attempt to do this was through what was known as "Mercersburg Theology," developed by John Williamson Nevin (1803–86) and Philip Schaff (1819–93), faculty at the German Reformed seminary in Mercersburg, Pennsylvania. Schaff, a church historian, stated in his inaugural address at the seminary that the "main question" for theology in their times was to pursue "the nature of the church itself in its relation to the world and to single Christians." Together, Schaff and Nevin sought to critique the individualism and emotionalism of revivalism by reviving the piety and theology of the Protestant Reformation. They presented a theology that was christocentric, making the incarnation, not doctrine or the death of Christ, the focal point of Christianity. They asserted that in the incarnation Christ took human nature upon himself and, in so doing, raised it into a higher sphere, uniting it with the nature of God. Through the Lord's Supper believers received the "spiritual real presence" of Christ. For Christians, the life of Christ was the foundation for an organic union of the natural and the supernatural, perpetuated in the world in objective, historical, and sacramental form through Christ's body, the church. These Mercersburg professors made the sacrament the center of worship, and the incarnate Christ the center of theology. They sought to counteract the subjective, revivalistic, voluntaristic, and rationalistic focus of popular Christianity by focusing on the objective, organic, sacramental, and liturgical reality of Christ and his work.

Outside of the German Reformed Church, the influence of Nevin and Schaff was negligible during the 1840s and 1850s. Many Protestants in the United States were ill at ease with immigrants, and with anyone who had a good word for Roman Catholicism. Revivalism and the common-sense realism of contemporary Scottish thinkers fit in much better with the prevailing religious temper.

Mercersburg Theology, however, persisted, and it caused great turmoil within the German Reformed Church. Some critics of Mercersburg thinking, looking at its efforts to recover the christological center of the faith and the organic nature of the church in its objective and historical continuity (including medieval Catholicism), accused it of "catholicizing." Mercersburg followers were labeled "crypto-papists," "Romanizers," "conspirators," and "traitors." These charges were especially incendiary in the light of growing anti-Catholic antagonism resulting from the presence new immigrants and from other domestic anxieties. Nevertheless, many of the most influential leaders of the German Reformed Synod, such as Thomas G. Apple and J. Spangler Kieffer, were loyal to Mercersburg Theology. They believed that it had a strong ecumenical thrust because it encouraged a solid, Christ-centered faith that sent Christians out to unite all of Christ's followers in one dynamic organism as the true church moving through history.

Mercersburg Theology's recovery of the Reformation emphasis on the christological center of the church and its appreciation of the organic development of the church through history enabled Mercersburg Theology to promote renewed interest in history, the awakening of sacramental concerns, and the return of German Reformed congregations to liturgical patterns of worship. It also gave the German Reformed Synod a strong theological basis for pursuing church unity.

Finally, Mercersburg Theology provided an organic and developmental model for the journey toward unity that served as a model for the future ecumenical movement. In its own commitment to the journey toward Christian unity, Mercersburg Theology insisted that Protestantism in the United States would be static and impoverished until an active dialogue was begun between Reformed and Lutheran believers. It did much to motivate the German Reformed Synod to try to make the unity of the Christian church more visible through union negotiations and participation in several national and worldwide ecumenical conversations (see vol. 6:42). This commitment of the German Reformed Synod finally bore fruit in the second half of the twentieth century, when a series of ecumenical dialogues lasting over three decades culminated in "The Formula of Agreement," a full communion agreement between the Evangelical Lutheran Church in America, the Presbyterian Church (U.S.A.), the Reformed Church in America, and the United Church of Christ.

The Dutch Reformed Church

A commitment to ecumenical work is deeply embedded in the history of the (German) Reformed Church. Early in its life, the (German) Reformed Synod made a good-faith effort to achieve union with the Dutch Reformed Church. The two churches were very similar: they had been nurtured by the same parent, the Reformed Church in Holland, and relations between the two groups were always very cordial, blossoming occasionally into specific plans for cooperation or union.

The first effort to achieve unity began in 1716 when the Reformed Church in Holland made a proposal on behalf of the growing numbers of German and Dutch immigrants settling in North America. Having heard that the first four presbyteries in the colonies had successfully constituted themselves into a single synod, the Reformed Church in Holland suggested that the Germans and the Dutch should unite with the Presbyterians and establish a single Reformed church in the colonies. Interest in this proposal waxed and waned over the next thirty-seven years. Finally, in 1753, the Reformed Church in Holland officially withdrew its proposal.

In 1804, a second round of discussions developed when "fraternal correspondence" began between the Dutch and the German Reformed churches, leading them to exchange delegates to their general synods beginning in 1813. By 1842, the time seemed ripe for closer relations, and an elaborate plan of cooperative union was worked out. Finally, in 1844, they jointly convened a Triennial Convention in Harrisburg, Pennsylvania, where five articles of agreement were adopted by the convention. They committed to mutual regard for their candidates for the ministry, similar instruction in their theological seminaries, use of the same textbooks for seminary instruction, a willingness to follow similar liturgies, and the blending of domestic missions as far as practicable. The convention planned to meet again in 1847, with high hopes that such cooperation would result eventually in organic union. By 1847, however, the fact that the German Reformed Synod regarded the Heidelberg Catechism as "symbol enough" while the Dutch church adhered also to the Belgic Confession and the Articles of Dort became an insurmountable barrier. The Dutch withdrew from the arrangement and relations were suspended.

However, when the German Reformed Synod became the General Synod of the Reformed Church in the United States in 1863, a third round of conversations with the Dutch commenced. One of the synod's first formal acts was to state its intention to enter into correspondence with five other denominations in the United States, including the General Synod of the Dutch Reformed Church (which became the Reformed Church in America in 1869). In 1872, the (German) General Synod appointed a committee of three from each of the five synods to confer with a similar committee of the Dutch church on union. The two committees on union met in Philadelphia in 1874, convening a committee to draft a paper expressing their shared sentiments on organic union. The report said that there were "likenesses sufficient to warrant the hope of an ultimate union," but that there were less easily adjustable differences. In fact, they were the same confessional differences that had thwarted their efforts at union almost thirty years earlier (see vol. 6:43).

In 1887, the General Synod of the (German) Reformed Church began a fourth and final round of union discussion with the Dutch Reformed Synod. A new committee, chaired by Thomas G. Apple, was appointed to negotiate with a similar committee from the Dutch church. Very positive meetings were held between the groups (see vol. 6:43). Apple kept German Reformed readership of the *Reformed Church Messenger* informed, reporting on the details of the meetings and sharing his own interpretations (see vol. 6:43). Members of Reformed congregations hailed the progress enthusiastically. A conference between the German and Dutch committees in Philadelphia in 1889 recommended a federal union. A few years later, in 1891, a plan was drawn up allowing for the judicatories of both churches to remain undisturbed, the mission boards to be consolidated, joint periodicals and Sunday school helps to be published, and a board of education to "consider the training of ministers for labor among immigrants of various nationalities." Both churches adopted the plan and preparations were made for a federal synod. Churchwide enthusiasm for the union among the Germans was expressed in more than fifty articles published in the *Reformed Church Messenger* between 1888 and 1892. An address by a German Reformed scholar, J. Spangler Kieffer, given to the General Synod of the (Dutch) Reformed Church showed how strong christocentric theology and a dynamic and organic understanding of the church universal were leading both denominations to embrace the possibility of a broader union (see vol. 6:44).

Unfortunately, the Dutch church postponed its vote on the federal plan for a year because some of its members feared that the German church was not sufficiently Calvinistic (since it had only one confessional standard), and had "made too much of the Sacraments" and of confirmation (see vol. 6:45). In 1893, when a Dutch vote was finally to be taken, a minority of the Dutch church presented such strenuous opposition to the plan that the national Dutch leadership was forced to drop the matter. The fourth round of union discussions between the Dutch and German Reformed churches in the United States—so alike in name, doctrine, and government—came to an end, although friendly relations between the two churches continued (see vol. 6:45).

Church Union: Vision and Reality

In spite of its unsuccessful negotiations with the Dutch Reformed Church, the (German) Reformed Church in the United States maintained its commitment to the struggle to make union with other Christian churches more visible. All ecumenical movements are fundamentally of scriptural origin, but sometimes the theology that flows from the Bible is not always central to the life of a church. With the (German) Reformed Church, however, the scriptural call to church union was fundamental. In a very special way this denomination was driven by its ecclesiology, or doctrine of the church. Because of the internal theological debates around Mercersburg Theology, German Reformed leaders were especially clear in their vision of the one holy catholic and apostolic church. They saw their church as focused on and rooted in the reality of the person of Christ, and its continuation totally dependent through all of history on that great organism which is the universal body of Christ. This view of the church gave the (German) Reformed Church in the United States a firm theological foundation that supported an extraordinary history of ecumenical negotiations (see vol. 6:46).

By the last decades of the nineteenth century, thoughtful German Reformed writers, such James I. Good, Thomas G. Apple, and J. Spangler Kieffer, had written extensively on the theological foundations for union and participated in a variety of union negotiations. In the early twentieth century Jacob C. Leonard and George W. Richards, president of Lancaster Theological Seminary, continued that work, becoming well-known in national and international ecumenical circles. Their efforts were supported by an increasingly detailed and extensive coverage of ecumenical issues and negotiations in the *Reformed Church Messenger* and in the *Christian Sun*. These newspapers contributed immeasurably to the ecumenical work of the (German) Reformed Church in the United States, keeping typical German Reformed readers well informed about ecumenical issues.

The list of ecumenical ventures attempted by the (German) Reformed Synod in the United States over its 150-year history was impressive. In addition to efforts with the Hungarians and the Dutch, other plans for union were negotiated but never consummated—such as one between the (German) Reformed Church in the United States and the Presbyterian Church in the U.S.A. (see vol. 6:47). Through it all, the General Synod of the (German) Reformed Church in the United States learned that all efforts toward union, even unconsummated ones, can turn out to be a blessing.

Part of a Global Ecumenical Movement

Even before the (German) Reformed Church in the United States became an active participant in the global ecumenical movement, articles in the *Reformed Church Messenger* reported on various church unions in Japan and India. These reports invited Reformed church members to imagine how such sweeping church unions and alliances might also be possible for them (see vol. 6:48–49). Soon thereafter, German Reformed leaders became enthusiastic participants in some of the most significant global ecumenical ventures of the late nineteenth and early twentieth century.

One of the earliest world denominational fellowships was the Alliance of Reformed Churches (1875), made up of churches throughout the world holding to the presbyterian system. There was also an offshoot of that global organization in the United States for churches governed by a presbyterian system. Although the U.S. churches finally did not develop a plan for the Federation of American (Reformed) Churches, which it created in 1894, it was an early sign of the enthusiasm for church union among Reformed people (see vol. 6:50).

In 1905, German Reformed denominational leaders who had participated in an interchurch conference on federation in New York City were convinced that the Spirit had been working on the hearts of God's people for fifty years to prepare them for a great occasion. Consequently, when the Federal Council of the Churches of Christ in America was formed, the *Reformed Church Messenger* published the entire plan of federation (see vol. 6:51), along with detailed reports and impressions from Reformed participants.

(German) Reformed Church delegates also attended the World Missionary Conference in Edinburgh in 1910. They reported, "Everyone felt at home . . . because the several thousands of delegates and friends met as brethren, and there was the same spirit animating every thought and desire. These were servants of the one Lord, and full of new hopes and ideals for their work. There came over the minds of many men and women in that vast audience a very happy sense of the real unity of the children of God, in spite of all their racial, social and denominational differences" (see vol. 6:52).

In the years that followed, the (German) Reformed Church in the United States continued to have its boundaries and horizons broadened through ecumenical contacts with the worldwide church: the Stockholm Conference on Life and Work in 1925, the World Conference of Faith and Order in Lausanne in 1927, and the International Missionary Conference in Jerusalem in 1928. Reformed leaders and members who had been speaking of the one holy catholic and apostolic church of Jesus Christ for their entire lives began to have a new sense of the depth and breadth of that reality.

The Formation of the Evangelical and Reformed Church

After participating in many international meetings that gave witness to the essential unity of the Christian church, the (German) Reformed Church in the United States renewed its commitment to the one church of Jesus Christ. After its participation in an ultimately unsuccessful series of negotiations with the United Brethren in Christ and the Evangelical Synod of North America in 1928–29 (see vol. 6:67), it discovered that it had a great deal in common with the Evangelical Synod. Both of these denominations were rooted in the sixteenth-century Protestant Reformation; both had originally been immigrant churches from German-speaking Europe; both had wrestled with their ethnic identity in the United States; both had developed a new denominational identity independent of their ethnic roots. Now both were feeling challenged by an even broader vision of the church. Formal negotiations between the two denominations were opened in February 1932, and within a year their joint commissions had unanimously approved a final plan of union.

Earlier, when the (German) Reformed Church in the United States had been in conversations with the Dutch Reformed Church, the fact that the Dutch church subscribed to two more confessions than did the German church was considered by both sides to be reasonable ground for terminating negotiations. Eighty-two years later, when the (German) Reformed Church in the United States began seriously exploring the idea of union with the Evangelical Synod—a denomination that claimed loyalty to the Augsburg Confession and Luther's Catechism, as well as the Heidelberg Catechism—its understanding of itself as a church had deepened. By the 1930s, such confessional differences were not seen by either side to stand in the way of an organic union. The preamble to the Evangelical and Reformed Church plan of union stated simply, "Under the conviction that they are in agreement on the essential doctrines of the Christian faith and on the ideals of the Christian life as contained in the Old and New Testaments and as defined by their respective standards of doctrine, [the two churches] do hereby declare their desire to be united in one body." The doctrinal section of the plan of union consisted of just one sentence: "We acknowledge and accept the historical confessions of the two churches as the doctrinal basis of union."

According to earlier thinking, confessional statements were understood to be repositories of truth. Now they were understood to be subordinate to the higher truth of the one holy catholic and apostolic church, in which divisions were overcome. In a sermon preached anticipating the formation of the Evangelical and Reformed Church, Reformed pastor William Leich of Dayton, Ohio, said, "Christianity has ever been in danger of hardening about organization, polity, buildings, rituals, dogmas and so on. But . . . Christianity has broken the fetters again and again and walked forth into new freedom of life. It has always proven itself alive by its freedom to act, grappling with the things that threatened to enslave and using them again as servants and instruments" (see vol. 6:53). In worship at the first joint session of the two denominations, Jacob C. Leonard capped the more than 130 years of ecumenical negotiations of the (German) Reformed Church in the United States by praying that the new Evangelical and Reformed Church might begin with "the exuberance of Christian youth . . . the morning faith, the morning courage, the morning vision—and also the joyous blessing of the evening calm that follows the day of successful service out in the Master's harvest" (see vol. 6:53).

Commenting on the new denomination, the *Christian Century* noted, "If the spirit which animated this union should become contagious and sweep across the world we should witness a vast crumbling of denominational walls." No descendants of Zwingli and Calvin, Schaff and Nevin, could pray for more.

The Language Question

40. German or English?

"Shall We Separate?" and "Anglicising Our Congregations"

(1894 and 1902)

Reformed Church Messenger; W. D. Happel

The Reformed Church in the United States was an immigrant denomination bound up with German history, culture, and religion. It was established by Protestants who came to North America in the great migrations of the eighteenth century, fleeing abject poverty, frequent wars, an unstable economy, and the invading armies of Roman Catholic France. In North America, German Reformed colonists settled in Pennsylvania and New Jersey, and along the fringes of the Appalachian Mountains in Maryland, Virginia, and the Carolinas. The earliest German Reformed congregations were organized in 1725 by a German schoolmaster from Worms, John Philip Boehm (1683–1749), who sought ordination three years later from the Dutch Reformed Church. Soon thereafter, some German-speaking congregations asked the Dutch Reformed Church for a German-speaking pastor, and a young Swiss German minister, Michael Schlatter, was sent to them. Schlatter organized the German Reformed ministers and congregations into a "coetus," according to a constitution in the Reformed tradition devised earlier by Boehm. After the Revolutionary War, in 1793 this coetus declared itself independent of the Dutch Reformed Church, and adopted the title "The Synod of the German Reformed Church in the United States of America."

Source: Editorial, "Shall We Separate?" *Reformed Church Messenger,* 4 October 1894, 2–3. W. D. Happel, "Anglicising Our Congregations," *Reformed Church Messenger,* 30 January 1902, 5.

In spite of the new church's proud German heritage, the use of the German language in the life of the synod became an increasingly divisive issue. Germans who had come to North America in the earliest migrations had been in the New World for seventy-five years. They were part of the United States and they spoke its common language, English. For them, the Heidelberg Catechism was translated into English in 1810, and the synod adopted English as its official language in 1825. However, more recent German immigrants still saw their identity primarily in ethnic terms, and they wanted to continue to use the German language to reinforce their identity. In 1819, the synod tried to accommodate both groups by dividing its congregations into two "classes," one using English and one using German.

Debates about the language issue were lively. Should the "German" churches (that were of German nationality and spoke German) and the "English" churches (that were also of German nationality but spoke English) organize separate general synods and become independent bodies? The issue came to a head 1894 when a new constitution of the German Reformed Church in the United States, which had been under construction for nearly a decade, was rejected by the German-speaking classes. Actually, the constitution had nearly been adopted six years earlier, but due to an oversight of several classes, the vote was taken again. Reasons for the opposition were not uniform: some believed (as it turned out, incorrectly) that the existence of the German classes would be endangered by its adoption; others maintained that the constitution would give the classes and synods too much power over congregations. In fact, the new constitution was no different in this respect from the presbyterial system that the Reformed church had always maintained. "Shall We Separate?" and "Anglicising our Congregations" are typical examples reflecting the issues arising between more and less "Americanized" members within the Reformed Synod. Similar questions arose nearly a quarter of a century later among members of the Evangelical Synod, another immigrant German church (see vol. 6:56).

Shall We Separate?

Shall the English and German portions of the Reformed Church in the United States organize separate General Synods, and become independent bodies? This question has recently been seriously raised in consequence of the rejection of the new Constitution. The defeat of this Constitution has produced a very serious shock in large sections of our Church. The great majority of ministers and intelligent laymen had confidently expected a different result. This new Constitution was the fruit of years of earnest study and faithful labor. The best and most judicious men had been engaged in the preparation of it for almost a generation, and the work had already cost the Church no small amount of money. When it was reported to the General Synod at Reading, it was received with general favor and adopted almost unanimously. In fact it had been adopted once before, not only by the General Synod, but also by two-thirds of the Classes. For the Constitution submitted at Reading was the same Constitution, without any important changes, that had been submitted at Akron, six years before, and that failed of formal adoption only in consequence of clerical negligence on the part of several Classes.

In these circumstances, then, it was confidently expected that it world now receive the almost unanimous approbation of the Classes. No serious fault was found with it either at Reading, and, as far as we know, afterwards. The defects which some have thought that they discovered therein, are either no defects at all, or they are of a trifling character, and could easily have been removed by means of amendments. It is, of course, not a *perfect* Constitution. The Church never will have a perfect Constitution, any more than she will have a perfect hymnbook or liturgy. And it may not meet exactly the wishes and desires of all individual ministers and members of the Church. No such Constitution can ever be framed; for no number of individuals will ever agree in their views as to what ought to be and what ought not to be in a Constitution. If we are ever to get a new Constitution, it must be on the basis of compromise, and, of course, some sacrifice of personal opinion. But while not perfect, the new Constitution is nevertheless a great improvement upon the old; and, if it had been adopted, it would doubtless have answered the wants of the Church for long time to come.

In these circumstances the rejection of it has naturally occasioned no little surprise and disappointment. And the feeling of surprise is increased by a consideration of the vote of the different Classes into which the Church is divided. Of the English portion of the Church all the Classes voted affirmatively, except Philadelphia, Tiffin, Lancaster (Synod of Ohio), and St. Joseph, while all the German Classes voted negatively, except three. Thirty-one out of the thirty-five English Classes voted for, and seventeen out of the twenty German Classes voted against it. Upon the German brethren, then, rests mainly the responsibility of having once more defeated the Church's long effort to get a new Constitution. It is true that four English Classes also voted in opposition to it, notable among which are Philadelphia and Tiffin; but we do not suppose that the German Classes simply followed blindly in the wake of these few English Classes, whose actions, moreover, must not by any means be supposed to have been *unanimous*. The German brethren must be presumed to have done their own thinking, and to have had reasons of their own for voting as they did.

What, then, is there in the new Constitution that could have been offensive especially to the Germans? It has been said that their vote was determined largely by the fear that the existence of German Classes and Synods would be endangered by its adoption. But this supposition certainly does no credit to the intelligence of our German ministers; as the new Constitution, by forbidding the formation of different Classes and Synods using the same language on the same territory, clearly implies the right of so doing on the basis of difference in language. It has also been suggested that the German opposition rose in part from the idea that the new Constitution gives to Classes and Synods too much power over Consistories and congregations. But it gives no more than is clearly implied by the conception of presbyterial government, and no more that has always been substantially exercised; for the government of the Reformed Church has always been presbyterial and not congregational. Besides, why should this fact of enlargement of government powers, if it were a fact, be supposed to bear especially hard upon the Germans? Would it not bear upon all alike? And does not the American portion of the Reformed Church have as clear an idea of religious liberty as the Germans have, and does it not love liberty as much?

It does not appear, then, as if the action of the Germans in this case had been determined simply by a spirit of opposition to their English or American brethren; for we will not do them the injustice of supposing that they have allowed themselves to be used as tools in the hands of a party belonging to the English section of the Church. And we are, therefore, not surprised to see that the question is raised whether it would not be better to separate in peace, as Abraham and Lot once separated; nor are we surprised to see that a strong current of feeling has set in in favor of separation. Those who remember the struggles of the past, and have not forgotten how parties then were made up and arrayed against each other, have no desire to see a repetition of the same thing in the future. The Church could not stand another strain like that which she sustained in years past. It was fondly hoped that the old spirit of partisan opposition was dead, and especially that it would not be possible again to array the German element in the Church as a body against either the whole or any part of the English element. There were no signs of such opposition visible in the General Synod at Reading. All seemed to be harmonious there. But this action on the new Constitution has again disappointed these hopes, and many are now in favor of a division of the General Synod, who would heretofore have opposed such a proposition.

Such a division would, undoubtedly, be an evil. And it would be unnatural. For the English option of the Reformed Church in the United States is itself of German origin. The great majority of its ministers and members are descendants of those Germans who a century and a half, or more, ago came to America because they had been persecuted on account of their religion and driven form their homes in the German fatherland. And while they now use the English language, they are still true to the original spirit of the Reformed Church, and in sympathy also, as they believe, with the best theological thought of Germany at the present time. There is no reason, therefore, why there should be any opposition between English and Germans among us, but the best reason why they should be united and work hand in hand in the upbuilding of our Reformed Zion. There can in the future be only one Reformed Church in this country, and that, of course will be English. A purely German church can have no permanent future on American soil. The Germans and their descendants will in the course of time themselves become English; and this end ought to be anticipated now by both the English and German portions of the Church, and they ought to be on the best of terms with each other.

But just here is the difficulty. The German is slow to see this inevitable tendency of things here in America. It was so with our own forefathers two or three generations ago; and this fact has been the cause of no small loss to the Reformed Church. The German loves his native tongue, and the possibility of seeing it die out makes him jealous and fretful. Hence German ministers, many of them at least, have no sympathy with English Reformed congregations in their immediate vicinity. They usually discourage the organization of English congregations. As evidence of this fact reference may be made to the cities of Buffalo, Cincinnati and Cleveland. German ministers have been known to advise their young people, who have grown English, to join any other English churches rather than those of their own denomination.

Now, if this spirit is to continue, then we think it would be better to separate in peace. In these circumstances the two sides can do each other no good. The English will not help the Germans in their missionary work, and the Germans will not help the English. And their association in the highest judicatory of the Church, in which questions affecting the interest and welfare of the whole Church continually come up for consideration, can only be a source of irritation and bad feeling. Why, for instance should the Germans have a voice in the preparation and adoption of English hymnbooks and liturgies, which they never expect to use themselves, and which they do not *want* even to see their children or children's children use? And so, on the other hand, why should the English have any say in the formation and adoption of similar ordinances in German.

Would it not in these circumstances be better to separate? The Lutheran Church exists in the form of many independent bodies. They are united only by the great name of *Luther*. Would the name *Reformed* be a bond sufficiently strong to keep alive the consciousness of spiritual unity in two independent Reformed bodies? It has not done so in the case of the Dutch and German churches. Would it be more effectual now in preserving the feeling of a common origin and fellowship between the German and American portions of the Reformed Church in the United States? We do not think so, and for our part at least we would regard such a division with unfeigned sadness. It would very much weaken our Reformed Church numerically. The whole body of our German membership would ultimately be found in English churches other than the Reformed. But it may be said that this will be the case even as it is now; that the mere fact of association in the General Synod does not serve to bring the young people of German congregations, as they become English, into English Reformed congregations; that the association is merely a source of friction and consequently of weakness to both sides; and hence that the least of two evils would be peaceful separation.

At any rate this subject is now up for discussion. Only let the discussion be carried forward calmly and in a Christian spirit. Let those who feel called to write on the subject, do so in the spirit of Christian charity. Let there be no excitement or passion, with its blinding influences. We are sorry to see that an editorial writer in the *Kirchenzeitung,* writing on this subject, betrays too much heated feeling. He frets himself into a state of excitement, and then uses language which is extravagant and irritating as, for instance, when a writer in the MESSENGER mildly suggests the possibility of amending the Heidelberg Catechism, he calls this a "murderous assault upon the Catechism." There can be nothing gained by yielding to such feeling in the present case. What is wanted is judicial calmness and fairness on both sides. The cause is too solemn and important a one to be approached in any other manner. Let us not whip ourselves into a rage when we approach the discussion of this question. Let us approach it, if we must deal with it all, calmly, fairly, and in the spirit of the Master.

W. R.

Anglicising Our Congregations

The German language is still used to a greater or less extent in the services of many of the congregations of the Reformed Church in this country. It would be interesting to know just what percentage of the services is German throughout our denomination. The writer has for a long time had the conviction that our congregations have clung too long and too tenaciously to a foreign tongue in the services of the sanctuary. In many congregations German services should be greatly reduced in number, and in many more, especially in the Eastern and more American part of the church, they should be discontinued altogether. A number of reasons urging action in this direction might be given.

One reason for making the change referred to is that the great majority of our people cannot be advantageously served and held to the church as long as the services are conducted in a strange tongue. The schools are English, and the education of those born in this country is therefore English. Newspapers are English. Business and civil and political affairs are all conducted in the same language. Being educated in English, and being accustomed to this language in all the spheres of life, it follows that the vast majority of our people cannot be interested and edified by German services. The writer has often observed their listlessness and indifference at these services. The result is that many become lukewarm in their relation to the church, and many more are lost to the church altogether.

Then, too, our ministers cannot do their best work in German. This applies, of course, to those born in this country. But they constitute by far the largest part of the ministry of our church. The colleges and seminaries of the church, with one exception, are English. Our ministers receive their training in the English language, and are qualified best to serve in this language. With Pennsylvania German as a basis, and with the additional knowledge of German acquired by study in college and general reading, they often preach it with considerable fluency, and yet it always remains the language of their left hand. They cannot give the people their best services through this language as a medium.

Moreover, a congregation limits its usefulness in a community by remaining altogether, or in part, a German church. It has the reputation of being a German church. Such a reputation is, of course, nothing of which a congregation need be ashamed. It is just as reputable to be German as English so far as that is concerned. But the matter does not end there. The point is that such a congregation draws to itself only those who are German or of German extraction.

Such a church can touch only a faction of the community in which it exists, and in many sections of our country this part is not large. And this holds true not only of a particular congregation, but of the church as a whole. In looking over the almanac of the Reformed Church in America the writer noticed that the reason given for the provincial character of that part of Reformedism is that the Dutch language was adhered to too long after New York had passed from the control of the Dutch to that of the English. This limited the spread and therefore the usefulness of this branch of the Reformed Church. This is true of the Reformed Church in the United States. Congregations have limited their usefulness and the whole church has remained provincial because of an unreasonable adherence to the German language.

Then, again, the continuance of the German language in our services has separated us from other denominations. The Reformed Church has something to give and to receive from other denominations. It is impossible to recount in this connection what we have to give in church government, customs, worship and theology. There is the consciousness throughout our denomination that we have something to give to others. On the other hand, there is something to be received, especially along practical activities, from the general church life of America by us. Throughout our history, the continuance of a European language has greatly lessened this reciprocal influence. We have held within the bounds of our own church influences that should have gone farther, and only after other churches had for a long time profited by certain practical measures did they receive recognition among us.

Finally, the continuation of German has made us less influential in our national life. According to the latest statistics of the Lutheran Church, the membership of that denomination is 1,750,000. It is numerically one of the largest denominations in the country, but its influence on the national life is far less than its membership and the type of Christianity which it represents would warrant. Why is this the case? Because it is a church which has had its existence very largely in foreign tongues. Its life is largely apart from that of the nation in which it finds itself, and, consequently, its influence is comparatively small. The English churches have stood closest to the nation's heart and life. How the Methodist Episcopal Church touched the national life in the administrations of Lincoln, Grant and McKinley is well known. It is by having an English Church at the national capital that for the first time we directly come into contact with the administration. It is only in the degree that we adapt ourselves to the language of the nation that our influence on the national life will grow.

The validity of these reasons for changing from German to English will perhaps be readily granted, but the question will arise, how such a change can be brought about without creating serious disturbances in our congregations. By going about the matter carefully and tactfully the change can ordinarily be made without serious injury to a congregation even for the time being.

The pastor and those who share his views should create a sentiment in favor of the change. This cannot be done by speaking on the matter from the pulpit. That will at once create opposition. It must be done in conversation with the people about the welfare of the congregation.

Having sufficient sentiment to sustain the change, care must be taken in making the change itself. A congregational vote on the question will most likely divide the congregation into factions, if it does not cause an actual division. It is better to talk the matter over with the consistory, and with their consent to drop the language quietly.

Even then certain objections will arise, and will have to be met.

It will be said that the church was built with the intention of being a German Church. To this it may be replied that what may have been a necessity years ago is not one now.

Some will say that German is a richer and more beautiful language than English. This no one will dispute. But a church does not exist to uphold a language, German or English, but to dispense the salvation of Christ. And to attain this end, that language must be used through which the largest number of people may be reached.

Others will raise the objection that there are some in the congregation who cannot get much benefit from an English service. But the few must try to adapt themselves to the many.

Then there will be a certain amount of prejudice. This will have to die away of its own accord.

This article is an account of the writer's experience in dealing with this problem. It gives some of the reasons which moved him to discontinue German in his congregation, the method of making the change, and the objections which were made. This congregation was organized twenty-nine years ago as an entirely German Church, with a German School in connection with it for the propagation of the language. When the writer became pastor over six years ago, forty out of the fifty-two morning services were German. The number was at once reduced to twenty-six a year, and last spring German was discontinued altogether. The change, although meeting with opposition from a few, has had a very salutary effect on the congregation as a whole.

What was done here could and should be done throughout a large part of the church. It is in line with the spirit of progress which is abroad in the church.

Wilkesbarre, Pa.

Hospitality for New Immigrants

41. The Hungarian Reformed Church: *"The Origin, History, Religion and Present Religious Needs of the Hungarian or Magyar People" and "The Hungarian Church Difficulties from an American Standpoint"*

(1892 and 1908)

Gustav Juranyi; Samuel McLanahan

In 1890, while still struggling with its own problems as a formerly immigrant church moving into mainstream United States society, the Reformed Church began missionary work among Hungarian Reformed immigrants. The Hungarians came to America in five waves of immigration between 1849 and 1956. Frequently, they settled in small communities where they tried to preserve the language and culture of their people. Although no ordained pastors were among them, many held to the Hungarian Reformed faith, and during those times of the year when they were accustomed to receiving communion, Hungarian Reformed immigrants worshiped in German Reformed churches. Eventually, the Reformed congregations offered hospitality and developed a ministry among Hungarians. By 1891, they arranged for the first of several Hungarian Reformed ministers, Rev. Gustav Juranyi, to come to the

Source: Gustav Juranyi, "The Origin, History, Religion and Present Religious Needs of the Hungarian or Magyar People," *Reformed Church Messenger,* 11 February 1892, 2–3; Samuel McLanahan, "The Hungarian Church Difficulties from an American Standpoint," *Reformed Church Messenger,* 6 February 1908, 7–8.

United States and help Hungarians organize into congregations. In order to increase the understanding of Reformed Church members about Hungarians, the Reformed Church Messenger *published "The Origin, History, Religion and Present Religious Needs of the Hungarian or Magyar People."*

However, after the Reformed Synod had been working with Hungarians for fourteen years, the Hungarian Reformed Church (in Europe) sent an emissary to the United States to organize an "American Classis" among the Hungarian people under the control of the European-based Hungarian church. This action produced mixed reactions. The (German) Reformed Church had done its best to support new Hungarian immigrants in their new country. Yet, many of the Hungarians, who found themselves lost in the predominantly German-speaking classes of the Reformed Synod, welcomed the possibility of a Magyar-speaking classis. Articles in the Messenger *outlined the problems between the groups.*

Then, when World War I made it impossible for Hungarians to move freely back and forth between the United States and Hungary, the Hungarian Reformed Church negotiated an agreement with the Reformed Synod called "The Tiffin Agreement." Under its stipulations, the Eastern and Western Classes of the Hungarian Reformed Church in America were received into "organic, legal and ecclesiastical" relation with the Reformed Synod. They were also assured of full privileges in the synod, payment of classis salaries in arrears, retention of their own properties, and free use of the Magyar language in their church life. Although this arrangement met the needs of many Hungarian immigrants, some members of the Reformed Synod felt betrayed by the Reformed Church in Hungary, even as they struggled to give their Hungarian neighbors respect and understanding.

Undoubtedly, the Reformed Synod expected that the Hungarian classes would eventually become "Americanized" as the synod itself had, and move into the mainstream church. However, Hungarian Reform immigrants did not choose the model of the melting pot, preferring instead to retain their cultural, linguistic, and ecclesiastical identity as Hungarians. Years of suspicion and resentment on both sides followed. Finally, after the Evangelical and Reformed Church was founded in 1934, an arrangement was made whereby the Magyar Synod of the Evangelical and Reformed Church was organized as a nongeographical synod within the larger denomination. After 1957, a successor to the Magyar Synod, the Calvin Synod, continued as an acting nongeographical synod within the United Church of Christ.

The Origin, History, Religion and Present Religious Needs of the Hungarian or Magyar People

We have now reached the period of the *Reformation,* and this is for me the best part of the Hungarian history, for it proves that the Magyar people had not only accepted Christianity as a mere outward form, but that it had been touched by its spirit; and this spirit, the spirit of God, operated in the hearts of this people, when its time was come, and opened their hearts to accept the glorious Gospel of the Son of God.

For, to begin with, Romanism had ripened in Hungary the same foul and rotten fruits as everywhere else. Nay it seem to me, that in that country the Roman corruption was more obvious than in any other community because nowhere the Roman prelacy had obtained such immense wealth and such an *immediate* influence upon the civil government as in Hungary. The Archbishop of Grau and Primate of Hungary was in fact that what is now a Prime Minister of State, and just in the decades going before the Reformation Archbishop Thomas Bakacs had made himself more than that: he was the non-controlled ruler of the kingdom.

So, when the time had come that the degrading yoke of Rome was to be shaken off from the necks of men: the Reformer's voice, departing from Wittemberg, was heard and hailed in Hungary too. The famous theses of Luther were at once spread over most cities of Hungary, and as the Reformation went on, as the Gospel came out clearer and clearer from the lips of the Saxon monk, there commenced a very pilgrimage of enthusiastic young men, of students and priests to Wittemberg, to hear the Reformer's own voice and to drink the water of pure Christian doctrine at its source. And then all these students returned home full of love to Christ and full of zeal to propagate His kingdom. With great fervor they preached the Gospel in all the various districts of the country, they translated parts of the Bible, they composed a great many hymns and they had disputations with the antagonists of Reformation. The foremost of these Reforming preachers of Hungary were: Michael Sztárai, Emeric Exzèki, Stephen Kis, John Erdösi, and most of all, Mathias Biro of Dèva. These were men of an intrepid mind and quite immovable courage. No prelate could stop their mouth, no dungeon could terrify them, no misery and distress was too hard for them. Driven out from one city they fled to another, just as the Lord had commanded His disciples to do. And their labors were not in vain, but its fruit was a most wonderful one. In a short space of time almost the whole nation embraced the Gospel: noblemen and vassals, citizens and farmers, all received with joy the glad tidings of liberty with Christ, and so much had these men and their successors done, that towards the end of the 16th century, when the Jesuits for the first time appeared in Hungary, one of their writers makes this avowal: that of all the great noblemen of the country only 3 families had remained in the Roman Church, and of the squires and citizens none.

I cannot, of course give you here a complete history of the Reformation in Hungary. This history is so full of interesting details, that even with a special lecture one could hardly do it justice. I must, therefore, be contented to draw a few outlines and mark the most conspicuous features of every epoch.

Towards the end of the 16th century almost the whole country, as stated above, had become evangelized, the real Magyars having embraced Calvinism, while the Germans and Slavonians remained with the Church of Luther. The Emperors of the House of Habsburg, who since 1526 had succeeded on the throne of Hungary, were Ferdinand I, a man without real conviction, but clinging rather to Romanism and doing the best he could to support the tottering edifice of the Roman Church, and his son, Maximilian II, who, as the perfect counterpart of his father, was in his heart fully convinced of the evangelical truth, and remained in the Roman Church only outwardly, for mere political reasons. Under these rulers, therefore, the Protestants had not to suffer by persecutions. But the son of Maximilian, Rudolf II, was again anything but like his father. Brought up in Spain, at the court of Philip II, he was in his whole life a mere puppet in the hands of the Jesuits. These were the real rulers, and now they commenced, with the help of the imperial mercenaries to drive away Protestant ministers from their homes, to deprive Protestant noblemen of their estates, and to violate openly the constitution and privileges of Hungary. The Protestants, after having tried all peaceable and legal means to come to their right, at last rose in arms against their perturbers, and forced upon them the *treaty of Vienna, in 1606,* by which free exercise of religion was granted to the Protestants, whilst the Jesuits were forbidden to own any land within the realm. This however was of no avail. The Jesuits did not think even to observe these articles of peace. They erected a big college at Tyrnou, and having slyly allured there the children of the highest Protestant noble families, they succeeded to make most of them backsliders to Romanism. And having thus caught the Lords, it was not too difficult to re-convert, by all sorts of vexatious, the poor vassals of those. Again and again the Protestants rose in self-defense, routed the imperial armies and imposed upon their adversaries new treaties of peace, those of Nicolsburg (1621), Pressburg (1626) and Linz (1645), embodying more detailed liberties of religion and worship. But the fanaticism of the apostate Lords and of the mighty Prelates was not to be coerced. The articles of peace hardly having been sworn to, the vexations and forcible conversions of Protestants commenced anew. The fiercest and most bloody persecution, however, of the Protestants began only in 1671 under Leopold I, when the Reformed princes of Transylvania, formerly the stronghold of the Protestants, had lost their power. Then the Jesuits thought the time had come to extirpate Protestantism wholly from the soil of Hungary. This time they directed their fury expressly against the pastors of Protestant congregations. It seems they called to their minds this biblical passage: *"I will smite the shepherd, and the sheep of the flock shall be scattered abroad."* In 1673 all Protestant pastors residing in Upper Hungary were summoned to appear before an arbitrary tribunal established at *Pressburg* with nothing but papists as judges and presided over by the Archbishop of Grau, George Szelepésenyi. The Protestant ministers, numbering 33 and mostly Lutherans, were tried for rebellion, blasphemy and high treason, and although they could not be convicted of any of these crimes, except to have popery styled as idolatry, they were all condemned to death, and only by special clemency of the king pardoned either to be exiled or to resign forever their ministry. The first murderous stroke against Protestantism having thus succeeded them, the Roman prelates thought how to repeat it with a still deadlier effect. As soon as the beginning of the next year all pastors of the whole country had to appear before the same court, and only those living in the great Turkish Dominion of Hungary disobeyed the summons. Of those 336 presenting themselves for trial the greatest part was exiled in the former manner, but 61 pastors, and among these 39 of the Reformed Church, refused in spite of torturing to accept by their own accord any punishment or to desert their flocks. These then after many months' imprisonment in moisty dungeons, were condemned to be dragged to Italy, and to be sold as galley-slaves to the Spanish squadron of Naples. In January of 1675 the first transport of 41 Protestant ministers crossed the Alps, fettered with irons, starving with hunger, half naked and continually beaten. From Triest they were brought over the Adriatic in the afterhold of a little ship and those who had not perished by these innumerable tortures were hurried over the Italian peninsula to Naples, and sold as slaves to the Spaniards. For two years were these ministers of the Gospel chained to the benches of several open vessels, and 10 of them died here the death of martyrs of the Truth, till at last the famous Dutch admiral De Ruyter, though an ally then of the Spanish crown, delivered the remaining sufferers out of the hands of the Spaniards and dismissed them to seek a refuge in different Protestant countries.

The second transport of 19 ministers (one having made his escape) could not be brought to Italy, as the Venetian authorities protested against them passing their territory, and therefore these were brought to the little town of Buccari, on the Hungarian shore of the Adriatic, and imprisoned for 80 days in dungeons without light, till those who had not perished yet were set free, several Protestant princes having interceded in their favor with the Emperor Leopold.

This is the dark picture of persecution of Protestants in Hungary. After this there followed only a few instances more of *bloody* persecution (especially the fearful execution of 17 prominent Protestant citizens of *Eperies,* who were altogether innocent of any offence)—but the unbloody vexations and forcible conversions took their course on through the whole of the long reigns of *Charles VI* and the empress *Maria Theresia,* and only the son of this latter mentioned, the enlightened prince *Joseph II* made them pause by his famous *Order of Toleration* (Toleranzpatent) in 1781. This then was indeed the dawn of a brighter epoch, for not more than 10 years after, in 1791, *the diet* assembled by order of *Leopold II* restituted to the Protestants most of their former rights, giving them a free exercise of their religion and an independent administration of their churches and schools. A few restrictions, this diet had still made, regarding marriages of Protestants and Roman Catholics, were removed in our days, by the laws of the year 1868, so that Hungarian Protestants now enjoy full equality of *rights* with the Roman Catholics, though, as we shall see, they are far from enjoying equality at state support.

The Hungarian Church Difficulties from an American Standpoint

In the present controversy between the representatives in the United States of the Reformed Church of Hungary and those representing the Reformed and Presbyterian Churches of the United States of America, each party, doubtless, believes in the justice of its own contention. In the hope that it may make the situation more clear, and perhaps tend toward a Christian adjustment of what is now a most unchristian state of affairs, the writer ventures to state the issue as it presents itself to him. He has no authority to speak for any one but himself, but he believes, after wide intercourse with Americans conversant with the facts, that he fairly states their position in general.

1. The matter at issue does not concern the character of the Reformed Church of Hungary. That Church is recognized as a sister church holding the Reformed faith, in so far as it has official symbols, and the Presbyterian system of church government, with this her permanent presidents, or "bishops," are not inconsistent. She is honored for her noble history. We only ask a like recognition of the American denominations named.

2. Nor does it turn upon the fact that the Hungarian Reformed Church is connected with the State in Hungary (being recognized by law, receiving State aid, having clerical and lay representation in the Diet, etc.), and is thereby exposed to political influences; although much of the present difficulty seems to have grown directly or indirectly out of this connection.

3. It is not whether the Magyar in America should cherish a love for his native soil and for his mother church, nor yet whether he should employ those forms and customs which use has made sacred to him. It is freely granted that he should; a bad son is not likely to make a good husband. But, on the other hand, a good mother ought not to try to come between her son and his wife.

4. It is not whether it is right for the Church in Hungary to send ministers and to establish churches in the United States. This is clearly her privilege, and may under certain circumstances be her duty. If this had been done earlier, or were being done now in a different way and with different motives from those which seem to characterize the present movement, there would be no conflict.

5. But when for more than fifteen years the American churches had been providing ministers, gathering congregations and helping to build churches for the Magyars in America, and the Hungarian Church had done nothing directly, was it right for the Hungarian Church authorities to send over and try to secure control of these churches and this property, without obtaining or even asking leave of the American Churches? When the Hungarian ministers at Johnstown almost unanimously, and the Magyar people of the congregations subsequently and repeatedly voted in the great majority of the congregations not to withdraw from their American connections, was it right to persist in the attempt through the second visit of Count Degenfeld and the successive missions of Drs. Antal and Bede, in direct disregard of the expressed wishes of the great body of these Magyar ministers and people? Is it not a fact that the whole effort of the representatives of the Hungarian Church in America, with perhaps one or two exceptions, has been to induce congregations already formed to desert their American friends, or, failing in this, to disrupt the congregation and set up a rival church in the same community? Are not the American

churches and the Magyars who prefer to be associated with them right in asking that their work be not interfered with in this way?

6. If this were done upon the ground that the Magyars were being taught false doctrine or immoral practices by the American churches, then there might be a justification for such an attempt. But this is not the case, according to Baron Banffy, lay president of the Convent, and his secretary, Dr. Nagy, who are directing the movement. Four distinct witnesses known to the writer testify, two in print, and two by private letters, that one or both of the persons named frankly declared to them that the motive was not primarily religious but political. One of these quotes the Baron as saying to him when he was sending him to America:

"I want to tell you that the home Church does not make all the great sacrifices and keep all those churches in America, because of our fear that the Hungarian Reformed emigrants might lose their faith, because if they want to remain Calvinists they can join the Reformed Church of America or the Presbyterian, which are both the same as ours, but the reason is a political one. We want them to remain good subjects of their old home; we want them to remain Hungarians and not to become Americans. Please remember this and work accordingly."

Is it right that the religious interests of the Magyars in America should be subordinated and sacrificed to the present and future exigencies of politics in Hungary? That they are being sacrificed as well as subordinated by the present movement is unquestionable.

7. Even if the general movement and the confessed motive of it could be approved, the methods employed by many representatives of the Hungarian Church would still be open to question. Ignorance and prejudice are appealed to by misrepresentation; as, for example, that to be connected with the Reformed Church of America is to become subject to the Germans, or that the Presbyterian is not a Calvinistic Church, or that the aim of the American churches is to get the money of the Hungarians, when as a matter of fact these churches have been and are spending large sums to aid the Magyars in securing churches, ministers and periodicals. Ministers connected with the American churches are repeatedly approached privately with offers of financial and other rewards if they will desert their American friends, and are warned of the evil results to themselves and their churches if they do not do so. When private solicitation fails, many of these same ministers are subject to attacks upon their private character and ministerial standing in the public prints. That there has been recrimination as well as crimination must be confessed and is to be deplored, but certainly the parties first attacked have the better excuse.

By their official representatives both the Reformed and Presbyterian churches have declared their willingness to seek an adjustment of the existing difficulties. Both churches assuredly stand ready to agree to anything which, in their view, will promote the true religious interests of their Magyar fellow citizens, will protect the latter in their right to form religious connections without dictation and molestation from outside, and will preserve the religious and pecuniary trusts, which have been committed to the respective denominations. Why should not the Conventus in Hungary meet the authorities of the American churches in the same spirit?

SAMUEL MCLANAHAN.

Lawrenceville, N.J.

Resisting Popular Culture

42. Mercersburg Theology:
"Denominationalism and Sectarianism"

(1893)

Philip Schaff

The revivals of the Great Awakenings and the great ideas of freedom and autonomy that permeated North America in the years leading up to the Revolutionary War produced a new and identifiably "American religious temper." According to this temper, individual personal religious experience and consciousness became the criterion by which all things in the church were to be judged. A congregation was defined as made up by the free association of those who had a religious experience, and a church, or denomination, was made up of groups of such experientially created congregations. This way of defining the church flew in the face of classic Reformed theology. In the tradition of the Heidelberg Catechism such subjectivist excess had always been balanced by the promise of God expressed within the church through word and sacrament.

Foremost among those concerned about this distorted theology of the church were two professors at the German Reformed Seminary in Mercersburg, Pennsylvania, John Williamson Nevin (1803–86) and Philip Schaff (1819–93). Nevin, a Scotch-Irish Presbyterian, was educated at Union College and Princeton Seminary, and taught at Princeton Seminary and Western Theological Seminary before accepting the call to Mercersburg, where he taught from 1840 to 1853. Nevin's theological focus centered on the doctrine of the church, which he developed in his great work The Mystical Presence *(1846) and in numerous articles in the* Mercersburg Review. *Schaff was a historian and theologian with a*

Source: Philip Schaff, "Denominationalism and Sectarianism," from *The Independent,* reprinted in *Reformed Church Messenger,* 23 November 1893, 3–4.

rich appreciation of Germany's new idealistic philosophy and its pietistic traditions. He left a promising career at the University of Berlin to come to Mercersburg, where he taught from 1844 to 1863.

Although the influence of Nevin and Schaff was negligible during the 1840s and 1850s, the Mercersburg Theology they developed has made long-standing contributions to the Reformed Church and to the history of Protestantism in the United States. Their work forcefully articulates three fundamental convictions: (1) the person of Christ is the ultimate and central fact of Christianity; (2) the incarnation is the essential starting point of Christian theology; and (3) the fullness of the life of Christ, perpetuated in objective, historical, and sacramental form, is presented through the richness and diversity of the history of the church.

Schaff's inaugural address, "The Principle of Protestantism, as Related to the Present State of the Church," was expanded by him, translated, and published with a strong introduction by Nevin, becoming one of the central manifestos of the Mercersburg movement. In the Mercersburg Review, *one of the great journals of pre–Civil War America under Nevin's editorship, the two professors offered insights from the ancient catholic church that Protestantism often ignored. Their writings gave new vitality to the doctrine of the church as the body of Christ and emphasized its objective and visible character. They were also among the first church leaders in the United States to urge greater dialogue between Reformed and Lutheran Protestants. "Denominationalism and Sectarianism," originally published in* The Independent, *appeared in* The Reformed World *shortly after Philip Schaff's death. In it, Schaff outlines a Pauline concept of the organic nature of the church, which was the motivation behind his lifelong support of the ecumenical movement and his long involvement in a United States branch of the Evangelical Alliance. The culmination of his thinking appeared in his famous address on "The Reunion of Christendom," delivered in Chicago at the World's Parliament of Religions shortly before his death.*

Denominationalism and Sectarianism

In recent discussions on Christian Union, denominationalism and sectarianism are frequently confounded and condemned together. Denominationalism, as such, may be perfectly compatible with Christian Union, as much so as different army corps are with the unity of an army and different monastic orders with the unity of the papacy. But sectarianism is essentially exclusive, and opposed to co-operation for one common purpose; it is nothing but extended selfishness under the garb of religious zeal. Denominationalism subordinated to catholic Christianity, and made subservient to it is a blessing. Sectarianism is a curse.

We must acknowledge the hand of Providence in the present divisions of Christendom. They are found in the most advanced and active nations of the world—in England and the United States. A stagnant Church is a sterile mother. Dead orthodoxy is as bad as heresy, or even worse. Denominations are a sign of life and interest in religion. The most important periods of the Church—the Nicene Age and the Age of the Reformation—were full of controversy. There are divisions in the Church which cannot be justified, and sects which have fulfilled their missions and ought to cease; but the leading denominations are historic forces and represent various aspects of the Christian religion which supplement each other.

As the life of our Saviour could not be fully exhibited by one Gospel, nor his doctrine fully set forth by one Apostle, much less could any one Christian body comprehend and manifest the whole fullness of Christ and the entire extent of his mission to mankind.

Every one of the great divisions of the Church has had and still has its peculiar mission as to territory, race and nationality, and modes of operation.

The Greek Church is especially adapted to the East, to the Greek and Slavonic peoples; the Roman to the Latin races of Southern Europe and America; the Protestant Churches to the Teutonic races of the North and West.

Among the Protestant Churches, again, some have a special gift for the cultivation of Christian science and literature; others for the practical development of the Christian life; some are most successful among the higher, others among the middle, and still others among the lower classes. None of them could be spared without great detriment to the cause of religion and morality, and leaving its territory and constituency spiritually destitute. Even the most imperfect Church is better than no Church.

No schism occurs in the Church without guilt on one or both sides. "It must needs be that offences come; but woe to that man by whom the offence cometh." Yet God overrules the sins and follies of man for his own glory.

The separation of Paul and Barnabas, in consequence of their "sharp contention" concerning Mark, resulted in the enlargement of missionary labor. If Luther had not burned the Pope's Bull, or had recanted at Worms, we should not have a Lutheran Church, but be still under the spiritual tyranny of the papacy. If Luther had accepted Zwingli's hand of fellowship at Marburg, the Protestant cause would have been stronger at the time; but the full development of the characteristic features of the two principal Churches of the Reformation would have been prevented or obstructed. If John Wesley had not ordained Bishop Coke we should have no Methodist Episcopal Church, which is the strongest denomination in the United States. If Chalmers and his friends had not seceded from the General Assembly of the Kirk of Scotland in 1843, forsaking every comfort for the sake of the sole headship of Christ, we should miss one of the grandest chapters in Church history.

All divisions of Christendom will, in the providence of God, be made subservient to greater harmony. Where the sin of past schism abounded, the grace of future reunion will much more abound.

Taking this view of the divisions of the Church, we must reject the idea of a negative union, which would destroy all denominational distinctions, and thus undo the work of the past. History is not the "empty fabric of a vision leaving no track behind." It is the unfolding of God's plan of infinite wisdom and mercy to mankind. He is the chief actor and rules and overrules the thoughts and acts of His servants. We are told that he has numbered the very hairs of our heads, and that not a sparrow falleth to the ground without the will of our Heavenly Father. The labors of confessors and martyrs, of missionaries and scholars, of fathers, schoolmen and reformers, and the countless host of holy men and women of all ranks and conditions, who lived for the good of their fellows, cannot be lost, but constitute a treasure of inestimable value for all future time. The Apostle encourages his brethren to be "steadfast, unmovable, always abounding in the work of the Lord," because their "labor is not in vain in the Lord" (1 Cor. 15:58). Whatever is built upon the foundation of Jesus Christ will stand.

Variety in unity and unity in variety is the law of God, in nature, in history and in His Kingdom. Unity without variety is dead uniformity. In variety is beauty. There is no harmony without many sounds, and a garden incloses all kinds of flowers. God has made no two nations, no two men, not even two trees nor two flowers alike. He has endowed every nation, every Church, yea, every individual with peculiar gifts. His power, His wisdom and His goodness are reflected in ten thousand forms.

"There are diversities of gifts," says Paul, "but the same Spirit, and there are differences of administration, but the same Lord. And there are diversities of operations, but it is the same God, who worketh all in all. But the manifestations of the Spirit is given to every man to profit withal." (1 Cor. 12:4–7)

We must, therefore, expect the greatest variety in the Church of the future. There are good Christians who believe in the ultimate triumph of their own creed or form of government and worship; but they are all mistaken and indulge in a vain dream. The world will never become wholly Greek nor wholly Roman, nor wholly Protestant, but it will become wholly Christian, and will include every type and every aspect, every virtue and every grace of Christianity, an endless variety in harmonious unity, Christ being all in all.

Every denomination which holds to Christ the head will retain its distinctive peculiarity, and lay it on the altar of reunion; but it must cheerfully recognize the excellencies and merits of the other branches of the Kingdom. No sect has the monopoly of truth; the part is not the whole; the body consists of many members, and all are necessary to each other.

Episcopalians may prefer their form of government as the best, but must concede the vitality of the non-Episcopal ministry.

Baptists, while holding fast to the primitive mode of immersion, must allow pouring or effusion as legitimate baptism.

Protestants will cease to regard the Pope as the antichrist predicted by Paul and John, and will acknowledge him as the legitimate Head of the Roman Church; while the Pope ought to recognize the respective rights and privileges of Greek patriarchs and evangelical bishops and pastors.

Those who prefer to worship God in forms of a stated liturgy, ought not to deny others the equal right of free prayer as the Spirit moves them.

Doctrinal differences will be the most difficult to adjust. When two dogmas flatly contradict each other, the one denying what the other asserts, one or the other, or both must be wrong. Truth excludes error and admits of no compromise.

But truth is many-sided and all-sided, and is reflected in different colors. The creeds of Christendom, as already remarked, agree in the essential articles of faith, and their differences refer either to minor points or represent only various aspects of truth and supplement each other.

Calvinists and Arminians are both right, the former in maintaining the Sovereignty of God, the latter in maintaining the freedom and moral responsibility of man; but they are both wrong when they deny one of these two truths which are equally important, although we may not be able satisfactorily to reconcile them. The conflicting theories on the Lord's Supper, which have caused the bitterest controversies among the medieval schoolmen and among Protestant reformers, turn, after all, only on the mode of Christ's presence; while all admit the fact that He is spiritually and really present and partaken by believers as the Bread of Life from Heaven. Even the two fundamental differences between Romanists and Protestants concerning Scripture and tradition as rules of faith, and faith and works as conditions of justification admit of an adjustment by a better understanding of the nature and relationship of Scripture and tradition, faith and works. The difference is no greater than that between Paul and James in their teaching on justification; and yet the Epistles of both stand side by side in the same canon of Holy Scripture.

We must remember that the dogmas of the Church are earthly vessels for heavenly treasures, or imperfect human definitions of divine truths, and may be improved by better statements with the advance of knowledge. Our theological systems are but dim rays of the Sun of Truth which illuminates the universe.

Each denomination should prepare a short, popular and irenic creed of the essential articles which it holds in common with all others, and leave larger Confessions of Faith to the theologians whose business it is to investigate the mysteries and to solve the problems of faith.

—*The Independent.*

The Dutch Reformed Church

43. Early Union Attempts: *"The Union Movement," "Conference on Union," and "The Union of the Two Reformed Churches"*

(1874, 1888, and 1889)

Reformed Church Messenger; Thomas G. Apple

The German Reformed Synod and the Dutch Reformed Church were very similar: both were Calvinist, having roots in the German and Swiss Reformed Churches of the sixteenth century; both were nurtured by the Reformed Church in Holland during the colonial era; and both underwent similar struggles to find their identity as immigrant peoples in the New World. Union between them should have been easily achieved. However, in spite of some informal discussions before the Revolutionary War and three formal efforts to unite between 1794 and 1893, they never did join together.

The first attempt to unite the two churches began when the Reformed Church in Holland, which was supporting both groups, heard that four colonial presbyteries had successfully become a synod. The Europeans suggested that the German and the Dutch churches ought to unite with the Presbyterians and establish a single Presbyterian church in North America. The inclinations of the two groups waxed and waned over

---

Source: "The Union Movement," *Reformed Church Messenger,* 9 December 1874, 1–2; "Conference on Union Between the Reformed Church in America and the Reformed Church in the United States, at Philadelphia, April 3 and 4, 1888," *Reformed Church Messenger,* 11 April 1888, 2; Thomas G. Apple, "The Union of the Two Reformed Churches," *Reformed Church Messenger,* 16 January 1889, 2–3.

thirty-seven years, and the Dutch church finally withdrew its proposal in 1753.

A second round of conversations was more official. Between 1804 and 1847 "fraternal correspondence" between the two groups led to an exchange of delegates and finally an elaborate plan of union worked out in 1844. A Triennial Convention was attended by both churches, and five articles of agreement were adopted about mutual instruction and the use of common textbooks in seminaries, shared liturgies, and a blending of domestic missions. At a second Triennial Convention in 1847, however, the Dutch church became alarmed that the German Reformed Synod regarded the Heidelberg Catechism as "symbol enough." Because the Dutch church demanded allegiance to the Belgic Confession and the Articles of Dort, they withdrew from the proposed agreement.

A third effort at union was initiated when the German Reformed Synod in 1863 changed its name to the General Synod of the Reformed Church in the United States. The new synod began corresponding with five other denominations about church union—including the General Synod of the Reformed Dutch Church (which became the Reformed Church in America in 1869). In 1872, German and Dutch committees on union met to draft a paper looking into the issue of union between them. Unfortunately, the committees found that the same confessional differences that had been a barrier nearly thirty years before continued to stand between them.

Finally, in 1887, a fourth and final effort toward union was attempted when the Reformed General Synod appointed a new committee chaired by Thomas G. Apple to meet with a comparable committee from the Dutch Reformed Church. An initial very positive meeting was held in Philadelphia where the issue of doctrinal difference was directly addressed and appeared to be surmountable. However, six months later, Apple made a cautionary report in the Messenger, *lamenting that the Dutch church did not seem to have the same sense of the organic unity of the church and the importance of the church catholic that the German Reformed Synod had.*

Nevertheless, a plan for federal union was drawn up by a joint committee in Catskill, New York, in 1891. It was adopted by both churches and plans were made for the first Federal Synod. Unfortunately, the Dutch church postponed its discussions for a year because of exactly the same doctrinal differences that had thwarted union in 1847. By 1893, when a vote should have been taken, there was so much Dutch opposition from a small but vocal group that both churches were forced to drop the matter for a fourth time.

The Union Movement

Some of the religious papers which have noticed the result of the late attempt to bring about a union between the two Reformed Churches, attribute the failure to the theology that prevails in our Church. One says, the Dutch were afraid that Mercersburg theology would spread in their Church, in case a union were effected, and another says, the Mercersburg men were afraid that, in a union of the two Churches, their theology would be endangered by the overwhelming majority that would then be arrayed against it.

These papers are wise above what is written. The report of the joint committee finds the difficulty in the way of union to lie, not in churchly usages, confirmation, keeping the festival days, liturgical worship, etc., but in the doctrinal difference between the standard of the two Churches. The German Church has but one doctrinal standard, the Heidelberg Catechism, while the Dutch Church holds, in addition, to the Belgic Confession and the Articles of the Dortrecht Synod. Neither Church is prepared to change its doctrinal standards. We take it, that the anti-liturgical party in the German Church are as much attached to the Heidelberg Catechism, and as little willing to bind themselves to infra-lapsarian Calvinism, as the Mercersburg wing.

The Dutch committee were not willing to yield an iota on this point. If there is to be a union, their Church could not tone down their Calvinistic views, but the German Church would be expected to come up to them. That, we believe, was the attitude of committee from the Dutch Church. Not even Dr. Bomberger and his friends were prepared to encourage the thought, that the German Church would be disposed to make any change in their doctrinal views on the subject of Calvinism. Hence the failure of the *great union movement* as the "Christian World" used to call it.

The only reference to any other doctrinal differences is contained in the statement, "In addition to this, the probable fact, that a body made up of these two denominations would include important differences in doctrinal views and ecclesiastical feeling, has appeared during the conference," which is somewhat vague. We do not see the force of the words "in addition to this" in the above, after stating that the difference is a doctrinal one. If this sentence does refer to Mercersburg theology, and the chief difficulty is made to hinge on this, then it would seem, that the Dutch Church think the anti-liturgical party in the German Church would be more ready to adopt their Calvinistic standards, than the Mercersburg men, an inference which that party would hardly be willing to admit, we presume. If we are to receive the statement of this committee as candid and full, then the cause of the failure cannot be attributed to the prevalence of Mercersburg theology in the German Church.

The truth of the case is, that this great union movement was started in a burst of an enthusiastic feeling, without considering properly the difficulties in the way. The Presbyterian, or the Dutch Reformed, either, would gladly incorporate our German branch into it, but neither think seriously of a union, which would involve any, the least, change on its part. Union must come spontaneously, as ripe fruit falls from the tree. Any attempt to force it, only tends to drive the bodies farther apart. We must be satisfied to wait till the time comes.

Conference on Union

Between the Reformed Church in America and the Reformed Church in the United States, at Philadelphia, April 3 & 4, 1888.

The First Session of the Conference was held in First Reformed Church, 10th and Wallace Streets, Rev. D. Van Horne, D.D., pastor. It was opened by Rev. J. I. Good, D.D., who announced the hymn, "Blest be the tie that binds."

Rev. A. R. Bartholomew read the Scriptures, John 17, and Rev. Dr. Drury, Editor of the *Christian Intelligencer,* led the Conference in prayer.

Rev. T. G. Apple, D.D., Chairman of the Joint Committee on Union, delivered the opening address:

Stating that the object of the meeting was to consider the question of a closer union of these two sister Churches, the one rising in the Netherlands, the other in Germany. Emigrants from Holland came to America as early as 1619 (a year before the Plymouth fathers), and those from Germany about 1684. For many years these Germans were under the care of the Church of Holland. These two Churches, more than any other in this country, represent the meaning of the broad, historic title, Reformed. In their earliest confessions they were substantially one; and historically these confessions were considered in entire harmony. The present differences between these Churches come from their independent development in this country. Now, shall these differences keep these two Churches apart?

Dr. Apple then called attention to two points: 1. The present divided state of the Protestant Church is abnormal. It may have historical justification in the past, but now is the day-dawn of union, and our two historic Churches should lead off in this coming together. Indeed, necessity may drive us to union against a common enemy. There must be a return to unity. The keynote to this has already been given in the union of Christian Churches in heathen lands.

2. As sacrifices were made in breaking into fragments, so union can come only by some sacrifice, not the sacrifice of principle or truth, but of denominational zeal and minor differences. We must subordinate what is only secondary to what is primary, uniting on truth that is central and then holding all other truths in right relation to this. Shall not the issues that once divided the Church now yield to those on which we are agreed?

But which denomination shall survive? Neither. There would not be an absorption of one but a union of the two in a better body than either alone, by a sacrifice of denominational pride and zeal. No one denomination will ever be the one Church of this county. The old generic title, "Reformed," is gaining its early place and meaning. This public meaning includes not only papers and discussions on Union, but especially devout prayer for divine guidance, imply dependence not upon human wisdom but rather upon that which is from above. Papers and discussions help us to think alike, but of greater avail is earnest prayer. Many eyes in other Churches look upon us today to see the result of this effort toward union.

Rev. Charles Scott, D.D., President of Hope College, Holland, Michigan, was then introduced.

He said he was in Philadelphia in 1853 at the meeting of the Synod of the Reformed Dutch Church, which passed the resolution suspending correspondence with the Synod of the German Reformed church. This act pained him then and had pained him during the thirty-five years since. Let us restore this correspondence, said he, and not hold separate what God had put together.

"Thy kingdom come" is, the normal prayer of the whole Church in all the world; and John 17th is the out-breathing of the Saviour's soul for the unity of the Church. Paul speaks of diversity in the Church, but also of unity, many members but one body. It is a plain historical fact that the early Reformed Church of Europe was but one body. France, Germany, Switzerland, Holland, Scotland, all were a perfect brotherhood in Christ, divided only by language and geography. The Catholics had their pope as head, and the Lutherans rallied around the name of Luther, but the Reformed had their *faith* as their basis of unity, and when they went from place to place they knew no partition. Holland became the life-heart of the Reformed faith. They knew only one Reformed Church. The Synod of Dort was the General Council of the Reformed Church of Europe. Yea, and when the Reformed came to America they knew only one Reformed

Church. How, then, did our Churches become separated? Let us again unite what so by history belongs together.

Dr. Scott then introduced Rev. E. T. Corwin, D.D., of Millstone, N. J., and afterward Rev. J. H. Dubbs, D.D., of Franklin and Marshall College, Lancaster, Pa., both of whom read papers on "The Historical and Doctrinal Relations of the Two Churches."

Dr. Corwin urged union among the Churches, 1) because it is right, 2) for the honor of Christ, 3) for the great work that may then be done. The signs of the times point to union. God is evidently leading the Churches together, and those most alike should be the first to take the step. The Reformed Churches of Europe were always considered one in doctrine and polity. They differed in language and minor matters, but were one over against Lutheranism. Surely the different branches of the Reformed Church today should be none the less a unit. Our two Churches especially should be one, because it would be simply restoring old relations. Stern necessity calls us to such unity, in order to do our work both in the home and in the foreign field.

Dr. Corwin then, in rapid outline, traced the history of the two Churches in America, and showed their close relation here. The Germans and Palatines who came to Pennsylvania before and after 1727 were under the Classis of Amsterdam until 1793. The first German minister ordained in America, was ordained by ministers of the Church of Holland; and did not the Synod of Holland send Schlatter to America as missionary superintendent? But the Revolution made great changes in our Church relations, and in 1793 the Germans became independent of the Church in Holland. But will it not be easy to come together again?

Dr. Corwin then gave a history of the correspondence between the two Churches. Early in the eighteenth century the Synod of Holland tried to unite the Dutch Reformed, the German Reformed and the Presbyterians in one body, but the scheme failed. In 1770 the great question arose in the Dutch Church, where to locate her institutions; and New Brunswick was chosen, because though on the border of her field, it was *near the Germans,* and so for their interest. Early and many were the longings for union. In 1812 began the exchange of delegates, and many references to union are found in the subsequent minutes of the Dutch Church. In 1842 Rev. Dr. J. F. Berg and Rev. Dr. E. Heiner of the German Church, urged union, and this gradually led to the famous Harrisburg Convention in 1844, which proposed conditions of union which were unanimously adopted by the Synods of both Churches; but the whole plan soon collapsed, and in 1853 the Dutch Synod discontinued even correspondence by delegates. In 1863 the German Church widely and wisely celebrated the tercentenary of the Heidelberg Catechism, in which the pastors took a deep interest, and soon after the old relations were renewed. In 1874 a conference looking to unity was held in Philadelphia between committees of the two Churches; and though union did not follow, yet great gain was found in harmonious discussions and a better acquaintanceship. Now we are again together for the promotion of union. Would it not be noble to unite these two Churches and so prepare the way for further union and greater victories? May God give us grace to act wisely.

Dr. Dubbs began by comparing the Reformed Church to the river Rhine, having her rise in Switzerland, her tributaries in France and Germany, and her course toward Holland. In all countries the Reformed Church bears witness to unity in diversity. Meeting here to revive the affection of other days is itself an evidence of a unity of faith and life. This essential unity is seen in four facts:

1. The Reformed Churches of Europe acknowledge the same founders and leaders. We both have Zwingli, Calvin, and the heroes of the Palatinate.
2. In confessional agreement. Our various confessions, for we have many, are not contradictory but only variations of the one great theme, their difference being confined to minor details. Local confessions emphasized some one truth, because of some attack upon it, but all are only different aspects of the great sum of truth.
3. The Reformed Churches are alike in external organization. It is easy to see how this came. The form of government that prevailed in Holland found its way into Germany and then was brought to this country.
4. The unity of the two Churches is seen in the mutual support each gave the other in time of need. Germany received the Hollanders who fled before the dreadful Alva; and Holland, a century later, repaid this debt by caring for the fleeing Palatines. And did not Holland also send men and money to the Germans and Palatines in America to build up the Church here? Indeed it is an interesting fact that the German churches of Pennsylvania were under the care of the Synod of Holland twenty-three years longer than even the Dutch churches of New York.

As to doctrine and life, however, there is a difference between the two Churches, not in appearance only, but real; and it is the work of this convention to see whether this difference forbids an organic union. Early in the history of the Church in Europe some differences were felt and expressed in its confessions. The Belgic Confession and the Articles of Dort were acknowledged by the Germans as Reformed; but they considered the Heidelberg Catechism an ample bond of union, and had no desire to increase the number of their symbols. Long ago, however, our relations were far more intimate than they now are: and a hundred years ago organic union could easily have been effected, except for the difference in language and geographical distance. The present time, however, seems very auspicious for a closer union. Both Churches must recognize and appreciate the principle of unity in diversity. Seeing that we should never have been separated, should we not now seek to come together?

Rev. A. P. Gieson, D.D., of Poughkeepsie, N.Y., then read an interesting paper on "The Canons of Dort."

The Catechism is for the young and therefore brief and concise. The Canons are more extended and precise, but none the less moderate. The Synod of Dort was made up of delegates from various parts of the Church and representing, of course, various views. The articles adopted, therefore, of necessity, excluded that on which they differed and included that on which they agreed. In regard to predestination, for example, the Catechism teaches an election, not in the Arminian but in the Calvinistic sense. "Chosen to eternal life." But beyond this it does not go, but allows freedom of belief. The Canons of Dort give the same freedom. The delegates represented three grades or views of the doctrine of election; but neither one of these views was adopted or condemned. All the members subscribed the Canons, none of its articles putting any one outside the pale of orthodoxy. This result was not a compromise, but the Canons were made broad enough to take in both extremes represented. They are not ambiguous, but liberal. As to election, their statements are as moderate as those of the Catechism. They assert what the Catechism implies, namely, that not all men are chosen, some are passed by.

As to the death of Christ, did he die for all or for the elect only? The Catechism says he died for all mankind, a universal redemption; but question 37 also gives a limit: namely, he died for believers. In fact the Catechism gives no definite decision but allows liberty of belief. Equal liberty is given by the Canons of Dort. Because of difference of opinion there was sharp debate; but all subscribed the Canons, i.e. they were so framed as to allow this divergence of view. They do not say Christ died only for the elect, but that the saving efficacy of his death becomes effective only in a certain class—which no one will deny.

On the subject of conversion the agreement of the Catechism and the Canons is very plain. The Catechism is even stronger than the Canons in reference to the work of the Holy Ghost, the Canons giving more prominence to the activity of the human will.

It is admitted that this representation of the Canons is different from that which is generally made; but it is nevertheless true. They are broad, liberal, moderate. Their language is most precise but in the interest of moderation. The very composition of the Synod made it impossible to agree upon any statements that were not broad enough to take in all the divergent views represented.

The Convention at 6 P.M. adjourned to the basement of the church where an abundant and elegant lunch was served by the ladies of the city churches. Members of the Convention and visitors, ladies and gentlemen were distinguished by a ribbon worn by each, the orange by the Dutch and the red by the German.

The Union of the Two Reformed Churches

There are doubtless many in our German Reformed Church who would like to know just what the situation is in regard to our union with the Dutch Reformed Church. While very little can yet be said positively, and while it might not be well to indulge in much speculation at this stage of the proceedings, yet our people are entitled to know just where we stand, so far at least as this can be clearly ascertained.

The Joint Committee to which the subject was committed for arbitration by the General Synods of the two churches, has held two meetings: one in New York, the other in Philadelphia. The result of these two conferences left the matter entirely undecided. The Committee of the Dutch Church simply reported progress to their last General Synod, and the whole matter now rests until the Joint Committee, or Commission, meets again to formulate a report to both General Synods; and as one General Synod does not meet again until May, 1890, the probability is that the subject will be allowed to rest for some time to come.

In the two conferences already held the two committees tried to persuade themselves that the conditions were favorable to a union of some kind, but there seemed to be no unanimity, in the first place, as to what kind the union ought to be, and in the second place, neither committee could feel fully assured that the Churches are as yet prepared for any union that may be proposed. My own impression is that the desire for union is more fully developed in ours than in the Dutch Church, but that the necessity for union is quite equal on their part to what it is with us. I believe that our peculiar theological development has produced among our people a stronger sense of the organic unity of the Church of Christ, and as deducible from this a stronger desire to abate the divisions in the same, so as to bring its outward form of organization into better agreement with this internal organic oneness. It is not with us so much a mere question of economy and utility, but a solemn duty pressing upon all Christians, and that in order to realize this union more and more it is a duty even to make some sacrifice of denominational preferences and denominational pride. We see, indeed, that the present denominational attitude of the Protestant Church has been overruled for some good, but still we regard it as an abnormal condition.

I do not think that this feeling exists to the same extent in the Dutch Church, because the idea of the church catholic, as an organization, has not been considered so fully among them as with us. They are inclined, it seems to me, to look more at the external advantages the union might bring, particularly in subserving their own denominational peculiarities. We look more at the internal necessity in the Church itself for a more adequate external union, while they regard the union as looking mainly, if not only, to certain external advantages. Of course these two views are not contradictory, for when properly considered it must appear that what is called for by the internal nature of the Church must, in the end, be productive of the greatest external advantages, and that which will steadily produce the greatest external advantages must, in the nature of the case, be consistent with the internal and spiritual constitution of the church; but there is a wide difference as to which of these is regarded as primary. It is the old problem of utilitarianism as compared to intuitive, or *a fortiori*, doctrine of right.

For this reason, as well as others that might be named, I do not believe there is as strong a desire on their part for union as on our part. In the absence of a sense of the closer internal and historical relationship of our two Reformed Churches, and the fitness, therefore, of the union, the Dutch Church is much embarrassed by their intimate *external* relationship with the Presbyterian Church. Hence the question of uniting with the Presbyterian Church has been much agitated among them, and though this project received a quietus for the time in the action of their General Synod next before the last, yet the feeling is still there, and ready to assert itself whenever a proposal is made to unite with our Reformed Church. On this account much allowance must be made for their hesitation and their exceeding carefulness, in bringing forward any positive recommendation of a union with our Reformed Church. We on our part are not trammeled with any such question. We feel our close relationship with the Presbyterian Church, as one member of the family of Reformed Churches, and look forward to the time when all the members of this Reformed family shall come into some closer union than that of the Alliance now in existence and operation, but our external relation to the Presbyterian Church is not such as to make our union with it, in any way, a barrier to the proposed union of the two Reformed Churches. We consider that our nearest alliance at present is with the Dutch Reformed Church. Hence, I think, we are more ready to enter upon a consideration of the terms of such union than the Dutch Reformed Church is. We are simply waiting for that Church to get ready, and the delay in pressing the union is to be more attributed to them than to us.

It may be a somewhat delicate question to consider, as to the comparative force of the external necessity for union in relation to each of the two Churches, but I speak candidly on this point for myself, and, as I think, for my Church also.

This necessity does not press *any more* upon our Church, to say the least, in my judgment, than upon the Dutch Church. So far as external advantages are concerned it will not make much difference to us whether this union is consummated or not. The German Reformed Church has a fair future before it, judging from the *data* at hand. Our growth and prosperity have been most encouraging. Within fifty years, or thereabouts, we have grown from one small synod, with no institutions of learning, to *seven synods,* with a number of growing colleges and seminaries. Our territory has extended much more rapidly than that of the Dutch Church, reaching now from the Atlantic to the Pacific coast, and having the majority of our Synods in the growing West. We have abundance of material all through the West for establishing missions, and ultimately flourishing, self-sustaining churches. It involves no reflection on any one to say that in this respect our advantages for denominational growth are greater than those of the Dutch Reformed Church. We have much to encourage us to go on our way, working out our independent denominational calling. Hence, if the present movement towards union should again prove abortive, it will make little difference so far as our work as a denomination is concerned, but it will, I think, close the door effectually for a renewal of any overtures on the subject, whether invited by ours or the Dutch Church, for many years to come; perhaps finally.

But now, when we consider the future either of the one or the other of these two Reformed Churches, it is plain that the prospect would be much brighter for a united Reformed Church than for each one separately considered; for we cannot close our eyes to the fact, that each one in its separate capacity must expect to continue among the smaller denominations of this rapidly growing country. This may be our calling, and if so no one should be dissatisfied with it. Nay, it may be a better portion for us to exercise this humility of being willing to labor on in a small, rather than in a large denomination. One need not love his own home less because it is a humble one.

But if it be in accordance with the will of Providence that one strong Reformed Church should occupy the place in this country of two separate branches, it is at once clear what a different future would be opened up before us. Considering how the two would compliment each other in the union, the one strongly entrenched in the metropolis of the nation, the other reaching out more over the rural districts, though not without strength likewise in some of the large cities, it is plain that the united body would take its place at once alongside the largest Presbyterian bodies of this country. Its influence would be vastly increased in reference to all the great problems that confront the Christianity of America. And as our means and appliances would be vastly enhanced our responsibilities would be proportionably enlarged. In the course of time, perhaps soon, the question of union with the other Presbyterian churches would, doubtless, be raised, and some closer union be formed of all the Reformed Churches in this country holding the Presbyterian system, that are now represented in the Alliance. This will, no doubt, come sooner or later, at any rate; the only question is, whether it would not be facilitated by a previous union of the two Reformed Churches. I, for one, believe it would be; hence I advocate it, both for what it would accomplish immediately and also ultimately.

Our present attitude, therefore, is simply one of waiting. The prospect at present does not seem to me to be very encouraging, mainly on account of the attitude of the Dutch Reformed Church. But still it is one in which we may labor and pray for the best, prepared however, to drop the whole subject if need be and continue to go on our way, working out, in the Providence of God, our own particular mission. And surely there is enough in this prospect to enlist our most earnest and diligent labor.

In the year 1897, our Church will have filled out just ONE CENTURY AND A HALF since our first *Coetus*, or Synod, was organized. Let us get ready to celebrate in a fitting manner this next epoch in our history, and if we turn it to proper account it will serve to give us a new impetus for standing with new vigor and brightened prospects upon another century (the XXth) of human history. Our jubilee celebrations of epochs in our history have been of the greatest benefit to us hitherto, because we are a historical Church, as the years 1847 (our first Centennial), 1863 (the Tri-Centennial of the Catechism), 1875 (the Semi-Centennial of the founding of the Seminary), and 1887 (the Centennial and Semi-Centennial of our College) abundantly testify. The ushering in of the XXth century will doubtless be a period of intense interest in all the nations of Christendom. The last decade of the XIXth will close one of the most noted records of all the centuries of modern history. Who can tell what great events in the closing of the present century will, in the order of Providence, prepare the way for a victorious transition to the next? One single decade is more now in the history of the world than were fifty, or even one hundred years, in the earlier times. Let our Church get ready to enter the XXth century with banners high uplifted and with songs of triumph upon our lips. Some of us are merely standing on Pisgah summits looking wistfully over into the promised land. Many will not live to see on earth the incoming of another century, but whether here or there, in the Church militant or the Church triumphant, we may witness, nevertheless, what our hands have been doing to prepare the way for a great future. Let the year 1897 be a great epoch, and its celebration be a glorious time, whether for our German Reformed Church separately, or for the Reformed Church in America unitedly, inasmuch as both Churches formed their organized Synods in the same year!

T. G. A.

44. The Theological Rationale:

"Address"

(1888)

J. Spangler Kieffer

After attending Mercersburg Seminary and drinking deeply of the theology taught there (see vol. 6:42), J. Spangler Kieffer (1843–1919) went on to share Mercersburg theology from his prestigious post as pastor of Zion Church in Hagerstown, Maryland. Spangler served as associate editor of the Reformed Church Messenger, *president of the Potomac Synod, and member of one of the committees that tried to negotiate union with the Reformed (Dutch) Church. In his "Address" to the General Synod of the Reformed (Dutch) Church in 1888, Kieffer spoke of the absolute centrality of the person of Christ in theology and the dynamic and organic nature of the church as the body of Christ throughout history. He affirmed the church as proudly connected to its roots through the creeds of the early church and through the Heidelberg Catechism. "We have our denominational attachment; we love our Church; but we love the one great Catholic Church of Jesus Christ a great deal more." This position supported repeated efforts by the Reformed Church in the United States to making the organic nature of the church more visible by uniting the various parts of Christ's body in one holy catholic and apostolic church.*

It fell to my lot at the last meeting of the General Synod of the Reformed Church in the United States, held at Akron, Ohio, in the month of June, 1887, to be appointed as the delegate to represent that Synod before this reverend body. And being present among you to-day, for the purpose of

Source: J. S. Kieffer, "Address" *Reformed Church Messenger,* 27 June 1888, 2–4.

discharging the responsible commission with which I have been honored, and speaking in the name of the Synod that has sent me and the Reformed Church in the United States which it represents, I bring to you, in the name of our common Lord and Master, their cordial Christian salutations. It is sufficiently known to you, I trust, from what has been said before this body on past occasions similar to this, that the Church for which I am speaking has at no time ceased to entertain for the Church represented by this General Synod sentiments of reverent, grateful and affectionate regard. It has not been possible for us to forget or to feel that we could adequately requite the sympathy and kindness manifested toward our Church during no inconsiderable portion of its earliest history in this country by the Church of the Netherlands.

Many congregations among us are the living witnesses of the loving care exercised and the obligations contracted in those days. I have the honor to serve a congregation, being the eleventh in a succession of pastors covering a period of 118 years from the date of the settlement of the first regular pastor, whose first pastor, the Rev. Jacob Weymer (a name highly honored along us and most worthy to be honored), serving the congregation from 1770 to 1790, connects us directly with the Church of Holland, by whom he was sent, and causes us often to remember those times. Though I dwell not upon these things, I beg to assure you that they are fresh in our recollection; we remember the past.

Remembering the past we rejoice the more over the present. We take sincere pleasure in the prosperity of that branch of the Reformed Church represented by this Synod. We rejoice in her ardor; her fidelity to the truth; her zealous activity in the work of extending our Redeemer's kingdom.

Speaking of that branch of the Reformed Church which I have the honor to represent here, I would say that, notwithstanding the existence of many hindrances to the progress of our work, we have much cause also for gratitude to God for his goodness and mercy, and his blessing upon our endeavors to promote the glory of his name and advance the Kingdom of our Redeemer. There are not wanting many evidences of the presence among us of him who said, "Lo, I am with you alway, even unto the end of the world." God has been with us to bless us; leading us by his Spirit; delivering us in the time of danger; opening for us the door of opportunity; giving us strength, and courage and hope. Peace and harmony reign among us; we are at one among ourselves. Perhaps at no previous time in our history has our work been in so prosperous and hopeful a condition.

The Church embraces, at present, under its one General Synod, eight District Synods, fifty-four Classes, 817 ministers, 1,481 congregations and

183,980 members. There are 1,432 Sunday-schools and 122,695 Sunday-school scholars. There are four colleges, four theological seminaries and, at different points throughout the Church, a number of classical schools or collegiate institutions. The work of home missions is vigorously and somewhat extensively carried forward; and our foreign missionary work in Japan, though of comparatively recent origin, is in a most prosperous condition.

At the last meeting of the General Synod of the Reformed Church in the United States, petitions were presented from four of the District Synods, asking that measures be adopted looking toward a closer union with the Reformed Church in America, and at the same time, our General Synod having learned of the appointment by this body of a committee to confer with a similar committee on its part in regard to this matter, was prompt to appoint such a committee.

Of what has been done within the past year by this joint Committee of Conference, touching the very important and responsible business committed to them, it does not belong to me to speak. But, though feeling great diffidence and embarrassment in speaking of so grave and critical a matter, I nevertheless feel obliged, as representing my Church at this particular juncture, not to pass by without mention the one question which above all others at present concerns and affects us.

I would say, then, (feeling myself both warranted and obliged to say) that there exists in the Reformed Church in the United States a strong desire for closer union with the Church represented by this body. Not only is this evident from the petition, I have spoken of as coming from so large a proportion of our District Synods, but it has also become apparent, in various ways, from what has occurred within the past year. The sentiment in favor of such union is general, if not universal; I know of the existence of no adverse sentiment. I would report this to be, as far as my knowledge and observation extends, the existing sentiment among us; corresponding, I would fain believe, to some similar sentiment in the Church represented by this Synod. We are not urgent, much less would we be precipitate. Still further would we be from asking any sacrifice which, or the equivalent of which, we should not be willing ourselves to make. We realize how grave the question is and how carefully it needs to be considered. We are willing to wait. But I feel warranted in saying that the Reformed Church is ready to move forward under the careful guidance of the committee having charge of this matter, and is desirous that some real progress may be made, lest there ensue discouragement and hopelessness in regard to an undertaking, seemingly so beneficent in character, and which, after having met with failure more than once in the past, has come up now, it would seem, for some final and conclusive judgment concerning it.

The ministers and members of the Reformed Church in the United States, I may be permitted to say, participate largely in that spirit which, within a few years back has spread so rapidly and come to prevail so extensively—the spirit which longs for a closer union than now exists among the several branches of the Church of our Lord Jesus Christ; which desires to lose no time in taking whatever steps may be possible towards the realization of that condition of the Church implied by our Saviour's prayer that his people might "all be one." And this feeling finds its immediate and most natural expression in the wish to be united to that branch of the Church from which it is separated by the smallest degree of separation, with which it once was, and in a certain way still is, in a remarkable manner identified by history and the Providence of God.

As regards the particular union proposed, it would seem that there ought to be found no insuperable obstacle to the accomplishment of it. Not only were these two denominations originally one, but, though now existing in a state of separation, it is a separation marked by the characteristic, that it stands for no antagonism, past or present. They were not rent asunder; there has been no strife between them; there is no bitterness to be forgotten; there are no wounds to heal. In such favorable circumstances, the problem of union it would seem, ought to be of a comparatively easy solution. Certainly, in such a case, there can be less apology for failure than where the divisions of the Church are the result of a violent rupture, and where the work of reunion is encumbered and widened by the remembrance and remains of ancient animosities and collisions.

Such an accomplished union between these two branches of the Reformed Church could not well fail to be beneficent in its character and results. It would put our theories into practice. It would transform our wishes, prayers, discussions, (which, in themselves are not without peril) into salutary action. It would be making a beginning there, where the beginning ought to be made, where the separating distance is least. It would be a beginning at least of that "healing of the divisions" of the Church for which we have long been accustomed to pray. It would be the setting of a good example, which would not be without following. It would result in one strong and influential Reformed Church of America. It would be a suitable preparation for a larger and more comprehensive union which should bind together in one body all the various branches of the Reformed Church in the country. For, it is proper to say that, by the Reformed Church in the United States, such a union as is proposed is desired, not simply and exclusively for its own sake, but largely also because of its looking towards, and being the natural beginning of, such a larger and more comprehensive union embracing in one body all those religious bodies which make up the Reformed household of faith.

Though having said that the suggested union ought to be of a comparatively easy accomplishment, I must add that we are by no means insensible to the difficulties by which the actualization of it is, in fact, found to be unavoidably attended, particularly as regards the agreement upon a common standard of doctrine. This is a point which it is proper we should refrain from discussing, leaving it to those to whose wisdom and calm deliberation it has been committed. I may be permitted, however, as tending to throw light upon the matter, as serving to remove wrong impressions should there be any such, and as serving to recommend the Church I recommend to your favorable and kind regards, to mention these several things touching her position in regard to doctrinal matters.

1. Fidelity to the Heidelberg Catechism. It is our one, simple, and, as it has seemed to me, sufficient standard of doctrine. To this standard the Reformed Church in the United States has been and continues to be faithful. We hold firmly its teaching of the utter helplessness of man, through the fall on the one hand, and the absolute sovereignty of God's grace in the work of his redemption on the other. We adhere faithfully to that system of Christian doctrine which it sets forth. Perhaps at no previous time in the three hundred and twenty-five years of its history has the Heidelberg Catechism been held in higher honor, or more diligently taught, than at present in the Reformed Church in the United States.

2. It is by the Heidelberg Catechism, of which the Apostles' Creed is the central feature, that we have been led more and more to the recognition of the absolutely central character of the Person of Christ in regard to the whole system of Christian truth. He *is* the truth. His Person is the centre and the substance of the whole Christian salvation. His incarnation is the central fact in the history of the world. He is "the end of a boundless past, the centre of a boundless present, the beginning of a boundless future." The Gospel consists not primarily of doctrinal (important as these are) but of the great redemption facts of our Saviour's life, His birth, sufferings, death, resurrection, ascension, out of which the Christian doctrines grow. Christianity is a *life,* rather than a doctrine; we are saved by the life of the crucified and risen Christ, of which we are made partakers through faith, by the Holy Ghost. The main movement among us for many years past, as regards theology and theological teaching, has been along the line of *the Christological principle.* This has seemed to us to be the line of the Apostles' Creed and of the Heidelberg Catechism; as it would appear also to be the line along which the thinking and teaching of the Church

have come within recent years to move. There has been in the Reformed Church of the United States no small amount of movement, discussion, and even controversy (in past years) as regards theology and doctrine, but, I beg you to believe there has been no movement among us except in this Christ-ward direction.

3. Along with the acceptance of what has been called the Christological principle, there grew in the Reformed Church in the United States, a strong sense of the historical and organic character of Christianity. We have been taught, we have learned to reverence the past; the nearer past of the Reformation, the remoter and greater past of Apostolic times. We would be bound to the past. We have no confidence in what is not firmly rooted and grounded in the past; in what has not come to us by process of historical development. I beg you to believe that we are not irreverent. We revere the past; but we reverence also the present and the future. We would be anchored to the past; but we would not be so anchored to it as to prevent our sailing forth into the future.

4. Amid many weaknesses and faults, a certain catholicity of feeling (I hope I may be permitted to say, and am not mistaken in saying) has been one of the characteristics of the Church I represent. We have our denominational attachment; we love our Church; but we love the one great Catholic Church of Jesus Christ a great deal more. It is the impulse of this feeling to seek after something larger and broader; to strive after that condition of the Church in which she shall be one outwardly as she is one in inward life and spirit. We would fain give up and get rid of our littleness and narrowness; our largeness and broadness we would keep and still increase. It would accord well with the existing spirit of the Church I represent, to enter into a union with a sister Church; a union which should be large and free enough to tolerate differences on more than one non-essential point; which should be based upon that common agreement in doctrine which we believe already exists in sufficient measure; whose bond of union, above all else, should be belief in Christ and reverent attachment and devotion to him. For we have learned that to believe in Christ is vastly more than to believe certain things about Christ; that to love him is more than all knowledge: that faith is great, and hope is great, but love is greatest of all.

45. Union Thwarted Again:
"Failure of Federal Union" and "The Christian Intelligencer *on the Failure . . . "*

(1892 and 1893)

The German Reformed Synod and the Reformed (Dutch) Synod had much in common: both were Calvinist, from the same Reformation roots; both had been supported by the Reformed Church in Holland during their early years in colonial North America; both had struggled to find their identity as immigrant churches in the New World. Nevertheless, although they explored church union four different times, they never did succeed.

In 1892, an article entitled "The Failure of Federal Union," originally appearing in The Independent, *a progressive newspaper published by a group of New York business leaders and Congregational ministers, was reprinted in the* Reformed Church Messenger. *It explained how confessional differences between the Dutch and the German churches prevented their union, reporting that the German Reformed adhered only to the Heidelberg Catechism, while the Dutch Reformed included the Belgic Confession and the Canons of Dort as normative. Furthermore, there was a suspicion among the Dutch that the Reformed Church "made too much of" the sacraments and confirmation.*

Another article in the Messenger *a year later reported how another newspaper,* The Christian Intelligencer, *reported that the German-Dutch union was thwarted because of "a fear of disunion" in the Dutch church*

Source: "Failure of Federal Union," from *The Independent,* reprinted in *Reformed Church Messenger,* 30 June 1892, 4–5; " 'The Christian Intelligencer' on the Failure of the Plan of Federal Union," *Reformed Church Messenger,* 11 May 1893, 9.

as well as "an innate repugnance to change and experiment" that was part of the Dutch character.

The real reason for the failure was probably more practical. The Independent *article noted that the Dutch would probably align themselves with their German Reformed cousins "if they could only get well enough acquainted with them to make the courtship agreeable." Yet, almost all of the discussions between 1794 and 1893 involved only church leaders and special committees, and when proposals came to a vote, they repeatedly generated grassroots suspicion because of the lack of information in the local churches. Apart from an important network of newspapers that tried to keep church members informed, there were no denominational structures to educate people in the churches about attempts at union, and no "ecumenical officers" whose specific job was to find ways to bring about church union. Furthermore, no mechanisms were in place to help local church members get to know the members of the other denomination—pulpit exchanges, shared Sunday school materials, common textbooks in theological seminaries, joint worship services on special occasions, or shared social action projects or social events.*

Failure of Federal Union

We are sorry, somewhat disappointed, that we are compelled to report this week the failure, or at least the delay, of the most important effort of the year, for Church union among our Northern Churches. We are very sorry that the two closely allied Reformed Churches, the former so-called German and Dutch Reformed, have found it more difficult to agree upon a federal union of their two bodies, which shall yet allow them to remain separate, than the two African Methodist Churches have found it to arrange for an organic consolidation of their two denominations.

In explaining the causes of the failure we are compelled to distinguish the two denominations by the discarded names German and Dutch. The German Church, with its chief congregations in Pennsylvania and the adjacent States, has been somewhat isolated from other denominations, while the Dutch Church, with its center at New York City has been brought into the closest relations with the Presbyterian and Congregational denominations. Ministers pass freely from one denomination to another, and, as between the Presbyterians and the Dutch Church, have not recognized any more difference of polity than of faith. Probably, considerably more than half the Dutch pastors were educated as Presbyterians or Congregationalists; and a good part of the members of the Dutch Churches are such by convenience rather than from principle. This has led necessarily to a conscious and confessed consideration of the wisdom of joining their smaller Church with one of the other Churches, either the Presbyterian or the German Reformed. The fellowships and the affections would draw them rather toward the Presbyterians who are their neighbors, while their name and their Confessions would rather ally them with their German Reformed brethren, if they could only get well enough acquainted with them to make the courtship agreeable. There is, however, a considerable opposition to union with the Presbyterians, having its center, perhaps, in the wealthy Collegiate Dutch Reformed Church of this city, which seems to have its explanation in a conservative and sentimental objection to having their honored Church, with its roots in a glorious past, swallowed up in a larger Church whose Standards are insular and do not go back of Westminster, while its own are older and are continental. This influence has been willing to coquet with, or even to form some sort of union with, the German Reformed Church, as something not so bad as absorption into the Presbyterianism of the Westminster Assembly.

Once before, a score of years ago or more, an attempt was made to form a sort of federal union with the German Church: but it did not succeed. This time the omens seemed more propitious. The Dutch Church made the advances, and the German Church responded encouragingly. Then the Dutch Church last year drew up and approved a plan for a Federal Synod, made up of an equal number of delegates from the General Synods of the two denominations, to which should be committed the missionary and educational work of the two denominations; and this plan was sent down to the thirty-four Classes, of which a handsome majority gave in their approval. Thus everything seemed to be in the most hopeful condition, and it seemed beyond question that a developed plan, fully adopted by the Dutch Church, would soon go into operation.

The committee of six which had the matter in charge for the Dutch Church reported everything favorable, and had no doubt that it would go through with no difficulty. They did not even know that one dissenting member, Mr. Zwemer, would present a minority report. It was a very shrewd report, dwelling on the lack of acquaintance with their German brethren, and of enthusiasm for the union, and the various doubts that have been presented, and urged delay. Then Dr. Van Giesen, who had signed the majority report, went over to the minority, and offered a substitute motion, putting the matter over for one year; and after some discussion this was done, much to the surprise and the chagrin of Dr. De Baun and the other members of the committee.

The discussion did not really bring out the objections which in the minds of so many of the Dutch brethren stand in the way of even federal union.

With some it is a real preference for union with the Presbyterians, and they fear that even federal union with the Germans will stand in the way.

With some the doctrinal reason is controlling. They do not think the German Church is sufficiently Calvinistic. The German Church has only one doctrinal standard, the Heidelberg Catechism. The Dutch Church has, besides this, two or three others—the Compendium, the Confession of Faith, and the Canons of Dort. These stiffen up the Heidelberg Catechism considerably; and those who love standards can hardly have too many of them, and they look with some suspicion on those who are slenderly endowed in this way. Connected with this is some feeling that there is in the German Church a strong party, of which Dr. Nevin was the father, which makes quite too much of the Sacraments, and also quite too much of Confirmation, receiving its young members rather by confirmation than on confession of their faith. That is, some of the Dutch brethren think there is too much of the Continental and Lutheran religious habit among their German brethren, and they do not care to unite with them, especially as the German churches considerably outnumber the Dutch churches in membership. The real point of all this is, that their sympathetic fellowship and community of habit is not so much with the German Reformed Church as with the Presbyterians.

All this was enforced by the active and vigorous opposition of the Dutch-speaking churches made up of late immigrants in Michigan and other Western States. These are the mission churches of their denomination, and are very pronounced in their Dutch theology. Besides, they are the recipients of the mission funds of the Church, and in case of union it might very well be that, inasmuch as the German Church has a great many poor congregations and not a large treasury, the common fund would not supply so generous a support for the Western missions. Whatever the reason these Western Classes are strongly opposed to union.

As the result of these various influences the approval of the plan of federal union was postponed for one year. We hope that this does not mean final failure, although we much fear it, and have little doubt that this was the wish of a large part of those who voted to postpone. It cannot be quite pleasant to the German Reformed Church to know that their orthodoxy and their liturgic methods are called in question in the Church which is wooing them. Fortunately it does not hold its General Synod annually, and as it will be two years before its next meeting, the Dutch Church will have time to correct any seeming discourteous suspicion. If we fear that the Dutch General Synod will next year be as far from union as now, we may gain some alleviating comfort from remembering that it leaves the way clearer for union with Presbyterians, for union of some sort is the inevitable blessed fate of the Dutch Reformed Church.

Now there are a great many other unions, federal or organic, which ought to be made. There is a call for grand ecclesiastical statesmanship in this matter. When will the Northern and Southern Presbyterians unite? Already they are talking about co-ordinating some of their mission work. Why are not the Cumberland Presbyterians asked to unite with the Northern Presbyterian Church? Must we wait for that "Consensus" of the faith of the Reformed Churches, before they can find a basis of union?

What about that union talked of between Congregationalists and Free Baptists? We hear of nothing done about it of late. Our African Methodist brethren are setting us all an excellent example.

—*The Independent.*

The Christian Intelligencer *on the Failure of the Plan of Federal Union*

It would not be profitable to inquire too strictly into the causes that have led to this result. Making every allowance for honest and sincere convictions and doubts as to the wisdom and feasibility of the plan, the deciding vote was largely due to a fear of disunion in our own Church, and that innate repugnance to change and experiment which seems inwrought in the Dutch character. That the plan was viewed with favor by our Church, and the Union earnestly desired, is proven by the large majority it received a year ago, and that in face of skilful appeals to ignorance and fear; the reversal of the earlier decision has been carried, if at all, by the change of comparatively few votes.

It is needless for *The Christian Intelligencer* to express its disappointment and sorrow at the result. While it would not have desired to push the plan through in face of an obstructive minority, since that would foredoom the experiment to failure, it has been both surprised and grieved that this attempt at Ecclesiastical Union on the federative principle has been overborne in the Church which by all historical and natural right should have given it welcome. We feel that our two Reformed Churches have missed the opportunity of leading in a movement the beneficent effects of which no one could forecast or measure. That our Church should be the obstructive one, fills us with shame as well as regret. Some, and may be a decisive number, voted against this proposed Union in the delusive idea that it stood in the way of a wider federation. If so, we fear they are doomed to disappointment, for how can those who advanced as their great argument that there was doctrinal unsoundness in the German Church, come with it and the still more tainted Presbyterian Church into any form of Union; or how can those who objected to the present plan as not worth its cost, accept a wider federation, which in the very nature of the case must be even more loose and general? However, we leave the future to answer these questions. Meanwhile, we are thankful to have had some part in promoting a plan of Christian Union, which will ultimately triumph even though at present defeated.

Church Union: Vision and Reality

46. A Christocentric Theology: *"The Growing Spirit of Christian Unity" and "Church Union"*

(1888 and 1890)

J. Spangler Kieffer; Thomas G. Apple

Enhanced by the substantive doctrinal discussions of the organic nature of the church universal stimulated by Mercersburg Theology in the 1840s and 1850s (see vol. 6:42), which was itself rooted in the theology of the early church, the (German) Reformed Church moved into ecumenical discussions in the last quarter of the nineteenth century with a clear theology informing its commitment to church union. The essence of its theological vision was a conviction about the centrality of the person of Jesus Christ—the sum of the gospel, the foundation of the church, the source of its faith, the center of the great creeds of the early church and of its theology. J. Spangler Kieffer (1843–1919), pastor of the prestigious Zion Church in Hagerstown, Maryland, wrote confidently in the Reformed Church Messenger *about "The Growing Spirit of Christian Unity."*

Reformed doctrine about the person of Christ led naturally to the central motif in the Reformed Church's ecumenical theology: its doctrine of the church (ecclesiology). According to this doctrine, the person of Christ was a foundation for the continuation of that life in the body of Christ, the church, expressed throughout history in a myriad of forms as the one holy catholic and apostolic church.

Another article, by Thomas G. Apple, further explained this theology of

---

Source: J. Spangler Kieffer, "The Growing Spirit of Christian Unity," *Reformed Church Messenger,* 18 January 1888, 9; Thomas G. Apple, "Church Union," *Reformed Church Messenger,* 29 May 1890, 2.

"Church Union." It was the Reformed Church's loyalty to the one church, grounded in the person of Jesus Christ, that required it to subordinate its own parochial denominational interests as an "individual organ" to the higher calling of making the true organic unity of the one body more visible. The very core of the Reformed Church's theology drove it to work to unite the divided churches of the world into the one catholic church.

The Growing Spirit of Christian Unity

We borrow the phrase from the programme appointed by the Evangelical Alliance for the Week of Prayer. Among the things for which Christian people were asked to give thanks to God, at the first of the services of that week was mentioned "the growing spirit of Christian Unity."

We believe that the implication is a correct one. The spirit of Christian unity has been growing with what seems to us a gradual healthy growth. The churches of the various denominations are much nearer together than they were a generation ago. There is less of rivalry and controversy; a stronger sense of the dangers which threaten denominationalism is expressed; an increasing consciousness of the necessity of "healing the divisions" of the Church; more of the spirit of fraternity and peace; more of the aspiration after the ideal condition of "one fold and one shepherd."

Among the causes of this increasing spirit of Christian unity, the chief without doubt has been the tendency, which of late years has become so prevalent and powerful to lay all stress, as regards theology and religion, upon the person of Christ. There has been a shifting of the emphasis. Some things are less highly, and others more highly regarded now than formerly. It is more clearly perceived that the divine-human power of our Lord Jesus Christ is the centre of all things; the sum and substance of the Gospel; and that our salvation is a matter of vital, personal, mystical union with Him. Men have learned that to "believe in Christ" is vastly more than to believe certain things about Christ. Attachment and devotion to a person is something incalculably more, and more influential, than belief in a doctrine. Faith, like all other great and deep things, has its seat in the heart, and not in the head. It is with the heart that man believeth unto righteousness. It is chiefly because of this we judge, because of the general tendency to magnify the person of Christ and to place the personal belief in Him far above the belief of any or all things about Him, that there has been an increase in the spirit of Christian unity.

We would not be understood to imply that this spirit is characterized by indifference as regards doctrine. For ourselves, we do not find this to be the case, and it would be a bad sign if it were. We believe there has been an increase of tolerance, not of indifference, which is something else. Men hold the peculiar and characteristic doctrines of their respective denominations still; but they do not receive as much emphasis as they once did. Men do not fight for them with the dogged obstinacy of former times. They no longer regard any doctrine in which they differ from their fellow Christians as the doctrine of a "standing or falling church." They distinguish, as perhaps at one time they did not do, between the personal Christ and the various doctrines concerning Him; between the great, radical and essential truth in words. They have an increased sense of the largeness of Christ and His Gospel, and the probable inadequacy of the very best attempt to explain the meaning of them.

We do not find indifference as regards doctrine to be characteristic of the spirit; but rather modesty in the holding of doctrine, a willingness to hear and consider the other side, the desire to preserve an open mind, and a readiness to admit that "now we know in part." As regards confessions, however, there is an unmistakable gravitation towards those, like the Apostles' and the Nicene, which have in them the most of the personal Christ and the least of metaphysical discussion concerning Him. And, as regards that higher and more perfect spirit of Christian unity, which we may expect to behold in the future, where ever its main root may be found to lie, it is certain that it will not be in the philosophical explanations.

J. S. K.

Church Union

The union of the Christian Churches of this country is, doubtless, only a question of time. Denominationalism need not entirely disappear, but it must change its character and motive. The different denominations now existing must come to regard themselves as simply organs of the one body. The love of denomination for its own sake must yield and be taken up in love for the whole Church. The ambition hitherto existing in each denomination to become great, if not the greatest, among the denominations of the land, must give way to a laudable ambition to see Christianity as a whole triumph over unbelief and sin in all its forms.

And this simply means that the prevailing motive for Church union must be faith in, and love for, *the Holy Catholic Church.* Church union must grow out of an advance in faith and love. It cannot succeed on the basis of mere utilitarian calculation. One of the dangers just now is that in such calculation, denominationalism, if not downright sectarianism, may really be fostered and strengthened by certain forms of union. Take for instance, federal, or co-operative union, in which several denominations join while the denominationalism of each retains its full autonomy. Such a union may be formed from a selfish motive, to strengthen each one against other denominations outside the league, and each one may use it to enhance its own denominational influence and power. In such union there is no sacrifice, no sacrifice of love for the denomination for love for the Church as a whole.

We do not mean this as an argument against federal union. The union that is to come may, and likely will, take something of that kind of form, like the union in our nation; but the poison of a narrow, selfish denominationalism must be first eradicated. Christians must learn to love the union, the whole Church, more than their own denomination.

But how is such love to be generated and fostered? I answer, by cultivating a true living faith in the article of the Creed, "I believe the Holy Catholic Church." The Church here meant must be a reality for our faith. There are many, it is to be feared, to whom the Church in this form is only an empty name. They believe in an invisible Church, they believe in the visibility of individual Christians, and in a visible Church in the form of a congregation, or a denomination; but of a visible Holy Catholic Church they have no conception. They do not see that spiritual unity requires outward, visible unity, also, in order that the former may adequately assert itself in the latter. To this outward unity the denominational form of the Church has been a hindrance. It may have been, doubtless was, a historical necessity, in order to conserve for the time being certain other interests; but the time has come when it ought to yield to the necessity for a broader union.

Hence one condition for the growth of faith in the Holy Catholic Church is, an acknowledgement that the present divided state of the Church is abnormal, an evil to be overcome. To overcome this evil requires sacrifice. Just as a man must be willing to sacrifice family interests for his country, so a Christian must be willing to subordinate the interests of his denomination for the whole Church. The evil now is, not that there are divisions in the Church, but that these divisions are not united under some proper headship.

We might enlarge and elaborate, but our purpose in these lines has been merely to set forth the motive that ought to rule in considering Church union. It should not be a selfish league of some portions over against other portions, like the league of Germany, Austria, and Italy against France and

Russia. It ought not to be ruled by love of denomination, but love for the whole Church. Faith in the Holy Catholic Church, and such faith working by love for the Church, is worth more than all utilitarian calculations. Church union will come, must come, as a growth from within, and its true basis is faith in the Holy Catholic Church of our Lord.

T. G. A.

47. Union with Presbyterians: *"Joint Report of Union" and "Report . . . on the Closer Union with the Presbyterian Church in the U.S.A."*

(1911 and 1912)

Joint Committee; George W. Richards

In 1911, after three years of meeting together, the Committee on Church Co-operation and Union of the Presbyterian Church in the U.S.A. and the Committee on Closer Union with the Presbyterian Church of the Reformed Church in the U.S. submitted a "Joint Report of Union" to the General Assembly of the Presbyterian Church in the U.S.A. and the General Synod of the Reformed Church in the U.S. The report made clear that it was only the "Concurrent Declarations" at the beginning of the report that were being submitted for official consideration and adoption by the General Assembly and the General Synod. The rest of the report consisted of the record of the negotiations concerning the name of the united church, which was still undecided, and the plan of union, which had been worked out by the committee, and which would be sent to the judicatories simply "for information and discussion" as a possible plan for action in the future.

Unfortunately, a newspaper, the Public Ledger, *caused great chaos among church members of both denominations by publishing a short,*

Source: Joint Committee of the Presbyterian Church in the U.S.A. and the Reformed Church in the U.S., "Joint Report of Union," in *Papers on the Relations and Status of the Reformed Church in the U.S. and the Presbyterian Church in the U.S.A.* (Philadelphia, 1912), 26–30; George W. Richards, "The Report of the Committee on the Closer Union with the Presbyterian Church in the U.S.A.," 95–111, pamphlet in the United Church of Christ Archives, reprinted from *The Reformed Review,* January 1912.

carelessly written piece claiming that the merger had already been favorably acted upon by the General Synod of the Reformed Church and by the Presbyterian General Assembly, and that it only required the approval of the synods. George W. Richards, a Reformed Church leader and member of the Committee on Closer Union with the Presbyterian Church, wrote an article for the Reformed Church Messenger *trying to explain the situation.*

Richards was a professor of church history at Lancaster Theological Seminary for forty years, nineteen of them as president of the seminary. For more than thirty years, Richards was known nationally and internationally as a strong advocate for church union, serving as a delegate to the founding meeting of the Federal Council of the Churches of Christ in America and to subsequent meetings, and as vice-president of the Federal Council from 1934–35. In 1937, he was a delegate to the Oxford Conference on Life and Work and the Edinburgh Conference on Faith and Order. Later, Richards chaired the Reformed Church's Commission on Closer Relations and Church Union, which recommended steps to bring about union with the Evangelical Synod of North America. He was elected first president of the Evangelical and Reformed Church.

Richards was steeped in the theology of the Mercersburg movement in the Reformed Church, and wrote three significant articles illuminating its history, as well as a history of Lancaster Theological Seminary and a volume entitled Creative Controversies in Christianity. *He also introduced the early works of Swiss theologian Karl Barth to American audiences by translating two volumes of Barth's early sermons.*

Richards was characteristically lucid in his report about the Presbyterians. He explained the true status of the joint report, and at the same time he questioned union with the Presbyterians. Although he was most certainly in favor of church union in principle, in this case he argued that the Reformed Church—with its German heritage and allegiance to the broad and irenic Heidelberg Catechism—needed to be careful: the Reformed Church should not give up its identity to be submerged in a Presbyterian denomination whose doctrinal adherence to the Westminster Confession represented a narrower expression of Reformation faith and life. Richards asked for what he called a "truly organic union," in which both churches deepened and widened their Christian consciousness to such an extent that their new life could no longer be contained in the old forms. Such a union would not be a "mere coalition, a merger, and a forensic transaction without spiritual value," but would come about through the Spirit of God.

Joint Report of Union

Adopted by the General Assembly of the Presbyterian Church in the U.S.A., and the General Synod of the Reformed Church in the U.S., May, 1911.

The Committee on Church Co-operation and Union, of the Presbyterian Church in the U.S.A., and the Committee on Closer Union with the Presbyterian Church, of the Reformed Church in the U.S., beg leave jointly to submit the following Report to the General Assembly of the Presbyterian Church in the U.S A., and to the General Synod of the Reformed Church in the U.S.

The Committees have met repeatedly, either in full session or by sub-committees, during the past three years. They rejoice in their cordial fellowship during this period of time, and in the respect and affection which their association together has produced. They have sought earnestly, by meditation and prayer, the welfare of both Churches, and have soberly recognized, at all times, the important interests affected by their deliberations. Humbly invoking the aid of the Holy Spirit, they submit their Joint Report, in the hope that it will commend itself to their respective supreme judicatories.

The Report, for clearness, as well as convenience, is divided into four parts: I. Concurrent Declarations; II. The Name of the United Church; III. The proposed Plan of Union; IV. Resolutions looking to further action.

I. Concurrent Declarations

As steps preliminary to further action in this matter of Closer Relations, the following Concurrent Declarations are submitted for consideration and adoption by both the General Assembly and the General Synod.

1. The Reformed Church in the U.S. and the Presbyterian Church in the U.S.A. represent the same type of evangelical Protestant Christianity, commonly known as Reformed or Calvinistic. The Churches of the Reformation in Europe, to which they are historically related, originated in different lands and passed through different experiences, which differences necessarily appear in the form of Standards of both Churches. We, therefore, with clear understanding of the nature of such differences, hereby declare our conviction that the Westminster Confession of Faith and Cat-

echisms, on the one hand, and the Heidelberg Catechism, on the other, are in essential agreement, and are different expressions of one and the same system of doctrine. This doctrinal agreement appears in the recognition, in both symbols, of the fundamental doctrines of evangelical Christianity as held by the Reformed or Calvinistic Churches, and also in the use made of the Apostles' Creed, the Ten Commandments, and the Lord's Prayer, in the Catechisms of the two Churches, for the instruction of the youth of their congregations.

2. In view of this historical kinship and doctrinal agreement, we also declare our conviction that the effort to unite the two Churches in one body should continue, and the General Assembly and the General Synod hereby recommend to the Presbyteries, Classes, and Congregations, to confer, in the spirit of comity, with reference to the proposed union, and to co-operate with one another during the coming triennium, whenever practicable, with a view to taking definite action for organic union, in the supreme judicatories of the two Churches, in 1914.

II. The Name of the United Church

The Joint Committee has been confronted with a serious difficulty in reference to the name of the United Church. With one accord, the members of the two Committees have recognized the importance of conserving the term "Reformed" and the term "Presbyterian." The difficulties which the Committees found in their way resolved themselves under two categories. (1) Traditional attachment. The attachment, in both Churches, on the part of the great masses of the membership, to the respective denominational names, is entirely natural, because three and a half centuries of history in Germany, Switzerland, and France, also in Scotland, England and Ireland, are vitally related both to the name "Reformed" and the name "Presbyterian." In the United States, also, a religious heritage of two centuries is connected with the names. (2) Legal considerations. The developments of many years have shown that the Constitution of the United States and of the several States, and the laws of all the States, so affect the corporate interests of the Churches, that it is wise carefully to consider and adjust, prior to a union of Churches, all legal questions. The Committee, accordingly, in Article I, of the Plan of Union, does not offer a name for the United Church, being convinced that it is far more desirable first to determine the feeling of the two Churches as to the general question of an organic union.

III. The Plan of the Union

I. Preamble

For the glory of God, the greater good of mankind, and the increased efficiency of the work of the Church of Christ, the Committee appointed on Church Co-operation and Union, by the Presbyterian Church in the U.S.A., and the Committee on Closer Union, of the Reformed Church in the U.S., propose to the General Assembly of the Presbyterian Church in the U.S.A., and to the General Synod of the Reformed Church in the U.S., the following Plan of Union between the respective Churches, for consideration.

II. Name

1. The Presbyterian Church in the U.S.A., whose General Assembly met at Atlantic City, N.J., May 19, 1910, and the Reformed Church in the U.S., whose General Synod met at York, Pa., May 19, 1908, shall be united as one Church, under a name and style hereafter to be determined. In forming the union, it is understood that the terms "Presbyterian" and "Reformed," used in the Constitutions of the two bodies, are equivalent one to the other.

III. Basis

1. The doctrinal basis of the Union shall be: The Scriptures of the Old and New Testaments, acknowledged as the inspired Word of God and the only infallible rule of faith and practice; with the Confession of Faith of the Presbyterian Church in the U.S.A., as revised in 1903, and the Heidelberg Catechism of the Reformed Church in the U.S.

2. The Form of Government and the Book of Discipline of the Presbyterian Church in the U.S.A. are also hereby made a part of the Basis of Union. Licentiates, ministers, elders, and deacons of the United Church may accept, as a term of subscription, either the Heidelberg Catechism or the Westminster Confession, or both, it being understood and agreed that the Confession and the Catechism are different expressions of one and the same system of doctrine.

3. The Directories for Worship, of both Churches, shall be a part of the Basis of Union, to the extent that each congregation shall have the same freedom in worship, both as to forms and usages, in the United Church, as it had before the Union.

IV. Organization

1. While the Form of Government and the Book of Discipline of the Presbyterian Church in the U.S.A. shall be the administrative standards of the United Church, it is provided and agreed, that the use of the terms "Spiritual Council," "Consistory" and "Classis"; also the relations which exist between the Classis and congregations, at present, in the Reformed Church in the U.S.; and the authority of the Consistories and Spiritual Councils in Reformed congregations, shall have full validity in the United Church; and it is agreed that, for a period of five years after the consummation of the Union, all appeals from decisions of Consistories, Classes and Synods, formerly a part of the Reformed Church in the United States, shall be adjudicated in accordance with the Constitution of the said Reformed Church. The General Assembly of the United Church shall be the final court of appeal.

2. All ministers and churches included in the two denominations, shall be admitted to the same standing in the United Church which they may have in their respective connections up to the consummation of the Union, and it is agreed that the congregations of the United Church may retain their present names or titles, subject to the authority of Classes or Presbyteries, and it is further agreed, that the Synods and Classes of the Reformed Church may retain the word "Reformed" in their titles.

3. The official records of the two Churches shall be preserved and held as making up the history of the one and United Church.

4. The corporate interests of the General Assembly of the Presbyterian Church in the U.S.A. and of the General Synod of the Reformed Church in the U.S., and of their Boards and Permanent Committees, as soon as practicable, shall be so readjusted as to carry out their several purposes as defined and permitted by law.

5. In the reconstruction and election of the various Boards of the two Churches, by the General Assembly of the United Church, an impartial representation of the membership and views of the two bodies constituting the United Church shall be observed and maintained. Until such readjustment of the several Boards has been completed, each of the Boards shall continue in the full performance of its functions, shall report annually to the General Assembly of the United Church, and the members of each of the Boards shall be chosen from the ministry and membership of the respective Churches with which they were connected prior to the Union. The status of the Boards of Publication in the Reformed Church, under the control of one or more Synods, shall continue as it is, until they are prepared to unite with the Board of Publication of the General Assembly of the United Church.

6. The boundaries of the several Classes and Synods of the Reformed Church in the U.S. shall remain, in the United Church, as they now are, provided, however, that the boundaries of any Classis or Synod may be changed by the General Assembly of the United Church, upon petition from the majority of the members of the judicatory interested, duly adopted in regular session.

7. The Presbyteries or Classes of the United Church, occupying to any extent the same territory, shall organize new congregations under the following regulations: In towns and rural districts, no new congregations shall be organized by either the Presbytery or Classis interested, without the consent of both judicatories, and, without such consent, a new congregation in a city shall not be located within five squares of an existing congregation in the United Church.

8. This Plan of Union shall not necessarily effect any change in the relations now existing between institutions of learning and any ecclesiastical organization of either Church, but these institutions and ecclesiastical organizations shall be free to effect such changes as may be permitted by law, and as circumstances may hereafter require.

Resolutions

The Committee, furthermore, submits the following resolutions to be adopted, provided the concurrent declarations be approved:

Resolved, 1. That the Plan of Union contained in this Report is hereby submitted by the General Assembly and the General Synod and to the subordinate judicatories, for information and discussion, as an acceptable plan for future action, subject to such modifications as conditions may require.

Resolved, 2. That the Committee on Church Co-operation and Union is hereby directed and empowered to confer with the Committee on Closer Union, of the Reformed Church in the U.S., and, on the basis of such information as may be received by both Committees, to make final report to the respective Supreme Judicatories in 1914.

Resolved, 3. That the following papers, prepared by the Joint Committees, be published by the Boards of Publication of the respective Churches, and distributed, in the discretion of the Committee, viz.: (a) The Historical Statement as to the Relations of the Presbyterian and the Reformed Church. (b) The Present Status of the Reformed Church in the U.S.,— Doctrine, Cultus, Polity and Usages; and (c) the similar statement for the Presbyterian Church in the U.S.A.

The Report of the Committee on the Closer Union with the Presbyterian Church in the U.S.A.

It is my purpose to offer an explanation of certain aspects of the Report on Union which was adopted by the General Synod at Canton, Ohio. The adoption of the Report involves the reference of the Plan of Union "to the Subordinate Judicatories for information and discussion as an acceptable plan for future action subject to such modifications as conditions may require." Statements which have appeared in the daily papers, assertions which have been made in conversation and in synodical discussions, and questions which have been asked by ministers and members in regard to the proposed union, have convinced me that neither the Report nor the General Synod's action on it are clearly understood.

While the Eastern Synod was in session in Philadelphia, the following squib appeared in the *Public Ledger:*

> Reformed Synod Takes Up Merger with the Presbyterians
>
> The merger has already been favorably acted upon by the General Synod of the Reformed Church at its meeting in Canton, Ohio, last May, but each of the six Synods will also have to take favorable action. The Presbyterian General Assembly voted for the union at its session in Atlantic City last May.

In the discussion of the report of the Committee of the Eastern Synod on the subject of union, the Joint Committee was criticized for not submitting a sufficiently definite plan of union, not even a name for the proposed United Church. Another question, frequently discussed in public and private, was whether the Plan of Union practically means a merger with the Presbyterians, or whether it is a modified form of federal union in which each church substantially maintains its identity after the union.

Since the Joint Committee and the Supreme Judicatories of the two churches invite discussion of every phase of this subject, I shall attempt to throw light on some points which seem to be obscure, and at the same time set forth my personal views; for I believe heartily in the principle presented by Pericles in his famous memorial oration, when he says: "The great impediment to action is not discussion, but the want of that knowledge which is gained by discussion preparatory to action."

The statement in the *Public Ledger* cited above is, of course, erroneous and misleading from beginning to end. Neither the General Assembly nor the General Synod acted favorably on the Plan of Union or "the merger."

Both these judicatories did act favorably on the Concurrent Declarations which affirm that "the Reformed Church in the United States and the Presbyterian Church in the United States of America represent the same type of evangelical Protestant Christianity, commonly known as Reformed or Calvinistic." While differences in the Confessions and the Catechisms are recognized, they are notwithstanding held to be in "essential agreement" and "different expressions of one and the same system of doctrine." Again, the two judicatories resolved, according to the recommendations of the Joint Committee in the Concurrent Declarations, that the whole report of the Committee, including a statement in reference to the Name of the United Church and the Plan of Union, be referred "to the Presbyteries, Classes, and Congregations, to confer in the spirit of comity with reference to the proposed union and to cooperate with one another during the coming triennium whenever practicable with a view to taking definite action for organic union in the Supreme Judicatories of the two Churches in 1914."

It is clear then that the General Assembly and the General Synod ask simply for a consideration and discussion of the material offered by the Joint Committee, for the purpose of finding out the feeling of the constituents of the two churches on the question of closer union. More than that the General Synod does not enjoin upon its subordinate judicatories or its officers and members. Every one, accordingly, is free to express his views without contravening General Synod's action; and nothing but a free, unbiased, and irenical discussion, from every point of view, will fulfill the resolutions of the Synod or the purpose of the Joint Committee. "Presbyteries and Classes and Congregations are to confer in the spirit of comity." The Standard Dictionary defines "comity" as "courtesy in private or public life; kindly consideration for others; friendliness in regard to rights."

A word now in regard to the nature of the report submitted by the Joint Committee. At its first meeting, December 4, 1908, in the Witherspoon Building, Philadelphia, Pennsylvania, it was conceded by all the members present that the sentiment for closer union between the two bodies was not sufficiently deep-rooted and widespread to warrant immediate and final action. Indeed, some of the members on both sides were of the opinion that we had about as much union in the form of alliance and federation as we could reasonably hope for at present. They were inclined to discontinue further negotiations. Others, however, felt that, since the two committees were duly authorized and assembled to discuss and devise plans of closer union, two things should be tried. First, the preparation of a tentative plan of union; second, the cultivation of a spirit of union in the two churches by written and oral discussions. The latter view prevailed, and the General Committee appointed a subcommittee of six, three from each of the two committees, for further consideration and action.

In the first meeting of the subcommittee it was unanimously agreed *"that no plan for closer relation between the two churches was to be considered and urged the adoption which was not accepted with practical unanimity by both Communions."* This resolution implies that, unless the sentiment, expressed by the Synods, Presbyteries, Classes, and Congregations of the respective churches during the coming triennium, is clearly and preponderatingly in favor of closer union, the Joint Committee will cease further negotiations.

It was further resolved by the subcommittee that, as a means of introducing the two churches to each other and of cultivating acquaintanceship and an intelligent union sentiment, three papers should be prepared by members of the subcommittee and, with the consent of the General Judicatories, be printed and distributed under the direction of the Boards of Publication of the respective churches. The subjects of the papers are as follows: First, "An Historical Statement as to the Relations of the Presbyterian and the Reformed Church"; second, "The Present Status of the Reformed Church in the United States, Doctrine, Cultus, Polity, and Usages"; third, "A similar statement for the Presbyterian Church in the United States of America."

After a number of meetings, a tentative plan of union was worked out with much labor and care, and finally submitted to the Joint Committee for adoption. At that meeting, however, it turned out that the *name* for the United Church was a stumbling block. Should it be called the "Reformed Church in America," or the "Presbyterian Church in America," the "Presbyterian and Reformed Church," or the "Reformed Presbyterian Church," or the "Presbyterian (Reformed) Church"? The reader will at once recognize that none of these names is satisfactory. The members of the Reformed Committee were too modest to ask the Presbyterians to relinquish their time-honored name, and to accept the historical name of "Reformed"; and the members of the Presbyterian Committee were too generous to ask the Reformed to yield their name and to accept the name "Presbyterian." Each one felt, however, that with the surrender of the name went also the thing for which the name stands; and to give up the name was practically to give up the church which one represents. But the question not only involves denominational honor but also serious legal difficulties. A change of name may invalidate enormous amounts of vested funds, and it will, under any circumstances, require action in the legislatures of the several states. Instead, however, of discontinuing further transactions because of this apparently insuperable difficulty, the Committee decided to make a frank statement to both churches in reference to the name of the proposed United Church. It was thought that, perhaps, if in other respects the churches desired closer union, the matter of a name might be amicably adjusted. It would clearly have been unwise for the Committee to attempt to solve legal difficulties in advance, as some one suggested on the floor of Synod, before the churches had given reasonable assurance of the desirability of union.

These facts account for the Committee's action as embodied in part two of the Report, entitled, "The Name of the United Church." It was not framed in the spirit of evasion or of compromise, but with the view of showing all concerned the difficulty of the problem. If neither church is willing to make a concession in regard to the name, then again further negotiations will prove futile. If some diplomatic genius will invent an appropriate title, which will meet the approval of both churches, he will render a notable service, and the Committee will gladly receive the suggestion.

The "Basis of Union" evidently has been carefully analyzed, since the publication of the Report, and also adversely criticized, at least in the Reformed Church. The absence of reference to the whole question in the Presbyterian Church papers indicates that the report was not discussed in the late sessions of Presbyterian Synods. In the General Assembly last spring it was passed without a word of discussion, with an ease born of the consciousness that the Presbyterian Church has little at stake. It is argued by some that the doctrinal standards of the two churches are not in essential agreement. The action of the late meeting of the Potomac Synod on this point says: "We do not agree with the 'Concurrent Declarations' especially that part which affirms that the Westminster Confession of Faith and the Heidelberg Catechism are in 'essential agreement' or sufficiently harmonious to be made the joint basis for a United Church."

A statement like this from so influential a body as the Potomac Synod requires careful consideration. The fact that a feeling of difference between the symbols of the two bodies exists, is, to say the least, significant, and is not without cause. In comparing the Confessions and Catechisms one must not only consider them as they were interpreted in the time of their composition by their authors and their contemporaries. But the difference of theological development in both churches, since their establishment in the United States, will also have to be taken into account. For, after all, it is not the Confessions in the abstract alone that ought to have weight, but the theological interpretation which they receive at the present time. No one, who knows the history of the two denominations in this country and their present theological status, will deny that there have been serious differences in the past, and it may be questioned whether they have been overcome in the present. These differences have arisen, not through hostility and opposition, but are traceable to national heritage, to the peculiar character of theological controversies, and to the genius of the leaders of the two denominations in the last two centuries. This fact undoubtedly is one reason, at least, why a synod and many thoughtful individuals in both churches, hesitate to declare an essential unity of doctrine. They feel that such a declaration can be made only with questionable evasion, equivocation, and compromise. Far more important than even church union is sincerity, loyalty to conviction, and honesty of profession. Whether Christianity is primarily doctrine, as some think, or life as others think, in either case a virtual agreement in theological interpretation of the standards is an indispensable necessity for a union in sincerity and truth.

To illustrate the difference which has manifested itself in this regard between the Presbyterian and the Reformed Church in the United States in the past, I shall quote two abstracts from the leaders of our church in the last generation. In a sermon before the alumni of the Mercersburg Theological Seminary, delivered at Reading in 1856, Dr. J. H. A, Bomberger said:

> Let us have it fairly understood, therefore, that it is not to Saybrook-platform Protestantism that we have plighted our faith and service, nor to the Protestantism of Hartford, Princeton, or New Brunswick, but to that form of it which is distinctly laid down in the standards already alluded to, and which may be easily ascertained by every candid inquirer. . . . As a church, therefore, or as an integral portion of the Evangelical Church we have not only a right to maintain our distinctive character, but we are placed by Providence under special obligations to do so. We are not German Presbyterians, as we are sometimes called. There would be far more propriety in the Presbyterian Church calling itself English Reformed. The title Presbyterian relates to a comparatively unimportant characteristic of the true Church. But we are German Reformed. The strong tendency of the more earnest theology of all the evangelical churches is towards those principles on which the German Reformed Church was originally founded, and for which she has from the first contended. This is the case, with reference to what are usually styled the five distinctive points of Calvinism. The preaching of our day savors far less of the Institutes of Calvin, of the Canons of Dort, or of the Westminster Confession, in reference to these points, than the mild, conciliatory, declarations of the Heidelberg Catechism. And so the Sacraments.

These words are quoted with approval in an article in the *Mercersburg Review,* July, 1872, by Dr. Thomas G. Apple, who adds:

> These Puritan and Presbyterian Confessions, including the Canons of Dort, are certainly a one-sided expression of the old Reformed faith, as expressed in so rich and catholic a spirit in the Heidelberg Catechism.
>
> The subject which we have considered, may serve to throw light on our relation to the Calvinistic churches around us. We have much in common with the Presbyterian and the Dutch Reformed Church. But it is clear that our own doctrinal position is more comprehensive than theirs, and better adapted to form a basis of union for the branches of the Reformed Church than theirs. Especially is there much in the history of both denominations to bind us to the Dutch Reformed Church. But we would consider it a great calamity, if we should think for a moment of giving up our broad, catholic position, for one that would give a one-sided expression of the old Reformed faith and life. Nothing would be gained, but much lost, by yielding to a temptation to gain some outward advantage, while at the same time we should surrender any of our internal strength of position.

In the face of such deep-rooted convictions so vigorously expressed, we may well ask whether the theological positions of the sons of these fathers have changed to such an extent, in the course of thirty years, that the men of the Reformed Church may now ignore all past differences, and, without even pausing for a thorough investigation, hasten to join a united general assembly.

Can church union be elected on the basis of sixteenth and seventeenth century confessions? And even if it were brought about by synodical action, would there be any gain for the constituent denominations concerned, or any real advance in the inner life of the Kingdom? IIave we not made progress in theological comprehension of the truth as it is in Christ Jesus these three centuries? Has not the Christian consciousness been enriched by the prayers, the labors, and the sacrifices of the descendants of the men of Heidelberg and of Westminster? Is there not an almost universal unrest among the ministry and laity of the Reformed and Presbyterian Churches because the old formulas no longer fit the new faith? Principal J. Oswald Dykes, Chairman of the Sub-Committee of the Eastern Section of the Alliance of Reformed Churches, on the present relation of British Churches to the Westminster Confession of Faith, Liverpool, 1904, says:

> Since 1877, nearly if not quite every Church in this Alliance which accepts the Westminster Standards has been endeavoring in one way or another, to adjust its relations to those doctrines. The avowed aim has in every instance been to remove hindrances out of the way of orthodox members accepting office by making it easier for them to profess adhesion to the existing Standards. It has been found that men who are intelligent and loyal as to the substance of the faith to confessional teaching, find it increasingly difficult to express their faith in the precise terms of the Westminster formularies, or to give an *ex animo* assent in their details to long and archaic documents which carry in every article the pressure and the colour of a period of English history which lies far behind us and was very unlike our own.

I have been told also, by one who is a reliable authority in the Presbyterian Church, that letters are received almost weekly from intelligent men inquiring about the authority and the meaning of certain articles of the Confession of Faith. A simpler and more comprehensible formula is asked for. Is not the Reformed Church ready to accede to such requests, and to prepare a brief Confession for the use of officials and members, as well as for a basis of union with the Presbyterian Church and even with other churches? May we not now, as members in committee have done, urge the Presbyterian Church to meet us in such a proposition; and, until they are prepared to do that, ought we not to labor peacefully side by side in alliance and in federal union, upon which relations we have already entered, and are now cooperating in the upbuilding of the Kingdom of God in America and in the Orient? Whenever the time is ripe for such a consensus statement, in which the essence of the old is conserved and the substance of the new is incorporated, then has the hour come for a union "which will be just and fair to both sides and will conserve the genius and spirit of both churches."

There are men in the Reformed Church, tried and true, who believe that there is no essential doctrinal difference between the standards of the two denominations; or, even if there is, that it may well be overlooked in the interest of the practical advantages of a united church. All these benefits, however, can be obtained through the Council of Reformed Churches holding the Presbyterian System, or the Federal Council of the Churches of Christ in America. The missionary territory in this country and abroad is being distributed among the churches so as to avert overlapping. Weak congregations in missionary fields of different denominations may be honorably merged by the Missionary Boards represented in the Council of

Reformed Churches. Reformed and Presbyterian publications can readily be brought to the attention of all bodies in the Council through the Boards of Publication, and cooperation in moral and social reform, in a systematic and authoritative way, may now be obtained both through the Council of Reformed Churches and the Federal Council of the Churches of Christ. All this can be accomplished without sacrificing denominational identity. May it not be well at this point to emphasize, also, that the churches are at present lured unduly by the snare of the economic and the practical to the neglect of the deeply intellectual and spiritual—those very things for which the Fathers and the Reformers became martyrs? We are in danger of a vague, colorless, and flabby theological latitudinarianism which is equally content with nothing or with everything, There is a sectarian bigotry which must be denounced in unmeasured terms. There is, also, a denominational loyalty, the decline of which will be a serious handicap to a vigorous pursuit of the work of Christ's Kingdom. The last sentence of the quotation from Dr. Apple's article, than whom there was no more ardent advocate of church union in America, keeps ringing in one's ears: "Nothing would be gained but much lost, by yielding to a temptation to gain some outward advantage while at the same time we should surrender any of our internal position."

Let us now consider the kind of union which is proposed in the Plan submitted by the Joint Committee. It has been interpreted in various ways by different men. Many do not profess to be in the clear as to its meaning. Some term it a form of organic union with federal modifications; others call it without hesitation a merger, or a submerger, or at best a sort of benevolent absorption. All seem to agree that, if the union involves the loss of our denominational existence, we are not prepared for the present to consummate it.

The Plan, which is now before us, is of course only tentative and subject to modification before its presentation for final action. Yet I am convinced, as a member of the subcommittee which prepared it after long deliberation and discussion, that it embodies about all that the Presbyterians can honorably grant and the Reformed can respectfully ask. In substance, then, the tentative plan may be regarded as the one which will be ordered for final adoption, providing the Joint Committee feels warranted to continue further negotiations.

What is the Reformed Church required to give up? First, it gives up its constitution and form of discipline. Second, it dissolves its General Synod, though for the present the subordinate judicatories remain intact. Third, it surrenders the permanency even of its Synods, Classes, and Congregations, for it opens the way for these bodies to be united with corresponding bodies in the Presbyterian Church by the United General Assembly. The same privilege is allowed the Judicatories of the Presbyterian Church. But that it will ever be exercised by the judicatories of the larger body is palpably improbable. Fourth, it abolishes, though the process may be gradual, all the Boards which are under the control of the General Synod, such as the Missionary Boards, the Sunday-school Boards, etc. In a word, the Reformed Church gives up its denominational existence; and an unprejudiced observer from the outside would regard it as a part of the Presbyterian Church.

What does the Presbyterian Church give up? It is easier to answer this question by asking a second—What does the Presbyterian Church retain? First, it keeps the Form of Government and Book of Discipline. Second, it retains the General Assembly, only in an enlarged form. Third, it preserves the Boards of the General Assembly with one or two additional members. Fourth, how much of a modification in the name it will allow remains to be seen. In short the Presbyterian Church gives up nothing, and in an enlarged form keeps everything it now has.

If it gives up nothing, it does, however, grant the Reformed Church certain privileges. It permits the General Synod to end its existence and to join the General Assembly. It allows the Classes to send their delegates to the United General Assembly. The historian will cease to write the history of the General Synod and will mark the beginning of the end of the history of the Reformed Church on the day that the United General Assembly opens. He will write, however, a new chapter in the history of the General Assembly enlarged by the addition of sixty Classes, or Presbyteries, formerly known as Reformed. It permits the addition of one or two men on the boards of the Church. It allows, also, that Reformed Synods and Classes may join similar bodies in the Presbyterian Church. It agrees that the Heidelberg Catechism be considered the equivalent of the Westminster Standards, and that the Reformed Congregations may continue their present mode of worship. In granting these privileges the Presbyterian Church neither surrenders nor sacrifices an iota of doctrine, polity, or worship. But in the acceptance of them, the Reformed Church surrenders its denominational existence and the autonomy which it enjoyed since the organization of the first synod in 1793. This is more than sacrifice; it approaches suicide. Far be it from us to cast a reproach on the Presbyterian Church or its Committee on Church Cooperation and Union, for the consequences of the proposed union. Thcy arc unavoidable and beyond the control of a committee or a church. Yet if that is the case, the Reformed Church has the right, if the convictions of her members disapprove it, to stand aloof from a union of this sort, without being chargeable with repudiating the Zwinglian hand or denying the authority of the prayer of our Lord (John 17:21).

A comparative study of the ratio of representation of the two churches in the United General Assembly will also serve to show the effect of the union on the Reformed Church. According to the Constitution of the Reformed Church, the ratio of representation of a classis in the General Synod, is one minister and one elder for every ten ministers or fraction thereof. According to the Form of Government of the Presbyterian Church the ratio of representation of presbyteries is one minister and one elder for every twenty-four ministers and "for each additional fractional number of ministers not less than twelve." The roll of delegates of the last General Synod contains the names of one hundred and fifty ministers and one hundred and fifty elders; that of the General Assembly of the previous year, four hundred and thirty-six ministers and four hundred and thirty-six elders. In the United General Assembly, according to the ratio of representation of the Form of Government, the Reformed Classes would have sixty-six ministers and sixty-six elders, and the Presbyteries, four hundred and thirty-six ministers and four hundred and thirty-six elders; or one Reformed minister to every seven Presbyterian ministers. It does not take a prophet's eye to foresee the part which the Reformed Church would play in the United Assembly. But even now the General Assembly is considered so large that it has become an unwieldy body. The question of reducing the ratio of representation has been seriously discussed; and if the reduction should be effected, which would be altogether reasonable, the proportion of Reformed representation would be reduced to an uninfluential minimum.

It may be argued, however, that for the present the Synods, Classes, and Congregations remain unchanged. But when the General Synod, the natural head of these subordinate judicatories is gone, who will not realize that denominational identity and independence are practically gone also? Headless as the Reformed Church then would be, it would be like the Church in Sardis of which it was said, "Thou hast a name that thou livest, and thou art dead." The supreme judicatory of a church plans the practical work of Synods, Classes and Congregations for each year. It controls, through its boards, the missionary operations, Sunday-school work, and other forms of benevolence, and is the court of last resort in all cases of appeal. If the General Synod of the Reformed Church is dissolved and united with the General Assembly, then the occupation of our Synods, Classes, and Consistories clearly is reduced to an acceptance of the action of the United Assembly, in which the Reformed representation is so small that it becomes practically insignificant. True, these judicatories still have the right of protest; a right, however, which they ought to be slow to use, and which, even if exercised, in the nature of the case could have little weight.

In the light of these facts it is not hard to answer the question, What will be the effect on the Reformed Church if the Plan of Union is adopted? It matters little what the Joint Committee may desire it to be. And here let it be clearly understood that not a member of the Presbyterian Committee, any more than of the Reformed Committee, seeks a union that would be unfair, disadvantageous, or dishonorable to the Reformed Church. Insinuations contained in current expressions, such as "they will take us in," or "they will swallow us up," or "they will let us come in," have no ground so far as the members of the Committees are concerned. Yet, by virtue of their numerical strength, their prestige, and the continuation of the Form of Government and Book of Discipline unchanged, the Presbyterian Church with its 1,339,000 communicants, could not help but absorb the 296,160 communicants of the Reformed Church. The smaller denomination would necessarily have to become Presbyterian. The character of a union of bodies of such unequal size can not be determined by the plan of a committee, or resolutions of synods. It would be controlled by a law higher than ecclesiastical constitutions; namely the law of organic life, by which the larger organism absorbs and assimilates the smaller. The smaller is merged in the larger. It matters little whether the merging is immediate or gradual; so far as the Reformed Church is concerned, it could not honorably accept a plan which would even ultimately work such a result. If in the words of Dr. Bomberger, spoken a generation ago, "We are not German Presbyterians," then surely at this stage of our history we can not become English Presbyterians.

Some one will say, if you favor church union as you profess to do, and yet are opposed to the union now under consideration, what sort of union do you want? I answer, there are different kinds of unions; and the kind which I strive for, I should term a *truly organic* union. Permit me to define it. When two churches of the same type, or of different types, have both advanced to a higher plane of Christian life and thought, by virtue of deep spiritual experiences usually under the leadership of an epoch-making personality, which have brought them into closer fellowship with the Christ and have deepened and widened their Christian consciousness to such an extent that the new life can no longer be contained in the old forms, and that the two bodies by spontaneous spiritual attractions are brought into one; then we shall have union without evasion, compromise, annihilation, or a one-sided sacrifice of the smaller body. Then both churches will become something different from what they were, without losing the essential truth for which they stood; they will rather conserve the old, and combine it with the new, truth that is continually breaking forth from God's Word and welling up in the hearts of His people. Out of the two there will come a new organism with a new life and a new name. A union on any other basis is doomed to be a mere coalition, a merger, and a forensic transaction without spiritual value. Such a union may be a "far off divine event," but, we believe, that toward it "the whole creation moves." It can not be made by might nor by power; it must come by the spirit of God in the churches.

The efforts for union, which are now made on two continents, are not wrong, undesirable, or fruitless; they are the unmistakable evidence of the activity of the glorified Christ in his church. As there were reformers before the Reformation, so there will be unionists before the Union. In a great movement like this, there always are pioneers who blaze paths; voices in the desert preparing the way for what we are now blindly groping, praying, and working. In the meantime we ought to possess our souls in patience, to cooperate in alliances and federal councils, and to abide in faith the fullness of the time for a union which will conserve diversity in unity and unity in diversity.

There is not a church in American Protestantism that has a juster claim than has the Reformed Church in the United States for the continuance of its denominational existence. It is not a sect nor a schism which has sprung up on American soil or even in a European land. It traces its origin to the very spring of Protestant Christianity in the sixteenth century. It has distinctive racial, temperamental, and doctrinal characteristics; all of which are so subtle and yet so real that they can hardly be defined in words. They are, nevertheless, so closely interwoven with the life of the Reformed ministers and people, both as a heritage and as an attainment by training in family, school and congregation, that they mold thought and life, word and deed. For us the Kingdom of God becomes historical and concrete, vital and personal, in the unique spirit and form of our denominational life. The church of our inheritance or of our adoption can be relinquished for another only when we have changed our deepest religious convictions, or when, through circumstances, we are compelled to adjust ourselves to the genius and forms of another denomination. It is one thing for an individual here and there, now and then, to change his denominational affiliations. It is an altogether different thing for a group of individuals to give up their denominational existence; for with it goes a part, not only of their own spiritual and ethical life but of that of their fathers for centuries before them.

Surely such a sacrifice is required or such a surrender should be made only under conditions which in the progress of the race are exceedingly unfrequent, and arise under the most extraordinary circumstances. When they do come, however, the call is so clear and the motive so powerful that instead of using argument and persuasion to consummate the change, its consummation could not be hindered by the most convincing logic or by the most powerful armies. Who could have prevented the Reformation when the hour of Protestantism struck? Who can hinder the higher union of churches when the historical time for union has come?

That the Reformed Church has a mission and a message for a union larger than the one now proposed, is powerfully set forth in. a sermon by Dr. Briggs, who will be regarded as an impartial and unprejudiced observer, when he says, "The German Reformed have the distinguished honor in this country of remaining undivided. There have been controversies among their churches, of much greater importance than those which rent asunder the Dutch Reformed and the British Presbyterians, but the German Reformed have ever remained true to the genuine type of the Heidelberg Catechism. The German Reformed Church has retained the comprehensive character of the original Reformed theology, rather than the distinctive Calvinistic peculiarities of that type. She has the graceful form and well-rounded proportions of a blooming daughter of the Reformation. One does not see in her as in so many Reformed Churches the sharp visage and the angular proportions of a venerable dame who has spent her days and wasted her strength in fruitless contention with her own flesh and blood. Wherefore the German Reformed occupy the best position in our country to mediate between the different churches of the Reformation and to take the lead in the Reunion movement."

Lancaster, Pa.

Part of a Global Ecumenical Movement

48. In Japan:

"Church Union in Japan"

(1888)

As Christians in the United States became more aware of Christian life in other parts of the globe, a reciprocal relationship began to develop between ecumenical events abroad and ecumenical life in the United States.

The earliest Protestant missionaries from the United States arrived in Japan in 1859, believing in cooperation and mission, and eager to share their convictions. The first Japanese Protestant church, known as the Japan Christian Catholic Church, was founded in Yokohama. It was closely affiliated with Presbyterian and Reformed missionaries, who regularly worked with Congregational missionaries to create united churches.

By 1888, efforts to create a united church involving Presbyterians, Reformed, and Congregationalists had made great progress. A report, which appeared in the Messenger, *was filled with contagious enthusiasm for Japanese church union. "If this union in Japan can be effected with the full and free approval of the home churches, directly interested, what is there to warrant them in refusing to 'go and do likewise' ?" Such united missionary churches began reflecting back an inspiring example of church union to Presbyterians, Reformed, and Congregational churches in the United States. Although the 1888 proposal was ultimately rejected by the Congregationalists, Japanese churches continued working toward union, forming a federation of Christian churches in Japan in 1911. Finally, on the eve of the Second World War, the United Church of Christ in Japan*

Source: "Church Union in Japan," *Reformed Church Messenger,* 29 August 1888, 8–9.

came about through the pressures of a militarist government seeking uniformity of Christians in the interest of wartime cooperation.

After the war, some Protestant denominations left the united church in Japan, but the Baptists, most Presbyterian-Reformed, Methodists, Congregationalists, Disciples, Evangelical United Brethren, and a few others remained in the union and sought to enhance ecumenical cooperation. The United Church of Christ in Japan was an ongoing inspiration for those who later worked so diligently to create the United Church of Christ in the United States.

The New York *Evangelist* gives a very interesting summary of the negotiations and proceedings, now happily nearing, it is confidently believed, a favorable consummation looking to the union of the United Church in Japan, (Presbyterian and Reformed) and the churches connected with the General Conference of the Congregational churches. These negotiations have been carried on for the last few years. After preliminary action had been taken by each of the bodies, a committee of twenty was raised, (ten from each side) to draw up in detail a basis of union, comprising the standard of doctrine and government. This committee has completed its work, and published its report in pamphlet form, establishing the union. This report awaits the final action of the two bodies, to be taken next November. The *Evangelist* summarizes the contents of this basis, as follows:

> This pamphlet has just reached us. We have examined it with care, and in our judgement, it has met the exigency admirably. After defining the Church invisible and visible, it sets forth the Article on doctrine. This, according to the basis of union before agreed upon, presents the Apostles' and Nicene Creeds, together with the Articles of the Evangelical Alliance, as the Confession of Faith of the United Church. It proposes also the Westminster Catechism, the Heidelberg Catechism, and the Plymouth Declaration as Confessions of recent times "that are to be held in veneration in the Church of Christ in Japan, and as having served a high purpose in the past, and still to be regarded as of lasting value for the instruction and edification of believers." Then follows the Form of Government, which requires Presbyterial oversight for all the churches under Bukwai (Presbyteries), Renkwai (Synods), and Sokwai (Assembly), and providing also in cases where the Presbytery or Synod shall so decide, for the trial of appeals by a regularly appointed Commission, whose judgment is to be final. And in order to meet the case of any church which may

prefer to manage its own internal affairs without a Session, it provides in the Appendix two forms for the churches: one, in which the officers of the church are to be a pastor and deacons (ordained for the purpose) and to assist the pastor in the administration of the worship and order of the Church, and granting authority to the church to elect a representative to the Bukwai (Presbytery) and Renkwai (Synod); while in the other form, the officers are to be pastor, deacons, and representative elders, etc., forming thus the Daiinkwai (Session). In all cases, however, as already stated, each church is under the supervision of Presbytery, and appeals from the church are tried by the Presbytery.

We rejoice with that paper, in the bright prospect of the consummation of this movement in the direction of the healing of the divisions in the Lord's Mystical Body. It ought, and may we not confidently expect, that this union once effected in the mission field, will teach us at home, our duty in this regard. If this union in Japan can be effected with the full and free approval of the home churches, directly interested, what is there to warrant them in refusing to "go and do likewise"? It will demonstrate that there is no fundamental hinderance in the way. And such being the case, how dare we allow our minor differences—our vested interests, our doctrinal and historical prejudices any longer to delay the answer to our blessed Lord's prayer! We should earnestly pray the Spirit of God to work in us the will, and we all know that once the will is wrought, a way will soon be found.

49. In India:

"Church Union in India"

(1890)

By the late-nineteenth century, there was a reciprocal dynamic between movements toward union abroad and growing enthusiasm about church union in the United States. Church unions in Japan and India challenged Christians back home to a higher vision of church union (see vol. 6:48).

Seventeen different Presbyterian missionary societies had sent missionaries to India between the 1820s and 1870s. By 1873, the Presbyterian Alliance of India and Ceylon, representing nine presbyteries, had been formed to promote sympathy and help, and to work toward an organic union of all Presbyterian bodies. In 1889, the Council of the Presbyterian Alliance appointed a General Committee on Church Union, which formulated a basis of union that was approved by the council and sent to all presbyteries for approval. It was also sent back to various sponsoring denominations in Great Britain, Canada, and the United States.

When the Reformed Church Messenger *reported on these developments, it noted that the mission churches in India were challenging their home churches on issues of church union. The* Messenger *asked, "What must they do if they would be consistent and logical, as regards their home churches? . . . Why might not all the Reformed Churches of the Presbyterial form of government, in the United States, agree upon some such a basis, and 'flow like kindred drops into one'? . . . What a glorious opening such a step would make for hopeful negotiations with other families of Churches, for larger union!"*

Unfortunately, the plan of 1890 was not successful in India. However, in 1908 nearly all of the Presbyterian and Congregational missions in

---

Source: "Church Union in India," *Reformed Church Messenger,* 20 March 1890, 8.

South India did join together in a federal union called the South India United Church (see vol. 6:11). In May of 1919, negotiations between this church and the Anglican and Methodist churches began, raising hopes all over the world that church union between churches holding to the historic episcopate and churches that did not have an episcopal system might be possible. In 1947, these negotiations finally reached their completion, creating the Church of South India. Unfortunately, Anglican churches in other parts of the world—even those that had originally sent missionaries to India—were not able to accept a union of churches with and without the episcopal system. This meant that the Church of South India was denied full communion with all other Anglican churches. Although the missionary churches tried to lead their "mother churches" along the road toward union, they sometimes had to leave them behind.

For some time past the movements in the direction of Church Union in foreign mission fields has awakened abiding interest in the Protestant world. Many pious hearts have been made glad in view of what has been accomplished, in this regard, in Japan, and at the same time moved with sorrow, and righteous disapproval of a defeat of a wider work in this direction, by the bigoted activity of a small, but unfortunately influential number of conservatives in the Congregational Church in this country. We will not cease to hope, however, that this narrow ecclesiasticism may yet be overcome as a hindrance in the way of a larger work of Christian Union, in that very hopeful and promising field.

Equally gratifying intelligence has recently reached us, of encouraging results towards obliterating denominational lines in India. Seventeen different Presbyterian missionary societies, are laboring in this field, including the Reformed (Dutch) Church. In 1873 the Presbyterian Alliance of India and Ceylon, in which nine Presbyteries were represented, was formed, for the promotion of mutual sympathy and help, and working ultimately to an organic union of all Presbyterian bodies. The Council of the Alliance meets every three years. The meeting held in Dec. 1889, proved to be the most important of the series. A number of Presbyteries appointed members of a General Committee on Church Union. This Committee formulated a basis of union which was submitted to, and approved by the Council. This basis now goes down to the Presbyteries for approval or rejection, as also to the home churches in Great Britain, Canada and the United States.

This basis comprises three main topics—polity, doctrine and local organization. The general polity is, of course, fashioned after the home churches. One feature, however, is rather amusing, which is, that in all meetings of church courts, in which the United Presbyterian Church of America is represented, *psalms only* are to be sung. The section on doctrine, however, is the most important, and ought to be instructive and suggestive, just at this time to the Presbyterian bodies in this country. It "proposes the adoption of the Apostle's creed, the Nicene Creed, and a modern statement of doctrine, such as that of the three Scottish Churches, entitled 'Doctrinal Basis of Union,' or the proposed creed of the English Presbyterian Church. In addition to these it is recommended that the United Church hold in veneration the Westminster Confession, the Westminster Shorter Catechism and the Heidelberg Catechism."

It is an interesting question how the home churches will act upon the adoption or rejection of this basis. The general principles of Union in the foreign field, has already received the approbation of their General Assemblies and General Synods, and should they now approve this basis for their missions, what must they do if they would be consistent and logical, as regards their home churches? May there not be a Providence in this whole movement? Why might not all the Reformed Churches of the Presbyterial form of government, in the United States, agree upon some such a basis, and "flow like kindred drops into one?" Leaving freedom of opinion upon debatable non essential points. Does the immediate vocation of the Church of Christ in this evening of the nineteenth century, require a continued emphasis of the metaphysics and dialectics of a controversial age? What a glorious opening such a step would make for hopeful negotiations with other families of Churches, for a larger union! Who knows but that a movement like this once inaugurated, the Spirit of the living God would open the windows of heaven and pour out such a blessing, that there would not be room to contain it?

50. Among Reformed Churches:

"Plan of Federation"

(1894)

As the worldwide ecumenical movement developed, various world denominational fellowships came into being. Such denominational "family" movements often had an ambiguous relationship to more general ecumenical efforts—sometimes supporting global ecumenism, and sometimes working at cross-purposes.

In 1875, the General Synod of the Reformed Church in the United States began an association with one of the earliest denominational fellowship organizations. It was invited to send delegates to the first meeting of the "Alliance of Reformed Churches throughout the World holding the Presbyterian System." According to J. I. Good, the General Synod expressed "satisfaction" with such movements, but—supposing that only those churches that held to the Westminster Confession could join—it did not send delegates. Nevertheless, sixty-four delegates representing twenty-one independent churches met together, affirming the supremacy of Holy Scripture, adherence to the Consensus of Reformed Confessions, and their general acknowledgment of Presbyterian principles. Two years later, in 1877, the first general Conference of the World Presbyterian Alliance was held in Edinburgh. Although the Reformed Church in the United States was not officially represented, one of its own scholars, Philip Schaff, read a paper entitled "The Harmony of the Reformed Confessions."

Schaff hoped that the World Presbyterian Alliance might produce a doctrinal statement to which all its constituent churches would be able

---

Source: "Plan of Federation," *Reformed Church Messenger,* 3 May 1894, 9.

to subscribe. According to Good, Schaff attended the General Synod of the Reformed Church in 1878, explaining more fully the object of the movement and correcting the misunderstanding that only churches holding to the Westminster Confession could join. As a consequence, the General Synod was pleased to appoint delegates to the next meeting of the World Presbyterian Alliance, held in Philadelphia in 1880, and to all successive meetings. The General Synod also sent representatives to what was called the "Western section of the Alliance."

In 1894, a formal attempt was made to bring together the Reformed Churches in the United States holding the Presbyterian system. On this occasion, committees of the Associate Reformed Synod of the South, the Cumberland Presbyterian General Assembly, the Synod of the (Dutch) Reformed Church in America, the Synod of the (German) Reformed Church in the U.S., the Synod of the Reformed Presbyterian Church, the General Synod of the Reformed Presbyterian Church, the United Presbyterian General Assembly, and the General Assembly of the Presbyterian Church in the U.S.A. came together and prepared a plan of federation "for the prosecution of work that can be better done in union than separately." They also created an ecclesiastical assembly that was to be known as "The Federal Council of the Reformed Churches in the United States of America holding the Presbyterian system."

Although the proposed plan did not reach fruition, it is an early example of the impulse to federate that eventually led to the formation of the Federal Council of the Churches of Christ in America fourteen years later.

The following is the Plan of Federation which the committees of the Associate Reformed Synod of the South; the Cumberland Presbyterian General Assembly; the Synod of the (Dutch) Reformed Church in America; the Synod of the (German) Reformed Church in the U.S.; the Synod of the Reformed Presbyterian Church; General Synod of the Reformed Presbyterian Church; United Presbyterian General Assembly; the General Assembly of the Presbyterian Church in the U.S. of America, at their meeting in Philadelphia on the 12th inst. agreed to recommend to their appointing bodies for adoption:

For the glory of God, and for the greater unity and advancement of the Church of which the Lord Jesus Christ the Head, the Reformed Churches in the United States holding to the Presbyterian system adopt the following Articles of Federal Union:

1. Every denomination entering into this Union shall retain its distinct individuality, as well as every power, jurisdiction, and right which is not by this Constitution expressly delegated to the body hereby constituted.
2. The acts, proceedings and records of the duly constituted authorities of each of the denominations shall be received in all the other denominations, and in the Federal Council, as of full credit and with proper respect.
3. For the prosecution of work that can be better done in union than separately, an Ecclesiastical Assembly is hereby constituted, which shall be known by the name and style of The Federal Council of the Reformed Churches in the United States of America holding the Presbyterian system.
4. The Federal Council shall consist of four ministers and four elders from each of the constituent denominations, who shall be chosen, with alternates, under the direction of their respective supreme judicatories in such manner as those judicatories shall respectively determine.
5. The Federal Council shall promote the co-operation of the federated denominations in their Home and Foreign Missionary work, and shall keep watch on current, religious, moral and social movements, and take such action as may concentrate the influence of all the churches in the maintenance of the truth that our nation is a Protestant Christian nation, and of all that is therein involved.
6. The Federal Council may advise and recommend in all matters pertaining to the general welfare of the Kingdom of Christ, but shall not exercise authority, except such as is conferred upon it by this instrument, or such as may be conferred upon it by the federated bodies. It shall not interfere with the creed, worship, or government of the federated denominations. In the conduct of its meetings it shall respect their conscientious views. All matters of discipline shall be left to the exclusive and final judgment of the ecclesiastical authorities of the denomination in which the same may arise.
7. The Federal Council shall have the power of opening and maintaining a friendly correspondence with the highest Assemblies of other religious denominations, for the purpose of promoting union and concert of action in general or common interests.

8. All differences which may arise among the federated bodies, or any of them, in regard to matters within the jurisdiction of the Federal Council shall be determined by such executive agencies as may be created by the Federal Council, with the right of appeal to the Federal Council for final adjudication.
9. The officers of the Federal Council shall be a President, Vice-President, Clerk and Treasurer.
10. The Federal Council shall meet annually, and on its own adjournment, at such time and place as may be determined. Special meetings may be called by a unanimous vote of the officers of the Council on thirty days' notice.
11. The expenses of the Council shall be met by a contingent fund to be provided by a *pro rata* apportionment on the basis of the number of communicants in each denomination; and the expenses of the delegates to the Council shall be paid from this fund.
12. Amendments to these articles may be proposed by the Federal Council, or by any of the supreme judicatories of the churches in the Federation; but the approval of all those judicatories shall be necessary for their adoption.

51. In the United States: *"The Inter-Church Conference on Federation . . . " and "Plan of Federation"*

(1905)

George W. Richards et al.; *Reformed Church Messenger*

On November 15, 1905, four thousand delegates from thirty denominations representing eighteen million church members joined together in New York's Carnegie Hall for The Interchurch Conference on Federation. It was, in the words of Reformed Church leader J. S. Kieffer, "a deeply significant, vital and permanent advance" in the history of Protestant Christianity in the United States.

Of course, the meeting was not without its antecedents: the Evangelical Alliance, the Young Men's Christian Association (YMCA), the State and International Sunday School Association, the Brotherhood of Andrew and Philip, the Young People's Society of Christian Endeavor, the Alliance of the Reformed Churches of the World, and, above all, the Ecumenical Mission Conference held in New York in 1900 had prepared the way. All of these organizations and events had raised awareness and raised hopes for a Christian church that could transcend denominational and even national boundaries.

The Interchurch Conference on Federation confirmed in new ways that the one church of which the Bible spoke was not simply a dream, unrealizable in fact because of theological, historical, denominational,

---

Source: George W. Richards, John Hassler Prugh, J. S. Kieffer, and Cyrus Cort, "The Inter-Church Conference on Federation at New York, Opened November 15th," *Reformed Church Messenger,* 23 November 1905, 5–6; "Plan of Federation Recommended for Approval by the Constituent Christian Bodies," *Reformed Church Messenger,* 23 November 1905, 7–8.

racial, and national differences. Rather, it proclaimed that the churches were on the way toward the realization of one church.

At the conference a constitution for the Federal Council of the Churches of Christ in America was completed. The preamble stated: "Whereas, in the providence of God, the time has come when it seems fitting, more fully to manifest the essential oneness of the Christian Churches of Christ in America in Jesus Christ as their Lord and Saviour, and to promote the spirit of fellowship, service and co-operation among them, the delegates to the Inter-Church Conference on Federation assembled in New York city, do hereby recommend the following Plan of Federation to the Christian bodies represented in this conference for their approval." By 1908, the various national assemblies of the participating denominations adopted the plan, and the Federal Council of the Churches of Christ in America became a reality.

The Inter-Church Conference on Federation at New York, Opened November 15th

When the Inter-Church Conference, on Federation was opened by Rev. Dr. Roberts on Wednesday evening, November 15th, delegates from thirty Churches were in their places. Most of these had come to New York early in the day and had been assigned to one or other of the fine hotels located in the neighborhood of Carnegie Hall, which is on the corner of Seventh Avenue and Fifty-seventh Street. Among the delegates were the following representing the Reformed Church: Revs. Dr. J. S. Kieffer, Dr. Cyrus Cort, Dr. A. S. Weber, Dr. G. W. Richards, Dr. J. P. Stein, Dr. J. H. Prugh, Dr. R. W. Miller, A. E. Dahlmann, S. W. Seeman, B. S. Stern and Dr. C. J. Musser. Besides these there were present also Rev. Dr. C. Clever, Dr. J. I. Good, Rev. E. E. Emhoff, Rev. F. W. Bald, Rev. P. S. Leinbach and Rev. Paul H. Schnatz. The audience numbered fully 4,000. The opening was simple and informal. The delegates came from that class who set little store by forms and ceremonies, and who in spirit and word and deed are great and impressive whenever the time and occasion demands.

The first evening was confined to addresses of welcome. But these already indicate the note and scope and importance of the cause in the interest of which this conference is held.

The chairman of the committee which brought the conference to pass,

Rev. Dr. William H. Roberts, of Philadelphia, read a letter from President Roosevelt, expressing sympathy with the purpose of the gathering and pointing out that its effect would be felt in increased measure of Christian unity in foreign lands. Mr. Roosevelt in his letter said:

> I have the very highest sympathy with the movement; for instance, I feel that indirectly in addition to the great good it will do here, it is perfectly possible that the movement may have a very considerable effect in the Christianizing of Japan, which I feel to be retarded by the divisions among ourselves and by the failure to recognize the fact that the Christian Church in Japan must, of course, assume essentially a Japanese national form.
>
> So you see I have a very real interest in what you are doing, and only wish it were in my power to attend the meeting as you request, but I regret to say that it is out of the question for me to do so.
>
> I am genuinely sorry to have to write you thus.

The Rev. Dr. Thompson spoke of the mission of the members of the conference, which, he said, was to encourage the great Christian bodies of the country to stand together and lead in the discussion of and give impulse to all great movements that make for righteousness. He said the conference believed that questions like those of marriage and divorce, Sabbath desecration, social evils, child labor, the relation of labor and capital, problems created by foreign immigration, and the moral and religious training of the young, demanded united and concerted action which the conference sought to afford.

On Thursday morning Rev. Dr. William Hays Ward, editor of the "Independent," reviewed the history of church work from the days of the apostles to the present. He traced the reasons for the success or failure of such movements, showing the development of the present situation through the general zeal for evangelism and foreign missions, as expressed in the interdenominational mission boards of the past century, through the Y. M. C. A. and Christian Endeavor, through the consolidation of churches in the foreign mission field, and through the various local federation enterprises.

Dr. Ward pointed out that the present union sentiment looks to the consolidation of allied denominations and to a general federation "in which there should be no compromise of the several creeds or forms of government, of the full right of each to serve God in its own way, while fellowshiping with and aiding all the others."

The spirit of the conference and its world-wide interest was shown in the thought of all the addresses. Even before Dr. Ward spoke Rev. Dr. Gladden struck a chord to which the conference enthusiastically responded. He offered a paper which was one of the finest expressions of Christian sentiment and world-wide sympathy heard in an assembly where every hour one hears things he would like to remember forever. It took the form of a plea, and was as follows:

> The Inter-Church Federation of the United States of America, representing 18,000,000 of communicants in the free Protestant Churches of America, sends greeting to the Christian rulers and the Christian ministers and the Christian people of Russia, beseeching them, in the name of our Lord Jesus Christ, to do what they can, without delay, to put an end to the dreadful cruelties which are now being inflicted on the Jewish people in many parts of the Russian empire.
>
> That those who bear the name of Jesus Christ should practice such cruelties, or tolerate them, brings pain to the heart and shame to the face of every true Christian in all the world. And what grief it must cause to the blessed Christ Himself, who pronounced His blessing on the merciful, who bade us love our enemies and bless them that curse us, and who gave us that parable of the Good Samaritan, who succored and befriended a suffering Jew.
>
> Our hearts go out to the Russian people in this day of their trouble and calamity. We are praying that peace and welfare may soon be restored to you, but our sympathy is chilled and our prayers falter on our lips when we read of this terrible carnage.
>
> The people of Russia must not in their time of need make it hard for their Christian brethren in all the world to think kindly of them.
>
> We speak, not as the representatives of any military or political power. We speak not as Americans to Russians, but as Christian men to Christian men, and we implore you, brethren, by the memories of Christ, that you will act at once, with one accord, and rise up and speak the word which shall restrain these atrocities and heal the reproach which they are bringing on the Christian name.

No further attempt will be made to report the addresses and events of the conference. The task would prove impossible. The program was followed as printed in a recent issue of this paper. The papers would fill a large volume. In passing, it may not be out of place, however, to say that our own Church was ably represented by Professor Richards, of Lancaster, who read a paper on Thursday afternoon on "Religious Education in the Family." It was full of the spirit and teaching of Reformed doctrine. He was followed by Mr. John Wanamaker, who said, "If the ideals of Professor Richards were realized, if the Christian house and the Christian home were everywhere established, there would be nothing left for me but to burn my paper."

The full proceedings of this great conference, with all the papers read, will be published in book form soon after the close of the conference, and at the moderate cost of $2.00. Time and space will allow nothing more than the adopted scheme of federation and a few paragraphs from several of our own delegates, who in this brief way give their impression of the conference.

Impressions of the Conference

The fact that a conference, in which thirty Protestant denominations, including 18,000,000 members, are represented, is more significant than any paper read or motion made. The gradual change which has been going on in the Protestant consciousness for the last fifty years has made such a meeting possible. It is simply an index of the currents that are coursing beneath the surface.

There is a spirit of frankness in the statements made by representatives of different bodies. No one is renouncing his specific convictions, and yet all recognize an essential unity. Unity itself requires diversity.

The formulation of a policy of future action is difficult. It must be both inclusive and exclusive. Yet the only way by which the Church can approach the question of co-operation is by continuous efforts to define some mode of procedure by which Churches may work together rather than think together.

The personnel of the assembly is strong. Leading men of all denominations are present. They are well-poised, earnest and have come here to do business. In that respect it is one of the most satisfactory general conventions I have attended.

GEORGE W. RICHARDS.

The Inter-Church Conference, in New York, was a great conference—great in its splendid aim, great in its manifestation of the spirit of Christian love, and great in its personnel.

When Jesus Christ laid the burden of missions upon the Church His great prayer was for the unity of His followers, to the end that the world might be evangelized. And these two things, the unity of Christ's followers and the evangelization of the world, greatly concern all branches of the Christian Church just now. And that is why the 500 delegates from thirty-two of the larger Protestant denominations in the United

States, representing 18,000,000 Christian communicants, manifested in New York such a beautiful fraternal spirit. Our fellowship was the beautiful comradeship of endeavoring unitedly to advance the kingdom of God.

The conference was not the work of a day. For fifty years God's Spirit has been working upon the hearts of His people, preparing them for it. Many previous movements contributed to the gathering of this conference and to the evolving of the proposed plan for a Federation of Protestant Churches in America. The Evangelical Alliance, the Young Men's Christian Association, the State and International Sunday School Association, the Brotherhood of Andrew and Philip, the Young People's Society of Christian Endeavor, the Alliance of the Reformed Churches of the World, the great Ecumenical Foreign Missionary Conference, in 1900—all these helped to deepen the conviction that those united to Christ by faith are one body. And, if the promises of the proposed Federation of Churches are realized, the wrongs in this country will be more effectively opposed, righteousness will more thoroughly be promoted, and the kingdom of Christ will be more speedily extended throughout the world.

Our Reformed Church, in the light of her history, pledges the hands, and hearts, and prayers of her members to this glorious movement.

JOHN HASSLER PRUGH.

The Inter-Church Conference on Federation bears the characteristic marks of a real and genuine movement. It has come in the way in which legitimate developments are accustomed to come. It was not without those heraldings, fore-announcements, pre-intimations; prophecies, by which all great consummations, have always been attended. In particular, there was not wanting, in the history of it, those preliminary, recurring, and at the time seemingly fruitless and futile attempts to accomplish the desired object, which are wont always to precede the attempt that is successful and final. Above all, the spirit of the conference itself would seem to suggest genuineness and legitimacy; to point to consummation and finality; to indicate an epoch; to betoken one of those conjunctures which, in the New Testament, are known as "the fullness of the time." The proceedings of the conference have been distinguished by the dignity, ability, and deep religious earnestness of its discussions, and, above all, by the unanimity of its spirit. Every genuine forward movement in the history of the Church will be found to be conditioned and characterized by a certain return to the beginning; for the beginning and the end are one; in a profound sense, the last thing is the first, and the first is the last. This sign has not been wanting to the present conference. There has been that in it which could hardly fail to remind one of the days of the apostles and the first beginnings of

Christianity. In particular, one has repeatedly been led to think of certain things said in the Acts of the Apostles, such as these: "They were all with one accord in one place"; "And the multitude of them that believed were of one heart and of one soul." These phrases "with one accord" and "of one heart and of one soul," may truly be applied to this conference. And, because of the spirit which they express, and the return which they imply to the beginnings of the Christian Church, they may well encourage the hope and belief that this conference represents, not an insignificant and transitory impulse, but a deeply significant, vital and permanent advance, amounting to nothing less, indeed, than a genuine epoch in the history of Protestant Christianity in America.

J. S. KIEFFER.

I have been very favorably impressed with the personnel and proceedings of the Inter-Church Conference on Federation. It is a notable convocation of representative men from all phases of evangelical American Protestantism. When leaders so diverse in doctrine, polity and customs can mingle together for days in harmonious fraternal communion and virtually adopt as their watchword the motto of our Reformation fathers, "Unity in essentials, freedom in non-essentials and charity in all things" a great stride has been made toward the millennium.

It vindicates the position of Ulrich Zwingli at Marburg 376 years ago in his conference with Luther. Calvin, too, although racked with disease, was ready to cross seven stormy seas to promote the peace and unity of divided Protestantism. Our Reformed fathers did all in their power to keep the unity of the Spirit in the bond of peace.

The addresses have been excellent and will make a volume worthy a conspicuous place in any Christian library.

I take special pleasure in the work and outcome of the conference because the plan of federation proposed to the thirty Protestant denominations represented here is substantially the same as that outlined last December in Pittsburg by the commissioners of seven Reformed and Presbyterian Churches. And that, again, was substantially the same as the articles that the two Reformed Churches formulated on the top of the Catskill Mountains a dozen years or more previously.

I have enjoyed the unique privilege of attending all of these meetings, and am the only person of whom this can be said. Besides, twenty years ago I offered resolutions in Mercersburg Classis urging General Synod to take steps to bring about the union of Reformed and Presbyterian Churches on the basis of the Heidelberg Catechism and Westminster Confession as interpreted by the U. P. Church of Scotland in 1879.

We led the way toward federation of American Protestantism, and now federation is in the air. Our work in those days was not all in vain. The evils of the sect spirit and the centrality of the Person of Jesus Christ, as the true basis and bond of unity and peace, have been emphasized in this conference in a way that seemed like echoes of the teachings of Drs. Nevin and Schaff at Mercersburg sixty years ago. The paramount duty of mission work in the home and foreign fields and the need of a united front of evangelical Protestantism in the face of the heathen world in behalf of missions have been duly recognized. The unification of missionary activity, the sanctity of the marriage relation, etc., for which some of us have labored earnestly for an entire generation, is now the prevailing note among all phases of American Protestantism. I thank God that I have, in His gracious providence, been permitted to see this day and to have an humble part in bringing to pass this blessed consummation. The formation of this Inter-Church Federation will doubtless inaugurate a new era in church history and mark an advanced stadium in the progress of American Christianity. For this we should all work and pray.

CYRUS CORT.

Plan of Federation Recommended for Approval by the Constituent Christian Bodies

Preamble

Whereas, in the providence of God, the time has come when it seems fitting, more fully to manifest the essential oneness of the Christian Churches of America in Jesus Christ as their Lord and Saviour, and to promote the spirit of fellowship, service and co-operation among them, the delegates to the Inter-Church Conference on Federation assembled in New York city, do hereby recommend the following Plan of Federation to the Christian bodies represented in this conference for their approval:

Plan of Federation

1. The name of the body shall be the Federal Council of the Churches of Christ in America.

2. The following Christian bodies shall be entitled to representation in this Federal Council on their approval of the purpose and plan of the organization: The Baptist Churches (North), the Baptist Churches (South), the

Free Baptist Churches, the Negro Baptist Churches, the Christian Connection, the Congregational Churches, the Disciples of Christ, the Evangelical Association, the Evangelical Synod, the Friends, the Evangelical Lutheran Church (General Synod), the Methodist Episcopal Church, the Methodist Episcopal Church (South), the Primitive Methodist Church, the Colored Methodist Episcopal Church of America, the Methodist Protestant Church, the African Methodist Episcopal Church, the African Methodist Episcopal Zion Church, the Mennonite Church, the Moravian Church, the Presbyterian Church in the U.S.A., the Cumberland Presbyterian Church, the Welsh Presbyterian Church, the Reformed Presbyterian Church, the United Presbyterian Church, the Protestant Episcopal Church, the Reformed Church in America, the Reformed Church in the U.S.A., the Reformed Episcopal Church, the Seventh Day Baptist Churches, the United Brethren in Christ, the United Evangelical Church.

3. The object of this Federal Council shall be—

I. To express the fellowship and catholic unity of the Christian Church.

II. To bring the Christian bodies of America into harmonious service for Christ and the world.

III. To encourage devotional fellowship and mutual counsel concerning the spiritual life and religious activities of the Churches.

IV. To secure a larger combined influence for the Churches of Christ in all matters affecting the moral and social condition of the people, so as to promote the application of the law of Christ in every relation of human life.

V. To assist in the organization of local branches of the Federal Council to promote its aims in their communities.

4. This Federal Council shall have no authority over the constituent bodies adhering to it; but its province shall be limited to the expression of its counsel and the recommending of a course of action in matters of common interest to the Churches, local councils and individual Christians.

It has no authority to draw up a common creed, or form of government or of worship, or in any way to limit the full autonomy of the Christian bodies adhering to it.

5. Members of this Federal Council shall be appointed as follows:

Each of the Christian bodies adhering to this Federal Council shall be entitled to four members, and shall be further entitled to one member for every 50,000 of its communicants or major fraction thereof. The question of representation of local councils shall be referred to the several constituent bodies, and to the first meeting of the Federal Council.

6. Any action to be taken by this Federal Council shall be by the general vote of its members. But in case one-third of the members present and voting request it, the vote shall be by the bodies represented, the members of each body voting separately; and action shall require the vote, not only of a majority of the members voting, but also of the bodies represented.

7. Other Christian bodies may be admitted into membership of the Federal Council on their request, if approved by a vote of two-thirds of the members voting at a session of this council, and of two-thirds of the bodies represented, the representatives of each body voting separately.

8. The Federal Council shall meet in December, 1908, and thereafter once in every four years.

9. The officers of this Federal Council shall be a president, one vice-president from each of its constituent bodies, a corresponding secretary, a recording secretary, a treasurer, and an executive committee, who shall perform the duties usually assigned to such officers.

The corresponding secretary shall aid in organizing and assisting local councils and shall represent the Federal Council in its work, under the direction of the Executive Committee.

The Executive Committee shall consist of seven ministers and seven laymen, together with a president, all ex-presidents, the corresponding secretary and the treasurer. The Executive Committee shall have authority to attend to all business of the Federal Council in the intervals of its meetings and to fill any vacancies.

All officers shall be chosen at the quadrennial meetings of the Council, and shall hold their office until their successors take office.

The president, vice-presidents, the corresponding secretary, the recording secretary and the treasurer shall be elected by the Federal Council on nomination by the Executive Committee.

The Executive Committee shall be elected by ballot after nomination by a nominating committee.

10. This plan of federation may be altered or amended by a majority vote of the members, followed by a majority vote of the representatives of the several constituent bodies, each body voting separately.

11. The expenses of the Federal Council shall be provided for by the several constituent bodies.

This plan of federation shall become operative when it shall have been approved by two-thirds of the above bodies to which it shall be presented.

It shall be the duty of each delegation to this conference to present this plan of federation to its national body, and ask its consideration and proper action.

In case this plan of federation is approved by two-thirds of the proposed constituent bodies the Executive Committee of the National Federation of Churches and Christian Workers, which has called this conference, is requested to call the Federal Council to meet at a fitting place in December, 1908.

[All the above items had not been finally adopted when the copy was mailed. Any amendments made will be reported later.—C. J. M.]

52. At Edinburgh:

"World Missionary Conference II"

(1910)

Allen R. Bartholomew

Although the World Missionary Conference in Edinburgh in 1910 was the outgrowth and culmination of a series of conferences extending back to 1854, its importance relates to the profound impact it made on the future of the ecumenical movement. The conference put into focus the common concerns of various Christians who wanted to take the Christian gospel to the non-Christian world.

In preparation for Edinburgh, eight commissions undertook intensive preliminary studies, which became major topics for the conference. These were: (1) carrying the gospel to all the non-Christian world, (2) the church in the mission field, (3) education in relation to the Christianization of national life, (4) the missionary message in relation to non-Christian religions, (5) the preparation of missionaries, (6) the home base of missions, (7) missions and governments, and (8) cooperation and the promotion of unity. Of these, the work of three commissions was of special importance in the later development of the ecumenical movement: the first, which represented the worldwide mission of the church; the second, which stressed the purpose of missions as bringing into being self-governing, self-supporting, and self-propagating churches; and the eighth, which promoted unity by claiming that "the aim of all missionary work [is] to plant in each non-Christian nation one undivided Church of Christ," in spite of the fact that missionaries occasionally tried to promote their own particular brand of Christianity. In order to nurture a sense

---

Source: Allen R. Bartholomew, "World Missionary Conference II," *Reformed Church Messenger,* 14 July 1910, 6–7.

of Christian unity, the leaders at Edinburgh decided that no potentially divisive questions of faith and order would be discussed.

Nevertheless, the agenda was ambitious. The greatest contribution to the later ecumenical movement made by the 1910 Edinburgh meeting was probably the way in which it affirmed and inspired leadership for the ecumenical movement, especially that of two men: John R. Mott and Joseph H. Oldham. Many who came to Edinburgh were young and charismatic leaders who had grown up in nondenominationally oriented student Christian movements and were passionately committed to world mission. Edinburgh galvanized them to explore a broad variety of ecumenical ventures over the next quarter century.

Mott was chair of the first preparatory commission for the conference, the one concerned about carrying the gospel to the non-Christian world. In this capacity he sent personal letters to some six hundred people from all over the world—many of whom he had met in his worldwide journeys as an evangelist among students—asking them to consider several questions. Their response led to a new global network among Christian leaders. Later, Mott chaired the all-important Continuation Committee of the conference, and its later outgrowth, the International Missionary Council (IMC).

Oldham, who became secretary of the Continuation Committee and the first secretary of the IMC, made the Edinburgh conference and its implementation in the life of the worldwide Christian fellowship his primary concern for twenty-six years. Later, he became chair of the Preparatory Committee for the Universal Christian Conference for Life and Work of 1937.

Others who attended Edinburgh in 1910 later played important roles in the ecumenical movement. For example: V. S. Azariah became the first Indian bishop of the Anglican Communion in India. Charles H. Brent declared from the floor of the conference that Christians could not remain content with Edinburgh 1910 but would have to meet in the future to address the potentially divisive questions of faith and order. He subsequently called for the first World Conference on Faith and Order. Edinburgh also shaped a young man named William Temple, later the archbishop of Canterbury and a prime mover in many subsequent ecumenical meetings.

Since the delegates to Edinburgh 1910 were not churches but individuals from organizations around the world sending missionaries to the non-Christian world, they could not legislate for their organizations or for their churches. Nevertheless, the conference invited Christian leaders to focus their common mind and to plan for future joint ventures. In addition, it opened new vistas of fellowship and cooperation among them, overcoming centuries of ignorance and misunderstanding. Allen R. Bartholomew's second report on the conference shows how the Edinburgh experience opened the minds and hearts of all who were there, so that they believed with new fervor that they were one body in Christ.

The Keynote to All Sessions

On the first Tuesday evening of the Conference, the opening session, there was not an empty seat in the vast assembly hall. The delegates were practically all in their places. Hundreds of missionaries from the galleries beheld a sight that must linger in their memories for many years. The scene was indescribable when Lord Balfour, of Burleigh, took the chair. On his right sat the Archbishop of Canterbury and Principal Whyte, and on his left Dr. Robert E. Speer, of New York, and Sir J. H. Kennaway. All sat with one accord. What an object lesson in Christian unity! Almost every shade of Christian belief was present on the platform and in the great assembly, and yet the unity in Christ, and obedience to His great commission was the glory of this unique enterprise. Can anyone conceive of any other attraction that could have brought all these into such a blessed fellowship? No: only the peculiar glories of missions could work such a divine wonder. The unity of the first evening was the keynote to all the sessions. To quote the words of Bishop La Trobe: "We have the one passion, and it is He and only He, the One who bids us carry out His gospel to bless the whole world."

Seldom has "Old Hundred" been sung by such a throng, never by so varied a throng, convened from all parts of the globe. No more appropriate word could be chosen for the opening hymn than:

> "All people that on earth do dwell,
> Sing to the Lord with cheerful voice."

These words were caught up by voices from the far West and the farther East, from Africa and the islands of the Pacific, from Christian and non-Christian lands. Did ever before so many different tongues unite to sing the simple and immortal paraphrase? Principal Whyte led in prayer. His very look is a benediction. Although his voice was low, yet the assembly settled into a great hush, and he was heard. The prayer was as simple in style as the occasion was great. It was touching, to hear this saintly soul pour out his very heart to God for a greater awakening of interest in the cause of missions. And the blessing came in untold measure during the conference sessions.

After the devotions, Lord Balfour sent a thrill of expectancy through the audience by telling us, "I am charged with a message from the King." Immediately the people sprang to their feet, and stood to hear it "with all honor and respect." The royal message expresses deep interest in the World Missionary Conference; the King is gratified at the fraternal co-operation of so many churches in the dissemination of Christianity throughout the world; he appreciates the supreme importance of the work, and hopes that the conference may be a means of promoting unity among Christians and of furthering the high and beneficent end in view. It was felt on every hand that the new sovereign had done a right kingly and Christian act in recognizing so cordially and sympathetically the work and aims of the Conference. The singing of the national hymn was impromptu, not a mere act of formality, but the prayer of thousands of Christian hearts that God would save the King.

Lord Balfour, in the opening address, spoke of "The Present Possibilities." He said: "We are no small and unimportant gathering. We are constituting the first meeting of a conference of which there are 1200 members representing 150 different churches and organizations, all with their representatives in the mission field. There are representatives here tonight from many countries on the Continent of Europe, in the United States of America and the British dominions. When we look at the list of those who constitute the Conference, two feelings are dominant in all our minds. Profound sorrow that our differences should make necessary so many different organizations, but there will also be a feeling of joy and thankfulness that we are drawing together now as perhaps we have never before been drawn together in the prosecution of the great enterprise in which we are all interested."

Throughout the address there was an emphasis laid on the need of co-operation in the work. "We want to get into closer touch with one another. We want to become more familiar with each other's methods, with each other's work, we want to rejoice in each other's successes, we want to sympathize in each other's failures and each other's disappointments, and, above all, we want to learn by the experience of both." The great awakening in the East was a new challenge to the Church. Now as never before the nations in the East are looking for enlightenment and liberty. "Christianity alone, of all religions, meets these demands in the highest degree. There cannot be Christianity without liberty, and liberty without at least the restraint of Christian ideals is full of danger. There is a power unique in Christianity of all religions to uplift and to ennoble, and it is for this reason that it has its roots and its foundations in self-sacrifice and love."

The final words of Lord Balfour evoked great enthusiasm. It was a plea for unity at home. "The hope has sprung up in my mind that unity, if it begins in the mission field, will not find its ending there. It is a thought not without its grandeur that a unity begun in the mission field may extend its influence and react upon us at home and throughout the older civilizations—that it may bring to us increased hope of international peace among the nations of the world, and of at least fraternal co-operation and perhaps a greater measure of unity in ecclesiastical matters at home."

The most remarkable address of the evening was that made by the Archbishop of Canterbury, coming, as it did from the head of the great Anglican Church. When he stood up in the United Free Assembly Hall to address a gathering which, to use his own words, was "an assembly without a parallel in the history of this or any other land," he received an ovation. With his first words he won his audience. "Fellow workers in the church militant, the society of Christ on earth," he began, and every man, however different his race and form of creed, felt that here was a fraternal greeting. The Church of England has lost much by its isolation in the past. May we not hope that the presence and participation of so many high churchmen at the Conference was the ushering in of a new day for that branch of the Church Catholic as well as for all the members in the Body of Christ. "The Central Place of Missions in the Life of the Church" was the theme of the Archbishop's address. Among the duties and privileges which are ours in the Church of Christ, the place which belongs of right to the missionary work is the central place of all. He said: "We meet for the most serious attempt which the Church has yet made to look steadily at the whole fact of the non-Christian world, and to understand its meaning and its challenge. We look at it from standpoints not by any means the same, geographical, racial or denominational. No one of us bates a jot of the distinctive convictions which he deliberately holds. Therein lies in part the value of the several contributions which will be made to our debates. But we are absolutely one in our allegiance to the living God. To Him we bring it all." Speaking of the present and promising opportunities, he said, the whole world was in closest, speediest touch; the millions of the furthest East awakening like some giant from the stupor of the ages, and deliberately, even eagerly, calling for the very knowledge which alone can make them wise unto salvation. A significant remark was this: "If the work is to be done we must make men know and feel; yes, and make them live as men who know and feel, not in abstract theory, but in living, burning fact, that there is none other name under the heaven, given among men, in whom and through whom we, or any other folk, can receive health and salvation, but only in the name of our Lord Jesus Christ." Such a labor calls for sacrifice on our part, which Christ looks for and demands. Thousands of Christians are shy and reticent on this point. It is ours to hearten them. Let people get hold of the truth that missions occupy a central place, vital to the very life of the Church, and it will tell on the work at home and for those afield. In his last words the archbishop made a profound impression. "Be quite sure," he declared, "that the place of missions in the life of the Church must be the central one, and none other. Secure for that thought the first place in our plans, our policy, our prayers, and then the issue is His and not ours. But it may well be that if that came true, there be some standing here who shall not taste of death till they see here on earth, in a way we know not now, the kingdom of God come with power."

The concluding address of the evening was given by Dr. Robert E. Speer. With clear, terse, powerful words, he spoke of the "Leadership of Christ" down through the ages in nations, churches and the lives of individuals. No one can follow Christ without following Him to the uttermost parts of the earth. When we follow Him perfectly we shall each be found walking with his Brother. Declaring this leadership summons us now to the achievement of the impossible, Dr. Speer quoted the words of a friend, who said: "What are Christians in the world for but to achieve the impossible by the help of God?" Who are we that we should set limits to the power of God in the redemption of men? If we believe that Christ is our Leader, we must believe that it is in the weakness of our faith that the hindrances lie which bar the coming of His kingdom. The headship of Christ was the most real fact in our common life. It was He who had assembled the delegates. They were not misled by any foolish optimism. They were looking sensibly at the facts. Let no one disregard the difficulties or belittle the foes or lessen the magnitude of the task. The true Christian will count the cost, but relying on Him who has all power in heaven and on earth will go forth to conquer in His name. These were mighty utterances, and one felt almost glad when the tensions of them were taken off the spirit by the closing hymn and by the parting benediction of the archbishop. Good it was to be there and glad the heart for the growing unity of the Spirit in the work of Christian missions.

"We are not divided. All one body we." This was the impressions made upon my mind on the first evening of the Feast of Missions.

The Formation of the Evangelical and Reformed Church

53. Finally Union: *"I Believe in the Holy Catholic Church, The Communion of Saints . . . " and "Prayer"*

(1934)

F. William Leich; Jacob C. Leonard

In a sermon preached at the opening of the special meeting of the General Synod preparatory to the joint session enacting the merger of the Evangelical Synod and the Reformed Church, F. William Leich offered an observation that applied not only to the ecumenical history of the Reformed Church, but also to the vicissitudes of every church that seeks to realize its ecumenical mandate while clinging to its denominational structure and identity. Musing on the difficulties that the Reformed Church had encountered on its way toward the union being celebrated, Leich said, "Christianity has ever been in danger of hardening about organization, polity, buildings, rituals, dogmas and so on. But . . . [it] has always proved itself alive by its freedom to act, grappling with the things that threatened to enslave and using them again as servants and instruments."

Certainly, throughout the history of the Reformed Church, theological doctrine had served both as an obstacle to and an incentive toward union. The sporadic union discussions with the General Synod of the (Dutch)

Source: F. William Leich, "I Believe in the Holy Catholic Church; the Communion of Saints," in *Third Special Meeting of the General Synod of the Reformed Church in the United States,* Cleveland, Ohio, 26 June 1934, 3–7; Jacob C. Leonard, "Prayer," in *Acts and Proceedings of the Joint Session of the General Conference of the Evangelical Synod of N.A. and of The General Synod of the Reformed Church in the U.S.,* Cleveland, Ohio, 26 June 1934, 145.

Reformed Church foundered repeatedly over the issue of the comparative Calvinism of the two churches (see vol. 6:43–45). Much later, in the negotiations with the Evangelical Synod and the United Brethren in Christ in 1928–29, doctrine became a decisive issue for many in the Reformed Church who suspected the Arminianism of the United Brethren in contrast to their own Calvinism (see vol. 6:67). At the same time, the theological commitment of the Reformed Church to the evangelical catholicity and organic unity of the church remained deeply ingrained and drove it on in search of church union—finally gaining that goal with the Evangelical Synod of North America.

The Prayer by Jacob C. Leonard was offered at the joint session of the general conference of the Evangelical Synod of N.A. and of the General Synod of the Reformed Church in the U.S. on June 26, 1934. The two denominations asked for God's blessing on the journey toward union that was yet to come.

Sermon Preached at the Opening of the Special Meeting of the General Synod

By the Rev. F. Wm. Leich, D.D., Dayton, Ohio

Ephesians 5:25–27: *Even as Christ also loved the Church and gave himself up for it, etc.*

"I believe in the Holy Catholic Church; the Communion of Saints."

This day and hour is of inexpressible significance to all of us here gathered and to the Church which for the last time we represent as a distinct unit in Christendom. Anyone who has given earnest thought to the matter will at once recognize that any attempt to give utterance to the thoughts and emotions which surge through our minds and hearts in the brief time allotted us would be futile and not even desirable. Language, even of the expert, is not adequate to give expression to the feelings which are stirred both by the backward as well as by the forward look. To any one attempting to portray the past we would be inclined to say: "Our glorious history is made; let him who will read the records that are written; it will ever remain a sacred record." And to him who would foretell the future it might be said by way of warning that prophesying is not every man's part and that it implies more than knowledge of and clever arrangement of present facts. So then perhaps to recall the things that are fundamental to our idea of the Christian Church may help us the better to evaluate our history as we know it and to determine our future as we work at it. May we find in this real food for constructive thinking.

That the Christian Church is dying is widely claimed and proclaimed in this age. And it is true, though not as these self-constituted executioners imagine. The Church is always dying only to rise again to a larger and more fruitful life. It is, as some one has said: "divinely unfinished, for in it man is cooperating with God for the hastening of the fulfilment of his redemptive world purpose. Its unfinished condition is not defeat or despair, but the joy, the hope, the glory of the task. It is the work of measuring up to "the stature of the fullness of Christ," as Paul puts it. Our opportunity lies in the possibility of completion, and this is the function of our religion."

In this process, together with other religions, Christianity has ever been in danger of hardening about organization, polity, buildings, rituals, dogmas and so on. But in distinction from all other religions and in evidence of its superiority, and this is especially true of Protestantism, Christianity has broken the fetters again and again and walked forth into a new freedom of life. It has always proven itself alive by its freedom to act, grappling with the things that threatened to enslave and using them again as servants and instruments. The disposition among men to take the way of least resistance tends to bind us to policies and rituals, to books and dogmas. To free ourselves from such bondage or to maintain the freedom we have achieved requires more than ordinary courage; it demands a more costly ministry and a more sacrificial spirit than a comfortable age produces, as well as a Spirit-guided purpose. I want to believe and I do believe that we as a Church with a glorious history are today at the point of demonstrating just this thing. It seems to me that our heart must burn for the union of all Christendom, though the ultimate achievement seems so far, far off, when we consider that great good might come from it—spiritual, moral and material, in fact, a complete reconstruction of our civilization. Our own Reformed Church together with the Evangelical Synod is about to make its contribution toward this goal. Let no one therefore belittle the effort, however much he may claim the right to criticize the method or the approach or to raise questions regarding the ultimate outcome.

Nowhere does the Christian religion grow out of purely natural soil. No one can become a Christian in and out of himself. For, as no other religion, the Christian religion is from beginning to end historical and rests upon facts, the knowledge of which comes only through communication and testimony. Therefore the Christian religion has been creative of a society as no other religion has ever been. Anyone who by the faith wrought by the Holy Spirit enters into personal fellowship with Jesus thereby also becomes part of a living whole which in Jesus finds head and center. And as surely as Christ offers himself to all men as the mediator of a fellowship with God, so he becomes also the mediator of a fellowship between those united with him. And, as among the twelve whom he chose surely not haphazardly but purposefully, he did not suppress the natural differences and peculiarities but rather transfigured and recreated them, so there is to be room for the same many-sidedness and differences in His society, the Church. True Apostolicity is one with true Catholicity—all-embracing power with universal compass. And the true Church will be able to receive into itself manifold differences and grant them their rightful place without detriment to the whole as long as the totality of apostolic testimony is its lifegiving power. But it is in danger of becoming a sect when one or the other apostolic emphasis becomes so dominant that only people who claim extraordinary knowledge or experience are permitted a place in it.

The nearest approach to the ideal is found in the early Christian Church recorded for us in the book of Acts. The history of the Church since that time witnesses to a continued falling short of attaining the ideal. Yet this is and has been the glory of its incompleteness, that so long as the Word is freely accessible as the source of lifegiving power and directing truth, the Church is ever receptive of and open to new growth and larger development. For a new humanity is its goal, a humanity which shall have lost nothing of all that with which God endowed it from the beginning; a new humanity in which all the possibilities of the divine creative purpose shall come to full fruitage and perfection.

This ethico-religious society, if I may term it so, is in the New Testament called the ecclesia, translated the Church. It resulted from the coming to earth and the ministry and work of Christ and has as its mission the establishment of the dominion of Christ forever—the mission of gathering men into a family and household of God, in which they shall be governed by the law of a supreme love to God and of an equal love for the brethren. We believe that it was a Church of this kind which Christ intended to found and which the apostles labored to establish. It is of this Church that Paul writes "even as Christ loved the Church and gave Himself up for it that He might sanctify it, having cleansed it by the washing of water with the word, that He might present to Himself a glorious church, not having spot or wrinkle nor any such thing; but that it should be holy, without blemish." Of this church believers throughout the ages have confessed "I believe in the holy, catholic church; the communion of saints."

This Church must be made worthy and kept worthy, for He is worthy. It is a holy church, called into being not by the will of man but by the Spirit of God. Holy—for the Spirit from above who rules in it would make holy men, a communion of saints, people who are permeated and motivated by the power and life of that Spirit; a holy church, not having spot or wrinkle or any such thing. And of this Peter writes in most eloquent fashion, "Ye are an elect race, a royal priesthood, a holy nation, a people of God's own possession, that ye may show forth the excellencies of Him who called you out of darkness into His marvelous light." So we maintain that the chief characteristic of the church is holiness—not mere spirituality, or mere charity or love. "The Christian revelation," says Forsythe, "is that the spiritual and personal God is holy and only therefore eternal; so that its answering religion is the religion of the Holy Spirit. And the site and the source of that revelation, that gift, is the cross of Christ, as the crisis of God's righteous judgment, holy grace and new creating conquest of the world. The supreme revelation of God is the holy; and the central meaning of the cross is less God's love than the holiness of it. And the great issue within Christianity is not between systems and doxies, but a battle for the holy as the one all-inclusive gift of Christ and for those ultimate powers and public features of Christianity which are indispensable to such revelation. Of this the Church is the one trustee."

This holy Church is the Christian Church, for Christ is its head and cornerstone, its master and Lord, its sure rock and foundation. The Word and the Gospel of Christ is the treasure it is to guard, the bread by which its members live, the salt wherewith it is salted and the light which it is to let shine, for the world.

It is one church. It is difficult to convince ourselves of this fact. Our human divisions have been so deepgoing and severe. We have even pleaded variety as a sign of life, which it is not. Variety does not indicate real life, but mere energy, mere vitality. The church begins with the individual but never ends there. And even that may be qualified when we recall that Christ came to redeem a race; it was a Church he saved. Believers are not one in consequence of being in Him, but in the very fact that He is. This has not yet appeared as an outward oneness in history, but there is an inner unity of the Gospel which will ultimately find by necessity a fitting outward expression.

It is also a catholic, universal Church. Israel of old was the covenant people. To its mind this meant the exclusion of all others, though the note of universality is not lacking in the Old Testament. Christ broke down the barriers and there is no doubt in the New Testament as to the universality of His church. The history of missions from Jerusalem down to the present attests to this.

This attempt at briefly setting forth the meaning and purpose of the Church in necessarily inadequate and broken sentences brings us face to face with the question—What are we in the Church? What does it ask and expect of us who claim to be members of it?

Clearly, the first requirement is a definite, living faith. To be a member of the Church of our Lord is not primarily a matter of a baptismal rite or of confirmation or of some form which expresses an experience or fact of filial relationship with God. In the nature of the case nothing is more indispensable to the relation and character of a true child than faith. Take away this faith and what we speak of as sonship is no longer worthy of the name. Christ himself continually emphasizes the virtue and indispensableness of faith and equal prominence is given it in apostolic teaching. And this simply means that the inner disposition is the fundamental condition of salvation, for which no amount of external performance can be a substitute, and that the proper inner disposition is that spirit of sonship which naturally comes from a real acceptance of the message of God in the Christ, who is the divine Word. This means more than mere intellectual assent, more than a certain knowledge. It denotes a practical positive relation and attitude of genuine self-committal to a divine person which the Heidelberg Catechism describes as a hearty trust. It is an act of self-committal to God as revealed in Christ. The foundation of this faith is the word of a positive Gospel, which means that it is a theological one, though not systematic. It can never rest securely on the basis of a vague Christian sentiment.

Then also the Church asks of us evangelical obedience, which denotes obedience to the ethical and religious codes of the Gospel. As faith is an inward obedience it becomes the disposition to specific acts of obedience. And as it tends to lassitude in a man's will power not to go out upon the field of this world's affairs and grapple with actual conditions there, so faith, not issuing in appropriate lines of activity lacks the requisite of healthy growth, indeed even of subsistence. Faith is all-sufficient in the sense that it puts us at once into normal filial relation with God. But it would deny itself if it did not inspire to good works with the coming of opportunities for their performance.

And the issue of it all is service in love. It is that the Church asks and expects of every member not only for the sake of its own life and work, but for the sake for the members themselves. In this service is included not only every form of missionary, charitable and benevolent enterprise, but all that is necessary to the achievement of the social ideal of the Gospel of our Lord. We need to note with great concern that the Christian Church is engaged in a great battle, a mortal conflict with paganism in thought, conduct and religion. There can be no compromise between the spirit of the selfish world and the Gospel of a holy sacrificial love, between the obedience which is the first thing with Christ and the self-will which is first with the world. It is war. And though we feel sure that the social order evolved by selfishness can never be stronger than the moral order and society of Christ, we dare not fail on our part which Christ has committed to us for our age by ignoring each other or working at cross-purposes with our fellows in the same battle. And this calls upon the loving loyalty of each man and woman who has named the name of Christ for all the best that is in them and for all they are and have.

We as the Church must realize in a greater measure than ever before that the Church is facing a new situation and that it must quickly learn to so dispose and use its forces as to really and adequately measure up to the task. To the world a divided Church means a divided Christ, no matter how insistently we may assert that he is our common Lord and Master and that the cause we are engaged in is a common cause. Is not perhaps one of the reasons for the sense of weakness in the present hour to be found in the fact that the Church has contented itself so largely with the commonplace motives and objectives and has failed in its appeal to the highest and best that is to be sought? "The day is done when we can approach the great problems of the time with a sectarian mind or face universal issues in the spirit of a religious group."

The ideal set before us is still afar off. Universal ideals always are. But it is coming nearer. The important thing is that we keep the ideal ever clearly before us, that it may be an ever growing challenge to the best we are and have for its achievement. While we speak of this day as the day of the last General Synod of the Reformed Church in the United States with deep and varying emotions, mostly of sadness, shall we not quickly learn to think of this last joyfully as the necessary step to the new first of tomorrow and all its larger promises? Do we perhaps see the end of the old, accustomed fellowship and spirit we have come to cherish? Let us note also that the Christian Church is always less concerned for itself than for God's cause and reign with the determination that if what is worth having may be better secured in the new and larger fellowship than in the smaller, as long as it remains a Church of the Word which cares everything for the Gospel of its Christ, we are ready and willing gladly to go the whole way. Let us not be afraid of actually realizing the ideal which we thought we had seen and which we have long talked about, lest the strength and power and glory of it go to those who have a poorer Gospel but put it in more effective form. May our love for the Church be the reflection of the love of Christ for it, who gave Himself up for its cleansing, that it might be glorious not having spot or wrinkle, that it should be holy and without blemish.

Prayer

We praise thee, O God, for the record that when the Day of Pentecost was fully come, the disciples were all with one accord in one place, and we thank thee for the manifestation of the presence and power of the Holy Ghost in the assembly of believers. Our hearts are filled with joy this very moment, while we bow before the Mercy Seat, in the conscious experience that in this union of two great Christian communions the Holy Spirit has descended upon us in comfort and grace and power. We glory in the blessed precepts of the Master, in His prayer that all disciples should be one as He and the Father are One. We glory in our Master by whose invasion the whole world is to be conquered, by whose presence the nations are to be awed, by whose rapture all people are to be thrilled, and at whose throne the whole creation is to bow. May the knowledge of thy truth find its way into the souls of all our people, and may our feet walk in the highway of Him who said: "Thine ears shall hear a word behind thee, saying: 'this is the way, walk ye in it' when ye turn to the right hand, and when ye turn to the left."

Great and Gracious and Merciful Heavenly Father, in this happy church union we are passing within new portals into wider fields. Give to us unlimited confidence in that Divine guidance which opens up undimmed vision and gives attainment of the measure of the stature of the fulness of Christ. Be thou our Sovereign Guide. Be thou to us the Bread of Life. Be thou to us the Rock of our Salvation. Give us grace to move in thy ways and in the paths of thy commandments, and keep our eyes turned towards the rising sun of promise and assurance.

We desire, our Father, as we pass through this new portal into Church Union and out into wider fields, the blessing of the sweet melody in the gentle whisper in thy voice. We pray thee to give to our new union, the Evangelical and Reformed Church, the exuberance of Christian youth. Give to us the morning face, the morning courage, the morning vision—and also the joyous blessing of the evening calm that follows the day of successful service out in the Master's harvest-field. Evermore cause the standard of thy truth and wisdom to be displayed before our vision, and cause the brightness of this standard to illuminate our way. This day and hour put anew into our hearts love for the pure and the true and the beautiful and the good, and upon our lips the law of kindliness.

We beseech, O Lord, give to us in this new ecclesiastical relationship faith that soars to high certainty of accomplishment in the name of Jesus Christ, the beloved Son of God, the only Savior of all mankind, that so we may rise above the level of our own poor understanding. So direct us that everything else shall give place to enthusiastic passion to serve.

And by thy Spirit, O Holy Father, enable us to walk willingly in the comforting shadow of thy sacred, blessed presence, through riches of grace in Christ our Redeemer. Amen.

PART IV

The Maturing "Unionist" Vision of the Evangelical Synod

The Evangelical Synod of North America had its roots in the complex economic, political, and religious situation of early-nineteenth-century Germany. Plagued by an economic depression and famine in the post-Napoleonic era, many Germans dreamed of an easier life in the United States of America—the land of plenty. Furthermore, the political oppression of absolutist and monarchical Prussia made democracy very attractive. Finally, among some immigrants there was a desire for greater religious freedom.

Early in the nineteenth century the Prussian government had forced Lutherans and Reformed Protestants together into one church, the Church of the Prussian Union. It provided compulsory religious education and prescribed rites for baptism, confirmation, marriage, and burial for all citizens. Those who rejected its creative blend of Lutheran and Reformed traditions wanted more freedom to preserve the purity of their specific traditions in the United States. Others, who actually came to appreciate the ecumenical blend of the Church of the Prussian Union, immigrated to the United States for economic reasons, but also wanted to keep the religious and theological values of the Prussian Union church alive.

The history and values of the Evangelical Synod of North America were dramatically shaped by the Church of the Prussian Union. The Prussian church was created by the king of Prussia, Frederick William III, a gentleman of Reformed background who took his religion seriously, and found himself scandalized by the bitter, sectarian bickering between Lutheran and Reformed citizens in his realm. Tensions among Protestants had been around since 1592, and by the nineteenth century the king, and many Protestants of all traditions, were simply tired of sectarian quarreling.

On the tercentennial anniversary of the Protestant Reformation in October of 1817, the king sought to put an end to all confessional distinctions in his realm. He issued a proclamation declaring that Lutheran and Reformed citizens from then on had to belong to a new Evangelical Church of the

Prussian Union. Unfortunately, three hundred years of religious warfare and argumentation do not vanish simply by fiat.

Some parishes insisted on remaining Lutheran or Reformed, even though they were union churches in name. Other churches embraced the unionist position. They were enthusiastic about the Prussian church and developed a serious unionist party committed to the idea of union. "Unionist" churches sought to follow the spirit of Jesus Christ, who never knew Luther or Calvin or accepted any human confession as an adequate embodiment of truth. For them, there was a spiritual unity underlying the diversity of Christ's followers that was of ultimate importance.

These Unionist Germans often looked to the Pietist movement, influenced by Philip Jacob Spener (1635–1705) and Nicholas Zinzendorf (1700–1760) to find alternatives to rigid scholastic Christianity or the rising tide of secular rationalism. Pietism emphasized the warm, spiritual experience of individual salvation, the holiness and primacy of the Christian life as opposed to knowledge about religion, and the avoidance of theological controversies on behalf of an underlying spiritual union. People influenced by Pietism considered all doctrinal controversies wrongheaded and trivial (see vol. 4:39).

The number of Germans that came to the United States in the first half of the nineteenth century was staggering. From 1830 to 1845, over forty thousand Germans left Europe *each year* to begin new life in the New World. These immigrants held a wide diversity of religious sentiments, from ultraorthodox Lutheran to anticlerical rationalist. And as these thousands of German immigrants settled on the North American frontier, they began to construct new lives for themselves. Germans of both Lutheran and Reformed background settled near St. Louis, Missouri, and in southern Illinois. They were ready for change and determined to avoid the doctrinal bickering they had known at home. They also wanted to get beyond the ecclesiastical paternalism of the Prussian government, which tried to force religious unity and harmony (see vol. 6:54).

To assist many of these German immigrants in their new life, pastors trained by the interconfessional and Pietist missionary societies of Basel and Barmen came to minister in German communities near St. Louis, Missouri. Their emphasis on the personal experience of salvation rather than on confessional agreement as the basis of church membership was welcomed. At a meeting in Gravois Settlement in Missouri on October 15, 1840, some of these German frontier pastors organized themselves as the Kirchenverein des Westens (Church Society of the West), a predecessor of the Evangelical Synod of North America, to address their common problems of living and being Christian on the frontier.

By 1848, the Kirchenverein was an important supportive society for both pastors and churches. It formulated its self-understanding in a *Bekenntnisparagraph* (Confessional Paragraph), which became the basic doctrinal standard of the Evangelical Synod (see vol. 6:55). Although it was produced in a frontier environment preoccupied with personal faith and subjective individualism, the Confessional Paragraph still identified the Kirchenverein with the great doctrinal statements of German Protestantism and the sixteenth-century Reformation. It made clear that no confessional statement, whether Lutheran, Reformed, or Evangelical, could be taken to be the whole truth. Rather, the "sole and infallible rule of faith and life" was to be found only in the Word of God, the Holy Scriptures, which always took precedence over any doctrinal position. At the same time, the interpretation of that Word was entrusted to the free Christian conscience, not to any ecclesiastical authority. Emphasis was put on the religious experience of individual Christians rather than on the theological dialectics of the academy.

This doctrinal humility served the German Evangelicals well, and echoes of the German Evangelical stance on doctrine reappear in the preamble to the constitution of the United Church of Christ more than a century later. Confessions are not regarded as absolute statements of truth, or as tests of faith, but as testimonies of the Christian community's experience of God to be affirmed by the conscience of each individual believer.

Although the early pastors of the Kirchenverein were not primarily concerned with building up a body of theological literature, in their denominational newspaper, *Der Friedensbote*, they had great appreciation for Luther and Calvin and for the Reformation history out of which their church had developed. Moreover, they also took great pride in their German heritage—the German theological and educational traditions, the focus on Christian education and religious piety, and the emphasis on the spiritual as a source for moral action. These principles produced an extensive network of voluntary organizations for Christian service.

Assimilation

The Evangelical Synod's earliest attempts at union were not across denominational lines, but with other German Evangelical groups. By 1877, the newly created Evangelical Synod of North America had an area of influence that stretched over Missouri, Illinois, Michigan, Indiana, Wisconsin, New York, Ohio, Pennsylvania, Iowa, and Minnesota. However, in spite of the scope of its oversight, new waves of German immigration that continued to pour into the United States stretched the resources and the resolve of their churches.

The Kirchenverein had been founded to minister to an immigrant German population, and it flourished by being committed to German-language worship, German customs, and German organization. At the same time, elements of its Pietist heritage tended to foster a quietist type of Christianity emphasizing the "inner experiential" qualities of Christianity rather than its more assertive and "expressional" ones. These characteristics served first-generation immigrant Germans well, and they survived and prospered.

However, with later generations, difficulties began to arise. Older generations became dismayed when young people, who were educated in English and wanted to "fit into" mainstream culture, were unwilling to be proudly German and different. Evangelical pastors were astounded when the very people they had been educated to serve wandered off into other more "Americanized" churches because they were no longer comfortable in a German-speaking service. Furthermore, congregations related to the Evangelical Synod were surrounded by more aggressive Protestant denominations deeply involved in mission and evangelism. Perhaps, Synod leaders mused, saving souls in the twentieth century required the church to adopt more aggressive methods.

In 1921, Carl E. Schneider, a professor at the Evangelical Synod's Eden Theological Seminary described the situation. He wrote that the need for the Evangelical tradition to adapt to its new life in the United States created an "Evangelical Problem" (see vol. 6:56). In the end, the synod recognized that it needed to expand its horizons. Therefore, in the late 1920s and throughout the 1930s it embarked upon a very careful process of introducing the English language in its newspapers, journals, and services of worship; providing college education and training in the best theological scholarship of the day to its pastors; and reaching out to join regional and national organizations of all kinds. The Evangelical Synod was very intentional, and successful, in its efforts to come out of ethnic isolation and take its place in contemporary North American society.

The Global Ecumenical Context

While the Evangelical Synod struggled to claim its identity in the religious climate of the United States, Protestant churches all over the world began to see themselves in new relationships. Evangelical leaders were easily caught up in the growing global ecumenical movement. When the Evangelical Synod joined in founding the Federal Council of the Churches of Christ in America in 1908, Evangelical participants heralded it as one of the most significant meetings the world had yet seen. *Der Friedensbote* and the *Magazin* reported faithfully on each of the Federal Council's meetings, as well as on the Conference on Organic Union (1918) (see vol. 6:57). Even synod members who remained in their local communities were able to catch a glimpse of what a nationwide church might mean.

In 1910, the World Missionary Conference in Edinburgh stretched the deep concern of the Evangelical Synod for Christian service, expanding its understanding of its responsibility to worldwide dimensions. The *Messenger of Peace,* an English-language version of *Der Friedensbote,* urged its readers to "rise to the height and breadth and depth of the conception of missions as revealed anew" through the Edinburgh meeting. As the global ecumenical movement began planning a conference on issues of faith and order, the Evangelical Synod published an important address by C. H. Brent, chair of the Preliminary Meeting of Faith and Order in Geneva in 1920 (see vol. 6:58). It sent the full message of the Stockholm Conference on Life and Work in 1925 out to its delegates (see vol. 6:66), and it covered in extraordinary detail the process by which the United Church of Canada came into being in 1925. Through all of this, Evangelical Synod members were encouraged to contemplate the possibility that someday soon, church union might actually involve them.

As the first quarter of the twentieth century drew to a close, the Evangelical Synod was no longer a regional, immigrant church. It was embracing many new relationships, attending international meetings, and coming to an awareness of itself as part of a church spanning the whole inhabited earth.

Church Union

The Evangelical Synod was always very proud that it did not come into being by splitting off from another church, as did so many new denominations in the nineteenth century. Instead, it had been a force that bridged the gap between Reformed and Lutheran camps by insisting on the fundamental unity of the Spirit that undergirded all Christians. The Evangelical Synod understood itself from its birth as the embodiment of the union spirit.

At the same time, memories and experiences of the theological backbiting among the Lutheran and Reformed factions in Germany made the people of the early Evangelical Synod shy away from theological statements, counterstatements, and general discussions seeking to arrive at common statements. They chose instead to witness to the one church by serving those people whom Christ himself had served. They developed an extraordinary network of hospitals, orphanages, homes for the "mentally handicapped," and "old folk's homes" during their ninety-four-year history as a separate denomination (see vol. 6:60).

Once the Evangelical Synod moved to live and work in the English language, however, it began to communicate more with non-German-speaking churches and movements, and its long-standing "spirit of unity" became more visible. Later generations of Evangelical leaders and theologians believed not only that the gospel sent them into the world to serve God's people, but also that they were called to unite the disparate churches in God's world.

This change was evident in 1916 when John Baltzer, president of the synod, appointed a Kommission für Beziehungen zu Anderen Denominationen und Kirchen im In- und Auslande (Commission on Relations to Other Denominations and Churches at Home and Abroad), to work out a position paper on union to be sent to all denominations of German origin that might be interested in the idea of German church union (see vol. 6:61). Furthermore, at the beginning of the First World War there was a deepened sense of unity felt by people of German origin in the United States who considered themselves patriotic citizens as their country went to war against Germany. Lay people were eager for contact with other immigrant Germans, as well as with the churches of the Prussian Union abroad. Baltzer had hopes of establishing a federation of German churches, since he felt that the newly formed Federal Council of Churches had little understanding of specifically German Christianity in the United States. This followed the long-standing commitment of the early Kirchenverein, whereby German Evangelicals had friendly relations with many Christian communities but went out of their way to seek closer ties with churches of German origin.

By 1928, after twelve years the Synod had become an English-speaking mainstream denomination involved in the national and global ecumenical movement, Baltzer appointed a new Commission on Relations with Other Church Bodies. The commission was chaired by theologian Helmut Richard Niebuhr of Eden Theological Seminary. As a result of its participation in the life and activities of the wider church the Evangelical Synod regarded union not simply as a means of increasing the Synod's strength in mission and evangelism, but as a primary Christian obligation. At its first meeting, the new commission decided to focus efforts to bring about closer relations between the Evangelical Synod and the Reformed Church in the United States—and with the Moravian Church (which was never pursued) (see vol. 6:62).

Soon thereafter, Eden Theological Seminary invited George W. Richards, president of the Reformed Church's Lancaster Theological Seminary, to give a series of lectures, and the possibility of closer relations between the Evangelical Synod and the Reformed Church was informally discussed by Niebuhr and Richards. A committee was formed by the Evangelical synod to address potentially difficult theological issues related to their loyalties to multiple creeds (see vol. 6:63). Other writings were published addressing all of the reasons that the Evangelical churches might hesitate to unite (see vol. 6:64).

Helmut Richard Niebuhr's contribution to the ecumenical work of the Evangelical Synod is noteworthy. As part of a well-known German Evangelical family, the brother of Reinhold Niebuhr, and a member of the Eden Theological Seminary board of directors, Niebuhr had served on the Eden faculty from 1919–22 and been president of Elmhurst College, the Evangelical Synod's undergraduate college, from 1924–27. He returned to Eden as dean (1927–31), and was highly respected throughout the Evangelical Synod. In his first book, *The Social Sources of Denominationalism*, Niebuhr maintained that separate denominational identities did not arise from the realities of faith, but from the sociopolitical situations in which people find themselves. Therefore, he argued, all Christians are called to reclaim their common faith and leave denominationalism behind in order to make the unity of the body of Christ more visible.

The Formation of the Evangelical and Reformed Church

The Reformed Church had never seemed a stranger to the Evangelical Synod. The first president of the Kirchenverein was a minister of the Reformed Church, Charles Lewis Daubert; the pastor of the oldest Evangelical church in St. Louis was Reformed, J. G. Buettner. Philip Schaff, of the Reformed Church (who had been a member of the Church of the Prussian Union before coming to the United States), came to St. Louis shortly after his arrival in 1844 to cultivate a relationship with Evangelicals in the Kirchenverein. Four years later, Schaff founded the *Kirchenfreund,* which he intended to be an interdenominational newspaper for Germans of Lutheran, Reformed, and Evangelical churches. In it he expressed his hope that a "German American" church might arise, uniting all three groups.

Because of these congenial relationships, the Evangelical Synod had always felt that there was a kinship between it and the Reformed Church in the United States.

In 1919, Reinhold Niebuhr, also a rising Evangelical theologian, looked more closely at the question of church union for the German Evangelicals in an article asking "Where Shall We Go?" He pointed out that Protestant churches in the United States were steadily reuniting in "family groups," and that it was likely that these unions would soon eliminate practically all so-called minor denominations, leaving only several large and distinctive churches. In the face of this situation, what should the Evangelical Synod do? Niebuhr argued that uniting with the Lutherans would require Evangelicals to become totally Lutheran, and destroy the "union" identity they so prized. Therefore, the only avenue Niebuhr saw was for the Evangelical Synod to unite with some moderate Calvinists.

Niebuhr's article was met with strong objections in a response by W. F. Henninger entitled "Why Go at All?" Henninger expressed the more commonly held view that the uniqueness of the Evangelical Synod's religious culture must not be sacrificed by merging with anyone (see vol. 4:61–62). Soon thereafter, Niebuhr published a rebuttal. Unfortunately, the Evangelical Synod was not yet ready to consider any merger (see vol. 6:65).

Eight years later, Niebuhr stated his case more strongly: there was now no justification for the separation between the Evangelical Synod and the Reformed Church. "A union of the two churches would bring fresh life and inspiration to both parties . . . [and] result in a denomination which could make a real contribution to American church life." An editorial in the *Theological Magazine* by H. Kamphausen supported Niebuhr, saying that if the Evangelical Synod wanted to unite, the Reformed Church was the only possibility. Once again a rebuttal was offered, this time by "Peter the Hermit," and entitled "Why Go, Why Not Stay?" This time, however, the Evangelical Synod was ready to entertain Niebuhr's suggestion, and several supportive editorials were published in the *Theological Magazine* (see vol. 6:66).

At first an informal meeting was held with George W. Richards, chair of the Reformed Church's Commission on Closer Relations and Church Union, and members of the Evangelical Synod's new Committee on Relations to Other Churches. Soon thereafter, the Evangelical Synod asked the Reformed Church for a more formal meeting to discuss union.

The Reformed Church responded cordially, but explained that it was already meeting with the Church of the United Brethren in Christ to explore the possibility of organic union, and it would not be "seemly" to interrupt one series of negotiations for another. However, at the same time, the United Brethren had received overtures from another Evangelical Church, a Pietist group of German origin based in Pennsylvania. When the commissions of the Reformed Church and the United Brethren met shortly thereafter to draft a plan of union, they unanimously agreed to expand their conversations by inviting three advisory members from the Evangelical Church and three from the Evangelical Synod of North America to their next meeting. It was hoped that by including such advisory members they would be able to work out a common basis of union that could be presented to all four churches.

The commission met in May, June, and July of 1928, appointing a special committee from each of the four denominations to analyze the problems, present their recommendations, and prepare a suitable preamble and statement of doctrine to accompany the proposed plan of union. Soon thereafter, representatives from the Pennsylvania Evangelical Church withdrew from the commission. By February 7, 1929, a plan of union had been drawn up for the three remaining denominations, adopted, and referred to those churches for action. Helmut Richard Niebuhr published articles in English and German summarizing the plan and calling attention to the similarities of the three groups (see vol. 6:67). J. H. Horstmann, also on the joint commission, explained that the doctrinal statement included in the plan was intended to demonstrate the agreement of the three denominations with regard to basic Christian teachings. Within a year the Evangelical Synod responded positively to the plan, and votes taken in various districts of the synod were overwhelmingly in favor of the merger.

Unfortunately, in September of 1930, a letter from George Richards of the Reformed Church reported that their classes had not been positive with regard to the merger, "especially those of five or six of the strongest classes in the East." The German Reformed members were particularly uncomfortable with the concept of "superintendency," so important to the United Brethren, who had an episcopal system. Ironically, although the General Conference of the United Brethren adopted the plan, in their system the congregations had the final voice, and the congregations voted against the plan. A report of the Evangelical Synod's Committee on Relations with Other Churches explained that it was the issues of "superintendency" and the "appointment of pastors" that had been the problems for the United Brethren, because they subscribed to the episcopal system and also practiced the itinerant ministry. In 1932, when the Reformed General Synod met, it received a report stating that further negotiations with the Commission of the Church of the United Brethren in Christ were not practicable at that time, and all plans for a threefold union were dissolved.

Nevertheless, the General Synod of the Reformed Church wanted to keep negotiations between the Evangelical Synod and the Reformed Church alive. Recommendations were made that their commissions should get together to prepare a basis of union, either by revising the old one or preparing a new one. On December 18, 1930, they met again in Pittsburgh to see what was possible.

During the same period, the Presbyterian Church invited some committee members from the Reformed Church to meet with it, and several Reformed synods stated their desire for closer union with the Presbyterian Church. At this point, for fear of hampering negotiations with the Presbyterians, the Commission on Closer Relations and Church Union of the Reformed Church decided to suspend negotiations with the Evangelical Synod. It assured the Evangelical Synod that it looked forward to negotiations being resumed. The Evangelical Synod's commission received this news with regret, telling the commission of the Reformed Church that it hoped that under divine guidance their several paths would reconvene in the future. Both statements were accepted, and negotiations ceased for the time being.

However, in May and June of 1931, when the General Synod of the Reformed Church and the General Assembly of the Presbyterian Church in the United States met, they decided not to continue negotiations. Soon thereafter, union talks between the Reformed Church and the Evangelical Synod resumed, with a joint meeting in Pittsburgh in 1932. At the Pittsburgh meeting, the plan of union that had been prepared originally for the three churches was revised and put into final form as the basis of union for the two remaining denominations. The editor of the *Theological Magazine,* H. Kamphausen, presented the plan of union to its reader/members in the Evangelical Synod (see vol. 6:68).

Things moved quickly. Within a year both churches approved the new plan, and members of the commissions on union of both churches called a special union meeting for June 26, 1934, in Cleveland, Ohio. The national synods of the two churches first met separately, presenting their decision to one another while in session. Among the Evangelical Synod delegates there was a strong and confident sense that the Evangelical Synod had come to this historic merger guided by the Holy Spirit, and that in choosing union they were choosing God's will for their church. President of the synod, Paul Press, invoked the "spirit of union" by which the Evangelical Synod had always so proudly identified itself, calling on the participants not to be concerned with "technical difficulties," but to enter into a *spiritual* union with the Reformed Church and to trust the Spirit of the living God to be with them (see vol. 6:69).

Hours later, delegations from the two denominations entered Pilgrim Congregational Church together amid the ringing of church bells. A new hymn, especially prepared for the occasion by Ambrose M. Schmidt, was sung (see vol. 6:69). Louis Goebel and George Richards, chairs of the commissions on union, declared the union in effect and proclaimed the birth of the Evangelical and Reformed Church. That evening, at the first worship service of the new denomination, Lee Redman, of Reading, Pennsylvania, preached a sermon on 1 Cor. 10:16, "The Bread Which We Break, Is It Not the Communion of the Body of Christ?" (see vol. 6:69). Those present celebrated the Lord's Supper together as a seal of their union—in Christ and with one another.

German Origins

54. A Local Unionist Congregation:

"The German Congregation in Cincinnati, Ohio"

(1834)

J. G. Buettner

In the early decades of the nineteenth century, immigrants from Germany who settled on the expanding frontier of the new Midwestern states of Ohio, Illinois, and Missouri were deeply affected by the economic, political, and religious situation that they had left behind in Europe. Some of the immigrants came to escape economic depression in Germany. Others were fleeing the political oppression of monarchical Prussia. Still others were tired of the perpetual discord between strict Lutheran and Reformed Protestantism and the ecclesiastical paternalism of the Prussian government. In 1817, the Prussian government had tried to dispel chronic Lutheran-Reformed discord by forcibly "uniting" all Protestants, or Evangelicals, into a single Church of the Prussian Union. Although initially this church was unpopular, as decades passed, some Prussians came to appreciate their union heritage.

Consequently, when some Prussian immigrants settled in Cincinnati, Ohio in 1834, rather than wanting to restore their loyalty to Reformed or Lutheran church life, they sought to found a union church in the United States. A pastor had been sent to Cincinnati to form a new German Reformed Church among recent arrivals. He had received his secondary education in a German Gymnasium *and his theological training at the seminary of the German Reformed Church in the U.S. When he got to Cincinnati, however, he found that the local people did not want a*

Source: J. G. Buettner, "The German Congregation in Cincinnati, Ohio," in Carl E. Schneider, *The German Church on the American Frontier: A Study in the Rise of Religion among the Germans of the West* (St. Louis: Eden Publishing House, 1939), 478–79.

Reformed church. They were immigrants from Prussia, and they wanted to belong to a union church similar to the Church of the Prussian Union. Many of them supported the "unionist" goals of the Church of the Prussian Union, and they were also deeply influenced by the Pietist movement in Switzerland and Germany. Pietism stressed the experience of salvation and the living of the Christian life rather than the doctrinal distinctions between orthodox Lutheran and "High Reformed" churches. It looked to a deeper, spiritual dimension of the Christian faith in which all Christians were united.

So it happened that a High Reformed minister ended up serving a congregation with members primarily of Unierte *(United) origin. In their church constitution they stated that "the welfare and the further progress of our congregation is inseparably dependent on a union," and they chose to minimize the dissension within their own families that would be caused by membership in either a Lutheran or Reformed "party" by giving up the use of the "Reformed" or "Lutheran" labels entirely. They called their church a Protestant-Evangelical-Christian Church. Furthermore, recognizing that there was not yet a church in the United States that united the Lutheran and Reformed traditions, they asked "the worthy synod of the High German Reformed Church of North America" to receive them into membership.*

Mr. Raschig, son of an eminent preacher of Saxony, received his first instruction in his parental home, continued his education by attending the *Gymnasium* at Meissen, and came to America for his theological training at the seminary of the High German Reformed Church. He distinguished himself as an able scholar and, after being ordained as a circuit preacher in 1834, was sent by the commissioning committee of Easton, Pennsylvania, to Cincinnati for the purpose of founding a German Reformed church. His sermons were well received, a goodly number of Germans gathered themselves around him and soon were ready to elect him as their pastor. Since the majority of these were Evangelical (*Unierte*) as compared with very few Reformed, and since all desired to be united on a Christian basis, constitution was drawn up and the newly founded church was given the name Protestant-Evangelical-Christian Church. I herewith list some of the articles of union:

1. Resolved, that we are not seeking a union of Lutherans and Reformed under a common name in order thereby to establish something new or in order to effect changes in our confessions of faith.
2. Resolved, that we do not recognize any need or occasion to effect changes in such matters.
3. Resolved, that this union proceed from the conviction that both confessions do not essentially differ in their articles of faith.
4. Resolved, that we especially desire this union since the majority of the members of this church enjoyed the benefits of the Union in Germany.
5. Since this circumstance was ever an obstacle to joining one or the other (Lutheran or Reformed) party;
6. Since without such a union dissensions easily, indeed inevitably, arise in our families;
7. Since we are convinced and know that many of our countrymen would gladly join us as soon as these divisive obstacles are removed;
8. Since the welfare and the further progress of our congregation is inseparably dependent on a union:
9. Resolved, that from this day on all use of the terms "Reformed" and "Lutheran" on our congregation cease.
10. Resolved, that in order to further a true Christian spirit among us and in order to maintain peace and harmony, we unite in the same way as did the Lutherans and Reformed in Germany under the name Protestant Evangelical Church.
11. Resolved, that without any changes we retain all church usages in vogue among us and only with respect to the Lord's Supper
12. Request our minister to observe the sacrament in the same manner as is customary in the Evangelical churches in Germany.
13. Resolved, that the choice of a suitable catechism for confirmation instruction be left to the discretion of our minister.
14. Resolved, that, as long as no union of both confessions exists in America, the worthy synod of the High German Reformed Church of North America be asked to receive us into membership.

55. A Testimony of Faith:

"*The* Bekenntnisparagraph"

(1848)

The small, interconfessional group of German pastors who founded the Kirchenverein des Westens (Church Society of the West) in Gravois Settlement in Missouri, on October 15, 1840, formulated their doctrinal self-understanding in 1848 in the famous Bekenntnisparagraph *(Confessional Paragraph).*

Although brief, the Bekenntnisparagraph *revealed much that was distinctive about the Kirchenverein. First of all, it was an objective, confessional statement, referring to the great confessional documents of German Protestantism (Lutheran and Reformed) rather than to the more subjective and Pietist dictates of much of frontier religion. At the same time, it stated clearly that no one of these confessions could contain the whole truth. Only the Word of God in Holy Scriptures could be said to contain that. The paragraph also upheld an important principle of Protestantism: the interpretation of God's Word was not entrusted to any ecclesiastical authority, but to the freedom of the individual Christian conscience.*

The Bekenntnisparagraph *remained the doctrinal standard of the Evangelical Synod of North America for many years. As late as 1928, the synod debated whether it ought to create a more elaborate creedal statement or whether the* Bekenntnisparagraph *was enough. The paragraph's affirmation that the confessions attested to the truth of God's Word in Holy Scripture, but were not themselves tests of that truth, undergirds the principle within the United Church of Christ that confessions*

Source: *"Bekenntnisparagraph,"* in Carl E. Schneider, *The German Church on the American Frontier: A Study in the Rise of Religion among the Germans of the West* (St. Louis: Eden Publishing House, 1939), 409.

and statements of faith are testimonies to the truth of God's Word, not tests of it.

"We recognize the Evangelical Church as that communion which acknowledges the Holy Scriptures of the Old and New Testament as the Word of God and as the sole and infallible rule of faith and life, and accepts the interpretation of the Holy Scriptures as given in the symbolic books of the Lutheran and Reformed Church, the most important being: the Augsburg Confession, Luther's and the Heidelberg Catechisms, in so far as they agree; but where they disagree, we adhere strictly to the passages of Holy Scripture bearing on the subject, and avail ourselves of the liberty of conscience prevailing in the Evangelical Church."

Assimilation

56. Getting Evangelicals Together: *"The Evangelical Problem"*

(1921)

Carl E. Schneider

The Kirchenverein des Westens (Church Society of the West) grew rapidly after its founding in 1840 by joining with other German Evangelical groups from around the country. In 1858, the Kirchenverein was joined by a group from Ohio, the German Evangelical Church Society, and in 1860, by the United Evangelical Synod of the East. In 1872, these groups merged with the German Evangelical Synod of the Northwest and the German United Evangelical Synod of the East to create the German Evangelical Synod of North America—with churches in Missouri, Illinois, Michigan, Indiana, Wisconsin, New York, Ohio, Pennsylvania, Iowa, and Minnesota.

In spite of this expansion, different attitudes toward assimilation among German immigrants created a problem for the Evangelical Synod. The Kirchenverein had been founded to minister to an immigrant German population—providing worship in the German language, preserving German customs, and maintaining German church organization. The Pietist background of many of its people caused the synod to focus upon issues of Christian religious life and service rather than on aggressive evangelism. With such support, the German immigrant community had grown and prospered in the New World.

However, as the church sought to serve the needs of second- and third-generation members, difficulties began to arise. Evangelical Synod young people, educated in English, wanted to fit into North American

---

Source: Carl E. Schneider, "The Evangelical Problem," *Magazin für Evangelische Theologie und Kirche,* n.s., vol. 23, no. 1 (January 1921): 431–49.

society instead of being proudly German and foreign. English-speaking members of German Evangelical congregations began feeling more comfortable in English-speaking churches. Moreover, the Evangelical Synod was surrounded by aggressive denominations that were flourishing in the mission fields and in evangelism, while the synod still seemed stuck in its past.

The issue was a delicate one. German identity had given the Evangelical Synod its heritage and pride. However, forward-looking leaders in the denomination became convinced that change was needed. In 1921, Carl E. Schneider, a professor at the denomination's Eden Theological Seminary and later author of the standard history of the denomination, The German Church on the American Frontier, *wrote candidly about the "Evangelical Problem." He was convinced that preserving the heritage of the German Evangelical Synod required changing to meet the times.*

. . . The manifold questions of policy and organization, and the most diversified and exacting synodical obligations—all closely linked together and demanding immediate attention—constitute the Evangelical problem. It is well for us to pause a moment in the whirlpool of purposes and methods, to discover, if we can, the method of correct adjustment to the ultimate purpose.

I. Definition and Realization of Purpose

The purpose of the Christian Church is conditioned on the one hand by absolute, never changing factors, and on the other hand by relative, variable factors. Pre-eminently the Church is a divine institution and does not consider herself a child of human limitations. She is built on the Eternal Rock, and assumes an unswerving loyalty *to* and dependence *on* Jesus Christ her only Lord. She understands that the world has not advanced beyond the revelation of God in Jesus Christ, and recognizes her purpose to be an agent in the spiritualization process instituted by the Christ. Thus the function of the Church lies along spiritual lines and in a spiritual realm. The Church, above all other institutions, may be expected to have a sense and an appreciation of the determining spiritual realities of life. Having a Kingdom mission she penetrates beyond anything which this world has to offer. Her very right of existence is given in her eternal purpose. At the same time she exists in the world, conditioned by the fluctuating circumstances of time and space, and is subject to all the vagaries and eccentricities of an historical development. Her countless divisions into denominations and sects is irrefutable proof of her subjection to the variable factors of history. Her historical development has taken place in the midst of an interminable interplay of causal factors which evidently did not spring from the realms of supranaturalism or metaphysical speculations, but from that complex which, in short, we may term world environment. Like the crucified Christ, she stands between heaven and earth, attempting, with temporal limitations, to accomplish an eternal purpose. . . .

As a part of the universal Christian Church our ultimate purpose can be nothing less than the ideal purpose of the Church at large. Our very existence is postulated by eternal factors. There is a general, cordial agreement regarding this, our function and purpose. Scripturally founded, Christ-centered, and God-ward directed, no one dares question our fundamentally evangelical position and destiny. It is, however, a more simple matter to agree to the purpose of life than to agree to the proper and best methods to achieve the purpose. The one involves the constant, the other the variable elements of our world view. Loyola, Luther, and Wesley were engaged in a very similar struggle, wrestling with practically the same spiritual religious problem, in the solution of which, however, they employed widely differing methods—Loyola emphasizing the method of spiritual exercises; Wesley accepting the method of conversion; and Luther insisting on justification by faith. It is not the most crucial problem of the Evangelical Church to understand her calling—she stands and falls by the purpose to seek and to save that which is lost. The Evangelical problem is largely a problem of method and involves the proper adjustment and correspondence to her God-given historical purpose. It is not so much a theological question, but rather a practical, historical problem and, therefore, demands that there be clear recognition of the historical factors which are involved. . . .

Without presuming to attempt an extended analysis of the genetic elements which contributed to the development of our ideals and world view, it must suffice to mention what seems to have been the one all-pervading and dominant factor which prevailed thruout our development, directly and indirectly affecting our thoughts, words and deeds—namely, the fact of our German origin. To what extent and in what specific manner the fact of our German origin and organic relation to German life, ideals and thought has been a determining factor may not at once be evident. Originally committed to the task of ministering to the needs of the German immigrants in America, it became the manifest destiny of our Synod to work out this purpose in the best possible manner. This was accomplished with direct reference to the German world view and found a correspondingly historical expression in the following three-fold attitude:

1. Adherence to German Theology

Adherence to German type of theology and religion of the Reformation was a prominent channel thru which we endeavored to fulfill our calling. We were a church of the Reformation, bound by confessional statements of the Reformation age. From the very beginning this was a vital part of the Evangelical world view. The cardinal doctrines of the Reformation which redirected the development of the entire Christian Church, placed a very strong emphasis on the individualistic and passive attitude of mind to faith, repentance, assurance of forgiveness of sins, certainty of salvation, etc. Pietistic tendencies assisted in the development, and fostered a quietistic type of Christianity which emphasized the inner experiential and impressional qualities of religion. To what extent this contributed to our hesitancy to assert ourselves and adopt more aggressive, expressional forms of activity will be referred to later. During the early part of her history the Synod fulfilled her destiny in an admirable manner.

2. Use of German Language

Exclusive use of the German language was another historical adaptation which was self-evidently necessary. It was the given function of our church to minister to a German constituency; and it was the most self-evident thing in the world that a German born pastor would address a German born congregation in the German language. It was a natural historical requirement, and indicated an ability for adjustment to a divine task which it was not possible for American church bodies then to accomplish. Carried on by the tide of such historical circumstances the Evangelical Synod flourished—committed to German language, German customs, German organization.

Ministration to the needs of the German immigrant, who did not belong to the most cultured or wealthy classes, also helped to determine our historical adjustment to the ultimate object of our existence. The coarse, vulgar, godless and degenerate German, and the simple, plain, Bible-loving and pietistically minded German immigrants were the early objects of our Synod's care. To supply the needs of these people, there was no need of a professionally theological and aesthetically cultured ministry. To what extent all this may have affected the development of our present day educational standards and ideals may be a question for further research. Suffice to say there were very definite and historically conditioned obligations to be fulfilled by the "grand old men" of our Synod, in the fulfillment of which, definite characteristics were developed. It is inspiring to read of the early experiences of our Synodical pioneers and of the wonderful contributions they made to the cause of the Kingdom in their own inimitable manner. . . .

The significance of this for us becomes evident when we view the enormous changes which have occurred since the early days of the Synod, previously referred to. It is on this point that the Evangelical problem becomes especially vital for us all at this time, deserves and challenges our careful attention. We must become reconciled to the fact that a proper and efficient correspondence in the past does not assure a present satisfactory adjustment to purpose. In the contemplation of this problem such questions as these will arise: To what extent, if any, are we committed to the preservation of past historical factors and elements? To what extent have we been deflected from our eternal purpose by the influences of the purely historical? Is a better correspondence possible between our thought and actions and the eternal purpose of God? Have we fearlessly thought our way thru to the final conclusions so as to be prepared to sacrifice everything and modify our thought and activity, if necessary, in order "to save some"?

It is on just this point that some very advanced positions are beginning to be taken, especially by a younger and progressive element of our Synodical family. It is suggested that, having fulfilled our historical purpose and made our contribution, we ought either in a more pronounced manner become adjusted to the needs and conditions of the modern day or surrender our right of independent existence and merge with some other church body and thus proceed to work out our destiny in new historical spheres. It is apparent that a new Evangelical world view is gradually developing, which will eventually challenge more serious attention than has hitherto been given to this subject. The question, in all fairness, deserves serious attention. To what extent may a reinterpretation of Evangelical purpose and principles be attempted and how may it be justified and undertaken?

II. Reinterpretation of Purpose and Principles

. . . A constant reinterpretation of Christian truth is also suggested by the conception of a progressive revelation of God. There is one constant terminus ad quem, one controlling purpose toward the realization of which the whole creation progressively moves by the grace of God. From the point of view of God, we may call this movement progressive or adaptive revelation; from the human point of view, it bears all the marks of continual reinterpretation. When the Israelites began their Exodus they were accompanied by God, who, during their nomadic journeyings lived among them in the tent of the tabernacle. God readapted himself to the changed, more settled condition of the Israelites in Canaan, and the temple was erected as the place of His habitation. Centuries later the same God appeared among men in hitherto unknown form and "we beheld His glory, glory as of the only begotten from the Father, full of grace and truth; as He tabernacled among us in the form of a man." John 1:14. Another reinterpretation, or readjustment, is revealed to the Samaritan woman who is told that "the hour cometh, when neither in this mountain, nor in Jerusalem, shall ye worship the Father." John 4:21. Then came the baptism of the Church with the Holy Spirit—making possible the subsequent period of interminable progress and development. The limitations of time and space were overcome. Racial, geographical, national and educational barriers were removed and Parthians and Medes and the rest of the motley group, "every man heard them speaking in his own language . . . the mighty works of God." Acts 2. The progress of the kingdom of God cannot be impeded by any formal or historical limitations. The historical past holds no normative restrictions for the development of the "things of God." Therein lies the inspiring prophecy for even our time, that the expressions of the Spirit will not be confined to, nor restricted by any given or existing forms. In the economy of God the forms most respected by men and hallowed by tradition may ruthlessly be surrendered for newer forms and more adequate interpretations.

. . . Having recognized the justification of a reinterpretation of purpose and methods the readjustment of thought and activity will follow as the night the day.

III. Readjustment of Thought and Activity

. . .

1. Readjustment of Evangelical Thought

The readjustment of Evangelical thought concerns itself with the thought life of our Synod and involves to a greater or less extent a new interpretation of our religious-theological concepts. We have already spoken of the doctrinal deposit of the Evangelical Synod referring especially to its Reformation inheritance and the present quietistic attitude of thought. We have acquiesced to the confessional statements and are largely committed to the theological positions of the Reformed and Lutheran Churches. The question has arisen whether the continued adherence to all this can be justified on merely traditional grounds. Has not, possibly, the time arrived in the course of the historical development of the Evangelical Synod when a reinterpretation of thought has become essential ? On this especial point the problem seems to be coming to a head with reference to the revision of our catechism. The terminology of the Lutheran catechism may have served its purpose in its time, but, becoming antiquated, and developing marks of monstrosity in the hands of our Evangelical children, one would think it to be the most self-evident thing in the world that it should be submitted to a recasting, not limited to questions of phraseology only.

It is indeed a serious criticism to be told that current Evangelical theology has not been kept abreast with modern German conservative theology. For many of us the nineteenth century with all its manifold influences—its development of physical, historico-biblical, psychological, philosophical, biological, and social sciences and the correspondingly enlarged conceptions of the scope, sacredness and unity of human life—might just as well never have existed. The new world-view is concerning itself with hitherto untouched materials and methods, and is making valuable contributions to the study of religion; assisting in a reinterpretation of Christian truth, more adequate and acceptable to the modern mind. The reinterpretation may affect some of the cardinal Christian truths—the atonement, inspiration, creation, miracles, etc. A single illustration may show what is meant and what may be involved. It is possible that an inherited conception of the verbal inspiration of the Bible, as it has been transmitted to us from the seventeenth century, may prevent us from entering into the spirit of any and all truly Evangelical forward movements. . . .

2. Readjustment of Evangelical Activity

Of more immediate and practical significance would be the second line of reinterpretation, which concerns itself with the organization and polity of the Synod, in which, of course, the causal relationship with the preceding cannot be denied. The newly evolving Evangelical world-view demands an expression or activity with a new emphasis on Americanization, education and assertiveness.

a) Assertiveness

It has been mentioned above that the older Evangelical conceptions resulted from our adherence to German type of theology and religion with their peculiar emphasis on passive or impressional religious piety. Very consistently have we developed this attitude in thought and conduct and gained for ourselves the somewhat enviable reputation of being a conservative church. We are averse to pushing ourselves into the foreground, and very cautious about participating in any aggressive movements which indicate too much the spirit of human assertiveness and initiative. The world is to be saved by the grace of God working in the hearts of man, and not by the religious movements of the day, nor by any methods of organization and devices. It thus became a characteristic mark of Evangelical piety to resign oneself to the grace of God; to be content, and—in our own quiet, unobtrusive way—to *begin* our little tasks by emphasizing the fundamental evangelical and biblical principles of individual salvation, consecration and regeneration, etc.

There is an enormous amount of truth and gospel in this attitude of resignation to the will and means of God. It marks the supreme achievement of the Christian to have completely surrendered his life to the power and influence of the Holy Spirit—passively receptive to the grace of God. But this is only a part of the method by which the world is to be saved and describes only one side of Christian piety. We are agreed that the Church is not to arrogate to herself the purpose of singlehandedly saving the world. She is only to *begin* to save. But right here we behold the danger of acceding to the *purpose* of beginning, while, on the other hand, we decline to accept the *method* of beginning. We emphasize that we are *only* to begin, and neglect to begin at all, seemingly not aware that there is a really definite starting point, and that it devolves upon us at some time and place to take the initiative and aggressively to assert ourselves. Heralded as our strength, may this not have become one of the weaknesses of our wonderful Evangelical Synod? Immersed as we are in a very valuable appreciation of the elemental expressions of Christian piety—faith, repentance, assurance of forgiveness and certainty of salvation—we are confronted by the danger of silently submitting ourselves to the dominance of these spiritual factors, without sufficiently comprehending the urgent need of more aggressive and active approach to the present day problems of the Church, nation and world. It was this kind of piety which has largely dominated German Christianity, where a main emphasis was placed on going to church; listening to the sermon; partaking of the sacraments; and otherwise enjoying the privileges and prerogatives of the communion of saints. Organized church life in Germany was marked by a corresponding lack of self-assertiveness; all the splendid achievements of German Christianity notwithstanding.

The modern Evangelical world-view would place a greater emphasis on the well grounded psychological maxim, "No impression without expression." The merely psychological and pedagogical principles at stake, in themselves, would urge a readjustment along these lines. More urgent, however, is the consideration that the modern world conditions call for a greater expressional activity than could be expected in any previous age. . . . Is it reasonable to assume that American Christianity would ever have accomplished this hitherto unheard-of task, solely by a passive reliance upon the Spirit to move the hearts of men and women to such service? Have we not ourselves experienced definite blessings as a result of modern methods in mission life enlistment? The day of the immediacy of the Spirit is past, and we need to adjust ourselves in true Evangelical fashion to a more aggressive activity, and thus offer the modern, socially conditioned man a greater opportunity for religious-expressional decisions, thereby creating for the Spirit the point of contact to work in the heart of man what it is His good will to accomplish. The new Evangelical world-view must be marked by this tendency to discard the mantle of resignation in order to work out the purpose of God in a more self-assertive and aggressive manner. Let us do this with fear and trembling under the tutelage of the Spirit.

b) Americanization

The proposed reinterpretation will involve an altered attitude toward our German traditions and antecedents, which, for the lack of a better word, may be termed Americanization. Due to the immediate purpose of supplying the needs of the early German inhabitants of America, the German language was used almost exclusively, and we, under the stress of this situation, developed into a consistently German-centered and German-oriented church. Thus did we interpret and fulfill our historical purpose. Having begun in this manner it was the line of least resistance so to continue, until now the question has arisen whether or not we have become tangled in the meshes of our tradition and have developed an unconscious tendency or inclination to retain German for tradition's sake. That this, in the nature of the case, would be a natural tendency is evident on the face of it. There has developed a serious temptation, in these last years especially, to retain the German language and German customs as a matter of policy or practical expediency; and the impression has gained ground that an undue emphasis has been laid on the retention of the German language where the best interests and welfare of the rising generation and the Church of tomorrow would advise a different procedure. Instances could be cited where, thru unjustified retention of the German language, our young people have been practically driven out of our churches to find welcome homes in American churches. Here and there a pastor, controlled by purely subjective considerations—among which could be mentioned prejudices engendered by the war, personal inclinations, and inability to use the American language—has insisted in following this suicidal course. He has at times, contrary to the wishes of his congregation, shown a lack of those spiritual qualities of prophetical leadership by which alone the kingdom of God is to be built. . . . That the time has arrived—or will arrive in all sections simultaneously—when the German language will become extinct, is not maintained; but that it is arriving cannot be denied, especially in the face of the rapid increase of our English confirmation classes. It is a readjustment called for by the change in time and conditions. At one time we were a *German* Evangelical Synod. We have long since realized our opportunities and obligations as a German *Evangelical Synod,* and are on the verge of accepting the challenge and enlarged opportunities of being the Evangelical Church in America . . . all of which is glowing, inspiring testimony that the Evangelical spirit cannot be fettered by any given historical forms. It can hardly be justified to let the language question develop into a serious Synodical problem, when its solution lies in the adoption of a simple principle. From the view-point of the consecrated Christian, possessed with the burning passion for saving souls for the Christ, it is almost inconceivable that this question could develop into a problem. . . .

. . . To the Evangelical thought of a quarter of a century ago all this would have been considered a betrayal of trust and a compromise; but it is the result of a new Evangelical world-view which is beginning to understand the necessity of a readjustment of activities to altered conditions, and shrinks not at the thought of Americanization. The revision of our statutes has been undertaken and should be approached from that point of view. The proposed change of name is indicative of the entire tendency.

The future calls for a more aggressive and active participation in the affairs of American Christianity, and it will be only thru a more sympathetic approach to interchurch or national and social obligations and responsibilities—in our own Evangelical manner, of course—that we may prove our right to a continued existence in the American commonwealth. If these questions are prayerfully faced in the presence of God, who then, overwhelmed by His love and grace, could think of compromising the divine, eternal bread of life for the passing satisfaction of a tradition? Recognizing our eternal purpose in the world, let us become all things to all men; prepared, if need be, to sacrifice our racial, historical and national pride so that some may be saved.

c) Education

The new condition of things has already achieved changes in our educational program and ideals. Inevitably it would be thus. The changes which have occurred in the last twenty-five years apply here with peculiar significance. The transition from an immigrant to an American, from a rural to a city constituency demands a corresponding adjustment in our educational system and ideals, all of which goes hand in hand with the aforementioned theological religious reinterpretation. . . . A decade or so ago it was a comparatively rare thing for an Evangelical young man or woman to attend a higher school of learning. Perhaps it did not fit immediately into the German point of view or more likely, let us assume, it was not compatible with the restricted financial means of the average German family. Today, however, especially in the city, but in ever increasing number also in the rural districts, the pastor is confronted on Sundays by college trained men and women. The man who has not been called upon to meet this situation knows nothing of the trepidation that it brings. To meet this modern situation nothing will suffice except a new emphasis on the education of our theological students. A merely consecrated, devout and sincere ministry will not suffice, for it cannot be the most efficient. If as a church we would make a fitting contribution to American Christianity, then we cannot afford to sink below the planes of the educational standard of the neighboring American church bodies. Is it too much to expect the Evangelical minister to be abreast of the best scholarship of the day? Distressing as it is to hear some of our city pastors tell of their experiences when they are called upon to fraternize with the more highly trained American pastor, it is even more humiliating to hear the plaintive cry of our theological students that they find little inspiration in the rank and file of Evangelical scholarship. . . .

. . . We conclude. That an Evangelical problem exists has been our assumption and we have attempted a modest analysis. That the new Evangelical world-view offers the solution to that problem is not our unqualified assertion, but that some readjustment or interpretation is absolutely essential, and in the order of the day is just as irrefutable as the principle upon which it is based; for "perfect correspondence is perfect life." Have we the courage to loosen the fetters of our traditions which bind us to a dead past! Fortunate is the church with a rich tradition. We can well be proud of ours. Yet the traditions of a church should be her inspiration, and not her limitation, in the effort to achieve God's ordained purposes. We fail in our purpose if we adjust our activities to our traditions, supposing that it is the purpose of the church to be the preserver of her past historical heritages. Tradition will not save the world; inherited doctrines and beliefs will not save the world; established organization, tested and tried tho it may be, will not save the world. May the Holy Spirit enlighten the church that considers it her purpose to preserve that which may only be the remnant of a past day. The Philistines are upon us, the power of sin has taken renewed possession of our people and is working havoc in their midst. When the time was fulfilled God revealed His purpose and His plan of salvation. Standing in the midst of this struggle the Evangelical church has been intrusted with only one controlling purpose and motive, namely: to seek and to save that which is lost. Shall we, Samson-like, continue to sleep securely in the false satisfaction derived from the triumphs and strength of the past, or shall we justify our existence in the world today by rising to the prophetical height of the New Testament principle of doing "all things for the gospel's sake" and becoming "all things to all men" in order "by all means to save some"?

The Global Ecumenical Context

57. The Federal Council of Churches: *"Conference on Organic Union"*

(1918)

William H. Roberts and Hubert C. Herring

In 1918, the General Assembly of the Presbyterian Church in the United States of America originated a proposal for some form of organic union among the evangelical churches in the United States. At its meeting in Columbus, Ohio, in May of that year, the General Assembly voted to invite evangelical churches in the United States to "meet and counsel together with a view to finding a way by which we may outwardly and concretely express the spiritual union which we believe already exists among the people of Christ."

Responding to this invitation, representatives of seventeen churches met in Philadelphia from December 4–6, 1918, for a preliminary "Interchurch Conference on Organic Union." There, the question of an appropriate basis for a practical plan of union was discussed and an "Ad Interim Committee" was empowered to formulate a plan of union on the basis of the December discussion. Soon thereafter, the Evangelical Synod published the report of the Committee on Business and Resolutions, which had been unanimously adopted by the Interchurch Conference in Philadelphia. The report celebrated the new spirit of union among churches in the United States, lifted up the new efforts for organic union in Canada, and looked toward the creation of its own plan of union by the Ad Interim Committee.

Since most of the participants from the Evangelical Synod had spent

---

Source: William H. Roberts and Hubert C. Herring, "Conference on Organic Union," *Magazin für Evangelische Theologie und Kirche,* n.s., vol. 21, no. 1 (January 1919): 135–37.

most of their church lives within a circle of fellow Germans with similar backgrounds and perspectives, the impact of these ecumenical meetings upon Evangelical leaders was profound. Suddenly, they found themselves working together with Christians from ethnic and denominational backgrounds that were very different. In fact the report of the Committee on Business and Resolutions, which appeared in the largely German-language denominational Magazin, *was published in English. The Evangelical Synod was beginning to understand itself as part of a widening ecumenical community.*

In February 1920, the Committee on Business and Resolutions called another Interchurch Conference on Organic Union, which amended the proposed plan of union slightly, adopted it, and sent it to the constituent bodies for ratification (see vol. 6:13). The plan, although it did not call for a full "organic union," nevertheless envisioned a more integrated structure than was already present in the Federal Council of the Churches of Christ in America, and it looked toward increased cooperation in mission. It also generated some new thoughts on the part of a young German Evangelical theologian named Reinhold Niebuhr (see vol. 6:65).

Unfortunately, in the end most of the churches did not ratify the plan, and it was dropped from consideration. Nevertheless, the Interchurch Conference on Organic Union was an important predecessor to the Consultation on Church Union, a larger group of Protestant denominations that would come into being in 1962.

Witherspoon Building, Philadelphia, Pa., Dec. 4–6, 1918
Report of the Committee on Business and Resolutions

The conference, composed of the representatives of seventeen churches, adopted unanimously on Thursday, December 5, 1918, the report of the committee on business and on resolutions. The report was adopted unanimously by a rising vote and is as follows:

As representatives of a number of the Protestant Evangelical Churches in America, convened in conference to consider questions looking toward Organic Church Union, we are grateful to God for the motion on the part of the General Assembly of the Presbyterian Church, in calling us to counsel concerning what may be done in the furthering of this great aim. In the same spirit of appreciation, we recognize that from many other sources there are calls challenging us to consider this question as a paramount duty of our day.

It is agreed among us, that the great world crisis thru which we have partially passed, and are still passing, has thrust upon us new obligations and duties, which we may not disregard. The common ideals and dangers, which have come to the front in the great war, have developed many latent forces which the Church must be quick to conserve. Moreover, the unanimity with which our people in the face of their many differing traditions, were able to fuse themselves into one body, for the common weal of the nation and the world, may be regarded as a hopeful prophecy and presage of our churches coming into a like unity, in the interests of that great kingdom dear to the heart of God and ourselves.

We believe in the oneness of the Church of Christ. We worship one God and own the Lordship of our Saviour, Jesus Christ. Our Lord admonished us that "One is our Master and all we are brethren." In His last prayer for His disciples, He prays that we may all be one, as He and the Father are one. We believe that the Church is one body, whose head is the Lord Jesus Christ, and whose life is the presence and power of the eternal and immanent Spirit of God. We are called in one hope of our calling; we have one Lord, one faith, one baptism, one God and Father who is above all, and thru all, and in all. It is His Divine Spirit which has been travailing thru our experiences, to bring us to a unity of the faith, a knowledge of the Son of God, and a cooperation in His will to bring in the kingdom of righteousness, peace and joy in the Holy Spirit. We recognize that under the enlightenment of the Divine Spirit, who brings us out of darkness into His marvelous light, that the several denominations of the Protestant Church have stood and do stand for the recovery and maintenance of some special treasures of truth and life, which treasures, however, are a heritage that belongs to the universal Church of God. We recognize with deep gratitude that these common heritages have to a large degree become the possession of all the different denominations.

Wc arc thankful for the growth and increase of the spirit of sympathetic and fraternal relations between us, which have enabled us to gather and inquire what may be the next step in the development of our common service. We believe that it is in accordance with the Divine purpose and in harmony with the will of Christ, that His Church should be one visible body to bear witness to Him among men. Being of one mind in those vital and spiritual verities which make us one body in Christ, we believe, that our Master now challenges us to conquer the divisive elements, which segregate us into various and sometimes conflicting bodies, and under the guidance of His Spirit to bring the manifold treasures which have been garnered in our several histories and experiences, to a common altar, and there devote them to our Lord and His cause. At this altar, we may unitedly pray for that grace which will enable us to discover the will of God, and the movement of His Spirit for this new day and generation; and also that we may aim as one body to move together and become effective means in God's hands for the establishment of His kingdom in the world. So far as we can see, there is light along the whole horizon which bids us to be hopeful of effecting some form of Organic Church Union.

In view of the wide opportunity and solemn obligation of the hour, the following action is taken:

1. That the members of this Conference from each communion, whether present in official or personal capacity, be asked as soon as possible to appoint representatives on an Ad Interim Committee to carry forward the movement toward Organic Union here initiated.
2. The Committee shall be composed of one member from each communion, and one additional member for each 500,000 communicants, or major fraction thereof. In addition, the Foreign Missions Conference and the Home Mission Council shall each be asked to name one member.
3. The same privilege of membership on the Committee shall be extended to evangelical denominations not represented here.
4. The members of the Committee appointed by the Presbyterian Church in the U. S. A. are asked to act as the nucleus and convener of the *ad interim* Committee.
5. This ad interim Committee shall be charged, with the following duties:

    (a) To develop and use at its discretion, agencies and methods for discovering and creating interest in the subject of Organic Union thruout the Churches of the country.

    (b) To make provision for presenting by personal delegations, or otherwise, to the national bodies of all the evangelical communions of the United States, urgent invitations to participate in an Interdenominational Council on Organic Union.

    (c) To lay before the bodies thus approached the steps necessary for the holding of such Council, including the plan and basis of representation, and the date of the Council which shall be as early as possible, and in any event, not later than 1920.

    (d) To prepare for presentation to such Council when it shall assemble a suggested plan or plans of Organic Union.

(e) To consider and report upon any legal matters related to the plan or plans of union which it may propose.

6. In addition to the above, the Ad Interim Committee is directed to report to the Interdenominational Council on any and all matters within the field of its inquiries. The Committee will be subject to the jurisdiction of the Council.

In requesting the Ad Interim Committee to undertake the arduous task outlined, the Conference desires the Committee to proceed with freedom at every point. As of possible assistance, however, in the deliberations, the Conference expresses its present judgment as to certain aspects of the problem to be faced.

1. The Conference is profoundly solicitous that the effort for organic union shall have first regard to those forces of vital spiritual life which alone give meaning to our effort. No mechanical uniformity must be sought, nor any form of organization which ignores or thwarts the free movement of the Spirit of God, in the hearts of His servants.

2. In line with this desire the Conference hopes the Committee will be able to devise plans so broad and flexible as to make place for all the evangelical churches of the land, whatever their outlook or tradition, temperament or taste, whatever their relationships racially or historically.

3. The Conference regards with deep interest and warm appropriation all the movements of our time towards closer cooperative relations between communions, especially the notable service rendered by the Federal Council of the Churches of Christ in America. While the Ad Interim Commitee's aim and function will lie in a field entirely different from those movements, it will be expected to maintain sympathetic relations with them, and to regard with satisfaction any reinforcement which its activities may bring to them.

4. The notice of the Committee is directed to the efforts for Organic Union represented in other lands, especially the Churches of Canada. The remarkable and significant statement recently issued by a joint committee of Anglican and Free Churches of Great Britain will also call for the study of the Committee.

5. The Conference calls attention to the fact that in its search for a plan of Organic Union, the Committee will not be precluded from considering plans of Federal Union such as are in varying forms present to the minds of members of this Conference. Our nation is a federal union but is not the less an organic union. Care should be used not to confuse the term "federal" as thus employed, with this meaning when used to signify "associated" or "cooperative."

6. Last of all, the Conference declares its hope and longing, that the evangelical churches may give themselves with a new faith and order to the proclamation of the gospel of Christ, which is the only hope of our stricken world, and to those ministries of Christian love and leading for the community, the nation and the nations, by which they shall reveal to men the mind of Christ and hasten the coming of His kingdom.

Attest:—

WM. H. ROBERTS, *Chairman Business Committee.*

HUBERT C. HERRING, *Secretary Business Committee.*

58. Faith and Order:

"A Pilgrimage Towards Unity"

(1920)

C. H. Brent

C. H. Brent (1862–1929), although a Canadian by birth, became an Episcopal bishop from the United States serving as missionary bishop of the Philippines. He was a humble man of prayer with a prodigious appreciation for other peoples and traditions. Brent had attended the World Missionary Conference in Edinburgh in 1910, which had intentionally excluded doctrinal discussion from its proceedings for fear of conflict (see vol. 6:12, 52). Before he left Edinburgh, however, Brent challenged his colleagues: "Whenever God gives a vision He also points to some new responsibility . . . you and I will go away with some fresh duties to perform."

Brent was serious. Within the year, he addressed a mass meeting of the Protestant Episcopal Church, sharing his own conviction that the time had come for a world conference to frankly discuss issues of faith and order. A resolution was passed by that Convention to appoint a Joint Commission to bring about such a conference, and to invite the cooperation of "all Christian communions throughout the world which confess our Lord Jesus Christ as God and Saviour."

Plans got underway, and as a significant leader in the creation and early growth of the Faith and Order movement, Brent delivered a stirring address, entitled "A Pilgrimage Towards Unity," to a preparatory conference for the world conference that was held in Geneva in August

---

Source: C. H. Brent, "A Pilgrimage Towards Unity," *Magazin für Evangelische Theologie und Kirche,* n.s., vol. 23, no. 1 (January 1921): 29–32.

1920. It was so inspiring that leaders from the Evangelical Synod of North America made sure that it was published in their denominational journal.

Unfortunately, planning for the conference was interrupted by the First World War. However, the conference elected a Continuation Committee, with Brent as chair, which did a great deal to ensure the continuity and ongoing plans for a World Conference on Faith and Order, which finally was held in Lausanne in 1927 (see vol. 6:15, 35).

This address by the "Preliminary Commission" bears at the head the names of all the Episcopal bishops of the United States. (They are dropped for practical reasons.)

Ten years ago a little group of Christians embraced the purpose, first conceived at an early Eucharist, of joining together in a special pilgrimage towards unity in the broken Church of Jesus Christ. It was not a man-made scheme but a humble endeavor to put ourselves in accord with the mind of our Lord expressed in His prayer THAT THEY ALL MAY BE ONE. From this modest beginning a world-wide movement has grown, so that at the preliminary meeting of the World Conference on Faith and Order which has just closed *at Geneva, eighty churches and forty nations were represented.* This Conference marks a stage on our journey and also exhibits the spirit of the pilgrims, some of whom, such as the *Germans* and the *Roumanians,* came at great cost to themselves.

Our journey is a long one. Christians have taken more than a thousand years to reach the far country of disunion where they now reside. We cannot return home again in a moment. Some of the pilgrims who first caught the vision a decade since had hardly hoped to get as far as they have in so brief a space of time. The temptation is to be content with slow progress, and to rest satisfied with something less than the goal of God's placing—a Church, on earth, among men, visibly and organically one. Partial unities seem more possible and federation has alluring features, but they fall far short of home. Then, too, impossibilities, according to God's design, are the only aim high enough for human capacity. We have allowed ourselves to take for granted the necessity of Christian disunion, blind to the fact that oneness is the first, not the last, requirement for God's firm foothold among men. The tinkling ambitions of separation are shocking in the face of a shattered, bewildered world that is looking for leadership and finding none. The performance of the churches, first and last, individually and collectively, is pitifully measured by their highsounding professions and claims. The failure of Christianity—and it has failed—is the inevitable failure of a Kingdom divided against itself. It will go failing until it manifests unity and all the privileges and wealth which each enjoys separately are placed at the disposal of all.

The pilgrims do not maintain that theirs is the only method of travel, by the way of Conference on Faith and Order, but they do contend that theirs is the only goal and that the spirit for which conference stands is the only spirit for a pilgrimage towards unity—the filial spirit which embraces God's purpose as its own and the fraternal spirit which claims each Christian as a brother beloved. Thru a long stretch of time controversy has burned with fierce flame in the churches, great and small, and has blackened and scorched many a fair subject. It is not extinguished yet. The spirit of controversy rejoices in a dialectic victory—what a hollow triumph it is—and gloats over a defeated foe. The spirit of conference is the slave of Truth and weeps because gulfs remain unbridged and good men are alienated from one another. Controversy loves war and conference loves peace. Controversy has great respect for its own convictions and little for those of others. Conference applies the Golden Rule to the separated and demands mutual respect for each other's convictions.

For a week the pilgrims were in conference in Geneva. Differences of thought were sketched in clear outline nor did any immediate reconciliation appear on the horizon, but never was there a word of harshness or self-will. The common conviction at the center of being, was that difficulties boldly expressed and openly met, were the only difficulties in a fair way of settlement.—What appear as contradictions have, as the secret to their strength, riches of being which, when at length put into harmonious relation to the whole of God's scheme, will be revealed as supplementary elements necessary to perfection. The study of the Church as it exists in the mind of God, of what we mean by unity, of the sources of the Church's inspiration, of the best expression in language of a living faith, occupied the prayers and thoughts of the pilgrims during the Conference, and for a long time to come will continue to occupy them. Faith first and then Order. The inner principle of life, the ideal, and then the mode of propagating and protecting by organic self-government of what is within.

The competition of churches received a body blow from the united action of the pilgrims. It is a sin against love to endeavor to detach a Christian from his own church in order to aid another church to increase its roll. Sheep-stealing in the cattle world is held to be a crime. How then ought it to be viewed by the under-shepherds of the Good Shepherd? That is a question as tho the whole world were evangelized or there were any dearth of opportunity anywhere. The number of unconverted and untouched in almost any given community form the majority of that community. A combined effort in the direction of those who know not Christ is our elementary duty.

The spirit of God was the strength of the pilgrims. He made us one in our fellowship. The Conference was a living body. Life touched life, nation touched nation, the spirit of the East held communion with the spirit of the West as perhaps never before. By invitation on the last day of the Conference we gathered together—it was the Feast of the Transfiguration in the Eastern calendar—in the Russian Orthodox Church in Geneva for the solemn worship of Divine Liturgy. Anglican, Baptist, Old Catholic, Presbyterian, Wesleyan, Lutheran, Quaker were all there, and all there to worship. The Metropolitan of Seleucia in a spiritual address spoke to the pilgrims of his own joy in the vision of unity, and told how, out of the transfigured troubles and pains of the present, would rise the glory of the future. We of the West need the fragrant, graceful worship of the East. The beauty of God filled His temple. We felt that we had been drawn within the pearly gates of the Apocalypse, and we came away, with pain béni and grapes in our hands, and sweetness in our souls, under the spell of the mystic East. It was fitting that we would forthwith consider certain proposals of the Orthodox Churches, sane and strong, touching on cooperation and fellowship. A few minutes later and the Conference became a fact of history, a hope and a vision.

The pilgrims go home with added inspiration, conviction and responsibility. No one departed unmoved. What another decade will bring forth in this movement who can say? But it is in the hands of God from Whom it came and to Whom it belongs. It is ours only so far as we recognize it to be His. Directly and indirectly it has already reached far. Its possibilities are measured only by our willingness to explore them. They will be realized fully if we pilgrims continue to aim to do our little share as God, Whose co-workers we are, does His great share. Some day there will be one flock under one Shepherd. We pilgrims register our active belief in this fact and promise to pursue our journey until we reach the Heaven where we would be.

C. H. Brent

Chairman of the preliminary meeting
of the World Conference on Faith and Order.

Geneva, Switzerland,
August 21, 1920.

59. Life and Work:

"A Message to All Christians"

(1925)

In April 1924, the German Evangelical Synod received an official invitation to send delegates to a Universal Conference on Christian Life and Work to be held in Stockholm in 1925. The invitation expressed beautifully the passionate vision of its primary architect, Nathan Söderblom, archbishop of Uppsala, Sweden, and of all Christians who were still shocked by a war-torn world and a divided Christendom: "No Christian can doubt that the world's greatest need is the Christian way of life not merely in personal and social behavior but in public opinion and its outcome in public action. . . . In short, we hope under the guidance of the Spirit of God, through the counsel of all, to be able to formulate programmes and devise means for making them effective, whereby the fatherhood of God and the brotherhood of all peoples *will become more completely realized through the Church of Christ."*

John Baltzer (1857–1930), president general of the Evangelical Synod of North America, and Samuel D. Press, president of Eden Theological Seminary, were among six hundred delegates from thirty-seven countries attending the conference. Presentations and discussions during the twelve-day meeting took place under six headings: (1) the general obligation of the church in the light of God's plan for the world—basic and fundamental questions; (2) the church and economic and industrial problems; (3) the church and social and moral problems; (4) the church and international relations; (5) the church and education; (6) ways

---

Source: "A Message to All Christians" from the Universal Conference on Christian Life and Work, Stockholm, 1925, in John Baltzer, "Report of the President General," in *Official Reports and District Resolutions to the General Conference of the German Evangelical Synod of North America* (St. Louis: German Evangelical Synod, 1925), 37–40.

and means for promoting cooperation between the churches, and for closer associations on federal lines. As in many international meetings, participants found that meeting people from different countries and religious and ethnic groups in informal conversations was often more valuable than the formal sessions.

"The Message of the Universal Christian Conference on Life and Work" was the only official statement of the meeting. It expressed penitence on behalf of the churches for their failure to do their duty, and affirmed their obligation to apply the gospel "in all realms of human life—industrial, social, political and international." Interestingly, it limited the mission of the church, which it proclaimed was "above all to state principles, and to assert the ideal, while leaving to individual consciences and to communities the duty of applying them with charity, wisdom and courage." Furthermore, unlike the optimistic tone of the social statements of the Federal Council of the Churches of Christ in America, the message ended on a somber note. Recognizing the devastation of the recent world war, the message noted, "The nearer we draw to the Crucified, the nearer we come to one another, in however varied colours the Light of the World may be reflected in our faith. Under the Cross of Jesus Christ we reach out hands to one another. The Good Shepherd had to die in order that He might gather together the scattered children of God. In the Crucified and Risen Lord alone lies the world's hope."

According to the Swedish ecumenist Nils Ehrenstrom, three particular areas in the Stockholm conference went beyond earlier ecumenical statements. First, whereas earlier world conferences had consisted of collections of concerned individuals or spokespersons for particular Christian interests, delegates were sent to Stockholm by their respective churches. Moreover, the presence of a strong delegation from the Orthodox churches stretched the participants' ecumenical conversations beyond the world of Protestantism. Second, prior to Stockholm there had been a "confessional cleavage," indeed, an "abysmal ignorance about one another" in the churches. Stockholm brought new understanding and Christian fellowship across denominational divisions, healing postwar national antagonisms. Third, Stockholm asserted the practical breadth and depth of Christian responsibility in the world by asserting that the universal sovereignty of Christ meant that the churches were responsible for the whole life of all God's people.

Although at the time the 1925 Universal Conference on Christian Life and Work was greeted around the world with mixed reactions, it kindled great hopes for new cooperation between the churches. It was an important step toward the formation of the World Council of Churches in

1948. Furthermore, the Evangelical Synod of North America, which had developed an extraordinary network of hospitals, orphanages, and "old folk's homes" to serve its neighbors at home, embraced an expanded vision. The Christian churches had a shared responsibility for all of God's people throughout the whole inhabited earth.

The Journey to Europe

Two reasons chiefly induced the General officers to send Dr. S. D. Press and the President General to Europe this year:

1. The visit of Dr. Dibelius, who had visited our General Conference in 1921 on behalf of the Evangelical Executive Committee in Germany required a return of such a courtesy, through which the existing relations, which of course are only spiritual and which must be regarded as entirely friendly, could be clarified and strengthened inwardly, so that we could become better acquainted with the organization of the Evangelical Church in Germany and establish closer fellowship with her. I will also add that Dr. Press at the same time had at heart other interests closely connected with his position as president of our theological seminary, which he was able to carry out satisfactorily.

2. We were also requested to attend the Conference on Christian Life and Work in Stockholm. Before I pass on to you the official message of this Conference, which met from August 19–30, I would like to say that the Conference cannot be called truly ecumenical, although it may be regarded as a sort of preliminary gathering to be followed in all probability by others, which may lead to a real ecumenical conference. Many questions of great importance for the life and work of the church of Christ have been considered seriously and from all possible angles and were illumined in a way which must issue a more effective work in building a Kingdom of God on earth not only for those who took part but also for all of Protestant Christendom.

It is manifestly impossible to give here even a selection of quotations from the very many addresses we have heard. I have therefore given to you only the official message of the great Conference, which was pervaded throughout by a thoroughly Christian—not all denominational—spirit. Perhaps an hour or two might be given to Dr. Press and myself in which we could relate our impressions and experiences in an informal manner.

The World Conference on Christian Life and Work

A Message to All Christians

The message which the World Conference on Christian Life and Work addresses to all Christians is as follows:

The Universal Conference for Christian Life and Work, assembled in Stockholm and composed of representatives of most of the churches in 37 different nations of the Old and New World, the Near and the Far East, herewith addresses a fraternal message to all followers of Christ with the urgent request to unite with the Conference in prayer, confession and thought. We regret that not all Christian churches deemed it necessary to accept the invitation to this Conference, for in view of the living and far-reaching problems which engage our attention we must hope for the cooperation of all portions of the church of Christ. Otherwise the testimony and the influence of the Conference were incomplete.

The struggles, losses and anxieties of the Christian church during and after the war have led to the humiliating acknowledgment that the world is stronger than a divided Christendom. Before God and the world we confess the sins and neglect of duty of which the church has become guilty through lack of love and sympathetic understanding. The call of this hour to the church must therefore be a call to repentance, and at the same time also a call for a cheerful new beginning through the inexhaustible source of power, Jesus Christ.

The Conference has recognized its duty to make the Gospel the decisive influence in all fields of human life, in the industrial, social, political and international life.

Thus in the realm of economic life we have acknowledged that the soul is the highest of all values of superior value and must not be subordinated to mere possessions or the mechanism of industry and that the soul has the right to its own salvation. Therefore we contend for a free and perfect development of human personality. In the name of the Gospel we have again emphasized that industry must not be based upon the mere desire for personal gain but that in the service for the common good property must be regarded as a trust for which we must give an account to God. Cooperation must take the place of selfish competition. Employer and laborer alike must be put in a position to regard their share in industry as the fulfilment of their calling.

We have also considered these moral and social problems: the lack of proper dwellings, unemployment, immorality, intemperance and crime. We have been led to realize that these different problems can not be really solved through the strength of any individual but that the community must assume the responsibility for them and exercise social control over the acts of the individual insofar as it may be necessary in certain cases for the common good. We have also occupied ourselves with questions which arise from the higher valuation of woman, childhood and labor in the field of education, the family and the every-day task. The church must not interfere in the rights of the individual but must represent the rights of the moral personality as well as anything else which enriches humanity through the complete enfolding of every individual soul.

We have considered in detail the Christian ideals which should govern international relationships, ideals which are so far removed from nationalistic self-glorification as they are from the mass-cosmopolitanism of any country, no matter what its importance may be.

We request the churches to give due consideration to the terrors of war and its inadequacy as a real solution for international disputes. We have not tried to present accurately formulated resolutions, nor have we set down the results of our friendly discussion by resolution or enactment. It was not only the sincere respect for the conviction of other persons and groups which induced us to choose this method, but chiefly the consciousness that the church sets up ideals and principles but leaves it to the individual and the community to seek lovingly, wisely and courageously the interpretation of these principles.

Therefore, we address this call first of all to all Christians. Everyone should, following his own conscience, recognize his whole responsibility for doing the will of God on earth and for the work in God's Kingdom. In addressing this appeal first of all to the churches we recognized gratefully that in this sacred way we seek for allies. We turn to the young people in all lands. With real joy, we have realized all the strivings and struggles of the youth of all nations for a better shaping of the social order. We would enlist the fresh strength and enthusiasm of youth at the height of its power for the service of the Spirit of God.

We address this message, in the name of the Son of Man, in the name of the Carpenter of Nazareth, also to the workers of the world, deeply grateful for all those who today under difficult conditions are allowing their conduct to be determined by the will of God. We deplore the causes of estrangement and lack of mutual understanding which still exist and shall seek to do away with them. We share the endeavor toward such a social order in which through righteousness and brotherly love there is made possible the development of the whole human race according to the will of God.

This Conference is only a beginning, but we cannot separate without providing in some way for the continuation of the work so happily begun. We have therefore undertaken to create a Continuation Committee which is to carry forward what has been here begun.

Church Union

60. Service First:
"A Chronology of the Evangelical Synod"

(1990)

Robert T. Fauth

In 1990, members of the United Church of Christ who traced their heritage back to the nineteenth-century immigrant German Evangelicals who founded the Kirchenverein des Westens (Church Society of the West) gathered to celebrate 150 years of ministry in the United States. A small booklet, edited by Robert T. Fauth, president of Eden Theological Seminary, was published, which contained a helpful chronology of German Evangelical history.

The story documented there shows the practical contributions of the Evangelical tradition to the ecumenical movement, highlighting an approach that Reinhold Niebuhr, Evangelical pastor and scholar, had lifted up in a sermon he had preached at the seventy-fifth anniversary of the Kirchenverein seventy-five years earlier: "The kingdom of God and the Christian Church will not achieve unity because of the uniformity of belief or action. We achieve unity because of our common purpose to bring about the coming of the kingdom of God. This purpose ought to be a holy zeal and the earnestness of our task ought to bring us together to work for a common end, though with different methods and various powers. Our highest ambition as a church ought to be that we may be an integral part of the Church that serves its master, an integral power by serving him according to the light God has given us to see the light."

Source: Robert T. Fauth, "Chronology of the Evangelical Synod" in *The Evangelical Synod: One Hundred and Fifty Years 1840–1990* (n.p., 199 0), 17–18. Used by permission of Edith L. Fauth.

1840 Der Kirchenverein des Westens (an association of pastors) formed at Gravois Settlement, Missouri.

1847 Publication of the first Evangelical catechism.

1849 St. Paul's Church, St. Louis, became the first congregation to join the Kirchenverein.

1850 German Evangelical Missouri College (now Eden Seminary) opened near Marthasville, Missouri.

1857 Good Samaritan Hospital established in St. Louis.

Ohio pastors join the Kirchenverein.

1858 German Protestant Orphans' Home established in St. Louis.

1860 United Evangelical Synod of the East joined the Kirchenverein.

1862 German Language Evangelical Hymnal published.

1866 Institution for training parochial teachers formed in Cincinnati.

Name of the Kirchenverein changed to German Evangelical Synod of the West with three districts: Eastern, Central, Northwest.

1867 Uhlich Children's Home established in Chicago.

1872 Elmhurst College founded, combining Melancthon Seminary and the Evansville (Indiana) Preparatory School.

Board for Home Missions created; its work officially funded by the General Conference.

1879 German Protestant Home for Orphans and Old People established in Detroit, Michigan.

1884 India Mission adopted by the denomination.

1886 Immigrant Mission established at Baltimore, Maryland.

1889 Evangelical Deaconess Hospital established in St. Louis.

1892 Evangelical Deaconess Hospital established at Evansville, Indiana.

Emmaus Home for Epileptics and Feeble Minded established at Marthasville, Missouri.

1894 German Evangelical Orphanage and Old Peoples' Home established in Bensenville, Illinois.

Evangelical Orphans' Home established at Hoyleton, Illinois.

1895 Denominational publication work incorporated in St. Louis.

1896 Evangelical Catechism published in English.

1899 Evangelical Companion (for children) began publication.

English Language Hymnal published.

1901 Sister institution to Emmaus Home established at St. Charles, Missouri.

1902 Evangelical Deaconess Hospital established at Lincoln, Illinois.

English journal, Messenger of Peace, began publication.

Jugendbund (later: Evangelical League) came into being.

1906 Pastors' Homes opened at Blue Springs, Missouri.

1908 Evangelical Hospital established at Fairbault, Minnesota.

1909 Evangelical Deaconess Hospital established at Milwaukee, Wisconsin.

1910 Evangelical Altenheim Community established at Indianapolis, Indiana.

All pension and relief plans centralized in a denominational program.

Eden Home for the Aged established in San Antonio, Texas.

1911 Evangelical Deaconess Hospital established in Chicago, Illinois.

Evangelical Deaconess Home established in Louisville, Kentucky.

1912 Evangelical Deaconess Association formed in Baltimore, Maryland.

1913 Caroline Mission established, St. Louis.

1914 Evangelical Deaconess Hospital established in Marshalltown, Iowa.

Evangelical Deaconess Hospital established in Cleveland, Ohio.

1915 Evangelical Deaconess Home and Hospital established in East St. Louis, Illinois.

1916 St. Paul's House established in Chicago, Illinois.

Fairhaven Home established in Upper Sandusky, Ohio.

1917 Evangelical Deaconess Hospital established in Detroit, Michigan.

1918 Evangelical Home for the Aged established at Sandusky, Ohio.

1921 Mission Work begun in Honduras.

Evangelical Women's Union organized.

1924 Eden Seminary relocated in Webster Groves, Missouri.

Evangelical St. Paul's Home established in Minneapolis, Minnesota.

1926 St. Paul's Evangelical Old Folks' Home established in Belleville, Illinois.

1928 Back Bay Mission organized in Biloxi, Mississippi.

1934 On June 26, the Evangelical and Reformed Church was formed at Cleveland, Ohio.

61. A FEDERATION OF GERMAN CHURCHES:

"A Letter"

(1916)

JOHN BALTZER

In 1916, John Baltzer (1857–1930), president of the General Synod of the Evangelical Church, responding to a mandate from the General Synod of 1913, appointed eight men and himself to a Commission on Relations with Other Denominations and Churches at Home and Abroad. The commission was charged with the task of contacting denominations of German origin open to the idea of union—for example, the General Synod of the Reformed Church in the U.S., the General Council of the Lutheran Church, and the Brüdergemeinde—with the purpose of uniting with them "on a positive evangelical basis." The commission also was instructed to contact evangelical churches in Germany about a celebration of the centennial anniversary of the founding of the Church of the Prussian Union.

President Baltzer indicated his hopes for a federation of Protestant churches of German origin in a personal letter to the members of the new commission. First of all, he hoped that a conference of these churches might be held to consider the preparation of a position paper around the question of whether union between these churches was reasonable in light of their political, social, educational, and economical situation. The paper needed to acknowledge that the recently established Federal Council of the Churches of Christ (1908) had little understanding of specifically German Christianity, and that the moment was ripe for a

SOURCE: John Baltzer, letter to establish the Commission on Relations with Other Denominations and Churches at Home and Abroad, 2 October 1916, in the Eden Seminary Archives.

federation of German-origin churches. According to Baltzer, the outbreak of the First World War had deepened the unity of people of Germanic origin in the United States. Lay people in many churches with German roots felt a need for closer relationships. Baltzer believed that a federation of German churches would have a positive effect on the moral situation in the country as well as on church life in general.

Finally, Baltzer wanted to increase the synod's ties to churches of the Prussian Union abroad. He hoped that German evangelical churches on both sides of the Atlantic would send representatives to each other's festivities surrounding the centennial anniversary of the founding of the Church of the Prussian Union, as well as exchange representatives to their synod meetings. Baltzer even suggested that the synod should develop relations with German immigrant evangelical churches in South America. As ambitious as these proposals were, Baltzer was still primarily concerned with German immigrant identity rather than the wider ecumenical calling of the church.

St. Louis, Oct. 2, 1916

Dear Brother.

re: Commission on Relations with Other Denominations and Churches at Home and Abroad

It is the mandate of this Commission, together with the Officers of the Synod, to find ways of implementing the ideas behind paragraphs #5 and #7, pages 301 and 302 of the minutes of the General Synod of 1913, and to determine which goals must be kept in mind.

The paragraphs read as follows:

#5.) The Officers of the Synod are instructed, with the aim of uniting with them on a positive evangelical basis, to contact denominations of German origin which are open to the idea of union, i.e. the Reformed Church, the General Synod, the General Council of the Lutheran Church, the Brüdergemeinde, etc.

#7.) . . . it is part of the mandate of this Commission to foster cooperation with Evangelical (territorial) Churches in Germany regarding the fourth centennial celebration.

Besides the Officers of the Synod, I have appointed the following brethren to serve on this Commission:

W. Becker, Director and Professor of Dogmatics, Seminary, St. Louis, Mo.

S. Press, Professor English Department, Seminary, St. Louis, Mo.

W. Th. Jungk, D.D., Editor of the "Friedensbote," St. Louis, Mo.

J. H. Horstmann, Editor Herald, St. Louis, Mo.

Paul E. Mensel, President of Foreign Mission, Washington, D.C.

Alf E. Meyer, Secretary of the Home Mission, Chicago, Ill.

J. U. Schneider, Ph.D., Pastor at "Zion," Evansville, Ind.

A. Mohme, Pastor at "Friedens" in Kewaskum, Wis. (Pastor of the German Landeskirche)

The meeting will take place on October 4, 1916 at 10 A.M. in the Seminary in St. Louis, Mo. Travel expenses will be paid. Most likely, it will be a day's work. I ask that you be on time. An agenda will follow or will be presented.

Cordially,

Yours

J. Baltzer
President of the Synod

62. Wider Conversations:
"Commission on Relations with Other Church Bodies"

(1928)

J. H Horstmann

Twelve years after he had appointed the Commission on Relations with other Denominations and Churches at Home and Abroad (see vol. 6:61), President General John Baltzer (1857–1930) appointed a second commission—the Commission on Relations with Other Church Bodies (the title varies slightly in different instances)—to be chaired by Helmut Richard Niebuhr. At first glance, the task of this commission was not much different from the one in 1916. This one was in response to a mandate presented in a General Conference resolution of 1925 "to study the historical, the doctrinal, and the administrative relationship between kindred communions and our Synod with the objective in mind to instigate and foster friendship between, and a more intimate and closer fellowship or eventual union with such communions and our Synod at home and abroad." However, a closer look suggests that twelve years of growth and participation in the national and global ecumenical movement had produced significant differences in the Evangelical Synod.

By 1928, the synod was conducting its business in English, a sign that most of its constituency was English-speaking. Furthermore, whereas two-thirds of the commission agenda in 1916 had to do with their German roots—celebrating their European (Prussian Union) background and coming together with other German people on the basis of their common

---

Source: J. H. Horstmann, "Minutes of the First Meeting of the Commission on Relations with Other Church Bodies," 15 February 1928, in the Eden Seminary Archives.

ethnic identity—by 1928, the commission was focusing on closer relations with an (albeit originally German) denomination that had been part of the United States for over a century. Talk of closer union no longer focused on the Germanic roots of the two denominations, but on the future and the practical joining together in faith, education, and action.

To prepare church leaders, George W. Richards of Lancaster Theological Seminary (then chair of the Reformed Church's Commission on Closer Relations and Church Union) was invited to give a series of lectures at Eden Theological Seminary. J. H. Horstmann, editor of the Evangelical Herald *and secretary of the new commission, wrote a series of educational articles preparing the Evangelical constituency for closer relations with the Reformed Church, and H. R. Niebuhr was asked to work out some cooperative plans with educational leaders in the Reformed Church.*

The Evangelical Synod had shifted in its self-understanding from looking primarily backward to its Germanic roots to exploring what it might accomplish in the future if it united with another denomination. New questions emerged: (1) What are the special difficulties standing in the way of "speedy and effective organic union"? and (2) How much are we prepared to give up for the sake of union doctrinally and economically? Years went by before the Evangelical Synod was able to answer these questions.

Eden Seminary, Feb. 15, 1928, 8:00 P.M.

All the members of the Commission (Dr. J. Baltzer, President General; Dr. H. R. Niebuhr, of Eden Seminary; Dr. F. Frankenfeld, Rochester, N.Y.; Rev. Louis Goebel, Chicago, Ill.; and Rev. J. H. Horstmann, Editor of the Evangelical Herald) were present.

After the opening prayer by Dr. Frankenfeld, Dr. Niebuhr was prevailed upon to act as chairman and Rev. J. H. Horstmann consented to act as secretary.

The task of the Commission laid down in the General Conference resolution (Minutes, 1925 pp. 48–8) [*sic*]. . . . "in order further to strengthen the spirit of mutual friendship and esteem be it resolved to encourage the exchange of delegates with kindred bodies at home and abroad," and interpreted by Dr. Baltzer in his letter appointing the Commission, "to study the historical, the doctrinal, and the administrative relationship between kindred communions and our Synod with the objective in mind to instigate and foster friendship between, and a more intimate and closer fellowship or eventual union with such communions and our Synod at home and abroad," was accepted by consent.

1. After some discussion it was decided that for the present the Commission would confine its efforts to an attempt to bring about closer relations between the Synod and the Reformed Church in the U.S., and the Moravian Church (Unity of the Brethren).

2. The chairman was asked to invite Dr. George Warren Richards, of Lancaster Theological Seminary, Lancaster, Pa., to pay a visit to Eden Theological Seminary for the purpose of delivering a series of lectures. On this occasion the possibility of closer relations between the Synod and the Reformed Church in the U.S. is to be informally discussed by Drs. Niebuhr and Richards.

3. The secretary, as Editor of the Evangelical Herald, was requested to write a series of educational articles preparing the Evangelical constituency for the objectives which the Commission has in mind.

4. The chairman was also asked to suggest to Rev. J. C. Keppel, Executive Secretary of the Board of Religious Education, that if possible he get in touch with educational leaders in the Reformed Church in the U.S. for 1928 E.L.T. Schools.

Adjournment then followed, the Commission to meet again at the call of the chairman.

J. H. Horstmann, Secretary.

63. Theological Issues:
"Committee on Creedal Statement and Relation to Other Communions"

(1928)

The famous Bekenntnisparagraph *(1848) (see vol. 6:55) remained the doctrinal standard of the Evangelical Synod during its entire existence. Produced by pastors who still felt the effects of the virulent theological dissension between Lutheran and Reformed that had characterized so much of church life in German history, the paragraph was astoundingly brief in comparison to the confessional standards of Lutheran and Reformed churches. Nevertheless, it succeeded in stating the central tenets of the German Evangelical faith—the roots of their faith in the confessional documents of the Protestant Reformation, their belief in the Bible as the Word of God, the historical and doctrinal criterion by which they interpreted the Word, and the freedom of conscience that they took to be their final judge when interpretations differed. However, the fact that they accepted the confessional documents of both the Lutheran and the Reformed traditions opened them to charges by their detractors that they were doctrinally undiscriminating or even theologically ignorant.*

Such charges were grossly unfair. Members of the Kirchenverein des Westens refused to enter into the arena of theological battle not because they did not stand for something doctrinal but because they chose to stand for something else. They were convinced that the important thing about being a Christian was how one lived a Christian life, not how one argued doctrinally. They saw themselves as taking their stand on a

---

Source: Minutes and agenda from the meeting of the Committee on Creedal Statement and Relation to Other Communions, 12 January 1928, in the Eden Seminary Archives.

level deeper than doctrinal agreement or disagreement, where differing opinions became one in the unity of the Holy Spirit.

Nevertheless, when the Evangelical Synod received a letter from the Reformed Church in the U.S. encouraging closer cooperation, the Evangelicals were wary. They knew that "what they stood for" would be reexamined from the outside. They did not know what the German Reformed theologians, especially those steeped in the christocentric thinking of Mercersburg Theology, would think of the Bekenntnisparagraph *(see vol. 6:42)*

Anticipating some concern, John T. Baltzer (1857–1930), president general of the Evangelical Synod, arranged a meeting on January 12, 1928, with "a number of brethren" to consider the matter of "creedal statement and relation to other communions." Baltzer raised his concern early in his agenda for the meeting. The Bekenntnisparagraph, *Baltzer proposed, was not comprehensive for several reasons, including that "it says not one word about the personal center of the Christian faith, the living Christ," and that "it does not reflect present days seeking and searching after the central truth of Christian religion."*

The creedal statement offered by Baltzer (though not written by him) as the original basis for discussion, as well as the "Confessional Proposal" made in the meeting by H. Niefer, and the suggestions made for its clarification, show that the committee was quite comfortable with a more christocentric emphasis. In the end, no official change in the Evangelical Synod's creedal basis was ever made. However, the concerns of the meeting show that Evangelical Synod leaders were already preparing for the kind of doctrinal reflection that they anticipated might be part of their discussions with the Reformed Church in the United States.

Webster Groves, Missouri
January 12, 1928

Dr. J. Baltzer, the Hon. President General, asked a number of brethren to counsel with him and his co-officers on January 12, 1928, 10 A.M., at Eden Theological Seminary, Webster Groves, Missouri.

Dr. S. D. Press opened the meeting with prayer and Dr. Baltzer called the meeting to order. The meeting was organized by electing Dr. Baltzer as chairman and P. G. Fischer as secretary.

The following were present:

Revs. J. Baltzer, D.D., A. H. Becker, D.D., G. Fischer, Tim. Lehmann, Paul Crosius, Prof. J. C. Keppel, J. H. Horstmann, H. F. Klemme, J. P.

Meyer, L. Goebel, H. Niefer, S. D. Press, D.D., H. R. Niebuhr, Ph.D., C. W. Locher.

The following were excused:

Revs. H. Bode, D. Bruning, Reinh. Niebuhr, P. A. Menzel, D.D.—

The President General, Rev. J. Baltzer, D.D., spoke a word of greeting and welcome and explained in short the kind and necessity of the meeting. After this he presented the following:

Agenda

For committee on creedal statement and relation to other communions.

1. *Whom are we formulating a creedal statement or expression for?* For ourselves, or others; or for us, and others?

* * * *

2. Where do we stand?

(a) Our present creedal statement depends our standing in the Universal Church and among kindred unions.

(b) It defines the biblical background for the organization, our conception of the Bible, the Word of God.

(c) It states the criterion for the interpretation of the Word of God with reference to historical documents of the 16th century.

(c) It declares freedom of conscience.

* * * *

3. Is our present creedal statement comprehensive or insufficient?

It may be termed not comprehensive,—

(a) Because it says not one word about the personal center of the Christian faith, the living Christ.

(b) Because its historical reference is not inclusive, but rather exclusive and not understandable to the laity, and therefore it is useless. (It says nothing about the coming of Christ.)

(c) Because it does not reflect present days seeking and searching after the central truth of Christian religion.

(d) Because it lacks clarity of statement.

* * * *

4. With the permission of the author, I herewith present a creedal statement which may be the basis of our discussion and for the formulating of a new version, or an explanatory statement.

– Confession –

The Evangelical Synod of N. A. confesses the living Christ as the dominant factor in Christian living without Whom there can be no salvation.

It accepts the Holy Scriptures of the New and Old Testament containing the historical record of Christ's coming and message, as the ultimate standard, by which the individual experience of the living Christ be measured.

It accepts the great creeds of the early church as the earliest and fundamental expression of the faith experience of the church.

As a daughter of the great Reformation of the sixteenth century, it recognizes its spiritual indebtedness to the two great branches of the Reformation, the Lutheran and the Reformed, as having shaped the evangelical expression of the Christian truths.

Seeking to keep the unity of the spirit in the bond of peace, it accords liberty of conscience for that individual interpretation of the churches compatible with the saviourship of Christ and the authority of the Scripture. Its motto is: "In essentials unity, in non-essentials liberty, in all things charity."

* * * *

5. Place of the Synod's creedal statement. Shall we leave it in the Constitution or take it out and place it at the head of the By-Laws or make it a special section with special ruling by the legislative body—or incorporate it in the Book of Worship—The Catechism or Song Book?

* * * *

6. Shall we encourage ventilation of problem in articles for the magazine or in papers for conference discussions?

* * * *

Part II
Relation to Other Communions
Unity of the Spirit in the Bond of Peace

1. Friendly and brotherly meeting with clergy and laity of other communions.

2. Exchange of pulpits with other communions.

3. Visitation of conferences and Synods of other communions.

4. A historical sketch of our creedal statements with a friendly word of introduction to kindred communions.

   Special letter of invitation to conferences on unity of the spirit and work, or on faith and work, or on faith and order between the Reformed, the Methodist, the Moravian Brethren and Congregationalists (German) of Central European extraction.

It was resolved, to take first the question of the creedal statement.—Then Reverend H. Niefer offered the following "Confessional Proposal":

> The Evangelical Synod of N. A. confesses Jesus Christ, the son of God, as the highest revelation of the essence and the will of God and as the sole mediator between God and man in whom our salvation is grounded.
>
> It confesses the Holy Scriptures of the New and the Old Testament as the God given witness to the divine revelation of salvation.
>
> As a protestant church, it is grounded in the reformation confessions, not in the sense of legalistic or literal adherence, but in the sense of treasuring the divine reality and eternal truth which has found its historical expression in them.
>
> It is in spiritual communion with and is prepared to cooperate with all Christian churches which share this foundation.

* * * *

This "Confessional Proposal" came now into discussion. Reverend J. H. Horstmann offered the following addition to insert on the end of section 3, after "historical expression in them": "In the spirit of holy scripture and protestant development it seeks to establish and extend the Kingdom of God on earth in spiritual inwardness and evangelical freedom."

The following suggestions were made:

1. By Dr. H. R. Niebuhr:
   It seeks to realize the mind of Christ in individual and social relationships—the kingdom of God on earth.

2. By Dr. A. H. Becker:
   In the spirit of Christ and in obedience to His command she labors to bring about the application of Christ's principles in all human relationships.

3. By Rev. J. P. MEYER:
   Following Jesus Christ and in the spirit of Holy Scripture it seeks to realize the Kingdom of God on earth, in both its ideal spiritual and its concrete social form.

Rev. NIEBUHR was asked to embody the ideas that came out in our discussion in the "Confessional Proposal" and to translate the whole matter in English.

The following recommendations of Dr. H. R. NIEBUHR were adopted: The advisory committee recommends that:—

1. The creed should be formulated on the basis of the Evangelical Protestant unity, not distinctions.
2. It should be a general statement, a guide to rather than a rule of faith, setting forth the continuity of our belief with the past.
3. We recommend the draft submitted by Rev. NIEBUHR as a basis for the further work of the commission with the addition of a positive reference to the ethical and social demands of our faith.
4. If a more detailed exposition of our faith is necessary for educational purposes it should be set forth in connection with some educational test of the Synod.

Reverend H. NIEFER was requested to write an article for the Theological Magazine concerning our creedal standpoint.

The meeting took then up the second part of the Agenda: RELATION TO OTHER COMMUNIONS:

RESOLVED to present the articles 1–4 to the commission on relation which will be appointed by the President General:—reading as follows:

1. Friendly and brotherly meeting with clergy and laity of other communions.
2. Exchange of pulpits with other communions.
3. Visitation of conferences and Synods of other communions.
4. A historical sketch of our creedal statements with a friendly word of introduction to kindred communions.

   Special letter of invitation to conference on unity of the spirit and work, or on faith and order between the Reformed, the Methodists, the Moravian Brethren and Congregationalists (German) of Central European extraction.

Dr. H. R. NIEBUHR reported about the intentions of the German Congregationalists (136 churches and 21,000 members) to unite the educational work of the German Congregationalists (Redfield College in Dakota), with Elmhurst and Eden.

Dr. BALTZER read a letter (written to Dr. Vollmer) of the Secretary of the Reformed Church in the U.S. concerning a union of both church bodies, and Rev. J. H. HORSTMANN read a paper of information giving in somewhat the history of the Reformed Church, also giving some statistical facts. Dr. Baltzer announced that he will appoint a committee to take up communications with the Reformed Church.

At 5 P.M. the meeting adjourned with prayer offered by Reverend TIM. LEHMANN.

C. FISCHER, Sec.

64. THE CASE FOR UNION:

"The Evangelical Synod and Church Union"

(1928)

CARL E. SCHNEIDER

In 1927 the Evangelical Synod Commission on Relations with Other Churches decided to pursue closer relations—"even union"—with the Reformed Church in the U.S. Many people in local Evangelical congregations were not enthusiastic about this possibility, preferring to keep their ecumenical identity connected with their early history as a bridge between Lutheran and Reformed camps.

Carl E. Schneider, a professor at Eden Theological Seminary, grew up in the Evangelical Synod and was already deeply involved in research for his 1939 history of the denomination's beginnings, The German Church on the American Frontier. *He understood why German Evangelical people took great pride in their irenic history of "union spirit" and service, and why they were reluctant to cast their lot with a Reformed denomination.*

Schneider, however, made the case for union with the Reformed Church in the U.S. He sketched out a theory about the way denominations rise up within the church universal to meet a specific need of the times. He described the denominational pride that naturally develops, but noted that it can run the danger of locking people into the old ways and keeping them from moving forward. Schneider reassured the Evangelicals. There is still a "genius for unity" present in the Evangelical Synod as there had always been. But now there was talk of union with the Reformed Church.

SOURCE: Carl E. Schneider, "The Evangelical Synod and Church Union," *Theological Magazine of the Evangelical Synod of North America* 56 (September 1928): 321–33.

Could it be, he asked, that this was the direction in which their acclaimed "genius for unity" was pointing them now? He urged Evangelical church members to inform themselves about the proposed union so that their decision would not be based on ignorance or prejudice. Perhaps there were "brothers" behind the eyes of these Reformed people, he mused. It was important to look carefully!

Schneider was a master at ecumenical persuasion. He spelled out the reasons Evangelicals had to be proud of their history, and then gently led them to consider whether that very history and identity now required them to enlarge their self-understanding to include "their brother" in the Reformed Church.

I. The Church of Christ Is the Organism in Which Christ's Spirit Resides and Effects a Unity Between All Its Members

Any consideration of Church union, whether it involves the union of numerous denominations or merely the merging of a few must make the distinction between the spiritual invisible organism of the Church and the physical, visible organization into denominational forms.

Primarily Jesus did not found an external institution. Jesus dealt more in principles than in precise programs. Throughout his ministry he pronounced the message and cared little for the mechanics. That, around which modern denominations revolve seek their right of existence—doctrine, organization, worship—was of little significance for Jesus. Certainly Jesus did not require creedal subscription or a finished theology in order to enter into the Kingdom of God. Nor did Jesus demand that members of the Church assume a definite form of external organization among themselves. He rather emphasized that the relations of the members to each other be on the basis of the Sermon on the Mount. Members of the Kingdom are not to be as deacons, elders or bishops but as little children.

And thus, in all this, the Church of Christ is primarily revealed as a qualitative entity. Beneath the historical, quantitative present-day sociological structure we perceive the qualitative functioning of free individuals constituting a spiritual unity by the binding power of an inner organizing energy. A reference to merely historical data for the explanation of the nature and the function of the Church is inadequate. We are confronted in the Church with a mystery the solution of which lies quite beyond any rationalization on our part. It is a spiritual mystery as marriage itself and it is not surprising, therefore, that Paul should speak of the Church as the Bride of Christ. Again he refers to it as the Body of Christ, the Heavenly City, the New Jerusalem, the Communion of Saints. The Church which Christ founded "was a family, with God as a common Father, its bond of union was that of a spiritual kinship, cemented by an affection, where obedience was obtained by personal and fraternal admonitions, counsel and persuasion. Its membership were 'brethren,' 'sons of God,' 'children of God' and they constituted 'the household of faith.' "[1]

In this sense the Church is a spiritual organism in which, by the common faith of its members, all believers, regardless of denominational affiliation, are bound together in the invisible Church through the bond of the Spirit. Although such a unity is invisible yet from the very beginning the Christians testified to their experience of "the holy catholic Church," and even as more definitely in the Nicene Creed we read "I believe in *one* holy catholic and apostolic Church." Jesus in his prayer that all may be one, certainly had in mind first of all this vital unity in the Spirit based on a common love and loyalty and purpose.

This has been the tacit position of Lutheran groups to the question of church union. Here, where the emphasis was placed on the faith-life of the individual which binds all believers together into the invisible Church, the whole question of church union becomes an anomaly for according to this view, "the united church already exists."[2] And indeed, the Lutheran position needs to be properly appreciated. There is such a thing as the invisible Church of the believers. Perhaps the outstanding Lutheran contribution to the religious life of the day consists in emphasizing the world of spiritual values which Luther summed up in the word "Faith" in the sense of "trust" or "fiducia." From this viewpoint the German scholar Sohm made an incisive indictment of the institutionalization of the Church, devoting his scholarly work on "Kirchenrecht" to the thesis that church law and church organization are inherently opposed to the essential nature of the Church. The Church of Christ represents the organism in which his Spirit resides and effects a unity between all its members. The genius of the Church lies in the nature of its spiritual organism and not in any attainment or efficiency of secular organization.

II. Denominations Are the Historical Expression of This Spiritual Organism of the Body of Christ Endeavoring to Meet the Particular Needs of Peculiar Situations

It is impossible, however, to remain standing on this proposition. An advance, or rather as some may claim, a retreat has taken place from the lofty position occupied by Jesus in the founding of his Church. The Church, beginning under the impetus of the staggering, spiritual personality of Jesus, when the immediacy of that spiritual presence disappeared, began to assume organizational forms. Denominational bodies were called into existence by the need to meet altered historical situations. We are confronted by the fact that the "idea" with which we begin wears off into an organization.

Such a process of development is not at all unique. It is the common experience in historical growth. The "idea" always comes first. The history of the world and of the church tells the romantic story of how sociological formations are the product of mental images and spiritual ideas. The question of whether it was inevitable that the "idea" of Jesus should materialize into a visible church and become institutionalized has been variously argued. Indeed it seems to lie in the logical course of sociological developments that individuals, imbued with the same loyalties and the same driving ideas, will inevitably band themselves into corporate groups in order the better to express themselves and propagate their ideas.

Already in the life time of Jesus the diversity of interpretation begins. The Apostolic church was denominationally divided into Gentile and Jewish Christians, the Corinthian church was divided into theological factions identifying themselves with their selected leaders Paul or Appollos or Cephas or Christ.[3] Similar divisions continued throughout the Middle Ages, strenuously combated by the Roman Church, but by their very existence testifying to the flexibility and plasticity of the Christian idea.

It is an unreasoned procedure, from our modern point of view, in *a priori* fashion to condemn the rise of denominations. We may see something beautiful in the spectacle the seed of the Kingdom shooting forth into many denominational branches. A strong historical defense may be urged for the rise of denominations. The freedom of the children of God is not to be curbed by artificial boundaries but is assured by the possibility of unfettered historical development.

The origins of the great denominations of today are not to be traced to foolish eccentricities of strangely-minded and half-souled man. They are rather the products of burning religious fires in the hearts of spiritually minded men who were strong enough to transcend the bound of tradition and convention and to step forth into a realm of the new and hitherto unexplored. Sometimes they met with rebuff and persecution. The little group at Scrooby, England which took its heroic stand against the popery of the Established Church was forced to leave the homeland and finally landing at Plymouth became the forerunners of American Congregationalism. Fourteen miles from Scrooby, in the town of Epworth, was born John Wesley, who, in an age when the church had become institutionalized, morally decadent and spiritually cold was destined to inaugurate a worldwide movement which recognized anew the power of Christianity as an internal force, manifesting itself in holiness of life and the immediate presence of the Spirit. Thus Methodism was born. In a day when liberty of conscience was suppressed, when state and church exerted unwarranted authority over individuals the Baptist principles of religious liberty, regenerate church membership and believers' baptism sprang into existence. In the early part of the 19th century when Reformed and Lutherans were viciously opposing each other in Germany the time was fulfilled for Frederick William III, to attempt to unite the two contending groups into what became known as the Church of the Evangelical Union. And when in the year 1840 a group of German Evangelical pastors, accidentally as it were, discovered themselves engaged in the similar task of ministering to the needs of the spiritually destitute German immigrants on the Missouri frontier, what more expedient step could they take than to band themselves together for the better performance of these tasks! And there resulted from this meeting in the little log-house parsonage at Gravois Settlement Missouri, on October 15th, 1840 "Kirchen-Verein des Westens"—later to develop into the Evangelical Synod of America.

We are tempted to lament the existence of many denominations. Yet such diversity in itself need not destroy the unity of the spirit. Existing side by side, they represent sincere and honest attempts to give expression to spiritual values which historically it has been their lot to receive, and which in a rather accidental manner in each case has taken on its own individual forms. Indeed it is just the unity of the spirit which tolerates and welcomes such a diversity for it honors the head, which is Christ.

III. The Unity of the Church of Christ Becomes Lost When Churches Insist on Retaining Their Denominational Forms When the Spiritual Need Therefore No Longer Exists

We have just maintained that denominations as such need not be considered an evil for they may testify to the working of the Spirit of God in the hearts of men. The shame of Protestantism does not lie in the diversity of its denominational forms. These are the product of the free historical development which is the genius of Protestantism. Such diversity may not be essentially incompatible with the spirit which binds all together. Indeed for the attainment of the unity of the fold it is not necessary to effect a uniformity of organization. There was less real unity of the spirit in the imposing unified structure of the medieval Catholic Church than may be found among smaller denominational bodies of our day who by some peculiar quirk of history are carrying on their separate existences perhaps unknown to each other.

And yet, although denominations may be the product of the Spirit, it is possible for them to develop in such a manner as to disturb the unity of the Church of Christ. Although the spiritual needs which called many of our denominations into existence no longer prevail, these selfsame denominations, riding on the high tide of the momentum of their glorious past and revered traditions, continue to nurture their ancient historical forms. Loyalty to the denomination is confused with loyalty to Christ. Is there a spiritual need for the Presbyterians, Methodists and Baptists to continue their north and south division on an issue which was settled more all 50 years ago? We are told that, "In one of the smaller cities of the Atlantic coast stand two Presbyterian churches facing each other, upon opposite sides of the street. They are the result of a division that occurred in one of them almost two generations ago because a portion of the congregation held to a 'mediate atonement' and the other to an 'immediate atonement,' distinctions which few Christians today would understand without recourse to a theological dictionary. At the beginning of the 18th century the Baptists of Delaware withdrew from fellowship with the Baptists of Philadelphia because the latter did not 'hold to the laying on of hands.' "[4] Or is there any valid justification for some Presbyterians of today to divide on the question of whether hymns *and* psalms should be sung or only psalms?

The long continued denominational inbreeding process tends to establish denominational loyalties apart from spiritual motives and values. All too frequently a kind of denominational chauvinism develops which frequently becomes obnoxiously manifest in others long before we discern it in ourselves. Ashworth suggests that the lukewarmness and indifference toward the whole subject of church union is frequently caused by the "fear of denominational sheriffs and editors and officials who are constantly occupied in keeping the denominational fences in repair."[5] Thus it has come to such a ludicrous pass that, "Neither Presbyterians, Methodist nor Baptists could ordain Martin Luther to the ministry if he were living. He could not so much as be made an elder or deacon in the Presbyterian church. And yet he is the father of Protestantism. Carey, Wesley, Spurgeon and hosts of the best ministers the world ever had, could find a place in but few of our denominations."[6] Alexander Campbell one of the earliest exponents of church unity in America should have said: "This plan of making our own nests and fluttering over our own brood; of building our own tents and of confining all goodness and grace to our noble selves and to the elect few who are like us, is the quintessence of sublimated Pharisaism. . . . To lock ourselves up in the bandbox of our own circle, to associate with a few units, tens or hundreds, as the pure church, as the elect, is real Protestant monkery—is evangelical Pharisaism."[7]

Indeed such an attitude is more than Pharisaism it is schismatic. Any Church which by its spiritual ministry does not at the same time challenge the validity of its purely temporal existence and is not willing to sacrifice its traditions and deny itself for the sake of the Kingdom of God and the greater unity of the invisible Church of which it is a part, any such church is, spiritually speaking, schismatic for it has fallen away from the ideals of the spiritual organism, the unity of which only theoretically or sentimentally it professes. "What right," asks Merrill, "has a 'denomination' to exist? Only as a serious attempt to realize the universal church of Christ. For any branch of the Church to hold as essential anything it does not consider essential to the universal church is a crime. It is insubordination toward Jesus Christ, the One Great Head of the Church."[8] This is the denominational schism of standing apart from the unity of the "one Lord, one faith, one baptism, one God and Father of all who is over all, and through all, and in all."[9] Such considerations as these, perhaps, led Bishop Anderson of Chicago to claim that in order to create the atmosphere in which unity shall thrive, "we must first confess the sin of schism—the sin, I say, not simply its economic disadvantage, its short-sighted policy, its unstatesmanlike methods, its unstrategic warfare with the world, but its sin."[10]

And so we repeat, the shame of Protestantism lies not in the diversity of its varied denominational forms, but in the reluctance to surrender these forms for the sake of the transcending spiritual values of the Church Universal.

It may be a comparatively simple matter to accept the principles discussed above. It is immeasurably more difficult to commit ourselves to some of the correlaries, especially if we should apply the principles to our own denomination. What attitude ought our denomination take with regard to church union? As is frequently the case in other matters, the theory of church union is far in advance of the reality. We may accept the theory in the abstract but find ourselves confronted by innumerable prejudices and seemingly insuperable difficulties when we begin to consider possible ways of procedure. Perhaps we find ourselves in the plight of Charles Lamb who, when asked by a friend if he was musical, replied "Sentimentally I am disposed to harmony, but organically I am incapable of a tune." We are all theoretically disposed to harmony. Just how incapable are we of a tune? Bearing in mind the distinction between the concepts of unity and union we may at least attempt to express our position in the form of several principles bearing respectively on these two points.

IV. The Evangelical Synod, True to the Ideals Which It Professes as a Member of the Body of Christ, in the Light of Its Historical Origin and Subsequent Development, Is Committed to the Principle of Church Unity

First of all then the Evangelical Synod is in accord with the Principle of Church Unity. We are a church which is full of the unity spirit. It is significant that as a motto we accept the Ephesian statement "giving diligence to keep the unity of the Spirit in the bond of peace." [11] The origin of our Synod is not found in any factional division within a previously existing body from which we split off. We do not represent a divergence from another church. Rather, in the light of our European background, we came into existence through the effort to unite two already diverging bodies whose organizational forms were at variance with each other. This merging was proposed on the assumption that the existing spiritual unity justified such a Union. The Union Church of Germany, called into existence in 1817 to bridge the yawning gap between the Reformed and Lutheran branches, was designed to comprehend the strengths of each and to issue liberty to both branches. There was not to be even so much as uniformness in doctrines and organization. The emphasis was placed upon the inner unity of the spirit which was thought to obtain between churches so organically akin to each other. In this respect we are a *unity* church perhaps more than a union church and therefore the ideals of spiritual unity should be close to our hearts and understanding. Indeed ours is not the problem of affecting a *return* or a *reunion* to some body from which we separated many years ago. Rather we were born under the auspices of the "will to unity" which, if truly genuine, will of innate necessity lead beyond the mere theory to visible expression.

Again, if we consider the American origin of our church in 1840 we shall find the same unmistakable evidence of the "will to unity." In the early decades of the 19th century German immigrants began to flood into the Mississippi Valley, colonizing in St. Louis and vicinity. Here were accumulated Germans of all classes and of all religious and irreligious complexions. It soon became evident that they were wantonly spiritually destitute. Who would care for their needs? To make short a long though exceedingly interesting story we find a number of German pastors, we know them by name and from memory, Nollau of Barmen, Riess, Gerber, Wall and Rieger of Basel, Heyer of the Rhein Society, Garlichs and Daubert ministering to these people mainly under the auspices of the Basel and Barmen mission societies. Accidentally, as it were, they discovered each other in their common task and organized into a society of pastors devoted to the cause of building the Kingdom of God. They were not interested in the founding of a new denomination but were led by the unity of their common spiritual interests to band themselves together. They believed more in making Christians than in persuading people to become members of the "Kirchen-verein." They were Kingdom-minded men and had nothing of the furor of denominationalism. Theirs was an irenic spirit, manifested in long continued relations with other church bodies. Fraternal delegates were exchanged at conferences with Presbyterians and other Eastern synods. We know particularly of the presence of a Rev. David Dimond of the Presbyterian Synod of Missouri at the Holstein Conference of 1850, and of his commendatory remark concerning German theological learning. We recall how the Marthasville Seminary was supported by members of other denominations. Gifts were received from "Yankee" men and women such as from Mrs. Webb's "Infant Sabbath School," and a Mr. Van Buren, a Mr. Urben, Mr. Scarrit. Particularly do we think of the relations maintained with Christian friends of the East, the Mr. R. Biglow of Hartford, Connecticut and the "Society for the Promotion of Collegiate and Theological Education in the West," which supported our struggling Seminary at Marthasville with notable gifts of money.

The genius for unity existing in the early days of our church is plainly evident. Our church fathers stood on a platform large enough to accommodate all denominations so long as they were interested in building the Kingdom of God in the spirit of Jesus the Christ. It is hazardous to argue against church union by reference to the traditions of our past and by claiming that to effect a closer union with some other church body would be contrary to the spirit of the founders of our church. Perhaps our eyes would be opened if we could interview some of these selfsame church fathers and have them tell us that they were never interested in the continued existence of the "Kirchen-verein" to the extent that a rapprochement with other bodies should be avoided. These men could join hands with men of diverse convictions. The Augustinian phrase was more than a mere abstraction to them. They themselves breathed the spirit of "In necessariis unitas, in dubiis libertas, in omnibus caritas." Indeed here, we find the noblest heritage which has come down to us from a glorious past. And being true to that condition, we find ourselves committed to the principle of unity.

V. The Evangelical Synod Committed to the Principle of Church Unity, Must Seriously Consider How the Logical and Spiritual Consummation of This Principle May Affect Its Independent Denominational Existence

In considering this proposition we may first of all raise the question of whether in last years and decades we have remained true to the best unity traditions, or whether we have not trended toward a denominationalism which does violence to this heritage of ours. So long as we were content to nurture unity ideals and labor for Kingdom causes, questions of doctrinal position and organization were shifted into the background.

However, as we grew larger in numbers and as we came to rub up against other closely organized denominations we were inevitably forced to answer such questions as, "Who are you?" "Why do you exist?" "What do you want?" "Where do you stand?" "Where are you going?" We were forced to probe into the question as to whether our church had outlived its right of existence. The German immigrant had ceased to come. Increasingly it became apparent that the reasons which underlay our origin would not longer sanction our present existence. Conditions of a new day seemed to require that we build new foundations. The literally spiritual position which in times past was our pride has recently come to be regarded as a liability. What we need today, some would claim, is a closely knitted creedal statement so that every one may know where we stand and on the basis of which it would be possible to conduct an intelligent promotional campaign, inspire loyalties and devotion and grow larger and stronger.

The same line of argument is followed in the field of organization. We are witnessing a development in our church which is moving from the spiritual basis to that of physical organization and which may involve the surrender of a spiritual principle for an organizational advance. Certainly we sense the danger of it. The very fact that recently under the auspices of the "Forward Movement" and through other channels a vigorous effort was made to place spiritual things first through the organization of committees for the deepening of spiritual life—I say this very fact showed that we sensed the danger lying in the trend toward organization and made attempts to overcome it.

However, in the light of our past we seem essentially to be more of a movement than an organization. As a movement we are seemingly in danger of being submerged by other more highly organized church bodies. In self-defense we have at times quite deliberately resorted to expansion programs and Forward movements. The "will to unity" which is indifferent to organizational niceties is capitulating to the "will to organize." With pride we consider our accomplishments, the New Eden, Foreign Missions, Home Mission, etc. In past years there have been sporadic demonstrations of brilliance so that other denominations seem to have sat up and taken notice. The vision rises in the minds of some of us that the future of our church is glorious with the promise of becoming a large and influential denomination which may take an honorable place in the councils of American Church bodies.

And yet, the virile strength of our church does not lie in this direction. The most distinctive thing about us is that we have no distinctive organizational or doctrinal features and that our strength lies in just that spiritual point of view which gave us birth as the Union Church in Germany and as the nonsectarian, interdenominationally minded "Kirchen-Verein des Westens" in 1840. We are so committed to the Spirit of Unity that we can best save our souls not by deflecting into the byways of denominationalism but by seriously endeavoring to follow through to the logical and spiritual consummation of these Kingdom principles, regardless of whither they may lead, and however they may affect our continued independent denominational existence.

Are we strong enough to draw the final conclusions? Surely we are agreed at least to the principle that the only justification for our denominational existence is the unsullied committal to the spiritual ideals of the Kingdom of God. The more this ideal is attained the less important does the continuance of our denominational existence become. We find ourselves confronted by the paradox of all spiritual values—that by the losing of life we gain it.

We have dealt with this subject rather abstractly from the point of view of principles. To visualize what we have in mind let us suppose that somewhere in the United States there existed a denomination which from almost every point of view is akin to us. Historically its roots run back into Germany and its pastors and members came from practically the same sections as ours and possess the same general racial memories having immigrated to this country under the same general conditions. In organization they may differ and in doctrinal standards they may not be identical but in their spiritual temper and religious zeal, in their theological trends and ethical ideals they coincide with us. Here we may find a type of preacher and congregation which represents the best of our hopes and expectations. In other words, we here discover a spiritual brother. Would it not be a tragedy if somewhere in the United States such a church should exist and continue to exist apart from any closer fraternal relations with us!

This is largely a hypothetical case. There are some who may say that such a church is found in the United Brethren, others will say it is a Lutheran church, others the Reformed. And indeed we need not immediately press the argument to fit the concrete case. First let us clear our minds with regard to the principle involved. Being committed to the principle of church unity we must seriously consider how the logical and spiritual consummation of this principle may lead to important readjustments in our denominational affairs, and may eventually require the dissolution of our present denominational forms.

This may not require merging to the extent that we dissolve or annihilate ourselves. Unity leads inevitably to union but it does not require uniformity. The unity of the fold is not discernable in the uniform sameness of the individual sheep, for physically they differ much from each other. The unity of the fold lies in the attitude toward the shepherd. May we not live in the hope that somewhere and sometime we may find a kindred group with whom we are so compatible that creedal distinctions become unimportant in view of the great spiritual consensus which unites. It is safe to suppose that any plan of union which may eventually be proposed which may bring us into closer relations with some denominational affinity, can never be founded on the basis of uniformity. Unity in variety and diversity must prevail. By analogy we think of the union which is found in the orchestra where it is not required that all instruments be alike. Indeed they must be distinctive and yet together effect a unison.

Such a unison based on love, and affection cannot be effected by blueprint methods but will develop spontaneously as we permit the Spirit of Jesus to become operative in our lives. As someone has said: "We do not want unity by machinery any more than we want truth by machinery or prayers by machinery."[12] Church Union will then result not so much from our acts nor will it be an act. It will rather manifest itself in the functioning of the Church and Churches and proceed from within—out. Without affection there can be no happy, lasting marriage. Love, the essence of religion, will alone be the basis of Church Union.

There is a legend in the Talmud of two brothers who owned in common a field upon the site of which King Solomon later built the first Temple at Jerusalem. One night, so the story runs, the younger of the brothers said, "My brother has a wife and children to support while I have no one to care for but myself. I will go into the harvest field and take some of the sheaves of grain that fall to me and put them with my brother's sheaves without his knowledge that he may have sufficient to provide for those he loves." On the same night the other brother thought, "God has blessed me with wife and children, while my brother lives alone. I will arise and take of my shocks of grain and lay them with my brother's share that he may be comforted in his loneliness." Thus, in the morning, to their surprise, each found his share undiminished. The next night each repeated his kind deed and with the same result. On the third night both brothers determined to watch, and, to their mutual surprise, they met in the middle of the field, each laden with his golden sheaves. And God said of the spot where they embraced, "This is the holiest spot I know: here I will build my holy Temple."[13] May the day soon come when denominations will thus discover themselves.

What should we do about it? A union with the Reformed Church is now being espoused in some circles. Meditate upon it and think it through as best we can. We all desire more information and without more knowledge our sentiment and feelings are apt to run riot. Certainly let no preconceived ideas prejudice us before we become better acquainted with what may be involved. Church union is not a manufactured product nor is it to be attained by a program of doctrine or organization. Church union is usually the consummation of a long period of development marked by various stages. Again the Talmud says "Walking on the mountain one day I saw a form which I took to be a beast; coming nearer I saw it was a man, approaching nearer still I found it was my brother." Let us take some definite and active steps whereby we may come nearer to and better understand the genius of the Reformed church. Now from the distance there may be nothing attractive in this vision, perhaps next year some of the objections may be removed and perhaps in the years and years to come gradually, step by step we may learn to so know and appreciate each other that our final verdict may be "This is my brother."

Notes

1. Sims, What must the Church do to be Saved? p. 117.
2. Brent (Editor), Can the churches unite? p. 193.
3. 1 Cor. 1:12.
4. Ashworth, The Unicorn of Christian Forces p. 68.
5. Ashworth, Ibid p. 65
6. Sims, Ibid p. 97.
7. Brent, Ibid p. 15.
8. Brent, Ibid p. 40.
9. Eph. 4:5.
10. Brent, Ibid p. 212.
11. Eph. 4:3.
12. Brent, Ibid p. 168.
13. Quoted by Ashworth, Ibid p. 98.

The Formation of the Evangelical and Reformed Church

65. Why the Reformed Church?

"In Rebuttal"

(1919)

Reinhold Niebuhr

Holding discussions about the possibility of union, or even raising the question as to whether such discussions should be held, invariably raises questions of identity and self-understanding. Whichever way the union issue is solved, denominations always emerge from such discussions clearer about what they have been and what they want to be.

In 1919, an interesting discussion appeared in the German Evangelical Magazin für Evangelische Theologie und Kirche. *The first article was written by Reinhold Niebuhr, who, after hearing of the merger of several Lutheran denominations into one United Lutheran Church and participating in the first "Conference on Organic Union" (see vol. 6:13, 57), wrote an article entitled "Where Shall We Go?" (see vol. 4:61). In that article he asked, What should the Evangelical Synod do? Denominations all around them were uniting in "family reunions," overcoming historic divisions. Niebuhr wondered, Should they stay as they were, proud of their history and tradition but an increasingly negligible force on the denominational scene, or should they unite with one of the larger denominational groups where they had historic ties? They needed to choose between the Lutherans and the Calvinists.*

Niebuhr was convinced that the Evangelicals would never be accepted

---

Source: Reinhold Niebuhr, "In Rebuttal," *Magazin für Evangelische Theologie und Kirche,* n.s., vol. 21, no. 1 (January 1919): 270–71.

into any Lutheran coalition without becoming totally Lutheran, which would mean being forced to give up their distinctive "union" identity. Therefore, he argued that the wisest thing for them to do was to unite with the Calvinists.

Not surprisingly, some people were outraged at this idea. W. F. Henninger wrote in response, trying to counter Niebuhr's position (summarized rather crudely as trying to "kill the Synod") point by point. He was convinced that the Evangelical Synod should stay as it was (see vol. 4:62).

Although most church members in the Evangelical Synod were probably more sympathetic to Henninger, Niebuhr wrote a rebuttal, calling attention to the "specious reasoning" of his attacker. The debate ceased at that point, but eight years later it erupted again (see vol. 6:66).

To the Editor:

With a good deal of interest I have read the answer to my question "Where Shall We Go?" in the form of a counter question "Why Go at All?" in the May issue of your magazine. I have no wish to prolong the argument indefinitely but I think you owe me a few words in the columns of your journal to call the attention of your readers to some very specious reasoning on the part of my opponent.

An attempt is made to refute my statement that we are a small denomination by pointing to the fact that we are 15th in a list of 165 denominations. The writer fails to say however that there are fifteen times as many communicants in the 14 denominations that are larger than we than in the 150 that are smaller. You can do anything with statistics. We are a small denomination. We need no statistical evidence for that. Every one of us actually engaged in the work of our church meets constant proof of our numerical weakness. If any more proof is needed than that which every one has at hand we might point to the fact that we do not even consider ourselves large enough to maintain adequate educational facilities for our young men and women. We are going to get a junior college now but my disillusioned and discouraged opinion is that it will be twenty years before we have a real A. B. college.

A similar attempt is made to refute my assertion that small denominations are disappearing. Again statistics are dragged in and evidence presented that in the past ten years small denominations have not decreased. That is all beside the point. The whole point of my argument rested upon the fact that in the past few months union movements, particularly family reunion movements, have been launched that bid fair to eliminate small denominations. What happened in the past ten years has nothing to do with the facts which we are facing now.

The writer of the article under consideration did me the favor of proving my contention that most of the pastors of our church regard only the Lutheran-Calvinistic division of Protestantism as legitimate, by going to great lengths to establish that all Protestant denominations have an element of either Lutheran or Calvinistic theology. What of that? A baptist might just as well point out that all churches are either immersionists or sprinklers and conclude from that that the question of the mode of baptism is the one fundamental one in protestantism. To what impossible conclusions such reasoning leads may be seen by the fact that it betrays the writer to describe Methodism as Calvinistic. Methodism, as everyone ought to know, is Arminian and not Calvinistic and the question of free will which divides Arminianism and Calvinism may be regarded as just as fundamental as the differences of opinion between Lutheran and Calvinistic theology. Precisely because we fail to have any sympathy for these other differences are we not fitted to play the role of mediator between many of the American denominations.

My final remarks in regard to confirmation were so completely misunderstood by Brother Henninger that one is persuaded that he did not try very hard to get their meaning. If there is anything in our Evangelical polity that I believe in it is confirmation, and I made the statement that we could never afford to part with the fundamental idea of confirmation which is that a Christian child need *not be converted* but should grow gradually into Christian convictions and decisions. I did assert however that confirmation should encourage spontaneous decisions for Christ and that the traditional way of conducting confirmation classes and confirmation rites did not provide for or encourage this element of spontaneity. From what Brother Henninger says about conversion one would judge that he does not believe in conversions at all. If he does not I can not help but call his attention to the fact that he is doubting a fundamental Christian and Biblical fact. If there is no such thing as conversion then all our preaching is vain. Just because we may not believe that violent and cataclysmic conversions are normal methods for children to enter the kingdom of God we ought not to permit ourselves to deny a fundamental religious fact. Incidentally it might also be observed that if all conversions do not prove "water tight" neither do all confirmations. Will Brother Henninger tell us whether fifty per cent of all young men and women he has confirmed in the past ten years are active church members? If they are he is more fortunate than most of us. In the past ten years we have confirmed more young men and women than the entire number of our active church members. That does not discredit confirmation in itself but it ought to teach us to be a little modest and refrain from adopting an air of superiority when reviewing religious methods other than our own.

R. Niebuhr

66. Which Partner Is Best?

"Letter," "Will It Be Luther or Calvin?" "Why Go, Why Not Stay?" and "Church Union"

(1928)

Reinhold Niebuhr; H. Kamphausen; Peter the Hermit; and H. L. Streich

Eight years after Reinhold Niebuhr raised the question of whether the Evangelical Synod ought to seek church union with the Lutherans or the Calvinists (see vol. 4:61–62; 6:68) he raised the issue again in a letter to the editor in the (by that time) English-language Theological Magazine of the Evangelical Synod of North America. *This time, readers were ready to entertain his question more seriously.*

Omitting the obligatory look backward to what the Evangelical Synod had come from and how it had historically understood itself, Niebuhr came right to the point. A 1918 merger of the Lutheran denominations had generated an "illiberal spirit." Now the only group remaining with which the Evangelical Synod had a common heritage was the Reformed Church in the U.S. (no longer referred to as "the Calvinists"). In fact, Niebuhr argued, so little still divided these two denominations that there was no justification for separate establishments. The union of the Evangelical Synod of North America with the Reformed Church in the U.S. would create a denomination of some six hundred thousand communicants to carry on common missionary and educational tasks, and union would bring fresh life and inspiration to both parties. Niebuhr asked if the

---

Source: Reinhold Niebuhr, "Letter to the Editor," *Theological Magazine of the Evangelical Synod of North America* 56, no. 1 (January 1928): 49–50; H. Kamphausen, "Will It Be Luther or Calvin?" ibid., vol. 56, no. 2 (March 1928): 131–33; Peter the Hermit, "Why Go, Why Not Stay?" ibid., vol. 56, no. 3 (May 1928): 189–90; H. L. Streich, "Church Union," ibid., vol. 56, no. 3 (May 1928): 297–300.

present temper of the Evangelical Synod was more congenial to this idea than it had been in 1919.

A somewhat guarded editorial by H. Kamphausen followed. It pointed out that significant changes had occurred in the Evangelical Synod since the first round of discussions in 1919: the synod had become a largely English-speaking body and had sought and found a place in contemporary Protestantism. Indeed, it seemed that the gaze of the synod had turned forward instead of backward. Younger people were eager to heed the challenge of the new age, to take a more creditable place in American Protestantism. It would not hurt to enter into negotiations with the Reformed Church

Not everyone agreed, however. The next issue of the Magazine *contained an article under the nom de plume "Peter the Hermit" (representing, perhaps inadvertently, the desire of the author and some others in the Evangelical Synod to remain solitary and untouched by happenings around them) expressing his unwillingness to "go" to the Reformed Church. He urged the people of the synod to stay where they were but to overcome their inefficiencies and to do what they should have done previously to become larger, more influential, better educated, more efficiently organized, and so on. "Why not remain and do something?" he urged.*

The merger issue dominated the denomination. Soon, H. L. Streich, the Evangelical Synod's executive secretary, took up Kamphausen's careful suggestions and spelled them out in detail. "Everyone" in the synod was talking about church union with the Reformed Church, from local pastors to state conferences. There was a demand for a commission on church union made to the general conference. Streich was enthusiastic. There were many reasons to commend the idea. Both denominations shared German origins. They were both children of the Reformation, evangelical in doctrine, with strong social emphases and a stress on religious education and confirmation. Even their liturgies were similar. Moreover, merger would not only give both churches increased power and prestige, but also would increase the efficiency of their work for the kingdom of God, with less waste of money and effort, and less overlapping and competition among local churches. Quoting H. R. Niebuhr, he noted that union would enhance their complementary educational institutions, spreading influence from the East to the West. As for a name, Streich proposed a remarkably prescient idea: simply, the Evangelical Reformed Church.

In less than a decade, the Evangelical Synod had grown dramatically in its understanding of itself and of church union. From a denomination threatened by change, seeing itself primarily in terms of German language and culture, European origins and an early frontier identity that it wished to conserve, it came to envision itself in terms of what it could become: a new Protestant denomination united with the Reformed Church in the U.S., secure in its historic Reformation identity, and with more power, prestige, money, and personnel to do God's work in the world.

Letter to the Editor

The drift toward unification of Protestantism is unmistakable. While no church union embracing all denominations is in sight there has been a considerable consolidation of smaller denominations. If this tendency continues what will be the position of our Synod in the future?

It is now ten years ago that three Lutheran bodies united to form the United Lutheran church. That union absorbed one body, the General Synod, which was probably closer to us in religious feeling than any other church body. The temper of the General Synod is no longer evident in the United Lutheran church. Some years ago there was some thought in a few circles of our church about the possibility of union with the United Lutheran church. There has been no evidence of such interest in late years. The United Lutheran church is a progressive church with tremendous energy, but its spirit is illiberal. Hundreds of our pastors and congregations would never find it possible to join this group.

The only other group remaining with which we have any common heritage is the *Reformed church.* Its membership is drawn from the same kind of people as our own and its whole temper is very similar to our own. Never as Calvinistic as the Presbyterian churches there is now so little to divide us from a group such as the Reformed people that there is no justification for separate establishments. The Reformed church may in time be drawn into a Presbyterian reunion. It might in fact prefer such a union, to one with us. But there is no certainty that it would. At least there are some elements in the church which would most certainly prefer a union with us. At least there would be no harm in occasional informal conversations between unofficial representatives to explore each other's minds.

A *union* with the *Reformed church* would create a denomination of some six hundred thousand communicants. A denomination of this size could carry on its missionary and educational tasks with much less waste than our respective denominations under present conditions. There would be more than this advantage in union however. A union of the two churches would bring fresh life and inspiration to both parties. It would result in a denomination which could make a real contribution to American church life.

Perhaps the idea is a wild one. When suggested some years ago by the present writer in the pages of this magazine it was hailed with derision. There is good reason however to believe that the present temper of the church is not so unsympathetic toward the proposal. At any rate the "Magazine" might render a real service to the church by exploring the problem of union and inviting the opinion of the ministers of the synod upon it.

R. Niebuhr

Will It Be Luther or Calvin?

Protestants have always been strong on disagreeing, on upholding personal opinion, on contending for intellectual integrity. That has been one secret of their success, they have furnished the leaven that started the dough of humanity into ever new processes of growth and activity. It seems no accident that the leading nations of the world have largely been Protestant.

Still the Catholic Church survives and is as powerful as it ever was. Authority that could enforce unity has held it together, and the strange combination of its inflexibility with a certain adaptability has again and again been the despair of its opponents.

Protestantism has at last learned the lesson that Rome in God's providence is destined to inculcate, namely, the lesson of the *one,* holy, *universal* Christian church. The organization of the *Federal Council* of the churches of Christ 20 years ago was an indication that American Protestantism was beginning to read the signs of the times. But the Federation of churches in the Council was for practical purposes only, it did not rest on uniformity of creed or affect the independence of the individual churches. More pretentious was the movement that called many Protestant churches together in Philadelphia in 1918, to consider ways and means for an *organic union* of all Protestant faiths. It was a by-product of war-time enthusiasm, and it had no sooner flared up than it died down again.

Since then there have been efforts for consolidation on a more modest scale. The Lutherans have combined three formerly independent bodies in the United Lutheran Church; and in Canada Methodists, Presbyterians and Congregationalists have founded the United Church of Canada.

Our own Synod has not remained untouched by the wind that has been stirring in the tree tops. To afford a spiritual home to those to whom Luther and Calvin were both servants of the same Lord, was its great ideal. It has never expected that it would convert all Lutherans or all Reformed of this country to this principle. In the days of its very beginning it encountered from extreme Lutheranism a hostility so bitter and so uncompromising that it would have blighted that hope had it ever been there. On the other hand, to win over the Reformed never even occurred to it. It was an importation from Germany, and in Germany the Reformed are a negligible quantity. They have developed, in the Western provinces, a vigorous church life, but the original stock from which our immigrants were drawn, did not come from there. The expectation of our fathers was that those who had brought from their old home a mild Lutheranism or a softened Calvinism might find with us just what they wanted. Our growth in the first period of our history was such that we had no reason to think that our principles had not sufficient drawing power. According to Schory ("Geschichte . . . ") we bad in *1888 55,000* families under our care. At six heads a family—then a modest scale—that meant over 300,000 souls. In the early nineties we grew again considerably, but when immigration stopped, we stopped to grow. In the last 25 years our numbers have remained more or less stationary.

In the mean time, however, we have grown to be largely an English-speaking body and have sought and found a *place* in *American Protestantism.* According to size we rank only fifteenth, or thereabouts, on the roll of American Protestant churches. In other words, we find that we are one of the less significant denominations. Hence the complaint that we have made no "appreciable contribution to American Protestantism." It would never have occurred to our fathers to grieve about that, for, first, they lived in days of phenomenal growth, and, second, they *did not expect* to make an impression on American Protestantism. Largely Lutheran in spirit, they were satisfied with the culture of the religious life; to impress the world with the numbers, the schools, the theology, the literature of the church, much less with its power in legislation and politics, would have seemed utterly *worldly* to them. They never tried to assert themselves, they were satisfied if they were left alone.

This somewhat quietistic spirit of the fathers was bound to be greatly modified by our immerging into the vigorous flow of American church life. The American churches are largely Calvinistic. By that we do not mean that they have Calvin's theology, least of all his predestinationism. We have in mind his emphasis on life rather than on doctrines; on work more than on faith; the freedom of the church from the state; the influence of the church on public life; the aggressive and assertive spirit of Calvinism in general. This spirit entered into a natural fusion with the genius of a vigorous race on a new continent, and the two together have produced the American church. More and more it has shed the swaddling clothes of orthodox theology and judges everything by the pragmatic test: does it work, will it pay? Long enough has the church wasted time on metaphysics, now let her show what she can do to give fulness of life to the individual and to realize the Kingdom of God in this world.

Our own Synod feels the pull of these vital forces. Our younger men, especially, are eager for her to heed the challenge of the new age. They are afraid if she persists in her policy of isolation, other churches will draw together and get strong and she will be left alone, bewailing her short-sightedness when it is too late and seeing before her the unenviable fate of gradual decay. What can we do under these circumstances, so asks R. Niebuhr (in his letter to the Editor, last January), to let in new blood and take a more creditable place in American Protestantism? He says, we can *unite with* the *Reformed Church.* They are a kindred body; they are probably willing; and, together, we should have 600,000 communicants.

N. knows well that our Synod, more Lutheran than Reformed in spirit, feels more drawn to Wittenberg than to Geneva, but, he says, the Lutherans don't want us. He is right in this. Only recently the Editor conferred with a representative man from the United Lutheran Church and was told that an organic union with them would be out of the question; there might possibly some sort of a looser relation be found, etc. There is not the shadow of a doubt but that the Synod and the Lutheran Church will not mix.

So if we want to unite, the Reformed Church is the only possible chance. Niebuhr made this suggestion once before, in 1919, and met with vigorous opposition. Many perhaps have not changed their attitude. All those of Lutheran lineage or leaning would strenuously insist that the *unionistic principle be not sacrificed* in a possible merger. If, for instance, the Reformed demanded the adoption of their name in the new denominator, that would seem to bar an agreement. The "United Evangelical Church of America" might satisfy the Evangelicals, but how would it strike the Reformed?

The Editor cannot commit himself on the question; he knows too little of the Reformed Church. It appears to have shared with us the fate that, so far, it has not contributed much to American Protestantism. If it had, our union with them would probably be in the nature of an absorption. This writer could get along with, and even in, the Reformed Church; he was brought up in it, although confirmed in the Lutheran church (in Germany).

At any rate, it would not hurt us to enter into negotiations with the Reformed. We could then more intelligently judge what a union with them would mean to us in obligations and in privileges.

Why Go, Why Not Stay?

By Peter the Hermit

This nom-de-plume is assumed so that the reader may forget the author but remember his message.

The message is, in part, comment and question to voices heard at times, most recently in the article, "Will it be Luther or Calvin?" appearing in the "Theological Magazine," Vol. 56, No. 2, Page 131ff.

The effort to catalog the reasons so far advanced and favoring the union of our *Evangelical Synod of North America* with some other and larger religious body or denomination has produced the following more or less pertinent points.

1. We are a small denomination, hence handicapped in many ways;
2. We have had relatively small growth in number of adherents;
3. We have been conservative in number and type of enterprises;
4. Being a "Union" church, we seem to lack "individuality";
5. For the same reason, there is little "historical antecedent" or reason;
6. We have no specific, discriminating doctrines;
7. We have no specific incentive;
8. We have no exceptional educational institutions or outstanding minds.
9. We have no comprehensive or perfect scheme of organization;
10. We have no definite program of work.

Correct or incorrect, and without further study or argumentation, it seems that the above ten points are actually *"confessions."* They appear to be the confessions of an *"Insufficiency"* as deplored by some.

But a closer study of these points and of past internal synodical history seems to indicate not *"Insufficiency"* but *"inefficiency."*

If the thoughts cataloged above are based on facts, we who make the statements and we about whom these statements are made have been remiss, are remiss, and, may be, will remain remiss, even under different surroundings, in the discharge of our simplest duties as Christians and members of an organized body of Christians.

Why, then, should we go elsewhere? Why not remain and do our duty?

The author is not ready to admit that the past of our Synod has been without some, and, perhaps, very definite profit to the Kingdom. The author admits some of the failings and shortcomings of our synodical fathers and of our present generation. The author recognized some things left undone and others which might have been done more skillfully. The author also admits the superiority of other denominations in the various lines of ecclesiastical and theological, educational and literary effort. But the author is not blind to the limitations of the larger denominations, to their failures, and to their shortcomings. Some of these larger denominations also make "confessions" to their constituency both in private and in public. Their very "forward movement," whatever the local denominational slogan and title, are such bold "confessions."

Why go elsewhere? Why unite with those suffering pro rata from the same maladies? Why not stay at home, learn from others, and do something worth while?

For, if we go, i.e., merge with others, we will need to relinquish these things: First—the principles and reasons for our organization as a separate church body; Second—the very ideal of "unity" between two great discordant church bodies, and, becoming part of one of these two discordant bodies, will need to promote discord instead of unity; Third—the very principle of the "Evangel" or Gospel of Jesus Christ by emphasizing the dictum of some leader.

The author is not unmindful of the fact that similar arguments, perhaps in varied forms, have been introduced otherwise when new alliances and mergers of church bodies were being effected. They may seem platitudes to some. The subject of church and denominational mergers has been most interesting to the author. He has seen and heard much pro and con, has witnessed conflict, experimentation, success and failure, also the heroic struggle of some who would not merge when ordered to do so by their erstwhile superiors. One question will not down, Why merge? Why go; why not stay and do a bit of constructive work of your own for the Christ and His Kingdom?

Honestly, Brethren, must we go? Is there no reason for remaining what we are and overcoming the very things we charge ourselves with? We had an opportunity to make a bold stroke when our constitution was undergoing repairs. We could have recast the present and the future into an efficient labor for the Lord of the church. Time and again suggestions have been offered and considered but without aggressive effort and active cooperation. Sometimes it has been our conservatism which held us back, sometimes the fear to undertake something new, and sometimes something worse than fear!

Why go? Why not remain and do something?

Church Union

Rev. H. Kamphausen, D.D.,
Editor Evangelical Theological Magazine,
Cleveland, Ohio.

Dear Brother:

I want to thank you for your timely and clear editorial on Church Union in the March issue of The Evangelical Theological Magazine, also Rev. R. Niebuhr for his challenging words on the same subject in a previous issue.

Everywhere throughout the Synod there are expressions and even movements toward Church unity. Our great principle of "unity" seems to be taking definite active form. Thank God for that!

Not only has the subject been favorably mentioned and a commission on Church Union demanded at the last General Conference, but District Conferences are passing definite resolutions on Church Union. About four years ago the Wisconsin District appointed a committee to interview the Lutherans regarding a possible merger. Two years ago our baby District—"a little child shall lead them"—the Southern, passed a resolution asking our Synodical officers to give the subject of Church Union their active attention. The same resolution was passed by the national Brotherhood Convention at Buffalo. Last year Church union was made the theme of the Missouri Conference ("The heart of the Synod"), Dr. A. H. Becker, speaking on the subject. And now comes Eden Theological Seminary with a convocation the latter part of this month at which Church Union is to be discussed by Dr. G. Richards, Chairman of the Commission on Church Union of the Reformed Church, U.S.A.

On my many travels I find "Church Union" is being discussed by our pastors everywhere. I am again and again asked what pastors and people in other parts of the Synod are saying on this vital question. Everywhere I find folks saying, "We ought to unite with some other denomination."

At Baltimore and Buffalo, I understand, our pastors are meeting with the Reformed pastors on this subject. This, is a very practical method of seriously dealing with the subject. By association we best learn to know folks. This makes for fellowship and friendship. This is how young folks come to marriage. Perhaps, if this practical example of our Baltimore and Buffalo pastors were followed elsewhere and by the officials of both groups a marriage here would also result.

You have correctly said that a merger with the Lutherans of any kind is impossible. That would mean submergence for the Evangelical Synod.

If any one doubts this, let him approach even the United Lutheran as you did. The above mentioned Wisconsin District Committee of four years ago had the same experience. Or let doubters read the article by Dr. Krumbine on "How Lutheranism Lapsed from Liberalism," in your March issue of the Evangelical Magazine, especially the last sentence. No, to unite with the Lutherans is out of question. It would mean submergence.

While we have a number of "Lutherans" in our Synod, people and especially pastors who claim to be "Lutheran" in doctrine and sentiment or by early training, the fact that they did not join Lutheran Synods proves they could not personally unite with any Lutheran Church in *America,* and yet there are over twenty shades or groups to choose from. The "Lutherans" in our Synod are not Lutherans of the American type. American Lutheranism and German Lutheranism are different.

But we have a very large number of Reformed or Calvinistic in our Synod who, like you, "could get along with, and even in, the Reformed Church." This Church like ours is of German extraction, children of the Reformation, evangelical in doctrine, with a strong social emphasis, stressing religious education and upholding confirmation. The form of service is also like unto ours. With all this likeness and kinship why couldn't we "get along with the Reformed Church"? And do we not in our Article of Faith say, we accept the Symbolical books of the Reformed Church?

Since the door to the Lutheran Church is closed to us, why not then turn to the Reformed Church in the United States?

Such a merger does not mean *giving up,* but *gaining* in power and prestige, in efficiency and effectiveness for the Kingdom. It would mean greater good from the same efforts. United efforts always multiply results. Five men singly could never lift a 500-pound bale of cotton, but five men together can easily. Together the Evangelical Synod and the Reformed Church could accomplish much more for the Kingdom than we are now doing separately. Surely that should be our concern. Everywhere human hearts are crying for spiritual help, millions are yet without the only Christ. Shall we not take every means of united efforts to reach a greater number of these needy, sin-sick souls? What loss of greater good this separated service! Two working together means much more than twice two. Here is the great argument for union of kindred forces,—the greater good accomplished. This is real Christian strategy and Church statesmanship.

Or consider it from the standpoint of economy and wastefulness and you come to the same conclusion of *the great good and usefulness resulting from Union.*

What two men are now doing at double the expense in two denominations, could in most cases—not in all—be done by one. This would mean the release of one man and the corresponding costs for other services. Instead of each denomination having an Executive Secretary for Men, Women, Young People, Religious Education, Home Missions, Foreign Missions, Editors for their Church Papers and Periodicals, one in many cases could do the work. What a saving of men and money for greater, more extended services, reaching larger number of God's unsaved children the world over. Yes, it would mean one President General less. Why all this waste? Does not Christian Stewardship also demand Church Union? How can we commit so great a sin, wasting men and money in the service of the Kingdom.

It will not mean giving less, but doing greater good, reaching more with what we give. Indeed it would mean more giving. Co-operation and united efforts with larger results always does. The United Church of Canada has larger receipts now than the three merged churches had. Some folks will simply not support wasteful methods.

A Union with the Reformed Church would also prevent overlapping and overlooking. Instead of an Evangelical and a Reformed Church, in many places, *one* "United Evangelical" would be sufficient. We do not, of course, mean, that where now an Evangelical and a Reformed Church in the same town or section of the City, they would merge. Many would, if not at once, eventually. But a Union would prevent both our Synod and the Reformed Church, each planting a Church in the same vicinity, as that is now possible. This unchristian competition would be eliminated. What a disgrace as well as waste this competitive denominational Church building is. There would be one denomination less, thank God!

With the released men and money many of the crying needs at home and abroad need no longer be overlooked. Now we must say to these repeated calls; We have neither men nor money.

Then as Dr. H. R. Niebuhr pointed out to me in a conversation on this subject, our educational institutions would complement one another. Most of the schools of the Reformed Church are in the East, excepting one in Ohio and one in Wisconsin. Ours are in the middle West. Our students in the East would have schools near at hand. Their folks in the middle West would have institutions close by. Indeed it might be possible here also to merge and save men and money. All this is another strong argument for merger.

But, dear Editor, I am writing more than I intended, I merely wished to commend you for discussing this vital and timely question in the magazine. Others may point out many more reasons for merger and how it may be brought about. There are few, if any reasons against a merger, except unwilling ones. Or as was reported in the case of the failure of two other groups to unite some years ago. The reporter said, "There were only eighteen reasons against merger." When asked to name these, reply "Eighteen Bishops."

As to name, why not simply write the names also; "The Evangelical Reformed Church."

Yours for Church Union,

H. L. Streich, Executive Sec.

67. Union Defended:

" 'The Plan of Union' Summarized"

(1929)

Helmut Richard Niebuhr

In the late 1920s, when a "Plan of Union" for a proposed "United Church in America" that would bring together the Evangelical Synod of North America, the Reformed Church in the U.S., and the United Brethren in Christ was published, reaction was positive among leaders in the Evangelical Synod. In an article in The Christian World, *Helmut Richard Niebuhr, chair of the Evangelical Synod's Commission on Closer Union of the Churches, reassured the members of the synod by summarizing the plan, drawing particular attention to its solution for the problems of the superintendency of the churches and the appointment of pastors.*

For the Evangelical Synod, the problem of superintendency was a minor one. It already had similar supervision provided by the president general and the district presidents. To reach agreement, however, concessions had been made by the United Brethren. They had agreed to drop the name of bishop from their supervisory function. In the Reformed Church, which had previously had no similar office, powers were carefully delineated. The appointment of pastors would be handled by a "stationing committee," but it was primarily advisory and directing rather than authoritative. The plan did not demand great changes for the Reformed and Evangelical churches, but the United Brethren would undergo considerable change. The practice of itinerant ministry, whereby the Brethren clergy were moved around by church leaders, was not in the plan.

In the end, nothing came of the proposal for a United Church in

---

Source: Helmut Richard Niebuhr, " 'The Plan of Union' Summarized," *The Christian World,* 30 March 1929, 7.

America. However, its plan of union eventually became the core of conversations that eventually produced the 1934 plan of union for the Evangelical and Reformed Church.

Rev. Prof. H. R. Niebuhr, Chairman of Committee on Relations with Other Churches, Evangelical Synod of North America.

The Plan of Union for the "United Church in America" is based on the conviction that the Reformed Church in the United States, the Church of the United Brethren in Christ, and the Evangelical Synod of North America, are not only allied by a common heritage from the German and Swiss Reformation and the evangelical revival, as well as from their common European homeland, but that they are essentially at one in doctrine and polity also. The Evangelical Synod has consistently emphasized its adherence first of all to the Holy Scriptures, secondly to the ancient doctrines of the church, as popularly set forth in the Apostolic Creed, and thirdly to the common and essential element in the various doctrinal standards of the Reformation. And in this we are at one with the other two church bodies represented in the negotiations. The doctrinal standards of the three churches are thus in agreement on all essential points and in a common confession of faith, in which the teaching of the word of God, the ancient doctrines of the early church and the evangelical doctrines of the Reformation are once more emphasized. . . .)

Very early during the negotiations it also appeared to the commissioners that these churches were essentially at one in matters of polity. All three are finally governed by a General Conference or General Synod, and are therefore, democratic in character. The problem to be solved was, therefore, only that of reconciling the differences within that general unity. The following brief summary of the plan of Union indicates in a general way how, in the opinion of the commissioners, this might be done.

It was agreed that the union contemplated should begin in the General Conferences and their work. These are to be united first of all, while the union of districts, classes, annual conferences or district synods is not to be undertaken until these organizations themselves desire union with each other. It is primarily the so-called "kingdom work" of the churches, that is, their foreign missions, home missions, educational work, their publication activities, etc., which is to be consolidated.

The plan of union does not contemplate any changes in the local congregations. These may retain their present names, but are to add a statement of their affiliation with the United Church in America. They are to retain their constitutions and their present liberty of worship. The Church which the commissioners contemplate is one which will be broad enough to contain different varieties of Christian expression and experience, but which will not sacrifice the depth of Christian doctrine in a universal tolerance without conviction.

In reconciling the differences in polity of the three churches it was discovered by the commissioners that, in their opinion, each one could make considerable concessions and yet profit greatly by a plan which seemed to retain the best features of each system. On two points especially considerable concessions were required from each church, while the outcome was one which appears to all the commissions to be an improvement on their present plans of church government. These points are the superintendency and the appointment of pastors.

So far as the superintendency is concerned, our Church needed to make only slight concession, for we are accustomed to the supervision exercised by the President General and by the district presidents. We agreed that a church so large as the United Church will be would require the services of more than one superintendent, the number being left to the General Council (equivalent to our General Conference) of the United Church to determine. The Church of the United Brethren agreed to drop the name of bishop for these superintendents and to give up some of the prerogatives of the office. The Reformed Church needed to make the largest concessions in this instance, for it has had no equivalent office in the past. Yet it also regards the new plan as an improvement on the old.

The paragraphs on the appointment of pastors represent a similar product of concession and agreement. The stationing committee which is provided for is to be regarded not primarily as an authoritative, but as an advisory and directing agency which will assist congregations to find the pastors they need and pastors the congregations they can serve best. In supplying a more effective directing agency for the whole task of the church, in supplying leadership for its congregations, the paragraph on appointment of pastors appears to many in our church to represent an improvement on our present practice. Negotiations on these points as well as on all others were marked throughout by a splendid Christian spirit of co-operation and a desire to find the best possible means for mutual accommodation and for the government of the united church.

The joint commissions in constructing the said plan of union have not been able to escape the conviction that the guidance of the Holy Spirit has been present in all the contemporary movements of the various Christian churches toward unity, and that this Spirit has not been absent from the events which have led to the formulation of the present plan. They are aware of its imperfections, they are aware that it leaves many problems for the future to solve, but they are also convinced that it seeks to express the divine ideal of the unity of Christ's disciples.

This is, briefly, the plan which our commission presents to our churches with its own complete and hearty recommendation and with the hope that its work will be found an effective step toward the achievement of the ideal for which our Evangelical Synod has always stood.

68. Partnership Affirmed:

"The Plan of Union" and an Editorial on the "Plan of Union"

(1932)

Reformed Church and Evangelical Synod; H. Kamphausen

After the plans for the United Church in America (to include the Evangelical Synod, the Reformed Church in the U.S., and the United Brethren in Christ) failed, the Reformed Church and the Evangelical Synod continued their conversations. Their commissions met in 1930 with the intention of preparing a basis of union.

Soon thereafter, however, the Reformed Church was invited to meet with the Presbyterians to consider the possibility of union. Not wanting to hamper these negotiations, the Reformed Church's Commission on Closer Relations and Church Union decided to halt its conversations with the Evangelical Synod, assuring the Synod that it looked forward to negotiations being resumed in the future. The Evangelical Synod assured the Reformed Church that it also hoped their paths would cross in the future.

By May and June of 1931, the General Synod of the Reformed Church and the General Assembly of the Presbyterian Church in the U.S. decided not to continue negotiations. Soon thereafter, the suspended conversations between the Evangelical Synod and the Reformed Church resumed. At a joint meeting in 1932, representatives from both denominations

---

Source: "The Plan of Union of the Reformed Church in the United States and the Evangelical Synod of North America," 12 February 1932, in the Eden Seminary Archives; H. Kamphausen, "The Plan of Union," *Theological Magazine of the Evangelical Synod of North America* 60, no. 4 (July 1932): 285–87.

decided to look at the "Plan of Union" that had been prepared for the stillborn United Church in America to see if it might be useful. They decided to dramatically shorten the doctrinal section, which had been a brief summary of the basic tenets of the faith, changing it to read, "We acknowledge and accept the historical confessions of the two churches as the doctrinal basis of union."

The section having to do with the election of general superintendents was changed to read simply that the General Synod will appoint or elect agencies for its administrative and promotional work. All of the sections originally written to deal with synods and conferences, appointments of ministers to congregations or charges, and the board of promotion were omitted. The only other change was to call the national governing body the General Synod, rather than the General Council.

An editorial in the denominational magazine in July 1932 drew attention to the similarity between the new doctrinal sentence and the statement of the Evangelical Synod's long-standing Bekenntnisparagraph, *or Confessional Paragraph. It recognized the Heidelberg and Lutheran Catechisms, and urged the General Synod to live up to its ancient (union) principles and to the "insistent call of the hour" (see vol. 6:55).*

The plan of union for the Evangelical and Reformed Church was unanimously approved at a joint meeting of the commissions on church union of both denominations on February 12, 1932, in Pittsburgh. A special meeting of both denominations was called for June 26, 1934, to formally declare the union (see vol. 6:69).

The Plan of Union

Introduction

It is evident that the Christian churches throughout the world are disposed to enter into closer fellowship and cooperation with one another. If the 17th and 18th centuries were the period of denominational rivalry and competition, the 19th and 20th centuries are the time of affiliation and cooperation among the churches.

The will to unite is shown by alliances, councils, federation and organic union of churches in Europe, in America, and on the mission fields of the Orient. More recent expressions of the deeply-felt need of union of the churches, in order to accomplish the work which their Lord gave them to do, are the World Missionary Conference at Edinburgh, 1910; the Stockholm Conference on Life and Work, 1925; the World Conference on Faith and Order at Lausanne, 1927; and the Jerusalem Conference, 1928.

In view of these facts and movements, in which one may see clearly the guidance of the spirit of our Lord and Saviour, who prayed for all "who believe in me" that they all "may be one," it behooves the churches, especially those of the same land and of the evangelical faith and order, to enter into negotiations for closer relationship with the purpose of attaining organic union.

Believing that each denomination exists not for itself but as an agency for the advancement of the Kingdom of God, which is greater than any single church or than all the churches taken together, and for which each denomination is to live and labor, and if need be, to die;

Believing, also, that in a union of churches the distinctive ideals of each, and the essential principles of the Christian faith and life common to all, would not only be conserved but be more effectually applied in the promotion of the Kingdom of God in the lives of individuals and of nations;

The Commissions on Church Union of the Reformed Church in the United States, and of the Evangelical Synod of North America present for consideration and action, to their respective judicatories and congregations, the following Plan of Union.

Plan of Union

Preamble. The Reformed Church in the United States Evangelical Synod of North America, under the conviction that they are in agreement on the essential doctrines of the Christian faith and on the ideals of the Christian life as contained in the Old and New Testaments and as defined in their respective standards of doctrine, do hereby declare their desire to be united in one body according to articles mutually agreed upon as follows:

I. Name

The name of the church formed by this union shall be "The Evangelical and Reformed Church." Congregations and institutions may retain their names, but they shall designate their membership in The Evangelical and Reformed Church.

II. Doctrine

We acknowledge and accept the historical confessions of the two churches as the doctrinal basis of union.

III. Supreme Judicatory

The Evangelical and Reformed Church shall establish, as its supreme judicatory for the prosecution of its work, a representative body to be known as "The General Synod of The Evangelical and Reformed Church."

IV. The General Synod—How Constituted

The General Synod shall be constituted of an equal number of ordained ministers and lay members, to be chosen by the Classes which are now in the Reformed Church in the United States and by the Districts of the Evangelical Synod of North America. The basis of representation shall be: one minister and one lay member for every 20 congregations or major fraction thereof. Each Classis and District shall have at least one minister and one lay member as representatives in the General Synod. A quorum shall consist of a majority of the members of the body. The members of the General Synod shall be elected by the Classes and the Districts in the same manner as these now choose delegates to their respective supreme judicatories until a uniform mode of election shall have been provided by the General Synod.

V. Functions of the General Synod

1. The General Synod, through boards and other agencies elected by it, shall carry on the general work of the church which is now conducted by the General Synod of the Reformed Church in the United States and the General Conference of the Evangelical Synod of North America.

2. The specific work of the General Synod shall be Foreign Missions; Home Missions; Education; Publications; Ministerial Relief; Benevolent Activities, and such other work as will promote the Kingdom of God and pertains to the Church as a whole

3. The work of foreign missions, of home missions, of education, of ministerial relief, and of publications shall be consolidated under the direction of the General Synod as rapidly as the laws of the State, the charters, constitutions, and the property rights of the boards of the respective churches will permit. In the original constitution of the boards of

the General Synod due recognition is to be given to representation of each of the consolidated churches.

4. The boards are to be governed according to their respective charters. At the regular meeting of the General Synod each board is to submit for review a report of its operations during the time elapsed since the last regular meeting of the General Synod.

5. The General Synod shall review proceedings of the Classes, the District conferences, and the Synods, which they shall submit to each regular meeting of the General Synod.

6. The General Synod shall have power to maintain correspondence with other denominations; to hear and determine complaints and appeals; to decide controversies between subordinate judicatories; and to give counsel to cases referred to it by one or more judicatories.

7. The General Synod shall promote the reorganization of Classes and Districts into conferences which shall be constituted on a territorial basis and shall have the same status as Classes or Districts. However, the General Synod shall not have power to unite subordinate judicatories of the consolidated Churches except at their request.

8. The General Synod shall meet in regular session quadrennially, or more frequently, as the General Synod may determine, and in extraordinary session at such time and place as it may determine.

9. The General Synod shall have authority to initiate action for the preparation of a constitution for The Evangelical and Reformed Church. The constitution shall be adopted by a two-thirds vote of the General Synod and shall be approved in such manner as the General Synod shall determine.

VI. Officers

1. The General Synod shall elect officers, who shall perform the duties that are customary in judicatories of that sort.

2. The General Synod shall appoint or elect agencies for its administrative and promotional work.

VII. Subordinate Judicatories

Until by regular action of the General Synod according to Article V, Section 7, it is otherwise determined, the Synods, Classes, and Districts shall continue; and each shall conduct its business in its own way. Whatever action is submitted to the subordinate judicatories by the General Synod shall be disposed of in the same way as these subordinate bodies disposed of such action by the General Synod or the General Conference prior to the union.

VIII. Rights of Property

1. The congregations, Classes, Synods, and Districts shall continue to exist and to do their work in the way it was done prior to the union; they shall also continue to hold and to supervise whatever property they possess and institutions they control. Congregations, judicatories, or institutions may unite by mutual agreement, and such union shall be confirmed, in case of congregations by the Classes or Districts, or by each as the case may require; in case of judicatories and institutions by the General Synod.

2. The theological seminaries, colleges, academies, and benevolent institutions that are under the control of the subordinate judicatories of the respective churches shall continue under the supervision of the Synods, Classes or Districts, which were in control of them before the union. Those institutions, however, which were under the control of the supreme judicatories of the uniting churches shall pass under the control of the General Synod. In the constitution of the boards of directors of these institutions the interests of the groups previously in control shall be properly recognized. A union of these schools may be effected according to the provisions defined in the previous paragraph of this article.

3. At the first session of the General Synod a committee on charters shall be appointed, which shall recommend the procedure to be adopted to safeguard the institutions and their charters.

IX. Authorizing of Ministers

Candidates for the ministry, after the union, and until a uniform method is prescribed by enactment of the General Synod, shall be authorized to perform ministerial acts by the Classes or Districts in the same way as they were authorized before the union. The ministers of the churches in the union shall be enrolled as ministers of The Evangelical and Reformed Church.

X. Members

Men, women, and children shall be admitted into the fellowship of The Evangelical and Reformed Church through baptism and profession of faith according to the custom and usage of each congregation prior to the union. When they shall have been admitted, they shall be enrolled as members of The Evangelical and Reformed Church.

XI. Worship

The freedom of worship at present enjoyed by the negotiating churches shall not be interfered with in The Evangelical and Reformed Church.

XII. Approval of the Plan of Union

1. The Plan of Union shall be submitted to the supreme judicatories of the Reformed Church in the United States and the Evangelical Synod of North America. Each church shall proceed according to its own constitution in the approval or disapproval of the Plan of Union. When the Plan has been approved by regular action of the two negotiating churches, the President and the Secretary, or stated clerk, of the Supreme Judicatory of each Church shall report the action to the Commissions on Union of the negotiating Churches, who shall then request the officers of the supreme judicatories to call a special meeting of each judicatory at the same time and place. In joint session of the judicatories the final report of the action of the Churches on the Plan of Union shall be made. The supreme judicatories of the churches that have approved the Plan of Union shall declare, by joint resolution, that the union of the churches is duly effected at that time. Then the delegates, duly elected by the churches entering into the union to constitute the original General Synod, shall effect an organization by the election of officers and proceed to the transaction of business. From the time of the organization of the General Synod until a constitution shall have been adopted, as heretofore provided, this Plan of Union shall be the fundamental law of The Evangelical and Reformed Church.

2. The number of delegates to which each of the uniting churches shall be entitled in the first General Synod shall be determined by the Commissions on Union and be announced to the stated clerks or secretaries of the Classes and Districts, three months before the meeting of the supreme judicatories for the consummation of the union.

3. Any part of this Plan of Union may be revised or amended by The

Evangelical and Reformed Church in the same way as the constitution of said church is revised or amended.

For the Reformed Church in the United States:	For the Evangelical Synod of North America:
Geo. W. Richards	Louis W. Goebel
Charles E. Miller	C. W. Locher
A. E. Dahlmann	S. D. Press
J. C. Leonard	H. R. Niebuhr
A. R. Bartholomew	F. Frankenfeld
Emory L. Coblentz	F. R. Schreiber
D. J. Snyder	J. W. Mueller
Reuben J. Butz	W. C. Hazelbeck
	J. C. Fischer
	J. H. Horstmann

The Plan of Union

When we were informed (Herald Jan. 8, 1931) that on December 19, 1930 the negotiations towards union with the Reformed Church in the United States had been broken off, we were not only disappointed but also very doubtful whether there was any hope that our ways would soon meet again. Our General Conference at Rochester, New York, had (in 1929) enthusiastically and unanimously accepted the "Plan of Union" and it looked in that year as though not only the Reformed Church but also the United Brethren would vote favorably on the proposed merger. But 1930 proved to be fatal to these hopes. First, the United Brethren disappeared from the picture. Their General Conference adopted the plan, but with them, so we were told, the congregations have the final voice and the congregations were against it. Then the Reformed Church surprised us. They had taken up again a scheme, previously considered, of uniting with the Presbyterian Church and kindred bodies. They sounded out our commissioners on that project, but were told that these had no authority to go on along this new line. So, on the date mentioned above, our men were notified by Dr. Richards, of the Reformed commission, that for the present everything was off. All the friends of the proposed union, and there were many, had a sinking of the heart when their high hopes were all at once so sadly frustrated. It is true that in some districts and with some individual pastors, the feeling of an affinity with the Reformed Church is not so pronounced. They would rather see a union with some more broadminded branch of the

Lutheran Church. Still, taken by and large, this Lutheran current doesn't seem very strong. It certainly has not so far found very decided expression.

As stated above, our hopes for a resumption of the efforts for a union were not very optimistic. We knew the Reformed pastors here in Cleveland were heart and soul with us, but we feared that the prospect of union with the large Presbyterian Church would prove more alluring to the Reformed Church than one with us. However, the plan of a merger with the Presbyterian bodies must have gone on the rocks, for towards the end of 1931 we heard that negotiations between the Reformed and our Synod had been opened again. It seems that circumstances—or shall we not say, providence?—were working in such a way that ultimate union would be the logical outcome. At any rate, the commissions of the respective churches have worked out again a "Plan of Union." It has been submitted to the churches and pastors of the Synod by its publication in the Herald of March 31, this year.

The Plan, as far as the organization of the future united church is concerned, follows very much the same lines as the former "Basis of Union." The name, "The Evangelical and the Reformed Church" is certainly not very satisfactory, but in the absence of a better one and in the hope that the future will provide an improvement—it may stand.

We notice that the Stationing Committee of the former plan has been omitted. We know it was objectionable to the Reformed; some of our own people also feared that it put too much power in the hands of the district president.

In this Editorial it is impracticable to discuss the whole Plan. We shall only make a few remarks on the "doctrinal basis." The former plan sought to provide such a basis in a brief summary of the tenets of our Christian faith. The present Plan does not make any such attempt. It only says, "We acknowledge and accept the historical confession of the two churches as the doctrinal basis of the union." We cannot see that there should be any difficulty for us to subscribe to this fundamental statement. Our own confessional paragraph recognizes the Heidelberg Catechism, the chief confessional standard of the Reformed Church, as a true interpretation of the Christian faith. Our position as a "Union" church pledged us from the very beginning to a Union program and policy. It may be conceded that our fathers, in adopting such a policy, were simply adapting the Prussian Union to their new environment without thinking particularly of the Reformed Church in the United States. But if Reformed and Lutherans could find a common basis and organic union in Prussia, why not here?

The Plan does not involve a surrender of conviction or viewpoint on either side. Calvin emphasized more the sovereignty of God, Luther the love of God. We can learn from both. As to the Lord's Supper, some of us may have the Calvinistic view and others may find more in Luther's interpretation. Can we therefore not both together go to the Lord's table? The Editor was born into the Reformed Church, was later confirmed by a rather strict Lutheran and has since then belonged to and worked in a "United" church. He has never felt that different views on the sacrament have made spiritual fellowship impossible; he will confess, though, that when the administering clergyman used the form: "this is the *true* body," he was compelled to make a mental reservation.

The Calvinistic (and Augustinian) double predestination doctrine has never been taught in the Heidelberg Catechism, nor in the Prussian branch of the Reformed Church.

In regard to the liturgy, the Lutheran Church has made a distinct contribution to the upbuilding of congregational worship. Here the Reformed Church, originally, practised a policy of rigid simplicity and extreme scripturalness (nothing but psalms to be used). Today we notice in all churches a growing desire for a richer worship program, one in which the congregation takes an essential part. Both our churches will cooperate here, in response to an evident need and in an increasing realization of very valuable ideals.

Both churches are more or less committed to the Social Gospel. Our very membership in the Federal Council (with its "Social Ideals") implies that.

Of course there will be difficulties and problems in plenty as we go on in carrying out the Plan and its implications. But consolidation is in the air. If Methodists, Presbyterians and Congregationalists could unite in the United Church of Canada and do it with the greatest success, we can't see why we couldn't unite with the Reformed, to the benefit of both of us.

The Plan will be considered by the General Synod of the Reformed Church this year, after which it will probably be sent down to the nearly sixty classes of that church body, which meet during the late summer and fall. The results of all these discussions on the part of the Reformed brethren, will then be gone over by the joint committee of both denominations and a report will then be submitted to our district conferences next year, from which the project goes on to our General Conference for final disposition.

We see every phase and aspect of the great Plan will be thoroughly threshed out. There will be no undue haste or failure to listen to dissenting or simply unconvinced opinions. Still, we are persuaded that our Synod is committed to a Union policy and we hope we shall live up to our ancient principles and to the insistent call of the hour.

69. Union Celebrated:

"Report of the President," "Awake, O Church United," and "The Bread Which We Break . . . "

(1934)

Paul Press; Ambrose M. Schmidt; Lee M. Erdman

There was a strong sense among all of the Evangelical Synod speakers and contributors to the various sessions declaring and celebrating the creation of the Evangelical and Reformed Church that God had guided them through their nearly ninety-four years of history in the United States to that place and to that event. They had begun their existence as the Kirchenverein des Westens, seeking to embody a "union spirit" that brought together Lutheran and Reformed faith and practice, and they believed that it was God's will that they further embody this spirit by uniting with the Reformed Church in the United States. Speaking in the light of a plan of union that entrusted many details to the future direction of the Spirit, the president of the Evangelical Synod, Paul Press, urged synod members to commit themselves "to a program and a mode of

---

Source: Paul Press, "Report of the President," in *Reports and Minutes of the Special General Conference of the Evangelical Synod of North America,* 6 June 1934, 78–81; Ambrose M. Schmidt, "Awake, O Church United," in *Acts and Proceedings of the Joint Session of the General Conference of the Evangelical Synod of N.A. and of the General Synod of the Reformed Church in the U.S.,* 26 June 1934, 189; Lee M. Erdman, "The Bread Which We Break, Is It Not the Communion of the Body of Christ?" in *Acts and Proceedings of the Joint Session of the General Conference of the Evangelical Synod of N.A. and of the General Synod of the Reformed Church in the U.S.*, 26 June 1934, 153–56.

procedure purely upon the basis of faith and trust, leaving the details to direction by the Spirit of God."

The Spirit was central to their sense of destiny. They raised their voices to sing a special hymn written in contemplation of the union. Ambrose M. Schmidt, author of the hymn, called the new church to awake and march into the future holding high the cross of Jesus, persevering until the whole world could join in worshiping Christ as "Lord and King."

Lee M. Erdman preached at the joint communion service of the uniting General Synod. He called the participants to understand their communion not only as a sacred feast of remembrance drawing them closer to their Lord and to one another, but as an act of renewed consecration "to work the works of God."

For the Evangelical Synod of North America, the "union spirit" that had brought them to this new act of union was sending them further along that path of union. They saw themselves as part of a united church committed to unite with other denominations until God's community spanned the whole inhabited earth.

Report of the President

To the Special General Conference of the Evangelical Synod of North America, in session at Zion Evangelical Church, Cleveland, Ohio.

My Esteemed Co-workers:

We meet today in solemn convocation to complete the preliminaries for an organic union with the Reformed Church in the United States. The occasion is rendered solemn by reason of the fact that by the consummation of the merger we relinquish our identity as the Evangelical Synod of North America. It is with mingled emotions that, as we traverse the development of our church in the well-nigh 94 years of its history, we pause in earnest contemplation of the past. Inadvertently our thoughts linger with men and their contributions of service and devotion, with events and their influence upon the thought-life of the church, with struggles and achievements, failures and victories, and over all with the firm conviction of the ever-present guidance of divine providence by which our church was sustained, blessed and prospered. May we ever remember the many mercies of God by which we were kept, held and enriched. It was the patriarch Jacob who said: "I am not worthy of the least of all the lovingkindnesses, and of all the truth, which thou hast shown unto thy servant." Surely these are also our sentiments.

We sincerely believe that God has guided us to this place and to this event in the development of our church life. Therefore we go forth to approach our task, though in different environments and with new associations with an abiding faith in the wisdom with which He has directed us and a sincere trust in His never-failing leadership. But ere we proceed on our way to assume higher tasks, to accept increased responsibilities and to enjoy extended privileges we stand at solemn attention bowed in grief over the peculiar manifestation of God's providence, who in His indiscernible wisdom saw fit to call the president and leader of our Synod from his task at a time when according to human judgment we could ill afford to spare him. When after having served his church as president for four years, Dr. C. W. Locher accepted a recommitment to this task at the General Conference last October, he seemed to possess a full equipment in body, mind and soul for the increased responsibilities incumbent upon his office in view of the approaching consummation of the merger. He applied himself diligently to complete the preliminaries attendant upon this event. Apparently without warning he was stricken down, the nature of his illness giving no immediate cause for alarm. As his physical powers failed him he succumbed very quickly. We revere the memory of our sainted leader and bow in humble submission to the will of God whom he loved and served and whose will to do he accepted as his choicest privilege. Dr. Locher brought to his task as president of the Synod an obedience to the call of his church which implied a willingness to render every possible service of which he was capable. His fitness for his office was represented by deep humility, sincere consecration to his calling, a sympathetic interest in the problems of his fellow-ministers, a spiritual analysis of Christ's message and the church's mission to the world. Increasingly he impressed the constituency of the church with the sincerity of his endeavor to maintain vital contacts with the spiritual resources of power. He excelled in unselfish devotion to His Lord and fully merited the encomium of the Lord, "in whom there is no guile."

The Board of Directors of the Synod adopted appropriate resolutions as a tribute of respect to the memory of Dr. Locher which were published in the Friedensbote and Evangelical Herald, a copy of which was fittingly engrossed and sent to Mrs. Locher and family.

Following the death of Dr. Locher it devolved upon me to assume the duties of his office. By reason of my incumbency of the office of first vice-president, the succession to the office of president became the mandate of my church. There was no alternative for me to take without proving myself disloyal to the confidence reposed in me. May I, however, say that I accepted the responsibilities of this position with positive reluctance, undisguised diffidence and pronounced misgivings, purely guided by a sense of duty.

The Board of Directors has appointed a committee to indicate the legal status of our Synod and the probable functioning powers in the interim until all legal and organizational adjustments have been effected.

The official call for this special session of the General Conference indicates the purpose for which primarily we are assembled. In consonance with the action of the 26th General Conference and in conjunction with the commission on church union the call was issued by the Board of Directors. As we enter upon the deliberations of the final details preliminary to the consummation of the merger may I remind you of the resolutions adopted by the 26th General Conference which are sufficiently significant and directive to be embodied in this report:

"Whereas, sincere and consistent disciples of Jesus have ever remembered their Master's fervent prayer, 'That they may all be one,' and

"Whereas, diligence to keep the unity of the spirit in the bond of peace has always been a cherished Evangelical tradition and a vital part of the program of the Evangelical Synod of North America, and

"Whereas, we are of the profound conviction that the Reformed Church in the United States is founded and grounded on the same essential Protestant doctrines of Christian faith and ideals of Christian life, and

"Whereas, more than the requisite number of Districts of the Evangelical Synod of North America have now wholeheartedly and unreservedly approved the Plan of Union with the Reformed Church in the United States, therefore,

"Be it resolved, that the General Conference of the Evangelical Synod of North America assembled in regular session at Cincinnati, Ohio, October 3–10, 1933, formally approves the organic union with the Reformed Church in the United States, as embodied in the Plan of Union submitted to it, and

"Be it further resolved, that the Board of Directors be instructed to call a special General Conference when requested by its Commission on Church Union for the purpose of consummating the above mentioned union."

In order that we may be assured of divine guidance as we approach the task which claims our interest and attention we as Christians instinctively turn to some scriptural truth. As a basis for our deliberations may I suggest the all-inclusive statement which the fearless leader, the head of the Christian Church, Jesus Christ himself made in John 6:38, "For I am come down from heaven, not to do mine own will but the will of him that sent me." This truth is self-explanatory and requires no commentary. To do the will of God was the life of Jesus. It was not necessary for him to adapt himself to the will of God as one accepts a mandate. In the inner self of his being, in the deepest consciousness of his soul he instinctively reacted to the will of God. He explains his attitude in the most succinct manner with another statement: "My meat is to do the will of him that sent me, and to accomplish his work." Jesus did not attempt to interpret the will of God in his life theoretically. He simply lived it out in every word, in every action, in every attitude.

Whether we can accept the consummation of the merger as being in accord with God's will depends upon us, upon the attitude of our soul toward His will. If God wills it, no other argument on our part will be necessary. It remains for us to ascertain the will of God. The mutual approaches of both churches to this vital consideration have proceeded from the endeavor to make the essential contacts with the will of God through earnest prayer which in turn have resulted in a visible guidance in the negotiations and which have finally developed into a deep consciousness and a firm conviction of God's approval. In all deliberations in the meetings of the commissions on church union, at the conferences of the respective Districts and in the action of the General Conference the answer seemed to be forthcoming by the unanimous assent to the proposed merger.

The deliberations have been concluded, the resolutions approving the merger have been adopted. Our purpose today is to enter upon the actual consummation of the merger. If our action today shall be in accord with the will of God, we will not be chiefly interested in the mechanics of the merger. We must not be unduly concerned about the technical difficulties which may disturb us. God forbid that we should stoop to means and methods to gain an advantage. Principally we enter into a spiritual union with the Reformed Church, and if our approach is made on the basis of the spiritual implications of the merger we need not become agitated about possible technical difficulties. As we have been guided by the spirit of God in the development of the negotiations so will we be directed by the same spirit into the correct organizational adjustments which will become necessary, which will not even preclude the safeguarding of the principles of our legal incorporation. Therefore we will do well to heed the suggestion of the commission on church union and I quote from the report: "It is obvious that the proposed union can be consummated only on the basis of mutual confidence and an abiding faith in the guidance of the Spirit of the living God."

For the peace of our mind and soul, and in order to clear us from all doubts and fears we need to subject ourselves, our hearts and souls to the most honest and searching scrutiny. May we explore the deepest spiritual resources of our soul to determine whether we are really so completely committed to the will of God to accept a program and a mode of procedure purely upon the basis of faith and trust, leaving the details to the direction by the Spirit of God.

By our union with the Reformed Church we are being merged into a new organization which calls for new adjustments, new attitudes and new endeavors. Unless we proceed from the right base of operations we may easily become confused, therefore it behooves us, individually and collectively, to approach the Throne of God in earnest prayer and in sincere consecration to the will of God pleading with him to "create in us a clean heart and to restore a right spirit within us," so that our spirit may be subjected to the will of God and renewed in the manner so that our approach to every task will be guided by the conviction that in the Kingdom of God and in the church we realize our aims "not by might or by power but by the spirit of God." May we be renewed into spirit-filled lives and in our attitudes become sincerely Christ-minded.

If time permits, the attention of the General Conference may be directed to several communications which have been submitted for consideration which I will refer to the Committee on General Resolutions and Findings. May I also request the General Conference to give earnest consideration to the financial situation of the Synod with special emphasis upon the Synodical Recovery Plan. The Treasurer of the Synod, Mr. F. A. Keck, has kindly consented to present a financial report and offer an explanation of the Recovery Plan.

It is an occasion of much joy and satisfaction to be privileged to report officially the accreditation of Elmhurst College as a four-year standard college by the North Central Association of Colleges. We rejoice with Dr. Timothy Lehmann, the president, and the Board of Trustees of Elmhurst College that this aim has finally been realized.

And now may the Christ, who is the head of the Church, guide us in our deliberations and fill us with His spirit so that we will be prepared to do His will in accepting the challenge for higher service in His Church and Kingdom.

Respectfully submitted,

Paul Press.

Awake, O Church United

Awake, O Church united,
Behold your new-born day!
Full-clad in God's own armor,
Go forth to fight and pray.
Against the Church of Jesus,
'Gainst nations bleeding sore,
The legion hosts of Satan
Are set in world-wide war.

Awake, O Church united!
Redemption's day has come;
Today the hard-fought battle,
Tomorrow comes the song.
Let prayer and intercession
Like holy incense rise,
While new-born consecration
Unites in sacrifice.

Awake, O Church united!
Like one great army go,
Let every line and sector
Full-armored face the foe.
Hold high the Cross of Jesus,
Rich days of service bring;
'Till all the world shall worship
The Christ, our Lord and King.

Ambrose M. Schmidt, D.D.

The Bread Which We Break, Is It Not the Communion of the Body of Christ?

Sermon preached by the Rev. Lee M. Erdman, D.D., Reading Pa., at the communion Service which followed the Joint Session of the General Conference of the Evangelical Synod of North America and the General Synod of the Reformed Church in the United States, on Tuesday, June 26, 1934, at 7.00 P.M.

1 Cor. 10:16, *"The bread which we break, is it not the communion of the body of Christ?"*

On this solemn, historic occasion when the desires of our hearts, long cherished, at length find consummation, it is meet and proper indeed that we should unite in the innermost sanctuary of worship, the celebration of the Holy Communion of the Lord's Supper. The unity which we desire above all else is the unity of the Spirit. The strength necessary for our tasks we know full well, is not from below but from above. We trust not the arm of flesh, but rather those hands that were pierced for us on the cross and are extended in constant benediction to those that believe. If this is, as we think it shall be accounted, a memorable day in the history of American Christianity, how appropriate it is that we should quicken our hearts and minds by remembering all that is high and holy in our heritage. Remembering thus whence we have come, we will know also whither we are going. In this sacred feast of remembrance we are conscious of those who have gone before and by whom we are compassed about as a cloud of witnesses. Others have labored and we have entered into their labors. Fathers and mothers who first guided us in the faith, pastors and teachers who nurtured us in the word, missionaries and apostles who laid foundations in the wilderness mid peril, toil and pain, reformers who regained for us the simplicity of the gospel and assured us the privilege of personal relations with our Lord, confessors and martyrs of whom the world was not worthy, but chief among all, the first begotten of the dead who is king of saints and who for us died upon the bitter cross and who asked that we should do this in remembrance of Him—all these draw nigh in these sacred, quickening moments to cheer and strengthen us on our way.

And thus this sacrament of sacred memories brings to us spiritual food, the bread of life. "I am the bread of life." "This is the bread that cometh down out of heaven that a man may eat thereof and not die." Men perish not primarily for lack of moral conviction which should move them to do those things which they know. And how shall the heart of man possess this certitude with its compulsions and its consolations. It is not the result of intellectual processes and philosophical speculation. Even George Santayana who follows theistic thought only afar off, describes the insufficiency of this method in words of haunting beauty:

> O world, thou choosest not the better part!
> It is not wisdom only to be wise,
> And on the inward vision close the eyes,
> But it is wisdom to believe the heart.
>
> . . . .
>
> And trust the soul's invincible surmise . . .
> Our knowledge is a torch of smoky pine
> That lights the pathway but one step ahead
> Across a void of mystery and dread.
> Bid, then, the tender light of faith to shine
> By which alone the mortal heart is led
> Unto the thinking of the thought divine.

But we know whence this faith has come and how it is begotten and nourished in our hearts. "Seeing it is God that said, Light shall shine out of darkness, who shined in our hearts, to give the light of knowledge of the glory of God in the face of Jesus Christ."

Yes, it is well to remind ourselves always, and especially in a time of uncertainty, of the testimony which our evangelical faith has borne to the gospel. We are saved by grace through faith. What man could not do God gave. The heinousness of sin, its reality and destructive power are revealed fully in the cross of Christ. And there also we behold the redemptive love of Him who spared not His only Son but delivered him up for us all. A broken body and shed blood pierces man's complacent idea of sin. No longer can he speak of it as mere error or good in the making which in some automatic way will be eradicated, as it was supposed, with the inevitable progress and development of the human race. We have heard less of this comfortable and superficial doctrine in recent years because side by side with the increase in intellectual and scientific attainments we have witnessed increase in the capacity to do evil. Science equips us with wondrous instruments but whether they shall be used for the healing of the nations or for their destruction depends upon that which is in the heart of man who possesses them. And have we not had glimpses, as it were, into the pit of hell as we have seen the increased power to destroy begotten of the insatiable greed and lust for power and fierce hatred of modern man? Yes, again out of the heart are the issues of life. And we turn with renewed confidence to him who alone cleanses our hearts of evil and prepares them to be the dwelling place of holy love. "In Him was life and his life was the light of men and as many as received him to them gave He the right to become the children of God." And thus as in faith we receive the Lord in our hearts the miracle of regeneration is renewed. We are brought into living fellowship with him. Old things pass away and all things become new. We are nurtured with living bread. How physical bread sustains mental processes no man knoweth because it involves the mysteries of the relationship between mind and matter. That there is much that passes understanding in the miracle of the new life we know full well, but this we know also with a certainty that is higher than all other forms of knowledge: as we remember his precepts to do them; as we remember his redemptive love finding its highest expression on the cross, we are quickened to new life and sustained in the same, participating through the miracle of grace in the life of the son of God. The broken bread, received by faith is thus the seal of oneness, communion in the body of Christ.

But as we draw near to the Lord we inevitably draw nearer one to another. Communion with Christ in spirit and in truth inevitably begets union among believers for we find that we hold in common that which is most precious, one faith, one Lord, one baptism, one God and Father of all who is over all, and through all and in all. As the radii of a circle draw near to each other in proportion as they approach the center, so do we experience the unity of the Spirit with our fellow-believers as Christ becomes the center of affections and hopes. To the ancient Christians the loaf was a symbol of this unity of believers in the body of Christ which is the Church. In the account of the Lord's Supper in the Didache we read: "And concerning the broken bread: We thank Thee, our Father, for the life and knowledge which thou hast made known to us through Jesus, Thy servant; to Thee be the glory forever. Just as this broken bread was scattered over the hills and having been gathered into one, so let Thy Church be gathered from the ends of the earth into thy kingdom."

It is our solemn conviction today that in the uniting of our two branches of the church we are giving expression to the symbolism of the loaf. What was widely scattered and separate has been brought into one. And now our prayer is that unity may follow union; that every portion may be leavened by the Holy Spirit; that being receptive to the movements of the Spirit the hand of God may move mightily upon us and knead us into one. Only thus shall we be sufficient for the more difficult tasks that are before us. Only thus shall we have the degree of patience, of mutual understanding and forbearance, that willingness to compromise in unessentials which is necessary for the further uniting of the fabric of the two organizations. The mighty compulsion of keeping the unity of the spirit in the bond of peace must be upon us if we are to bear witness to the world that we are of the body of Christ and severally members one of another.

But there is another way in which we bear witness and that is by our works. This sacrament is not only a sacred feast of remembrance in which we are drawn nearer to our Lord and of brotherhood by which we are united the more closely one with the other in His body, but of renewed consecration to work the works of God while it is day. In one of the ancient prayers of the Communion office is this collect "And be pleased . . . graciously to receive at our hands this memorial of the blessed sacrifice of Thy Son; in union with which we here offer and present unto Thee, O Lord, the reasonable sacrifice of our own persons, consecrating ourselves upon the altar of the Gospel, in soul and body, property and life to thy most blessed service and praise." The purpose of bread is to nourish life and sustain labor. But again we remember that it is broken bread. How significant. We who are many are gathered into one that we may know the one true God, again we separate going our several ways each to bear his testimony in his particular sphere. There are these two rhythmic movements the one centripetal and the other centrifugal. The one brings us together that we may be inspired and strengthened and refreshed; here we shall see visions into deeds and that the kingdoms of this world may become the Kingdom of the Lord and of His Christ.

But if we in turn are to be bread to those that feed on husks, we must be broken bread. The secret of the cross and the power of the cross must be ours. We must be ready and willing to spend and be spent, and with Paul say "Now I rejoice in my sufferings for your sake, and fill up, on my part, that which is lacking of the afflictions of Christ in my flesh for his body's sake, which is the church." The secret of the cross is the secret of the saints. It is they who attain to joy through suffering; it is they who are removed to deepest compassion because they suffer in the presence of the ignorant, the willful and the vicious; it is they who are moved to the heights of moral indignation as they feel the evil that men do to the innocent and the weak; it is they who pour out the last full measure of devotion, accounting all that the world holds dear but as refuse, that they may serve the brethren and bring men into living union with the Son of God.

In this day when many who ask for bread receive but a stone, when many loudly proclaim that the multiplying of physical bread, the production of material things in plenty will meet the needs of men, may we have grace unitedly to show men the more excellent way. May we ever guide them to the living Lord of Life who is the true bread which cometh down from heaven, that bread which was broken for us. And as we receive it in faith we are able to bring something of heaven into the world despite its heartbreak and its sin.

"And He shall see of the travail of His soul and be satisfied."

PART V

The United Church of Christ

Only six years after the Congregational Christian Churches of the United States came into being and three years after the Evangelical and Reformed Church was formed, an event occurred involving certain members of these new denominations that launched the ultimately successful union negotiations between them. In January 1937, Truman Douglass, a prominent Congregational Christian minister in St. Louis, invited a small group of local ministers and professors to meet together—including George M. Gibson, who wrote the syllabus for the discussion, and Samuel Press, president of Eden Theological Seminary—"for the purpose of redefining and clarifying the bases of [their] faith and work." After several months of working together on the fundamentals of their faith and ministry, the group came to feel that they had "a strong unity of thought and mind" around the primary things of importance, and that perhaps their denominational fellowships might also be able to come together in unity (see vol. 6:70).

In 1938, knowing that his Congregational Christian colleagues Douglass and Gibson were in Beloit, Wisconsin, attending a meeting of the General Council of the Congregational Christian Churches, Press, who was chair of the Evangelical and Reformed Church's Commission on Closer Relations with Other Churches, sent them a telegram. In it he asked, "What about a rapprochement between our communions looking toward union?" Soon thereafter, an informal meeting was held in Chicago between Press and Douglas Horton, minister of the Congregational Christian General Council. Horton sent an overture to George W. Richards, president of the Evangelical and Reformed Church, proposing official conversations between the two denominations. Thus began fifteen years of union negotiations between the Congregational Christian Churches and the Evangelical and Reformed Church, two denominations which at first glance seemed unlikely partners for church union.

About the same time, another discussion emerged that invited denominations based on congregational principles (Congregational Christian, Baptist, and Disciples) to envision church union. During the second World Conference on Faith and Order, held in Edinburgh in 1937, two editorials in the *Christian Century* raised important questions about congregational polity. Did the Congregational emphasis on the autonomy of every local church hold congregational denominations back from affirming the doctrine of the catholic and organic unity of the church that undergirded ecumenical discussion? Could the two doctrines be reconciled (see vol. 6:71)? These editorials raised the issue that Washington Gladden, a progressive Social Gospel leader and Congregational pastor, had raised thirty years earlier, namely, whether Congregationalism had sufficiently clarified the issue of autonomy versus fellowship (or "connectionalism") in its denominational self-understanding (see vol. 6:3). The different perspectives on this issue, and the differing views of Congregationalism that they generated, dominated the ecumenical work of Congregational Christian leaders for the next twenty years.

During the early stages of union conversations between the Congregational Christian Churches and the Evangelical and Reformed Church, each recognized the potential to create something radically new for church unions in the United States: organic union between two denominations quite different from each other. There were economic and social differences when the Congregationalists and the Christians united in 1931, and they differed considerably in style of worship. Nevertheless, each insisted upon local church autonomy and rejected creedal authority, while upholding the freedom of individual conscience. Each had a relatively informal intradenominational power structure and an intense commitment to union. Their union brought together distant relatives within the ecclesiastical world.

So also did the 1934 union between the Evangelical Synod of North America and the Reformed Church in the United States. The Evangelical and Reformed Church united people with a common heritage rooted in the German and Swiss Protestant Reformation. Both of these German immigrant denominations had evolved to gain status as mainstream denominations; both had a constitutional tradition where lines of authority within church government were clear. Like the Congregational Christian Churches, the Evangelical and Reformed Church was a union of ecclesiastical relatives.

Although at first glance a union between the Congregational Christian Churches and the Evangelical and Reformed Church could have been viewed as an unlikely partnership, these two denominations had both developed a deep concern for church unity. By the late 1930s they were ready for a new challenge.

Union Negotiations

Official endorsement to enter into union negotiations came from the Evangelical and Reformed General Synod and the Congregational Christian General Council in 1942. A Joint Committee on Union began its work shortly thereafter. Reporting on the beginning of these negotiations, an editorial in the *Christian Century* on October 21, 1942, first described the two churches with language that would become very important to the United Church of Christ: "It is a significant and heartening fact that these two churches which have had a taste of union want more of it! They are not content to be merely *united* churches, but wish to be *uniting* churches. The impulse for unity, once it has been released in action, tends to take the form of a mission, with the Holy Spirit (which is the Spirit of unity) increasingly in charge."

Leaders in both denominations had learned the tools of their craft well during the years in which they had represented the four antecedent denominations, and they entered energetically into the task of providing a broader forum for their union discussions. George W. Richards, president of Lancaster Theological Seminary, continued an extraordinary ecumenical career, which he had begun in the Reformed Church in the United States, by publishing an article in the Congregational Christian magazine *Advance,* introducing the Evangelical and Reformed Church to Congregational Christian readers. At the same time, he touched lightly upon what would become the most sensitive area between the churches. "If you will permit me to use my autonomy, without authority, I venture to affirm that in due time it may be possible to deauthorize the Evangelical and Reformed Church at the top and to deauthorize the Congregational Christian Church at the bottom, without interfering with the Lordship of Christ" (see vol. 6:72). Douglas Horton, minister of the General Council of the Congregational Christian Churches, prepared a companion article for *Advance* on the differences between the two denominations in faith and practice (see vol. 6:73). During 1947 alone, the monthly Congregational Christian magazine *Advance* published more than thirteen substantive articles discussing the advantages and disadvantages of union, followed the next year by articles on the spiritual, social, and sociological aspects of union. The *Messenger,* the comparable journal of the Evangelical and Reformed Church, also sought to stimulate interest in union by thoroughly addressing the issues and publishing articles detailing the pros and cons of union. Open letters were solicited by the newspaper giving opinions on the merger (see vol. 6:74). *Advance* published prayers for those on both sides of the union discussions and articles showing how local churches were presenting the prospective union to their church members (see vol. 6:75). *Youth* magazine, a journal of the Evangelical and Reformed Church, introduced its young people to the youth organization of the Congregational Christian Churches, discussed theological and practical grounds for union, and outlined for its readers the most significant points in the "Basis of Union." By June 1948, *Youth* celebrated the union of the Pilgrim Fellowship of the Congregational Christian Churches and the Youth Fellowship of the Evangelical and Reformed Church to create "The Youth Fellowship of the United Church of Christ" (see vol. 6:76). The *Messenger* even published part of a presidential address by Hampton Adams to the International Convention of the Disciples of Christ. In that speech Adams anticipated the union of the Congregational Christian Churches and the Evangelical and Reformed Church "within the next two or three years," and he made the first mention of what years later would become a "partnership" between the United Church of Christ and the Christian Church (Disciples of Christ). Church leaders did their best to educate and involve members in all settings of both denominations in issues of union.

At the same time as the denominations got to know each other better, the Joint Committee on Union worked to prepare and revise drafts of the Basis of Union and to send out periodic reports highlighting the points of debate that were beginning to emerge. The final draft of the Basis of Union was finished in 1947 and adopted by the General Synod of the Evangelical and Reformed Church in July of that year (see vol. 6:77).

Eager to make sure that the Basis of Union was not misunderstood, the Joint Committee of the two denominations published a "Primer of Union" giving information about the historical background of both denominations, statistics, polity, the understanding of ministry, and answers to commonly asked questions regarding the union (see vol. 6:78). As early as 1944, the Joint Committee had drawn up a proposed schedule for the consummation of the union, including a two-year period of getting acquainted in local, regional, and national settings; a joint meeting of the national assemblies in 1946; and final preparatory steps for the consummation of the union in 1947. The Congregational Christian General Council and the Evangelical and Reformed General Synod approved the steps as proposed, and the goal of union seemed well prepared and assured.

Agitation Against Union

In spite of all this educational work on all sides, the old debate within Congregationalism about local congregational autonomy became increasingly heated. Congregational Christian opponents of the union maintained that Congregational Christian principles would be violated by the proposed union. Their primary and most overarching concern was that the union would produce what they called "an authoritarian church"—overrunning the autonomy of local churches by forcing them to become "one church," controlling their property rights, choosing their minister, and even telling them what to believe by requiring assent to a statement of faith. Connected with this was the conviction that the General Council of the Congregational Christian Churches was overstepping its role in an authoritarian decision to allocate to itself the right to determine the way in which the decision would be made. Critics argued that such a decision was the responsibility of autonomous local churches themselves. Lesser fears concerned whether the proposed constitution for the new denomination, to be written after the new church was born, would further restrict the autonomy of local churches after union had become fact and it was too late to redress such restriction. Finally, it was feared that the proposed union of the various mission boards and agencies of the Congregational Christian Churches with the comparable boards in the Evangelical and Reformed Church would put funds meant for Congregational use under "alien" control.

Fears within the Congregational Christian Churches were exacerbated by a strong negative statement produced by a meeting held in Evanston, Illinois, in November 1947 (see vol. 6:79); by the prolific antimerger pamphleteering of Malcolm K. Burton, Midwestern defender of congregational principles (see vol. 6:80); by Marion J. Bradshaw, leader of a group seeking to continue the work of the Evanston meeting through "The Committee for the Continuation of the Congregational Christian Churches" (see vol. 6:81); and by the efforts of Henry David Gray, a pastor in Hartford, Connecticut, who saw himself as "a mediator" in the controversy (see vol. 6:82).

The intensity of these antimerger activities continued to raise doubts among Congregational Christian people. The League to Uphold Congregational Principles and the Committee for the Continuation of Congregational Christian Churches of the United States joined forces for some particularly virulent pieces (see vol. 6:83). It soon became clear to those who believed that this particular church union was a good idea that they needed to focus discussion within the denomination on the central issues raised by the opposition: the meaning of autonomy in Congregationalism and the nature of relationships between local congregations and regional or national entities, as well as with other denominations.

Addressing Concerns

Proponents for the union heard all of these concerns and mounted a well-organized campaign to educate members and alleviate fears. The Congregational Christian General Council, meeting in Oberlin in 1948, added a set of "Interpretations" to the Basis of Union to explain points in the latter that had given rise to misunderstandings (see vol. 6:84). The Oberlin meeting endorsed the Basis of Union with Interpretations by an overwhelmingly positive vote of 1000 to 11 (some reports say 12).

Unfortunately, the Interpretations led to difficulties within the Evangelical and Reformed Church. It was not clear to the Evangelical and Reformed Church whether the Interpretations changed the meaning of the Basis of Union in any particulars; and furthermore, once the Interpretations were added, the General Synod and the regional synods of the Evangelical and Reformed Church needed to vote again.

Evangelical and Reformed Church members were concerned that a new concept had been introduced in the Interpretations, a concept that at first seemed quite unacceptable. Paragraph (a) of the Interpretations read, "The Basis of Union calls for a union of the General Council of Congregational Christian Churches and the General Synod of the Evangelical and Reformed Church to form the General Synod of the United Church of Christ." For the Evangelical and Reformed Church, this narrow definition of union was theologically thin. Organic union took place between whole churches, not between the executive committees of churches. The Interpretations clarified for Evangelical and Reformed leaders how the principle of the "local autonomy" of every congregation in the polity of the Congregational Christian Churches made it impossible for the Congregational Christian General Council to act for all the congregations. Yet, theologically it also affirmed that the General Council of the Congregational Christian Churches was itself called together as "church." The General Council, as church, could make decisions for itself and invite local churches to affirm or reject them. The Interpretations led both denominations to deeper understandings of their differences in polity, and eventually the additional language was accepted by the Evangelical and Reformed Church.

Proponents of union among the Congregational Christians tried to allay fears by answering every conceivable question. They pointed out places in the Basis of Union where local church autonomy was positively guaranteed, and noted that the Interpretations specifically said that the General Council of the Congregational Christian Churches "acts only for itself" and not for the local churches. They also sought to allay constitutional fears by pointing out that the constitution, yet to be written for the new denomination, would "define and regulate" the role of the new General Synod, but it would only "describe" the "free and voluntary relationships" that local churches, associations, and conferences might choose to enter. They tried to reduce financial anxieties by asserting that merged boards in the new church would all remain independent in administering their funds.

Finally, in 1948 the General Council adopted "Comments on the Interpretations of the Basis of Union," written by Evangelical and Reformed leader George W. Richards, lest anyone misunderstand the purpose of the Interpretations. To reassure Congregational Christian congregations, a pamphlet was prepared and circulated by respected Congregational historian Frederick L. Fagley, explaining to local church members that the United Church of Christ would not compromise the autonomy of any local congregation (see vol. 6:85).

During the campaign to convince local Congregational Christian churches to vote for the Basis of Union with Interpretations, it had been stated repeatedly that the union would not be consummated unless it was supported by a 75 percent favorable vote of local congregations. This was not a legal stipulation, but it was considered a good faith promise. Therefore, after the General Council submitted the Basis of Union with Interpretations to local congregations, conferences and associations for advice, it faced a procedural crisis when only 72.8 percent of voting local congregations endorsed the merger. After some soul searching, and in spite of the less than 75 percent vote, the Congregational Christian leadership decided to move ahead, confident that God was with them on their long journey toward unity. The leadership of the anti-merger movement, however, felt just as strongly that God opposed the union. Many of them could not understand how any continuation of the union process could be justified when the vote had failed to reach 75 percent.

Nevertheless, at its meeting in Cleveland in February 1949, the General Council of the Congregational Christian Churches once again approved the "Basis of Union with Interpretations," this time by a vote of 757 to 172. And a few months later, in May 1949 the Evangelical and Reformed synods voted their approval of the same. Once again, a uniting General Synod was scheduled to give birth to the proposed United Church of Christ, this time it was to be June 26, 1950.

Church Union around the World

It is important to note that while these two United States denominations struggled toward union with one another, Christians all over the world also were increasing their commitment to church unity. The global ecumenical movement created an exciting atmosphere of hope and expectation among all Christian churches and increased the pressure within all denominations to seek church union. Leaders of the Congregational Christian Churches and the Evangelical and Reformed Church were pioneers in international union efforts, even as they labored to bring their own small union into being at home.

When Willard L. Sperry, dean of Harvard Divinity School, participated in the World Conference on Faith and Order in Edinburgh in 1937, he told the readers of *Advance* that world movements for Christian unity were no longer an "academic elective," or an "ecclesiastical luxury"; the situation in the mission fields, and the "organized and fully self-conscious theories of race, class, and state which [were] candidly anti-Christian" springing up within Christendom itself, made a united voice in the church "a spiritual and moral necessity" (see vol. 6:86). An editorial in *Advance* the same year declared that the "common peril from war, materialism, racial and national dominations, and political and economic dictatorships" had made imperative a Life and Work Conference in Oxford, England, on "Church, Community, and State." Churches around the globe were coming to a visceral awareness that if the church of Jesus Christ was going to make a compelling witness in their threatened and divided world, churches not only had to act as one, they had to be one. The "Affirmation of Union" sent out to the churches by the Edinburgh meeting made this point with passion.

Both the Evangelical and Reformed Church and the Congregational Christian Churches had participated (in their earlier denominational forms) in the Federal Council of Churches from its inception in 1908. At the same time, Henry Smith Leiper, the United States secretary of the World Council of Churches, regularly broadened the horizons of *Advance* readers by reporting on "Ecumenical Milestones" such as the Second World Conference of Christian Youth in Oslo; the Provisional Committee of the World Council of Churches, which met with the International Missionary Council to plan the first World Assembly of the Churches; the meeting of the most representative conference of theological seminary students ever held in Oxford, Ohio; and the International Missionary Council meeting in Whitby, Canada. All of these events made 1947 an astonishing year.

In 1938, the Congregational Christian Churches and the Evangelical and Reformed Church had greeted the provisional formation of the World Council of Churches of Christ enthusiastically. Although delayed by World War II, when the first assembly of the World Council of Churches finally was held in 1948, they were there. Meeting under the theme "Man's Disorder and God's Design," churches from forty-four countries sent 351 official delegates, and hundreds of alternates, consultants, accredited visitors, youth delegates, and representatives of the press to Amsterdam. It had taken almost thirty years for churches around the world to accept responsibility for a permanent ecumenical body.

Members of the Evangelical and Reformed Church and the Congregational Christian Churches took key leadership roles in this new ecumenical organization. H. Richard Niebuhr, well-known Evangelical theologian, presented a major address to the section of the assembly dealing with "The Universal Church in God's Design," and Douglas Horton, minister of the Congregational Christian Churches, served as chair of the American Committee for the World Council, and of the nominating committee of the World Council's Central Committee. After the assembly, Horton said, "The actual meeting of the churches is more important than anything which was done. The spirit making for union has achieved a body. The churches that participated are one in a new sense. The ecumenical movement at last has a roof over its head. We can stand up to the forces about us in a way which was never possible before." For many, the extraordinary significance of the event was best expressed at the moment when the "Message of the Assembly" was adopted: "Christ has made us His own, and He is not divided. In seeking Him we find one another. Here at Amsterdam we have committed ourselves afresh to Him, and have covenanted with one another in constituting this World Council of Churches. We intend to stay together."

The fact that 147 churches so separated by history and tradition could actually come together and stay together made the participating churches strikingly conscious that the central point around which they all gathered was Jesus Christ and his saving work. They affirmed that "the World Council of Churches is a fellowship of churches which accept our Lord Jesus Christ as God and Savior"; its stated goal was "to call the churches to the goal of visible unity in one faith and in one Eucharistic fellowship expressed in worship and in common life in Christ, and to advance toward that unity in order that the world may believe."

The Evangelical and Reformed Church and the Congregational Christian Churches were euphoric over the first Assembly of the World Council of Churches. For months the pages of *Advance* and of the *Messenger* were full of glowing, eyewitness accounts and assessments of this historic occasion. Local church federations and ecumenical gatherings were newly inspired to do their work as part of, and necessary to, a growing worldwide ecumenical movement (see vol. 6:87).

The World Council of Churches set about offering counsel and providing opportunities for united action, but it had no power to legislate for the churches. Its authority consisted simply in the truth and wisdom of its pronouncements. Nevertheless, questions were soon raised about the meaning of membership in the World Council. Within several years, it sought to explain itself without doing violence to the diverse understandings of the Christian church held by its members. At a meeting in Toronto in 1950, a statement on "The Church, the Churches and the World Council of Churches" was received by the Central Committee and commended for study and comment to the churches (see vol. 6:88). The statement did two things: it acknowledged that the World Council "deals in provisional ways with divisions between existing churches, which ought not to be, because they contradict the very nature of the Church," and it recognized that there was a place in the World Council "for those churches which recognize other churches as churches in the full and true sense, and for those which do not." All member churches might not be able to accept each other as true and pure churches, but they had decided not to remain in isolation and they had come together to explore their differences in mutual respect, trusting in the Holy Spirit. This "Toronto Statement" set a new tone for ecumenical relationships around the world and provided important support for the ongoing union efforts of the Congregational Christian and Evangelical and Reformed churches.

As already noted, the Congregational, Christian, and Evangelical and Reformed denominations were founding members of the Federal Council of Churches in 1908 and supported it continuously for forty years. George W. Richards of the Evangelical and Reformed Church was a key leader in the Federal Council during most of those years. In 1950, when the Federal Council was reconstituted into the National Council of the Churches of Christ in the United States of America—with twenty-nine participating denominations and eight participating interdenominational agencies—the Congregational Christian Churches and the Evangelical and Reformed Church were founding members (see vol. 6:89).

The creation of the World Council of Churches and the National Council of Churches were important ecumenical milestones. Yet, even as they came of age, the seeds for deeper understandings of church union were being sown. When the Congregational Christian General Council met at Grinnell, Iowa, in June 1946, a resolution was passed asking the Federal Council of Churches to invite those denominations that recognized each other's ministries and sacraments to send official representatives to a plenary conference to explore the possibility of developing an even closer union. Twelve years later, in May 1958, eight of the largest denominations in the United States met at the first Greenwich Conference on Church Union and developed an ambitious plan of union for what they tentatively named a "United Church in the United States" (see vol. 6:90). This action was an inspiration in the formation of the Consultation on Church Union (COCU), which came into being in 1960.

The story of the Consultation on Church Union has carried forward the ecumenical vocation of the Congregational Christian Churches and the Evangelical and Reformed Church beyond their own union. From 1960 to 2000, four major COCU unity proposals were developed. Understandings of church union shifted from a 1984 consensus statement that "covenant communion" was an "interim step" on the way to organic union, to a conviction that even though covenant communion might not find expression in forms and structures, it was a visible and organic kind of union. The historic distinction between federal and organic union began to blur as churches gained an appreciation of each other through "communion in sacred things." This stance has led COCU denominations to seek mutual recognition of one another's ministries, and the "reconciliation of ministries." In 1999, after nearly forty years of theological dialogue, the nine major denominations belonging to COCU affirmed a "new relationship" to be called "Churches Uniting in Christ."

In the 1940s, however, such collaboration was only a dream as the Congregational Christian Churches and the Evangelical and Reformed Church negotiated their union. They took each step as it came, but they believed that they were part of a movement that would eventually unite churches around the world.

Years in Court

Unfortunately, on April 18, 1949, the vision of Christian unity that informed the Congregational Christian and Evangelical and Reformed union had another setback. On that date the Cadman Memorial Church in Brooklyn, New York, and the Cadman Memorial Congregational Society filed suit against Helen Kenyon, moderator of the General Council of the Congregational Christian Churches, challenging the right of the General Council to negotiate the union. This court case and its appeals took four long years to resolve. During those years, the Congregational Christian advocates for union struggled to keep a positive momentum going, while their Evangelical and Reformed colleagues sought to stand faithfully by them. It was a very difficult time.

In 1950, a lower court in New York supported the Cadman Memorial Church in its decision, and issued a permanent injunction against any collaborative or joint activity between the two denominations. While still under injunction, the Congregational Christian General Council reaffirmed its hope that union could be effected between the two bodies, and appealed the decision. In 1952 the courts ruled in favor of the denominational leaders, but the reversal was immediately appealed by the Cadman Church. Once again the General Council of the Congregational Christian Churches reaffirmed its desire for and intention to consummate the union, while the Evangelical and Reformed Church patiently waited.

In the course of the legal/ecclesiastical arguments of the case, different understandings of Congregationalism were formulated and upheld, and efforts were made to resolve the differences. As minister of the General Council of the Congregational Christian Churches, Douglas Horton in 1950 reminded the General Council that John Robinson, minister to the Pilgrims in 1620, had spoken "Of Equability and Perseverance in Well Doing" needed by people on both sides of the debate they were having with the Church of England, calling for a redoubling of energies in those ministries where God's will remained clear to all. The General Council tried to make peace. It appointed a Committee on Free Church Polity and Unity with representatives from both sides of the issue, who were asked to study the historic documents and current practices of Congregational polity in order to find some way out of the impasse. Unfortunately, a "reconciling conclusion" was never reached. The General Council published the report of the committee in 1954 "for information only," carrying neither the approval nor the disapproval of the General Council or of the Executive Committee. There was no need to say more, because on December 3, 1953, the New York court of appeals upheld the position of the General Council and dismissed the Cadman case. The legal appeals to stop the formation of the United Church of Christ had run their course (see vol. 6:91).

The United Church of Christ

Once the issues were settled in the courts, union advocates sought to regain their earlier momentum toward union and overcome new fears that had developed within the Evangelical and Reformed Church that the proposed church would need to place too much emphasis on congregational principles. Both churches were delighted to discover that in spite of the court case, their joint commitment to union was still strong. By mid-1954, negotiations were renewed. Seasoned committee members were optimistic, but they were not naive. They knew that success would depend upon cultivating genuine ecumenical dialogue among all of their members again.

For the next few years, the leaders of both churches developed an exhaustive program to prepare the two denominations for union, bringing into action all the techniques and procedures that their ecumenical experiences had taught them. "Get acquainted" meetings were held for lay leaders of both churches in Indiana, Texas, California, Washington, Pennsylvania, and Massachusetts. A joint committee was formed to set up a shared stewardship project "to help demonstrate the added strength which a united church will have." Congregational Christian and Evangelical and Reformed leaders took joint action on recommendations for getting acquainted, including suggestions that local churches, commissions, boards, conferences, synods, associations, and other denominational groups invite fraternal delegates and observers to each other's meetings "to foster fellowship and understanding"; and that the Executive Committee of the General Council of the Congregational Christian Churches provide subscriptions to *Advance* for members of the General Council of the General Synod of the Evangelical and Reformed Church, and the latter reciprocate with subscriptions to the *Messenger.* Some two hundred Evangelical and Reformed clergy voluntarily exchanged pulpits with an equal number of Congregational Christian ministers in what the *Messenger* referred to as "the most extensive get-acquainted program ever attempted by Protestant bodies in America." Most of the spring meetings of the Evangelical and Reformed synods in 1956 invited representatives of the Congregational Christian Churches to address them, and set aside time to consider problems that had to be met before union could be effected.

At the annual convocation of Eden Theological Seminary in 1956, Albert Buckner Coe, moderator of the Congregational Christian Churches, gave four lectures introducing Congregationalism to the more than two hundred ministers in attendance. A remarkable series of informative articles appeared simultaneously in *Advance* and the *Messenger,* describing the history, programs, and organization of the two communions. Members of the Executive Committee of the General Council of the Congregational Christian Churches and the General Council of the General Synod of the Evangelical and Reformed Church issued a joint "Report to the Churches," urging church members to be controlled by their faith and not their fears, and expressing their resolve to go forward toward union. Prominent church leaders who had been part of the union movement from the beginning began to collect little-known details "for the archives," and once again published personal statements enthusiastically supporting union. It is difficult to imagine any further step that could have been taken to secure union in the minds and hearts of people in the local congregations of both denominations.

Some remaining opponents to union among the Congregational Christians founded the National Association of Congregational Christian Churches to provide an alternative national body for concerned congregations, but in the end only 5 percent of local Congregational Christian congregations joined.

When the votes were taken in 1956, both denominations voted overwhelmingly to move toward a "Uniting General Synod" in 1957, trusting each other enough to allow the writing of a new constitution, the preparation of a statement of faith and the merging of the national boards of the two churches to occur at a later date.

The interval between 1956 and the Uniting General Synod in 1957 was marked by one last skirmish between the Congregational Christian General Council and antimerger groups. A final attempt was made to halt the union through the civil courts, but that legal maneuver was unsuccessful.

When finally convened, the Uniting General Synod was a carefully orchestrated event culminating more than fifteen years of effort. It was filled with gratitude, joy, and celebration that God had stayed with everyone throughout the process, and that they were finally able to consummate a union that they believed to have been God's will from the beginning. Not surprisingly, some of the most profound moments of the synod were expressed in worship.

The formal "Declaration of Union" preceding the service of worship on the evening of June 25, 1957, expressed eloquently the conviction of both churches that God had called them together and been active on their behalf. Recalling the biblical mandate to make Christ's church one, Fred Hoskins, minister and secretary of the General Council of the Congregational Christian Churches, used language reminiscent of the 1804 "Last Will and Testament of the Springfield Presbytery" and echoed in the preamble to the Basis of Union: "moved by the conviction that we are all united in spirit and purpose and are in agreement on the substance of the Christian faith and the essential character of the Christian life; affirming our devotion to one God, the Father of our Lord Jesus Christ, and our membership in the holy catholic church, which is greater than any single church and than all the churches together; believing that denominations exist not for themselves but as parts of that church, within which each denomination is to live and labor and, if need be, die; and confronting the divisions and hostilities of our world, and hearing with a deepened sense of responsibility the prayer of our Lord 'that they may all be one even as thou, Father, art in me, and I in thee, that they are also may be in us, so that the world may believe that thou hast sent me.' "

Short addresses were given by James E. Wagner, president of the Evangelical and Reformed Church, and Hoskins, both speaking to aspects of the participants' feelings of the moment. Wagner addressed the nostalgia of those looking backward at the denomination they had loved so much, anxious about all the change and newness that the United Church of Christ would certainly bring, fearful suddenly about whether they were really doing God's will. He expressed confidence that, as one denomination, God would bring them all "some better thing" that neither of the two had possessed alone, and that they would all be further enriched by the oneness and fullness they would share together in Christ (see vol. 6:92). Hoskins's address was predominantly a jubilant thanksgiving to the triune God, who had supported them throughout their struggle toward union. Carrying the spirits of all of those present with him, he began and ended his address with the declaration "God be praised for this hour! Christ be exalted for this joy!" (see vol. 6:92).

The following morning, delegates to the Uniting Synod came together in the Old Stone Church (Presbyterian) located on the square in downtown Cleveland for a celebration of the Lord's Supper, "conceived in this instance," as explained in the program, "not only in terms of its traditional significance but also as the symbol of dedication of the delegates to the solemn responsibilities which are theirs and of their acknowledgment that, without the blessings of Almighty God and the guidance of his Holy Spirit, all their doings are nothing worth and shall be brought to nought."

The heady joy and gratitude for the day found expression in several hymns, inspired by the union, that had been composed by pastors William C. Nelson and Gerald H. Hinkle, and in eloquent prayers offered at different times in the proceedings by Douglas Horton, former minister and secretary of the General Council of the Congregational Christian Churches; Gerhard Grauer, Chairman of the Commission on Closer Relations with Other Churches; and Samuel Press, president emeritus of Eden Theological Seminary, who was recognized along with Truman Douglass as having begun the movement toward union so many years earlier. (See vol. 6:93)

At the conclusion of the festivities, the General Synod of the new denomination sent out a "Message to the Churches from the Uniting General Synod" (see vol. 6:94). Addressed to "the Members of our Fellowship and to the Whole Church of Jesus Christ throughout the World," the message was signed by the leaders of the new denomination: Moderators Louis W.

Goebel and George W. Hastings; Co-presidents Fred Hoskins and James E. Wagner; and Co-secretaries Fred S. Buschmeyer and Sheldon E. Mackey.

Fully aware that the United Church of Christ was an unusual accomplishment for Protestantism in the United States—a union of two denominations with different national and cultural origins, different church polity and intradenominational structures—the message made clear that the forces behind their union were theological, indeed christological. They came together "because the two companies of Christians have held and hold the same basic belief, that Christ and Christ alone is Head of the Church. From Him derive the understanding of God as Father, the participation in the same Spirit, the doctrines of faith, the influence toward holiness, the duties of divine worship, the apprehension of the significance of Baptism and the Lord's Supper, the observance of church order, the mutual love of Christians, and their dedication to the betterment of the world. To be drawn to Him is to be drawn to one another, and to acknowledge Him as Head is to feel pain in dismemberment one from the other." The message also affirmed that union was not a state once and for all achieved, but "a process, informed by growth and adventure" and leading finally to "communion fulfilled in Christ."

The Plain Dealer, the local Cleveland newspaper, the joy and significance of the union. In a cartoon entitled "Blessed Event," the newspaper pictured the arrival of the United Church of Christ as the birth of a baby brought by the proverbial stork. This baby would continue to grow and develop along its whole life's journey—in this case, toward the union of all of Christ's followers throughout the whole inhabited earth (see vol. 6:94).

Setting the Stage

70. An Invitation:
"Letters"

(1937)

Truman B. Douglass

In January 1937, when the Congregational Christian Churches had been a denomination for only six years, and the Evangelical and Reformed Church for only three years, an event occurred that stands in the lore of the United Church of Christ as that which precipitated eventual union discussions between the Congregational Christian Churches and the Evangelical and Reformed Church. Truman Douglass, minister of Pilgrim Congregational Church in St. Louis, and George Gibson, of Eden Seminary in St. Louis, had been meeting together on an informal basis to discuss matters of faith. They shared the conviction that "the only real and permanent basis of Christian unity must be theological—a unity of belief," and they decided that they wanted to think about these theological matters together with a small group of ministers who also were interested in clarifying the theological foundations of their life and work. To that end, Douglass sent invitations to about a dozen ministers and professors in the St. Louis area, including Samuel Press, president of Eden Theological Seminary, an Evangelical and Reformed seminary in Webster Groves.

After the group had met together for several months, the participants began to feel "a strong unity of thought and mind." One member remarked that if their group was any standard, the two denominations they represented could come together in unity. Press told the group that

---

Source: Truman B. Douglass, letter to Samuel D. Press, 26 January 1937, in the Eden Seminary Archives; idem, letter to Charles C. Merrill, 20 October 1955, in the Eden Seminary Archives.

he was the chair of the Commission on Closer Relations with Other Denominations of the Evangelical and Reformed Church, which had blanket authorization to enter into unofficial conversations to discuss possibilities for church union with anyone. After Douglass had departed for the General Council meeting, Press sent him a telegram inviting an appropriate committee from the Congregational Christians to enter into informal conversations with his committee in the Evangelical and Reformed Church. The telegram was turned over to Douglas Horton, the new secretary of the Congregational Christian General Council, who had heard about this possibility from Douglass. He in turn passed it on to the Commission on Interchurch Relations of the Congregational Christian General Council. In this quiet way, union conversations began between the two denominations.

Years later, when Douglass reflected on the matter, he still was able to declare, as he had in that little St. Louis discussion group, that there was no essential difference of spirit between the two groups, even after all the intervening years.

Letter to Samuel D. Press

January 26, 1937

Dr. S. D. Press
Eden Seminary
Webster Groves, Mo.

My dear Dr. Press:

I am wondering if you would be interested in meeting with a small group of ministers—most of them the younger men—for the purpose of redefining and clarifying the bases of our faith and work.

The project is one which George Gibson and I have been talking about for some time. We have been led to see the necessity for such a fellowship by our growing conviction that the only real and permanent basis of Christian unity must be theological—a unity of belief; and also by the hope that some of us might unite ourselves in a simple order or brotherhood wherein we can attempt a serious and disciplined application of the Christian rules of life.

The object of the meetings which we are proposing is not so much "discussion" as it is to reestablish the grounds of our witness to Christian truth. This would seem to be especially needful for those of us who have been wandering in a vague liberalism and have discovered the sterility of that approach.

As a basis for our thinking—at least at the outset—I am suggesting that we use a most valuable statement prepared by George Gibson under the title: "Seven Teachings and Seven Rules—Notes on the Classic Tradition in Christian Revelation and Its Faith and Order."

We are to meet at the First Congregational Church, Webster Groves, on Tuesday, February 2, at 12:30. We shall have a sandwich together and then talk over this project. The first chapter of George's statement will be distributed at that time.

I shall appreciate a line from you, saying whether you are interested and can join us on that day.

Fraternally,
Truman B. Douglass

Letter to Charles C. Merrill

October 20, 1955

Dr. Charles C. Merrill
74 Kirkland Street
Cambridge 38, Massachusetts

Dear C.C.:

As the events which preceded the formal discussion of the C.C.–E. & R. union receded in time the less secure my recollection of them becomes. I was therefore pleased when my secretary found in our files a copy of a letter to you under date of June 2, 1947 in which I tried to answer the questions you have more recently asked about the beginnings of the union interest.

The relevant paragraphs from the letter are as follows:

> "The beginnings of the interest which led ultimately to the proposal for union of our denomination with the Evangelical and Reformed Church were all very simple. While I was minister of Pilgrim Church in St. Louis a group of about a dozen ministers met weekly over a period of six or eight months. All of us had been out of seminary for ten years or more and we were concerned to do some solid thinking about the basis of our faith and message. We met weekly for a study period of about three hours—following a syllabus which, by the way, was prepared by Dr. George M. Gibson. The group was composed

chiefly of Congregational ministers and professors at Eden Theological Seminary. Dr. S. D. Press, then President of the seminary, was one of the most helpful members of the group.

"After some months of this regular thinking together about the fundamentals of our faith and the nature of our task as ministers, the members of our comradeship came to have a high regard for one another, and to feel a strong unity of mind and heart around the things of primary importance. The awareness of this community of thought and purpose led one of us to remark quite casually that what we had discovered in our small company might be taken as an indication that the two denominational fellowships which we represented could come together in unity.

"Dr. Press was at this time chairman of the E. and R. Commission on Closer Relations with Other Denominations. He remarked that his commission had blanket authorization to enter into unofficial conversations with any other ecclesiastical body interested in discussing the possibility of church union. I mentioned this fact in a letter to Dr. Horton, who I knew was presently to be nominated as Secretary of the General Council.

"At the end of our season of studying together in St. Louis I went to the General Council meeting at Beloit. While there I received a telegram from Dr. Press (which I am told has been lost from the files of the General Council) inviting an appropriate committee from our denomination to enter into informal conversation with his committee. This telegram was turned over to Dr. Horton, who had just been elected Minister of the General Council. It is my recollection that he brought it to the attention of the Business Committee, but the Council was so far along in its proceedings that there was no time to give the matter adequate attention. It was therefore referred to our Commission on Interchurch Relations.

"This, I believe, is the gist of the story. I cannot claim any significant part in it except that of being an intermediary between Dr. Press and Dr. Horton and of warmly commending to Dr. Horton and our Commission the E. and R. people as I came to know them in St. Louis and especially at Eden Seminary.

"I can still say, as I said at the beginning, that I believe there is no essential difference of spirit between us. My friendship with Dr. Press, who has strongly influenced a whole generation of E. and R. ministers, has been an authentic benediction to me. He is as much a Congregationalist as I am—which is saying a good deal, as I am the third generation of our family in the Congregational ministry. In addition he is—as I hope I am—a member of the Holy Catholic Church *before* he is a representative of any denomination. It is my own belief that we shall find this expression of our real unity around this larger Catholic loyalty rather than in a reconciliation of politics and administration, important as this may be."

Thanks for your generous word about my article in *Advance.*

Warm regards.

Sincerely,
(signed) *Truman B. Douglass*

71. Autonomy as Weakness?

"Congregationalists and Other Congregationalists" and "Congregationalism and Catholicity"

(1938)

The Christian Century

In 1904, Washington Gladden raised an issue in The Congregationalist and Christian World *that, although not given much attention at the time, haunted Congregational efforts at church union for more than half a century. Gladden was one of the first Congregational ecumenists. He participated in the preparation of the first proposal for union between the Congregationalists and the Christians in 1897 (see vol. 6:18), and served as chair of the joint committee preparing the (ultimately unsuccessful) Act of Union between the Congregationalists, Methodist Protestants, and United Brethren in 1904 (see vol. 6:3). In an address to a joint meeting of the three denominations, Gladden noted that whereas Congregationalists had always been very proud of their concept of the autonomy of the local church, this concept had actually become a weakness. By focusing upon autonomy, the principle of fellowship, which ought to have been coordinated with it, had not been properly developed. The result was that Congregationalists had a lopsided understanding of their own identity*

Source: Editorial, "Congregationalists and Other Congregationalists," *The Christian Century,* 19 January 1938, 70–72; copyright 1938 Christian Century Foundation; reprinted by permission from the 19 January 1938 issue of *The Christian Century.* Editorial, "Congregationalism and Catholicity," *The Christian Century,* 26 January 1938, 102–4; copyright 1938 Christian Century Foundation; reprinted by permission from the 26 January 1938 issue of *The Christian Century.*

that hindered their ability to cooperate with other churches and gave them problems in working out the implications of organic unity in the church.

In 1938, two editorials appeared in The Christian Century *discussing the very "weakness" identified by Gladden. The concept of congregational autonomy was a problem for Congregationalists, and also for Baptists and Disciples, who likewise prided themselves on their congregational polity. Perhaps, the articles suggested, this "weakness" was limiting their participation in the burgeoning, worldwide ecumenical movement—in particular, the Second World Conference of Faith and Order held in Edinburgh in 1937. At that conference, delegates from these denominations had been peculiarly silent, making no mention of their cherished principle of congregational autonomy, and seeming to go along with the "catholic" notion of the one church universal on which the meetings were based.*

However, as the editorials pointed out, Congregationalism had arisen in the sixteenth and seventeenth centuries in protest against *a catholic conception of the church. Early separatist and Puritan writers had rejected the idea that the church required some universal earthly organization within which the headship of Christ could be realized. Congregational dissenters had rebelled against all ecclesiastical organization from above, and declared that the true basis of church organization was the individual congregational unit. In fact, they actually denied that any other unit existed! One of the editorials quoted from the Savoy Declaration of 1658, which asserted, "Besides these particular churches, there is not instituted by Christ any church more extensive or catholic entrusted with power for the administration of his ordinances, or the execution of any authority in his name."*

Nevertheless, as that same editorial noted, Congregationalism itself had "never been satisfied with its own theory," but had been drawn by necessity into "connexional relations—for counsel and help, for missionary expansion, for the training, standardizing and pensioning of the ministry, for education, for the care of the poor and aged and for ordaining ministers." Moreover, Congregationalists had composed their own ecumenical marching orders in the Burial Hill Declaration (1865) (see vol. 6:1) and the Oberlin Declaration on the Unity of the Church (1871) (see vol. 6:2), which committed them to the one holy catholic and apostolic church. They had become steadily more involved in the worldwide ecumenical movement seeking to make that one church more visible.

Congregationalists, and other denominations that followed a congregational polity, were living on the horns of a dilemma that would have to be addressed before they could make their full contributions to the ecumenical movement. The question remained: "How to bring together the catholic principle and the congregational principle in one united body?"

Unfortunately, the Congregational Christian Churches made no attempt to focus on this apparent dilemma in their self-concept. The issue continued to smolder and finally played a key role in the shaping of the United Church of Christ.

Congregationalists and Other Congregationalists

As the movement for the ecumenical unity of non-Roman Christendom takes more definite shape, it becomes clear that the burden of responsibility for the outcome rests primarily upon the so-called free churches of Protestantism. Up to the present, these churches have contributed more than their share of stimulus and encouragement. It can fairly be said that they have been the chief source from which the movement has drawn its inspiration. The older churches of the East, the Continent and Great Britain have been drawn into the movement on initiatives which were taken by America's free churches, including the Protestant Episcopal. It was in the United States that the longing for unity was first crystallized into definite overtures. The movement has now reached the point where the longing is universal, and each church is confronted with the problem, first, of envisaging the goal and, second, of deciding what place, if any, its own doctrinal and ecclesiastical features should be given in the united church.

Upon Congregational and other congregational churches this responsibility rests in a peculiar manner. It has become evident that congregationalism as an ecclesiastical polity is not an adequate basis for unity. The congregational bodies themselves have been moving steadily during the past fifty years away from the extreme form of local independency toward a system approaching, in fact, if not in name, the presbyterial order. At the Edinburgh conference, no attempt was made by any of the very numerous delegates from congregational churches to set forth the congregational order as a solving conception of the problem of unity. The conference met, continued and ended in an atmosphere of catholicity. The major premise of all its deliberations was the conviction that the church of Christ on earth is, by divine intention, one, holy and catholic, and that it is this character of the church which the ecumenical movement is seeking to recover and to embody in a living organization.

Where does congregationalism, with its emphasis upon the autonomy and independence of each local church, fit into this picture? Do the congregational denominations of Great Britain and America desire to impose their type of organization upon the church universal? Do they ask, as a condition of unity, that those communions which hold to the catholic conception of the church shall dissolve their ecclesiastical structures and disperse their church order into independent local units, each clothed with autonomy as Baptist, Congregational and Disciples churches now are? This, stated very sharply, is the question which the free churches confront by virtue of their participation in the ecumenical movement. So far, they have not advanced any such demand. Their silence at Edinburgh, their tacit acceptance of the catholic presuppositions around which the entire discussion revolved, their gracious acquiescence in the findings, leave them in an ambiguous position. Are these congregational churches really willing to go into a united church whose organization rests, not upon the local unit, but upon the catholic unity of the whole body of Christ?

The consideration of this crucial question should not be put off indefinitely either on account of preoccupation with denominational concerns or by obscurantist drifting with the ecumenical movement. At the next World Conference on Faith and Order, those communions holding the congregational system should be represented by a body of delegates who have something to say. What they may say is not now the question. But having affirmed the congregational principle for several centuries, these bodies stand in an anomalous position when they allow the ecumenical movement to go forward without paying even a gesture of respect to their historic contention. Mayhap their contention has been erroneous. Possibly it represents a half-truth. Possibly, again, it represents the only sound basis of ecclesiastical organization and should be pushed with vigor upon the conscience of the whole church. In any case, these congregational denominations owe it both to themselves and to the ecumenical movement to define in their own thought the witness which their representatives in an ecumenical conference should bear.

Since the Edinburgh conference, the issue has arisen rather sharply in at least one of these congregational bodies. We refer to the denomination which wears the name Congregational. Like the Baptist and Disciples denominations, it was silent at Edinburgh so far as this fundamental question was concerned. But even while the conference was assembling, there broke out in British Congregationalism a lively and wholesome controversy over certain implications of congregational faith and order in relation to the ecumenical movement. This controversy heated up in two brochures, one entitled, *Inevitable Congregationalism,* by Rev. Dr. Albert Peel, editor of the *Congregational Quarterly,* the other entitled *Congregationalism Today,* by Principal Nathaniel Micklem, of Mansfield College, Oxford.

Dr. Micklem takes sharp issue with his fellow Congregationalist, Dr. Peel, and presents an interpretation of congregationalism which he regards as at once loyal to the historic tradition and hospitable to the catholic ideal. Dr. Peel's booklet includes numerous addresses which he has made during the past two decades, mostly before gatherings of his own denomination. Not unnaturally, statements could be found in these addresses which were none too well considered. To so discerning a critic as Dr. Micklem they lent themselves as foils against which he could thrust his own clarifying interpretation. It is not our present purpose to take sides or to prejudice their discussion, but it seems doubtful from this distance that the difference between these two Congregational leaders is so great as Dr. Micklem's selection of texts from Dr. Peel's addresses would make it appear. Our sole interest at the moment is in the fact that congregationalism as a polity for the Christian church has become the subject of serious discussion.

The discussion has spread to the United States. A movement is on foot, prompted chiefly by Dr. Ernest Graham Guthrie, Congregationalism's "Bishop" of Chicago, and supported by the best minds of the denomination, including Dean Sperry of Harvard to arouse Congregationalists in this country to prepare for the International Congregational Council, which meets here in 1940, by becoming intelligent on the subject of their own faith and order. Referring to an editorial in The Christian Century as "taunting us with the fact that at Edinburgh there was no great voice that spoke for the churches of the congregational order," Dr. Guthrie tells his own brethren that "it will be nothing less than a confession of permanent inferiority if British Congregationalism comes to that council with fully articulated convictions . . . and we [American Congregationalists] come as confused, uncertain and dumb as we were at Edinburgh."

Such a challenging call is irresistible, and we may expect the Congregational denomination to begin and to carry through a fruitful process of rethinking its historic witness. But what of other congregationalists? No sign of such activity has appeared among the Disciples and Baptists. Both of these bodies are larger than the Congregationalists. The ecumenical movement now commands more of their devotion and hope than ever before. Manifestly, they cannot avoid a reconsideration of their respective positions as congregationalists. The program makers for the conventions of these two denominations have here at hand the theme which should occupy their gatherings until definite convictions about the order of the Church of Christ have become the common and intelligent possession of all their churches. This rethinking of congregationalism is the only adequate way to prepare for the next conference on Faith and Order in 1947.

But the project of rethinking congregationalism cannot be completed by each of these denominations working separately. Left to itself, each group will no doubt reach conclusions not reached by the other two. Does this not suggest the desirability of a kind of "ecumenical" conference of Baptists, Congregationalists and Disciples to consider their common congregationalism in the light of their several traditions? There are differences even among congregationalists! These differences may not be of great importance, and yet they may. Perhaps the Congregationalists have the more flexible order and have advanced farther toward an organic consciousness and an organic procedure than the other two. The Disciples, notwithstanding their thoroughgoing Protestantism in external form and procedure, are more catholic than Protestant in their ideology. The Baptists, taking them as a whole, North and South, are at the extreme left, so to speak, of congregationalism.

Each of these bodies has something to contribute to the others. Their witness for their historic order, a witness competent to find voice in the ecumenical movement, can be better presented if it is conceived in a unity of their own than in separation. Besides, these three denominations have engaged in the fraternal exercise of throwing out "feelers" toward one another during many years, looking toward a closer unity. There is no Christian reason why they should not achieve actual unity, especially now that the longing for unity pervades the whole Church of Christ. A small preparatory conference of their ablest scholars and leaders to consider their common congregationalism, with its implications of faith and doctrine, would have more than academic results. It would at least lead to a larger representative conferencc with an agenda based upon the findings of the preparatory conference, and the results of this larger gathering might be far more substantial and significant than we can envisage in advance of the event.

As we see it, congregationalists may take one of three attitudes toward the ecumenical movement. They may surrender their congregationalism, and allow their several traditions and their churches to be absorbed in the catholic conception and structure of the church as this conception and this structure may be wrought out by the churches now holding the catholic ideal. It is difficult to imagine such an outcome. It is difficult, because not even the more explicit catholic communions would affirm that the congregational witness was wholly without merit and value. But it is unthinkable that, even if a majority of each group were willing to be so absorbed, there would not be an intransigent minority unwilling to sink its historic identity in such a union. The principle informing the whole ecumenical movement is the principle of going forward *together,* in contrast to the false principle of dividing the now existing churches in order to form a new church.

The second attitude is one of indifference and aloofness. Some no doubt there are who assume such an attitude. Their number, however, is growing beautifully less. But it is a possible position, especially in view of the catholic lines along which the ecumenical movement is plainly developing. The congregational mind is none too familiar with the concept of catholicity. What familiarity the concept has in many minds is associated with feelings of repugnance and fear. It is so closely associated with "Roman Catholic" that there will be some readers of these paragraphs who will not have observed that the word "catholic" is spelled uniformly with a small "c," and that it refers not to anything upon which Rome has a monopoly, but to a generic conception of the church of Christ. The form and structure of a non-Roman catholicism are not necessarily decided in advance, and when decided, we may be sure that there will be no compromise with Rome. Happily, we have reached the point in the non-Roman churches where we are able to claim for ourselves the dignity and divinity of the catholic ideal and to strive for its embodiment without arousing the unintelligent fears which once would have been conjured up by such a movement.

The third attitude which congregationalists may take—and we believe should take—toward the ecumenical movement is one of responsibility for the character of the church which may issue from it. This attitude of responsibility implies generous participation, and an actual contribution toward the outcome. Congregationalists have no need to be apologetic for their congregationalism. It has been faultily conceived, no doubt, and its embodiment has left much to be desired in the structure of the living church. But cannot the same be said of the more explicitly catholic communions? And may it not be true that there is in congregationalism a principle belonging to the very genius of the Christian faith for the want of which the catholic churches are weak, as congregationalism itself is weak for the want of catholicity?

The Christian Century holds that congregationalism, though it has erred in conceiving itself as an ecclesiastical polity, has not erred in conceiving itself as an indispensable factor in a soundly Christian ecclesiastical polity. No part of the ecumenical church has more to contribute to the whole than have these congregational bodies. What that contribution is to be is the essence of the problem which the Congregational denomination of England and America is out to discover and formulate. Baptists and Disciples must not be behind them in studying the question. And altogether they must see to it that another world conference is not held in which they stand "confused, uncertain and dumb."

Congregationalism and Catholicity

Looking toward the unity of non-Roman Christendom, it now becomes the concern of every denomination to decide what treasures in its own tradition it regards as worthy to offer to a united church. These treasures will not emerge automatically in any world conference. They must be brought there. They must be brought in the spirit of loyalty to one's own tradition, and in all humility laid before the ecumenical mind for its consideration. This is the course which has been pursued by the great communions of the East, the Continent and Great Britain. It has not been the course pursued by the free churches of America. The result is that the ecumenical movement has developed one-sidedly in terms of the catholic principle in Christianity. The congregational principle has so far been disregarded. Many are therefore asking whether, if the congregational bodies go into the united church, they must go with empty hands.

It is probable that this one-sided development is all to the good. Progress toward unity can hardly be made on all fronts simultaneously. No progress at all could be made without first establishing the principle of catholicity. This required that the congregationally minded churches should humbly expose themselves to the full impact of the catholic ideal. The virtual silence of congregationalism in the initial world conferences is a tribute to its open-mindedness. It is also a tribute to its logical instinct; for unless the catholic principle can establish itself there is no basis on which to erect a united church. It is fortunate, therefore, that in the ecumenical movement the churches which cherish the catholic ideal have had the right of way in the first stages of the discussion. The effect of this was happily expressed by Dr. Edgar DeWitt Jones, president of the Federal Council of Churches, when he said at Oxford: "We came here thinking of our churches; we return home thinking of the church."

But it is not to be assumed that congregationalism has no positive thoughts of its own as it silently contemplates the emerging outlines of a catholic Christendom. It cannot forget its own history or the causes of its secession from the historical order of the church. Sitting now in a calm Christian conference with non-Roman catholicism, and sharing in the general penitence for the divisions which exist in the body of Christ, congregationalism does not easily forget the circumstances which produced the initial rupture and drove it into a status of separatism. Nor is it willing to concede that its secession was due solely to the corruptions which existed in the church, and that, inasmuch as these no longer exist, it is ready to return.

On the contrary, congregationalism was a protest against something structural in the historic church, as well as against temporary abuses. Those left-wing Puritans who despaired of reforming the church from within and proposed as their motto, "Reformation without tarrying for any," saw something which the very order of the church lacked, something which they held to be of the essence of the Christian faith, and which could not be restored within the existing order, something which required independent action in defiance of the established system. No doubt the gross abuses were the precipitating cause, but these provided the occasion for affirming a living principle which Baptists and Congregationalists embodied in their local churches and have maintained to this day.

The ecumenical movement will be wise if it indulges in no illusions at this point. It is in search of catholicity, but it will not find a catholicity acceptable to congregationalism if it seeks for it only in the past, if it assumes that union is merely re-union—the reinstatement of the *status quo ante bellum.* The search for catholicity must be in large measure a constructive activity. It will have the greatest respect for history, and it will maintain continuity with the historic church by the most sensitive regard for venerable Christian institutions; but it will also sit at the feet of history to learn the lessons which history teaches. And among these lessons none is more important or vital to the character of a united church than that which is contained in the historical dissent of such bodies as Baptists, Congregationalists and Disciples.

The re-emergence of the principle of catholicity will evoke the reassertion of congregationalism. For congregationalism arose in protest against the catholic conception of the church—against the conception that the church as a whole requires organization. Against this catholic theory of the church the Dissenters of the sixteenth and seventeenth centuries affirmed that the true basis of church organization is the congregational unit, and in their radicalism they denied that there was any other. "Besides these particular churches," said the Savoy Confession of 1658, "there is not instituted by Christ any church more extensive or catholic entrusted with power for the administration of his ordinances, or the execution of any authority in his name."

Congregationalism has never been satisfied with its own theory. In spite of its theory, its churches have been drawn into connexional relations—for counsel and help, for missionary expansion, for the training, standardizing and pensioning of the ministry, for education, for the care of the poor and aged and for ordaining ministers. Among Baptists, Congregationalists and Disciples, the longing for an intercongregational fellowship and for an organization to implement it, has been irresistible. But in each of these denominations the development of such an organization has had to take place against the grain of the earlier tradition of radical independency. Missionary societies have been resisted on the theory that each church (congregation) is its own missionary society. Ordination by a representative council of neighboring local churches has been resisted on the theory that the minister can be ordained only by the local church—his ordination consisting of his election as its pastor by a specific congregation, accompanied by the laying on of hands by officers of the electing congregation, and conferring no status beyond the boundaries of that particular congregation.

This atomistic congregationalism has steadily surrendered to at least a skeleton connexionalism, involving a considerable sacrifice of autonomy to the general interests and responsibilities of the denomination. A sort of denominational "catholicity" has taken the place of the original theory of stark congregational independency. And now these churches confront the larger catholicity—that of the Church of Christ as a whole, whose unity is being sought in the ecumenical movement. In the light of their tradition and the values which it carries, what is to be their attitude toward this holy Catholic church which, if it please God, will one day come into being? This is the problem which congregationalists must set themselves to solve during the decade before another world conference on faith and order is held.

We make no pretense of offering a solution in this place. Each denomination must work out its own solution. But the three leading congregationalist bodies can help one another, as we suggested in these pages last week, by recognizing that they face a common problem and by conferring together to define their position and to separate the wheat of congregationalism from its chaff. As a start toward such an undertaking, we offer three statements which we believe will reflect, in the most general terms, the present spirit of the congregational bodies.

In the first place, Congregationalists are now ready to admit that congregationalism is not an adequate basis for the organization of the Christian fellowship. The fathers were mistaken in claiming so much for their principle. The Christian community exists in congregations, but it is not bounded by these congregations. There is a church which includes all the local churches. This church by divine intention has a unity of its own—it is a spiritual reality, and as such rightfully demands a body in which to live and through which to function. Congregationalism as a polity is weak in that it cannot mobilize the church's forces for making the Christian impact upon civilization on a wide front and under a persistent strategy. Not only so, but it is weak in its inability to provide for the free flowing of the spiritual resources of the whole church to all its members. It is always in peril of the smugness of localism. Christianity is a community; but congregationalism has been in error in taking the conception of "two or three gathered together" as the norm of the Christian community. This is not the norm—it is the minimum. The norm of the Christian community is the whole body of those who profess the Christian faith. To build a church polity on the minimum conception of a "gathered church," a local congregation, and to exclude all other polity is to falsify the character of the Christian society.

The second statement flows from the first: The Christian community as a whole can exist as an actuality only through organization. Christian community is not sentimentalism. It is the cooperative life of all Christians and all Christian congregations through organic relationship; it is the actual sharing of Christian values and responsibility in one corporate body of which Christ is the head. The early congregationalists made Christ the head of each local church in a manner which, in effect, denied his headship of the whole body of the faithful. True, they attributed to him a certain transcendental headship—he was head of the *invisible* church, which was conceived as including the faithful dispersed through all the churches. But the only visible church of which he was the head was the local congregation. This theory was the *ne plus ultra* of sectarianism—it made a sect of each local congregation which was thus a complete church in itself. Christ was divided into as many headships as there were local churches. The resort to an "invisible" church was the good old Protestant device for escaping this predicament. But it left the church *on earth* without a head, and restricted the Christian community to the "two or three gathered together."

Intelligent congregationalism in our day cannot tolerate this conception. For a hundred years it has been slowly developing a connexional corporateness within its several denominations, emphasizing increasingly the interdependence of local churches as over against their earlier claim of independency. But now it is becoming clear that their intradenominational interdependence is not enough. They cannot stop there. If they can no longer claim that the headship of Christ is exhausted by his headship of the local church, they cannot claim that Christ is the head of their *denomination*—the very idea is repugnant. It not only still leaves Christ divided, but it smacks of arrogance and partyism, which is condemned by

Scripture and by every instinct of the Christian faith. The doctrine of the headship of Christ cannot be applied to any part of his church save as it reflects his headship over all his church. This, however, spells catholicity. And congregationalism has now come to the point where it is willing to make the concession, so long withheld, that the headship of Christ over all his church requires a catholic body in which his living presence may be known and through which his redemptive work may be accomplished.

What, then, becomes of the congregational principle? This brings us to the third statement which we believe congregationalism will surely affirm, namely, that in the organization of the catholic body of Christ, room must be made for that which is essential and sound in the congregational tradition. Though congregationalism may recede from its earlier claim of local independency as an adequate basis of church polity, it will hardly recede from its claim that the united church shall recognize the freedom and autonomy of the local church in a degree not recognized in the historic church from which the Dissenters came out.

Congregationalism stands over against the parish conception of the local church. The history of the church after the apostolic period was marked by the gradual draining off of spontaneous initiative and responsibility from the local congregation into a super-congregational authority, reducing the local church to a mere parish, consisting of all those in the particular vicinity who were baptized. The effect of this development was to formalize church membership, to stifle spontaneous religious exercise, and to neutralize the sense of personal and local obligation. It destroyed the power of initiative and thus enfeebled the spiritual life of the local community and of the whole body of the church.

Congregationalism is, historically, a protest against this weakening of these living centers of the Christian community. It may yield its doctrine of radical independency, but its doctrine of the responsibility of the local church to have an autonomous life of its own, and to participate in the life of the whole Christian community by its spontaneous contribution to the whole body, will not be surrendered. Congregationalism will insist upon the guarding of this local responsibility in any organized expression of catholicity. It will do so, not merely because it is determined to assert the freedom of the local church, as a legalistic right, but because this congregational freedom is necessary to the bearing of a responsible witness to the faith that animates every local Christian community.

The freedom of a local church is not a principle of isolation, but of responsibility. In the luminous words of Principal Micklem, "it is the principle of the responsibility of each local fellowship before God for its own witness and discipline." Speaking for his own Congregational denomination, Dr. Micklem adds that "this is perhaps our greatest ecclesiastical contribution to the church catholic. So vital is this principle entrusted to us that, so far as we are concerned, there can be no healing of the church's schism till this principle for which we stand is accepted by the reunited church."

Thus the problem of church union is defined for us in terms of its two extremes: How to bring together the catholic principle and the congregational principle in one united body? That this can be done is the hope and faith of those who are working at the great task. But that there has yet been drawn a blueprint of such a structure, none would claim. Those who are working from the catholic side know their own minds. It is important beyond all else that those who work from the congregational side know theirs.

Union Negotiations

72. An Introduction:
"The Evangelical and Reformed Church"

(1942)

George W. Richards

George W. Richards (1869–1955) began his church life as a member of a union church near Reading, Pennsylvania, and he continued to serve the cause of union long past his retirement in 1939. He was professor of church history at Lancaster Theological Seminary for forty years, nineteen of them as president of the seminary. In 1905, he was a delegate to the earliest preliminary meetings leading to the formation of the Federal Council of Churches—delivering the first address on the program. He continued faithful to that organization, serving as its vice-president in 1934–35. He attended several European ecumenical conferences that were precursors to the World Council of Churches: the Faith and Order Conference in Lausanne in 1927, and the Oxford Conference on Life and Work and Edinburgh Conference on Faith and Order in 1937. He chaired the Reformed Church's Commission on Closer Relations and Church Union, which recommended union with the Evangelical Synod of North America, and he was the first president of the General Synod of the Evangelical and Reformed Church. He chaired the committee that undertook the first union negotiations between the Evangelical and Reformed Church and the Congregational Christian Churches. In the course of his extraordinary ecumenical career, he also helped to prepare six other bases for union involving other denominations.

His article, published in Advance *to acquaint the Congregational Christian Churches with the Evangelical and Reformed Church, carefully*

Source: George W. Richards, "The Evangelical and Reformed Church," *Advance,* 1 September 1942, 400–402.

presents the differences between the denominations and addresses the problematic issues of autonomy and authority that were central to union with the Congregational Christian Churches.

The Evangelical and Reformed Church

In this time when paradoxes, as always, are more perplexing than enlightening, I shall venture only one. History repeats itself; history never repeats itself. In 1814 the Synod of the German Reformed Church in response to an overture, voted that two ministers be sent as delegates to the meeting of the General Synod of the Dutch Reformed Church to be held in New York City, June next. It was stipulated that, "Each Synod shall receive the delegates of the Sister Church in a brotherly and becoming cordial manner, and provide them with suitable lodgings during the session of Synod (in 1941 that would mean a suite of rooms and meals at the Waldorf Astoria); the delegates shall have voice but not vote on the issues before the Synod."

Furthermore, during the first decade of the 20th century, the Rev. William Hayes Ward, Editor of the *Independent,* wrote a letter to me in which he proposed an informal meeting of the committees on union of his church and mine. Unfortunately I did not keep the letter and therefore cannot recall the date when it was written. Suffice it to say, it was favorably received not by me only but by my colleagues in the Faculty of the Theological Seminary at Lancaster. Action, however, could not be taken because the Presbyterian Church in the U. S. A. and the Reformed Church in the United States were preparing a plan of union. It was not deemed prudent to enter into courtship with two attractive maidens at the same time. Since 1814 and 1910, times have changed and the condition of the churches have changed with them.

Let me add a third prefatory statement. The churches, which we represent, have always, at least in the last three generations in America, been disposed to unite with other churches by way of alliance, federation, and organic union. So much one may infer from the names they now bear: Congregational Christian; Evangelical and Reformed. Both churches are looking forward to a larger and more comprehensive union than has yet been attained.

The Congregational Christian Church and the Evangelical and Reformed Church were widely separated in space both in Europe and in America. The one had an English, and the other a German, background.

The Congregational Church in America dates back to 1620 and was located in New England. The first congregation of the Reformed Church in the United States was organized in 1725 in Pennsylvania. The first congregation of the Evangelical Synod was organized in 1833 on the Femme Osage Creek, not far from St. Louis. The distributing center of the pioneers was the State of Missouri. Each group was separated by more than a century and occupied wholly different portions of territory in the colonial and national periods. Yet they were not widely separated in spirit—far less in America than in Europe. The process of Americanization was also a process of unification. The Foreign Mission Board of the Reformed Church organized in 1838 supported Missionary Schneider at Broosa and Aintab, Turkey, from 1842 to 1866, through the American Board. The Congregational Board of Home Missions sent not only ministers to serve the German churches in the Mississippi Valley but also provided subsidies for the support of ministers and congregations while they were courageously organizing churches for the German Evangelical pioneers of the Old World to the New in the mid-nineteenth century. Not a few young men of the Evangelical & Reformed Church have been trained for the ministry, in whole or in part, in Congregational seminaries, for example, in Hartford, in New Haven and in Cambridge.

I shall discuss five aspects of the Evangelical and Reformed Church: 1. Doctrinal Standards; 2. Theological interpretation; 3. Government; 4. Worship; 5. Work.

I. Standards of Doctrine

In the Constitution, Part I, Section 3, the doctrine of the Evangelical and Reformed Church is officially defined as follows:

> The Holy Scriptures of the Old and New Testaments are recognized as the Word of God and the ultimate rule of Christian faith and practice.
>
> The doctrinal standards of the Evangelical and Reformed Church are the Heidelberg Catechism, Luther's Catechism and the Augsburg Confession. They are accepted as an authoritative interpretation of the essential truth taught in the Holy Scriptures.
>
> Wherever these doctrinal standards differ, ministers, members and congregations, in accordance with the liberty of conscience inherent in the gospel, are allowed to adhere to the interpretation of one of these confessions. However, in each case the final norm is the Word of God.

The order for baptism, for confirmation, for ordination of ministers, elders, and deacons, and for the inauguration of Teachers of Theology—each requires in brief form an affirmation of the Article on Doctrine in the Constitution.

The sensitive spot, that may provoke controversy between the two churches now engaged in informal conversation, is not the *content* of the Article on Doctrine; but the *fact* of this required affirmation, which is equivalent to a pledge of acceptance of the doctrinal standards. They are a *professio fidei* dangerously close to a *lex fidei.* This however, is a specter that can be met and laid; an assurance that I base upon the union of Presbyterians, Congregationalists, and Methodists, under the name of the United Church of Canada. For two decades they have been peaceably living and working together, notwithstanding the differences which once divided them and for which some of their forefathers fought and died.

II. Theological Interpretation

The horizon widens and one may breathe more freely, when one considers theological interpretations of the doctrinal standards. The latter, though subject to revision, as a rule remain static; the former change with the years and the climates of opinion. Thus a distinction must be made between standards of doctrine and theological interpretations—"between the things fundamental, instrumental and accidental" (John A. Comenius). The Constitution of the Evangelical and Reformed Church therefore provides freedom, within certain limits, for difference of interpretation of the doctrinal formulas. The Evangelical and Reformed Church is, in spots, conservative, liberal and mediational. There is no considerable trend toward fundamentalism or toward secular humanism. The dominant interest of ministers and members is in Christian activity—evangelism, national and international missions, benevolence, the application of the gospel both to the individual life and to the economic and the political order of the nation and of the world at large. It is officially committed to the ecumenical movement of Oxford, Edinburgh, and to the World Council of Churches.

Theologically it is progressively evangelical. It is free from ecclesiastical shibboleths, because it distinguishes the essential elements from the ephemeral forms of Christianity. It differs from Roman Catholicism but it has the catholicity of the Apostles' Creed; it differs from ultra-Lutheranism but it has the mystic depths of Luther's doctrine of grace. It does not teach the Calvinistic doctrine of double predestination, but it preaches trust in the sovereignty of God and zeal for the glorification of God through obedience to His will. It does not hold a dogmatic view of inspiration, but it feels bound by the authority of the Word of God as manifested in Jesus Christ. It does not accept the theory of apostolic succession, but it believes in the historical continuity of the Church Catholic and a ministry duly authorized and thoroughly educated for the preaching of the gospel, the administration of the sacraments, the exercise of Christian discipline, and the perpetuation of the Christian life in the community. It does not prescribe a method of conversion but insists on its necessity through the grace of God appropriated by the faith of the individual and confirmed by a daily life of trust, hope, and love.

"The article of the standing and falling Church" is the experience contained in the confession: "I believe that Jesus Christ is my Savior and Lord." When men have that conviction in the heart and make confession with the mouth, they have passed from the bondage of ordinances and the rudiments of the world into the liberty of the sons of God. They are then free to work out statements of doctrine, forms of worship, and ways of life which are true to their experience, to the spirit of the glorified Christ, and to the conditions of the age in which they live.

The Evangelical and Reformed Church welcomes the accredited results of biblical criticism, of scientific study, and of philosophic thought, and is ever striving to reconstruct theology in the light of a new age; yet while it is convinced that the gospel must always be related to the thought and life of the time when it is proclaimed, it is equally certain that Jesus Christ is the same, yesterday, today, and forever; the Alpha and the Omega, the One who was and is and is to come. Theologies change, but the gospel is constant and eternal. Our faith is not assent to the contents of a book, a symbolic statement, a theory of inspiration, but trust in a person, which at the same time involves a complete commitment of one's whole life to the living God incarnate in Jesus Christ.

III. Government

The difference between the two churches, not only in their origin in Europe, but also in their present status in America, is most evident in the forms of Government. The Evangelical and Reformed Church does not regard government as a part of the *esse* but of the *bene esse* of the church. That form of government is *jure divino* which enables judicatories, officers, and members to carry on most effectively what "Jesus began both to do and to teach." The church may have preference for its specific polity, which is largely determined by the traditions that come from the founding fathers. But it does not equate the government or organization with the Gospel of God, that is with allegiance to the Saviourhood and Lordship of Jesus Christ, or, even in a less degree, to the summary of the faith in the Apostles' Creed. From the point of view of the Evangelical and Reformed Church different forms of polity may exist side by side in the same country and each, for its adherents, is *jure divino*—a pragmatic rather than a dogmatic test.

The Preamble of the Constitution of the Evangelical and Reformed Church may cause the Congregational Christians to pause for a moment; but, I hope, not to cease conversations or to despair of union. It reads as follows:

> For the maintenance of truth and order in the proclamation of the gospel of our Lord Jesus Christ and the advancement of the Kingdom of God in accordance with the Word of God, the Evangelical and Reformed Church, formed by the union of the Evangelical Synod of North America and the Reformed Church in the United States, ordains this constitution to be its fundamental law and declares the same to have authority over all its ministers, members, congregations, and judicatories.

I call special attention to the last clause, "and declares the same to have authority over all its ministers, members, congregations, and judicatories." Aye, there's the rub! It is a constitution for the whole church, all its members, congregations, officers—not merely for the control of the General Synod or the General Council. The church is governed by judicatories, but their members are chosen by the congregations. Two principles are maintained—that of *autonomy* and that of *authority;* these blend within limits prescribed by the Constitution. There is autonomy of members, ministers, congregations, judicatories of congregations (the Consistory or Church Council and the Spiritual Council), of the local synod and of the General Synod. Whether it be a member, an officer, or a judicatory, when he or it feels aggrieved, the right of appeal, of complaint, and of reference is granted. Of course the General Synod is the court of last appeal. From its decisions one would have to seek redress in a civil court, which has not happened once in a century. Each member, officer, or judicatory is pledged to abide by the Articles of the Constitution and the By-Laws. Thus autonomy is limited by authority which is voluntarily vested by the members and the officers in the several judicatories.

If you will permit me to use my autonomy, without authority, I venture to affirm that in due time it may be possible to deauthorize the Evangelical and Reformed Church at the top and to deauthorize the Congregational

Christian Church at the bottom, without interfering with the Lordship of Jesus Christ. Again, I cite the United Church of Canada in which this somewhat difficult problem has been satisfactorily solved.

IV. Worship

I feel somewhat unleashed when I turn from polity to cultus or worship. Indeed at this point we might stop a minute, catch our breath, and even drink tea together; for we have gone over the roughest portion of our journey. The Constitution of the Evangelical and Reformed Church contains three brief, liberal statements relating to Worship:

1. Congregations are allowed freedom of worship. The forms and order of worship that are set forth in the Book of Worship and in the hymnal approved by the General Synod shall be followed as accepted norms.

   The Lord's Day and the festivals and seasons of the Church year shall be observed with appropriate services in the House of God.

2. The sacraments of the Church, instituted by Christ are Holy Baptism and the Lord's Supper.

3. The rites of the Church are confirmation, ordination, consecration, marriage and burial.

There are three different groups so far as worship is concerned: 1. Those who, through long usage, prefer the free service; 2. those who blend the free service and liturgical forms; 3. those who are zealous advocates of a more or less highly liturgical service. None of these forms, however, is mandatory; nor could one be censured for using or not using one or the other. Here, also, the congregation is granted the freedom of the Sons of God. There is a growing tendency toward a liturgical service.

A paragraph written by a minister of the Evangelical Synod before the union describes an aspect of the spirit and mode of worship which prevails in the Evangelical and Reformed church at present:

> Evangelical churches are accustomed to observe the Church Year as a systematic method of keeping the divine plan of salvation and Jesus' work of redemption constantly before their people. Lent in particular is very generally observed as a season of special personal devotion and consecration and of intensive evangelistic effort, and most of the additions to the Church are obtained at that time. Confirmation is practiced, not as a rite or a sacrament but as a method of Christian

instruction and nurture and of winning young people for Christ and the Church during their early adolescence.

The Evangelical and Reformed Church has been, and is, committed to the educational method of the cultivation of the Christian life. Baptized children of Christian parents are brought up in the nurture and admonition of the Lord in the home, the school, and the congregation. Under oversight of the pastor through instruction in the fundamentals of the faith, the youth are prepared for full membership and are admitted to the Lord's table by the rite of confirmation. It is assumed that faith is begotten in the heart by the Holy Spirit through the preaching, teaching, and practicing of the gospel—is confirmed by the use of the sacraments and by good works which are the fruit of faith.

While the Evangelical and Reformed Church regards the ordinary means of grace—the preaching and teaching of the Word, Christian nurture in home and school, pastoral visitation, instruction and oversight, the sacraments, and fellowship in worship and work—as the normal way of begetting and developing the Christian life in children, in men and women, it by no means is averse, or indifferent, to special evangelistic efforts. The Constitution requires the election of a Commission on Evangelism, which, however, does not encourage the independent, sporadic unchurchly methods of many self-appointed revivalists. It favors and supports the kind of evangelism that is true to the evangel and the Scriptures, to approved evangelistic traditions, and to the conditions and needs of men of each generation.

The Evangelical and Reformed Church is in full accord with the *Social Ideals,* at first published as the *Social Creed* of the churches in the Federal Council. It does not accept two gospels; but two implications of the one Gospel, which is good news from God to men through his Son Jesus Christ for the salvation of the individual and the transformation of the social order of which the individual is an organic part.

V. Work

I shall not describe in detail the work of the Evangelical and Reformed Church. It is essentially the same as that of the Congregational Christian Church. It follows in the steps of its Master who came preaching, teaching, healing. It is obedient to his last mandate—Make disciples of all nations. Its missions are in the United States, Canada, and Honduras, in Japan, China, India and Mesopotamia. it supports academies, colleges, theological seminaries, in this and other lands. Its orphanages, homes for the aged and the poor, hospitals for the physically and mentally ill, are generously maintained by voluntary gifts from year to year. Its ministers and members cooperate with other churches in works of mercy and relief, and in the maintenance of welfare institutions in the community. Our Lord's commandment of love is measurably observed by the set purpose to please God by serving fellowmen who are of every nation, class, color, and condition, and reach to the ends of the earth.

The Church is, also, militant toward men and conditions which hinder and oppose the purpose of God in Christ; the weapons of its warfare however, are not carnal but spiritual.

VI. Conclusion

In conclusion, permit me to add that the two branches of the Evangelical and Reformed Church are the oldest Protestant churches; perhaps none is more evangelical and more liberal. On account of its German-Swiss origin, its comparatively late establishment in America, the strange language and manners of life of its founders, it has not grown numerically as rapidly as the churches of the British pioneers. But it has taken a noble part, in the face of almost insuperable obstacles and in the day of small things, from colonial times, in the Christianizing and Americanizing of a substantial portion of our Republic, especially of those who came from Germany, Switzerland, and, to a less extent, of those who came from Holland and France. It is no longer a foreign church in an alien country; it is a Christian church whose members are not only devoted to their Saviour and Lord but are loyal citizens of the land which their forbears adopted and who in the sweat of their brows made the wilderness to blossom as the rose.

VII. Statistical Statement

a. Membership—approximately 658,000.

b. Congregations—2,860—congregations in 40 states and Canada; 870 in Pennsylvania; 372 in Ohio; 228 in Illinois; 214 in Missouri; 147 in Indiana; 111 in New York.

c. Institutions—13 educational institutions in the United States; 35 benevolent institutions (orphanages, old folks' homes, hospitals, etc.).

d. Ministry—1,885 pastors and 595 ministers—approximately one hundred in the general work of the Church, including theological seminaries; one hundred more in other forms of Christian service; most of the rest without charge or retired.

e. Mission abroad—Japan, China, India, Irak and Honduras.

f. Missions in America are nearly all in the United States, just a few in Canada.

One word more—My experience in working for Church Union, for 30 years, has convinced me that more is required for a *Christian* Union of Churches than agreement on doctrine, theological interpretation, government, worship, and work. It is the indefinable thing that Paul in his letter to the Philippians asks of his readers: "So by all the stimulus of Christ by every incentive of love, by all your participation in the Spirit, by all your affectionate tenderness, I pray you give me the utter joy of knowing you are living in harmony, with the same feelings of love, with one heart and soul, never acting for private ends, or from vanity, but humbly considering each other the better man, and each with an eye to the interests of others as well as to his own. Treat one another with the same spirit as you experience in Christ Jesus."

The mind of Christ in us alone can effectively accomplish that which we so ardently seek—a closer fellowship of all who call themselves Christians, of every land and clime, of every name and creed. When we contemplate this high ideal we are humbled to the dust because we fall short of it. Yet, in the same epistle, we read words which exalt us to the heights: "In him that strengthens me I am able for anything." (4:13).

73. Compare and Contrast:

"A Brief Study of the Differences . . . "

(1942)

Douglas Horton

Douglas Horton (1891–1968) probably was the preeminent ecumenist of the Congregational Christian Churches. In many ways he was the Congregational counterpart of his friend and colleague in the Evangelical and Reformed Church, George W. Richards. Horton was active not only in the activities of his own denomination, but also in nearly every ecumenical venture during the first half of the twentieth century. He played prominent roles in the development of the Evangelical Alliance, the Federal Council of Churches, the National Council of Churches, the World Missionary Conference in Edinburgh (1910), and the World Council of Churches. He was moderator of the Faith and Order Commission of the World Council from 1957 to 1963. He was an ecumenical observer at the Second Vatican Council. As minister and secretary of the General Council of the Congregational Christian Churches from 1938 to 1955, Horton worked with his Evangelical and Reformed counterpart, Louis W. Goebel (president of that denomination from 1940 to 1955), to bring the two denominations together to form the United Church of Christ. With his Congregational Christian colleague, Truman B. Douglass, Horton articulated a new understanding of Congregationalism that regarded wider church bodies (such as the General Council of the Congregational Christian Churches and, later, the General Synod of the United Church of Christ) as "a kind of congregation" distinct from local congregations

---

Source: Douglas Horton, "A Brief Study of the Differences Between the Evangelical and Reformed Church and the Congregational Christian Churches in Respect of Faith and Practice," *Advance,* 1 October 1942, 447–49.

but neither superior nor subordinate to them. This interpretation of Congregationalism enabled the General Council to rule itself rather than simply act as a representative arm of local churches. His understanding of the General Council as "church" also made a significant contribution to the final court rulings that allowed the union of the General Council of the Congregational Christian Churches and the General Synod of the Evangelical and Reformed Church to come together to create the United Church of Christ (see vol. 6:91).

In his "Brief Study of the Differences Between the Evangelical and Reformed Church and the Congregational Christian Churches in Respect of Faith and Practice," Horton sought to explain that the differences between the two churches in doctrine and ritual were more apparent than substantive. He pointed out that differences in polity, specifically the freedom or autonomy of individual Christians and local congregations, were misunderstood. Freedom, according to the early Congregationalists, made possible the individual and church's direct response to the perception of God's will. It was "not the kind of freedom which is mere license: it is freedom in the Holy Spirit, freedom to be as Christlike as possible, freedom to refuse to adhere to what may be regarded as un-Christlike direction from ecclesiastical authorities, freedom to adopt reforms without tarrying for lagging ecclesiastical governments." Horton emphasized a balanced view: God speaks through individual saints and through the congregation, through an individual congregation and through the General Council.

In the faith of the Evangelical and Reformed Church are strains of inheritance from four of the most celebrated of the Sixteenth Century Reformers, Luther and Calvin, Zwingli and Melanchthon. Before the merger of the Evangelical with the Reformed branch of the church, each one had had a notable history as an agency of reconciliation between the two great Protestant Churches of the Continent, the Lutheran and the Reformed. In the Evangelical Synod the spiritual descendants of Luther and Calvin had united under the teaching of missionaries from the Barmen and Basel Societies in the spirit fostered by the Administrative Union of Prussia; and the Reformed Church had drawn into one body sons of Zwinglian Switzerland and of the Melanchthonian Palatinate. The Evangelical and Reformed Church is the guardian of treasures drawn from all of Continental Protestantism.

It is not strange, therefore, that in the section of the constitution of that church which is entitled "Doctrine" the great symbols of both the Lutheran and the Reformed schools of thought should be named as standards—the Heidelberg Catechism, Luther's Catechism, and the Augsburg Confession.

In the faith of the Congregational Christian Churches, on the other hand, are to be found inheritances not from Continental but from English and Scottish Protestantism. Congregationalism, though it broke with Anglicanism ecclesiastically, shares with Anglicanism many theological premises and practical attitudes. It was a mildly Puritan rather than an iconoclastic Anabaptist movement which settled New England. Similarly, the three branches of the Christian Connection brought with them into their united church more than they left behind of the characteristics of the Baptist, Methodist, and Presbyterian groups from which they severally came. The General Council of Congregational Christian Churches in its own way unites the Protestantism of the British Isles, as the Evangelical and Reformed Church unites the Protestantism of Europe proper.

When one seeks, however, in the constitution of the General Council today reference to the great symbols of British Protestantism, he seeks in vain. The Cambridge Platform of 1648, in which the Congregationalists of that time adopted *in toto* the doctrines of the Westminster Confession, and so declared themselves Calvinists, would seem, for instance, to provide an admirable historical standard to which Congregationalists might point today. All the principles of Congregational polity are set forth therein. But no: there is no mention in the constitution of any creed, ancient or modern, whatsoever, and instead and to the contrary it is explicitly stated that the churches find their union in "the acceptance of Christianity as primarily a way of life" and not in "uniformity of theological opinion or any uniform practice of ordinances." For a definition of that way of life, one is referred simply to "the Bible" in which is to be found "the supreme rule of faith and life."

From the fact that the two constitutions differ at this point, the one citing, the other omitting mention of, historic confessions, it might be inferred that there is an underlying difference between the two communions in matters of faith, but this, I believe, would be a conjecture without foundation. The difference lies not in the area of faith itself, but in the attitude of the two denominations to formal statements of faith. That, however, is a matter which does not call for consideration until the practices of the two communions engage our study.

The fact that the Congregational Christian General Council does not set forth a particularized statement of faith at the head of its constitution does not argue that Congregational Christians are not interested in creeds and do not have any. The plain historical fact is that they have been prolific creed makers and ready creed users. They have known that the gospel, in order to be made socially available, must be expressed in terms intellectually apprehensible, and have not hesitated to cast it in mnemonic creedal form when necessary.

Generally speaking, every Congregational Christian Church has its own creed: *quot ecclesiae tot confessiones.* It has been said that every individual Congregational Christian has his creed, and there is a measure of truth in the remark. It is at least because of multiplicity of creeds rather than of any distrust of them that no one of them is selected to be named in the constitution of the General Council—no one, that is, except the Bible itself.

In spite of this multiplicity of form, however, there is an indubitable consensus of thought among Congregational Christians. The communion is one of the few in America which is not distraught by theological controversy. The creed of 1913 is generally acceptable to all, and is used in the Sunday morning worship of many churches. So well recognized is this consensus that the General Council (1940) has set apart a Commission to draw up a thoroughgoing Statement of Faith as soon as possible.

If the Heidelberg Catechism, Luther's Catechism, and the Augsburg Confession be taken for general substance of doctrine, especially with the proviso that at their points of difference any one of them may be followed, and the presupposition that all are to be conceived as expressing the Word of God, they may fairly be said to represent the consensus of Congregational Christian opinion.

It is true that few contemporary members of Congregational Christian Churches could be found who could accept every thought which is common to these Sixteenth Century symbols. They could not, for instance, answer the question, "Whence then proceeds this depravity of human nature?" in quite so pre-Darwinian a manner as does the Heidelberg Catechism: "From the fall and disobedience of our first parents, Adam and Eve, in Paradise." They would probably feel that any attempt to interpret this answer in modern terms would pervert the meaning it had for those who originally wrote it and would therefore be impossible for men of integrity today. Such instances of dissent in secondary matters might be multiplied.

But is not this attitude, which balks at accepting certain details of the Confession, while gladly embracing the Confession as a whole, as prevalent among the people of the Evangelical and Reformed Church as it would be among Congregational Christians? We believe so. The Catechism is significant today to most of us, not for its *minutiae* but for its exposition of the broad and fundamental relationships of God and man and the world. The people of the Evangelical and Reformed Church and those of the Congregational Christian Churches read the same books, follow the same spiritual leadership, send their children to the same kinds of school and college. They are both alike the offspring of the Protestant Reformation. Their history as agents of union between churches has given each a certain catholic breadth of outlook. It would be strange indeed if they did not hold a common faith.

It is in the realm of practice that differences are more likely to appear.

Little divergence is seen, however, either in the realm of ritual or ministry. By the constitution of the Evangelical and Reformed Church, "congregations are allowed freedom of worship." Here again a consensus of opinion among Congregational Churches may be taken for granted, for they have enjoyed freedom of worship from of old.

Both communions use this freedom to the same ends. In some churches in each communion may be found the simple and austere worship of early American frontier life, In others the impulse of the liturgical movement has been felt, and numerous forms suggested by the more Catholic traditions are employed. In all of the churches on both sides of the denominational line, however, the Reformers' insight that it is by faith and not by works that we are justified, is the presupposition of worship. This, and the further insight that the Church is a priesthood of believers, gives to Evangelical and Reformed as well as to Congregational Christian churches, whether they be more or less ritualistically inclined, a forthrightness of devotion in an unclerical atmosphere which marks them as belonging to one great tradition. Ministers of the two communions find it easy to exchange pulpits, and lay people to worship in the churches of either denomination.

Little of difference is to be found in the two communions as they face the vast needs of the world in the Spirit of Christ. Each one is committed to the Christian education of youth. Each one regards the Christian family as the fundamental unit of the Christian Church. Each believes in an educated ministry. Each one is sensitive to the social needs of the passing generations. Each one has developed missions at home and abroad. Both believe that the one great need of the world and the only hope of the world is Jesus Christ. This shared consciousness has caused the two denominations to create and sustain similar ministries.

If any difference in basic attitude is to be found between the two communions, it is probably in the realm of polity, and that not in the legislative or administrative branches, which follow the pattern of a representative democracy, but in the area of personal and group relationships, which our fathers called *disciplina.*

If the Evangelical and Reformed Church is a highly connectional system in which majorities or appointed executives rule the whole, leaving the minorities and the masses who do not enjoy executive positions to obey as best they may, there is a difference between the two systems.

But, though it must be left to a qualified member of the Evangelical and Reformed Church to describe the actual working of its polity, I, as a somewhat intimate observer of that communion from outside, should be more than astonished to learn that any such degree of centralization prevailed. From the outside, the minorities and the people in general seem to enjoy as many privileges as they do in the Congregational Christian fellowship.

In the latter fellowship, however, freedom is of the very essence. It is not the kind of freedom which is mere license: it is freedom in the Holy Spirit, freedom to be as Christlike as possible, freedom to refuse to adhere to what may be regarded as un-Christlike direction from ecclesiastical authorities, freedom to adopt reforms without tarrying for lagging ecclesiastical governments.

According to Congregational Christian theory, God may speak through the individual saint to the congregation, or through the congregation to the saint. Normally He uses both channels. Correspondingly, He may speak to the fellowship of churches, that is, the synod, through the individual church, or to the individual church through the synod—and normally he speaks through both. He may speak to the conference of churches or synod through the General Council or General Synod, and vice versa.

On these premises, through three and more centuries, a theocracy has been developed and maintained in Congregationalism. The only head of the church is Jesus Christ, but He is not conceived to have chosen any hierarchy or majority to be His special vice-regents on earth: He may at times choose to place in the humblest member of the church more authority, because He speaks through him, than in any humanly appointed or elected governor. It is for this reason that all persons and groups of persons within the Church are conceived to be on an equality under Christ. There are no "higher" and "lower" judicatories. No commands are issued by the General Council to the Conferences of Churches, or by the Conferences themselves to the individual churches. Authority is freely delegated by one body to another, but only so long as the former judges the latter to be acting in conformity to the authority of Christ. The situation never arises wherein a Congregational Christian believes he has no right to appeal from a ecclesiastical ruling to the judgment of Christ Himself. The whole body of the church is held together by mutual loyalty, and the key word is cooperation.

It will immediately be asked what course is followed when a minority deems it unwise or wrong to cooperate with the majority, any part with any other part. Acting upon the premise that loyalty to Christ is the first consideration, the two groups endeavor to hold their differences in abeyance until through mutual consultation and discussion, the Holy Spirit has revealed to them a higher synthesis in which their disagreements may be resolved. If the nature of the disharmony is such, however, that they cannot continue in the common worship and service of Christ, they have recourse to brethren who represent a wider fellowship, precisely as in a presbyterial system disputants turn to a higher "court." This body attempts to reconcile them. If it fails to do so, appeal may be made to a body representing a still larger fellowship, etc. If all attempts at reconciliation finally fail, there is nothing for it but that the two groups in disagreement should separate, but if they are Congregational Christian at heart, they do not leave the fellowship, nor do they part without a continuing hope that in due time the Holy Spirit will reveal His will with sufficient clarity to allow them to enter once more into full cooperation with one another.

This type of discipline may not appear to be essentially different from that which is employed in the more closely connectional systems of church government; but as a matter of fact it does have two effects which are unique.

The standing of each body as over against all other bodies in Congregationalism allows usages to grow up in that body which are peculiar to itself. When these prove to be the occasion of tension between that body and others in the denomination, some unifying synthesis must be discovered, as already suggested. Often enough, however, the tension is felt to be of a health-giving kind, or does not exist at all; often it is felt that the peculiar circumstances of the group in question warrant a deviation from customary practice; and a duality or multiformity of practice is established within the communion, such as would be the despair of any denomination interested especially in uniformity.

There is no better illustration of this development of variety within unity than that already mentioned: the attitude of the communion toward creedal forms is that any such form is permissible provided it adequately symbolizes the great truths of the Bible, and that any individual church may discover a way of wording its creed which is peculiarly well suited to it. This of course does not outlaw the great historic creeds, which have their own place in the larger church. The result is multiplicity but not chaos, for the creeds are not testimonies to individualism but individual witnesses to a common loyalty. This is a practical result of the cooperative type of discipline which informs the Congregational Christian churches.

The psychological result is quite as interesting. In a system in which no group is conceived as being inferior to any other group and wherein no group needs to accept the communications of any other group as binding mandates, the possibilities of bitter feeling against ecclesiastical superiors is largely scotched at the start. Now and then I run across resentment in the minds of men who feel they ought to have been "promoted" by the denomination to more influential pulpits, but this unhappy state of affairs is the result not of a system but of a difference of estimate. Men of a freedom-loving turn of mind are happier in a fellowship where recommendations rather than imposed regulations are the order of the day, and where the atmosphere is rather that of a family than of a state. Paradoxically enough, in situations where protest is at all times possible, less impulse to protest arises. It is a matter of fact that heresy trials or trials of any sort have been almost unknown in Congregationalism for two or three generations and yet during that time Congregationalism has steadily grown.

It is probable that in actuality the Evangelical and Reformed Church functions almost exactly as does the Congregational Christian Church. Its constitution theoretically seems to place greater emphasis on the idea of the judicatory than would be fostered in a Congregational system, but my own observation is that each judicatory wields its authority with such Christian forbearance as to make itself indistinguishable in the manner of its functioning from the corresponding Congregational Christian legislative or administrative group. There seems to be in all parts of the communion the same apprehension of the dangers of over-centralization that one finds written into the very constitution of the Congregational Christian Churches.

The key to a plan of union between the two communions is found in the constitution of the Evangelical and Reformed Church. Section 3 reads in part "Wherever these doctrinal standards (the Heidelberg Catechism, Luther's Catechism and the Augsburg Confession) differ, ministers, members and congregations, in accordance with the liberty of conscience inherent in the gospel, are allowed to adhere to the interpretation of one of these confessions."

The beauty of the principle which underlies such a plan is that unity is arrived at without call for compromise and without severing the cords which unite the members of the union to their own past. If the church which might be created from the two denominations we represent honored that principle in all parts of its constitution, it would conserve all the value of its traditions and yet in union find new strength for Christ. We have indicated that there is no fundamental discrepancy between us in matters of faith. Again, the practices of the two communions are in very large measure identical. If the differences are in areas of secondary importance, it might well be left to the people "in accordance with the liberty of conscience inherent in the Gospel" to follow the way of the erstwhile Evangelical and Reformed or Congregational Christian Church.

If the differences are in the stratum of basic principle, the union could hardly be consummated, and we should, with infinite regret on my own part, have to forgo the thought of it. But I do not believe they are. The only possible divergence I discern is, as I have said, in the realm of discipline, the general manner of our ecclesiastical life. It would perhaps be a test of our own thought upon this matter if we asked ourselves whether, in the spirit of another sentence of section 3 of the Evangelical and Reformed Constitution—"In each case the final norm is the Word of God"—it would be acceptable, in the preamble to any constitution which might be adopted by the combined churches, to make a statement to the following effect: "This constitution is set forth as a witness to the faith and practice of the church, but it is at all points subject to the judgment of God, made known or yet to be made known, and the refusal of any member or members of the church on the ground of Christian principle to adhere to it at any point by no means dissolves their fellowship with the church but only announces the need for mutual enquiry into the mind of Christ upon the point of issue."

I know that the Congregational Christian and I believe that the Reformed and Evangelical Church would find no stumbling block in such a statement. If that is the case, it is safe to say that there are no differences between the two communions so great as to prevent organic union. On the divine side and on the human, union is called for. *Ut omnes unum sint!* We cannot with impunity disregard the words of our Lord, if we are to do His work well. And we know that the future belongs to those churches sufficiently widespread to look after their members wherever they may go. "Unto him that hath shall be given." The union of the two communions, the one with its Continental, the other with its Anglo-Saxon, ancestry would proclaim the Supra-national character of the Church and fulfil a dream of the Reformation. If there is to be in the United States of America a United Church of America, I know no communions better prepared to establish it than the Evangelical and Reformed and the Congregational Christian Churches.

74. The Choice:

"*Shall General Synod Vote for Union with the Congregational Christian Churches? (Yes/No)*"

(1947)

Frederick W. Schroeder and Erwin H. Bueneman

Once the Congregational Christian Churches and the Evangelical and Reformed Church officially entered union negotiations in 1942, church leaders of both denominations were far too experienced to let union be negotiated purely "from the top." Immediately they developed various ways to inform and energize local constituencies about the issues involved. Every church member was invited to have an opinion.

The periodicals of both denominations published a wide variety of articles explaining the doctrinal standards, theology, polity, worship, and service patterns of each denomination and pointing out issues that might be troublesome. They created forums where differing opinions could be expressed and compared.

For example, The Messenger, *published by the Evangelical and Reformed Church, printed a pair of articles by Frederick W. Schroeder and Erwin H. Bueneman containing pro and con arguments on the proposed union. Frederick W. Schroeder, president of Eden Theological Seminary in Webster Groves, Missouri, spoke out strongly on behalf of union. Acknowledging that the two denominations had different cultural*

Source: Frederick W. Schroeder and Erwin H. Bueneman, "Shall General Synod Vote for Union with the Congregational Christian Churches? (Yes/No)" in *The Messenger,* July 8, 1947, 12–16.

origins and somewhat different church polity, he believed that none of those differences were sufficient to separate the two groups. Indeed, he argued, the point was not where the two groups had come from, but where they wanted to go. They needed to "go together" for three reasons. First, there were no irreconcilable differences in their church polity, since church polity was a device invented by people for governing the church, not something divinely ordained. Second, although the theological positions of their leaders might have been far apart in the past, contemporary church leaders spoke the same theological language. Third, Protestants needed to give substance to their professed belief in the unity of the church.

Erwin Bueneman's perspective on the proposed union was very different. He acknowledged that differences in cultural origins and differences in church polity were insufficient reasons to oppose union. However, there were theological differences that justified resistance. He stated that it was not clear whether the two denominations were worshiping "the same Christ." To make his point, Bueneman reported that certain Congregational Christian Churches were meeting with Unitarian churches, and that one Congregational pastor even sought joint recognition in both churches. This was evidence that the two denominations were not serving "the same Christ," and therefore the Evangelical and Reformed Church should not pursue union with the Congregational Christians.

"Yes" by Frederick W. Schroeder

It is not difficult to find some plausible reasons why General Synod should not approve the pending merger proposals. For one thing, the two churches have a different cultural background. The Congregationalists, for the most part, stem from Anglo-Saxon stock whereas our forefathers came from Germany. To be sure, the Anglo-Saxons came from Germany, too, but that was back in the sixth century, and much has happened in the intervening years. Moreover, the Congregationalists came over in the "Mayflower" a full century or two before our progenitors came to this land in search of religious freedom and economic opportunity; and it is conceivable that by virtue of their longer residence in the land they may have acquired certain social graces and educational advantages which are not yet ours. But if love laughs at locksmiths this cultural difference—fancied or real—might not be an impossible barrier to the merger.

Then there is this matter of church policy. While neither of the two churches can claim to have followed either a pure congregational or a strict presbyterial system of government, there is considerable difference in our respective forms of church government. In Congregational Christian churches the principle of local autonomy, though modified, is held to be inviolate; we, on the other hand, have vested the synods and the General Synod with legislative powers to which local congregations are amenable. For both church bodies the lines have fallen into pleasant places, and I suspect there are those for whom the one or the other system with which they feel most at home has become so sacred as to be unalterable.

The merger might also be opposed because of certain theological differences. The constitution of our church, for example, has a doctrinal statement setting forth in clear and unmistakable terms what we believe. The clause which guarantees the individual "the liberty of conscience inherent in the gospel" does not nullify this statement but merely allows latitude for differences of interpretation within the framework of the accepted doctrinal standards. Our Congregationalist friends have no such statement. Although they are said to be quite prolific in writing creeds, they have never considered any confession definitive for either clergy or congregations. This in itself tends to make them suspect in certain quarters. Moreover, one might be able to make a reasonably good case for the claim that traditionally the theological position of Congregationalism has been more liberal than that of the Evangelical and Reformed Church.

Reasons such as these might be advanced in opposition to the merger; and, if you think primarily in terms of where we have come from—that is, in terms of origins and traditions—these reasons will seem to be very important. But I submit this merger is not proposed on the basis of traditional similarities but rather on the basis of present and potential affinities in faith and order. Surely in this crucial moment of the world's history we do not want to imitate the legendary "worry bird" that flies backward because he does not care where he is going but would like to find out where he has been. Considering, then, not so much where we have come from—culturally, ecclesiastically or theologically—but whether we are going, I, for one, support this merger; and I do it for at least three good reasons that I should like to enumerate.

I

First of all there is no such fundamental difference in polity as to make our respective types of church government irreconcilable; even if there should be there is nothing inherently sacrosanct about any form of church government. The manner in which churches are organized is a matter of custom or convenience. The New Testament emphasizes the importance of doing all things "decently and in order" but it prescribes no pattern for any particular order, whether it be congregational, presbyterial or episcopal. Every form of church government is a man-made arrangement, and not something divinely ordained; and what man has made he can remake or unmake. To be sure, that is not always easy. Congregationalists, for example, may be reluctant to modify their cherished principle of local autonomy; we, on the other hand, may be afraid that order will be sacrificed on the altar of too much freedom. Obviously there will need to be give an take; and one must expect that "growing pains" will be felt as the new church develops a polity that does justice to the two principles of freedom and order. But if our forefathers were endowed with sufficient wisdom to perfect an order adequate for their time and needs, surely we, who are the heirs of their product, should have the resourcefulness to create a form of organization that will express our spirit and serve our purposes. To deny this is to confess an intellectual and a spiritual poverty that would malign the church and the churchmen of our day.

II

My second reason for supporting the merger is that theologically the two churches are not as far apart today as some seem to think they are. If you survey the theological climate of the seminaries in which the future ministers of the church are studying you discover at once that the pendulum is swinging to the right, much to the dismay of the few remaining "unregenerated" liberals. This means that such differences of thought and belief, which might still prevail among the older clergy of the two denominations, are on the wane; the oncoming generation of ministers in the two churches speaks pretty much the same kind of theological language. And what if there are some differences of interpretation; have we not always adhered to the principle: "In essentials unity, in nonessentials liberty, in all things charity!" In essentials there is unity. Jesus Christ is acknowledged to be Lord and Savior in both denominations; the statement of faith in the *Basis of Union* is unequivocably Trinitarian; it also bears witness to our spiritual kinship with the faith enshrined in the ecumenical creeds of the ancient church and the evangelical confessions of the Reformation. Can anyone ask for greater guarantees than these? Of course, there will be differences of interpretation in regard to this doctrine or that; such differences can be found within our own denominations even now. But certainly no one would want to claim that his faith is better or that his loyalty to Christ is deeper simply because his theological definitions are more orthodox than those of another.

III

The third reason for supporting the merger is rooted in the conviction that it is imperative for Protestants to give substance to their professed belief in unity and ecumenicity. We are reminded now and then that the way to do this is to extend the areas of cooperation which reach across denominational lines or to increase the scope of church federation on the community, national and international level. Such efforts are indeed commendable but they do not relieve us of the responsibility of effecting organic union between churches wherever that is possible. Cooperation and federation are not enough to convince the world that the church is really sincere in its declaration: "We are not divided, All one body we, One in hope and doctrine, One in charity." The plain truth of the matter is that the church is "by schisms rent asunder"; and all the world knows it.

Those without the church are confused and disturbed by the existing divisions; the average person finds them meaningless if not actually giving the lie to our professions of oneness. To speak of the "una sancta" when we do everything in our power to preserve our ecclesiastical entities is not very convincing. This does not mean that all divisions can or should be abolished at once, but it does mean that wherever two or more churches can find a common ground of faith and order on which the principles for which they live can be fused into a higher synthesis, they are morally obligated to unite. Churches must be willing to die in order that the church may live.

Churchmen have spoken with considerable feeling and conviction regarding the urgency of establishing one world; they will, however, forfeit their right to leadership in this matter if they do not set their own house in order in the matter of church unity. And then there is this prayer of our Lord "that they may all be one." Try hard as we may it is difficult to reconcile our divisions with this petition. No exegetical studies of the text made thus far have in any way refuted what appears to have been the obvious intent of Jesus, namely that all of his followers were to be united in one church. The proposed merger is a step in that direction.

"No" by Erwin H. Bueneman

Church mergers may be *favored* for a variety of reasons, none of them more compelling than the one—to quote from the *Basis of Union*—which reminds Christian people that they find themselves today "confronting the divisions and hostilities of our world, and hearing with a deepened sense of responsibility the prayer of our Lord 'that they may all be one.' " It would certainly be too bad if such matters as name or polity, however large they may loom in the thinking of many people, were to prove the *insuperable* obstacles to the achievement of the merger of our two denominations.

There is only one basic obstacle to church merger that has a valid claim upon our consideration, and that is the doctrinal one. It is because of this reason alone that the writer of this article has consistently opposed the proposed merger of the Evangelical and Reformed Church and the Congregational Christian Churches, since this was first suggested in 1942. It is still the reason why he conscientiously believes that General Synod should not approve of the pending merger proposals.

It is that reason to which we are bound in one of the "evangelical confessions of the Reformation" tacitly acknowledged in the *Basis of Union,* mentioned explicitly however as one of "the doctrinal standards of the Evangelical and Reformed Church," namely the Augsburg Confession, which states: "The church is the congregation of saints in which the gospel is rightly taught and the sacraments rightly administered. . . . To the true unity of the church it is enough to agree concerning the doctrine of the gospel and the administration of the sacraments."

It is the writer's considered conviction that between our two churches we do not have this basic agreement; and no matter how successfully we may iron out any other difficulties and overcome all other obstacles that might stand in the way of a merger of our two churches, we do not have real unity to start out with and to build upon, and in the end we shall not therefore have achieved a real union!

Now it will immediately be protested that this assertion completely ignores the lofty sentiments and affirmations expressed in the *Basis of Union.* And, admittedly, the article on faith would seem to provide a very comprehensive testimony of faith, which is putting it mildly. For taking it at its face value, it world appear to embrace within its scope three ecumenical creeds, six Lutheran confessions, more than thirty Reformed confessions, according to Schaff; and then, as a sort of summary of all that, the Congregational Kansas City Platform of 1913 rewritten! This is certainly "being all things to all men"!

The difficulty lies in the fact that one can apparently do a lot of things with words, and the fact that here we seem to have evolved a satisfactory formula unfortunately won't actually guarantee that we have thereby achieved agreement! Let's face the facts! The "evangelical confessions of the Reformation"—Reformed as over against Lutheran—are not themselves in agreement, not only in their teaching on the sacraments, but in their comprehension of the very nature and character of the gospel of which their divergent teaching about the sacraments is only an end result. This article on faith no more accomplishes real agreement than did the confessional paragraph of the Evangelical and Reformed Church. In matters which concern the very heart of the Christian faith, because of which the historic Protestant churches went separate and different ways, no formula however well-intentioned would ever be able to manufacture a basic unity between them that wasn't there in the first place. The explicit proviso, twice mentioned in the *Basis of Union,* "This statement shall be regarded as a testimony, and not as the test of faith," still leaves unanswered the question, What would be the faith of the United Church?

It is the obligation of the church to give a clear, unequivocal, witness to the world. She is called into the world to witness to the truth in Christ as she has received it. The Christian religion is not just a mater of private or inner personal conviction. It has been planted, watered and ordered, in a church established by Christ himself, in which the Holy Spirit works through Word and sacraments. Wherever a number of personal wills are united in one organism, as in the church, there must be one fundamental authority—the conviction of faith that unites them! What must always be considered by the church is her obligation to witness, with a clear and unequivocal voice to the truth in Christ as she has received it. Therefore the doctrinal element is always fundamental, and a church cannot be indifferent to the teaching in her pulpits and schools.

I

The theological reason is therefore the only valid reason why General Synod should not approve of the pending merger proposals. I am quite aware that this rejoinder will immediately be made, "To me, helping to answer Jesus' prayer 'that they may all be one' means very much more than any theological debate." There is a tremendous appeal in the current slogan, "A divided world needs a united church," and who would dare to deny the truth of that statement? There is a tremendous emotional appeal in another slogan, "From theology we must go back to religion." And in the abstract it is perfectly legitimate to distinguish between religion and theology. But, as one authority has pointed out, there is something misleading in the manner in which this distinction is employed, particularly by the advocates of church union now! What is overlooked is that theology is indispensable in expressing and communicating religion to people, and that it depends upon the character of the theology whether the religion communicated is pure or adulterated, true or false, scriptural or unscriptural. Yes, it is desperately true that "a divided world needs a united church!" But the question still needs to be answered, What would be the faith of the United Church?

To this question advocates of church union give Dr. Morrison's answer, that belief in the lordship of Christ is both a sufficient faith, and a sufficient basis for union, and that it is all we need for the proposed merger of our churches. But, as Dr. Otto Piper points out in the current number of *Theology Today,* the lordship of which Christ? He concludes, "Christ then would be a convenient symbol for the object of everybody's belief, while each one would be free to implement it with whatever content he wished."

II

Doesn't our proposed *Basis of Union* affirm a very positive conviction about Christ, and doesn't it exalt his lordship in a very definite way? Apparently it does! It should be remembered, however, that faith is expressed not only in affirmation, but also in practice. In the June 7 issue of the Universalist *Christian Leader,* there is published notice of the Central Fellowship Committee of the Universalist Church, announcing the acceptance into "reciprocal fellowship" with the Universalist Church of America of a clergyman of the American Unitarian Association, and also of a clergyman of the Congregational Christian Churches! Before me is a published announcement of the Isle of Shoals congregational Conference to be held in August at Portsmouth, New Hampshire, with the statement that at "the tenth laymen's week-end conference, Congregational and Unitarian laymen will unite in a joint gathering." Another bulletin before me announces a world fellowship conference, of which Rev. Dana McLean Greeley, prominent Unitarian clergyman, and Rev. Carl Heath Kopf, pastor of Boston's Mt. Vernon Congregational Church, will be co-chairmen.

In the light of such examples of practice, how now is it possible to exalt the lordship of Christ, while at the same time engaging in fraternal fellowship with those who deny that lordship in the sense that we understand that term; whose position was recently stated by Dr. Frederick May Eliot, president of the American Unitarian Association, in these words: "Christianity has been guilty of spiritual arrogance on a world-wide scale, labeling all other religions false; . . . that amounts to spiritual imperialism, and is as out of date our world today as any form of imperialism."

All this just "doesn't add up"!

It should certainly be obvious that, despite our stated affirmations, we do not in practice have agreement in the doctrine of the gospel, and so the question still remains to be answered, What would be the faith of the United Church?

General Synod needs earnestly and prayerfully to consider whether this proposed merger of our two churches is really going to help get answered our Lord's prayer "that they may all be one." Not in terms of increased numerical strength, nor in terms of enhanced worldly influence, but on the only true basis on which the followers of Christ can ever be really one—in the unity of faith in Jesus Christ, and him crucified, "the power of God unto salvation unto every one that believeth."

75. The Grassroots Debate:

"An Open Letter on the Merger," "Prayers Concerning the Merger," and "Pilgrim, St. Louis, Presents the Merger"

(1948)

Ruth Isabel Seabury; Frederick Groetsoma; and *Advance*

Once the Congregational Christians Churches and the Evangelical and Reformed Church entered serious union discussions, their church leaders began to utilize a broad variety of means to inform and energize their people.

*The main periodicals of both denominations (*Advance *and* The Messenger*) published articles by recognized leaders introducing the doctrinal standards, theology, polity, worship, and service patterns of the other denomination and pointing out areas of concern. Ruth Isabel Seabury, who worked for the Congregational Christians in student work and Christian education, contributed to a "Forum on the Merger" by sharing her enthusiasm about the prospective union. She spoke of her conviction that God was sending a "new directive" to the people of God to express the oneness of Christ's people more fully.* Advance *also published two prayers by Frederick Groetsoma concerned with the merger, and gave space for a report from a church in St. Louis that was successful in introducing local church members to both sides of the union issue.*

Source: Ruth Isabel Seabury, "An Open Letter on the Merger," in "Forum on the Merger," *Advance,* May 1948, 30; Frederick Groetsoma, "Prayers Concerning the Merger," *Advance,* April 1948, 5; "Pilgrim, St. Louis, Presents the Merger," *Advance,* January 1948, 47.

Forum on the Merger

An Open Letter on the Merger

Dear Joe:—

You have asked me quite frankly and with a bit of urgency what I think about the merger, and you have voiced some of your most urgent fears hoping I would have an answer. Now, I am sure you must realize that I am decidedly enthusiastic about the merger.

I am, to be sure, an hereditary Congregationalist. All my forebears in New England in our part of the family on both sides have been Congregationalists. I found among my great-grandfather's papers deeds to pews in five churches, which make them my property and the property of my heirs "for the rest of time." Though some of those churches have long since ceased to exist, I am intrigued by the thought of "belonging" that they gave me. Nevertheless, I feel just as keenly my warm connection with the Evangelical and Reformed Church—Christians too!

I have been lucky beyond most Congregational Christians because, for the past 15 years I have become increasingly well acquainted with the leaders and members of the E & R Church. I am as much at home in their women's organizations, in their pulpits, in their theological seminaries even, as in our own. I count some of their leaders among my closest friends. I like them and delight in their fellowship. I am proud to know them.

Of course it's trite to say that on the human side there is no basic difference between us. We are the same kind of people, for the most part, many kinds, all kinds, with the same point of view toward life and work and the church, though they, perhaps, the ones I know best have more education about their faith than the corresponding people on our side. The discussions I have been in with them have the same liberal spirit as any with the best of my Congregational friends.

In the second place, I believe in the great freedom of their churches. It is essentially an even greater freedom than any enjoyed in CC circles. Their secretary of missionary education tries just as wistfully as I do to guide his people in their programs and with, I should gather, just as uneven success! They cannot be pushed any more than our people can, or commandeered even into education. They are, to be sure, a warmer fellowship in some respects. They know their leaders better, and treat them with more enthusiasm! Perhaps they also, in some cases, have a warmer expression of faith, though that I fancy is a bit overrated. There is just as much reserve among them as among our people and freedom seems far more responsible than with us, because perhaps it does delegate its authority freely.

One of my definite and constant contacts has been at the point of student work in both fellowships. We are already experimenting in united student work. We have joint work at the University of Missouri and at the University of Illinois, and it is impossible to tell, of course, who belongs to which! It works; that's the one thing we know. Our young people work perfectly together and are inspired by the contact. I am impressed with the fact that wherever we have come together we have made a larger unit and a more progressive and forceful unit with programs better led and better planned, so that we can take a bigger share in the work of the campus. The same would be true, I think, all down the line. If our women's work were one, it could do a better job in the Kingdom. So also with our laymen's work.

Our friends of the E & R Church have a swift response to human need, and often a less cumbersome way of telling the story of need which impresses me. They have in some ways better field work on the national side; we, perhaps, better strength at the state angle. We shall supplement each other in that and many other ways.

All this has come by a growing awareness on my part that we are alike pretty much, and therefore we ought to be together. Afraid? No, I'm not a bit afraid. I believe that the *Basis of Union* as presented to our people is quite consistent with Congregational polity. I believe, too, that it has provided soundly for the freedom of the congregation, caring for the greatest elements of our program and for the careful use of our funds for the purposes for which their donors intended them. Aside from that, I believe it provides a good basis for a constructive, growing, experimental church life which will attract more and more individuals, groups and even churches into the fellowship, the "unity of the spirit in the bonds of peace" which our Master demands of us.

I have always thought of Jesus as a great breaker from tradition and one bound by righteousness, not by fear of the law, held by the Spirit of God, not by the fear of men. I can never forget his words to the anxious Pharisee who wanted to fulfill the letter of the law in forgivings of his brother. "How many times must I?" said he, "Seven?" And Jesus said, "Till seventy times seven." I feel sorry for the poor calculating mind with its notebook in hand trying to keep that record, instead of seeing that freedom to live with God in a great outmoving experience of life at its highest and best. That's just the way I see it personally.

Of course, my chief reason for favoring the merger is that I believe we have a fresh insight in these days, a new indication of the will of God for men, a new revelation of our need for penitence, that the church presents to the world so divided a front! I shall never forget the man in Switzerland, a leader in world affairs, to whom I put the question, back in 1928, "What has gone wrong that the world is heading straight into war?" He answered me, "I think there are two chief factors which ought to concern you as an educator in the church. The first is the inertia of good, bright people! The second is the divided church." "I think," he said, "God cannot witness to men or to nations through so divided a body." It is my firm belief that whereas back in the day of our forefathers there were reasons of conviction and faith which expressed themselves in the separation of Church from State, and Church from Mother Church, today we are seeing a new directive, a call to express the oneness of our fellowship and the union under God of Christ's people.

Ruth Isabel Seabury

Boston, Mass.

Prayers Concerning the Merger

For Guidance

O thou without whom nothing is strong, nothing is holy, be with thy church in this hour. We acknowledge thy guiding hand in the past. Our fathers dared the wild seas and forbidding wilderness that we, through their faithfulness, might have a blessed heritage of freedom. Now thou has led us into this hour of decision. Grant unto us, O Lord, the guidance of thy holy spirit that we use this freedom to further thy cause. Keep us from any cheap and sentimental attachment to the past; but let no false glamour of tomorrow lure us into any hasty and unwise speaking or thoughtless actions. Keep us from mistaking our own selfish prejudices and desires for thy holy and blessed will. In quietness possess us; still our confused and beleaguered minds. Reveal thy will to us now, and as thou didst lead our fathers, so lead us in thy true ways. Holy Father, let thy kingdom come, and thy will be done in thy church through Christ our Lord and to him be glory and power for ever and forever. Amen.

For Those in Disagreement

Behold us in mercy, O God. Differences of personal opinion now threaten the unity of the spirit and the brotherly fellowship we so cherish. Let not our eagerness to accomplish thy will become a means of rending again thy seamless robe even as we seek to mend it. Give us again and always that due sense of comradeship with all our brethren who honestly differ with us and joining heart and mind with them, let us again be humbly led forth by thy spirit into any new truth thou hast for us. Forgive us, if in our pride at being led of thee, we have become blind to thy true light and deaf to thy true voice. We pray for humility and desire above all else that blessedness that comes when we all dwell together in the bonds of the spirit of Christ. Amen.

Frederick Groetsoma

Newton Highlands, Mass.

Pilgrim, St. Louis, Presents the Merger

A committee on church union was created consisting of two deacons, two trustees, two deaconesses, two from the Women's Association, two from the Missionary Committee and one from the Religious Education Committee. Under their direction the following procedure was followed as reported by Deacon D. Howard Doane:

"We requested our minister, E. Paul Sylvester, to preach one sermon on a phase of the subject, being careful to avoid either a pro or con position. His sermon topic was 'The Historical Background of the Congregational Christian, and the Evangelical and Reformed Churches.'

"We sent out a letter to all church members, enclosing the *Basis of Union.* This letter urged 'study' and 'attend the meetings.'

"The first of four Wednesday night dinner meetings was devoted to the presentation of factual material and the answering of questions on points not clear in the minds of the church members. We had broken up the whole subject and assigned parts to different individuals who were to answer the questions related to their assigned subject.

"It was our intention next to present the affirmative side of the question but, due to conflicting dates for our invited speakers, this became impossible. Consequently, President A. C. McGiffert, Jr., of Chicago Seminary, spoke first on why we should not favor the Union. We made it clear that we wanted a complete statement of all reasons he could give for not merging. We did not want him to attempt to balance his subject, but rather develop to the limit all the negative aspects. He did a complete and credible job. We made a recording and transcription of his remarks for others to hear and read who could not be present. We asked for questions but not arguments following Mr. McGiffert's address.

"At the next weekly meeting, Ferdinand Q. Blanchard, pastor of Euclid

Avenue Church, Cleveland, and National Chairman of the Merger Committee, spoke. We had requested that he deal exclusively with reasons why we should merge. We wanted as strong a presentation as he could give. We asked for questions but not arguments at the end of his address. He did an excellent job also. His talk was transcribed and made available for later study.

"Our final meeting was devoted exclusively to discussion. We asked for questions, statements of viewpoints and as complete participation by members as possible. At other meetings we had discouraged discussion but at this meeting we encouraged it. This was a very interesting meeting and both sides were discussed on a high plane and without rancor.

"Following the last of the four meetings, every member of the church was mailed a ballot. They were returned to the Committee without identification—the ballot was secret. Accompanying the ballot was a short letter of instructions and condensed copies of the Blanchard and McGiffert talks. This gave every member an opportunity to hear or read both sides. The ballots were not called for return until they had been in members' hands during two Sundays. A deadline for return was set.

"The Committee did all within its power to avoid the implication of a 'wrong' or 'right' side of the question. The Committee as such carefully avoided stating individual views. Of course, at the last meeting each committeeman had an opportunity to express his or her individual position. The Committee however, did not take a stand either for or against."

76. Youth:

"The Faith That Will Unite Us" and "The Basis of Union of the Pilgrim Fellowship . . . and the Youth Fellowship . . . "

(1946 and 1947)

Gerson S. Engelmann; Joint Committee

Youth *magazine, published by the Evangelical and Reformed Church, presented excellent materials dealing with the anticipated union between the Congregational Christian Churches and the Evangelical and Reformed Church. For example, in 1946* Youth *began a series introducing young people in the Evangelical and Reformed Church to the history, theology, and polity of the Congregational Christian Churches and the history and function of its youth group, The Pilgrim Fellowship. In the third program of the series, Gerson S. Engelmann presented the "common faith" of the two denominations as it was shown in the Statement of Faith in the Basis of Union (see vol. 6:77) and discussed what a united church might mean to youth. In 1947,* Youth *also published a new* Basis of Union *created for the Union of the Pilgrim Fellowship of the Congregational Christian Churches and the Youth Fellowship of the Evangelical and Reformed Church.*

Source: Gerson S. Engelmann, "The Faith That Will Unite Us," in "Let's Look at the Merger," *Youth,* 5 May 1946, 10–12; Joint Committee on the Basis of Union, "The Basis of Union of the Pilgrim Fellowship of the Congregational Christian Churches and the Youth Fellowship of the Evangelical and Reformed Church," *Youth,* 27 July 1947, 6–7.

The Faith That Will Unite Us

Our Common Faith

In the last stanza of one of the hymns at the end of our worship service, we sang:

> One common faith unites us all,
> We seek one common goal.

These words certainly express the theme of this statement of faith. It starts with what we believe and ends with our purpose. Thus our faith is the creed and the goal is the deed.

As young people, we are inclined to minimize belief. Usually it is a young person who says, "It doesn't matter what a man believes, what really counts is what he does." Examine this, is it a true or false statement? Doesn't what we do depend upon what we believe? Will a man live a good and moral life if he does not believe in God and the moral law? Everything that we do in life can be traced ultimately to some prior belief that we hold to be true.

This statement starts with God. He is the beginning of our faith. Herein we find the value of the Old and the New Testament Scriptures, for they set forth this faith in God. And it is interesting to notice the progression of thought that is contained in this opening paragraph of the statement of faith. This faith in God is (1) set forth in the Bible; (2) expressed in the ecumenical creeds (i.e., the general creeds of the church such as the Apostles' creed); (3) restated by the Reformation leaders; and (4) should be restated by us according to the inspiration given by God.

And what a challenge there is in the closing sentence of that first paragraph. It is by the restatement of that faith whereby we learn all that we have in common with all those who have gone before us in our Christian way. Thus, we can preserve a unity of mind and spirit not only with them, but it also tends to bind us closer together with all those who are now working toward the same high objectives and purposes that are ours.

We Believe

From lines thirty-one to forty-three, we have a restatement of the Apostles' Creed. One of our purposes of saying this in its original form in our worship service, was to give us this as a source of comparison with this present restatement. Can you find any of the essential items of the creed missing or are they all here? You will not always find the exact words, but the ideas seem to be present.

We still believe that God is creator and ruler of the world. He is the same for us as he was for our forefathers. In these days when nothing seems stable, he is the same from everlasting to everlasting. He is the only sure thing in this uncertain world and we can truly say with the hymnwriter:

Our God, our help in ages past,
Our hope for years to come,
Our shelter from the stormy blast,
And our eternal home.

We still believe that Jesus Christ, the son of God, is the only Savior for our generation as he was for those who have gone before us. He lived and died for us, and he still lives to challenge men to walk in his way.

We still believe in the Holy Spirit. Only if God is manifest in our world can the souls of men be renewed, comforted and inspired.

We still believe that there is a Holy Catholic Church. Let us be sure that we do not confuse this with the Roman Catholic Church. We are speaking of that pure and universal church that transcends and includes all churches and groups who call themselves Christian. Among all of these you can find souls who belong to the universal church. Any church that claims that she alone is catholic, immediately proves that she is not, for the word is inclusive rather than exclusive. We want to have a part in this universal fellowship and so we must be willing to grant it to others as well. All belong to the church universal who profess this faith and follow Jesus Christ as Lord and Savior.

Our Purposes

Now let us look at the purposes contained in the second last paragraph of this statement of faith. There is a reason for the church. It has not been established just to perpetuate itself, but to do some things that have to be done. Man, created in the image of God, has rebelled against his Father. He seeks to satisfy his selfish desires. With the freedom that God has given him, he violates his laws, and profanes his holy places. Man must be called to repentance and faith. He has to reestablish his relationship with God through public worship, through the creed he professes and through the life that he lives. He continues this relationship by the use of the sacraments which bring him the grace of God that was in Christ Jesus, in whom we are reconciled to God.

Naturally, if these things are dear to us, they ought to be just as meaningful to us. The gospel cannot be true for just one class, group or race, it must apply with equal effect to all. Christianity is not true to its Lord unless it insists that the gospel is for all men.

There are four final goals, knowledge, justice, peace and brotherhood. Knowledge, for we are convinced that the truth alone can make us free. Justice, for though the kingdom of God goes beyond it, justice must be a necessary part of that kingdom. Peace, for we worship the Prince of Peace. Brotherhood, for God is the common Father of us all.

We Look for the Kingdom

The Christian ever works and prays for the kingdom of God. Because of Jesus Christ, we are assured that the final outcome of this world is with God. No matter how strong evil is, or how well the organized principalities of wrong seem to endure, we know that God must triumph in the end. As Lowell once expressed it:

Truth forever on the scaffold,
Wrong forever on the throne,
Yet that scaffold sways the future,
And, behind the dim unknown,
Standeth God within the shadow,
Keeping watch above his own.

The Final Word

Let us ever remember that as Christians we are commanded to keep the fellowship of the unity of the spirit. We may disagree in ideas, but our hearts must maintain the unity of the love of Christ. Faith is not an argument. Instead, when the final statement of faith is drawn up, it "shall be regarded as a testimony, and not a test, of faith."

The Basis of Union of the Pilgrim Fellowship of the Congregational Christian Churches and the Youth Fellowship of the Evangelical and Reformed Church

Preamble

We, the regularly constituted representatives of the Pilgrim Fellowship of the Congregational Christian Churches and the Youth Fellowship of the Evangelical and Reformed Church, moved by the favorable action of our two parent bodies toward union;

BELIEVING that all Christian youth should be united in the ways of the Lord Jesus Christ in order to fulfil his prayer, "that they all may be one";

REALIZING that upon our generation rests the attainment of a united and peaceful Christian world, and, with a sincere desire to bring this about to the best of our ability;

DO NOW DECLARE ourselves to be one in body, and do set forth the following articles of agreement as the basis of our life and fellowship in Christian work.

I. Name

The name of the body formed by this union shall be "The Youth Fellowship of the United Church of Christ."

II. Purpose

THE YOUTH FELLOWSHIP UNITES ALL YOUNG PEOPLE OF THE UNITED CHURCH OF CHRIST IN THIS PURPOSE:

> To know God in our lives as revealed by Jesus Christ, to worship him only, to study his truth, and to dedicate ourselves to do his will.
>
> To extend the Christian fellowship and the message and mission of the Church to all people, working with all who seek to fulfil this purpose.
>
> To serve the world in the name of Christ, striving toward the establishment of brotherhood, justice and peace.

III. Organization

Membership

The Youth Fellowship shall be comprised of all young people between the ages of 12 and 24 who are affiliated with the United Church of Christ.

National Council

The national body of the Youth Fellowship shall be the National Council. It shall meet every two years. The first meeting of the National Council shall be composed of two hundred members, one hundred of whom shall be representatives of the former Pilgrim Fellowship, and one hundred shall be representatives of the former Youth Fellowship, each of the two fellowships to determine the method of election of its representatives, recommending that they include members of their student constituencies, and to authorize the entire body to constitute the first National Council. Eighty-five of each delegation are to be young people.[1] The functions of the Council are:

1. To speak with a united voice for the Youth Fellowship of the United Church of Christ.
2. To initiate, develop and recommend the general youth program of the United Church of Christ in co-operation and in accordance with the accepted principles and practices of the Division of Christian Education of which the Youth Fellowship is a recognized agency.

Youth Cabinet

The Youth Cabinet which will be elected by the National Council, taking into consideration the geographic areas of the United Church, will be comprised of the following:[2]

1. Officers
   a. Chairman
   b. Vice-chairman
   c. Secretary
   d. Treasurer

---

1. The Joint Committee feels that further discussion is needed on this matter of adult representation at the meetings of the National Council, particularly as voting privilege is concerned.

2. In the event that a number of Commissions are set up, it is recommended that provision be made to include the chairmen of these Commissions as members of the Youth Cabinet, reviewing the above specifications if necessary.

2. Sixteen Representatives-at-large
3. There shall be the following staff members of the Division of Christian Education: four from the Department of Education in Church and Home; and two from the Department of Christian Higher Education.

One-half of the first Cabinet shall be composed of members from the former Pilgrim Fellowship and the other half from the former Youth Fellowship, i.e., two of the officers, eight representatives-at-large, and three staff members from each denomination.

No member of the Youth Cabinet is to exceed twenty-four years of age during his term of office.

IV. Approval of the Basis of Union

The Basis of Union shall be submitted to the executive committees of the Congregational Christian Pilgrim Fellowship and the Evangelical and Reformed Youth Fellowship. Each group shall proceed in the approval or disapproval of the Basis of Union. When the Basis has been acted upon by the two groups, they shall report this action to the Joint Committee on Basis of Union, who shall put the Basis of Union in its final form and then request the calling of the first meeting of the National Council at the time, or shortly after, our parent bodies unite. In this joint session of the two Fellowships the final report of the Basis of Union Committee shall be made. The National Council shall declare by joint resolution that the union of the two Fellowships is duly effected at that time. Then the delegates, duly elected by the Fellowships entering into the union to constitute the National Council, shall be led in a constituting prayer, effect an organization by the election of officers, and proceed to the transaction of business. From the time of the organization of the National Council, until a constitution shall have been adopted, as heretofore provided, this Basis of Union shall be the fundamental law of the Youth Fellowship of the United Church of Christ.

This Basis of Union may be amended by action to be determined by the National Council.

JOINT COMMITTEE ON THE BASIS OF UNION

Roy Lausman, Co-chairman
Ernie Rueter, Co-chairman
Mrs. Eugene Wehrli, Secretary
Irene Meehan
Richard Trotter
John Trnka
Robert D. Brodt, Adviser
Oliver Powell, Adviser

77. Union Affirmed:

"The Basis of Union— Without the Interpretations"

(1947)

Ten years after Truman Douglass of the Congregational Christian Churches and Samuel Press of the Evangelical and Reformed Church first suggested that their denominations might come together in unity, a final draft of the "Basis of Union" between the two churches was published jointly by the Executive Committee of the General Council of the Congregational Christian Churches and the General Council of the Evangelical and Reformed Church. Official endorsement for the negotiations had come from the churches in 1942, and a Joint Committee on Union had begun its work shortly thereafter. In the end, the Basis went through ten drafts before reaching its final form.

The preamble to the Basis gave clear indication of the theological commitments that had brought the two denominations together and that would sustain them through another ten years of struggle toward union. They affirmed their common devotion to "one God," declared their commitment to the sovereignty of Christ, and confirmed their existence as parts of "the holy catholic Church, which is greater than any single Church and than all the Churches together." They confessed that as they confronted the divisions and hostilities of their world, they heard with a deepened sense of responsibility the prayer of Jesus Christ "that they may all be one" and they felt called to declare themselves one body.

Source: "The Basis of Union of The Congregational Christian Churches and The Evangelical and Reformed Church," pamphlet published jointly by the Executive Committee of the General Council of the Congregational Christian Churches and the General Council of the Evangelical and Reformed Church, 1947.

In the section "Faith," the Basis affirmed that the faith to which the uniting churches bore witness was that set forth in the Old and New Testaments and sustained by the ancient church in the ecumenical creeds, which were themselves reflected in the evangelical confessions of the Reformation, and which they felt called to express in the words of their time. A brief footnote indicated that the confession "expressed the content and meaning of the faith held generally by the members of the two uniting communions," but that it was designed to be "a testimony, and not a test, of faith."

When the two churches came to examine the Basis, the General Synod of the Evangelical and Reformed Church approved it in July 1947, and its action was ratified by the regional synods in the spring of 1948. Among the Congregational Christian Churches, approval was not so easily achieved. Questions about the meaning of Congregationalism surfaced and generated debates among Congregational Christian leaders and members that went on for ten years.

The material regarding the faith of the new United Church of Christ was not the problem. Rather, concerns revolved around those sections of the Basis dealing with the polity or governance of local churches, associations, the General Synod, and unified mission boards,

Critics of the Basis were fearful that the autonomy of the local churches was not sufficiently protected. They worried that the proposed General Synod would have authority or power over local congregations incompatible with congregational polity. And finally, they claimed that local churches would not have sufficient control within the national boards, which were supposed to "represent" them. Arguments over the Basis of Union were personal, political, and legal. It took ten years, and thousands of words of interpretation, before it finally became (with interpretations that were written later) the basis for the United Church of Christ.

"The Basis of Union of The Congregational Christian Churches and The Evangelical and Reformed Church"

First issued in March 1943 with subsequent revisions in August 1943, March 1944, October 1944, September 1945, October 1946 (not printed), and November 1946 (not printed).

Now finally revised at a meeting of the Joint Committee held in Cleveland, Ohio, on January 22, 1947, and presented for official action by the two communions.

THE JOINT COMMITTEE

Congregational Christian

Ferdinand Q. Blanchard, *Chairman*
Simon A. Bennett
William F. Bohn
Mrs. Henry B. Davis
Noble Strong Elderkin
David K. Ford
Harold B. Frame
David McKeith, Jr.
Charles C. Merrill
J. Chester Molyneux
Wilhelm Pauck
Herman F. Reissig
Frank Milton Sheldon
Russell Henry Stafford
Alfred Grant Walton

Evangelical and Reformed

George W. Richards, *Chairman*
Roberts R. Appel
John C. Gieser
L. W. Goebel
G. W. Grauer
John R. C. Haas
Nevin C. Harner
John Lentz
John W. Mueller
S. D. Press
Paul N. Schaeffer
Paul M. Schroeder

The present members of the Joint Committee desire to express their grateful appreciation to their predecessors on that committee for their very effectual labors and to the representatives of the Boards and others for assistance without which the work could not have been completed.

Table of Contents

PROCEDURES

The Congregational Christian Churches

In March, 1947, the Congregational Christian Churches intend through the Conference offices to send the Basis of Union to all of their delegates to the General Council inviting them to meet by Conference groups as soon as possible thereafter to discuss the Basis and appoint from each Conference group one of their number as a representative to advise the Executive Committee of the General Council in person at its next meeting as to whether or not to send the Basis officially to the churches.

On April 30, 1947, at Columbus, Ohio, the Executive Committee will meet with these representatives sent by the Conference groups of General Council members and decide whether to send the Basis of Union officially to the Conferences, Associations, and churches.

If that decision is affirmative, it is proposed that before April 1, 1948, the churches and their members, and before June 1, 1948, the Conferences and Associations, vote approval or disapproval of the Basis of Union.

In late June 1948, at the regular meeting of the General Council, the delegates will vote, on the basis of the previous votes taken by the Conferences, Associations, churches and members, on the question of effecting the Union.

It is recommended that the General Council vote approval of the Union if seventy-five per cent of the Conferences voting, seventy-five per cent of the Associations voting, seventy-five per cent of the churches voting, and seventy-five per cent of the members voting have already approved the Basis of Union.

The actual union would probably follow in the early Autumn of 1948, the first step being the official uniting of the General Council of the Congregational Christian Churches and the General Synod of the Evangelical and Reformed Church. This ceremony would take place in some appointed city and other gatherings celebrating the union would probably be held in other important centers throughout the country.

The Evangelical and Reformed Church

The Basis of Union will be presented to the General Synod at its triennial meeting at St. Louis, Missouri, July 9–16, 1947. If adopted by a two-thirds vote of the members of the General Synod voting it shall be submitted to the thirty-four Synods. If two thirds of the Synods vote approval the General Council shall declare it adopted.

The Committee on Closer Relations with Other Churches shall then request the General Council to call a special meeting of the General Synod to conclude whatever business it needs to transact. This meeting shall be held at the same time and place as a similar meeting of the General Council of the Congregational Christian Churches. Then the General Synod of the Evangelical and Reformed Church and the General Council of the Congregational Christian Churches shall meet in joint session in order to consummate the union. The Chairmen of the Committees on Union of the two Churches shall announce the vote of the Congregational Christian Churches and of the Synods of the Evangelical and Reformed Church, and the United Church of Christ shall be constituted by prayer and the election of officers.

Basis of Union
of the
Congregational Christian Churches
and the
Evangelical and Reformed Church

Adopted by the Joint Committee 22 January 1947

Preamble

We, the regularly constituted representatives of the Congregational Christian Churches and of the Evangelical and Reformed Church, moved by the conviction that we are united in spirit and purpose and are in agreement on the substance of the Christian faith and the essential character of the Christian life;

Affirming our devotion to one God, the Father of our Lord Jesus Christ, and our membership in the holy catholic Church, which is greater than any single Church and than all the Churches together;

Believing that denominations exist not for themselves but as parts of that Church, within which each denomination is to live and labor and, if need be, die; and

Confronting the divisions and hostilities of our world, and hearing with a deepened sense of responsibility the prayer of our Lord "that they all may be one";

Do now declare ourselves to be one body, and do set forth the following articles of agreement as the basis of our life, fellowship, witness, and proclamation of the Gospel to all nations.

I. Name

The name of the Church formed by this union shall be UNITED CHURCH OF CHRIST.[1]

This name expresses a fact: it stands for the accomplished union of two church bodies each of which has arisen from a similar union of two church bodies.[2] It also expresses a hope: that in time soon to come, by further union between this Church and other bodies, there shall arise a more inclusive United Church.

II. Faith

The faith which unites us and to which we bear witness is that faith in God which the Scriptures of the Old and New Testaments set forth, which the ancient Church expressed in the ecumenical creeds, to which our own spiritual fathers gave utterance in the evangelical confessions of the Reformation, and which we are in duty bound to express in the words of our time as God Himself gives us light. In all our expressions of that faith we seek to preserve unity of heart and spirit with those who have gone before us as well as those who now labor with us.

In token of that faith we unite in the following confession,[3] as embodying those things most surely believed and taught among us:

We believe in God the Father Almighty, Creator and Sustainer of heaven and earth; and in Jesus Christ, His Son, our Lord and Saviour, who for us and our salvation lived and died and rose again and lives for evermore; and in the Holy Spirit, who takes of the things of Christ and shows them to us, renewing, comforting, and inspiring the souls of men.

We acknowledge one holy catholic Church, the innumerable company of those who, in every age and nation, are united by the Holy Spirit to God in Christ, are one body in Christ, and have communion with Him and with one another.

We acknowledge as part of this universal fellowship all throughout the world who profess this faith in Jesus Christ and follow Him as Lord and Saviour.

We hold the Church to be established for calling men to repentance and faith, for the public worship of God, for the confession of His name by word and deed, for the administration of the sacraments, for witnessing to the saving grace of God in Christ, for the upbuilding of the saints, and for the universal propagation of the Gospel; and in the power of the love of God in Christ we labor for the progress of knowledge, the promotion of justice, the reign of peace, and realization of human brotherhood.

Depending, as did our fathers, upon the continued guidance of the Holy Spirit to lead us into all truth, we work and pray for the consummation of the Kingdom of God; and we look with faith for the triumph of righteousness and for the life everlasting.

III. Practice

A. The basic unit of organization of the United Church of Christ is the Congregation; that is, the local church.

B. The Congregations, through their ministers and through delegates elected from their membership, may organize Associations for fellowship, mutual encouragement, inspiration, and such other functions as may be desired.

C. The Congregations, through their ministers and through delegates elected from their membership, constitute Conferences for fellowship, counsel, and cooperation in all matters of common concern. The Conferences exist to make cooperation effective (a) among their Congregations and (b) between their Congregations and the General Synod, the Boards, commissions, agencies, and instrumentalities[4] of the Church.

D. The Conferences, through delegates elected by them from the membership and ministers of the Congregations located within their respective bounds, constitute the General Synod.

E. Officers, Boards, councils, commissions, committees, departments, agencies, and instrumentalities are responsible to the bodies that elect them.

F. The government of the United Church is exercised through Congregations, Associations, Conferences, and the General Synod in such wise that the autonomy of each is respected in its own sphere, each having its own rights and responsibilities. This Basis of Union defines those rights and responsibilities in principle and the constitution which will be drafted after the consummation of the union shall further define them but shall in no wise abridge the rights now enjoyed by Congregations.

G. Individual communicants have the right of appeal, complaint, or reference to their Congregations, Associations, Conferences, and ultimately to the General Synod. Ministers, Congregations, Associations, and Conferences have similar rights of appeal, complaint, or reference. Decisions rendered in consequence of such appeals, complaints, or references are advisory, not mandatory.

H. Each Congregation, Association, and Conference has the right of retaining or adopting its own charter, constitution, by-laws, and other regulations which it deems essential and proper to its own welfare. This right includes the holding and operation of its own property.

I. The freedom of worship and of education at present enjoyed by the Congregations of the negotiating communions will be preserved in the United Church. Other freedoms at present enjoyed are not hereby abridged.

J. Men and women enjoy the same rights and privileges in the United Church. It is recommended that at least one third of the members of the national administrative bodies be women.

K. Baptism and the Lord's Supper are the recognized sacraments of the Church.

IV. Functions of the General Synod

A. The General Synod shall initiate action for the preparation of a constitution of the United Church. This constitution shall be based upon the principles set forth in this Basis of Union. When prepared, it shall be submitted to the General Synod; and the General Synod shall declare it in force when it shall have been ratified by not less than two thirds of the former Congregational Christian churches voting, and by not less than two thirds of the former Evangelical and Reformed Synods.

B. The General Synod shall elect its officers and assign them their duties.

C. The General Synod, directly or through an executive committee, commissions, and other committees, shall carry on the general work of the Church which is now conducted by the General Council of the Congregational Christian Churches and the General Synod of the Evangelical and Reformed Church; and through the instrumentality of Boards, commissions, and other organizations as needed, shall meet the responsibilities of the Church for foreign missions, home missions, education, publication, the ministry and ministerial relief, evangelism, stewardship, social action, and institutional benevolence.

D. The General Synod shall have power to receive overtures and petitions; to give counsel in regard to cases referred to it; and to maintain correspondence with other communions.

E. The General Synod shall promote the reorganization of Conferences, Associations, and Synods into Conferences and Associations which shall be constituted on a territorial basis and enjoy a status similar to that of the former Conferences, Associations, and Synods. This reorganization shall be effected by the Conferences, Associations, and Synods concerned, with the counsel and confirmation of the General Synod.[5]

F. If and when the Basis of Union is regularly adopted, the General Synod shall appoint a commission composed of an equal number of representatives of the two uniting communions to prepare a statement of faith based in principle upon Article II of this document, which shall be submitted for approval to the General Synod, Conferences, Associations, and Congregations. This statement shall be regarded as a testimony, and not as a test, of faith.

G. The General Synod shall meet in regular sessions, determine their time, place, frequency, and program, and provide for extraordinary sessions as may be necessary.

H. The executive committee of the General Synod shall be called the Executive Council. Its function shall correspond to those of the present Executive Committee of the Congregational Christian General Council and of the present General Council of the Evangelical and Reformed General Synod. While it shall not be charged with the administration of the Boards and other agencies and instrumentalities of the communion, it shall be its duty to consider their work, to prevent duplication of activities, to effect all possible economies of administration, to correlate the work of the several organizations, including their publicity and promotional activities, so as to secure the maximum of efficiency with the minimum of expense. It shall have the right to examine the annual budgets of the several national organizations and have access to their books and records. It shall make report of its actions to the General Synod at each stated meeting of that body and present to that Synod such recommendations as it may deem wise for the furtherance of the efficiency and economical administration of the several organizations. It shall study the relative needs of these organizations, including the Conferences, and recommend the apportionment percentages for the distribution of benevolent contributions.

I. For the interim between the effecting of the union and the adoption of the constitution, the membership of the Executive Council shall be twenty-four, with equal representation of the uniting communions.[6]

J. This Executive Council shall have a budget under its control, with income for it derived from the present sources of revenue of the General Council of the Evangelical and Reformed Church and the Executive Committee of the General Council of the Congregational Christian Churches. It shall carry out faithfully all obligations of both of these bodies and conserve as separate funds all funds of both bodies until otherwise provided.

K. There shall be a central receiving treasury for all funds contributed to the General Synod and all the national agencies and instrumentalities. Each Conference will decide whether its Congregations shall be encouraged to send their moneys for these organizations direct to the central treasury or through the Conference treasurers.

L. No attempt will be made to set up a detailed plan for the solicitation, collection, and disbursement of missionary, benevolent, and administrative funds before the union is effected, but the General Synod shall be requested at its first meeting to appoint a special committee adequately representing all interests to deal with these matters and to report at a later date. In any plan it is understood:

1. That all property rights and trust funds shall be scrupulously protected as provided in Article IX, Sections A and C, of the Basis of Union.

2. That an adequate budgetary system will be established which will be voluntary in character on the part of the Congregations, Associations, Conferences, and Synods but in which due emphasis will be placed on the moral responsibility of all to support the general work of the Church.

M. Pending the report of the committee to be appointed by the General Synod and until new policies are adopted, present practices in apportionment allocations, per capita assignments, and kindred matters shall be maintained.

N. The choice of location of headquarters for the United Church of Christ shall be left until after the union is effected.

V. Conferences, Associations, and Synods

Until, according to Article IV, Section E, it is otherwise determined, the Conferences, Associations, and Synods shall continue; and each shall conduct its business in its own way. Whatever action is submitted to them by the General Synod shall be disposed of in the same way as these bodies respectively disposed of such action by the General Council of the Congregational Christian Churches or the General Synod of the Evangelical and Reformed Church prior to the union.

VI. Ministers and Congregations

A. The ministers of the two communions shall be enrolled as ministers of the United Church. Candidates for the ministry, after the union, and until a standard method is provided by the constitution, shall have the same status, and be licensed or ordained as ministers by the Associations or Conferences and Synods in the same way, as before the union. The standard method shall provide for ordination by authorization of the Conference or Association and normally upon the call to a Congregation. Similarly the formal induction of a minister into his parish, which is recommended as normal procedure, shall be by authority of the Conference or Association at the request of the Congregation.

B. A minister of another denomination shall not be accepted by any body of the United Church in which ministerial standing is held without recommendation from the body to which he belongs; if, however, a denomination refuses to recommend a minister in good and regular standing, he may be accepted after proper examination by the Conference or Association in which his standing would be held.

C. The calling of a minister to a Congregation is a concern of the Church at large, represented in the Association or Conference, as well as of the minister and the Congregation. Ministers and churches desiring to maintain a system of pastoral placement in which the Conference or Association shall have little or no part, shall be free to do so; but the recommended standard of denominational procedure shall be one in which the minister, Congregation, and Conference or Association cooperate, the Conference or Association approving candidates, the Congregation extending and the minister accepting the call. The new communion will appeal to all Congregations not to call or dismiss their ministers, and to all ministers not to respond to calls or resign, until the Association or Conference shall have given approval. In all relationships between minister and local church or Congregation, the freedom of the minister and the autonomy of the church are presupposed.

VII. Members

All persons who are members of either communion at the time of the union shall be members of the United Church. Men, women, and children shall be admitted into the fellowship of the United Church through baptism and profession of faith according to the custom and usage of each congregation prior to the union. When they shall have been admitted, they shall be recognized as members of the United Church.

VIII. Organization of Boards

[*This article has been ratified (subject to the adoption of the entire Basis of Union by the negotiating communions) by the Executive Committee of the Congregational Christian General Council, by the Evangelical and Reformed General Council, and severally by the governing authorities of all Boards, agencies, and instrumentalities involved.*]

A. The Boards, commissions, and other agencies and instrumentalities shall proceed to correlate their work under the General Synod as rapidly as their charters, constitutions, property rights, the effectiveness of their program, and the laws of the State will permit. In the original personnel of the Boards, commissions, and other agencies and instrumentalities, when consolidated, due representation shall be given to each of the consolidating communions.

B. At each regular meeting of the General Synod each Board and commission shall submit for review a report of its operations during the time elapsed since the last regular meeting of the General Synod.

C. Except in the case of the Pension Board, the members of the Boards shall be nominated and elected by the General Synod. They shall be represented through corresponding members, with voice but without vote, in the General Synod itself. They shall elect their own officers. The executive committees or other governing groups of the Boards shall have a sufficient number of members to provide for geographical distribution, representation of both of the uniting Churches (*see Section A above*), and the inclusion of persons qualified to render specific services, as for example in the field of investment, medicine, education, etc., as the Boards may require.

D. The American Board of Commissioners for Foreign Missions and the Board of International Missions shall be united under the name of the AMERICAN BOARD OF COMMISSIONERS FOR FOREIGN MISSIONS.[7]

1. The Board thus constituted shall from the time of the consummation of the union until the adoption of a constitutional plan of organization consist of two hundred and twenty-five members, one hundred and thirteen of whom shall be chosen from the Evangelical and Reformed Church and one hundred and twelve from the Congregational Christian Churches, all to be elected by the General Synod of the United Church. One third of these members shall be women.

2. This body is smaller than the present Congregational Christian Board and larger than the present Evangelical and Reformed Board. Through its members its work will be related to the Congregations and Congregations. The traveling expenses of members incurred in connection with meetings will be borne in part by the Board and in part by the members themselves. It is believed that the additional interest and effectiveness in promoting the program resulting from these large group meetings will immeasurably outweigh the cost involved in the proposed plan of organization.

3. On the adoption of a constitution and by-laws for the United Church, the term of office of all Board members elected under these provisions shall terminate on the date designated by the General Synod for their successors to take office under the permanent plan of organization of the Boards.

4. Among the duties of this Board shall be the following:

a. To receive and consider the reports of the board of directors (*see Paragraph 5 following*) and the executive officers and to give them any necessary directives.

b. To determine long-range policies to be adopted by the Board.

c. To nominate and elect the general officers of the Board, the members of the board of directors, and the executive officers.

d. To report fully to the General Synod of the United Church concerning operations and finances of the Board (*see Section B above*).

5. The Board shall elect forty-five members who, with five persons ex officio, shall serve as a board of directors. The members ex officio shall be the President and the two Vice-Presidents of the Board and the two highest administrative officers of the General Synod of the United Church.

E. The homeland Boards, agencies, and instrumentalities of the Congregational Christian Churches and of the Evangelical and Reformed Church, exclusive of the Pension Board and the agencies for social action, from the time of the consummation of the union until the adoption of a constitutional plan for their organization, shall function by means of a single corporate body. The name of this corporate body shall be the BOARD FOR HOME MISSIONS OF THE UNITED CHURCH OF CHRIST. In order to provide the appropriate corporate structure for this enlarged and consolidated work, the charter of The Board of Home Missions of the Congregational and Christian Churches shall be amended so that it may be used for this purpose.

Corporate Membership

1. There shall be two hundred and twenty-five corporate members of the Board for Home Missions of the United Church of Christ elected by the General Synod of the Church.[8]
2. These corporate members shall represent the United Church of Christ in the promotion and administration of the work of home missions. The term "home missions" as here used shall include the founding, support, and building of churches, education, educational institutions, publication, ministerial relief, evangelism, stewardship, institutional benevolence, and other home services.
3. They shall elect a board of directors as hereinafter provided.

4. They shall meet periodically, but at least annually, to review the proceedings of the board of directors, to study the status of the work of home missions, and to plan for its further development. In the interim between meetings they shall be alert to inform themselves as to the progress of the work and shall individually seek opportunity to bring the work to the attention of the Congregations and members of the United Church of Christ.
5. The corporate members shall give careful consideration to all recommendations from the General Synod or its Executive Council, and in the field of home missions, as defined above, shall have responsibility for determining matters of promotion, administration, and policy.
6. The terms of these corporate members shall be six years and they shall be elected in three classes of seventy-five each, one class being elected every second year at the regular biennial meeting of the General Synod of the United Church of Christ. At the first meeting of the General Synod of the United Church, the two hundred and twenty-five persons shall be divided into three classes of seventy-five each, one class designated to serve two years, one class designated to serve four years, and one class designated to serve six years; provided however that, on the adoption of a constitution and by-laws for the United Church, the term of office of all Board members elected under these provisions shall terminate on the date designated by the General Synod for their successors to take office under the permanent plan of organization of the Boards. This paragraph is subject to amendment if it is decided that the General Synod shall meet otherwise than biennially.
7. In order that there may be continuity of operation during the years of reorganization the first list of corporate members shall include persons who are members of the Boards, agencies, and instrumentalities of the two uniting bodies at the time the union is consummated, as follows:

Members of the Board of National Missions of the Evangelical and Reformed Church	14
Members of the Board of Christian Education and Publication of the Evangelical and Reformed Church	12
Members of the Commission on Evangelism of the Evangelical and Reformed Church	10

Members of the Board of Business Management of the Evangelical and Reformed Church	12
Members of the Commission on Benevolent Institutions of the Evangelical and Reformed Church (excepting the representatives appointed by the institutions)	4
Members of the Commission on Higher Education of the Evangelical and Reformed Church (excepting the Presidents of Colleges)	12
Forty-eight persons elected at large, from the membership of the Evangelical and Reformed Church	48
Sub-total	112
The President, three Vice-Presidents and thirty-six other members of the Board of Directors of The Board of Home Missions of the Congregational and Christian Churches	40
Members of the Commission on Evangelism of the Congregational Christian Churches (excluding the four persons elected to the Commission by The Board of Home Missions)	12
Three persons designated by the association of Congregational Christian Colleges	3
Fifty-eight persons elected at large from the membership of the Congregational Christian Churches	58
Sub-total	113
TOTAL	225

8. The particular class to which each individual belongs will be indicated by the General Synod at the time of election.

Board of Directors

9. The board of directors, as constituted at the time of union, shall consist of the Chairman and the two Vice-Chairmen of the Board for Home Missions of the United Church of Christ, the two highest administrative officers of the General Synod of the United Church of Christ, and forty-five members who shall be chosen from and elected by the corporate members of the Board for Home Missions. At least one third of those elected shall be women.

10. In order that all interests may be represented, the first board of directors shall be nominated by a joint committee composed of an equal number of persons to be designated in advance by the appropriate bodies of the two uniting communions.

11. Of the first board of directors, twenty-four shall be chosen from the Evangelical and Reformed Church and twenty-four from the Congregational Christian Churches.

12. The board of directors shall immediately elect committees as follows:

   a. An executive committee composed of thirteen persons, among whom shall be the chairman of the board of directors and the chairmen of the divisional committees. At least four of this committee shall be women.

      This executive committee shall exercise such powers as are conferred upon it from time to time by the board of directors.

   b. An investment committee consisting of five members, including the Treasurer, at least three of whom shall be members of the board of directors, who shall have power to invest and reinvest the funds of the corporation, or trust funds held by them, and to select investments and reinvestments of the said funds, and to change the investments of such funds, and such other powers as may be given them by the Board.

   c. Such divisional committees[9] which specialize in the founding, support, and building of churches, education, educational institutions, publication, ministerial relief, evangelism, stewardship, institutional benevolence, and other home services, as the interests of the work require, who shall have such powers as may be given by the directors.

   d. Such other standing committees as the interests of the work require, who shall have such powers as may be given by the directors.

F. The Commission on Christian Social Action of the Evangelical and Reformed Church and the Council for Social Action of the Congregational Christian Churches shall be united under the name, the COUNCIL FOR CHRISTIAN SOCIAL ACTION.

Membership

1. From the time of the consummation of the union of the communions until the adoption of a constitutional plan of organization, there shall be twenty-four members of the Council for Christian Social Action elected by the General Synod of the United Church of Christ. Of the first members of the Council, twelve shall be chosen from the Evangelical and Reformed Church and twelve from the Congregational Christian Churches. The terms of these members shall be six years and they shall be elected in classes of eight each, one class being elected every second year at the regular biennial meeting of the General Synod of the United Church of Christ. At the first meeting of the General Synod of the United Church, the twenty-four persons shall be divided into three classes of eight each, one class designated to serve two years, one class designated to serve four years and one class designated to serve six years. On the adoption of a constitution and by-laws for the United Church, the term of office of all Council members elected under these provisions shall terminate on the date designated by the General Synod for their successors to take office under the permanent plan of organization. This paragraph is subject to amendment, if it is decided that the General Synod shall meet otherwise than biennially.
2. The Council for Christian Social Action may choose as advisory members, with voice but not vote, representatives of other Boards, agencies and conferences, and of the men's, women's and youth fellowships.

Committees

3. The Council for Christian Social Action shall immediately elect such standing committees as the interests of the work require. They shall have such powers as shall be given to them by the Council.

Functions

4. The Council for Christian Social Action shall be an agency under the General Synod of the United Church of Christ, and shall have power to take over, unify, and operate the activities carried on by the Council for Social Action of the Congregational Christian Churches

and the Commission on Christian Social Action of the Evangelical and Reformed Church.

Staff

5. The Director and other staff members shall be elected by the Council for Christian Social Action.

G. The pension activities of the United Church shall be administered by one corporation, the name of which shall be left for later decision by mutual agreement. It is here referred to as the MERGED FUND.

1. Provision shall be made in the by-laws of the Merged Fund whereby the General Synod of the United Church shall from time to time make examinations of the practices and developments of the Merged Fund.
2. The Trustees shall be chosen from eligible persons whose names have been presented to and approved by the General Synod of the United Church.
3. The Merged Fund shall be a non-profit membership corporation in which control lies in the members of the Fund through a Board of Trustees, elected by the members. Congregations and other employing agencies shall be included as participating members.
4. The maximum annuity[10] provided by the Pension Fund of the Evangelical Synod, the Sustentation Fund of the Reformed Church, and the Original Plan of the Annuity Fund for Congregational Ministers (hereafter referred to in this statement as the three "original plans") shall be in each case $500.00.
5. The liability of the Merged Fund to the members of the three "original plans" shall be set up on the books of the new corporation for the funded portion of their respective annuities only.
6. Sufficient money shall be designated in advance by the United Church as a prior claim upon apportionment to meet the indicated annual requirements for the unfunded portion of the annuities under all three "original plans" and to make cumulative provision for their funding.
7. This prior claim upon the apportionment[11] shall be for not less than $500,000 in each year in which the apportionment giving of the United Church for the year immediately preceding equals or exceeds $3,300,000. The prior claim may be proportionately reduced

in any year in which the apportionment giving for the preceding year is less than $3,300,000, but the prior claim shall in no case be for less than an amount sufficient to meet the requirements of the year in question for the unfunded portion of the annuities under all three "original plans" plus the necessary expense of promotion and administration. The prior claim upon the apportionment shall continue until the total liabilities of the three "original plans" are completely funded.[12]

8. Liability for payment of the unfunded portion of "original plan" annuities in any year shall be limited to the money received as applicable to such unfunded portion. In the event that in any year there shall not be sufficient money to pay the annuities which the denomination has designated, the legal liability of the Merged Fund shall be completely satisfied and fulfilled when such applicable money as is available has been disbursed to the "original plan" annuitants.

9. The assets and liabilities in the Merged Fund pertaining to members of the Ministers' Retirement Annuity Fund of the Evangelical and Reformed Church and of the Expanded Plan of the Annuity Fund for Congregational Ministers shall be consolidated as completely as legal requirements and considerations of equity permit.

10. Ministers enrolling in the Merged Fund other than those who are members of one of the present plans at the time of the union, shall be received under a new form of certificate.

11. The assets received by the Merged Fund from the present funds shall all be pooled into a common unit of investment and, together with investment of future receipts, shall be collectively available from time to time to meet the liabilities of the various Departments of the Merged Fund. No particular assets shall be segregated against the balance in any particular fund, except for conditional gift accounts and other accounts which may be required to be segregated by law.

Pilgrim Memorial Fund Income

12. In the operation of the Merged Fund the Pilgrim Memorial Fund[13] Income received in any year shall be allocated in the succeeding year in the following manner:

    a. A specific sum determined before the merger shall be allocated to the Original Plan of the Annuity Fund.

b. A further specific sum determined before the merger shall be allocated to the Merged Fund to meet the expenses incurred in the operation of the Original Plan of the Annuity Fund.

c. An amount determined from year to year shall be allocated to the Merged Fund to meet the expenses incurred on account of Congregational Christian members of the consolidated "expanded plan."

d. Such an amount shall be allocated for the benefit of the members of the Expanded Plan of the Annuity Fund, as shall provide $45 for each unit sharer among the members of such Expanded Plan, according to the rules of the Annuity Fund, or as nearly this amount as can be provided after allocations a, b, and c have been made.

e. Any balance after the above four allocations shall be used for the strengthening of the whole Merged Fund, or in such manner as the Trustees believe most beneficial for the benefit of ministerial members of the Merged Fund and their families who do not fall within the four following categories:

I. Congregational Original Plan members

II. Evangelical Pension Fund members

III. Reformed Sustentation Fund members

IV. Congregational Christian Expanded Plan members

f. If allocations under heading e shall exceed $45.00 per member, members under heading d shall be entitled to further allocation.

13. The pension boards of the two denominations shall give careful attention to the continuance and extension of a plan to provide retirement income for lay workers of the churches and other organizations of the United Church.

IX. Legal Obligations

A. The property rights of all bodies such as Congregations, Associations, Conferences, Synods, and corporations shall be scrupulously observed.

B. The theological seminaries, colleges, academies, denominational boards, benevolent institutions, and other corporations shall be controlled under the terms of their respective charters and other governing documents. Those institutions, however, which were under the supervision of the national bodies of the uniting communions shall, at least until the constitution is adopted, pass under the supervision of the General Synod. While they are under the supervision of the General Synod, the interests of the previously supervising groups shall be properly recognized.

C. Due protection shall be given all trust funds, including pension funds.

X. Approval and Implementation of the Basis of Union

A. The Basis of Union shall be submitted to the General Council of the Congregational Christian Churches and the General Synod of the Evangelical and Reformed Church. Each shall proceed according to its own polity[14] in the approval or disapproval of the Basis of Union. When the Basis has been approved by the regular action of the two bodies, each shall designate an equal number of its membership, approximately three hundred, with power to represent it at a joint meeting which shall constitute the first meeting of the General Synod of the United Church of Christ.

B. The joint meeting being duly called and assembled, to it the final report of the action of the communions upon the Basis of Union shall be made; and by joint resolution it shall be declared that the union of the communions is effected at that time, the General Synod of the United Church of Christ being the successor to the General Council of the Congregational Christian Churches and the General Synod of the Evangelical and Reformed Church, the joint meeting becoming the first meeting of the General Synod of the United Church. Then the delegates shall be led in a constituting prayer, effect an organization by the election of officers, and proceed to the transaction of business. From the time of the organization of the General Synod of the United Church until a constitution of the United Church has been adopted, this Basis of Union shall regulate the business and affairs of the United Church.

C. At the joint session referred to in the foregoing paragraph when the Union shall be formally effected, such action shall be taken as will unite the General Council of the Congregational Christian Churches and the General Synod of the Evangelical and Reformed Church: the further union of Conferences, Associations, Synods, and other bodies within the uniting communions shall proceed with the approval of the groups concerned, according to the principles laid down in this Basis of Union.

D. The General Synod of the United Church of Christ at its first meeting shall also take any and all appropriate steps necessary to insure the continuity and to effect the consolidation of the Boards, commissions, and other agencies and instrumentalities as described in Article IV, Section C, and to make effective an interim plan for their consolidation and operation, as more explicitly set forth in Article VIII.

E. The General Synod at its first meeting shall be made up of representatives elected as set forth in Article X, Section A; but at subsequent meetings, until a constitution shall have been adopted, the General Synod shall be composed of delegates elected by the present Conferences and Synods, or their successors, one delegate representing each three thousand communicants or major fraction thereof, so that the total number will be about six hundred.

F. Upon the consummation of the union the general officers of the former Congregational Christian General Council and the former Evangelical and Reformed General Synod not connected with the Boards shall become the staff of the General Synod of the United Church of Christ until other arrangements are perfected by the General Synod.

G. Revisions and amendments of the constitution shall be made by the General Synod and ratified by the Conferences in collaboration with the Associations and Congregations.

XI. Revisions and Amendments

Revisions and amendments of the Basis of Union while it is in force before the adoption of a constitution may be made by consent of ninety per cent of the members of the General Synod of the United Church of Christ duly assembled.

Notes

1. If the name "United Church of Christ" seems presumptuous, it should be remembered that any good general name must seem so, since it would apply equally well to other groups. A name, however, quickly becomes a mere means of classification, and it is hoped that the world will soon come to know that the Churches uniting under this name do not pretend to be more than they actually are.

(The purpose of this and other footnotes in this instrument is purely explanatory. They are designed to throw light on the text, but are not part of the Basis of Union.)

2. See the brief history appended to this basis of union.

3. This confession expresses the content and meaning of the faith held generally by the members of the two uniting communions. It is not to be considered a substitute for any confession of faith which may be used in any congregation today. Like the ampler statement called for in Article IV, Section F, it is designed to be a testimony, and not a test, of faith.

4. The Basis of Union employs both the word "agencies" and "instrumentalities" in order to meet legal requirements.

5. It is expected that the Conferences and Synods will take the first steps necessary to this reorganization as soon as practicable after the consummation of the union, forming non-competitive units without overlapping boundaries capable of continuing all the work carried on by the present Conferences and Synod, together with such other work as may prove to be desirable. The formation of Associations, as deemed advisable, would follow.

6. Paragraphs describing arrangements for the interim between the consummation of the union and the adoption of the constitution, while constituting part of the Basis of Union, are printed in smaller type to distinguish them from the rest of the text.

7. It is the intention of the present American Board to amend its Charter and By-laws to conform to those of the Board of the United Church.

8. Note that this Board, in size and structure, parallels and complements the American Board of Commissioners for Foreign Missions (see Article VIII, Section D, Paragraph 1).

9. It is at present believed that the Board for Home Missions will require the following Divisions in order to care for all the interests involved:

Division of Christian Education—continuing

CC Division of Christian Education
ER Board of Christian Education and Publication (education and curricular editorial functions only)
ER Commission on Higher Education
ER College and Seminary interests
CC College and Seminary interests

Certain aspects of the higher education interests to be lodged with a College-Seminary Council composed of representatives of the Division of Christian Education, the American Missionary Association Division, and of the Colleges and Seminaries.

Division of Ministerial Relief—continuing

ER Relief functions of the Board of Pensions and Relief
CC Division of Ministerial Relief

Division of Evangelism and Church Extension—continuing

CC Church Extension Division
CC Commission on Evangelism
ER Board of National Missions
ER Commission on Evangelism

American Missionary Association Division—continuing

CC American Missionary Association Division

Division of Publication—continuing

CC Pilgrim Press Division
ER Board of Business Management

The Division of Publication (*continuing the Pilgrim Press Division and the Board of Business Management*) will proceed forthwith to develop and recommend particularly to the board of directors, of the Board for Home Missions a plan for consolidating and unifying the publication and merchandising interests of the United Church.

10. By "maximum annuity" is meant the annuity paid to a member who has completed the full term of service or membership defined by the rules of the fund to which he belongs. The annuity of a member who has completed less than the full term of service or membership is a percentage of the maximum, stipulated by the rules of the fund in question. The annuity of the widow of a member of any of the "original plans" shall be 60% of the annuity to which her husband would be entitled.

11. In 1945 the amounts received from apportionment of the two denominations for similar purposes were as follows:

From the Evangelical and Reformed Churches	$210,741
From the Congregational Christian Churches	117,025
Total	$327,766

This amount does not include $176,846 contributed by the Congregational Christian Churches through the Unit Plan.

12. It is estimated that the time required to fund the "Original Plan" annuities upon the above basis will be approximately thirty years.

13. The Pilgrim Memorial Fund, consisting of about $5,500,000, is an endowment fund held for the benefit of The Annuity Fund for Congregational Ministers, the income of which is at present used for the administrative expenses of the Annuity Fund and the benefit of its members.

14. See Procedures, p. 3.

78. A Primer of Union:

"Questions and Answers Regarding the Proposed Union . . . "

(1947)

Talks between the Congregational Christian Churches and the Evangelical and Reformed Church began very informally in 1938. In that same year, the Christian Century *raised a question that had long been simmering below the surface in denominations of congregational polity (see vol. 6:71). It was the same issue that Washington Gladden (1836–1918), an important Congregational leader, had noted back in 1904. In his ecumenical work, Gladden had come to perceive an imbalance between autonomy and fellowship among Congregationalists, with the result that the cherished notion of local congregational autonomy had actually become a "weakness" (see vol. 6:3). This weakness seemed to prevent Congregationalists from joining in cooperative action and ecumenical ventures. In fact, after the second World Conference on Faith and Order, in 1937, some people wondered if the Congregational emphasis on the autonomy of the local church was holding congregationally ordered denominations back from affirming the catholic and organic unity of the church.*

Although the original ecclesiastical understanding of autonomy in New England Congregationalism had protected local congregations from hierarchical church interference so that they would be free to

---

Source: Joint Committee of the Congregational Christian Churches and the Evangelical and Reformed Church, "A Primer of Union: Questions and Answers Regarding the Proposed Union Between the Congregational Christian and the Evangelical and Reformed Churches," pamphlet published by the Congregational Christians Churches and by the Evangelical and Reformed Church, 1947.

respond directly to the bidding of the sovereign God, autonomy, after the Revolutionary War, became a secular concept often equated with personal or political liberty. The response of many Congregational Christians to the "Basis of Union" for the proposed United Church of Christ was filled with concern about autonomy. Groups opposed to the union began publishing dissenting pamphlets and arguments (see vol. 6:79–83).

In response, a joint committee of the Congregational Christian Churches and the Evangelical and Reformed Church produced a pamphlet entitled "A Primer of Union." It tried to clarify issues that were causing discomfort. It spoke directly to four concerns raised in an antimerger meeting (held in November 1947, in Evanston, Illinois), that those who had prepared the Basis of Union were (1) moving from congregational to presbyterial polity; (2) taking away the autonomy of the local church; (3) altering the regularization of relationships between ministers and churches; and (4) asking for a vote on the Basis of Union before a new constitution and bylaws and a new statement of faith had been presented to the churches (see vol. 6:79).

Historical Background

1. **Whence the Name "Congregational"?**

   In 1620 the Mayflower brought the Pilgrims to Plymouth and during succeeding years other vessels brought many Puritans to Massachusetts Bay. They and their like-minded friends in England called themselves "Congregationalists" because they believed that each congregation should govern its own inner life.

2. **Whence the Name "Christians" (as a distinctive denominational title)?**

   At the end of the eighteenth and the beginning of the nineteenth century three unrelated movements took their start in Virginia and North Carolina, in New England, and in the Ohio Valley, and in 1820 were united under the simple name "Christian" as a protest against denominationalism.

3. **Are Not the Disciples of Christ Often Known as "Christians"?**

   Yes. The founders of that denomination were familiar with the name as used by the group already established, and adopted it in many places.

4. When Were the Names "Congregational" and "Christian" United?

In 1931, when a union was effected between the General Convention of the Christian Church and the National Council of the Congregational Churches. (The title Congregational Christian is hereinafter abbreviated to C.C.)

5. Whence the Name "Evangelical"?

This name, the general equivalent of "Protestant," was taken by a group whose members began coming into the Middle West in the early nineteenth century from Germany and Switzerland, some of them having formerly been of the Lutheran Church, which dates from 1517, and others of the Reformed Church of Zwingli and Calvin.

6. Whence the Name "Reformed"?

This stems from the Reformation in the 16th century. It was brought from the Palatinate and neighboring German provinces and Switzerland when, beginning in 1710, the spiritual descendants of the great Swiss and Palatine Reformers settled in Pennsylvania and the surrounding colonies and founded churches there.

7. When Were the Names "Evangelical" and "Reformed" United?

In 1934, when the Evangelical Synod of North America and the Reformed Church in the United States became the Evangelical and Reformed Church (hereinafter abbreviated to E. and R.).

8. Would These Four Honored Names Be Lost in a Union?

No: the local churches would retain their former names, and add, above or below them, United Church of Christ.

9. Where Did the Idea of the Proposed Union Have Its Start?

In St. Louis, where the ministers of the two communions have long enjoyed close cooperation. The matter was presented to the members of the C.C. Commission on Interchurch Relations and Christian Unity in 1940, and they waited upon the E. and R. General Council, inviting informal conversations with the E. and R. Committee on Closer Relations with Other Churches. These conversations were made official by the national bodies of the two communions in 1942. In 1944 the national bodies voted to carry forward a process of mutual acquaintance looking toward possible union.

Statistics

10. How Many Congregations Belong to the C.C. Churches?

The last Year Book, with statistics for 1943, shows 5,891.

11. How Many in the E. and R. Church?

The last Statistical Tables, for the year ending December 31, 1943, show 2,835. This makes a combined total of 8,726.

12. How Many Members of the Two Communions Are There in the United States?

1,093,325 C.C. members, and 675,958 E. and R. members not counting the baptized who are not yet communicants. The total of the two is 1,769,283.

13. Where Are the C.C. Churches Strongest?

There are more than 25,000 members in each of the following states, shown in the order of their strength: Massachusetts, Connecticut, New York, Illinois, Ohio, California, Michigan, Iowa, Wisconsin, Minnesota, Maine, and New Hampshire.

14. Where Does the Numerical Strength of the E. and R. Church Lie?

There are over 200,000 members in Pennsylvania alone, and more than 25,000 in each of the following states, taken in order of their strength: Ohio, Illinois, Wisconsin, Missouri, Indiana, and New York.

15. Are the Two Communions Growing?

Yes, each is adding about one per cent per annum, though each has shown losses in Sunday School enrollment.

16. How Do They Stand on Benevolences and Congregational Expenses?

Their giving is about the same, as follows:

	Benevolences	**Congregational Expenses**
C.C.	$2.66	$14.80
E. and R.	3.11	14.71

17. Compared to Other Denominations Is This Good or Only Fair?

The giving of both church groups is a little below the average of American denominations for benevolences and a little above the average for congregational expenses.

18. What About the Value of Property Held by the Churches?

The C.C. total is about 167 million dollars, the E. and R. total about 91 million dollars. The combined total is about 258 million dollars.

19. What Debts Have the C.C. Churches?

They regard as a first charge upon their resources the payments of ministerial pensions under a system now superseded which will call for about $120,000 per annum until about 1950, after which the demand will lessen annually.

20. What Debts Have the E. and R. Church?

None as such, though there are liabilities of about $900,000 in a denominational church building account, matched by assets of over $1,500,000, and mortgages in process of liquidation on a building in Philadelphia and a publishing house in Cleveland.

Polity

21. How Are the C.C. Churches Organized?

In Associations which, roughly speaking, are county units, in Conferences which are usually state units, and in the General Council, which is the national body.

22. How Is the E. and R. Church Organized?

In Synods, which are generally larger than Associations and smaller than Conferences, and in the General Synod, the national body.

23. How Are the Members of Associations, Synods, Conferences, and National Bodies Chosen?

The two denominations are similar in being representative democracies, the Associations, Synods, and Conferences being made up of delegates from the congregations; and the national bodies, of representatives from the Conferences (and Associations) and Synods.

24. Who Owns the Property of the Local Church?

In both denominations it is usual for the local church to own it, but in the E. and R. constitution there is a provision whereby every congregation uniting with the denomination after 1950 must include in its constitution a clause to the effect that in case of later withdrawal its property shall revert to the denomination. The Reformed congregations have long since followed the latter practice.

25. Who Would Own Local Church Property Under the Proposed Union?

The local church, unless it made it over to the Conference.

26. Who Are the Lay Officers of a Congregation?

In the E. and R. Church they are the elders, deacons (who give special attention to the benevolent side of the church life), and trustees. In the C.C. churches they are the deacons (who combine the office of elder and deacon) and trustees. In all cases they are elected by the congregation. These are the traditional offices: in both churches other positions, like that of Church School Superintendent, have come to assume great importance.

27. Who Admits and Dismisses Members in a Local Church?

In a C.C. church, the adult membership, on recommendation of a committee composed of the ministers and deacons (and sometimes a few other members at large), in an E. and R. church, the Spiritual Council made up of the Minister and Elders.

28. How Often Do the Associations, Conferences, and Synods Meet?

The Associations from two to six times a year, the Conferences once or twice a year, the Synods twice a year.

29. How Often Do the General Council and General Synod Meet?

The former every two, the latter every three, years.

30. What Bodies Look After the Interests of the Denominations Between These Meetings?

Committees: the General Council's Executive Committee and the General Synod's General Council.

31. Do Any of These Bodies, Except the Local Churches, Have Full-Time Executives?

The C.C. Conferences usually employ full-time "Superintendents," who enjoy the authority given to executives but not that traditionally assigned to bishops. The Presidents of Synods are ministers who give only part of their time to the Synodical work. The C.C. Churches have their Minister (who is also Secretary) and Associate Secretary of the General Council, the E. and R. Church its President, Secretary, and Treasurer of the Church. The Minister of the General Council and the President of the Church have corresponding duties. The Moderatorships in both cases are honorary offices. The duties of the E. and R. Moderator begin and end with the triennial meeting over which he presides, but the C.C.

Moderator usually spends part of his biennium in travel among the churches, exerting a wide influence. The Treasurership of the C.C. General Council is also an honorary position.

32. What Kind of "Polity" or Church Government Do the Two Denominations Employ?

The C.C. Churches may be said to have a congregational polity (rule by congregations) with presbyterial elements (rule by presbyteries, or committees representing groups of churches), and the E. and R. Church a presbyterial polity with congregational elements. Both contain episcopal elements (rule by leaders chosen by Conferences or Synods) but without connotations of "Apostolic Succession."

33. Is There Any Common Ground in the Two?

Yes, both groups believe that the ultimate authority in a denomination under God is not in the executive officers, nor in any particular group of any kind, whether it be a General Council, General Synod, Conference, Synod, or an individual church, but rather in the denomination as a whole: which is to say that each individual and each congregation carries part of this authority. The Boards and other national representative bodies of the denomination are assigned their authority by the denomination as a whole.

34. What Is the Principal Point of Divergence?

In general, there has probably been greater centralization of assigned authority in the E. and R. than in the C.C. communion.

35. In the Proposed Union Would Any Part of the Denomination Be Under the Control of Any Other Part, As, For Instance, the Local Churches "Under" the Conferencc?

No: each part would have its rights and responsibilities and no other part could take them away. These rights and responsibilities are described in principle in the Basis of Union and are to be more fully defined in the constitution of the United Church.

36. Could a Majority Vote of the Churches In a Conference Bind the Minority?

It could not bind the minority churches in their internal life, but it could bind them in their Conference relationships as for instance in the matter of the number and kind of delegates attending stated Conference meetings.

37. Would Not the System of Appeals in the United Church Vitiate This Condition?

No: for the body to which an appeal was made would have only reviewing powers: if for instance the General Synod were called upon through a committee to consider whether a minister had been justly treated by the body wherein he held standing, it could after examination declare its approval or disapproval of the action of that body, and in the event of disapproval request a re-trial, but it could not give the minister a re-trial itself nor take over the matter of his standing.

38. Whence the Proposed System of Appeals?

The idea of appeal from one unit to a more broadly representative unit has been developed chiefly in presbyterial churches. The idea that the unit from which appeal is made may devise its own constitution, on the basis of which alone its action may be judged, is largely congregational. The principle of fellowship in both congregational and presbyterial systems would call for working harmony in the constitutions of the various units.

39. Who Would Own Property Now Held by Conferences, Theological Seminaries, Synods, etc.?

All existing charters would remain intact.

40. What Would Happen If a Congregation Did Not Pay Its Apportionment?

As now, it would have only its own conscience to reckon with. It would not be subject to discipline or penalty by a higher body.

41. Would the United Church Be Truly an Organic Fellowship?

Yes, it would be capable of moving ahead as a unit.

The Ministry

42. Under the Present Systems Where Does the Minister Hold His Standing?

C.C. ministers have their standing in the Association or Conference, E. and R. ministers in the Synod.

43. Under the Proposed Plan for Union How Would Ministers Be Ordained?

By the body in which they would have their standing, that is, the Conference or (where desired) the Association.

44. What About the "Vicinage" Council in Congregationalism, Whereby Neighboring Churches and Not Necessarily the Association Ordained a Minister?

In the few remaining areas in which vicinage councils are employed, the ministers they "ordain" do not acquire standing in the denomination until they are accepted by the Association.

45. Under the Present Systems Who Calls the Minister?

In both denominations the local church does so, but in the E. and R. Church he must be approved by the Synod or in the interim of the annual meetings of the Synod by a committee responsible to the Synod.

46. How Would a Minister Be Called in the United Church?

By the local church. The aid and approval of a Conference committee on placement would undoubtedly be strongly advised by the denomination as a whole.

47. Would the Minister Be Installed, and If So, How?

When elected by a Congregation, the minister would be installed by an Association or Conference at the request of the Congregation.

48. What Would Become of Ministerial Pensions?

Both the C.C. and the E. and R. pension systems would persist, those who are already members being duly protected, but no new members being admitted. For the latter a third system would be set up, which would eventually supersede the other two.

General

49. What Right Have We to the Name "United Church of Christ"?

We should be in fact a united church of Christ, though not the only one. "Church" here has the meaning of "denomination." If the name seems too presumptuous, it should be remembered that any good general name must seem so, since it would apply equally well to other groups. A name, however, quickly becomes a mere means of classification, and it is hoped that the world would soon come to know that we did not pretend to be more than we actually are.

50. How Many Bodies Would Be Brought Together in the "United Church of Christ?"

Each of the two uniting bodies is itself the result of previous unions of "movements" and corporate groups. In the C.C. Churches are united (1) The Pilgrims, (2) the Puritans, (3) the Congregational Methodists, (4) the Evangelical Protestants, (5) the Christian Church of Virginia and North Carolina, (6) the Christian Connection of New England, (7) the Christian Church of the Ohio Valley. In the E. and R. Church are united (8) the Reformed Church in the United States, (9) the National Hungarian Reformed Church, (10) the Evangelical Union of the West, (11) the Evangelical Union of Ohio, (12) the United Evangelical Synod of the East, and (13) the United Synod of the Northwest. To these might be added (14) the German groups from Russia which have united with both the C.C. and the E. and R. Churches.

51. Would It Not Be Better to Draw Up a Complete and Detailed Constitution Before We Attempt to Unite?

There would be advantages to this plan, but the best procedure of all seems to be the one being followed:

1. To agree upon the general principles of the union by publishing, discussing, improving, and re-publishing the Basis of Union.
2. Simultaneously to get just as well acquainted with each other as possible.
3. To unite at first only the C.C. General Council and the E. and R. General Synod, and this only after a thorough referendum in each denomination.
4. To allow the mission boards, conferences, synods, and other bodies within the denominations to unite at their own preference and convenience.

52. How Can a Congregation Get in Touch with Members of the Other Denomination?

Each denominational headquarters stands ready to suggest ways and means, if called upon.

53. Would This Union Shut Out the Possibility of Union with Other Denominations Later?

On the contrary, our enlarged size would make union with our larger contemporaries more possible.

54. Should We Be Cut Off from Our International Affiliations?

We should be members (if admitted) both of the Alliance of Reformed Churches throughout the World Holding the Presbyterian System and of the International Congregational Council.

55. In the Event of Union, What Would Happen to Congregations Which Voted Not to Enter?

The services of the United Church would be made available to them as to any congregation in regular standing. It would be hoped that they would eventually decide to enter. If such a church's association or synod entered the union, the minister of the church would be a minister of the United Church, since his standing is held in those bodies.

56. What Advantages Are Claimed for the Union?

Among others, the following:

Spiritually the union would announce to the world that the Church of Christ is a unitive and not a divisive or a static body.

Practically it would permit the church to preach the necessity for unitedness among the nations, etc., without the reproach that she is unwilling to move in that direction herself.

Sociologically the increase in the number of local congregations would tend to control the chief cause of denominational losses, viz., the removal of members to localities where the denomination is not represented.

Strategically the uniting of similar traditions of faith, liberty, and fellowship would multiply their power in the service of Christ, since in union there is strength.

57. What Arguments Are Presented Against the Union?

Chiefly the following:

The discrepancies in **polity** (cf. the more rigid and the less rigid manner of protecting the churches from unworthy ministers from other denominations) are too great to be overcome.

The traditional attitudes to written **creeds** would hold the two groups apart.

The loose relation of C.C. mission boards to the denomination differs too widely from E. and R. relationships.

The **cultural backgrounds,** the one chiefly Anglo-Saxon, the other chiefly Continental, cannot be melted together.

58. What Creed Would Be Used by the New Church?

A large committee would be asked to make a thorough study of all shades of thought within the Church and draw up a comprehensive statement setting forth our common belief.

59. Would Such a Creed Be Authoritative?

It would be a testimony of our faith but would not be used as a test which ministers and members would have to accept verbally.

Missionary and Other Denominational Agencies

60. What Relation Would the Mission Boards Have to the Denomination?

They would be the arms of the denomination and controlled by it, but would have the same liberty of action they enjoy today. Boards having the same objects would unite when feasible.

Agitation Against Union

79. The Opposition Organized: *"The Evanston Meeting"*

(1947)

In July of 1947, the General Synod of the Evangelical and Reformed Church adopted the final draft of the Basis of Union by a vote of 281 to twenty-three, and sent the document to the thirty-four synods to ratify at their spring meetings of 1948. This action intensified the opposition to the Basis of Union that had been growing among the Congregational Christians.

One dramatic expression of this opposition was a meeting held on November 4–5, 1947, in Evanston, Illinois. The meeting was called by Neil E. Hansen, secretary of the Chicago Missionary Society; Arthur Cushman McGiffert Jr., president of the Chicago Theological Seminary; and Hugh Elmer Brown, pastor of the First Congregational Church of Evanston. It brought together 190 Congregational Christian clergy and laity from twenty-seven states who were opposed to the Basis of Union and the plan of merger.

The primary objection to the Basis of Union voiced by the Evanston meeting was that it "constituted a threat to the traditional autonomy of the local church within Congregationalism." The meeting deplored the actions of the Executive Committee and the General Council, which they considered to be accepting authority that they did not and should not have according to Congregational polity. The meeting also raised questions about other provisions in the Basis: the acceptance of both the Congregational Christian and the Evangelical and Reformed procedures for regularizing ministers; the provision whereby some money given for

Source: "The Evanston Meeting," pamphlet, November 1947, in the Yale Divinity School Archives.

mission work would be used for ministerial annuities; and, the proposal to unite the respective Foreign Missionary Boards, Home Boards, and other national agencies. In addition, the meeting claimed that if the merger were pursued, crucial time, energy, and leadership would be lost. Energy that should be devoted to Christian service would be lost. They lamented that individual Congregational Christian churches were being asked to give up essential rights.

The Evanston meeting called upon the finance committee of the General Council to provide a condensed comparative statement of the assets and projected annual commitments of the Evangelical and Reformed Church and Congregational Christian Churches so that members might assess the corporate interests involved in the proposed merger. And finally, it suggested that local congregations undertake a historical study of Congregationalism, in light of which the Basis of Union should be reexamined. It urged a federative union of the churches instead of the proposed organic union.

We reject the present Basis of Union

- It is a defective instrument for accomplishing its purposes of organic union
- We believe the kind of union it proposes is short-sighted and ill-timed
- We hold that the genius of Congregationalism calls for a federative rather than an organic union of churches

190 members of our Congregational Christian Churches from twenty-seven states, having grave questions concerning the proposed merger of the Congregational Christian Churches and the Evangelical and Reformed Church, met at the First Congregational Church of Evanston, Illinois, November 4 and 5, 1947.

Their deliberations are presented in the following findings which were unanimously adopted at this meeting.

(This is a summary. Numbers at the end of sentences refer to longer statements on the following pages.)

WE ARE UNITED in the Evanston Meeting in the conviction that, in view of the fact that the Basis of Union proposes a change from the congregational to the presbyterial polity, organic union with the Evangelical and Reformed Church according to this Basis of Union is undesirable and should not be consummated.

WE BELIEVE the Basis of Union must be accepted or rejected according to its printed word, without reliance upon the oral or written interpretations of anyone. (1)

WE ARE CONVINCED that the Basis of Union, if accepted with its ambiguities, contradictions and omissions, will, among other things, take away the autonomy of the local church. (1, 2, 3)

WE BELIEVE the Executive Committee of the General Council adopted uncongregational procedure for which it had no justification when it agreed to receive the Basis of Union from the Joint Committee; and that it assumed authority it did not possess when it sent the Basis of Union to the churches and set a date on or before which the churches must vote. (4)

WE POINT OUT serious defects concerning the Basis of Union such as the following:

It includes two contradictory methods of calling and accepting resignations as ministers. (5)

Though our time in history demands the largest possible expenditure for Christian work at home and abroad, a large amount of missionary giving will be used annually for thirty years to fund ministerial annuities. (6)

Though the uniting of the Home and Foreign Mission Societies of the two groups may be legally effected, the legal question remains whether this could be done if some of our churches do not vote or vote "No." (7)

The uniting of the societies of the two groups will not increase Christian service or giving. It will bring heavy, time-consuming tasks in this grave hour in the world when the present vital force of all our national societies should be used to the utmost in Christian service rather than in organizational rearrangements.(8)

There will be very little consolidation of local churches of the two groups in any given community because of cultural, geographical and other differences. (9)

Legal difficulties exist in the proposed merger which need to be explored professionally by all churches inclined to vote favorably. (10)

A comparative financial statement of assets and liabilities of the two groups has never been published. (11)

WE BELIEVE it is essential that a constitution and by-laws and a statement of faith, if we are in favor of either or both, be presented to our churches *before* a final vote is taken on the *Basis of Union,* if the proposed United Church and General Synod need anything more than the minimum constitution of our General Council. (12)

WE RECOMMEND the following to churches before they vote on the *Basis of Union:*

That they postpone voting until adequate opportunities have been given their members to study the reasons for and the reasons against the merger. (13)

That full recognition be given the right of Christian people to differ or dissent without penalty. (13)

That ministers and laymen, before voting, consider with wisdom the wider interests and possibilities under our present fellowship. (14)

That the Executive Committee of the General Council arrange for adequate education concerning the proposed merger for the members of our churches, and take responsibility for eliminating one-sided official propaganda for and promotion of the merger. (15)

That churches in voting on the proposed merger use the secret ballot. (16)

WE BELIEVE a person who opposes the merger as proposed in this *Basis of Union* cannot justly be understood to be opposing church unity. (16)

WE REPORT without prejudice a proposal acceptable to many in the Evanston Meeting that churches voting "no" on the proposed merger and those which refrain from voting should indicate their right and purpose to continue as Congregational Christian Churches and to seek fellowship with like-minded Congregational Christian Churches if the United Church of Christ is formed according to the Basis of Union. (17)

WE ASK our young people to realize that the proposed merger, if voted, will take from them their inheritance of a place among the free churches, and deprive them of a position of leadership in bringing about and working out in their generation a new formation of American Protestantism—the federative union of many denominations. (18)

WE BELIEVE a "No" vote on the proposed merger will maintain for our churches the opportunity to help bring into existence a new pattern of federative union among many denominations. We believe this pattern to be of vastly greater importance for American Protestantism and the life of the World Council of Churches than the organic union of the Congregational Christian Churches and the Evangelical and Reformed Church. (19)

WE ARE UNITED in the Evanston Meeting in the hope and prayer that our fellowship of churches, beginning with the meeting of the General Council at Oberlin in 1948 will seek the guidance of Almighty God to lead us in ways wherein we may help bring into existence the federative union of many denominations. This is the time in church history when American Protestantism should form new bonds of fellowship for more cooperative Christian work to advance the Christian life of our country and forward the Kingdom of God in all the world.

80. Classic Congregationalism Defended: *"Why the Basis of Union Is Not a Valid Document"*

(1949)

Malcolm K. Burton

By the mid-1940s, Malcolm K. Burton, James E. Fifield, Marion J. Bradshaw, Warren S. Archibald, Raymond A. Waser, Arthur Acy Rouner, and a small group of key Congregational leaders began to actively oppose all plans for union leading to the United Church of Christ. For his part, Burton, in October 1945, launched what by his own admission was "voluminous pamphleteering" against the merger, publishing over 350 pamphlets, circular letters, leaflets, and books.

In 1950, Burton was elected to the Committee on Free Church Polity and Unity. Between 1950 and 1954, this committee conducted a thorough study of the source documents and practices of the churches, associations, conferences, boards, and the General Council of the Congregational Christian Churches. The committee then submitted its findings to the state superintendents and two hundred other leading Congregationalists, asking in what respects, if any, practices had departed from the findings in the written documents. Burton also served on the central committee of the Committee on Free Church Polity and Unity, and on its subcommittee on polity. He wrote a large portion of the committee's report on possible forms of church union.

Source: Malcolm K. Burton, "Why the Basis of Union Is Not a Valid Document," address to the General Council of the Congregational Christian Churches in Cleveland, Ohio, 4 February, 1949, in the Yale Divinity School Archives.

After the General Council of the Congregational Christian Churches met in Oberlin, Ohio, in 1948, and agreed (by a vote of one thousand to eleven) to adopt the Basis of Union with Interpretations, Burton wrote a four-page leaflet entitled "What Really Happened at Oberlin?" and sent it out to all the churches. Soon James W. Fifield Jr., a pastor in southern California, was moved by the pamphlet to organize a national "Anti-Merger Committee," which later became the "Committee for the Continuation of the Congregational Christian Churches." In November 1954, Burton was elected director (later called executive vice-chairman) of the Committee for the Continuation of the Congregational Christian Churches.

When the Cadman Memorial Church in New York City filed a lawsuit in 1949 against the General Council of Congregational Churches to stop the merger, Burton sat with the Cadman Church attorney throughout the trial, identifying witnesses for him. Burton was also one of ten individuals and four churches who were the plaintiffs in an unsuccessful federal lawsuit filed in June 1957. Burton described his view of these court cases in two books, Destiny for Congregationalism *(1953) and* How Church Union Came *(1966).*

Burton represented the wing of the antimerger movement that sought to preserve "classic Congregationalism." He was committed to protecting the absolute autonomy of the local church to govern itself without interference (or suggestion) from outside ecclesiastical power, and to control its properties, finances, funds, and services. For Burton, no other gathering of persons or groups apart from the local congregation could serve as a vehicle through which God's will could be exercised.

The Basis of Union, dated Jan. 22, 1947, is the fundamental document of this whole proposal for a merger of our Congregational Christian Churches with the Evangelical and Reformed Church. Is it a valid document?

Our churches were told that they could remain the same under the Basis of Union as they are now. In like manner the people of the Evangelical and Reformed Church were told that the merger would mean no fundamental change for them. Here is our whole difficulty. What are the rights and freedoms under the two systems? Can they be combined through the Basis of Union without loss to either side?

The Nature of the Evangelical and Reformed Church

The Evangelical and Reformed Church, as a national denomination, is a body politic and corporate. It is clearly recognized in the courts of the land as a "general" type of church, to which certain definite powers and authority accrue.

That the denomination as a whole is a "body politic and corporate" is shown first of all in its name. It is a "Church," spelled with a capital "C" and in the singular, of which all of the parts are but subsidiary units before the law. The local unit is a "congregation," not a church.

Secondly, this national "body politic and corporate" is bound together by a central constitution, which declares that the E. and R. Church "ordains this constitution to be its fundamental law and declares the same to have authority over all its ministers, members, congregations, and judicatories."

Third, the E. and R. Church is incorporated under the laws of the land as a single, national "body politic and corporate," and its constitution is recognized in the courts as having authority over its constituent parts.

Fourth, the E. and R. Church, as a national "body politic and corporate," recognizes a system of legislation by which its fundamental law and other regulations can be amended and altered for the entire church. It operates under a system of representative assemblies, as a kind of ecclesiastical republic, along lines commonly recognized as presbyterian.

Fifth, the Evangelical and Reformed Church, as a national "body politic and corporate," recognizes a series of judicatories, through which a constant pressure can be maintained upon its members and constituent organizations to keep them in conformity with the central laws and purposes of the church.

Because of the foregoing character of the Evangelical and Reformed Church, as a national "body politic and corporate," certain advantages accrue to persons who like that kind of set-up. It makes for the law and order of which Presbyterians have always been proud.

In the realm of faith this law and order finds its expression in a Creed for the church as a whole.

Another advantage, for those who like this system, is that no minister can be called to a congregation without the approval of the Synod. Such approval becomes a matter of routine with ministers who have proved themselves obedient servants of the denomination. But it also stands as a threat for those who might be led by conscience in some new or unapproved way.

Lastly the congregations themselves can be kept in line. They cannot, according to a recent court case in New Jersey, divert their missionary giving simply to objects of their own choice. Neither can they withdraw from the denomination and get out from under the authority of this national, corporate church without the probable loss of their property.

Within such a framework of law and order many freedoms can be enjoyed at the discretion of the church as a whole. Through its constitution the denomination can set forth certain rights and liberties as the prerogatives of semi-autonomous units. In their own spheres they can enjoy whatever range and latitude of freedom is assigned to them by the "body politic and corporate,"—that is, by the denomination as a whole. All such freedoms and autonomy, however, are within the basic framework of the church as a whole. These rights and freedoms can be amended, revised and limited by the same "body politic and corporate" which grants them in the first place, without the necessity of approval by each local congregation. Elected assemblies of a so-called representative nature have the final say.

The Nature of Our Congregational Christian Churches

Having considered the essential rights and responsibilities within the Evangelical and Reformed Church, let us now look at the facts concerning our own fellowship.

Congregational Christian Churches are not a "body politic and corporate" on a national scale. Not even the General Council is incorporated.

We are not a Church, in a single national sense, but Churches, voluntarily associated together.

No central constitution has authority over our ministers, members, Conferences, Associations or churches.

We have no system of legislatures, nor do we recognize the authority of any representative assemblies over our independent churches. As Mr. J. D. Fackenthal has pointed out, "There is as to a Congregational Church no higher authority than the membership of the particular church in meeting assembled."

We recognize no system of judicatories. Historically our churches have taken their stand against any ascending series of ecclesiastical courts. As the Year Book of our Congregational Christian Churches has long pointed out, the local church "is the final arbiter of all questions relating to its own life."

Because we are not a "body politic and corporate" in a denominational sense, or on a national scale, and because we do not have a central framework of law, nor any legislatures capable of amending that law, nor any judicatories to enforce that law, certain definite benefits accrue to persons who like our kind of voluntary fellowship.

Our freedom and autonomy are not limited or defined by any central constitution. We are not asked to approve any denominational creed or statement of faith. Our churches are not required to get approval on their choice of ministers. Our churches cannot be penalized by any ecclesiastical authority for any cause whatsoever, nor can their property be confiscated through the courts if they refuse to follow denominational directives. In all of the foregoing our set-up is the direct opposite of the Evangelical and Reformed Church. The advantages of law and order which accrue to its members are absent with us. In like manner the advantages and rights of our independent churches are of a different order from those which accrue to the Evangelical and Reformed Church.

The essential genius of Congregationalism depends upon the whole series of negatives which we have suggested above. Congregationalism is like a mighty "double negative" whose great positive force is compounded out of the many restrictions which it denies. We want to be free,—not just within certain limits prescribed by a national church,—but free under God. We can do this only by denying the powers of a national church, by denying the rights of judicatories, by denying the validity of elected assemblies, by denying the imposition of creeds or man-made laws,—in short by denying the concept of a church as a national "body politic and corporate."

Does this make Congregationalism a negative thing? Think for one moment of how we try to explain to a little child the infinite powers of God. We explain to that child that God is not limited according to time. He is not limited in space. He is not limited in wisdom or love. To unfetter our concept of God, we are compelled to resort to a whole series of negatives, so that we can free Him from all sense of ordinary human limitation. Does that mean that God is a negative? No. God is the most positive, creative force in all the world.

In like manner Congregationalism gains its most creative freedom by those negatives which protect it and describe it as completely unfettered. We may be weak on the order and law of presbyterianism but our genius is freedom, unlimited and uncircumscribed, under God.

When our forefathers drew apart from the established order of their day they did so with deep conviction that Christ is the only Head of His church. They believed that, "Where two or three are gathered together in His name," there Christ is. True ecumenicity is that Spirit which binds together all Christians, whatever their name or sign, under the one true Headship of our Lord.

Organization is never the Church. The more organized it gets, the more dangerous it becomes to those freedoms which are in Christ. Our forefathers insisted on their right to establish churches "gathered" with our sanction of Bishops, Presbyteries, or Synods. Their doctrine of the Church is ecumenical and all-inclusive. It is a valid doctrine.

This freedom under Christ—without benefit of Bishops, Presbyteries, or National Church—has been the guiding principle of Congregationalism these three hundred years.

Dr. Gaius Glenn Atkins sums up the meaning of this, our freedom, in his brief little account, "Adventure in Liberty." He declares that:

"If one stands far enough away from the massive and entangled action of Protestantism, he sees throughout its course a growing quest for realization of the independence of the spirit-guided Christian life, both in theory and practice."

"Protestantism," continues Dr. Atkins, "was bound by the very genius of it, when the right time came, to try the experiment of the liberty of a Christian man with all its implications and issues, completely and at all costs."

This liberty, of which Dr. Atkins speaks, tried out in all its implications and issues, completely and at all costs, is Congregationalism; and, continues Dr. Atkins, "Whatever else is built, must be upon this foundation."

Let us see whether the Basis of Union builds on this foundation.

Main Framework of the Basis of Union

What are the principal features of the Basis of Union?

Art. I. The name, "United Church of Christ," in the singular.

Art. II. Beginnings of a Creed, to be submitted for approval by General Synod, Conferences, Associations, and "congregations."

Art. III. 1. Congregations as subsidiary units.

2. Limited spheres of autonomy, with definite powers for the Synod.

3. Government for the entire church.

4. Provisions for representative assemblies.

5. System of judicatories.

Art. IV. 1. Powers of General Synod over entire church.

2. Provision for central constitution.

Art. VI. Standard procedures for the calling and ordination of ministers.

Art. VII. Membership in a national church.

Art. VIII. Centralized powers over all Boards.

Art. X. Power to amend the constitution through representative assemblies.

Art. XI. Amendments to Basis of Union by General Synod.

What Do These Provisions Mean?

Are these provisions Congregational? Are they intended to insure the liberty of a Christian man with all its implications and issues, completely and at all costs? Or are they the provisions for the establishment of a Church, on a national scale, which shall be a "body politic and corporate" with recognized powers before the law? All the principal features of the Evangelical and Reformed Church are incorporated in this central framework of the Basis of Union. Is this the foundation on which Dr. Atkins would have us build?

Words about Congregational usages and practice (which were lifted out of their anomalous position in the Basis of Union and quoted so freely while our churches were voting) lose their meaning when dropped back into this framework of the Basis of Union. The change from a fellowship of free and independent churches into a "body politic and corporate" makes all the difference in the world.

A "congregation" is not the same as a "Congregational Church."

"Autonomy in its own sphere" is not the same as "autonomy."

For a congregation to "hold and operate" its property within a "general" Church is not the same as all independent church that owns its property.

It is not enough to say that we shall retain all "our present rights and freedoms." The Basis of Union would give the power to define these rights and freedoms to the future constitution, which could be progressively amended without consent of the individual church.

Elected assemblies which write or amend a central constitution derive their powers from a "body politic and corporate." For us to recognize such powers is to accept the principle which would creatively determine all the rest and would put an end to our present kind of freedom.

These changes reflect a concept of Church which is alien and hostile to Congregationalism. They make the framework for a denominational Church with power (and let's not be fooled on that point),—with real power over all of its constituent parts.

Neither the Oberlin Interpretations, nor any other promises or assurances can alter this main framework of the Basis of Union. They cannot restore to Congregational words and phrases therein the meaning which these concepts enjoy in our free and voluntary fellowship.

Our churches were told that they would remain the same under the Basis of Union as they are now. They were asked to vote on such phrases as seemed to prove this point, not upon the main framework of the Basis of Union (which they did not understand) or upon any realistic proposition for merger.

The Basis of Union is contradictory and self-nullifying. It cannot perform according to its promises. It is not it valid document. It never solved the fundamental problem confronting it,—the conflict between two contradictory and mutually exclusive polities. It never told our people that they would have to give up anything. Neither did it indicate to the E. and R. members any fundamental change for them. Since it is not a valid document, the so-called votes obtained upon it cannot be valid either. We have, therefore, no valid proposition before us upon which to proceed.

Comments on the Cleveland Council

At the Cleveland Council the proponents of merger claimed that an overwhelming majority favored the union and that this majority is steadily increasing. But at the same time they insisted (to quote Dr. Truman Douglass) that "any further delay means rejection of the union."

Laying aside for the moment all other questions, ask yourself whether the above is valid from the standpoint of either sanity or religious conviction.

If an overwhelming majority wants the union, and if that majority is increasing, a delay which permits working out a better plan could not possibly endanger the union. In like manner if God wants this merger He will not abandon it if we pause momentarily to get more light from Him.

To insist that both God and the majority wants the merger, and at the same time to express intense fear of its rejection if delayed, is to show neither sanity nor faith in God. Rather it is like an unstable person who is filled with his illusions of grandeur and strength at one moment and then seized by the terrors of persecution and fear of death in the next. The vote at Cleveland was a sign of weakness and not of strength on the part of those who want the merger. It sprang from fear and a sense of imminent defeat, not from confidence and a trusting faith. There was no applause when the result was announced. The vote of 757 to 172 was the kind of "statistical victory, and moral defeat" against which Dr. Fred Meek warned us at Oberlin.

Add to the above the following and then decide for yourself how much validity the Cleveland decision really enjoys:

1. Only 51% of the total number of Congregational Christian Churches approved the merger on any terms.
2. Most votes for the merger were obtained on the understanding that 75% approval (among churches voting) would be required, which percentage was not obtained.
3. Congregational Christian Churches are not a body politic, and therefore any so-called voting among them has no more power over them than a Gallup Poll would have.
4. The General Council has no authority to merge either our churches or itself into any new denomination, particularly not if the polity is different.
5. It has never been either affirmed or denied whether the "United Church of Christ" would incorporate as a national body.
6. The whole merger action will be reviewed in the courts and all fundamental questions (which have thus far been evaded) will ultimately have to be explained.
7. Opposition within the General Council increased from 12 votes at Oberlin to 172 at Cleveland; all suggestion that harmony had been reached or a solution found has disappeared; and in trying to force a union on their present ill-conceived plan the proponents of merger have shown themselves willing to create a new division within Protestantism,—in the name of church unity!

MALCOLM K. BURTON

27 Broad Street, New London, Conn.

81. A Dangerous Ecumenical Moment:
"On the Denominational Divide"

(1950)

Marion J. Bradshaw

Marion J. Bradshaw, a professor of philosophy of religion at Bangor Theological Seminary for thirty years, joined Malcolm K. Burton as one of the determined pamphleteers against the merger of the Congregational Christian Churches with the Evangelical and Reformed Church. Central to his critique was a defense of "classic Congregationalism"—the belief that the absolute autonomy of the local church must be ensured at all costs, so that it may be free to govern itself, free from any outside ecclesiastical pressure, and free to make its own choices about its money, programs, funds, and services. Bradshaw served as chair of the Maine and New England Committees for the Continuation of the Congregational Christian Churches, and as a member of the executive committee of the national committee by the same name.

His pamphlet entitled "On the Denominational Divide" was a response to Douglas Horton's address to the General Council of the Congregational Christian Churches in Cleveland in June 1950. Horton's address, entitled "Of Equability and Perseverance in Well Doing," was itself a response to the decision of Justice Steinbrink, of the New York Supreme Court, against the merger of the Congregational Christian Churches and the Evangelical and Reformed Church (see vol. 6:91). Horton disagreed with the judge and argued that in contemporary Congregationalism, the General Council itself needed to be considered as a "kind of congregation," distinct from

---

Source: Marion J. Bradshaw, excerpt from "On the Denominational Divide: Being a Reply to the Address Given by the Minister of the General Council, Cleveland, June, 1950," pamphlet, 1950, in the Yale Divinity School Archives.

a local church and neither subordinate nor superior to it. According to Horton, the General Council had the legal right to rule itself, and not be controlled by the will of the churches. Horton later developed this understanding of congregationalism in his book, Congregationalism: A Study in Church Polity.

Bradshaw's "On the Denominational Divide" began by applauding Judge Steinbrink's legal decision against the merger, and repeatedly scorned Horton for his "unwillingness to recognize the jurisdiction of the courts." He further decried the stipulation in the Basis of Union that local congregations had to be members of an association, arguing that this was interference with the free decision-making capacity of local churches. He considered any decisions made by a General Council to be an even more egregious interference with local church autonomy.

Bradshaw insisted that Horton's "emotional disturbance" regarding the nature of the General Council could be blamed on Horton's experience at the World Council of Churches in Amsterdam in 1948, where the existence of the separated churches (i.e., denominations) was spoken of as a "weakness and shame before God." To Bradshaw, this statement seemed to suggest that autonomous local churches were a "shame before God." "The heart and mind of Dr. Horton vibrate to this ecumenical emotion, and he holds intensely the Presbyterian persuasion that mere spiritual unity is insufficient and must be supplemented, or even supplanted, by one united and visible Body of Christ, the Una Sancta at long last made obvious to those who cannot walk as seeing the invisible."

Bradshaw saved his most barbed prose for the last section of his pamphlet, seizing upon a phrase in Horton's address, "the exciting ecumenical movement." He argued that the efforts of the ecumenical movement to make the union of the churches more visible was a "surrender of Congregational principles," whereby its advocates were pursuing a "campaign for increased power over the local churches," and thus for "control over the church members who furnish the money and have the votes."

Ironically, Bradshaw saw the 1948 affirmation of the World Council of Churches calling all member churches to accept Jesus as Lord as a creedal statement, while failing to remember that the autonomy of local congregations that he so zealously sought to protect was originally conceived as the means whereby local churches could preserve their capacity to respond to that very Lordship.

The Exciting Ecumenical Movement

Considering the extensive use Dr. Horton makes of reference to "the exciting ecumenical movement, which is the growing edge of Christianity today," it is fair to raise the question whether in his excitement he has not forgotten his facts. According to the latest statistics which the Christian Century has brought to my attention, the Southern Baptists are the most rapidly growing body in American protestantism, and they are not in the World Council of Churches, perhaps in part because of the subscription to a non-Biblical creed which Council membership requires.

In the light of Dr. Horton's strong criticism of fixity in religious organization, it is interesting to note how far Amsterdam went in fastening this non-Biblical statement upon "the exciting ecumenical movement" as its permanent creedal basis. It is true, of course, that the separate elements of the required creedal basis may all be found in the Scriptures, yet even William Adams Brown called this ecumenical statement a "near-heresy." And yet there are at least 28 acts and entries in the Amsterdam *Report* which show the determined effort to freeze the creedal basis of the ecumenical movement. They voted that it is adequate for the present purposes of the World Council; that possible changes be kept within the Christological principle set forth in the present basis; that the Presidents of the World Council shall not even discuss the creedal statement publicly. I confess to some surprise that Dr. Horton is so very fearful of the fossilizing effects of fixity in organization, yet apparently expresses no misgivings about freezing the Council's creedal basis. Is it only when frozen in *organizational* matters that "we become religiously static in a changing world which cries for an alert Christianity"?

Dr. Horton's present statement well typifies the thinking of many active leaders in the drive for organic union of the churches. And it clearly reveals the formula under which liberalism loses out in the church union moves. We must have a powerful organization, it is said, "to out-guess and out-maneuver anti-Christian forces," and to get it we are willing to freeze the creed, group action being regarded as more important than freedom of thought in religious matters. This not only involves a sharp reversal of our historical emphasis, but is also close to a surrender of Congregational principles.

What is it that we have really become when we are encouraged to think our task is "to out-guess and out-maneuver" some other social or political group? In the Hibbert Journal, January, 1950, J. M. Lloyd Thomas found that "There is disturbing ground for fearing that the movement for re-union has gone astray and become, in the face of our atheisms and paganisms, a diplomatic game of power politics." And where the campaign for increased power over the local churches is so obvious and so determined, the official denials that the union moves are aimed at organizational power will continue to be suspect.

"With Authority over Itself"

Finally, Dr. Horton's idea of a national church unit becoming truly effective through sufficient "authority over itself" seems remarkably like an army staffed with a more than adequate complement of generals but with no privates. The pretence may be continued for a time that "authority over itself," with its membership changing every two years, is all that such a national unit desires and seeks. Observers who have "gone to school to the children of this world" may safely assume, however, whatever be said, that what is really aimed at is some kind of secure control over the church members who furnish the money and have the votes.

There is both here and abroad an intense desire, a prayerful and zealous purpose, to weld the churches into one organized church. It is precarious, indeed, to state positively its primary purpose. Some would make out that it is basically an endeavor to make each church conscious of its spiritual ties to all other churches through the common relation of all to Christ. Often it shows signs of being an endeavor to make the church politically powerful through its claimed monopoly of God, or at least of God-in-Christ. To many competent observers of the earthly scene, this latter purpose seems so obvious, and the threat of it so alarming, that one of England's greatest preachers in a long generation took recent occasion to say that the political churches are the gravest danger in the present world.

In expressing his opinion of the dangers which inhere in churches becoming political,—that is, in their allowing themselves to become organized agencies for out-guessing and out-maneuvering other organized groups,—Dean Inge quoted grave words from Amiel's *Intimate Journal:* "All the great religious and political edifices have crime for their foundation, injustice and fraud for their masonry, and human blood for their cement." The great dean adds, "This is too strong, but it is what I am tempted to say when I let myself go. . . . Political religion in its various forms is our most dangerous foe."

MARION J. BRADSHAW

Bangor, Maine
August, 1950

82. MEDIATORS:

"Central Convictions . . . Daring Deeds"

(1955)

HENRY DAVID GRAY

Henry David Gray (1908–1994) served several influential pastorates in Congregational Christian churches in Massachusetts and Connecticut, and authored a book, The Mediators, *in which he told the story of the arguments surrounding union between the Congregational Christian Churches and the Evangelical and Reformed Church from the standpoint of a self-styled "middle group" of "mediators." Gray and his friends sought to mediate between the ardent advocates of union, Douglas Horton and Truman Douglass, and the equally ardent opponents, Malcolm K. Burton and Marion J. Bradshaw. He was convinced that the vast majority of the Congregational Christian Churches and their members did not support either of the extremes, but were simply trying to find a middle way as thinking Christians.*

"Central Convictions . . . Daring Deeds" originally was an address given to the Twin Cities Congregational Christian Association in Minneapolis, Minnesota, in October 1955. It was a response to an article by Truman Douglass that had appeared in the September 1955 issue of Advance, *"Great and Honorable Actions (and) Answerable Courages" (the title was taken from Governor Bradford's account* Of Plimouth Plantation*). Typical of Gray's approach, this address was thoughtfully theological rather than being focused strictly on bureaucratic or political issues.*

In "Central Convictions . . . Daring Deeds," Gray set forth a position

---

SOURCE: Henry David Gray, "Central Convictions . . . Daring Deeds: A Reply to Truman B. Douglass," pamphlet, 1950, in the Congregational Library Archives.

that the oneness of the church is a spiritual oneness arising from the living, personal Word of God known through the teachings, work, and life of Jesus Christ; the oneness is not institutional or organizational, nor should it be. Furthermore, he did not believe that the proposed union of the Congregational Christian Churches and the Evangelical and Reformed Church was "under the guidance of the Spirit." Unfortunately, Gray lamented, the union of denominations was being heralded as if it were the Gospel for the day, but really it was a "counsel of despair" trusting the size of an organization to lend it influence and prestige rather than relying on God alone.

The great issues at stake in the proposed union of the Congregational Christian Churches with the Evangelical and Reformed Church are religious. They concern our central Christian convictions. It is strange that there has been no debate on these issues; and that instead our discussions have dealt chiefly with matters of organization. Dr. Truman Douglass' September article in "Advance," which modified very considerably the earlier position in his other statements, such as the Feb. 4, 1948 "Christian Century," is a first mild attempt to seek theological justification for a type of church union which is primarily a rather late example of the sociological tendency to centralization characteristic of the twentieth century.

Since the aim of all church union is the furtherance of God's purpose for His people, it follows that we should consider the value of any church, union in the light of "central convictions" which inspire "daring deeds" for Christ and His Kingdom.

I. Points of Beginning

It needs to be stated clearly and unequivocally that what we Congregationalists are concerned about is the Church as the fellowship of those who worship the God and Father of our Lord Jesus Christ.

It needs to be said, also, that like our forefathers, we turn to the New Testament for our understanding of *how* we are to further the life and work of Christ's Church.

It needs to be added that we rely upon the guidance of the Holy Spirit in the New Testament sense, as the Spirit of God that was in Christ, now present in those who are Christ-like; yielding "the fruits of the Spirit" which are "love, joy, peace, good temper, kindliness, generosity, fidelity, gentleness, and self-control."

It needs to be proclaimed that our Christian Hope, for this world or for the next, is *not* in belonging to any organization at all—church or otherwise—but is in faithfulness to God who, in Christ, has promised that those who believe in Him shall experience a new life here and now so glorious in character that we can begin to live, and can continue to live a life that is eternal.

These points of beginning bring us directly to the central convictions of our Churches, and the daring deeds into which those convictions should lead us.

II. God and Man

The first central conviction to be faced in the proposed union of the Christian Congregational Churches and the Evangelical and Reformed Church concerns the Christian concept of God and of man's relationship to God.

We believe in the God and Father of Our Lord Jesus Christ.

This means that a moderator of the General Council who assures a court that the Council may unite at will with a Jewish synagogue is talking foolishly, on the basis of a thin legal misinterpretation of a basic Christian fact. We *can* unite with any person or group of persons who have in them the same mind and spirit of God which is made known to us in Christ—and with *no others.* Our Christian dedication is more fundamental than our legal rights.

The centrality of allegiance to God "in Christ" means that the one-ness of the Church of Christ is *not* institutional or organizational; The one-ness of Christ's Church is the shared spirit of Christ. "Wherever the Spirit of Christ is *there* is the Church." Dr. Douglass characterizes spiritual unity as "thin air." But Jesus himself said "Worship the Father in spirit," and the New Testament bears ample witness to the reality of the Spirit. The plain fact seems to be that many people are no longer willing to accept the teaching of Jesus concerning spiritual one-ness. They no longer *believe* that the best way to "stay together" is to be *drawn together* by a common allegiance to a common Lord. They *say* that the one-ness of the Church must be outward and visible; but *in fact* the only one-ness worth having is one-ness in Christ. Any and all outward *forms of union* are empty shells unless and until there is a consecrated heart; unless and until there is a "unity of the spirit in the bonds of peace." So long as we remain committed to the conviction that we are related to the God and Father of our Lord Jesus Christ, our *one-ness is spiritual;* it will, of necessity, be one-ness "in Christ." If it is not, no amount of organizational unification will either create or sustain real one-ness.

III. Christ's Church

The second central conviction concerns the question, "What is Christ's Church?" "What is the measure of its power and what is its task?"

The Church is the fellowship of those who follow Christ, seeking to do His will in at least four ways: (1) through ever richer experiences of worship; (2) through enlarging experiences of personal growth; (3) through wider and nobler service to others in Christ's name; and (4) through the proclamation of the Gospel "into all the world." Just to state this Congregational concept of the Church is to declare that with us churchmanship and discipleship are identical. We believe that the Church is the fellowship of believers committed to Christ. This view has roots in the New Testament. There are just two meanings of "Church" in the New Testament. The word is used 105 times; 86 of these clearly refer to the local Church, and 18 refer to the universal company of believers in all ages and places. Not one refers to any denomination or to any body comparable to the united Protestant or Roman Catholic, or Eastern Orthodox Churches.

The vitality and power of the Church of Christ is to be measured by the worth of the worship, work, and witness of His followers. When the people of Christ are living their faith daily, when the worship of the Churches is sincere, when the ministry of the Churches is the eager dedication of men and women to the service of their Master, when the extension of Christ's Kingdom is gladly accepted as a privilege of discipleship, when the life of contemporary society is permeated by Christ-like standards in human relationships—when these things are true, *then* "the vast company of Christians outside our two denominations," for whom Dr. Douglass pleads, will be given *real hope* and *real encouragement,* for then our Churches will be going forward in the power of the Spirit of God in Christ, and not in the weakness of ecclesiastical machinery.

Both the New Testament and Christian history testify to the truth that the work and witness of the Church of Christ depends upon Christian commitment rather than ecclesiastical unification. When Kenneth Scott Latourette wrote his monumental *"History of the Expansion of Christianity"* two full volumes were devoted to "The Great Century." That Century was the nineteenth, in which the Gospel spread more rapidly than in many other centuries combined. In that century the London Missionary Society, The American Board, the American Missionary Society, the Y.M.C.A. and uncounted other Christian enterprises arose. The record of their work and witness makes us feel humble and unworthy. Now, mark you, this very same century saw the rise of many denominations. It was not an era of ecclesiasticism; it was a time of evangelism; it was a day when central convictions bore fruit in daring deeds.

If what we seek is a fresh endowment of the Spirit and new power for Christian witness, as Dr. Douglass suggests, then, what we most need is *new consecration* and *not added centralization.* Suppose we contrast the daring deeds of the nineteenth century Congregationalists with the record of our Churches in the decades just passed, in which there has been a drift away from a voluntary fellowship of Churches toward central organization with wide powers affecting the life and work of the Churches. Has centralization strengthened and extended the work of the free Congregational Churches? The answer is NO.

The answer NO needs to be stated in specific terms. In the decades just passed the Congregational Christian Churches have rarely had the vitality to produce even one-half the leaders needed for ministerial and missionary service. In the 1930–1940 decade we had ebbed as low as to have only 50% of our ministers, 40% of our foreign missionaries, and 33% of our home missionaries coming from our own Churches. Our former leadership in publication of religious literature has almost disappeared. The number of our Churches, missionaries, and local ministers has decreased in about the same ratio as the number of our national and conference officials has increased. Where we have retained a vigorous Christian witness, it has been as much or more due to the work of individuals and local Churches, as it has been to the work of wider bodies. And the lost opportunities in expanding America are, in very large measure, the result of our inner confusion and our tendency to leave to the conference or national bodies tasks which we ought to have done as individuals, as Churches, or as Associations of Churches.

There is a lesson in the fact that the Park Street Church in Boston and the Lake Avenue Church in Pasadena, both of which do their work spontaneously, have *expanded* their direct and independent work at home, have founded new missions abroad, and are contributing to such causes much more in dedicated leaders and in dollars than any other Churches of our order.

In short, the claim that ecumenicity is the modern equivalent of evangelism is false. Yet, if you study the "answerable courages" said to emanate from ecumenicity you will see that union of denominations is being heralded *as if it were the Gospel for our day.*

The fact seems to be that desire for union is a counsel of despair, a desire to trust size of organization to lend influence and create prestige; when the only real power of the Church of Christ (as our forefathers, and presently the Quakers amply demonstrate) lies in utter dependence on

God. It staggers the imagination to think of what God might have wrought through our Churches in the past decade if we had given to the worship, work and witness of Christ all the time, energy and money which we have devoted to the organizational type of ecumenicity, a form which has no rootage in the Gospel and which in our own fellowship, has brought division and distress instead of refreshment and power.

IV. The Church and Its Lord

A third central conviction concerns the question: How is Christ's Church related to its Lord?

"Modern Congregationalism is the legitimate outcome of a consistent application to Church polity of the principles of the Reformation"; these are the opening words of Williston Walker's authoritative collection of *"The Creeds and Platforms of Congregationalism."*

What is here stressed is the fact that *we believe Christ is the sole Head of the Church.* Congregationalists reject *all* authority save that of the Word of God, the living, personal Word known in the teachings, the work, and the life of Jesus Christ.

Jesus himself said, "No man can have two masters." This is as true of Churches as it is of individual Christians. *If* we profess to believe in "the triumph of an idea, a movement, a spirit, a style of life," then we ought *to trust that idea* and *trust that spirit.* The Pilgrim tradition is a present adventure which the great, learned, and lovable Albert Peel, foremost Congregational historian of the century, described as "the most courageous and most scriptural venture of faith possible to Christian communities, for it takes the promises of God seriously and, depriving believers of all external support or control, casts them wholly upon the Spirit. The depths to which it can fall corresponds to the heights to which it aspires. It gives full, practical expression to the undeniably scriptural view that the Church is the people, and holds it better to run all risks than to sacrifice the principle which makes the congregation of believers responsible for the quality of their own spiritual life." Dr. Peel accurately reflects the influence of a lifetime spent with the diaries of Congregational leaders, the findings of Councils, and the study of the Scriptures.

"One is your Master, and you are all brothers"—that One is the God and Father of our Lord Jesus Christ. We *can own* NO other Master, not even our own Association, Conference or General Council.

If our Churches are true to the principle of the sole Headship of Christ, then locally there will be no test of membership except the sincere desire of the applicant to accept the covenant or statement of purpose which testifies to the allegiance of a people to God. No "dues" or "assessments" are in order in such a fellowship. When sole allegiance is to Christ, then *responsibility* means being true, at all costs, to the voice of God in Christ as the Spirit speaks to conscience. We are false to our convictions when we fall to fulfill our Christian duties, *NOT* because we have broken an ecclesiastical rule, *BUT* because we have been untrue to our Lord Himself. We are false to our convictions when we do whatever we are told to do by ecclesiastical organizations unless we believe that we are called of God so to act.

To put Dr. Douglass' words in fitting context, the "spiritual toughness, organizational resiliency, (and) capacity for adaptation" which makes our Congregational way "relevant and serviceable to the deepest needs of men and to the supreme tasks of the Church in the present," or in any other generation, is rooted In the conviction that Christ, and Christ alone, is Head of the Church.

It is for this religious reason that we hold each local Church to be a true Church in its own right, "Where Christ is—there is the Church."

To accept the *sole* Headship of Christ in His Church means to deny any *other* Headship.

When Baptism is set down as a condition of Church membership, as it is in the "Basis of Union," it symbolizes a fundamental change in our concept of Church membership as a covenant relationship of Christian people in a community for worship, work, and witness. Allegiance shifts from Christ as Head to Sacrament or Creed as Head. Nearly all our members are baptized but when a conscientious person from the Society of Friends wishes to join one of our Churches his sincerity is likely to be accepted in place of baptism.

When the relationships of pastor to people are supposed to conform to a "standard" procedure, then allegiance shifts from Christ as Head to the Placement Bureau as Head.

When program planning in Churches, in the youth, women's and men's fellowships, and in the associations of Churches is the acceptance of what has been planned at a "Mid-Winter Meeting" at which the Churches as such are not even represented, then allegiance shifts from Christ as Head to "the Board" as Head.

When theological schools, orphanages, and other institutions are under the control of a Synod, so that curricula, faculty, administration, student body, licenture, and ordination are subject to central oversight, then allegiance shifts from Christ as Head to Synod as Head.

When *any* constitution or other fundamental document, subject to amendment by *any* body outside the local fellowship is accepted by a Church, then that local Church has shifted its responsible relation from Christ as Head to the constitutional body as Head. Once *any* such constitution is accepted by a local Church, power is thereby given *over* the local Church.

A precise illustration may make clear this transfer *from* allegiance to God in Christ *to* allegiance to a body outside the local Church. A few years ago a nationally-known Presbyterian leader was minister of a nearby Church. One day he called to ask if I would perform a marriage between two members of his Church, one a divorced man whose wife had gone to live with other men. The session of his church and the ministers of that Church unanimously agreed that the young man and his bride-to-be were just the sincere, earnest kind of a couple whose marriage should be performed in the Church. The Presbytery disagreed. The wedding took place in a Congregational Church where God's love for his children took precedence over the powers of any ecclesiastical body.

The sole Headship of Christ is the true source of stamina for our Congregational Way. Our strength is in Him. The true resiliency of our Churches is their ministry to the needs of men and communities as Christ speaks to their consciences. The true relevance of our Churches to the needs of our age is our eagerness to adventure in ever new ways of service in response to the inner leading of the Holy Spirit.

There is a lack of nerve and courage in the weak assumption that we cannot trust the Headship of Christ in a super-organized age. "Why are you afraid, have you still no faith?"—no faith, after the witness of all the ages since Jesus was here among men, a witness often made most clearly (as in St. Francis, St. Teresa, Grenfell, or Frank Laubach) when it most defies organizational circumscription. Why are we running for cover under the roof of ecclesiasticism in the face of the example of the ages in an over-organized Church of Rome or Roman Empire, and in the light of the principle of decentralization already evident in contemporary society? The yen for "one big organization" is the sociological backwash of a secular practice which has had its day, and is presently being modified in business and government to resemble more closely the kind of voluntary fellowship which is the native climate of our free Churches.

As one who has been interested in history from childhood days, and as one who has had some relation to the polity developments in our Churches in recent years, I have been rather surprised at the attempt which has been made to re-write Congregational history in order to provide a setting for mid-twentieth-century ideas of "one big Church." The names of Jacob, Barrow, Cotton, and sometimes Owen are often quoted. And the name of a modern English Congregationalist, who holds no position of importance among English Congregationalists, Jenkins, is added for good measure. Much is said in some circles about the years of "Consociation" in Connecticut. It is almost incredible that careful scholars should allow themselves to speak of a somewhat Puritan thread as if it were the whole cloth of Congregationalism.

There are *many* threads in our history. But if you wish to follow the central pattern then turn to the great Councils, to the records of the Churches themselves, and to the balanced scholarship of men like Williston Walker. Or, if you wish, turn to the carefully documented study made by the Committee on Polity and Unity which gives you *the actual documentary position of our Churches* as of the year 1954. When careful scholarship is applied, either to our history or to our contemporary documents, there is no doubt but that we have been, and that we say we still are, a voluntary fellowship of free Churches, organized "to do and to promote the work of these Churches."

The Headship of Christ has been and is a conviction so central to our Congregational way that a change in this allegiance represents a fundamental change from our historic witness and from our present way of working.

V. One, Holy, Catholic, Apostolic

A fourth central conviction is raised by this question: What do we mean when we say that Christ's Church is one, holy, catholic, and apostolic.

These are ancient words, but they are words with which we shall have to become familiar in the years of great Church power into which the American Churches have now entered.

One-ness means a common allegiance to Our Lord as we have already pointed out.

Holiness means that the Church of Christ is righteous and just, like its Lord. Its "great and honorable actions" are *honorable.*

When a local Church mistreats its organist, its minister, or its caretaker it is not *holy.* When a minister fails to keep his high trust as an ambassador of Christ, both he and the Church he serves are *not holy.* When "officials" introduce favoritism or power-politics into Church affairs the Church is not holy.

So, too, in the wider relations of our Churches, fairness, honesty, integrity, and honor are the marks of righteousness. When printed assurance is given that a ballot will be taken and that 75% approval will be required to consummate a union, that assurance should be scrupulously kept. No "tenth inning" should be played because only 63% have scored "yes." No "umpire's decision" to make 72.8% acceptable instead of 75% should be made. No funds given by all should be used to bring even 27% "into line." No "Committee on Information" should function as a bureau of propaganda for one viewpoint. Honesty is honesty. "Honorable actions" must be *honorable.* The Church local *and* the wider representatives of the Churches must be *holy,* if their "answerable courage" is to be other than a hollow pretense.

The Church is to be *catholic.* In the New Testament the word Church is used 18 times to refer to the Church universal. Catholic means universal, not only worldwide today, but in all previous times, and for all ages to come. The Church universal is far more than the small sized ecumenical goal of those who seem hungry for organizational power and for the false safety of size.

To be catholic or universal the Church needs to include in its fellowship *all* who choose to follow Christ. This is the Church as a universal fellowship—not as a worldwide organization. The Church Universal is not made up of many denominations, Protestant, Roman Catholic, or Eastern Orthodox; it is created by God and depends solely upon the Spirit of Christ which upholds, strengthens, and guides the representatives of the Churches in Council.

Church Councils are a means of fellowship. Their powers are moral and declarative. It is deplorable that most of our recent Council meetings have been "business sessions" devoted to everything but the great Christian convictions and their relevance to the needs of our time. The Churches in Council have all the powers that inhere in the intrinsic worth of their actions and recommendations. They have no power *over* the Church. *They are not the Church Catholic. They are not even a Church at all in the New Testament* sense of the word "Church." If we choose to speak of the General Council as a "Church" we should honestly state that we are changing the New Testament usage, the usage of our Churches for hundreds of years; and that we are re-defining the word "Church" to mean a body of people elected for two years by other bodies, and passing out of existence every two years.

Apostolic. The word means that we share the same faith as did the apostles. It can be, and is, twisted to mean that chosen men, ordained by some set procedure, are the representatives of Christ among men. And there has been a tendency toward this view among us in recent years. Early Congregationalists ordained their ministers in *a* Church to serve *that* Church, and only that Church. This is still practiced among us, though very rarely. We ordain most men now by the invitation of the Church, through the Association of Churches, and such ordinations are customarily accepted by other Associations. An Association could, however, refuse to accept the credentials offered, and once in a long time this actually occurs.

Our ministers are men and women, called of God in their own consciences, and called by a group of Christian followers to minister to them. The apostolic power of a Congregational minister is his Christ-like character—as much or as little of it as he possesses.

These are the ways in which the Church of Christ is *one, holy, catholic, and apostolic.*

VI. Summary

To sum up, let me say again that Church union is essentially related to our central convictions—

1. Our belief in God, the Father of our Lord Jesus Christ
2. Our belief that the Church is Christ's Church, and its task his work
3. Our belief that the Church can hold no other allegiance than that which it has to Jesus Christ as Lord.
4. Our belief that the Church must be one in Christ, holy in character, catholic in inclusive witness, and apostolic in its faith.

VII. Reasons for Union

In conclusion, then, let us ask, For what reasons would anyone want union with the Evangelical and Reformed Church, or with any other fellowship or denomination?

Much of the discussion of the issue before us, on all sides, has seemed to move on the plane of expediency, and has been related to overhead costs, size, publication ventures, and lobby influence on government, on the one side; and to institutional responsibilities and safe guarding of funds on the other. These issues are important, but they are not as important as the ends they are designed to serve. What do we want the union for?

Surely there could be only one basic reason for any church union, namely to help men and women to become Christians, or to become better Christians.

Church order is important not to provide an efficient organization, or dignified assemblies, or even adequate sustentation and church extension funds, but in order to bear witness to the gospel. The criterion by which it is judged should always be the gospel; but the Congregational Christian fellowship is in no condition to act under sure guidance of God's Spirit. Yet, it is only as we are able to follow that Spirit that we shall rise from level of expediency to the level of Christian action. Too often power has gone out of our church Councils because we have sought to settle matters with our own judgment in terms of what seems to us to be the best policy at the moment, rather than to probe the apparent issues to their proper depth and submit them to Christ's judgment. We talk about "pushing a motion through" rather than about finding and following the guidance of God's Spirit. Our goal seems to be to "get our own way" rather than to find and follow Christ's way.

Over the months and years of our difference, debate has seemed to center on the issues of procedures which are the expression of principles, rather than on the principles themselves. Some of us have longed for and pleaded for some word which would rise above our selfish fears and cares. *There is yet time to face the fundamental issues with wisdom, understanding, and charity. Nothing is ever lost when honest men face their differences and take time to find God's answer to their needs. Conclusions are too often only the point at which we grow weary of thinking.*

Surely our unhappy divisions are to be healed, not by search for a lowest common denominator, or by any device of expediency, but rather by universal penitence, by a common understanding of the things we most surely believe and by a more faithful obedience to the Word and Will of God.

In the final analysis all church unions must be spiritual unions. That we all have failed to find the guidance of the Spirit in the proposed Union of the Congregational Christian Churches and the Evangelical and Reformed Church is painfully clear. On every side of the fruit our controversy has been bickering, misunderstanding, impatience, strife, bitterness, and broken personal relationships. But the "fruit of the Spirit is love, joy, peace, good temper, kindliness, generosity, fidelity, gentleness, self-control." Those who belong to Christ have crucified the flesh with its emotions and passions. "As we live by the Spirit let us be guided by the Spirit." So reads the book we all profess to follow. Here is the central conviction which leads to daring deeds for Christ and His Church.

83. Ecclesiastical Lobbying:
"They're Planning to Take Your Church . . . "

(1956)

The League to Uphold Congregational Principles

The Committee for the Continuation of Congregational and Christian Churches in the United States

The Joint Committee for Union between the Congregational Christian Churches and the Evangelical and Reformed Church began its work in 1942. From that time on, church leaders from both denominations worked diligently to educate their constituencies about what would happen when the two churches came together. In 1947, the two denominations jointly published "A Primer of Union" (see vol. 6:78) to provide answers to frequently asked questions and to allay fears and correct misinformation among their congregations. Denominational leaders from both churches had written voluminously about the union. Hundreds of forums and discussions had been held for youth and adults.

Nevertheless, people were still afraid and the educational program had not been completely successful. In 1956, a pamphlet entitled "They're Planning to Take Your Church . . . " was published by several antimerger organizations. It reflects the astute observation made by Congregational ecumenist Washington Gladden in 1904 that the balance within Congregationalism between fellowship or community and local autonomy had tipped too far in the direction of autonomy. Local

---

Source: "They're Planning to Take Your Church . . . ," pamphlet published jointly by The League to Uphold Congregational Principles, Hartford, Connecticut, and The Committee for the Continuation of Congregational Christian Churches of the United States, Chicago, Illinois, 1956.

autonomy, long considered a strength of Congregationalism, had become its weakness (see vol. 6:3).

"They Are Planning to Take Your Church . . . " is a prime example of how resistant fears are to education. In spite of ten years of effort to explain the proposed union, fears about the loss of autonomy and the imposition of external ecclesiastical authority were still alive and well.

They're planning to take your church . . . into a new and different kind of denomination!

"June 25, 1957 has been chosen as the date on which the Congregational Christian churches and the Evangelical and Reformed Church will unite to form the United Church of Christ."—Quoted from official magazine "ADVANCE," Sept. 7, 1955, p. 8.

What does this mean to your church?

Here are the answers, based on material being circulated in connection with the merger ("The Basis of Union," "Step by Step," etc.). . . .

•

The new denomination will be an <u>authoritarian</u> church.

The plan of union calls for the writing of AN OVERALL CONSTITUTION.

Such a constitution is LAW—the fundamental and controlling law over THE WHOLE DENOMINATION—including all its members, ministers, congregations, and instrumentalities.

Congregationalists have always rejected the control of any such over-all constitution. Each church has had its own by-laws, and no outside ecclesiastical body has had any authority over the local church.

An over-all constitution would mean a radical change for the Congregational Christian churches. It would mean a sharp curtailing of Congregational freedom of action.

Do you want to be bound by an over-all authoritarian constitution?

•

Your church will lose its present freedom.

If the merger goes through, your church will lose its long-established freedom to determine its mode of fellowship, and will have controversial doctrines of medieval character pressed upon it.

The Basis of Union sets forth what we are getting into, and according to it:

- We are "duty bound" to say the things which "the ancient Church expressed in the ecumenical creeds" and which were later included in "the evangelical confessions of the Reformation."
- A statement of faith based on these creeds and confessions, *to be worked out after the union is completed,* "shall be submitted for approval to the General Synod, Conferences, Associations, and Congregations."

Congregationalism stands for freedom in matters of faith. . . .

Do you want a creed-bound church?

•

Your church will be under pressure to change to a narrow, extremist view of Christian faith.

In Congregationalism, free minds have traditionally found a frank, honest, and *natural* approach to religion. Spiritually sensitive people have been able in our free churches to work out honest and satisfying understandings of the Christian faith. Now this would be all changed.

According to President James E. Wagner of the Evangelical and Reformed Church, we are turning away from "liberalism" and "breezy modernism" and are being "transformed" in our theological character by the "sterner doctrinal assumptions" of Barth, Brunner, and Reinhold Niebuhr. Dr. Wagner affirms that the men on the theological committee (which is already at work) have probably all been "influenced" by this new theology.

To accept these "sterner doctrinal assumptions" in place of the simple teachings of Jesus means for Congregationalists A RADICAL CHANGE IN DOCTRINE. It means a narrow and extremist view of the Christian faith, a renewal of warfare between science and religion, a rejection of reason in our approach to God, and a minimizing of ethics.

Do you want a narrow-minded faith?

•

Your church will lose its identity as a free, independent church.

Instead of sharing in a fellowship of free churches, such as we now enjoy in our Congregational Christian fellowship, your church would become a mere "congregation" in this new, national, unitary CHURCH.

Instead of being an independent and sovereign body in its own right, your church would become a mere "unit of organization" in a single national structure and would lose its status and rights as an independent Congregational or Christian church

All of its rights as an independent church will be jeopardized if your church accepts a status as a "congregation" in this new denomination!

•

Your church will lose its real autonomy.

In the new denomination your church would have "autonomy in its own sphere." This is *not the same* as the complete and genuine autonomy which your church now enjoys.

According to The Basis of Union, the future constitution would *define the rights and responsibilities of your church.* In other words, the over-all constitution would set the limits to your "sphere of autonomy." It would tell you what things you could still decide for yourselves.

DEFINING THE RIGHTS OF YOUR CHURCH, AND SETTING FORTH ITS "RESPONSIBILITIES," IS AN ABRIDGMENT OF YOUR RIGHTS. IT VIOLATES THE REAL AUTONOMY OF YOUR CHURCH.

The independence of your church is not now limited or circumscribed by an over-all constitution. You will lose this priceless right if you accept in its place this deceptive substitute of "autonomy in its own sphere."

•

The new denomination means government from the top.

The proposed General Synod would be a smaller body than our present General Council, but with far more power. The General Synod would have power to draw up the future constitution and even TO CHANGE ANY PARTS OF THE PRESENT BASIS OF UNION.

Conferences would take from local Associations their present power of electing delegates. They would also take over powers of ordination and of ministerial standing. Ministers would be under the authority of the tightly organized upper bodies.

This is all part of the "government" that will be set forth in the over-all constitution. As President James E. Wagner of the E. & R. Church has said about the law of his own Church, "It has been good to know, however, that in case of extreme necessity the law was there to resort to."

Are you willing to submit to centralization of authority?

•

We will lose our bodies of free fellowship.

In the new denomination the General Synod "shall promote the reorganization of Conferences, Associations, and Synods" on a "territorial basis." This means that our Associations and Conferences would merge with the Synodical bodies of the E. and R. Church and take on their functions.

E. and R. Synods exercise both *legislative* and *judicial* powers which our Conferences and Associations are forbidden to exercise. The Basis of Union provides for such governmental powers in the reorganized bodies. Hence the plan of union would *carry over the Synodical form of government.*

Free churches cannot long survive when unevenly yoked with authoritarian bodies.

•

The new denomination will require your church to act as an ecclesiastical court.

The Basis of Union says that, "Individual communicants have the right of appeal, complaint, or reference to their Congregations, Associations, Conferences, and ultimately to the General Synod."

This means that your church would have to act as an ecclesiastical court whether it wanted to or not—hearing complaints of petty grievances by members against other members or against their pastor.

Furthermore, the decisions of your church would no longer be final in matters relating to its own affairs. Local disputes would be subject to review by Conferences and the General Synod on appeal.

This would set up the machinery which could be used in the future for heresy trials and other disciplinary action against the free mind and conscience of ministers and church members.

•

Here is your church now . . . in a free fellowship:

- *Governs Its Own Affairs under the direct "Headship of Christ"*
- A "complete" church in its own right, with full independence and sovereignty over all its affairs and relationships.
- Can choose its ministers from any source with entire freedom, and without authoritative pressure from anyone.
- Writes its own statement of faith or purpose without pressure from the denomination, nor against a background of a nationally-approved creed.
- Has complete and undisputed ownership and control of its own property as a free and independent church.
- Is a direct and constituting member of a Congregational Christian Association and conference created to serve free churches.
- Has purely voluntary relations with local Association, state Conference, General Council and national Boards.
- Makes contributions on a voluntary basis and in response to needs genuinely felt by the local church.
- Is *not* under any national constitution, nor is it constrained by legislative or judicial bodies.
- Is *not* required to act as an ecclesiastical court, nor is it subject to any review of its own actions by any synodical or denominational body.
- Importance of local free churches clearly recognized: "We stand for the autonomy of the local church and its independence of ecclesiastical control."
- Rights of conscience protected: "We hold sacred the freedom of the individual soul and the right of private judgment."
- Related to other churches through "faith, freedom, and fellowship" in a non-authoritarian community of interest.

Here is your church as a "congregation" of the new denomination:

THE GENERAL SYNOD (Taking over functions of E. and R. General Synod, plus those of our General Council.)

- THE GENERAL SYNOD will write Constitution which will be "fundamental law" of entire denomination.

- Will have power to amend any portions of the present Basis of Union with Interpretations.
- Will act as top governmental, legislative, and judicial body of the new denomination.
- Will speak "authoritatively" for the entire denomination.
- Symbolizes shift of emphasis from the local church to *The Church* as a whole, making the *denomination* the chief consideration rather than the welfare of local churches.
- Will have power to increase its own authority at will.

THE SYNODICAL CONFERENCES (E. and R. regional Synods "reorganized" to take in the C.C. Conferences and Associations.)

- THE SYNODICAL CONFERENCES will carry out laws and regulations of the General Synod and of *The Church.*
- Will control standing of ministers and congregations.
- Will exercise such legislative and governmental functions as are assigned to them under the future Constitution.
- Will "farm out" the apportionment goals which the congregations are expected to raise for *The Church.*
- Will seek means of bringing adherence to the "standard" and "normal" procedures outlined for the calling of ministers, etc.
- Will act as first courts of appeal on complaints and other cases coming up from local "congregations."
- Will have sole power of electing delegates to the General Synod.

Your Church as a "congregation" of the new denomination:

- YOUR CHURCH will have only such "rights and responsibilities" as are defined for it under future constitution.
- Will be subject to "advisory" opinions from the higher ecclesiastical courts of *The Church.*
- Will choose its ministers in accordance with "normal" and "standard" procedures, or else be considered *abnormal* and irregular in its conduct.
- Will be under synods instead of governing its own affairs.

- Will have "autonomy in its own sphere"—being permitted to hire its own janitors, paint its own building, pay its own bills, etc.
- Will adopt its own creed—subject to the pressures that come from a nationally adopted statement on faith.
- Will have some of its present rights left "unabridged" for as long as it is able to resist the pressures toward conformity in the new *Church.*

•

The United Church would take on E. & R. contingent liabilities.

The Basis of Union provides that the United Church would assume as a "prior claim" on denominational money the funding of the original annuities of ministers in the two denominations. Since Congregational Christian churches have met almost all of their own obligations in this regard, this means that the United Church would accept as a "prior claim" on its missionary money the funding of E. and R. ministers' annuities *only.*

This prior claim "shall be for not less than $500,000 in each year," provided the missionary giving is $3,300,000 a year or more. A footnote in the Basis of Union estimates that 30 years would be required to meet this obligation.

The benefit that would accrue to E. and R. ministers by this underwriting of their annuities is not matched by any benefits for Congregational Christian ministers or churches.

•

The plan for the new church is confusing and contradictory.

The Basis of Union with Interpretations is so confusing that no one can say for sure what it is intended to mean. It may take ten years or more to write the future constitution. Meanwhile the General Synod would have a free hand in shaping the organization of the new Church.

Congregationalists have repeatedly asked for a more satisfactory and definitive document before going into the union. The E. and R. leaders, however, have insisted that we be committed to the union first. They want things "all sewed up" before we know what we are getting into.

Justice Steinbrink, an eminent trial judge who heard 23 days of testimony in a lawsuit over the merger (the Cadman Case), stated:

"The Basis of Union connotes and points toward a centralized body whose limitations are not yet defined because of clauses to which attention has been and will later be directed.

"The Basis of Union is a conglomeration of confusion and conflicting statements with a cacophony of ideas."

Congregationalists have a right to know more about what they're getting into before making a decision.

•

Proportional representation in the new church will not be allowed until after policy has been established.

Compared with the E. and R. Church, the Congregational Christian denomination has more members (1,310,570 to 775,000), more churches (5,570 to 2,750) and more institutional funds (probably ten times as much or more). Yet the proposal is that the first General Synod be composed of an equal number of members from each side. However, the *second* General Synod will be set up on a proportional representation basis.

The first Synod will have authority to initiate action for the preparation of a constitution. If proportional representation is considered fair for the later Synods, why not for this first policy-making body?

Even more important, the Executive Council which will act for the General Synod for the intervals between meetings is to be made up equally of C.C. and E. & R. people until the constitution is adopted. The same situation exists as to the boards of the merged home and foreign missionary agencies.

Why is proportional representation delayed?

•

Your church may lose the undisputed control of its own property.

According to laws governing church bodies the property of local congregations becomes "dedicated to the uses of" the kind of church with which it is affiliated, and a local congregation cannot really withdraw without forfeiting its property.

There is not one word in the Basis of Union or Interpretations about any church having the right to withdraw, or about having the right to retain its property if it does withdraw.

If your church accepts status as a congregation in the United Church it will automatically *give up its status and rights as a free and independent Congregational Christian church.* If it later seeks to withdraw from the United Church, it will have only the rights of a dissident congregation of that Church. *It will also forfeit all property rights in C.C. boards and instrumentalities.*

Getting out of the United Church cannot restore the rights you will lose on being taken in!

•

They claim you will be in the union whether you take action or not!

"NO ACTION is required by any bodies save the national denominational bodies and their delegates . . . "

—Quoted from official leaflet, "Step by Step"

"All persons who are members of either communion at the time of the union shall be members of the United Church."

—"Basis of Union," Article VII.

"At the time of Union every member of every congregation would be assumed to be a member of the United Church."

—"Letter Missive" of Dec. 16, 1955

These statements challenge your right to determine your own religious future.

•

Stay out, if you want to "wait and see."

The only safe way to "wait and see" what the merger would be like, before making your decision, is to *stay out of the union.*

There is danger in the merest act of cooperation with the United Church, even after having voted against the union. A legal principle of "estoppel" might be held to apply here. This means simply that "actions speak louder than words" in determining whether you have assented to membership in the United Church.

Officials keep trying to lure the churches into the union with assurances that they can "get out later" if they don't like it. As we have already shown, your church would lose its rights as an independent Congregational church if it were to go into the union and then try to withdraw. It might also lose its property.

Even COOPERATION with the United Church may result in absorption of your church.

•

The present merger plan has no legal basis.

The General Council of Congregational Christian Churches has NO POWER WHATEVER to take the churches into the union. Its lawyers and witnesses have repeatedly admitted this in court. The highest court dealing with the Cadman Case stated clearly that "there is no power . . . and none is claimed" by which the General Council can unite the churches. Yet the officials and Executive Committee of our General Council are trying to do the very thing which was repudiated most emphatically in court.

Officials have presented only one side of the merger question since the beginning. They have used denominational funds to bombard the churches with propaganda favoring the merger and the salaried officials have gone around promoting it. They have claimed that the merger was "undebatable." They have urged churches not to discuss the issues for fear that it would divide their memberships. They have discouraged full and free discussion at state Conferences and local Associations. They have frowned on all who dare to oppose their plan. Methods used bespeak the authoritarian nature of the plan itself. If officials would stoop to these methods before the plan goes through, what power will they *not* seek to exercise once they get our churches into their new denomination?

The time to take your stand against this plan is NOW!

•

Steps your church should take now.

Don't let your church be taken into a new denomination by default. Allow no one to "assume" that your church is a member without its own action.

1. Adopt a Protecting Resolution. (See next page for a suggested motion.)
2. Avoid any cooperation with, or participation in, the new denomination which might be construed as having given consent to its formation.

3. Avoid any act which could be construed as having made you a member of the new Church.
4. Stay OUTSIDE of the union if you want to WAIT AND SEE what it is like before making a final decision. (Your church could join later if the future Constitution met with its approval, but *it could not get out later without loss of valuable rights and standing as a free Congregational Christian church.)*
5. Join the new National Association of Congregational Christian Churches. This is made up of Congregational Christian churches which intend to remain Congregational Christian. Membership in this Association does not require any change in the present relations of your church with other Congregational Christian bodies. (Write Dr. Harry Johnson, Executive Secretary of the National Association of C.C. Churches for further information. His address is 1301 N. 15th Street, Boise, Idaho.)

A suggested resolution for your church.

"MOVED:

"That this church reaffirms its adherence to the Congregational principles of independency and of voluntary fellowship as among the churches, and

"That it declares that no action of local Association, State Conference, or General Council of Congregational Christian Churches can make this church a part of any other denomination, or of the proposed United Church of Christ, and

"That the election of delegates by this church to local Association or State Conference meetings is not to be interpreted as indicating approval of the proposed United Church of Christ, or as making this church a part of said United Church of Christ, and finally,

"That any delegates elected by this church to local Association or State Conference shall cease to represent this church officially, and shall cease to be delegates thereof, at such time as said local Association or State Conference shall become a part of the United Church of Christ."

•

References and documentation for statements made in this book

Page 4 Basis of Union,* article IV., A, and Constitution and By-laws of E. and R. Church**

Page 5 See Dr. James E. Wagner's letter to E. and R. Synodical members, "Looking Forward to The United Church of Christ,"* Apr. 2, 1955 and Dr. Marion J. Bradshaw's book, "Baleful Legacy"***

Page 6 B. of U., article II and article IV., F.

Page 7 B. of U. III., A.

Page 8 B. of U. III., F.

Page 9 B. of U. IV., X., A. and E., XI. and III., D. Also James E. Wagner, "Toward Clarifying Some Misunderstandings," ADVANCE, May 2,1956.

Page 10 B. of U. IV., E. III. F., G. and Constitution and By-laws of E. and R. Church.**

Page 11 B. of U. III., G.

Page 12 See report of Committee on Free Church Polity and Unity* pp. 23, 24, 40, 41, 42.

Page 13 B. of U. I, II, III, IV, VI, VII, XI.

Page 14 B. of U. VIII., G., esp. 5, 6, 7 (inc. footnote 12), 8, 9, 11, 12.

Page 15 See testimony in Cadman trial and original opinion of Justice Meier Steinbrink;** Minutes of General Council, 1952,* p. 23; and "Newsletter to the Churches" dated Jan 7, 1955.**

Page 16 B. of U. X., A and E; IV., A, H, and 1; VIII, D. 1., E. 7. and 11. For comparative statistics of membership and churches see "United in Christ" leaflet of May 15, 1955.* For comparison of assets see "Frazier Report" published by the League to Uphold Congregational Principles.**

Page 17 Decision of Supreme Court of South Dakota, Reformed Bethanien Church v. Ochsner, Feb. 20, 1948.**

Page 19 See Truman Douglass, ADVANCE, Mar. 21, 1956, p. 26 and James E. Wagner, ADVANCE, May 2, 1956, p. 12 for assurances about withdrawal. For answer to these assurances see "Toward Clarifying some 'Clarifications' "** and "An Answer to the Statement that 'You Can Get Out If You Don't Like It'."**

Page 20 New York Court of Appeals decision, Dec. 3, 1953.* See also "Brief Review of Merger Procedures."**

Page 21 For other protective resolutions send for four-page folder of "Resolutions on the Merger."**

**Documents marked with single asterisk are obtainable from General Council of Congregational Christian Churches, 287 Fourth Ave., New York 10, N.Y.*

***Documents marked with double asterisk are obtainable from the Committee for the Continuation of Congregational Christian Churches, Room 2308, 100 N. LaSalle, Chicago 2, Ill.*

****The book "Baleful Legacy" is obtainable from Modern Publishers, 532 N.W. Second St., Oklahoma City, Okla., price $2.50.*

This book published by The League To Uphold Congregational Principles, Box 628, Hartford 1, Conn. and The Committee for the Continuation of Congregational Christian Churches of the United States, Room 2308, 100 North LaSalle Street, Chicago 2, Ill.

Addressing Concerns

84. Union Explained: *"The Interpretations of the Basis of Union"*

(1948)

In July of 1947, the final draft of the "Basis of Union" between the Congregational Christian Churches and the Evangelical and Reformed Church was adopted by the General Synod of the Evangelical and Reformed Church and sent to its thirty-four synods for consideration at their spring meetings. At the same time, opposition to the merger intensified within the Congregational Christian Churches, and a great flurry of publications against the union appeared (see vol. 6:79–83).

The joint committee that had written the Basis of Union circulated "Comments on the Basis of Union by the members of the Joint Committee which drew it up," seeking to reassure readers about issues that seemed problematic. Soon thereafter, the Executive Committee of the Congregational Christian Churches developed and circulated a set of "Interpretations" concerning the Basis of Union.

At first, some Congregational Christian opponents seemed satisfied, but soon it became clear that the Interpretations also created more problems. Members of the Evangelical and Reformed Church became concerned that the Interpretations changed the meaning of the Basis of Union that they were being asked to vote on. They were voting only on the Basis of Union, not on the Interpretations. To clarify this, the General Council of the Evangelical and Reformed Church sent a letter to its synods saying that no interpretive material on the Basis of Union was binding.

Source: "The Interpretations of the Basis of Union," excerpt from "The Basis of Union Between the Congregational Christian Churches and the Evangelical and Reformed Church," published jointly by the Executive Committee of the General Council of the Congregational Christian Churches and the General Council of the Evangelical and Reformed Church, 1948.

At the same time, members of the Congregational Christian Churches were becoming fearful of schism within their denomination. An antimerger statement from a 1947 meeting held in Evanston, Illinois, had said that churches voting for the merger would, in effect, be leaving the fellowship of the Congregational Christian Churches (see vol. 6:79).

Finally, in 1948, the General Council of the Congregational Christian Churches, meeting in Oberlin, Ohio, formally adopted the Basis of Union with Interpretations, and agreed to resubmit it to the churches for voting. This seemed to have positive results among the Congregational Christian Churches, and the General Council passed it by a vote of one thousand to eleven. However, the president of the Evangelical and Reformed Church, Louis Goebel, who was present in Oberlin, made it clear that the new interpretations meant that the Basis of Union with Interpretations would have to be resubmitted to the General Synod of the Evangelical and Reformed Church and approved by its thirty-four synods.

In addition, the wording of the Interpretations itself caused new problems. First, paragraph (a) stated that the Basis of Union calls for a union of the General Council of Congregational Churches and the General Synod of the Evangelical and Reformed Church to form the General Synod of the United Church of Christ. This emphasis alarmed Evangelical and Reformed leaders, who understood "organic union" in terms of churches and not simply councils or synods. It was difficult for the Evangelical and Reformed Church to understand that in Congregational polity, autonomous churches could not, by their very nature, act together as church.

Second, paragraph (b), section (4), contained another troublesome concept. Speaking of the constitution of the United Church of Christ, it said that the constitution "would define and regulate" the new General Synod, but only "describe the free and voluntary relationships which the churches, associations, and conferences shall sustain with the General Synod and with each other." In the Evangelical and Reformed Church, a constitution was understood to be "the guarantor of orderliness, justice, and freedom in all organizational relationships, and therefore binding for all." The notion of a "descriptive constitution" was almost incomprehensible.

At its General Council meeting in September, 1948, the Evangelical and Reformed Church tried to raise the mentality of the conversation above the level of politics by proposing the introduction of a new sentence in the problematic paragraph (b) (4) of the Interpretations: "We hope that the Constitution of the United Church may, through the guidance of the Holy Spirit and the experience of the new church, not merely develop a compromise of the two former polities but may bring a new polity and plan of organization to the United Church." This change, however, could not be left standing because it could not be included in the Interpretations that the General Council of the Congregational Christian Churches had adopted at Oberlin and sent back to the churches. In the end, the action of the Evangelical and Reformed General Council was rescinded at a special meeting in November of 1948.

United Church of Christ historian Louis H. Gunnemann has pointed to that sentence as being highly significant. It explained the differences between the two denominations as they looked toward union. The Evangelical and Reformed Church understood the institutional church as an organism that assumed new forms according to how it could best do God's work in the world at a particular time. For them, the idea of "a new form" of church government was perfectly in order.

For the Congregationalists, however, the ongoing lack of clarity about the relationship between the autonomy of the local churches and the power that was or might be exercised in the Executive Committee and the General Council made any action of those bodies suspect.

The Interpretations of the Basis of Union

(a) The Basis of Union calls for a union of the General Council of Congregational Christian Churches and the General Synod of the Evangelical and Reformed Church to form the General Synod of the United Church of Christ.

(b) The constitution for the United Church of Christ provided for in Article IV-A of thc Basis of Union: (1) will not come into force until it has been ratified by two-thirds of our churches voting; (2) is to be based on the principles set forth in the Basis of Union; (3) is in no wise to abridge the rights now enjoyed by the churches; (4) will define and regulate as regards the General Synod but describe the free and voluntary relationships which the churches, associations, and conferences shall sustain with the General Synod and with each other.

(c) The Basis of Union calls for a union of the Boards of Home Missions, the Boards of Foreign Missions, the Annuity Boards, the Councils for Social Action, and similarly all related Boards, commissions, agencies, and instrumentalities of the two denominations.

(d) Churches, associations, conferences, and the General Synod, being self-governing fellowships, possess autonomy in their own spheres, which autonomy is acknowledged and will be respected.

(e) Synods, conferences, associations and churches are to retain their present status until they are united by their own action and when mutually agreeable.

(f) Congregational Christian churches do not go out of existence at the time of the union of the two communions. In consummating this union the Congregational Christian Churches and the Evangelical and Reformed Church are uniting without break in their respective historic continuities.

(g) The United Church of Christ will be a union of two denominations joined in fellowship and cooperation without involving any invasion of the rights now enjoyed by local churches or congregations.

(h) With the constituting of the General Synod of the United Church of Christ, the General Council of the Congregational Christian Churches [and the General Synod of the Evangelical and Reformed Church] will remain in existence in order to fulfill necessary legal functions, but shall transfer to the General Synod all of its functions which do not for legal reasons need to be retained.

85. Not to Worry!

"The Status of the Local Congregational Christian Church as Proposed in the Basis of Union"

(ca. 1949)

Frederick L. Fagley

Between 1942 and 1947, the Basis of Union being developed to bring about the union of the Congregational Christian Churches and the Evangelical and Reformed Church went through ten drafts. In 1945, longtime Congregational church leader and historian Frederick Louis Fagley (1879–1958) wrote a brief history on the role of a constitution in the history of Congregationalism. In it, Fagley quoted the original constitution of the Congregational Churches: "the National Council shall never exercise legislative or judicial authority, or consent to act as a council of reference." In light of this history, Fagley suggested that it might be advisable for the Congregational Christians to seek a revision of their existing constitution whereby the churches would confer the necessary authority upon the General Council and give it power to vote on the Basis of Union. "For if the free churches *of our fellowship are to unite with* a church, *with a centralized authoritative nature, . . . these independent churches should first become* a church *themselves with corresponding authority, rights and duties comparable to the body with which they seek to unite. Then the Congregational Christian Church thus*

Source: Frederick L. Fagley, "The Status of the Local Congregational Christian Church as Proposed in the Basis of Union," pamphlet published by The General Council of the Congregational Christian Churches, New York, n.d., in the Congregational Library Archives.

created could transfer to the new body, the General Synod, the autonomy in its own sphere and the authority over the boards and agencies of the fellowship which are implied in the Basis of Union."

Although Fagley's paper was sent to the Executive Committee of the General Council of the Congregational Christian Churches, there is no indication that the Executive Committee ever discussed it. The paper was referred to the Commission on Interchurch Relations, and the questions it raised were kept on the agenda for further study.

In the meantime, a leading opponent of the merger, Malcolm K. Burton, received a copy of the paper from Fagley and made much use of it (see vol. 6:80). Burton sent copies "to all the superintendents and all the leading people in the denomination." He quoted from it liberally in his own pamphlets, citing it as evidence that it was impossible for any merger to be legally consummated by the Congregational Christian Churches under their present constitution.

Even as Fagley's writing was being used by opponents of the merger, the General Council also made use of Fagley's expertise to support the union cause. It published a pamphlet by him entitled "The Status of the Local Congregational Christian Church as Proposed in the Basis of Union." There, Fagley quoted extensively from the Basis of Union as evidence for the assurance "that the wider agencies of the churches may not invade the sphere of congregational authority" since their decisions would be advisory and not mandatory. Fagley reassured his readers that in the Basis of Union, the freedom of the minister and the autonomy of the church were presupposed, and that the authority to determine church membership rested with the congregation. These were issues that opponents of the union continued to interpret differently even when a reputable authority, such as Frederick Fagley, tried to convince them that the Basis of Union could be trusted.

Fagley was employed as an executive in the national leadership of the Congregational Christians Churches for many years. In 1918, he organized a Department of Evangelism for the denomination, and in 1922, he became secretary of the Commission on Evangelism and Devotional Life. After his retirement in 1948, he became the founder and first secretary of the Congregational Christian Historical Society. Fagley had a longstanding interest in the continuing education of clergy, drawing groups of clergy together to read books and discuss papers. His small volume The Congregational Churches *was widely read, and* The History of American Congregationalism, *which he coauthored with Gaius Glenn Atkins, remained the standard history of American Congregationalism until 1992.*

How Would the Basis of Union Affect the Local Church?

The distinctive element in the Congregational Christian heritage is the local church, in which each member has his spiritual responsibility and the whole fellowship constitutes a self-governing body of followers of Jesus Christ. Consequently a central issue in the proposed union of our churches with the Evangelical and Reformed Church is whether the Basis of Union would safeguard the freedom and democracy of the congregation. Each church and each member must face this question. We here summarize some of the pertinent considerations as we see them.

The effort to unite two Christian fellowships with similar aspirations but differing traditions requires intelligent compromise, that is, some changes in the polity of both denominations. Do these changes jeopardize essential Congregationalism, or do they affect only non-essentials?

Adoption would not preclude revision in the Basis of Union, if 90 per cent of the General Synod agree, or in the proposed constitution of the United Church, if authorized by the General Synod in collaboration with the Conferences, Associations, and churches.

The Autonomy of the Local Church

The Basis of Union recognizes the full freedom of the congregation. "Each Congregation . . . has the right of retaining or adopting its own charter, constitution, by-laws, and other regulations which it deems essential and proper to its own welfare. This right includes the holding and operation of its own property." (III-H) "The freedom of worship and of education at present enjoyed by the Congregation . . . will be preserved in the United Church. Other freedoms at present enjoyed are not hereby abridged." (III-I) "The constitution . . . shall in no wise abridge the rights now enjoyed by Congregations." (III-F) These commitments covering both the Basis of Union and the proposed constitution are central. The God-given freedom of the covenant fellowship is clearly acknowledged.

Is this freedom limited in the Basis of Union by the proposed grant of autonomy in their "own sphere"—to Associations, Conferences, and the General Synod? The categorical statements about the freedom of the congregation noted above offer assurance that the wider agencies of the churches may not invade the sphere of congregational autonomy.

The Authority of the Local Church

The essential democracy of our churches derives from the authority vested in the whole fellowship of the congregation under Christ, and in the responsibility of the wider agencies to the whole fellowship of congregations. Would the Basis of Union alter, in the proposed government of the United Church, this traditional democracy? The government would be "exercised through Congregations, Associations, Conferences, and the General Synod in such wise that the autonomy of each is respected in its own sphere, each having its own rights and responsibilities." (III-F) The meaning of this section seems clearer when seen in the context of other sections. "The basic unit of organization . . . is the Congregation." (III-A) The Congregations would as now directly organize Associations (III-B), and constitute Conferences (III-C), and indirectly, through the Conferences, constitute the General Synod (III-D). While the Basis of Union does not specifically so state, the Associations and Conferences would presumably be responsible to the Congregations, and the General Synod to the Conferences, just as "officers, boards, councils, commissions, committees, departments, agencies, and instrumentalities are responsible to the bodies that elect them." (III-E)

Furthermore, the proposed extension of authority to the wider agencies of the churches beyond that already delegated in present practice appears limited. "Individual communicants have the right of appeal, complaint, or reference to their Congregations, Associations, Conferences, and ultimately to the General Synod. Ministers, Congregations, Associations, and Conferences have similar rights of appeal, complaint, or reference. Decisions rendered in consequence of such appeals, complaints, or references, are advisory, not mandatory." (III-G) The advisory character of these so-called "decisions" would not seem to negate the fundamental principle of our polity; they would not contravene the principle enunciated by the Planning Committee for the International Congregational Council, "that in all the organization of the church at every level, all authority is spiritual or, as our fathers put it, ministerial, not legalistic, coercive, or magisterial."

The Responsibility of the Laity

The priesthood of all believers is another guiding principle of Congregational polity. It is reflected in the institution of the church meeting, as the ultimate human authority in the church. Negatively, it is expressed in traditional fears over a clergy-dominated church. The Basis of Union recognizes the responsible role of the layman. The democracy of the local congregation is clearly declared by Article III-H, cited above. The Associations are to be organized, and the Conferences constituted, by Congregations, "through their ministers and through delegates elected from their membership." (III-B, C) The General Synod likewise is to be constituted by Conferences, "through delegates elected by them from the membership and ministers of the Congregations." (III-D) This emphasis on equality within the church is also reflected in the principle of Article III-J: "Men and women enjoy the same rights and privileges in the United Church. It is recommended that at least one-third of the members of the national administrative bodies be women."

The Freedom of the Minister

The direct relationship between pastor and congregation is a cherished part of our heritage. Two commitments of the Basis of Union are clear. "In all relationships between minister and local church or Congregation, the freedom of the minister and the autonomy of the church are presupposed." "Ministers and churches desiring to maintain a system of pastoral placement in which the Conference or Association shall have little or no part, shall be free, to do so." (VI-C) The Article also sets forth, however, a "recommended standard of denominational procedure" to be urged upon churches and ministers, involving approval by the Association or Conference before a minister is called or dismissed. What effect the proposed appeal to the ministers and Congregations might have on their freedom remains to be seen.

Similar "standard methods" are proposed for ordination and induction, namely, "by authority of the Conference or Association at the request of the Congregation." (VI-A) These are proposed, not for the interim period when current procedures would prevail, but as provisions in the constitution. The use of the terms "standard" and "normal" in this connection seems by implication to preserve the right of the local church to call a council of the vicinage.

Membership in the Local Church

Article VII provides that "men, women, and children shall be admitted into the fellowship of the United Church through baptism and profession of faith according to the custom and usage of each congregation prior to the union. When they shall have been admitted, they shall be recognized as members of the United Church." This last sentence makes it fairly clear that admission to the covenant fellowship of the local church would continue as heretofore, but would carry with it recognition of membership in the wider fellowship.

This Article also contains the statement that "all persons who are members of either communion at the time of the union shall be members of the United Church." This statement requires qualification, since in our communion each local church would need to decide whether to participate in the new fellowship. It means that all members would be carried over into the new fellowship unless their churches voted to sever their connection with it. The authority as to church membership resides in the congregation.

The Local Church and the Merger Procedure

Since the Basis of Union would affect more than the administrative agencies of the two communions, the decision as to its adoption or rejection by our denomination is placed squarely upon the local churches. They alone have the authority to alter their own polity. If the General Council and Evangelical and Reformed General Synod declare the Basis of Union adopted, all churches of the two denominations will be included in the United Church unless by definite vote a church separates itself from the fellowship. Conscientious consideration of the issues by the largest possible number of churches is indispensable if the decision is to be democratic, and the existing fellowship of our churches conserved.

The General Council will necessarily have to assume authority in judging the mind of our churches with regard to the merger, since no authorized procedure has been established by the local churches. To aid the Council in reaching a judgment, Associations and Conferences as well as local churches have been asked to vote on the Basis of Union. While votes by the Associations and Conferences do not have the same status as votes by local churches, they will help the Council in estimating the sentiment of our churches. This does not lessen the importance, however, of action by every church.

The local churches have the final decision for our denomination as to the adoption of the constitution of the United Church, if and when it is presented. The Basis of Union provides that "the General Synod shall declare it (the constitution) in force when it shall have been ratified by not less than two-thirds of the former Congregational Christian Churches *voting,* and by not less than two-thirds of the former Evangelical and Reformed

Synods." (IV-A) This formulation seemed necessary if a decision were to be reached at all. Its flexible character increases rather than decreases the importance of the whole-hearted participation by local churches, at every stage of the decision, that it may be as representative as possible.

Local churches will retain their own names, using the further title "United Church of Christ" if and as they desire.

Church Union around the World

86. Faith and Order:
"The Edinburgh Conference" and "Affirmation of Union"

(1937)

Willard L. Sperry; Second World Conference on Faith and Order

The Second World Conference on Faith and Order began in Edinburgh on August 3, 1937. It was composed of representatives from 123 churches with 344 delegates, 84 alternates, and 15 Continuation Committee members—in all, 443 persons appointed by their churches—along with 8 guests and 53 members of the youth group, making a total of 504 persons. The conference built upon the euphoric First World Conference on Faith and Order, held in Lausanne in 1927 (see vol. 6:15, 35, 58).

The second conference was divided into four predetermined commissions: (1) the grace of our Lord Jesus Christ; (2) the church of Christ and the world of God; (3) the church of Christ: ministry and sacraments; and (4) the church's unity in life and worship. These commissions were further divided into groups at the conference that worked together for ten days to prepare reports for the plenary. In the end, there were actually five commission reports, because the members of commission 4 asked that a special additional report be given on the "Communion of Saints."

When the groups made their reports, the report of commission 1, on "the grace of our Lord Jesus Christ," stated, "There is in connection with this subject no ground for maintaining division between Churches."

Source: Willard L. Sperry, "The Edinburgh Conference," *Advance,* 1 November 1937, 484–86; "Affirmation of Union," reprinted with the permission of Scribner, a Division of Simon & Schuster, Inc., from *The Second World Conference on Faith and Order,* edited by Leonard Hodgson (New York: The Macmillan Company, 1938), 275–76. [Note: There are various reports about the exact number of persons in attendance.]

Commission 3, on the ministry and the sacraments, was less encouraging. That report highlighted differences that dominated Faith and Order discussions for the next fifty years.

Willard L. Sperry, dean of Harvard Divinity School and a Congregational Christian delegate, agreed with Canon B. H. Streeter that one of the most important functions of such a conference was to educate those who participated. After Edinburgh, Sperry stated, "Church union is no longer an academic 'elective' or an ecclesiastical luxury; it is a spiritual and moral necessity" in response to the critical situation in the mission fields and to the " 'principalities and powers' which live as reasoned systems of unchristian thought in the minds of men."

Sperry was particularly struck by a distinction made about churches in the Edinburgh report. On the one hand, there were "authoritarian" churches, which rest their case for religion upon "a divine givenness in the Scriptures, in orders, in creeds, in worship"; and on the other hand, there were churches more concerned about the "personal," which rest their identity upon "the individual experience of Divine grace as the ruling principle of the 'gathered' Church, in which freedom is both enjoyed as a religious right and enjoined as a religious duty." As Congregational Christian participants grew in their understanding of this distinction, they grew in their capacity to imagine church union with Christians rooted in very different understandings of the church. An eloquent "Affirmation of Union" was heartily adopted by all the participants at the conclusion of the conference.

The Edinburgh Conference

A gleam that points the way
toward mystical experiences of a common life.

[Editor's Note: Dean Sperry, of Harvard Divinity School, in addition to being a representative of the Congregational and Christian Churches in the World Conference on Faith and Order has had a prominent part in the Movement and in the recent Edinburgh Conference as a member of the Executive Committee, and as Chairman of Commission IV, dealing with The Church's Unity in Life and Worship.]

Most Christians are apathetic toward the reunion or further union of the Churches. They are happy in their own Churches and often convinced that their particular communions compass all that is "necessary for salvation." The native provincialism of the human mind, its instinctive fear of the unknown, and its habitual self-righteousness, all put stumbling stones in the way to one Holy Church Universal.

Any one who attended the Edinburgh Conference on Faith and Order must have been disabused of his denominational self-sufficiency. No single Church exhausts the richness of the varieties of Christian experience. The late Canon Streeter (Canon Streeter and his wife were killed in an airplane crash in Switzerland, in September, 1937) said to me, just before I started for Edinburgh, that the main function of ecumenical conferences is to educate those who take part in them. We, who were there, were agreed that our Christian education had been greatly advanced by the experience.

But these world movements, looking to a united Church, are something more than a costly means of educating a few hundred fortunate delegates. They are at the present time witness to a need that is so urgent as to become imperative. Church union is no longer an academic "elective" or an ecclesiastical luxury; it is a spiritual and moral necessity.

That necessity has two origins. It rises, in the first instance, from the critical situation on the mission fields. Divided Christian churches in countries like India and China, where Christians are still an almost negligible minority in the midst of vast non-Christian populations, cannot face and meet, in their divided state, the aggression of the new nationalism, and the secular economics of the time. We are no longer confronted with old, dying religions in the Orient; we are faced by new and powerful religions of political and racial nature. A divided Christian voice is no answer to their challenge.

Furthermore, within Christendom itself, we are now confronted by organized and fully self-conscious theories of race, class, and state which are candidly anti-Christian. Our enemy is no longer the animal man, the old Adam. It is "principalities and powers" which live as reasoned systems of unchristian thought in the minds of men. The Christian Church must achieve, what as yet it lacks, something like a common answer as to its faith and its ethics, which with a single voice may be given in the present perilous situation. United we may stand, but divided we are ineffectual and perhaps in actual danger.

Did the Edinburgh Conference achieve anything? Did it make any advance on the previous Conference held at Lausanne in 1927? In one sense of the word we at Edinburgh did less than might have been expected of us. Technically we were forbidden to "do" anything official. We were met simply to share our experiences and to discuss our differences with a view to overcoming them. The constituent churches appointed and sent delegates on the definite understanding that the Conference was a conference, and not a formal Church council in disguise. We had, therefore to keep faith with those who had come, and steadily to resist the temptation to assume anything like authority.

Personally, I do not think I ever spent a fortnight in any Church gathering in which there was more deliberate patience, more honest effort to achieve imagination, and less suggestion of ecclesiastical politics at work behind the scenes. The occasion was fully democratic, and the fact that it was kept so is due in no small part to the Christian humility and charity of its wise presiding officer, the Archbishop of York.

Albert Schweitzer on his return to his African mission, after his first furlough found his work disorganized and in sad disrepair. He set manfully about reorganizing it, but said, "The prose of Africa is heavy on me, and it will be a long time before it passes." The statement implies that his first term in Africa had been the poetry of his missionary life. Lausanne was the "poetry" of church union, our first, clear, modern glimpse of the ideal. Edinburgh was its "prose." It was none the less true on that account and none the less important. Every great religious movement passes from its apostolic to its sub-apostolic age. Not until it has lived through its second period can it know whether its initial vision was merely a sentimental hope—"such stuff as dreams are made of"—or an insight into the eternal reality of things.

We came away from Edinburgh convinced that while, in many of its technical aspects, the problem of Church Union will prove more difficult than we had at first expected, there is already existing a widespread and genuine spiritual Christian unity among us, and that this fact is our warrant for going on with the task. Furthermore, we bowed our heads to the simple and oft-repeated statement that "God wills unity." How can believers in one God think otherwise? Delegates who had been at both Conferences were agreed that in its earnest and honest "prose" attack upon the problem Edinburgh marked a great advance on Lausanne. We now know better than we have ever known before what the issue is, as between the various Churches, and we can see what must be done even though we do not see at the moment how to do it.

The ecumenical (world-wide) movements of Christianity have outgrown the earlier assumption of such projects, that it may be possible to find some minimum of faith and practice on which we can all agree, and build the reunited Church on that basis. The trouble with this suggestion is that it is itself irreligious. Religion is not a minimal view of life, it is the maximum view. The moment you begin trimming down your beliefs or your ethics you destroy their religious spirit. In a reunited Church each constituent body must be allowed to keep to the full its faith and practice. Nothing characteristic of any denomination must be left out, all must be included if the ideal of a "universal" Church is to be realized.

The Lausanne meeting took form, as an inspired thought, in the mind of Bishop Brent when he was attending the great missionary gathering held in Edinburgh in 1910. He then conceived the World Conference on Faith and Order. Let us give honor where honor is due. The vision first came to a member of the Anglican communion, and most of the patient, preparatory work was done by members of that communion. It was not a Congregationalist who set the process in motion. The Anglican Church—both in England and America—has been from that time to this active in the leadership of the Movement. Its presiding officer and its executive secretary have been for some years, and still are, prominent English churchmen. In this country it has been our own Episcopal Church which has been most zealous in behalf of the cause. These facts have inevitably given to the terms in which the issues are stated an Anglican coloring, which all concerned have now come to recognize. They have, further, led in many quarters to the suspicion that the Faith and Order Movement is, to use a vernacular description, an attempt "to get us all into the Episcopal Church."

I have been a member of the Executive Committee of the Movement in recent years, sharing, therefore, in many of the preliminary meetings which preceded the full session at Edinburgh. As a Congregationalist, I should like to state with conviction that our Anglican leaders are fully aware of the suspicions to which their official prominence in the Movement gives rise, and are earnestly anxious to make the Movement fully and freely interdenominational. The situation has been mentioned openly and often, and officially the Movement has no interest furthering Anglican and Episcopalian interests to the neglect of the equal place and claims of other Churches. If we Congregationalists do not take our rightful place in the Church Union program, the fault is our own. There is no least desire to exclude us, and every wish that we shall be included. Many private and wholly candid conversations with the Archbishop of York have set my mind at rest on this point. I feel that I have only myself to blame if I do not work with him.

Meanwhile the technical difference between the Anglican Church and the non-Anglican Churches has furnished one of the talking points of both the Lausanne and the Edinburgh Conferences. There is, superficially at least, more theological agreement among evangelical Churches than we might suppose. To their surprise the delegates at Edinburgh found substantial unity on the question of the "grace of God" Our differences—at least those which are most apparent—concern our several conceptions of the nature of the Church and its ministry. How is a man properly ordained to the Christian ministry? The Episcopal Churches, and with them others like the Greek Orthodox, require ordination at the hands of a bishop. Others of us defend Presbyterian or Congregational ordination. This matter has been under constant discussion, and, in spite of many mediating proposals, such as the South India Plan, is still a difficulty.

We Congregationalists who have been familiar for some years with tentative proposals back and forth with Episcopalians as to the possibility of closer union are accustomed to think that the Episcopalians are the only Church people who will not recognize our Congregational ordination. It came to me as something of a surprise and shock to learn that neither does the newly reunited Church of Scotland recognize our orders. If any one of us wished to become minister of a parish in the Church of Scotland, he would have to be reordained. The Episcopal demand that a man have ordination by a bishop is for us the most familiar instance of the technical difficulty in the path toward reunion or further union. No one of us, as a Congregational minister, could submit to such reordination if the rite were intended to imply that in so doing he conceded that his Congregational ordination was inadequate or invalid. Quite naturally, we make this issue a test case. But it is not fair to ask the Episcopal Church to bear what is, from our standpoint, the whole onus of this responsibility. The Church of Scotland thinks of us in much the same way and would require of us what would be for us a meaningless repetition of our ordination.

I am persuaded that this whole question of Episcopal *vs.* non-Episcopal orders is simply one specific statement of a deeper underlying problem, which at Edinburgh we began to grasp for the first time in modern church history. Churches, like individuals, are divided into two types, those in which the conception of religion is in the first instance a matter of outward-mindedness, and those in which it is a matter of inward-mindedness. The Roman Church at one extreme and the Quakers at the other make the distinction plain—a distinction which is blurred in the mid-world where most of us live our Church lives.

We have, in the words of the Edinburgh report, "authoritarian" Churches which rest the case for religion upon "a divine givenness in the Scriptures, in orders, in creeds, in worship." We have, on the other hand, "personal" types of Churches which insist upon "the individual experience of Divine grace as the ruling principle of the 'gathered' Church, in which freedom is both enjoyed as a religious right and enjoined as a religious duty."

The Edinburgh report, as originally drafted, described these Churches as being "objective" and "subjective" in their religious emphasis and their ecclesiastical polity. The words were, very properly I think, cut out of the final report as being too technical and psychological. Nevertheless, they indicate to those who are familiar with such a vocabulary the distinction which we have in mind.

We Congregationalists belong to a "personal" and "gathered" ("where two or three are gathered together") type of Church. For us the individual reception of God's grace, our private right of conscience, our independence and initiative as single congregations lie very near our whole understanding of Christianity. To deprive us, one by one, as individual Christians or single congregations, of this interpretation of our religion would be to impair our whole grasp of our religion. We recognize ourselves as being, in our Churchmanship, "subjective" in our conception of the Church.

We must concede, however, the existence of Churches in which this personal element is not the point of departure and not the chief characteristic of corporate Christian life. There are Churches whose outward-minded, objective, authoritarian conception of something given in the first instance by God is expressed through a papacy or an episcopate. That outward fact exists whether the individual likes it or not, and in the first instance quite independent of his personal appropriation of it.

But this outward-minded authoritarianism is by no means confined to Churches which cherish the institution of the historic episcopate. It exists, in another form, in all those Churches which rest the case for Christianity—its Churches included—upon "the sole authority of Scripture." That phrase was introduced into the Edinburgh report at the insistence of certain of the French Churches of the Continent, who care little for the objective authority of the episcopate, but much for the objective authority of the Bible. I became convinced that, as the member of a "personal" Church, I should have just as much technical difficulty in being formally united to what I felt to be a rather extreme type of Fundamentalism as to an "Episcopal" Church. I can no more accept the old theory of verbal inspiration than I can accept the historic episcopate as the warrant for my ministry.

The Faith and Order Movement must follow this lead given at Edinburgh and attempt something like a comprehensive description of these two types of Churches which emerged from the dust of its discussions. If it prove that the distinction suggested at Edinburgh is faithful to the facts, we have in the corporate and organized life of Christianity a difference with which we have long been in single individuals. There are these two well-recognized human types, with their representation within the field of religious experience. We seem to have in the life of Churches a social duplication of individual types that at are beginning to understand.

Is there any hope of reconciling the outward-minded and the inward-minded types, or must they be set over against each other semipermanently? Apparently in the experience of the saint, the prophet, and the mystic, the contrast and the felt strain between the world within and the world without is relaxed, and men consciously achieve a unified life. I hazard the guess that the success of the cause of Church Union lies, not so much in the prospect of technical readjustments of rival claims, as in the hope of mystical experiences of a common life when we are together with persons of the type other than ourselves. The Edinburgh Conference came, at times, to the verge of such an experience. The gleam points that way.

Affirmation of Union

In Allegiance to Our Lord Jesus Christ,
Adopted by the Conference [at Edinburgh] by a Standing Vote
on 18th August 1937, Nemine Contradicente

The Second World Conference on Faith and Order, held in Edinburgh in August 1937, brought together four hundred and fourteen delegates from one hundred and twenty-two Christian communions in forty-three different countries. The delegates assembled to discuss together the causes that keep Christian communions apart, and the things that unite them in Christian fellowship. The Conference approved the following statement *nemine contradicente:*

We are one in faith in our Lord Jesus Christ, the incarnate Word of God. We are one in allegiance to Him as Head of the Church, and as King of kings and Lord of lords. We are one in acknowledging that this allegiance takes precedence of any other allegiance that may make claims upon us.

This unity does not consist in the agreement of our minds or the consent of our wills. It is founded in Jesus Christ Himself, Who lived, died and rose again to bring us to the Father, and Who through the Holy Spirit dwells in His Church. We are one because we are all the objects of the love and grace of God, and called by Him to witness in all the world to His glorious gospel.

Our unity is of heart and spirit. We are divided in the outward forms of our life in Christ, because we understand differently His will for His Church. We believe, however, that a deeper understanding will lead us towards a united apprehension of the truth as it is in Jesus.

We humbly acknowledge that our divisions are contrary to the will of Christ, and we pray God in His mercy to shorten the days of our separation and to guide us by His Spirit into fulness of unity.

We are thankful that during recent years we have been drawn together;

prejudices have been overcome, misunderstandings removed, and real, if limited, progress has been made towards our goal of a common mind.

In this Conference we may gratefully claim that the Spirit of God has made us willing to learn from one another, and has given us a fuller vision of the truth and enriched our spiritual experience.

We have lifted up our hearts together in prayer; we have sung the same hymns; together we have read the same Holy Scriptures. We recognise in one another, across the barriers of our separation, a common Christian outlook and a common standard of values. We are therefore assured of a unity deeper than our divisions.

We are convinced that our unity of spirit and aim must be embodied in a way that will make it manifest to the world, though we do not yet clearly see what outward form it should take.

We believe that every sincere attempt to co-operate in the concerns of the kingdom of God draws the severed communions together in increased mutual understanding and goodwill. We call upon our fellow Christians of all communions to practise such cooperation; to consider patiently occasions of disunion that they may be overcome; to be ready to learn from those who differ from them; to seek to remove those obstacles to the furtherance of the gospel in thc non-Christian world which arise from our divisions; and constantly to pray for that unity which we believe to be our Lord's will for His Church.

We desire also to declare to all men everywhere our assurance that Christ is the one hope of unity for the world in face of the distractions and dissensions of this present time. We know that our witness is weakened by our divisions. Yet we are one in Christ and in the fellowship of His Spirit. We pray that everywhere, in a world divided and perplexed, men may turn to Jesus Christ our Lord, Who makes us one in spite of our divisions; that He may bind in one those who by many worldly claims are set at variance; and that the world may at last find peace and unity in Him; to Whom be glory for ever.

87. A World Council:
"World Council Constituted," "A Toi La Gloire," and "Ecumenicity in a Village"

(1948–1949)

David D. Baker; Barbara Deitz; and Charles H. Gilbert

On August 23, 1948, delegates from 147 churches and forty-four countries came together to form the most ambitious ecumenical organization in the twentieth century, the World Council of Churches (WCC).

The formation of the WCC is often described as ecumenical streams flowing together into an ongoing river. Initially, the Faith and Order and the Life and Work movements joined to create the WCC. The first assembly had to be postponed because of World War II, but it finally convened in 1948. In 1961, the International Missionary Council joined, and in 1971, so did the World Council of Christian Education.

The idea of a world council was first suggested in an encyclical letter of January 1920 from the Orthodox Ecumenical Patriarchate, or Church of Constantinople. It called "all the churches of Christ everywhere" to a "League of Churches" (Koinonia ton Ekklesion) *similar to the proposal after World War I for a League of Nations. Key Protestant leaders, such as Nathan Söderblom, Lutheran archbishop of Sweden, and J. H. Oldham, a leader of the Life and Work movement and a founder of the International Missionary Council, also called for a global ecumenical organization.*

Source: David D. Baker, "World Council Constituted," *The Messenger,* 14 September 1948, 3–7; Barbara Deitz, "A Toi La Gloire," *The Messenger,* 26 October 1948, 12–14; Charles H. Gilbert, "Ecumenicity in a Village," *Advance,* May 1949, 13–14.

The name for the council was chosen years before the first assembly. At a meeting in July 1937, on the eve of the World Conference on Life and Work in Oxford, and the World Conference on Faith and Order in Edinburgh, representatives of the two movements met in London and proposed to bring the two organizations together and set up a fully representative assembly of Christian churches around the world. In that meeting, a church leader from the United States, Samuel McCrea Cavert, "timidly" suggested the name "World Council of Churches." William Temple, soon to be archbishop of Canterbury, replied, "Why not? This is what we really need and want."

Soon a committee of fourteen was chosen. It met in Utrecht in May 1938, and created a provisional committee to oversee the WCC "in formation." Temple, the archbishop of York and later of Canterbury, was chair, and W. A. Visser 't Hooft, of the Netherlands, was general secretary. Over the next several years, the provisional committee resolved constitutional questions concerning the basis, authority, and structure of the new organization and planned the first World Council of Churches Assembly for August 1941. Unfortunately, because of World War II, the inaugural assembly was not held for another seven years.

Nevertheless, during the war years, a provisional WCC office was set up in Geneva under the leadership of Visser 't Hooft. His office organized a chaplaincy service, contributed to work among prisoners of war, provided assistance to Jews and other refugees, relayed information to the churches, and, by keeping up contacts with Christian leaders on all sides, prepared for postwar reconciliation and interchurch aid. When the delegates finally came together in 1948 in Amsterdam for the long delayed first assembly, they had a strong practical basis for their ecumenical vision.

The 1948 assembly of the World Council of Churches declared: "The World Council of Churches is a fellowship of churches which accept our Lord Jesus Christ as God and Saviour." For those first delegates, the WCC was not itself a church, still less the church universal or an incipient "world church." "They understood the council to be an instrument whereby the churches bear witness together in their common allegiance to Christ, search for that unity which Jesus Christ wills for his one and only church, and co-operate in matters which require common statements and actions." As William Temple declared, "Any authority the Council will have consists in the weight which it carries with the churches by its own wisdom."

Representatives from the Evangelical and Reformed Church and the Congregational Christian Churches who were part of that first assembly in Amsterdam were filled with enthusiasm over what they had experienced. David D. Baker, from the Evangelical and Reformed Church, rejoiced about all those people who had come "from the ends of the earth" to meet together. It was "something new under the sun."

Baker's excitement was echoed by youth delegate Barbara Deitz, whose article "A Toi La Gloire" ("Thine Is the Glory") expressed the wonder of all the participants as they contemplated "a new conception of what God can do as he lives in the hearts of individuals . . . a new understanding of Christian unity and the bond that holds Christians together all over the globe . . . and . . . a new awareness of what . . . unity may mean for the future."

Back home, church people in the United States had a new awareness of their shared unity in Christ as they heard about the World Council of Churches. It was a milestone. However, one Methodist pastor, serving in a Methodist/Congregational federated church in Maine, New York, wrote to Advance *to say that his church was already "a miniature World Council of Churches." Charles H. Gilbert wrote, "I have come to know and work with some of the finest Christians this side heaven. These saints have delightfully human qualities with a certain touch of heaven in them. Some are Methodists and some are Congregationalists; both belong to 'my' church."*

World Council Constituted

Major Christian groups except Roman Catholic and Russian Orthodox unite in world-wide organization

On August 23 in Amsterdam, Holland, the World Council of Churches was officially formed. Approximately 400 delegates of 135 churches from 40 countries voted it into existence in Amsterdam's great *Concert-Gebouw* when they adopted unanimously a resolution presented by Pastor Marc Boegner, of France, declaring the formation of the World Council of Churches "to be and hereby is completed." Thus after ten years as a provisional body due to the hindrances of a world war, the World Council of Churches came into existence. Whereupon, the assembly arose and was led in prayer by the Archbishop of Canterbury who was presiding.

From a seat in the front row of the press gallery of the *Nieuwe Kerk* I looked down on the procession of men and women who had come from the ends of the earth for the opening meeting of the assembly on Sunday, August 22. From New Zealand and New York, from Switzerland and Sweden, from Java and Japan, from France and Germany and the Argentine, from Korea and Czechoslovakia and West Africa; from the Northern Hemisphere and the Southern, from before the iron curtain and from behind it, from the great universities of the Western World and from the cultural centers of the age-old philosophies of the East, in academic robes and the prescribed gowns and headdress of ecclesiastical orders, in the *saris* of the East and the sandals of Africa, the four hundred delegates to the meeting of the World Council of Churches were marching, two abreast, through the aisles of the crowded church. Three thousand persons were gathered in *Nieuwe Kerk* and many thousands more packed the square outside to watch the colorful procession.

Here was something new under the sun. The church which began with a few believers in a remote province of the Roman Empire twenty centuries ago had now been planted in all the earth. To the strains of the anthem, "All people that on earth do dwell," these representatives of the peoples of the earth were witnessing to a common faith in their common Lord. Hearts were beating as one to the words of St. Paul, read by Dr. K. H. E. Gravemeyer, of the Reformed Church of the Netherlands, "God, who commanded the light to shine out of darkness, hath shined in our hearts, to give the light of the knowledge of the glory of God in the face of Jesus Christ." And the deep-seated hope of the assembly voiced in prayer by the Archbishop of Canterbury was a common hope, "O Lord of heaven and earth, who hast promised to reveal thy glory of Jesus Christ among all nations, remember, we beseech thee, thy holy church throughout all the world. Unite all who profess and call themselves Christians in the bond of a living faith as the body of Christ."

It was fitting that the opening address of the first meeting of the World Council of Churches should be delivered by John R. Mott. For sixty years this Christian citizen of the world has been helping to weave the fabric of humanity in the pattern of Jesus Christ. He sketched the past, running over the landmarks of previous world Christian gatherings. He paid tribute to the great prophets of a united Christendom who have gone on before. And then he looked to the present and future. "I have never known such a time of open doors," he declared. "I would find it impossible to mention a door which I honestly think and believe—note my language—is closed today to the friendly ministry of Jesus Christ."

Following Mott, came a minister from a Methodist Church on the island of Ceylon, Dr. D. T. Niles. Catching up Dr. Mott's idea of open doors, he declared that "the Christian witness recognizes no barrier and allows no partiality." In insisting upon our Christian task as a world task, he specifically stressed that "we are witnesses to the Negro in the same way as to the white. We are witnesses within the Western democracies as well as the Eastern republics. We are witnesses among peoples of all religions and no religion. We are witnesses among the outcaste, the refugee, the displaced person—witnesses unto the uttermost part of the earth."

Monday and Tuesday, following the opening and organizational meetings, were given over to presentation of the major areas of study to which leaders of the churches have been giving profound attention for the past two years in preparation for these two weeks.

The addresses introducing the areas of study were profound. Simply to mention the names of the men and women who delivered them is to call the roll of some of the great Christian scholars of the world church: Prof. Karl Barth, of the University of Basel; Prof. C. H. Dodd, of the University of Cambridge; Prof. C. T. Craig, of Yale; Prof. Georges Florovsky, of the Academy of Orthodox Theology, Paris; Prof. R. Prenter, of the University of Aarhus, Aarhus, Denmark; Bishop Stephen Neill, Assistant Bishop to the Archbishop of Canterbury; Prof. T. C. Chao, of Yenching University, Peiping, China; Mrs. Kathleen Bliss, editor of the *Christian News Letter,* London; Prof. Jacques Ellul, of Bordeaux, France; Mr. John Foster Dulles, of the United States, and Prof. Joseph Hromadka, of the John Hus Theological Faculty, Prague, Czechoslovakia. The themes on which these scholars spoke were the headings under which the assembly has been divided into sections for study and discussion and for formulation of statement:

I. The Universal Church in God's Design

II. God's Design and the Church's Witness

III. The Church and the Disorder of Society

IV. The Church and the International Disorder

Because of his eminent position in the theological world, Dr. Barth's words were heard with profound respect by the assembly. He suggested that the over-all theme of the Amsterdam meeting "Man's Disorder and God's Design" ought to be considered in the reverse order—that we first seek God's kingdom and his righteousness so that all we need in relation to the world's disorder may be added unto us. Modern man, he said, must guard against forgetting that human existence has no meaning without faith in a transcendent truth, goodness and love which man himself has not created and by which he can only let himself be bound. He then went on to clarify the term "God's Design," pointing out that it did not mean the existence of the church visible in the world, or "something like a Christian

Marshall Plan." It was the plan of God himself high above all our Christian ecclesiastical life. Barth deplored that in the material prepared for the assembly there were too few reminders of the living Christ, of the already founded kingdom, the already established reconciliation of the world, the Holy Spirit and even the glorious second coming of Christ.

That this Amsterdam assembly is a meeting of great minds with differing conceptions of eternal truth was evident as one address followed another. Barth's emphasis was countered, for example, by that of Mrs. Bliss. The church's task begins, she said, "by declaring even when men begin to despair of society that the struggle to build societies is part of God's purpose for men, that God *meant* men to explore the treasures of the universe and use its riches, that he intended them to work and find satisfaction in the work, meant them to trade and build, to make laws, to govern and to be governed." "If with the blinkers off we could look anew at the tragedy of our society, which is going to live in disorder perhaps for decades," she concluded, "we might see that the renewal of the church and the renewal of society come from one source, from the healing power of the love of God operating through men in open and courageous encounter with the world."

The presentation of areas of discussion came to climax of interest in the addresses of Mr. Dulles and Prof. Hromadka, the former being an adviser on foreign affairs to the leaders of the Republican Party in the United States and the latter a member of the Central Action Committee of Czechoslovakia—both of them world Christians. These leaders from opposite sides of the iron curtain agreed on some things. The Christian church and its members have a special responsibility in the present divided world. Another war would be futile. Mr. Dulles even admitted that there are some similarities between the social and economic ends that Communists profess and those that Christians seek. But Mr. Dulles deplored Communism's rejection of the concept of moral law and its denial of human rights.

Admitting that modern Communism carries in itself many perils for the sacredness of human personality and the majesty of justice and love, Prof. Hromadka declared that Communism represents, "although under an atheistic form, much of the social impetus of the living church." The church's task, he insisted, is to summon all her members and others to "make a new beginning, to start from the bottom and to work for a new society, a new order, that will stand in some continuity with the past, but which, however, will in a more adequate way respond to the real needs of the present moment and reflect more genuinely the invisible glory and majesty of the Crucified and Risen."

Mr. Dulles pleaded for the churches to "expose the evil of war and its futility," declaring that "another world war would engulf all humanity in utter misery and make almost impossible the achievement of the good ends for which, no doubt, the combatants would profess to be fighting." While Communist power now limits what can be done internationally, Mr. Dulles went on, those limits have not nearly been approached. "If we will do what now is possible, in a spirit of universal brotherhood, we can be sure that present limits will constantly recede. They cannot withstand such unifying influences as we can thus set in motion." And Mr. Dulles saw in this opportunity for Christian action the necessity for just what the churches of the world are now doing in establishing this World Council of Churches. "If, in the international field, Christians are to play their clearly indicated part," he declared, "the churches must have better organization. They should be able to speak more impressively with greater unity. They should put more emphasis on Christianity as a world religion, remembering that God gave his Son because he loved the world, not merely the West."

Introductions over, the assembly broke up into sections. At this writing it is devoting itself to discussion of the issues in the light of the wealth of material that has been prepared so carefully during these past two years. Reports of the sections will be heard by the assembly in plenary sessions again next week, and statements will be issued before adjournment, which, it is prayerfully hoped by millions on all the continents, will help men to know and to follow the design of God for his troubled world.

A Toi La Gloire

In whatever language, the youth delegates at Amsterdam expressed appreciation of eternal perspectives.

"A Toi La Gloire" will ever re-echo in my mind as the song of the youth section at Amsterdam, as I remember the many times we fervently sang its words of praise, "Thine is the glory." It symbolizes, to some extent, the spirit of earnestness and humility with which we youth delegates approached our work as advisers to the Youth Department Committee of the World Council of Churches. Actually, we were the guests of the assembly, for we had no voice or vote in the official proceedings; but we tried to make our witness to the total group by our insistence on democratic procedures in the Youth Department activities, and our desire to build fully committed Christian lives as the true foundation for the ecumenical church.

The youth section was in some ways more representative than the delegate group at the World Council assembly. There were one hundred young people from about forty-five countries—three more countries than the delegates represented! We also boasted of the fact that one-third of our group were women, which fact may indicate something for the future World Council meetings, since there were only fifteen women among the 352 delegates at this 1948 meeting. The sixteen young people from the United States constituted the largest group in the youth section. There were two each from the Evangelical and Reformed, the Methodist and the Episcopal Churches; and one each from the Northern Baptist Convention, Society of Friends, Church of the Brethren, Disciples of Christ, Congregational Christian, Evangelical-United Brethren, Presbyterian U. S. A., Presbyterian, U. S. and Lutheran Churches. Although we represented our denominations first, we, in a sense, represented all the Christian youth of the United States, since many of us were chosen because of our background in interdenominational work.

Under the leadership of Jean Frazer, secretary of the Youth Department, the youth section met two days before the assembly opened in order to have time to get acquainted with each other, and to hear of the work of the Youth Department throughout the past year. We had a unique opportunity to develop friendships and to build a cooperative spirit because we lived and ate together in a Dutch youth hostel. The members of the Dutch ecumenical youth groups were very good to us in welcoming us to the youth hostel, and guiding our confused wanderings on the Amsterdam trams! And many times we were rescued by a kind Dutchman when we couldn't make a taxi driver understand our pronounciation of *Lauriergracht,* the name of the street where we lived!

We sat together as a youth section at all main sessions and plenary meetings of the assembly, and we had a vantage point on the platform behind the speakers' heads, but in full view of the delegates seated on the main floor. We participated in all the worship services of the assembly, and we sang as a choir on a few occasions.

At the same time that the delegates were busy with their commission discussions and committee reports, we held our own study groups on the same topics. The reports from our four groups were not voted on by youth plenary sessions, but were only received as the work of particular groups to be passed on to the proper delegates' study commissions. Many of us had the feeling that the youth reports were given scant consideration by the delegates; even so, our work was certainly not in vain, for just the fact that we discussed these topics, aired our opinions, learned from each other, and crystallized everything on paper means that a process of growth and maturing was going on for every one of us each day of the assembly.

Our first group on "The Universal Church" was not so concerned with definitions of the church as with the task of renewing the church. It felt that unity can come only after renewal, which will come by keeping the church Christ-centered. The group affirmed the necessity for a renewal in theology, especially by the churches studying each other from the viewpoint that no theology is infallible.

Section II, studying "The Church's Witness to God's Design," felt that, in order for the church to fulfill its missionary task, it must seek to identify itself with and take a vital interest in the whole life and environment of the people to whom it proclaims the gospel message. This would involve a study of the non-Christian religions, and of modern ideologies which are coming to have a semireligious manifestation, so that the gospel may be presented in a language more relevant and meaningful to the hearer. This group felt that the task of taking the gospel to the workers in industrial areas was one of the most vital challenges confronting young Christians today. They acknowledged the work rendered by the YWCA and YMCA, and believed that these associations should be used by the Christian community in the service of evangelism, particularly in non-Christian lands where other means of communication are difficult.

"The Church and the Disorder of Society" was studied from the point of view of the failure of the church to keep alive to the social and economic changes now taking place all over the world. The need for repentance was deeply felt by this group who believed the church has all too often acquiesced in un-Christian attitudes, such as racial segregation and discrimination, and in class distinctions, and has lent support to international war, thus adding to the disorder of society. The task of the church must be to build a strong sense of community among its members to counteract the depersonalization of our industrial society, and to build a deeper sense of "Christian vocation" in each church member. The group was convinced that there is a Christian witness which can be made in the profession or job where one finds oneself, by the fellowship and cooperation in love which the Christian can manifest to his fellow worker.

Group IV on "The Church and the International Disorder" was clear that "disorder and chaos will be inevitable until the nations learn to discern God's design in the salvation which is freely offered in Jesus Christ." This lays the responsibility on the churches which, by their proclamation of the gospel, will help to bring about international order. The churches must constantly proclaim the Word of God that transcends national, racial or ideological barriers, and stems directly from the Bible. "Christians need to be made more aware of the tension created between moral claims of a sovereign God, and the political claims of a sovereign state." While realizing that relations between nations are necessarily regulated by the use of power, Christians must proclaim its corrupting influence when it is not controlled by international law.

In the youth plenary sessions, many felt that the most important item of business was to ratify the constitution of the World Christian Youth Commission, a cooperative instrument set up in July by representatives of the World's YWCA, YMCA, the World's Student Christian Federation, the World Council of Christian Education, and the Youth Department of the World Council of Churches. This instrument will help to further cooperation on the world level between those organizations concerned with Christian youth, who can recognize their underlying unity in their common determination to proclaim the lordship of Jesus Christ over all realms of life.

In general, the youth delegates looked at issues *as Christians,* rather than as members of a particular denominational group. Of course, differences in church background did come to the front at times, and we were always conscious that we came from a great variety of confessions and denominations. But it was in this very fact, in the tragedy of our deep traditional differences, that we saw our unity. We all knew, deep down within us, that our common loyalty to Jesus Christ was the only thing that could transcend our human differences and draw us closer together. We sensed, somehow, that we must speak *as Christian youth* to the world, if we are ever to understand what our Christianity means for the world.

Our opportunity to live together as a youth delegation brought us many occasions to have informal "bull sessions" and to make friendships with "kindred spirits"—other young people from distant parts, all concerned about the same problems. Actually, it is not the decisions we made in commission study groups, important as they may be, but the friendships we made and the experiences and thoughts we shared with other Christian young people that we will cherish long after Amsterdam's written reports are forgotten.

We American young people especially benefit by getting away from our own prosperous, self-satisfied type of Christianity and coming face to face with Christian youth who struggle in countries with overwhelming majorities of non-Christians and who have a strength and conviction we sadly lack. Amsterdam will mean to us, particularly, a new conception of what God can do as he lives in the hearts of individuals. It will mean a new understanding of Christian unity and the bond that holds Christians together all over the globe, each working in his own way. And, in the years to come, it will bring a new awareness of what the fact of our unity may mean for the future of our individual, local churches and our lives together.

Ecumenicity in a Village

How church union really works

Ours is a miniature world Council of Churches. Our Federated Church has been a practical, functioning concern for years. Ours is a smaller world than Amsterdam's, but it is our world. Names on our rolls indicate Polish, French, German and Armenian ancestries. Our culture is a blending of old New England settlers and new industrial workers, an active college dean, the head of an art department, a former Hollywood star and operatic singer, some excellent potato growers, competent dairymen, a florist, a school principal and teachers and just plain people. Our participating denominations are two: Congregational and Methodist. Our town has also a non-participating fundamentalist group and also a Roman Catholic group—just like Amsterdam!

I like to think that what has just been done on a world scale is here epitomized in our local Federated Church. This is our standing witness to the fine thing that was done in Amsterdam. For that reason my opinion is that our federation has more than a temporary value. It is a testimony.

This is written with full knowledge of paragraph 276 of the Methodist *Discipline:* "An effective denominational church serving every rural community is our primary objective. Federated and union churches have afforded expedient temporary service as acceptable alternatives in some fields but should obtain denominational entity as soon as possible. Mutual exchange, denominational withdrawal, and affiliated membership are among the methods found helpful."

If denominational boards could just play checkers with church members, there is a town to the north of us with a small Methodist and a small Congregational society. They are linked together in an "Association" instead of a federation like ours. Half the year they all go to one end of the village to church; the other half the year they go to the other. The denominational boards could just do some swapping and come out with "denominational entity" in each of our towns just close up Methodism in the northern town, and the Congregationalists in ours.

Just like that! Only neither Methodists nor Congregationalists are checkers. The very loyalties that make good church members make people too deeply rooted to shift readily from one denomination to another. Why try to take away their denominational tag? Let them work together.

So here we are classified, I hope, as one of the "acceptable alternatives in some fields." We are not even trying to attain "denominational entity." Neither denomination loses anything by this arrangement as can be ascertained in both year books. We work together arm in arm, partake of the same elements, baptize at the same altar, unite with whichever church we like at the same communion table. We pray the same prayers, study together in the same Sunday school classes. At the annual Fourth Quarterly Conference of the Methodist Society recently the Congregational women took it on themselves to serve the covered dish supper to Methodists so the Methodist women could attend the business meetings. When the annual meeting of the Congregational society came along it was a joyous thing to see the Methodist women taking full charge of the dining room.

The Methodist people are perfectly happy in the former Congregational building. I say former, because when the Methodist edifice burned two years ago the Congregational people invited the Methodists to use their house of worship. The result was that when the Methodists collected their insurance, it happened to be the same amount the Congregational church building and grounds was appraised at. So the Methodists put their money into a federation with the Congregationalists and now it is federated property.

The two societies agreed that the minister should live in the Methodist parsonage and the federation takes care of the upkeep. The Congregational parsonage remains the property of the Congregational society and the Methodists have nothing to do with it. Neither Methodists nor Congregationalists have their tongues in their cheeks over this federation; they want it to work, and it is working.

Not that all the machinery of operation is perfect. It seems to me some more simple arrangement could be effected. When money is needed for some special project I have to stop and think which treasury to approach: the Methodist church treasury, or trustee treasury, or the Congregational church treasury, or the Federated Council treasury which handles the Improvement and Current Expense funds. But changes are not made overnight. If anyone thinks twenty years of working together as a federation is a temporary expedient, let him try to change something from the way it was set up at the time of federating. "We have always done it this way!"

My head has always been under too small roofs. I never knew anything about other denominations before. My Methodism was quite sufficient to keep me busy and I never bothered to cooperate much with other churches. I'd mind my business and let them mind theirs. But being pastor of this Federated Church has compelled me to get interested in the church of my New England ancestors. It must have been an enriching experience for those who attended the World Council in Amsterdam. It is enriching to me to read the monumental book, *Man's Disorder and God's Design* which came out of Amsterdam. I'm beginning to see the church in new light.

My mail is voluminous. After looking it all over for usable suggestions I consign about the usual proportions of both denominational matter to the waste basket. I can't use everything that comes along. I can't do everything that these two great denominations would like to have done. I'm still only one minister!

But when the Congregational *ADVANCE* comes along I devour it. Fortunately I can do it before the next issue comes next month. It has been exciting watching the merger and the antimerger forces at work. I took delight in leading my people to vote for the merger one hundred per cent and voted for it myself at the Association meeting. We Methodists aren't quite so much afraid of the bugbear to Congregationalists: "losing our local autonomy." In spite of Methodism's centralization we have been moving in the direction of more local autonomy than we in local churches have known what to do with. And I find it not always easy to get our Congregationalists to use the local autonomy they are afraid of losing!

My Methodist *Christian Advocate* comes so fast I never get it read through unless I'm sick abed! But I skim it. And the Congregational *Ministers' Quarterly* I find very helpful and stimulating. Then one day last year I read that the Congregationalists had come out with a *Book of Worship* similar to our Methodist volume, only more compact.

From a communion service in this new book I have made a mimeographed adaptation for use in our federation. I noted that the service in our Congregational book was adapted in part from the Methodist *Book of Worship.* My local adaptation was used first at the January communion service and judging from the comments it was an enrichment to both our peoples.

I have come to know and work with some of the finest Christians this side heaven. These saints have delightfully human qualities with a certain touch of heaven in them. Some are Methodists and some are Congregationalists; both belong to "my" church.

One big advantage of this arrangement is that no one dare get mad enough at the Methodists to quit and join the Congregationalists.

One of the finest young men in college is a Congregationalist. He's just the kind we Methodist ministers are on the watch for to lead into the ministry. And this young man did change his course from pre-medical to pre-theological. I was aware that there must be certain procedures he should go through. I almost itched to get him licensed as a local preacher in the Methodist church and introduce him to our Annual Conference! But I'm really trying to be fair to both sides of this federation and so I learned what had to be done, introduced this young man to our Credentials Committee, and subsequently had the pleasure of taking him to the Association and introducing him there to "placed in the care of the Association."

It was a great day when that happened. I suggested to our Congregational people that they elect his mother a delegate to that Association. So in my car that day was this boy and his mother. Some day he will go to theological seminary, will apply for licensure and eventually there will be a Congregational minister born and reared in the Congregational fold of a Federated Church who took his first step under the direction of a Methodist pastor.

The World Council of Churches in Amsterdam, Holland, needs its witnesses in small American communities. Here is one in the Church of Maine, New York. Come and see us when you are near Binghamton!

88. Ecclesiology for the World:

"The Church, the Churches and the World Council of Churches (Toronto Statement)"

(1950)

When the World Council of Churches was founded in 1948, it gave reassurances that it had no power to legislate for the churches. Its effectiveness depended on the truth and wisdom of its work. Within a few years, churches began to ask for more clarification—not simply on the powers of the WCC, but on what it meant for a church to belong to such a council.

This was no small task. Churches define themselves as churches in many different ways. It was important for the WCC to develop an ecclesiology that would strengthen its own work and yet not do violence to the diverse understandings of the Christian church held by its members.

At a meeting in Toronto in 1950, a statement on "The Church, the Churches and the World Council of Churches" was received by the Central Committee and commended for study and comment to the churches. The statement did two things: it acknowledged that the WCC "deals in provisional ways with divisions between existing Churches which ought not to be because they contradict the very nature of the Church"; and it recognized that there was a place in the WCC "for those churches which recognize other churches as churches in the full and true sense, and for those which do not." Even if member churches might not be able to accept each other as true and pure churches, when they joined the WCC they had

---

Source: "The Church, the Churches and the World Council of Churches: The Ecclesiological Significance of the World Council of Churches," in *Documents on Christian Unity: Fourth Series, 1948–57,* ed. G. K. A. Bell (London: Oxford University Press, 1958), 215–23.

decided not to remain in isolation, but to come together to explore their differences in mutual respect, trusting in the Holy Spirit. The "Toronto Statement" set a new tone for ecumenical relationships around the world. It helped the Congregational Christian Churches and the Evangelical and Reformed Church see themselves in the larger context of the global ecumenical movement.

I. Introduction

The first Assembly at Amsterdam adopted a resolution on "the authority of the Council" which read:

> The World Council of Churches is composed of Churches which acknowledge Jesus Christ as God and Saviour. They find their unity in Him. They do not have to create their unity; it is the gift of God. But they know that it is their duty to make common cause in the search for the expression of that unity in work and in life. The Council desires to serve the Churches, which are its constituent members, as an instrument whereby they may bear witness together to their common allegiance to Jesus Christ, and co-operate in matters requiring united action. But the Council is far from desiring to usurp any of the functions which already belong to its constituent Churches, or to control them, or to legislate for them, and indeed is prevented by its constitution from doing so. Moreover, while earnestly seeking fellowship in thought and action for all its members, the Council disavows any thought of becoming a single unified church structure independent of the Churches which have joined in constituting the Council, or a structure dominated by a centralized administrative authority.
>
> The purpose of the Council is to express its unity in another way. Unity arises out of the love of God in Jesus Christ, which, binding the constituent Churches to Him, binds them to one another. It is the earnest desire of the Council that the Churches may be bound closer to Christ and therefore closer to one another. In the bond of His love, they will desire continually to pray for one another and to strengthen one another, in worship and in witness, bearing one another's burdens and so fulfilling the law of Christ.

This statement authoritatively answered some of the questions which had arisen about the nature of the Council. But it is clear that other questions are now arising and some attempt to answer them must be made, especially in the face of a number of false or inadequate conceptions of the Council which are being presented.

II. The Need for Further Statement

The World Council of Churches represents a new and unprecedented approach to the problem of inter-church relationships. Its purpose and nature can be easily misunderstood. So it is salutary that we should state more clearly and definitely what the World Council is and what it is not.

This more precise definition involves certain difficulties. It is not for nothing that the Churches themselves have refrained from giving detailed and precise definitions of the nature of the Church. If this is true of them, it is not to be expected that the World Council can easily achieve a definition which has to take account of all the various ecclesiologies of its member Churches. The World Council deals in a provisional way with divisions between existing Churches which ought not to be because they contradict the very nature of the Church. A situation such as this cannot be met in terms of well established precedents. The main problem is how one can formulate the ecclesiological implications of a body in which so many different conceptions of the Church are represented, without using the categories or language of one particular conception of the Church.

In order to clarify the notion of the World Council of Churches it will be best to begin by a series of negations so as to do away at the outset with certain misunderstandings which may easily arise or have already arisen, because of the newness and unprecedented character of the underlying conception.

III. What the World Council of Churches Is Not

1. *The World Council of Churches is not and must never become a Super-Church.*

It is not a Super-Church. It is not the World Church. It is not the Una Sancta of which the Creeds speak. This misunderstanding arises again and again although it has been denied as clearly as possible in official pronouncements of the Council. It is based on complete ignorance of the real situation within the Council. For if the Council should in any way violate its own constitutional principle, that it cannot legislate or act for its member Churches, it would cease to maintain the support of its membership.

In speaking of "member Churches," we repeat a phrase from the Constitution of the World Council of Churches; but membership in the Council does not in any sense mean that the Churches belong to a body which can make decisions for them. Each Church retains the constitutional right to ratify or to reject utterances or actions of the Council. The "authority" of the Council consists only "in the weight which it carries with the Churches by its own wisdom" (William Temple).

2. *The purpose of the World Council of Churches is not to negotiate unions between Churches, which can only be done by the Churches themselves acting on their own initiative, but to bring the Churches into living contact with each other and to promote the study and discussion of the issues of church unity.*

By its very existence and its activities the Council bears witness to the necessity of a clear manifestation of the oneness of the Church of Christ. But it remains the right and duty of each Church to draw from its ecumenical experience such consequences as it feels bound to do on the basis of its own convictions. No Church, therefore, need fear that the Council will press it into decisions concerning union with other Churches.

3. *The World Council cannot and should not be based on any one particular conception of the Church. It does not prejudge the ecclesiological problem.*

It is often suggested that the dominating or underlying conception of the Council is that of such a Church or such and such a school of theology. It may well be that at a certain particular conference or in a particular utterance one can find traces of the strong influence of a certain tradition or theology.

The Council as such cannot possibly become the instrument of one confession or school without losing its very *raison d'être*. There is room and space in the World Council for the ecclesiology of every Church which is ready to participate in the ecumenical conversation and which takes its stand on the Basis of the Council, which is "a fellowship of churches which accept our Lord Jesus Christ as God and Saviour."

The World Council exists in order that different Churches may face their differences, and therefore no Church is obliged to change its ecclesiology as a consequence of membership in the World Council.

4. *Membership in the World Council of Churches does not imply that a Church treats its own conception of the Church as merely relative.*

There are critics, and not infrequently friends, of the ecumenical movement who criticize or praise it for its alleged inherent latitudinarianism. According to them the ecumenical movement stands for the fundamental equality of all Christian doctrines and conceptions of the Church and is, therefore, not concerned with the question of truth. This misunderstanding is due to the fact that ecumenism has in the minds of these persons become identified with certain particular theories about unity which have indeed played a role in ecumenical history but which do not represent the common view of the movement as a whole, and have never been officially endorsed by the World Council.

5. *Membership in the World Council does not imply the acceptance of a specific doctrine concerning the nature of church unity.*

The Council stands for church unity. But in its midst there are those who conceive unity wholly or largely as a full consensus in the realm of doctrine, others who conceive of it primarily as sacramental communion based on common church order, others who consider both indispensable, others who would only require unity in certain fundamentals of faith and order, again others who conceive the one Church exclusively as a universal spiritual fellowship, or hold that visible unity is unessential or even undesirable. But none of these conceptions can be called the ecumenical theory. The whole point of the ecumenical conversation is precisely that all these conceptions enter into dynamic relations with each other.

In particular, membership in the World Council does not imply acceptance or rejection of the doctrine that the unity of the Church consists in the unity of the invisible Church. Thus the statement in the Encyclical *Mystici Corporis* concerning what it considers the error of a spiritualized conception of unity does not apply to the World Council. The World Council does not "imagine a Church which one cannot see or touch, which would be only spiritual, in which numerous Christian bodies though divided in matters of faith, would nevertheless be united through an invisible link." It does, however, include Churches which believe that the Church is essentially invisible as well as those which hold that visible unity is essential.

IV. The Assumptions Underlying the World Council of Churches

We must now try to define the positive assumptions which underlie the World Council of Churches and the ecclesiological implications of membership in it.

1. *The member Churches of the Council believe that conversation, co-operation and common witness of the churches must be based on the common recognition that Christ is the Divine Head of the Body.*

The Basis of the World Council is the acknowledgment of the central fact that "other foundation can no man lay than that is laid, even Jesus Christ." It is the expression of the conviction that the Lord of the Church is God-among-us who continues to gather His children and to build His Church Himself.

Therefore, no relationship between the Churches can have any substance or promise unless it starts with the common submission of the Churches to the Headship of Jesus Christ in His Church. From different points of view Churches ask "How can men with opposite convictions belong to one and the same federation of the faithful?" A clear answer to that question was given by the Orthodox delegates in Edinburgh 1937, when they said: "In spite of all our differences, our common Master and Lord is *one*—Jesus Christ who will lead us to a more and more close collaboration for the edifying of the Body of Christ." The fact of Christ's Headship over His people compels all those who acknowledge Him to enter into real and close relationships with each other—even though they differ in many important points.

2. *The member Churches of the World Council believe on the basis of the New Testament that the Church of Christ is one.*

The ecumenical movement owes its existence to the fact that this article of the faith has again come home to men and women in many Churches with an inescapable force. As they face the discrepancy between the truth that there is and can only be one Church of Christ and the fact that there exist so many Churches which claim to be Churches of Christ but are not in living unity with each other, they feel a holy dissatisfaction with the present situation. The Churches realize that it is a matter of simple Christian duty for each Church to do its utmost for the manifestation of the Church in its oneness, and to work and pray that Christ's purpose for His Church should be fulfilled

3. *The member Churches recognize that the membership of the Church of Christ is more inclusive than the membership of their own church body. They seek, therefore, to enter into living contact with those outside their own ranks who confess the Lordship of Christ.*

All the Christian Churches, including the Church of Rome, hold that there is no complete identity between the membership of the Church Universal and the membership of their own Church. They recognize that there are church members "extra muros," that these belong "aliquo modo" to the Church, or even that there is an "ecclesia extra ecclesiam." This recognition finds expression in the fact that with very few exceptions the Christian Churches accept the baptism administered by other Churches as valid.

But the question arises what consequences are to be drawn from this teaching. Most often in church history the Churches have only drawn the negative consequence that they should have no dealings with those outside their membership. The underlying assumption of the ecumenical movement is that each Church has a positive task to fulfil in this realm. That task is to seek fellowship with all those who, while not members of the same visible body, belong together as members of the mystical body. And the ecumenical movement is the place where this search and discovery take place.

> 4. *The member Churches of the World Council consider the relationship of other Churches to the Holy Catholic Church which the Creeds profess as a subject for mutual consideration. Nevertheless, membership does not imply that each Church must regard the other member Churches as Churches in the true and full sense of the word.*

There is a place in the World Council both for those Churches which recognize other Churches as Churches in the full and true sense, and for those which do not. But these divided Churches, even if they cannot yet accept each other as true and pure Churches, believe that they should not remain in isolation from each other, and consequently they have associated themselves in the World Council of Churches.

They know that differences of faith and order exist, but they recognize one another as serving the One Lord, and they wish to explore their differences in mutual respect, trusting that they may thus be led by the Holy Spirit to manifest their unity in Christ.

> 5. *The member Churches of the World Council recognize in other Churches elements of the true Church. They consider that this mutual recognition obliges them to enter into a serious conversation with each other in the hope that these elements of truth will lead to the recognition of the full truth and to unity based on the full truth.*

It is generally taught in the different Churches that other Churches have certain elements of the true Church, in some traditions called "vestigia ecclesiae." Such elements are the preaching of the Word, the teaching of the Holy Scriptures and the administration of the sacraments. These elements are more than pale shadows of the life of the true Church. They are a fact of real promise and provide an opportunity to strive by frank and brotherly intercourse for the realization of a fuller unity. Moreover, Christians of all ecclesiological views throughout the world, by the preaching of the Gospel, brought men and women to salvation by Christ, to newness of life in Him, and into Christian fellowship with one another.

The ecumenical movement is based upon the conviction that these "traces" are to be followed. The Churches should not despise them as mere elements of truth but rejoice in them as hopeful signs pointing towards real unity. For what are these elements? Not dead remnants of the past but powerful means by which God works. Questions may and must be raised about the validity and purity of teaching and sacramental life, but there can be no question that such dynamic elements of church life justify the hope that the Churches which maintain them will be led into fuller truth. It is through the ecumenical conversation that this recognition of truth is facilitated.

6. *The member Churches of the Council are willing to consult together in seeking to learn of the Lord Jesus Christ what witness He would have them to bear to the world in His name.*

Since the very *raison d'être* of the Church is to witness to Christ, Churches cannot meet together without seeking from their common Lord a common witness before the world. This will not always be possible. But when it proves possible thus to speak or act together, the Churches can gratefully accept it as God's gracious gift that in spite of their disunity He has enabled them to render one and the same witness and that they may thus manifest something of the unity, the purpose of which is precisely "that the world may believe" and that they may "testify that the Father has sent the Son to be the Saviour of the world."

7. *A further practical implication of common membership in the World Council is that the member Churches should recognize their solidarity with each other, render assistance to each other in case of need, and refrain from such actions as are incompatible with brotherly relationship.*

Within the Council the Churches seek to deal with each other with a brotherly concern. This does not exclude extremely frank speaking to each other, in which within the Council the Churches ask each other searching questions and face their differences. But this is to be done for the building up of the Body of Christ. This excludes a purely negative attitude of one Church to another. The positive affirmation of each Church's faith is to be welcomed, but actions incompatible with brotherly relationship towards other member Churches defeat the very purpose for which the Council has been created. On the contrary, these Churches should help each other in removing all obstacles to the free exercise of the Church's normal functions. And whenever a Church is in need or under persecution, it should be able to count on the help of the other Churches through the Council.

8. *The member Churches enter into spiritual relationships through which they seek to learn from each other and to give help to each other in order that the Body of Christ may be built up and that the life of the Churches may be renewed.*

It is the common teaching of the Churches that the Church as the temple of God is at the same time a building which has been built and a building which is being built. The Church has, therefore, aspects, which belong to its very structure and essence and cannot be changed. But it has other aspects, which are subject to change. Thus the life of the Church, as it expresses itself in its witness to its own members and to the world, needs constant renewal. The Churches can and should help each other in this realm by a mutual exchange of thought and of experience. This is the significance of the study-work of the World Council and of many other of its activities. There is no intention to impose any particular pattern of thought or life upon the Churches. But whatever insight has been received by one or more Churches is to be made available to all the Churches for the sake of the "building up of the Body of Christ."

None of these positive assumptions, implied in the existence of the World Council, is in conflict with the teachings of the member Churches. We believe therefore that no Church need fear that by entering into the World Council it is in danger of denying its heritage.

As the conversation between the Churches develops and as the Churches enter into closer contact with each other, they will no doubt have to face new decisions and problems. For the Council exists to break the deadlock between the Churches. But in no case can or will any Church be pressed to take a decision against its own conviction or desire. The Churches remain wholly free in the action which, on the basis of their convictions and in the light of their ecumenical contacts, they will or will not take.

A very real unity has been discovered in ecumenical meetings which is, to all who collaborate in the World Council, the most precious element of its life. It exists and we receive it again and again as an unmerited gift from the Lord. We praise God for this foretaste of the unity of His People and continue hopefully with the work to which He has called us together. For the Council exists to serve the Churches as they prepare to meet their Lord Who knows only one flock.

89. A National Council:

"Act of Constituting the National Council of the Churches of Christ . . . " and "Inaugural Message . . . "

(1950)

The National Council of the Churches of Christ in the United States of America came into being when representatives of twenty-nine different American denominations and eight interdenominational agencies met in Cleveland, Ohio, on November 29, 1950. It was the culmination of a process that had begun with the founding of the Federal Council of the Churches of Christ in America in 1908.

Back in 1908, the Federal Council marked a new level of ecumenical cooperation in the United States. It was created by the action of the highest authorities of its member churches to express the catholic unity of the Christian church and to empower a Christian body to serve Christ and the world together. Major activities of the Federal Council focused on social service and temperance.

By 1948, the Federal Council had grown until it was almost unrecognizable. Within the Federal Council there were units in field administration, evangelism, international justice and goodwill, race relations, religious radio, Christian social and industrial relations, marriage and the home,

---

Source: "Act of Constituting the National Council of the Churches of Christ in the United States of America," *The Christian Century,* 13 December 1950, 1483–84; copyright 1950 Christian Century Foundation; reprinted by permission from the 13 December 13 1950 issue of *The Christian Century.* "Inaugural Message of the National Council," ibid., 1484–85; copyright 1950 Christian Century Foundation; reprinted by permission from the 13 December 1950 issue of *The Christian Century.*

just and durable peace, the ministry, religion and health, and worship. Outside of the Federal Council numerous interchurch organizations, federated denominational mission boards, and administrative agencies of the churches tried to work collaboratively: the Foreign Missions Conference of North America; the Home Missions Council of North America; the International Council of Religious Education; the National Protestant Council of Higher Education; the Missionary Education Movement of the United States and Canada; the United Stewardship Council; and the United Council of Church Women. It was time to bring all of these subunits and organizations together into a larger ecumenical body.

The Federal Council itself formally proposed a larger organization in the early 1930s. In 1941, the idea was approved at a conference in Atlantic City and formally endorsed by twenty denominations. However, it was not until November of 1950 that the National Council of Churches (NCC) officially brought together the twenty-nine denominations, representing over thirty-two million Christians, and practically all organized aspects of their common life in an ecclesiastically constituted organization for common action in the name of Jesus Christ. At the time it was the longest ecumenical step, short of organic union, taken by any one country toward the union of its churches. The Congregational Christian Churches and the Evangelical and Reformed Church were active in the Federal Council and became enthusiastic supporters of the new NCC.

Act of Constituting the National Council of the Churches of Christ in the United States of America

The Auditorium, Cleveland, Ohio, November 29, 1950

PRESIDING: Dr. Franklin C. Fry

HYMN— "The Church's One Foundation"

ROLL CALL OF THE DELEGATIONS

(The chairman called upon the denominational delegations to rise. He then asked them the following question:)

Do you, as members of the constituting denominations, declare that your communions have approved the formation of the National Council of the Churches of Christ in the United States of America and have agreed to become members thereof, and do now authorize your representatives sign the official documents?

(Delegations replied in unison:)
We do.

(The denominational delegations were seated.)

(Chairman)
Consent having been given, and authority having been invested in twenty-nine denominational representatives to affix their names to the official documents, I now call upon each of these duly appointed representatives to come forward and sign such official documents as the name of his communion is announced:

African Methodist Episcopal Church
African Methodist Episcopal Zion Church
American Baptist Convention
Augustana Lutheran Church
Church of the Brethren
Colored Methodist Episcopal Church
Congregational Christian Churches
Danish Evangelical Lutheran Church
Disciples of Christ
Evangelical and Reformed Church
Evangelical United Brethren
Evangelical Unity of Czech Moravian Brethren in N.A.
Friends—Five Years Meeting
Friends of Philadelphia and Vicinity
Methodist Church
Moravian Church (North and South Provinces)
National Baptist Convention, U.S.A., Inc.
National Baptist Convention of America
Presbyterian Church in the U.S.
Presbyterian Church in the U.S.A.
Protestant Episcopal Church
Reformed Church in America
Rumanian Orthodox Episcopate of America
Russian Orthodox Church in America
Seventh Day Baptists General Conference

Syrian Antiochian Orthodox Church
Ukrainian Orthodox Church of America
United Lutheran Church in America
United Presbyterian Church of N.A.

(After all had signed the chairman declared:)

The Act of Constitution

The representatives of the communions have now certified their official intent to be members of and to share in the work of the National Council. Therefore, as your presiding officer, I declare that the National Council of the Churches of Christ in the United States of America is officially constituted. Let us now dedicate it to the glory of God and to the service of mankind.

(The people then stood and joined in the following expression of dedication in unison with the chairman:)

The Dedication

And now, as a fellowship of Christian churches,
In the communion of the saints,
In love and good will toward all,
In gratitude for the labors and sacrifices of our fathers,
In loving remembrance of those who have finished their course,
Acknowledging that without us their work is not made perfect,
We invoke the blessing of God upon this National Council of the
Churches of Christ in the United States of America
And dedicate the council to his glory and the service of mankind,
In the name of the Father,
and of the Son
and of the Holy Spirit.
Amen.

(The people were seated.)

Demonstration of New Allegiance by the Interdenominational Agencies

(The chairman turned to the representatives of the following interdenominational agencies and asked them to stand:)

The Federal Council of the Churches of Christ in America
The Foreign Missions Conference of North America
The Home Missions Council of North America

The International Council of Religious Education
The Missionary Education Movement of the U.S. and Canada
The National Protestant Council on Higher Education
The United Council of Church Women
The United Stewardship Council

(Chairman)
As a demonstration of your relationship within this National Council of Churches, which has come into being as the result of your joint initiative, and as a visible sign of the delegation of your responsibilities to the newly formed organization, will you place in my hands official documents indicating that you are now united in this new organization of cooperative Christianity?

(Agencies)
We will.

(Each representative of the agencies handed the chairman a document which he placed beside the other official documents. The representatives were then seated.)

(Chairman)
State, county and city councils of churches cooperate with the National Council in communities throughout the nation. As an expression of their new relationship to this council, and of their devotion to the cause of Christian cooperation, their representatives will lead all of us in the prayer of consecration to new tasks.

(All representatives of state, county and city councils of churches stood during the following prayer:)

PRAYER led by Dr. Hugh C. Burr as representative of the Councils of Churches:

Almighty God, our heavenly Father, whose wisdom is everlasting and whose patience is very great, we thank thee for this hour of achievement and promise. As we bow before thee, kindle our imagination that we may more clearly envision the possibilities which thou hast set before us, and more quickly think thy thoughts after thee. Inspire us with a holy zeal for the new tasks, and a renewed determination to press on in our high calling in Christ Jesus.

As we go forward together, grant us, most loving Father, new insights into thy truth and a deeper understanding of one another. Lead us into new experiences of unity, new paths of service and new areas of victory. Mindful of thy steadfastness beyond our weakness and thy resources beyond our frailties, may we be strengthened to fulfill thy expectations for us.

Accept from us, our gracious Father, unworthy though we be, all that we have and are as an offering upon thine altar.

This we ask in the name of Jesus Christ our living Savior and Lord, to whom with thee and the Holy Ghost we give adoring praise, world without end. Amen.

(The people rose.)

HYMN— "God of Grace and God of Glory"

RECESSIONAL

Inaugural Message of the National Council

Adopted at Cleveland on December 1
by the First General Assembly

To the People of the Nation
The National Council of the Churches of Christ
in the United States of America
Sends Greetings:

This Council has been constituted by twenty-nine churches for the glory of God and the well-being of humanity. It manifests our oneness in Jesus Christ as divine Lord and Savior; his is the mandate we obey and his the power upon which we rely. It is designed to be an instrument of the Holy Spirit for such ministries of evangelism, education and relief as are better achieved through Christian cooperation than by the labors of separated groups, It coordinates and continues the work of eight interdenominational agencies ministering in as many fields of Christian usefulness.

Ecumenically Related

The council is linked in spirit with the worldwide ecumenical organizations which provide for interdenominational cooperation at the international level. It is likewise similar in purpose to the federations of churches in state, county and city through which the several communions do their common work in our land. So it becomes the national unit of a system of unified Christian enterprise which circles the inhabited earth.

For the denominations which compose it, the council opens an avenue for mutual confidence, a widening way along which potential controversy among them may be wrought into concord, and unhappy competition into emulation in pursuit of whatsoever things are true, honest, just, pure, lovely and of good report.

The council itself, however, is not a denomination, not a church above the churches. The autonomy of each communion is assured by constitutional provision. The council is an agency of cooperation—not more but magnificently not less.

The Functions of the Council

In behalf of the denominations the council continues and develops many services. It assists in the preparation of materials for the church school, and through its scholars is making ready for the world the Revised Standard Version of the Bible; it serves as a clearinghouse for full reports and statistics bearing upon church membership, denominational organizations and programs, and social trends of interest to Christians; it seeks to aid the churches in undergirding and coordinating their home and foreign missions; it searches out and trains leadership for Christian undertakings; it lifts up its voice in behalf of the Christian way of life in messages to the people of the country; it provides a single inclusive agency through which, if they wish, the denominations may nominate and support chaplains and minister to the men and women of the armed forces of the United States; it offers a means of approach to agencies governmental and civil in matters of justice and good will; it devotes itself to the presentation of Christian ideals through radio, television and motion pictures; it is an organ of evangelism both specifically and broadly conceived, standing ready to serve the cause of Christ in every area as need arises, to the end that the entire country may be permeated by the blessings of his gospel. Through these and other means it gives help to the churches, bringing the experience of all to the service of each.

The council has nothing to fear from the times, though it has much to desire of them. Being the servant of One who holds in his hand all the nations and the isles as a very little thing, it is free from the apprehensions of those who, taking counsel of men alone, forget that no age is isolated from God's ageless purpose. We call our fellow citizens to Christian faith: this will defend them from groundless social dreads and lift them to concerns worthy and productive.

The Spirit of the Council

The council stands as a guardian of democratic freedom. The revolutionary truth that men are created free follows from the revelation of God in Jesus Christ, and no person who knows that God as Father has given him all the rights of sonship is likely to remain content under a government which deprives him of basic human rights and fundamental freedoms. The nation may expect in the National Council a sturdy ally of the forces of liberty.

The council stands for liberty with the richest content. It stands for the freedom of men to be as the Lord God meant them to be. It stands for Christian freedom—including the freedom to pursue happiness and with justice and sympathy to create conditions of happiness for others. It therefore stands against the misuse of freedom. The nation may expect from the National Council, in the name of One who suffered death upon a cross, an unrelenting, open-eyed hostility, as studious as it is deeply passionate, to all of man's inhumanity to man.

The council opposes materialism as an end in itself. It is the foe of every political system that is nourished on materialism, and of every way of living that follows from it. From that smug idealism which is a form of selfishness, the council prays to be protected; but danger on this hand does not lessen the necessity it feels to fight a constant fight against all kinds of secular materialism which demolish the slowly built edifice of Christian morality and fair dealing.

Churches the Soul of the Nation

Through the council the churches, as they are dedicated to the doing of God's will, must increasingly become a source of spiritual power to the nation. The American churches, of which the council is one of the visible symbols, are in their true estate the soul of the nation. When those churches take their true course, they draw their standards not from the world around but from the guiding mind of Christ. The church is not the religious phase of the civilization in which it finds itself; it is the living center out of which lasting civilizations take life and form. In this sense, the council will be an organ through which the will of God may become effective as an animating, creative and unifying force within our national society.

The council gives thanks to God for all those forces which make for harmony in our society. When, for example, science employs its ingenuity to knit the world together in bonds of communication, when business and industry make a like contribution through the life-bringing mutuality of commerce, when the arts depict the beauty and the tragedy of our existence which draw us into unity with one another, when the many professions and occupations recognize themselves as callings to human usefulness, then the council salutes and supports them. By word and deed and in the name of Christ who gave his life for all mankind it affirms the brotherhood of men and seeks by every rightful means to arrest those forces of division which rend the nation along the lines of race and class and stay its growth toward unity.

The Present Crisis

Because clouds arising at this moment from the war in Korea threaten to darken the entire sky, the time is big with peril and with opportunity.

To the leaders we have set in authority in our government is committed the solemn and momentous task of making necessary choices in the political and military spheres.

We who are the people of the country, however, have a part to take as well. The call of Christ to us all seems clear, that we take it with calmness, self-control, courage and high purpose, as becomes those whose lives are in the hands of God. Without hysteria, without hatred, without pride, without undue impatience, without making national interest our chief end but shaping our own policies in the light of the aims of the United Nations, without relaxing our positive services to the other peoples of the world, and in complete repudiation of the lying dogma that war is inevitable, let us live and, if need be, die as loyal members of the world community to which Christ summons us and to which we of the council are dedicated.

Larger Significance of the Council

We of the National Council of the Churches of Christ in the U.S.A. begin our work in humility as we see the magnitude of the task ahead. We are conscious of our own shortcomings. Knowing that men too often dream in marble and then build with straw, we whose very human lives are not separate from sin and ignorance can make no boast of past or future excellence.

But this we have done: by God's grace we have forged an implement for cooperation such as America has never seen before. Into it have been poured the thoughts of wise and noble men and women, the prayers and consecration of the faithful, and the longing of all the participating churches to serve the spiritual needs of all the people. The council is our churches in their highest common effort for mankind.

Our hope is in Jesus Christ. In him we see the solution of the world's ills, for as human hearts are drawn near to him, they are drawn near in sympathy and understanding to each other. The council itself is a demonstration of his power to unite his followers in joyous cooperation. Let nation and nation, race and race, class and class unite their aims in his broad purposes for man, and out of that unitedness there will arise new strength like that of which we ourselves already feel the first sure intimations.

In this hope we commend you, our fellow citizens, to God's mercy, grace and peace.

Later Revision

By direction of the Assembly, a sentence is to be inserted affirming the responsibility of the National Council for Christian higher education, but this was not available at the time of going to press.

90. Another Plan: *"A Plan for a United Church in the United States"*

(1953)

Greenwich Conference on Church Union

Although during most of the 1940s the Congregational Christian Churches and the Evangelical and Reformed Church worked diligently to develop an acceptable basis of union for the bilateral union that they intended to call the "United Church of Christ," they continued to remain involved in other ecumenical ventures.

In 1946, the Congregational Christian Churches passed a resolution asking the Federal Council of Churches to invite those denominations that "recognize one another's ministries and sacraments" to send official representatives to a plenary conference to explore the possibility of closer union. When the invitation was seconded the following August by the International Convention of the Disciples of Christ, the invitation was broadened to include "those communions which are in sufficient accord in essentials of Christian faith and order to give promise that such a conference would result in further and effectual achievement of Christian unity."

Nine denominations responded favorably: Methodist, Presbyterian USA, Presbyterian US, Congregational Christian, Disciples of Christ, Evangelical and Reformed, African Methodist Episcopal, and the Association of Community Churches. At that time these denominations

Source: The Greenwich Conference on Church Union, "A Plan for a United Church in the United States," pamphlet, 22 May 1953. From the library of John von Rohr.

represented sixteen million church members, some 40 percent of the Protestants in the United States.

With high hopes, representatives from these churches met in Greenwich, Connecticut, in December of 1949. Those who came decided from the beginning that they would aim at nothing less than "organic union," which they defined as "a fellowship and organization of the church which will enable it to act as one body under Jesus Christ who is the Head of the Church." They called themselves "The Conference on Church Union" and elected officers to lead them into the future: president, Ivan Lee Holt of the Methodist Church; vice-president, William B. Pugh, stated clerk of the General Assembly of the Presbyterian Church USA; treasurer, John Lentz of the Evangelical and Reformed Church; and acting secretary, Douglas Horton, minister of the Congregational Christian General Council.

By 1950 a drafting committee had drawn up a "Plan of Union," which was presented to a plenary session of the conference in October of that year, where it was approved with minor changes. It was then brought to a joint convocation of the conference and sent to various commissions on interchurch relations in the nine denominations. No formal action was taken at the joint convocation, held in Cincinnati in January of 1951, but amendments were suggested to the drafting committee.

The drafting committee considered the proposed amendments in New York in November of 1952, and presented a revised text to a plenary session of the conference on May 22–23, 1953. At that meeting the conference voted to submit the revised plan for study to the various commissions on Christian unity of the member churches, as well as to other interested organizations, groups, and theological seminaries, specifically requesting guidance for the future of the conference.

The theological sections of the plan, included here, asserted that the call for a united church was a "divine imperative," bringing the churches together as one body. Recognizing that they were living in a world of secularism, atheism, and religious indifference, they declared that God had called them to transcend the barriers separating them from one another and to make common cause in a world that needed their concerted action. Furthermore, they looked forward in faith and hope to a union more comprehensive than their present undertaking. The proposed plan also contained a statement of the "common faith" that had brought them together.

By 1953, the efforts of the Congregational Christian Churches and the Evangelical and Reformed Church to consummate their union had been suspended by a court injunction. Antimerger groups within the Congregational Christian Churches were doing all they could to stop that union (see vol. 6:79–83). The leadership of the two denominations, however, remained convinced that God was calling for church union one way or another. As they waited for their earlier efforts to be affirmed or denied in the courts, they kept alive their vision of a United Church of Christ.

In the end, the Greenwich Conference on Church Union never went any further. In December 1953, when the highest court in New York State ruled that the union between the Congregational Christian Churches and the Evangelical and Reformed Church could move ahead, denominational leaders did exactly that (see vol. 6:91).

I. The Divine Imperative

We, the Conference on Church Union, consisting of officially appointed representatives of our several Churches, gratefully recognize the initiative and guidance of God in the movement among Christian people for a united Church. The call for unity is a divine imperative and we believe that union is an indispensable means to that end.

We have long known that in essentials of faith we are already one. We now rejoice in the growing realization that the practical operations of our several polities are strikingly similar. Over many years there has been a steady growth of fraternal fellowship, mutual cooperation, and the spirit of unity among us. This has prompted us earnestly and prayerfully to inquire what may be the next step in the development of our responsibility for one another. Through our common faith in Jesus Christ as Lord and Savior we are made one body in him and, in penitence for our present unhappy separation from one another, we believe that our Master now calls us to transcend those barriers which divide us into various and often competing denominations and churches.

Today, Christians confront a world situation which demands that the churches shall make common cause. In our own and many other sections of the world, secularism, atheism, and religious indifference are strongly entrenched and militant. These evil forces stand sharply over against the Christian Church with its eternal gospel of redemption. They cannot be effectively resisted and overcome by separate churches, but only by the corporate witness and the concerted action of Christians united. In the broad perspective of the world scene, and in view of our great common convictions and concerns, our denominational differences appear relatively inconsequential.

In our meetings together, in prayer and prolonged deliberations, we have reached a common conviction that the time has now come when all the churches must take with profound seriousness both the divine mandate and the practical need for a united Church. Even though this union of Churches may mean some adjustment of denominational traditions and emphases, yet all will be enriched by the varying practices brought into the union. If at any point we must decrease that the Cause of Christ may increase, we shall count our loss as gain.

We look forward in faith and hope to a more comprehensive union than that envisaged by our present undertaking. Holding this faith and this larger hope, but not waiting for its full realization, we are convinced that we should now form ourselves into an organic union; and that our union must be so truly ecumenical in spirit and structure that it may be not only a Church united in itself but so manifestly inspired with a fervent desire and intention to be used of God that it will bring about a more comprehensive union. To this end, we offer a statement of the ecumenical evangelical faith to which such a united Church should bear witness, and propose a Plan of Union.

II. The Common Faith

We Are One in common faith of the Christian Church and in our desire to share as a common heritage the various historic and treasured expressions of that faith.

We Are One in our common belief

in God our Father;
in Jesus Christ, his only Son, our Savior;
in the Holy Spirit, our Guide and Comforter;
in the Holy Catholic Church, through which God's eternal purpose of salvation is proclaimed and his Kingdom comes on earth;
in the Scriptures of the Old and New Testaments as disclosing the Word of God for men, from which new light is evermore breaking forth for us and for our world;
in the forgiveness of sins;
and in the life everlasting.

We Are One in our faith that the Church is of God and in the deepening sense of obligation with which we hear the prayer of our Lord for his disciples, "That they may all be one; even as thou, Father, art in me, and I in thee, that they also may be in us, so that the world may believe that thou hast sent me."

WE ARE ONE in that spirit of love which, owning the same Lord, recognizes diversity of gifts, concerns, and ministrations, and assures to all freedom in ways of worship, and of witness.

WE ARE ONE in our purpose that this United Church of Christ be dedicated to our Lord for the furtherance of his redemptive work in the world.

Years in Court

91. Legal Arguments: *"Decisions of the Courts in Regard to the Proposed Union . . . "*

(1953)

In April of 1949, antimerger sentiment within the Congregational Christian Churches finally came to a head. A group within the Congregational Christian Churches attempted to stop the union of the Congregational Christian Churches and the Evangelical and Reformed Church by filing a suit against Helen Kenyon as moderator of the General Council of the Congregational Christian Churches of the United States. The plaintiffs in the litigation were the Cadman Memorial Congregational Society of Brooklyn and the Cadman Memorial Church, filing on behalf of themselves and other Congregational Christian congregations that objected to the proposed union. The core of the dispute had to do with the autonomy and power of the General Council of the Congregational Christian Churches and the extent of its authority to make decisions regarding church union for local congregations.

Witnesses from the Congregational Christian General Council told the court that the General Council was similar to a local congregation in its autonomy and power, and that it was accountable only to itself as a gathering of Christians under the Lordship of Christ. The antimerger plaintiffs insisted that the General Council was a "representative body" accountable to the churches from whom its delegates were elected. They called the General Council a "national agency of fellowship," deriving

---

Source: "Decisions of the Courts in Regard to the Proposed Union of the Congregational Christian and the Evangelical and Reformed Communions," pamphlet, in private collection. [Note: the appeal and the final opinion of the court appeared in the pamphlet in reverse order.]

its existence from the will of the churches, and therefore needing the approval of the churches for its decisions. They also insisted that in the event that the proposed union was consummated, congregations choosing not to become a part of the United Church of Christ had a rightful claim to the assets of the various Congregational Christian missionary boards and pension funds.

On January 26, 1950, Meier Steinbrink, a justice of the New York State Supreme Court, decided in favor of the plaintiffs and issued a permanent injunction against any collaboration or joint activity between the two denominations. Steinbrink ruled that the General Council of the Congregational Christian Churches was without power to unite itself with the Synod of the Evangelical and Reformed Church or with any other body; that the General Council had no authority to make any legally binding commitments upon local congregations; that, in consequence, it could not take any action that would bring independent and autonomous congregations into the proposed United Church of Christ unless these churches individually voted themselves into such a united church; and that any actions previously taken by local churches in favor of the merger did not commit them to union in the present. In addition, the court stated that the polity of the Congregational Christian Churches was a "system of church organization which recognizes the independence and autonomy of the local church in all matters temporal and spiritual," and "that the association of churches through voluntary, independent organizations devised for fellowship and cooperation is without ecclesiastical authority." Clearly, this definition of Congregationalism was debatable.

The most decisive opinion of the court was its judgment that the General Council of the Congregational Christian Churches had no power to make decisions binding upon local congregations—a ruling that made the proposed union between the Congregational Christian Churches and the Evangelical and Reformed Church illegal. Finally, it appeared, this was the answer to the question raised by the Christian Century *in 1938 as to whether, according to congregational polity, any congregationally ordered denominations were empowered to unite with anybody. The answer now was simply, "They were not." (See vol. 6:71)*

In the aftermath of his decision, journalists asked whether substantial majorities had any standing at all in courts of law, and whether they had any means at all to accomplish what they wanted. Some observers asked whether the membership of the Congregational Christian Churches in the Federal Council of Churches and in the World Council of Churches was rendered invalid by Steinbrink's decision. They debated whether the ruling had any power retroactively with regard to church unions that had already occurred: specifically, the union in Canada in 1925 that brought the Congregational Christian, the Methodist, and the Presbyterian churches together to form the United Church of Canada (see vol. 6:14); and the union in 1931 of two congregationally ordered denominations, the Congregational Churches and the Christian Churches (see vol. 6:39). Finally, in the light of the Steinbrink decision, questions were raised about whether two other congregationally ordered denominations in the United States, the Disciples of Christ and the Northern Baptists (later known as American Baptists), could legally conduct negotiations for union, which in fact they were doing at that time.

Not surprisingly, the General Council appealed the Steinbrink decision to a higher court. In May of 1952, the Appellate Division of the Supreme Court, Second Judicial Department, State of New York, reversed the decision of the lower court by an opinion of four to one. That decision was in turn appealed to the highest court of New York State, the Court of Appeals. Finally, on December 3, 1953, the high court rejected the request of the union opponents that it overturn the decision of the Appellate Division, and it reaffirmed the position of the General Council on union. Once this appeal process was completed, the leadership of the Congregational Christian Churches and the Evangelical and Reformed Church moved ahead to plan a uniting General Synod.

Appellate Division of the Supreme Court
Second Judicial Department
State of New York

CADMAN MEMORIAL CONGREGATIONAL SOCIETY OF BROOKLYN and THE CADMAN MEMORIAL CHURCH, suing on behalf of themselves and other Congregational Christian Churches similarly situated,

Respondents

vs.

HELEN KENYON, as Moderator of the General Council of the Congregational Christian Churches of the United States,

Appellant

279 App. Div. 1074

The Court's Decision
May 5, 1952

Appeal by defendant from a judgment which, inter alia, declares as between the parties the rights of the plaintiffs and certain other Congregational Christian Churches similarly situated, with respect to funds and property alleged to be held by defendant and certain corporate societies and agencies, not parties to this action, in trust for specified religious purposes, declares that such funds and assets held by defendant and such corporations, except as otherwise required by express trusts, are held in trust for such purposes, states the rights of said parties, and defendant's authority, with respect to the "Basis of Union of the Congregational Christian Churches and the Evangelical and Reformed Church," alleged to have been adopted by defendant without authority on behalf of the churches comprising the Congregational Christian Churches of the United States, and grants injunctive relief as against defendant, its members, present and future officers, attorneys, employees, agents and instrumentalities, and all other persons acting with knowledge of the terms of the judgment.

In controversies such as this, ecclesiastical or doctrinal questions may be inquired into only in so far as it may be necessary to do so to determine the civil or property rights of the parties. The civil courts do not interfere with ecclesiastical matters in which temporal rights are not involved. Plaintiffs have failed to establish any right or interest in or to the funds and other assets which plaintiffs asserted were held in trust, which requires or permits a determination of the ecclesiastical issues presented. The action was not brought upon the theory that the rights of the plaintiffs or other churches similarly situated, with respect to ownership and control of their individual properties and funds, would be in any way threatened or endangered by the proposed church union complained of. As to such rights and as to funds held under express trusts, there is no dispute between the parties. As to other funds held by or under the control of the defendant, it was not established that they were received in any way other than as absolute gifts or contributions, to be expended for specific objects or for defendant's usual purposes. Neither does the evidence establish that the funds or assets held by the corporate societies and agencies, other than those held under specific trusts, are held under any trust, except in the general sense in which all corporations hold their property for the execution of their corporate purposes, cf. *Corporation of Chamber of Commerce of New York v. Bennett,* 143 Misc., 513. 257 N.Y. S 2; *Wetmore v. Parker,* 52 N.Y. 4.50; *Bird v. Merklee,* 144 N.Y., 544, 39 N.E. 645, 27 L.R.A. 423:

Sherman v. Richmond Hose Co., No. 2, 230 N.Y. 462, 130 N.E. 613, nor has it been established that any fiduciary obligation imposed by corporate charters or certificates, or directions given to limit the use of such funds, cf. *St. Joseph's Hospital v. Bennett,* 281 N.Y., 115, 22 N.E. 2d 305, 130 A.L.R. 1092 will he violated by the consummation of the "Basis of Union" approved by defendant, or that any such violation is threatened or imminent, cf. 1130 *President St. Corp. v. Bolton Realty Corp.,* 300 N.Y. 63, 69, 89 N.E. 2d 16, 16 A.L.R. 2d 617; *People v. Canal Board of N.Y.,* 55 N.Y., 390. If such violation shall be threatened, protection to donors and beneficiaries is provided through an action by the attorney general, who may compel the use of such funds for the purposes for which they were given. *St. Joseph's Hospital v. Bennett,* supra; *Trustees of Sailors' Snug Harbor in City of New York v. Carmody,* 158 App. Div., 738, 144 N.Y., 24, affirmed 211 N.Y., 286, 105 N.E. 543; *Female Association of N.Y. v. Beekman,* 21 Barb., 565. In any event there should have been no declaration of the rights of plaintiffs with respect to the funds and assets held by the corporate societies and agencies. If any declaration is to be made with respect to plaintiffs' rights in or to such funds, or if it is to be determined that such funds are subject to a trust which may be enforced at the instance of plaintiffs, such determination should be made only in an appropriate action or proceeding in which such corporate societies and agencies may be before the court as parties. A declaratory judgment serves a legitimate purpose only when all persons who may be affected thereby and who may question in a court the existence and scope of the rights declared are parties to the action and have opportunity to be heard. A court may, and ordinarily must, refuse to render a declaratory judgment in the absence of such parties. *Manhattan Storage & Warehouse Co. v. Movers & Warehousemen's Association of Greater New York,* 289 N.Y., 82, 43 N.E. 2d 820; *Wood v. City of Salamanca,* 289 N.Y., 279, 45 N.E. 2d 443. Findings of fact, express and implied, inconsistent with the foregoing, except such findings as were made expressly or by implication, upon questions of doctrine, polity and other ecclesiastical matters, are reversed. For the reasons heretofore stated, this court has not considered and has made no determination upon the questions of fact arising upon the issues as to such ecclesiastical matters. (Judgment reversed on the law and the facts, with costs, and plaintiffs' complaint and defendant's counterclaim dismissed, with costs to defendant.)

Court of Appeals
State of New York

No. 338

CADMAN MEMORIAL CONGREGATIONAL SOCIETY OF BROOKLYN and THE CADMAN MEMORIAL CHURCH, suing on behalf of themselves and other Congregational Christian Churches similarly situated,

Plaintiffs-Appellants,

vs.

HELEN KENYON, as Moderator of the General Council of the Congregational Christian Churches of the United States,

Defendant-Respondent.

306 N.Y. 151

The Court's Decision
December 3, 1953

This controversy, here in an appeal as of right, concerns the methods and procedures under which the Congregational Christian Churches of the United States and the Evangelical and Reformed Church plan to unite under the name of United Church of Christ. Both are Protestant in faith and polity and both possess a rich heritage from the past.

The Congregational Christian Churches trace their origin to the Reformation in England dating to 1581, and in this country dating to the Puritans in 1620. By tradition and usage the approximately fifty-eight hundred churches in America are independent, self-governing fellowships without any central ecclesiastical control. They have, however, in order to carry on a religious program commensurate with present-day requirements, organized themselves into district associations, state conferences and conventions and a general council national in scope.

The Evangelical and Reformed Church is a Protestant denomination of national scope consisting of congregations, synodical units and an ecclesiastical governing body having jurisdiction and control over such congregations and their members, ministers and organizations. It was founded in 1934 by the union of the Reformed Church in the United States dating to 1725, and the Evangelical Synod of North America dating to 1840. It presently comprises approximately twenty-eight hundred churches having a membership of over seven hundred thousand persons.

The two uniting groups thus aggregate about eighty-six hundred churches with a membership of about one million eight hundred and fifty thousand persons.

The action is in equity. It is brought by the Cadman Memorial Congregational Society of Brooklyn, a New York religious corporation, and the Cadman Memorial Church, an unincorporated religious body affiliated with the Cadman Memorial Congregational Society. The former has custody and control of the temporalities and property and the latter conducts services of worship and other religious activities and meetings in the church edifice located in Brooklyn. For convenience, the plaintiffs will hereinafter be referred to either as the "Cadman Church" or "plaintiff."

According to the record, the Cadman Church occupies a unique place among Congregational Christian churches being not only one of the oldest in America, but one of the largest. It is a union of the former Central and Clinton Avenue Congregational Churches of Brooklyn in which the members of the Simpson Methodist Church have joined for purposes of worship only. Its name honors the memory of a distinguished former preacher, the Reverend S. Parkes Cadman. It is congregational in polity and, like other Congregational Christian churches, is concededly independent and autonomous and not subject to the control of any other ecclesiastical authority. It is a member of the New York City Congregational Church Association, Inc., and the New York Congregational Christian Conference, Inc., and is represented in the voting membership of the defendant General Council.

The defendant General Council of the Congregational Christian Churches of the United States, sued in the name of its Moderator and Presiding Officer, is an unincorporated association with its principal office and place of business in New York City. Whenever referred to hereinafter it will be called either the "General Council" or "defendant."

The General Council is a voluntary association, national in scope, having a constitution, by-laws and standing rules. According to its constitution, membership is made up of both laity and clergy representing individual congregational churches, local associations and district conferences or conventions and affiliated colleges and theological seminaries, as well as certain other designated groups or classes of persons, such as ex-officio members of the conferences or conventions, representatives of home and foreign missions, honorary members, ecumenical members and certain others, by invitation, the latter enjoying the privilege of the floor but having no vote.

By constitutional pronouncement it stands "for the autonomy of the local church, and its independence of ecclesiastical control," "the fellowship of churches, united in district, state, and national bodies for counsel and cooperation," "the unity of the Church of Christ." It recognizes such local independence in matters of Christian faith and dogma by declaring that it finds "in the Bible the supreme rule of faith and life, but recognize[s] wide room for differences in interpretation. We therefore base our union upon the acceptance of Christianity as primarily a way of life and not upon uniformity of theological opinion or any uniform practice of ordinances" (Constitution).

The General Council has for its purpose:

> "to foster and express the substantial unity of the Congregational Christian churches in faith, purpose, policy (sic) and work; to consult upon and devise measures and maintain agencies for the promotion of the common interests of the kingdom of God; to cooperate with any corporation or body under control of or affiliated with the Congregational or Christian churches or any of them; and to do and to promote the work of these churches in their national, international, and interdenominational relations, and in general so far as legally possible to perform on behalf of the united churches the various functions hitherto performed by the National Council for the Congregational churches and by the General Convention for the Christian churches, it being understood that where technical legal questions may be involved the action of the separate bodies shall be secured."

The Basis of Union with Interpretations constituting the subject matter of this controversy, is the result of several years of study and negotiation between the Commission on Interchurch Relations and Christian Unity representing the General Council (By-Law, No. III, Subd. 8) and a committee representing the Evangelical and Reformed Church, its final form being adopted at a joint meeting of the commission and the committee held at Cleveland, Ohio, on January 22, 1947. Thereafter the General Council submitted it to the individual Congregational Christian churches and state conferences for advice. Notwithstanding that the recommended seventy-five per cent of the individual churches entitled to vote did not formally approve, nonetheless more than seventy-two per cent of those voting did approve, as did ninety per cent of the associations and district conferences. Regarding this as substantially affording the advice which was sought, the General Council, at its meeting held in February 1949, voted (757 for and 172 against) to consummate the plan and so advised the Evangelical and Reformed Church which likewise approved. Such action by the latter church is mentioned by way of interest, although of no consequence in this litigation as it is not a party to the within action.

According to its express terms, the Basis of Union recognizes the local church as the basis of organization, and that the conferences, conventions and associations shall "conduct its business in its own way" by providing that each congregation, association and conference "has the right of retaining or adopting its own charter, constitution, by-laws and other regulations which it deems essential and proper to its own welfare"; in other words that there will be no intrusion in or abridgment of traditional congregational polity and usage through fellowship of independent autonomous congregations, free of authoritative control.

The plaintiff seeks a judgment declaring that the General Council has no power or authority to consummate the Basis of Union on its behalf or other Congregational Christian churches, and that any Congregational Christian churches uniting with the proposed United Church of Christ, as proposed in the Basis of Union

> "will cease to be churches of that (Congregational) fellowship and denomination and cease to have any right or interest in or in connection with the corporations, commission, board, agencies and instrumentalities representing or acting for or under the direction and control of the Congregational Christian Churches or the funds and properties thereof" and that any Congregational Christian churches who do not join with the United Christian Church, will "remain the Congregational Christian Churches entitled to all the rights and privileges presently possessed and enjoyed by such churches" including "the control and benefit of all the corporations, commissions, boards, agencies and instrumentalities which now represent and act for or are under the direction of the present Congregational Christian Churches" and that the United Church and all those who join with it shall have no interest therein.

As an incident thereto it seeks injunctive relief to restrain the General Council, its members and officers, from consummating the Basis of Union and to restrain the General Council, its agencies and instrumentalities from merging or transferring and mingling their funds and assets with the Evangelical and Reformed Church or with the United Church of Christ.

According to its complaint the plaintiff is proceeding upon the theory that the proposed United Church of Christ is and will be so alien and different in structure and polity that fundamental congregational usage and practice will be wholly lost and destroyed. By way of showing such fundamental difference it points out that the United Church of Christ will be a general or authoritative church governed through various ecclesiastical bodies having degrees of sovereignty as distinct from the existing voluntary and advisory association, conferences, conventions and general council; that the individual churches and members will be subordinate to control providing, as it does, for a central authority for the engaging and dismissal of ministers, the establishment of a system of church judicatories and for a united or uniform confession of faith in place of the absolute independence and freedom now and heretofore enjoyed in such matters by Congregational Christian churches. The plaintiff objects also to the prospect of a constitution for or applicable to Congregational churches as well as other differences which more fully appear in the Basis of Union. This, in sum, is to say that because of the difference in structure and polity of the two uniting bodies such a union will destroy or materially alter the nature of Congregationalism.

The General Council in its answer concedes that under the Basis of Union the plaintiff and any other Congregational Christian church, association or conference, or their members, would not be subject in respect "to either their spiritual or temporal affairs to any control by the proposed United Church of Christ,"—that the proposed expression of faith set out in the Basis is not to be considered a substitution for any confession of faith which may be used in any congregation and "shall be regarded as a testimony and not as a test" and that freedom of worship and education at present enjoyed "will be preserved in the United Church * * * [and] not * * * abridged." These clear and unequivocal admissions afford assurance that the proposed union will in no way change the historical and traditional pattern of the individual Congregational Christian church. They serve to remove all fear that any action taken by the General Council leading to a consummation of the Basis of Union will in any way obligate the individual church to join in the Union except through its own voluntary action. Every possible assurance is given that each member church will continue to possess the same freedom of faith and manner of worship as heretofore enjoyed—that there will be no interference in or abridgment of Congregational usage and practice. In short, there is no power and none is claimed by which the General Council can compel or intends to compel the plaintiff Cadman or any other non-assenting church to join the Union unwillingly or impose upon them a change of faith or doctrine. Union depends on voluntary action freely taken by independent autonomous churches. If any doubt remains, it seems abundantly clear from this record, that the very nature of Congregationalism, surviving as it has, the vicissitudes of time for nearly four hundred years, assures the integrity of the individual Congregational Christian church, its faith and independence. Under these circumstances no ecclesiastical question is presented, cf. *Watson v. Jones,* 13 Wall, 679, 20 L. Ed. 666.

We turn then to a consideration of whether the consummation of the Basis of Union will interfere with any alleged property right possessed by the plaintiff in and to funds and assets now held and controlled by the General Council, its boards, agencies and instrumentalities which, it is estimated, aggregate approximately $60,000,000.

The plaintiff alleges that if the Basis of Union is consummated such funds and other assets will "be diverted from the uses and purposes for which they were set up, created and established and for which they have heretofore been used." The complaint goes on to allege that such diversion will deprive the plaintiffs of representation in the General Council to which they are presently entitled; will deprive them of their interest in the administration of the funds and assets, by mingling such funds with funds and assets of other and unrelated religious organizations, impose upon them liabilities and burdens alien to and different from those now incident thereto and deprive the plaintiff of its lawful right in the application and use thereof.

Before proceeding to a discussion of the merits of the allegation thus made, we note that the parties agree that funds and properties held by the Cadman Church are in no way involved in or threatened by the proposed union; that the funds held by the General Council and any of its agencies, boards and instrumentalities under express trusts, including pension funds, will not be affected. (Basis of Union, Art. III, §H; Art. IV, §L, subd. 1; Art IX, §C).

The dispute concerns rather the appellants' alleged beneficial interest in general funds belonging to and used by various boards and agencies in carrying on their respective functions. Such funds are raised through per capita and apportionment systems applicable to individual churches and their members. No individual church or member is required to contribute anything—it is entirely voluntary and, in fact, the Cadman Church for years has refused to pay per capita dues on the ground that it is not obliged and cannot be compelled to do so. It has, however, concededly contributed other amounts "in lieu of" the per capita assessment. The apportionment plan is also entirely voluntary and benevolent. The general practice, we are told, is for the individual churches to send their voluntary general contributions to the State Conference and the funds which the State Conference does not use are turned over to the General Council, its agencies, boards and instrumentalities, who use such funds in carrying on a world-wide program of Christian outreach. This has many aspects and to assure successful results, the work in its various categories is done through boards, agencies and instrumentalities created for the express purpose of performing a specified phase of the program. They are usually corporate in form and while the name "Congregational" appears in most of such agencies, their express purposes are nonetheless very broad and in no way limited to furthering any particular religious viewpoint, dogma or confession of faith. For instance, the American Board of Commissioners for Foreign Missions (a Massachusetts corporation) has for its purpose the extension of Christ's Kingdom abroad, without making any reference to Congregational Christian churches, to the General Council or any denomination whatsoever but, on the contrary, and it is significant here, it may unite with others in the manner provided in the by-laws including "election by a council, synod * * * representing any churches * * * located within the United States."

The Board of Home Missions of the Congregational and Christian Churches (a corporation chartered in New York, Connecticut and Massachusetts) is much the same. It too may carry on its work "either directly or through other corporations having similar objects in the United States and in other countries." We may note also that the Congregational Board of Ministerial Relief (a Connecticut corporation organized by Special Act in 1885 and amended in 1933) has for its purpose the relief of needy Congregational ministers. In addition, its benevolences are available to "ministers of other churches affiliated, merged or consolidated with the Congregational Churches and after their decease for the benefit of their needy families, in accordance with resolutions and declarations adopted or made, from time to time by the General Council * * * or by any body which may succeed to the present functions of that Council; and said corporation may cooperate with any other corporation or body which is under the charge and control of the Congregational and Christian Churches in the United States or of churches at the time affiliated with them."

In fact the Corporation for the General Council of the Congregational Christian Churches of the United States, a financial corporation organized under a Special Charter given by the Legislature of Connecticut for the purpose of providing and administering a pension fund for retired Congregational ministers, (its principal asset being the Pilgrim Memorial Fund, a trust which all agree will not be affected by the proposed Union) provides that:

> "If hereafter any other body of Christians shall have united with the Congregational and Christian churches by union, merger, affiliation or otherwise effected by or with the consent of said General Council, said Corporation may exercise its powers for the use and benefit of the churches or other institutions of the united or merged denominations, or of such affiliated body."

Other corporations may be mentioned such as The American Missionary Association, The Congregational Home Missionary Society, The Congregational Church Building Society and The Congregational Sunday School Extension Society, all New York corporations, The Congregational Education Society, a Massachusetts corporation, The Annuity Fund for Congregational Ministers and The Retirement Fund for Lay Workers, both New Jersey corporations, but need not be discussed more than to say that in most instances their charters give them very broad and general powers which would not be violated by uniting with any other similar charitable and religious organization. The principle of voluntariness has long been a motivating force in Congregational fellowship.

Notwithstanding that the above listed boards and agencies are corporations authorized and existing under the laws of several different states, the plaintiffs nonetheless contend that such boards and agencies have in fact no separate and independent status because their boards of trustees, officers and administrators are drawn from the membership of the General Council and that their activities are, for all practical purposes, controlled and supervised by the General Council—that diversion of their funds and assets and mingling of same with the funds of others is an interference to its detriment in a property interest belonging to the Cadman Church and other non-assenting churches. This, however, is not established in fact as the proof shows and, it is conceded, the Cadman Church has not contributed any funds, except as we have seen, for other than a general corporate purpose and these voluntarily and without restriction as to use or application. Under such circumstances it must be assumed that such funds were general gifts for use by the corporations in connection with their general corporate purposes. Such voluntary unrestricted contributions for a general charitable and religious purpose create no proprietary or beneficial interest warranting the civil courts in interfering in their expenditure so long as it appears that such use and application is not violative of charter purposes. As this Court has previously observed:

> "Gifts to religious and charitable corporations to aid in carrying out the purposes for which they are organized, whether by expending the principal of a bequest or the income of a bequest to be invested in perpetuity, do not create a trust in any legal sense." *Bird v. Merklee,* 144 N.Y. 544, 550, 39 N.E. 645, 646, 27 L.R.A. 423; see, also, *Wetmore v. Parker,* 52 N.Y. 450; *Johnson v. Hughes,* 187 N.Y. 446, 80 N.E. 373.

Furthermore, and we repeat, all agree that no trust funds or assets, including pension funds, held by or under the control of the General Council or any board or agency or by any non-assenting church are in any way affected by the proposed union. Absent a showing that any fiduciary obligation imposed by the charters or certificates of incorporation of any board or agency will be violated or that such violation is imminent or threatened, there is no basis or necessity for a declaratory judgment enjoining the General Council in any respect, nor, may any restraining order issue against the various corporate boards and agencies, the Evangelical and Reformed Church or the United Church of Christ, as they have not been made parties defendant and are not before the court. Such a remedy is available only in an appropriate action, which this is not, (Civil Prac. Act, §§193, 473; *Manhattan Storage & Warehouse Co. v. Movers & Warehousemen's Ass'n of Greater New York,* 289 N.Y. 82, 43 N.E. 2d 820; *Ivory v. Edwards,* 304 N.Y. 949, 110 N.E. 2d 887. On this record, the proof having established that the Basis of Union is voluntary and in no way interferes with Congregational faith or manner of worship, and the plaintiffs having failed to establish any direct or beneficial interest in and to the unrestricted funds of the General Council, its various boards, agencies and instrumentalities, and having failed to show that any such general funds are to be used for other than authorized charter purposes, the complaint was properly dismissed on the merits.

The judgment [of the Appellate Division of the New York State Supreme Court] appealed from is affirmed, without costs.

The United Church of Christ

92. The Uniting General Synod: *"Addresses"*

(1957)

James E. Wagner; Fred Hoskins

On Tuesday evening, June 25, 1957, at Cleveland, Ohio, the Congregational Christian Churches and the Evangelical and Reformed Church took a step that was unique in the history of Protestantism in the United States: two quite different denominations with differing cultural and ethnic origins, and differing church polities and differing intradenominational power structures, came together to form a new denomination on the basis of one intense, common conviction that their union was God's will. This conviction had sustained them through nearly twenty years of negotiation, legal injunction, and delay, and it found its full expression in the Uniting General Synod of the United Church of Christ. At that synod, representatives from the two denominations celebrated their union in the context of worship, expressing their gratitude for God's presence with them throughout their journey, and their commitment to continue, with God's help, to seek other unions in the spirit of Christ's prayer "that they may all be one."

In his short address at the opening worship service on Tuesday, June 25, James E. Wagner, president of the Evangelical and Reformed Church, spoke of the normal feelings of hesitation that were part of that moment. Acknowledging every human animal's unwillingness to give up the old, familiar, and precious for new and unfamiliar things, Wagner

---

Source: James E. Wagner, address at the opening session of the Uniting General Synod," in *Minutes of the Uniting General Synod of the United Church of Christ,* Cleveland, Ohio, 25–27 June 1957, 64–66; Fred Hoskins, address at the opening session of the Uniting General Synod, in ibid., 61–63.

reminded the gathered delegates of Peter's indecisiveness about whether Gentiles could become Christians. Wagner assured those present that Peter's vacillation, like their own, was only natural in the face of newness and change. What would carry them forward on the venture of faith was the same discovery that Peter experienced in the first century. "The best we have known will not have been lost at all, . . . [but] enriched by the new (or different) which each of us brings to our common life, that God himself will introduce 'some better thing' neither of us possessed of himself alone, and that . . . in whatever way and measure each of us decreases we will find both of us increasing in that oneness and fullness which we have in Christ."

Wagner also recognized the anxiety of some participants who feared that they were being presumptuous in their confidence that they were doing God's will. "Men have to act as if *they knew the mind of God, submit each prayer to God with the clear recognition that God may enter a discipline or a demurrer by means of His own. And as, in the spirit of prayer, they check their plans and proposals freely with one another, the people of God have historic ground and precedent for believing that in the free interplay of mind with mind God has the best opportunity men can give Him to have His own mind be more freely known."*

In a parallel address, Fred Hoskins, minister and secretary of the General Council of the Congregational Christian Churches, confessed to a "new convert's zeal to give a testimony." The long years of travel together toward union had generated "a spacious mutual trust," and in that trust both churches could approach tasks ahead with complete confidence. Together they would bear a stronger and better witness to Christ than either of them had done separately. They could be confident that God would provide them with the light, guidance, and strength required. Finally, the years of struggle had made them impatient to press forward together to carry out the mission of the church.

Hoskins ended his address with a jubilant, thanksgiving to the Triune God with which he began his speech:

> *God be praised for this hour!*
> *Christ be exalted for this joy!*
> *The Holy Spirit be thanked for His*
> *gracious leading!*

Address by Rev. James E. Wagner

Tuesday, June 25

As I looked forward to the assignment which Dr. Hoskins and I share in addressing briefly the opening session of this Uniting General Synod, I found my mind turning again and again to two Scriptures which at first mention will seem to have no conceivable pertinence to our assembly here tonight.

One is to be found in Galatians 2:11–13 where, in a highly suggestive autobiographical passage, St. Paul wrote: "But when Peter was come to Antioch, I withstood him to the face, because he was to be blamed. For before that certain came from James, he did eat with the Gentiles: but when they were come, he withdrew and separated himself, fearing them which were of the circumcision. And the other Jews dissembled likewise with him."

That was a time, said St. Paul, when St. Peter was a fence-straddler and a hypocrite. I venture to speak a word in defence of St. Peter. To understand his predicament it is necessary to recall that the first Christians were all Jews, but that as the full implications of the revelation of God in Christ began to take hold and the Holy Spirit was let loose at Pentecost it was inevitable that Gentiles would seek what Jewish friends and neighbors were finding in Christ. Even those first Jewish followers of Christ could not completely disentangle themselves from the perverted "chosen people" psychology they had inherited, so the first crucial, controversial issue in Christian history was: Can Gentiles be admitted into the fold of Christ? And if so, under what conditions? Or, as we put it looking back on the controversy, was Christianity to turn out to be just another Jewish sect or was it to yield to the impact and leading of God and become that "fellowship of the forgiven and the forgiving" in which all God's children, penitent and trusting, would find redemption and themselves at home?

A fundamental change—expansion and expansiveness—was about to take place in the Christian fellowship; and St. Peter, whose fisherman's eye had learned to read the signs of changing weather, must have known the change was coming—and inevitably so. His hesitancy and wavering may be understood, therefore, as not unlike our own at this juncture or as we have looked forward to it,—the realization that some old, familiar, precious things,—names, procedures, structures, and so on,—are about to give way to successors new and unfamiliar. What will steady and sustain us, indeed carry us forward in this venture of faith, will be the safely-predictable day-by-day discovery which St. Peter experienced in his day, namely that the best we have known will not have been lost at all, that it will be enriched by the new (or different) which each of us brings to our common life, that God himself will introduce "some better thing" neither of us possessed of himself alone, and that, as in another classic Scripture, in whatever way and measure each of us decreases we will find both of us increasing in that oneness and fullness which we have in Christ.

The second Scripture which suggested itself in anticipation of this occasion is found in 1 Samuel 7:12, "Then Samuel took a stone, and set it between Mizpeh and Shen, and called the name of it Ebenezer, saying, Hitherto hath the Lord helped us."

Certainly that sentence, "Hitherto hath the Lord helped us," will epitomize the glad and humble gratitude with which the Congregational Christian Executive Committee and the Evangelical and Reformed General Council look back on their experience since negotiations were resumed three years ago, and with which now they submit the fruit of their labors to this Uniting General Synod.

But the words, "Hitherto hath the Lord helped us," appropriated to our gathering here, reflect an assurance without which our being here together would be an empty and pathetic masquerade. That assurance is that this union is of God's making and it is God who has brought us to this hour.

There is always an element of presumption,—presumptuousness, really, —in making an affirmation like that. For who can know the mind of the Lord, whose ways are past finding out? And how easy it is in "the pride of life" to become so enamoured of our human schemes and strivings that we identify them with the will and mind of God.

But if devout men were not willing to make this assumption, to act for a moment in the faith that having prayed for God's guidance the step they felt led to take was of God's leading,—then no human venture in the doing of God's will would ever have been, would ever be now, attempted. Men have to *act as if* they knew the mind of God, submit each prayer to God with the clear recognition that God may enter a discipline or a demurrer by means of His own. And as, in the spirit of prayer, they check their plans and proposals freely with one another, the people of God have historic ground and precedent for believing that in the free interplay of mind with mind God has the best opportunity men can give Him to have His own mind be more fully known.

Born out of such a concept of the way God leads His children, the plans and proposals for this Uniting General Synod are offered to the delegates here assembled as, forty-eight hours hence, they will have to offer their actions and decisions to the synods, conferences, associations and congregations of our two fellowships.

What authority will what we do here have with the regional judicatories, the local churches, the individual pastors and lay members of our respective fellowships?

Legalistically the answer would vary (in theory at least), actions of a General Synod in the Evangelical and Reformed Church carrying more authority for regional synods and the local church than would be characteristic of Congregational Christian tradition.

But "the household of God" is not primarily a legalistic, but a moral and spiritual, corporate life in which "the tie that binds" is that of "Christian love" and wherein "the fellowship of kindred minds is like to that above."

On the authority of this General Synod, of the constitution we shall eventually adopt, of programs and procedures we may approve from time to time for the guidance of our common life, I venture to offer in closing this paragraph from my sermon to the General Synod at Lancaster (changing only the number of delegates):

> In the Protestant tradition no ecclesiastical body can speak with arbitrary or dogmatic authority. Likewise, in the true Protestant tradition, no ecclesiastical body will seek to compel men's conformity or submission against their conscience and intelligence and the free and voluntary assent of their minds and wills. This General Synod will labor with the prayer and in the faith that the Holy Spirit will be guiding it. That, and the fact that the cooperative thinking of seven hundred and fourteen of the most competent and devout and most highly trusted pastors and lay delegates, chosen by their peers to represent them, will have brought about the decisions we reach and the pronouncements we utter,—all this lends a weight and a compulsion to what we say and do here which no thoughtful person will lightly discount or ignore. For the deliberations we engage in throughout this week there is an added reason for our praying, "Not my will but Thine be done."

Some of us will have to continue working on the problems incident to the ordering of our common life. Let no man look upon this work lightly, or despise those of us who must burden ourselves with it. This task is inherent in the nature of the Church as a social institution. And it is not improbable that those of us who have worked and must continue to work at that more prosaic task of the union are for that very reason made more keenly aware that our ultimate unity will be found, not there in the complexities—and perplexities—of structure and procedure, but in mission. We will find ourselves increasingly one through the loving zeal with which now we reinforce each other in our witness for Christ, find ways of working together while the processes of constitution-making go on, seize every opportunity of fellowship and worship with each other, and each for the other pray that once again in our time the Lord of the Church may do what He did long ago: make both one, breaking down the middle wall of partition between us, so that we shall be no longer strangers and foreigners to each other but fellow-citizens in this new unit of the household of God which we are now privileged to help establish,—builded, it is our prayer, as is the universal Church, upon the foundation of the apostles and prophets, Jesus Christ himself being the chief cornerstone.

Address by Rev. Fred Hoskins

Tuesday, June 25

Fathers and Brethren:

> God be praised for this hour!
> Christ be exalted for this joy!
> The Holy Spirit be thanked for His
> gracious leading!

Our hearts are filled with gratitude to friends in many churches for the prayers, labors, and kindly encouragement they have so generously offered to and for us through the years as we have moved toward the consummation of this union.

We acknowledge a heavy indebtedness to our fathers who not only taught us to love our respective denominations and to regard highly our church family traditions, but also to honor all the branches of Christ's universal Church. We are thankful that our fathers stirred up in our hearts a restlessness which will not quiet until the visible Church shall effectively illustrate and reflect the oneness men may have in Christ.

Furthermore, we wish to acknowledge that this which we do tonight is but building on foundations laid by older and wiser persons than we. Years ago it was they who were able to see over and through the walls, sometimes superficial and sometimes artificial, which separated our two communions. It was they who had the perspicacity to see and the courage to report how similar our two denominations really are in origins, loves, in emphases, in practices, and in understanding the mission of the Church to our world. They it was who understood that, with reference to the unity of the Church, the time had come to cease merely calling, "Lord, Lord!" and to get busy demonstrating the unity of God's people.

Possibly we of the present would not have had the vision, or the skill, or the courage, to propose or to move into this exciting adventure of taking a further and longer step toward the fulfillment of our Lord's great prayer. But the vision has been revealed, the proposal has been made, the foundation has been laid. We pray that we may be guided and strengthened to build on the foundation with prayer and intelligence and vigor.

A Union of Trust

We have a new convert's zeal to give a testimony. We wish to witness before the whole world that the parties to this union come to it with a spacious mutual trust. To be sure, each of our communions comes with its peculiar values and each is insistent that its essential values shall be preserved and in no wise cut off in any truncated, makeshift arrangements.

In the many years of planning and of cultivating acquaintance we have developed a full trust in each other. We do not have to know all the questions and problems which will arise in the future, much less to know in advance what the answers and solutions will be. We have agreed upon the principles of polity and program. We trust one another. As Christian brethren we shall seek the appropriate answers and solutions as the need arises. There is time enough to write a constitution and by-laws. We unite in mutual trust and not anywise in fear.

A Union with Faith

We feel so jubilant about it that we are eager for the entire world to know that the parties to this union come to it in and with faith. Long since, we realized that if it be taken up without faith *The Basis of Union with the Interpretations* would never suffice to effect a union which would glorify the Head of the Church. (Just as early, we recognized that no other plan for Union which the mind of man might conceive would be adequate to honor God if it should be adopted without faith.) Far back, the Joint Planning Committee saw that its work could never be successful if it centered only upon structures. It saw that it would have to do its work within a clear-cut Christian frame of reference. It set such a frame of reference when it declared its purpose to do all its work in a manner that would enable us in the United Church to make a better witness to Christ. We shall not presume to more than we have achieved, but we come to this union in and with faith that God had His hand in it all and that we shall bear a stronger and better witness to Christ than either of us has done separately.

A Union of Hope

We have a zeal to testify to the entire world that the parties to this union come to it with a vigorous and built-in hope. Our hope is of the same essence as the hope St. Paul so extravagantly commended. Our hope is not of the "pious wish" type. Ours is earnest expectation, the kind of expectation upon which a man will bet his life. We move in the hope, which is to say expectation, that God will provide us light according to our need, guidance according to the demands of the time, and strength according to the requirements of each situation. Our hope is that we may keep ourselves enough out of the way that God can move in and find us useable instruments for doing His will. This is not a union of fear, it is a union of hope.

A Union for Mission

We want to publish to the world that we are nerved by faith, that we are secured by hope, that we are poised by our mutual trust, and further, we are impatient to press forward to prosecute the mission of the Church. It is the mission of the Church to be the tool for a divine penetration of the world. The Church is under orders to confront and penetrate with the gospel of Jesus Christ every dimension of life. Overseas ministry, homeland witness, social action, religious education, evangelism, stewardship, divide the mission up as you will, call the parts what you may, there still is but one mission for the Church. It is the mission which God endorsed by the resurrection, the same one upon which God sent Jesus Christ.

We are aware that the Church itself stands under the judgment of the cross as surely as does the world, but for this cause we bow our knees unto our Lord Jesus Christ and vow to devote our prayers and strength and gifts to the mission of our Lord Jesus Christ. We vow to take seriously His prayer, "As Thou has sent me into the world even so have I also sent them into the world."

God be praised for this hour!
Christ be exalted for this joy!
The Holy Spirit be thanked for His
gracious leading!

93. The Celebration:

"Hymns and Prayers"

(1957)

William C. Nelson and Gerald H. Hinkle; Douglas Horton; Gerhard W. Grauer; and Samuel Press

After struggling toward union for nearly twenty years, the Congregational Christian Churches and the Evangelical and Reformed Church set the dates for the Uniting General Synod of the United Church of Christ as June 25–27, 1957, in Cleveland, Ohio. After all they had been through, the two denominations might have experienced their final coming together as somewhat anticlimactic. The experience, however, was quite the opposite. There was a strong, even heady, feeling within both denominations that God had been with them throughout their journey, and the final union had come to pass through God's grace.

Prior to the Uniting Synod, The Messenger *published two "hymn-poems" written by pastors William C. Nelson of Akron, Ohio, and Gerald H. Hinkle of Willow Street, Pennsylvania, expressing the wave of joy and gratitude flooding local churches. It was proposed that the hymns be sung in all local Congregational Christian and Evangelical and Reformed congregations on the final day of the Uniting Synod.*

At the synod itself, most of the proceedings took place in the context of worship, where worshipers were overwhelmed with heartfelt gratitude for what God had done for them and in spite of them. There was a recurring

---

Source: William C. Nelson and Gerald H. Hinkle, hymns in editorial "Celebrating Union," *The Messenger,* 4 June 1957, 4; Douglas Horton, "The Uniting Prayer," *The Messenger,* 23 July 1957, 2; Gerhard W. Grauer, "The Constituting Prayer," in *Minutes of the Uniting General Synod of the United Church of Christ,* Cleveland, Ohio, 25–27 June 1957, 74–75; Samuel D. Press, "A Prayer for the Church," *The Messenger,* 23 July 1957, 8–9.

invocation of the Holy Spirit, asking the Spirit for guidance so that they might continue to do God's bidding in the future.

At the opening worship service of the synod on Tuesday evening, June 25, 1957, the United Church of Christ was formally created by the official action of representatives of the Congregational Christian Churches and the Evangelical and Reformed Church. After they had unanimously approved a joint resolution declaring the "Basis of Union with the Interpretations" adopted and the union in effect, Douglas Horton, formerly minister and secretary of the General Council of the Congregational Christian Churches, led the participants in the "Uniting Prayer." In it, he asked the Almighty to seal their covenant and bless their communion, that they might continue to be instruments for the propagation of the gospel and the furthering of Christ's reign in all the nations, and that they might become a ready channel of blessing to the whole church of Jesus Christ.

The next morning, all the delegates, associate members of the synod, and fraternal delegates joined in the celebration of the Lord's Supper, "conceived in this instance," as the program explained, "not only in terms of its traditional significances but also as the symbol of the dedication of the delegates to the solemn responsibilities which are theirs and of their acknowledgment that, without the blessings of Almighty God and the guidance of the Holy Spirit, all their doings are nothing worth and shall be brought to nought."

The service was held at the beautiful Old Stone Church, Presbyterian, located on the public square in downtown Cleveland. After a communion meditation given by Boynton Merrill, the "Prayer Constituting the General Synod" was offered by Gerhard W. Grauer, pastor of St. Paul's Church, Chicago, Illinois, and chair of the Committee on Closer Relations with Other Churches in the Evangelical and Reformed Church. He, too, touched upon the note of trust and gratitude for God's presence throughout their twenty-year journey toward union, noting, "Our differing heritage kept us apart; our common heritage in Christ unites us."

Samuel D. Press, of Clayton, Missouri, president emeritus of Eden Theological Seminary, was recognized, along with Truman Douglass, as having begun the whole process so many years before (see vol. 6:70). Press offered a "Prayer for the Church," asking that the United Church of Christ be not merely a human invention, but God's creation, a petition in harmony with Grauer's prayer: "We have covenanted together, but we cannot create, we cannot unite, we cannot constitute a United Church of Christ. . . . Send Thy Spirit upon all congregations of our fellowship that we may become an actually United Church of Christ which shall know no higher purpose than to grow together, pray, worship and work together, to the end that Thy name may be glorified and Thy kingdom may be established in every department of life over all the earth."

Celebrating Union

Several attempts at the writing of hymn-poems inspired by the pending establishment of the United Church of Christ have come to our attention. The hymns are printed here with the permission of the writers.

One was written by Dr. William C. Nelson, pastor of Trinity Church, Akron, Ohio. His hymn can be sung to any C.M.D. tune, but he recommends "All Saints, New," which is used in *The Hymnal* for "The Son of God Goes Forth to War" (No. 288).

When from the shores of other lands,
Through perils of the sea,
Came men oppressed, and Pilgrim bands
In quest of liberty,
They kept their faith though sorely tried;
They humbly knelt to pray.
O Thou who blessed them, stand beside
And strengthen us today.

We differ, Lord, in many ways,
With many voices sing,
Yet tune our souls to common praise,
And one devotion bring.
O grant us now the zeal that fills
With courage from above;
Unite our hearts and move our wills
To common works of love.

O heal the rifts of Christendom,
That other men may see
One spirit in our midst, and come
To share our unity.
Teach us to love beyond our creed,
To care beyond our kin;

Turn noble thought to valiant deed,
The whole wide world to win.

Rev. Gerald H. Hinkle, pastor of the Evangelical and Reformed Church of Willow Street, Pennsylvania, has written a hymn which he says is to be sung by his choir and congregation on the Sunday nearest the Uniting General Synod. He suggests that it be sung to "Lancashire," the tune used in *The Hymnal* for "Lead On, O King Eternal" (No. 299).

In this glad hour of union,
We hail thee, Lord and King;
And humbly we beseech thee,
Accept the praise we bring
For thine inspired Commission,
That all thy saints be one;
And for the grace to answer,
"Thy will, O Lord, be done!"

We thank thee for thy servants
Who, years before their time,
Did see the vision glorious,
Did dream the dream sublime.
We ask thy benediction,
As now we seal in thee
Their fondest hopes, their passion,
Their love for unity.

O may thy wondrous Spirit
Dwell in thy church, each part,
Until thy call to one-ness
Abides in every heart;
Until with thee in glory,
Around thy throne of grace,
One fellowship eternal,
We hail thee face to face!

"These and other attempts at hymn-writing," says President James E. Wagner, "make their own unique contribution to the stuff of which Christian union is made; for one has the feeling that, while some are engaged in the more prosaic and difficult tasks of union negotiation, the hearts of others are being moved to sing of the hope and promise the union offers."

On Sunday, June 25, Evangelical and Reformed and Congregational Christian congregations throughout this country will remember the Uniting

General Synod in prayer. Many of them will also voice their prayer in song, using one of these hymns, perhaps, or one which they themselves will be inspired to compose.

The Uniting Prayer

On Tuesday evening, June 25, 1957, in Cleveland, the United Church of Christ was brought into being by the joint action of representatives of the Congregational Christian Churches and of the Evangelical and Reformed Church assembled for the Uniting General Synod.

Following the formal and unanimous approval of the joint resolution declaring The Basis of Union with the Interpretations adopted and the union in effect, Dr. Douglas Horton, former minister and secretary of the General Council of the Congregational Christian Churches, led in the Uniting Prayer which follows.

Almighty God, who in Jesus Christ givest thy Spirit to the church, to create and preserve, to renew and to create afresh, we stand in thy presence in all humility and reverence, acknowledging thy incomprehensible goodness. We beseech thee for pardon for all that is in us amiss and call upon thee now to do for us a work which we are utterly unable to accomplish of ourselves.

We who are children of fathers who called for reformation in the church when men justified themselves of their own righteousness and gave glory not to thee alone, and of fathers who found Christ in his completeness in every congregation of his people, have now entered into covenant to be the United Church of Christ.

A company of thy people who trace their sources to one part of the earth and to peoples of one tongue have met with others deriving from another place and other peoples, and both of them together have now declared themselves to have entered into one communion within thy holy church.

So now, O Lord, we who cannot finally shape events nor order destiny turn to thee, the Maker of the future, in the confidence of thy exceeding precious promises, to beg that thou wilt seal unto us this covenant so made and communion entered into. Speak peace and ever deeper mutual understanding to us in the years to come, turn us from every way of darkness into light, and so prepare for us, we pray, an inheritance that passeth not away.

Seal our covenant and bless our communion as we yield ourselves to thee to be an instrument to thy hand for the propagation of the gospel and the kingdom of Christ in all the nations. Grant us to be a ready channel of thy blessing to the whole church of Jesus Christ. To that end establish in us all thy ordinances in purity, give our ministers to speak thy word in fullness, prevent and remove from us ignorance, schism, and unfruitfulness, and help us, with thy whole church, to be to our nation and to the world as the soul to the body, whence the light of thy Spirit, invisible and eternal, may shine upon and transform the things which are visible.

Hear our prayers for every particular church. Impart to each one of them thy gracious and effectual assistance; pour out upon them the riches and excellency of the gospel; and draw them all into the perfect knowledge of him at whose hand are joys for evermore.

In this moment of union, when we taste the first fruits of the glory which is to be revealed, we bring thee thanks that may not be uttered for that thou hast called us to this hour; and we ask not with our lips alone but in the dedication of our lives that thy grace, which gives liberty and power, may rest upon the United Church of Christ, through Jesus Christ our Lord. Amen.

The Constituting Prayer

Almighty and most gracious God, who of Thy loving kindness and tender mercy didst send forth Thy Holy Spirit to establish Thy Church, Christ Jesus being the chief cornerstone, and didst preside at the first assembly of the apostles and elders at Jerusalem and hast promised to be with Thy Church always, even unto the end of the world: Send Thy Spirit upon us, O Lord, that we also may be impelled to do Thy will and accomplish Thy purpose.

Our fathers in their pilgrimage walked by Thy guidance and were mindful of Thy continuing revelation. Remind us of those who walked before us and renew our kinship with them. Thou hast blest our fellowships: Thou hast borne with our sinfulness, our narrowness and our prejudices. We have blessed traditions. Help us to be true to them and yet cause us to await new truths that shall break forth from Thy word and from our experiences. For our blessed heritage, we give Thee thanks. Our differing heritage kept us apart; our common heritage in Christ unites us.

We face this momentous occasion with trembling, not with fear, but with eager anticipation, for we believe that Thy hand hath led us to this moment. We have long acknowledged the sin of our divisions. . . . We have joined with others in confessing that we have clung to ways which are merely our own and have caused the Church to continue in division.

We have offered our thanks to Thee for those who are striving to draw nearer to each other and to Thee and thus heal the disunity of the Church. And now we stand before this godly event. We confess our insufficiency, but we remember Thy promises. We heed Thy call. Take our imperfect minds and wills and enable us to face this new and imposing summons which seeks to strengthen the witness of Thy Church.

Deliver us from error, pride and prejudice. . . . From narrow self-sufficiency. Forgive us if we are tempted to think merely of bigness and greater efficiency and bring to our remembrance that we unite to strengthen our faith, enlarge our vision and broaden our Christian witness to God's love in Christ.

Take our feeble efforts . . . the things we have done . . . the things we hope to do, and purge them of anything false and mediocre, anything superficial and partial and help us to know that we are not merely joined together by resolution and legal action, but by Thy Spirit.

We have covenanted together, but we cannot create, we cannot unite, we cannot constitute a United Church of Christ. What we propose, do Thou perform. What we haltingly seek to do, wouldst Thou bring to pass by the might of Thy Holy Spirit. We would be constituted as a General Synod in the name of the Father, the Son and the Holy Ghost. Make us willing humbly to learn from each other and from Thee. We would be building a more glorious and united Church, but only by Thy direction and only according to Thy plan. Make this not our invention, but Thy creation, O Lord. Humbly we ask that the inspiration of Thy presence may guide us and those who through the years shall seek to continue to build a United Church of Christ. Send Thy Spirit upon all congregations of our fellowship that we may become an actually United Church of Christ which shall know no higher purpose than to grow together, pray, worship and work together to the end that Thy name may be glorified and Thy kingdom may be established in every department of life over all the earth.

Awaken us to the crying needs of our world. Keep us sensitive, keep us aware of our oneness with the whole body of Christ. Deepen our faith in Thee as the hope of the world and enable us with Christians all over the earth, to spread Thy life-giving Gospel, that by Thy grace the day may come when every knee shall bow and every tongue shall confess Thee as Lord.

We lift up our voices in sincere and humble gratitude that we have been privileged to witness the outpouring of Thy Holy Spirit upon us in the experiences of last night. Verily the place whereon we stand is holy ground.

And now unto Him that is able to do exceeding abundantly above all that we ask or think, according to the power that worketh in us, unto Him be glory in the Church and in Christ Jesus unto all generations for ever and ever.

A Prayer for the Church

The prayer which follows was offered by Dr. S. D. Press, of Clayton, Missouri, president emeritus of Eden Theological Seminary, who, with Dr. Truman B. Douglass, is recognized as having released the first impulses which led at long last to the formation of the United Church of Christ.

O thou whom we worship as our Savior and Lord, thou art indeed the true king of all humanity.

In thy divine love we have our being. By thy unspeakable love, by the giving of thyself for us and our salvation, we have been redeemed from our state of lostness in sin. Through the continuous action of thy Spirit in our lives we becomc sons of God by grace.

Thou, who reignest in the power of the resurrection, who canst make the dead live, hast created in our world of space and time thine own realm of the Eternal Spirit: the miracle of thy world-conquering church, the Tree of Life, whose leaves are for the healing of the nations.

Unto thee, O Lord, we lift up our hearts in praise of thy holy name, in thanksgiving for all thy wondrous deeds of loving-kindness to thy children in the world. In faith and love we would be thine. Thy living presence in our midst is our joy and strength; in thee heaven is linked to our earth as the harbinger of a new humanity.

In thy divine kindness, O Lord, thou hast granted us high moments during these days. We would give testimony in this blessed hour of our oneness in thee on the deepest level of our lives.

Thy ardent prayer for the unity of thy followers has become a solemn commission laid upon us all. It incited the noble venture which has brought us together into one communion. We beseech thee, O God, let the oneness of thy people become under thy guiding hand a holy mission for us all within thy covenant of truth and grace, as a testimony to the world of the new humanity founded on earth. Let it bear the authentic marks of him, our Savior, who in deep compassion took our infirmities upon himself and healed our diseases.

This precious grace in making us co-workers with thee, seeking to gather into one family all thy erring children scattered throughout the world, thou bestowest upon us notwithstanding our limitations manifested in all we do. In thy holy presence we are filled with a deep sense of awe and are overcome by a feeling of profound humiliation of self, because of the sin which clings so closely to us. Help us, O God, in the fellowship of the Holy Spirit to conquer our selfish ambitions and our personal pride. We pray thee, cleanse us in the inward parts and put a right spirit into us.

We have given ourselves to this glorious endeavor for the oneness of the church, our Lord, not with a sense of our own fitness and sufficiency. We acknowledge our constant need of thee lest we work in vain, laboring for things that perish. Help us to labor with thee for substance that endures eternally. We ask thy guidance for every step of the way we have only begun to travel. Against the hardest tests yet to be met, equip us with the spiritual armor of a conquering faith, an affectionate love, and an enduring patience.

O God, help us to see the world in us and around us less in its opposition to the truth in Christ and more in its sore need of him. Grant us the spiritual wisdom to measure the strength of our United Church not in terms of success or greatness but in the striving of her members to grow daily in Christ's likeness. We pray thee earnestly, let her ministry in all of its agencies proclaim only him who saves by his fervent love of every man, woman, and child in the world and by his divine power to remake them in the image of God.

O Lord, thou hast said, "I will build my church." We pray thee, build thy kingdom and its righteousness deep into our souls: thy steadfast love, thy compassionate, tender regard for all our brothers in the world. Heal the brokenness of the Christian fellowship throughout the world. Purge us from the dreadful vice of arrogance and expunge from our midst every form of the devastating curse of racial and national unbrotherliness.

Our Father, let Christ be formed in us: his unfeigned humility, his full sharing of our creaturely lowliness, his spirit of self-giving for others, his redemptive suffering for those in sin, seeking tirelessly to restore the fallen and to bring back home the prodigals. O God, make us, thy servants one and all, heirs to his prophetic spirit, by keeping the fires burning which he kindled on earth. Give us his fearlessness and boldness in resisting unto blood the wrongs and injustices of our society, like the martyrs in all ages who followed in his wake.

Keep us humble, O God, and obedient to thy will. Let us never in our own fellowship yield to the temptation to lord it over thy people. Guide us in helping them all to grow up into the free manhood of Christ: to become God-taught sons in a God-directed church. Constrain us to recognize in reverence the peculiar dignity of every individual soul: the traces of thy creative design and the workmanship of thine own Spirit.

We thank thee, O God, for the spiritual freedom we have received in Christ, for the recreated, unfettered will empowered by the Holy Spirit to choose the way of obedience—"not my will but thine be done." Restrain us from seeking delusive selfish freedoms which do not liberate, but enslave. Strengthen us in the true freedom: to be the hirelings of none, yet the servants of all, especially of the weak and the meek, the lowly and the lonely.

Lord of the church, we pray thee, let thy church in her earthen vestments strain toward the fulfillment of her high spiritual calling: to be the holy temple of thy body in full splendor, a church without blemish. Pour into our hearts thine all-inclusive love, keeping thy church a house of prayer for all peoples, a place where they may find thee, the Author and Perfecter of our faith.

Let us keep the door of the kingdom open in the wideness of thy mercy. With our eyes riveted on thee, let us work and pray for the coming of thy kingdom in glory, in a renewed world: one flock, one Shepherd. Keep us in thy love. Thine is the kingdom, the power, and the glory forever. Amen.

94. Union in Christ:

"Message to the Churches from the Uniting General Synod" and "Blessed Event"

(1957)

General Synod of the UCC; *The Plain Dealer*

At the conclusion of the Uniting General Synod, in which the Congregational Christian Churches and the Evangelical and Reformed Church celebrated the birth of the United Church of Christ, those in attendance sent out a "Message to the Churches from the Uniting General Synod." Addressed to "the Members of our Fellowship and to the Whole Church of Jesus Christ throughout the world," the message was signed by the leaders of the new denomination: moderators Louis W. Goebel and George W. Hastings; co-presidents Fred Hoskins and James E. Wagner; and co-secretaries Fred S. Buschmeyer and Sheldon E. Mackey.

Fully aware that their union was something extraordinary in the history of Protestantism in the United States, a union of two denominations with different national and cultural origins, different church polity and intradenominational structures, the synod's message affirmed the conviction that they had come together for theological, indeed christological, reasons. The two denominations had joined "because the

---

Source: "Message to the Churches from the Uniting General Synod," in *Minutes of the Uniting General Synod of the United Church of Christ,* Cleveland, Ohio, 25–27 June 1957, 130–31; "Blessed Event," cartoon in *The Plain Dealer,* 27 June 1957.

two companies of Christians have held and hold the same basic belief, that Christ and Christ alone is Head of the Church. From Him derive the understanding of God as Father, the participation in the same Spirit, the doctrines of faith, the influence toward holiness, the duties of divine worship, the apprehension of the significance of Baptism and the Lord's Supper, the observance of church order, the mutual love of Christians, and their dedication to the betterment of the world. To be drawn to Him is to be drawn to one another, and to acknowledge Him as Head is to feel pain in dismemberment one from the other."

The message also stated forcefully that although the General Synod enjoyed the new richness and depth that the union was bringing them, union was not a state once and for all achieved. Rather, it was "a process, informed by growth and adventure" and leading finally to "communion fulfilled in Christ."

The Plain Dealer, *the local Cleveland newspaper, also understood that the formation of the United Church of Christ was a new beginning. In a cartoon entitled "Blessed Event," the newspaper portrayed the arrival of the United Church of Christ as the birth of a baby brought by the proverbial stork—a baby that would grow and develop over a lifetime. In this case, the United Church of Christ had embarked upon a journey toward the union of all Christ's followers throughout the whole inhabited earth.*

Message to the Churches from the Uniting General Synod

To the Members of our Fellowship
And to the Whole Church of Jesus Christ throughout the world,
The United Church of Christ wishes grace and peace
From God the Father and from our Lord Jesus Christ.

Today for two hitherto separate communions of the Church of Jesus Christ the first step toward full union has been taken. Representatives of the General Council of the Congregational Christian Churches and of the Evangelical and Reformed Church, meeting in the City of Cleveland in the State of Ohio in the United States of America, have bound themselves together in the presence of God to form the United Church of Christ.

The Evangelical and Reformed Church stems from the Protestant Reformation on the continent of Europe in the early sixteenth century. The Congregational Christian Churches trace their spiritual ancestry through the Pilgrim Fathers and the Puritans of the late sixteenth and early seventeenth century in England and to later reform movements on this side of the Atlantic. Both have their Christian lineage through the Western Church, but they have not been members of the same body since Western Christendom ceased to be one. Their centuries of separation have now come to an end.

The Congregational Christian Churches belong to the International Congregational Council, the Evangelical and Reformed Church to the Alliance of the Reformed Churches Throughout the World Holding the Presbyterian Order. Now, following happy precedents in Canada, South India and elsewhere, two classical polities of Christian history have adjusted themselves to each other through union in such a way as to leave intact and effective the excellences of each. Differences in ecclesiastical procedure, which in sundry places and times have occasioned tensions and disorders, are appointed their secondary place and divested of evil effect.

This union has been made possible because the two companies of Christians have held and hold the same basic belief, that Christ and Christ alone is the Head of the Church. From Him derive the understanding of God as Father, the participation in the same Spirit, the doctrines of faith, the influence toward holiness, the duties of divine worship, the apprehension of the significance of Baptism and the Lord's Supper, the observance of church order, the mutual love of Christians, and their dedication to the betterment of the world. To be drawn to Him is to be drawn to one another, and to acknowledge Him as Head is to feel pain in dismemberment one from the other. So the union has come.

At this moment of the joyous new access of life imparted by the union, the United Church of Christ is stricken in conscience at its continuing separation from the rest of the Church, and it prays for the day when the greater Church of Jesus Christ, now hindered and weakened by many divisions, will come to visible reality, one flock, one shepherd, through the influence of One who is alive in every part of His Church. To the elimination of useless and hurtful separations within the greater Church the United Church of Christ offers itself and its resources. Active participation in both the National Council of the Churches of Christ in the United States of America and the World Council of Churches has been an expression of this concern on the part of both of the uniting groups. Now united, but recognizing that we are still under the judgment of an unfinished task, we pledge a continuance of that participation.

It is the belief of the United Church of Christ that all within the greater Church should accord to each other the fullest possible recognition and, where the Lord seems ready to bless organic union, should enter into that happier estate which answers radically and essentially His prayer that they all may be one.

We remind our, membership that the union of churches is in itself an empty objective save as it is made the means of conveying Christ's redemptive purpose to man in the realm both of personal and social life. In every particular church let us pray that there may be not only a new awareness that God has appointed us for a special witness in this day, but also that we are summoned to outdo our past in every ministry of worship, of Christian nurture, and of dedication to the broadening and deepening of God's kingdom in and among all men. We hold that when a church extends its duties only to its own members and assemblies, it has fallen away from the principal end of its institution: its very purpose on the human side is to edify the Church Universal, making disciples of all nations through a vital and enlightened missionary program.

We should instruct ourselves continually in the truth that union is not a state once and for all achieved. It is a deliberate process, informed by growth and adventure. A thousand new relationships must yet be woven into the fabric of the United Church of Christ. This cannot be without pain and tribulation; but with every day of patience and imaginative courage marking the emergence of the completed pattern, the time will come when our union shall be communion fulfilled in Christ.

The spiritual richness made available to us in our union is already unmistakably and deeply apprehended. We have suddenly become the heirs not of one line alone but of two lines of inheritance. Our minds have become the meeting place for two abundant streams of thought and practice. There are none of us who cannot feel, at this confluence, an enhancement of our inner life.

While we do not begin with the ultimate in all the dimensions of our hope, God has covenanted with His people that when they give His word free course and glorify it, as our union is designed to do, He is faithful: He "shall establish you, and keep you from evil." Our union brings forth treasures old and new. The old treasures we intend to conserve; we turn toward the new in limitless anticipation, praising God for the beginnings of the United Church of Christ.

"Now unto Him that is able to do exceeding abundantly above all that we ask or think, according to the power that worketh in us, unto Him be glory in the Church by Christ Jesus throughout all ages, world without end. Amen."

By the Co-Secretaries:
FRED S. BUSCHMEYER
SHELDON E. MACKEY

The Moderators:
LOUIS W. GOEBEL
GEORGE B. HASTINGS
The Co-Presidents:
FRED HOSKINS
JAMES E. WAGNER

The twenty-fifth day of June in the Year of our Lord 1957

The General Synod of the United Church of Christ

Blessed Event
The Plain Dealer
June 27, 1957

Postscript

Thomas E. Dipko

The longing for unity among the followers of Jesus Christ is as characteristic a mark of the Christian church across the generations as it was in the first century. The documents in this volume are compelling evidence of the tenacity of that longing. The story they tell makes no sense apart from the irrepressible discomfort separated Christians feel when they remember that Jesus' prayer "that they may all be one" remains the preeminent unanswered prayer of the New Testament.

Our forebears in the last half of the nineteenth and the first half of the twentieth centuries lived in a world fractured by clashing ideologies and global warfare. Their confession that the unity God wills for the church is a gift already given and waiting to be claimed was not dimmed by the crucible of a world divided against itself. What can we learn from the ecumenical diary that we find in these remarkable pages?

Unity and Mission

A preponderance of evidence reminds us that Christians in so-called mission lands, where they were clearly a minority, were particularly passionate for thc unity of the church. The principal argument given is now familiar. How can the gospel be shared credibly with persons who are hearing it for the first time if those who announce it are themselves divided? In spite of the sending churches' confusion of the gospel with Western culture, and the spiritual colonialism that sometimes resulted, the church in so-called mission lands became a prophetic ecumenical voice to the older churches in Europe and North America. The younger churches raised questions and dreamed dreams that demanded the birth of the modern ecumenical movement.

Leaders, both lay and clergy, from the sending churches quickly realized that the vision of Christian unity in receiving lands would make demanding claims on the divided sending churches back home. One voice at the

Edinburgh World Missionary Conference in 1910 expressed the hope that "unity, if it begins in the mission field, will not find its ending there."

What was less clear to the churches in the West was the emerging hostile environment that rendered their own nations into new mission fields for the gospel. It was easier to see the minority status of mission churches in non-Christian lands than to recognize the shrinking influence of the church in the face of anti-Christian totalitarian ideologies at home. Fascism, communism, consumerism, and racism in various guises became brutal evidence that the frontier of God's mission is local everywhere.

Youth in churches throughout the world seemed to recognize this universal locality of mission before many adults did. Their discontent with disunity among Christians rendered their domestic and international gatherings classrooms for preparing uncounted servants of the cause of Christian unity. John R. Mott and Willem A. Visser 't Hooft, began their journey to prominent ecumenical leadership through the work of the Young Men's Christian Association (Y.M.C.A.). The World Student Christian Federation and the Young Women's Christian Association (Y.W.C.A.) became early platforms for welcoming the leadership of women and for inviting Roman Catholic and Eastern Orthodox members. Suzanne de Diétrich, so influential in the founding of Comité Inter-Mouvements auprès des Évacués (C.I.M.A.D.E.) during the Second World War, was among the advocates for this expansive and inclusive global ecumenism.

Personal Encounter and Church Transformation

Those who acted on their convictions about the unity that God wills for the church did not go to ecumenical gatherings with rigid blueprints in hand. They felt called by the Holy Spirit to a venture open to the surprises of God. Again and again their testimony discloses a conversion of heart that came about through the simple privilege of being together with other baptized sisters and brothers.

After the Lausanne World Conference on Faith and Order in 1927, Willard L. Sperry, dean of the Harvard Divinity School, summarized the experience of many when he noted that the real value of ecumenical encounter was "not in any statement that it might issue." Echoing the sentiments of others, he treasured "the mingling together of representatives of all the churches" and resulting relationships that opened the way both to acknowledge and transcend differences. One sign of this conversion of heart was and remains the move from a mere tolerance of diversity in the church to a capacity to celebrate diversity as a gift from God.

In church union negotiations that failed during this period, one of the deficits often cited was the lack of direct encounter between members of the participating churches. This often occurred when "representatives" at the negotiating tables were not able to replicate their positive ecumenical experiences when they got back home. In conversations between the Reformed Church in America and the Reformed Church in the United States, one leader lamented that members of the two churches had not met adequately "to make courtship possible." In some instances, this shortcoming was seen as a consequence of inadequate or nonexistent ecumenical staffing that was needed to further unity endeavors within the churches.

The importance of truly meeting others across denominational or confessional boundaries was treasured all the more as the circle of exposure became global. Without the enduring bond of these personal relationships, the survival of the ecumenical movement through the abyss of two world wars would not have been possible.

Hidden behind the published stories of the power of these personal relationships are uncounted names and faces of saints whose witness made advances possible in ecumenism long after they were gone. The friendship between the United States Episcopal layman Silas McBee and Italian Roman Catholic bishop Geremia Bonomelli is one example. History books have cited properly the unprecedented letter sent by Bonomelli to the World Missionary Conference at Edinburgh in 1910 as a consequence of that friendship. His influence on young Angelo Roncalli, later to become Pope John XXIII, is less well known. His counsel to the young priest in 1908 was that the Roman Catholic Church needed to call an ecumenical council to respond to the new opportunities for unity among Christ's followers. Perhaps Bonomelli would have said the same thing without the benefit of his friendship with McBee. The fact remains that this friendship helped shape the ecumenical vocation of both men and touched the pope responsible for calling the Second Vatican Council.

Particular Churches and the Universal Church

At the heart of the ecumenical movement stand Jesus Christ and the question of how historic churches relate to each other and to the one holy catholic and apostolic church. Nothing is more injurious to evolving relationships among the churches than the claim that one of them exhausts the fullness of the universal church. Actions on the part of any one church that place all others "outside" the universal church make ecumenical dialogue untenable. In spite of claims that seem to approximate that exclusive status for one church, the reality is that ecumenical dialogue continues because even claims to catholic fullness leave room for churchly elements in other Christian communities of faith.

Congregational synods early found ways to assert that their local churches were true and full expressions of the church of the New Testament without denying the larger family of believers embraced by the catholic church. In a similar way, this understanding of particular confessional churches within the universal church was affirmed by the continental reformers of the sixteenth century. The pioneers of the ecumenical movement in the eighteenth and nineteenth centuries implored the various churches not to identify absolutely and exclusively any one church as the catholic church of the creeds. The Toronto Statement of 1950 is the eventual fruit of this commitment to respect the ecclesiology of each church while not requiring any church to grant full recognition to others (see vol. 6:88).

The genius of this document is that it kept open the possibility of acknowledging vestiges or elements of the universal church in other communities of faith without denying claims to catholic wholeness in a given historic church. This openness, limited to be sure, was of critical importance to the Eastern Orthodox churches as they sought a place in the work of the World Council of Churches.

This openness to the catholic church that embraces one's own communion while somehow including others tempered confessional and denominational pride before and after the Toronto Statement. It inspired Truman Douglass of the Congregational Christian Churches to say of Samuel Press of the Evangelical and Reformed Church, "In addition, he is—as I hope I am—a member of the Holy Catholic Church before he is a representative of any denomination."

What Douglass and others defined as "catholic loyalty" is similar in intent to the purpose of the Toronto Statement. The ambiguity of this text, like the unresolved elements in many ecumenical documents, is less anomalous than the scandal of disunity among the followers of Jesus Christ. Across the decades, some of the unresolved differences have proven to be signs of the diversity of gifts entrusted to the churches. They are, in the mystery of God's grace, not obstacles to union but riches waiting to be shared. They require not that any particular church give up what is cherished, but rather, that the churches learn to receive into their lives charisms treasured by other churches within the universal church.

Contrary to expectations that "like" churches would find it easier to consummate union agreements than those of differing polities, the opposite was often the case. The Reformed Church in America and the Reformed

Church in the United States, both parented by the Reformed Church of Holland, were unable to reach agreement on union proposals. The same is true of the Christian Churches and the Christian Church (Disciples of Christ). Although various ethnic Lutheran churches were able to unite, shared Lutheran confessions have not been adequate to bring all bodies of that tradition into one church in the United States. The reintegration of the divided churches does not always follow the return route of the road that led to disunity. The birth of the United Church of Christ is an example of reconciled diversity that bridges the reform movements of England, Holland, Switzerland, Germany, Hungary, and the United States across presbyterial and congregational polities and, in the instance of the Hungarian Calvin Synod, embraces a form of episcopacy.

Visible Unity and Structural Plurality

In this period of ecumenical history, federative plans of union were often understood as inferior to organic union that included the institutional merger of existing denominations. On reflection, this is surprising because even the Chicago-Lambeth Quadrilateral does not require institutional structural oneness as a condition of full communion. Conversations on organic union, however, like one held in 1918, regarded "fullest possible recognition" among churches as less than the organic union that is "that happier estate which answers radically and essentially [Jesus'] prayer that they may all be one." One observer called federation "a makeshift of the opportunist and a compromise with ecclesiastical arrogance."

Other voices, also committed to church union, saw mutual recognition among the churches as opening the way to relationships that were organic without being monolithic. The civil structure of the United States was used as an example of "a federal union [that] is not the less an organic union." The possibility of seeing various churches as similar to distinct monastic orders was also explored. Even the advocates of this approach, mutual recognition that invites "reconciled diversity," were cautious about its abuse. If it involved "no sacrifice" on the part of separated churches for the sake of the "church as a whole," then it would be unworthy of their ecumenical vocation. Lesslie Newbigin, a bishop of the Church of South India, warned that rapprochement of this kind "costs us nothing and achieves what it costs."

This struggle with the relationship between visible unity and structural oneness has prepared the churches today to consider the possibility of covenanted life among the churches as a form of organic union. "Communion in sacred things," with full recognition and reconciliation of ordained ministries, is key to this understanding of visible unity that may not require but also welcomes structural oneness where it serves the cause of unity. Where full communion in sacred things is declared among churches, there is consensus that shared structures to enable the new relationships are appropriate but do not displace the institutional life of the respective churches. Unity of this order is understood to be organic and visible without being structurally monolithic.

This understanding of organic unity presumes eventual consensus about the exercise of oversight (*episkope*) in the several churches. Some churches that claim and value the sign of the historic episcopate expressed in the personal office of bishops indicate a willingness to share this sign where it is welcomed. Those churches that understand oversight in more collegial or conciliar ways, while offering their traditions to churches accustomed to bishops, will need to determine whether the sign of the historic episcopate is truly an ecumenical gift and whether it is possible to receive it. The discussion of this ministry of oversight is increasingly cast in the larger context of the priesthood of all believers that is affirmed by all the churches. The universality of the priesthood of all the baptized holds great promise for resolving how ordained ministries may one day be affirmed in common by the respective churches.

The Unfinished Reformation

What is evident in this volume is the continual need of the universal church to respond to the guidance of the Holy Spirit on the road to reform required by faithfulness to the gospel. There are millions more persons in the world today—many of them in the northern and western hemispheres—who have not heard the gospel than there were when the modern ecumenical movement was born in the nineteenth century. The churches who claim to be expressions of the one holy catholic and apostolic church are painfully aware of their need for repentance and reform for the sake of God's mission to humankind. In addition to the historically documented sins of racism, anti-Semitism, nationalism, and classism of the past, there is a new awareness today of the failure of the church to affirm the equality and welcome the leadership of women, include more credibly those who are differently abled, and celebrate the presence and gifts of those who are gay, lesbian, bisexual, or transgendered.

On the difficult path to reform that the quest for Christian unity requires, the past can illumine our way without inhibiting the work of Holy Spirit.

One of the saints of the Reformed Church urged that "the traditions of a church should be her inspiration, and not her limitation, in the effort to achieve God's purposes." Our forebears in the nineteenth and twentieth centuries knew and loved their traditions, and again and again offered them to the larger service of the universal church. They acted on their willingness to see denominations die in order to open a way for the universal church to become more visibly manifest in history. Their legacy to a future that they could not clearly see is an unshakeable trust in God's care for the church across all time, the church always reforming, the church catholic against which the gates of hell will not prevail.

Index

Scriptural Index

Old Testament

New Testament